CAMBRIDGE GREEK *

APOLLONIUS OF RHODES
ARGONAUTICA
BOOK IV

EDITED BY

RICHARD HUNTER

Regius Professor of Greek, University of Cambridge, and Fellow of Trinity College, Cambridge

CAMBRIDGE
UNIVERSITY PRESS

CAMBRIDGE
UNIVERSITY PRESS

University Printing House, Cambridge CB2 8BS, United Kingdom

Cambridge University Press is part of the University of Cambridge.

It furthers the University's mission by disseminating knowledge in the pursuit of
education, learning and research at the highest international levels of excellence.

www.cambridge.org
Information on this title: www.cambridge.org/9781107636750

© Cambridge University Press 2015

First published 2015

Printed in the United Kingdom by Clays, St Ives plc

A catalogue record for this publication is available from the British Library

Library of Congress Cataloguing in Publication data
Apollonius, Rhodius, author.
[Argonautica. Book 4]
Argonautica: Book IV / Apollonius of Rhodes; edited by Richard Hunter.
pages   cm. – (Cambridge Greek and Latin Classics)
Includes bibliographical references and indexes.
ISBN 978-1-107-06351-8 (hardback)
1. Argonauts (Greek mythology) – Poetry.   2. Jason (Greek mythology) –
Poetry.   3. Medea, consort of Aegeus, King of Athens (Mythological character) –
Poetry.   4. Epic poetry, Greek.   I. Hunter, R. L. (Richard L.), editor.   II. Title.
PA3872.A13   2015
883′.01–dc23
2014048899

ISBN 978-1-107-06351-8 Hardback
ISBN 978-1-107-63675-0 Paperback

CONTENTS

ACKNOWLEDGEMENTS

The Introduction and Commentary have benefited from the perceptive suggestions of Pat Easterling and Neil Hopkinson. Thanks to the kindness of Dr Amin Benaissa, the courtesy of the Egypt Exploration Society and the advice of Professor Peter Parsons, I have been able to make reference in the Commentary to some unpublished readings preserved on Oxyrhynchus papyri; I am very grateful for this generous help. My debt to my predecessors, most notably Hermann Fränkel, Enrico Livrea, and Francis Vian, will, I hope, be very obvious. Michael Sharp and Elizabeth Hanlon of Cambridge University Press have been supportive and helpful as always.

REFERENCES AND ABBREVIATIONS

References to *Arg.* 1–3 are by book and line number only, e.g. 2.700; references to Book 4 are by line number only. Vian's Budé edition of *Arg.* (Paris 1974–1981) is cited by volume and page number, e.g. Vian III 165. Other commentaries and editions of *Arg.* are cited by author name, e.g. Mooney, Paduano-Fusillo. References to notes on Book 3, e.g. 3.661n., are to R. Hunter, *Apollonius of Rhodes, Argonautica Book III*, Cambridge 1989. Fragment numbers for Callimachus follow Pfeiffer, unless stated otherwise. Σ indicates 'scholium' or 'scholia'.

Barrington	R. J. A. Talbert ed., *Barrington atlas of the Greek and Roman world*, Princeton 2000
Beekes	R. Beekes, *Etymological dictionary of Greek*, Leiden 2010
CA	J. U. Powell ed., *Collectanea Alexandrina*, Oxford 1925
CEG	P. A. Hansen, *Carmina epigraphica Graeca*, 2 vols., Berlin 1983, 1989
Chantraine	P. Chantraine, *Grammaire homérique*, Paris 1948–1953
Denniston	J. D. Denniston, *The Greek particles*, 2nd edn, Oxford 1954
D–K	H. Diels and W. Kranz, *Die Fragmente der Vorsokratiker*, 6th edn, Berlin 1951
FGE	D. L. Page ed., *Further Greek epigrams*, Cambridge 1981
FGrHist	F. Jacoby, *Die Fragmente der griechischen Historiker*, Berlin 1923–1930, Leiden 1940–1958
FHG	C. Müller and others, *Fragmenta historicorum Graecorum*, Paris 1848–1885
GGM	C. Müller, *Geographi Graeci minores*, Paris 1855–1861
GP	A. S. F. Gow and D. L. Page, *The Greek Anthology. The Garland of Philip*, Cambridge 1968
HE	A. S. F. Gow and D. L. Page, *The Greek Anthology. Hellenistic epigrams*, Cambridge 1965
Heitsch	E. Heitsch, *Die griechischen Dichterfragmente der römischen Kaiserzeit*, Vol. 1, 2nd edn, Göttingen 1963
IG	*Inscriptiones Graecae*, Berlin 1873–

K–B	R. Kühner, *Ausführliche Grammatik der griechischen Sprache*, I, 3rd edn, revised by F. Blass, Hanover 1890–2
K–G	R. Kühner, *Ausführliche Grammatik der griechischen Sprache*, II, 3rd edn, revised by B. Gerth, Hanover/ Leipzig 1898–1904
KRS	G. S. Kirk, J. E. Raven, and M. Schofield, *The Presocratic philosophers*, 2nd edn, Cambridge 1983
LfgrE	*Lexikon des frühgriechischen Epos*, Göttingen 1979–2010
LIMC	*Lexicon iconographicum mythologiae classicae*, Zurich 1981–1999
LSA	F. Sokolowski, *Lois sacrées des cités grecques. Supplément*, Paris 1962
OLD	P. G. W. Glare and others, *Oxford Latin dictionary*, Oxford 1968–1982
Pfeiffer	R. Pfeiffer, *Callimachus*, 2 vols., Oxford 1949–1953
PGM	K. Preisendanz, *Papyri Graecae magicae. Die griechischen Zauberpapyri*, 2nd edn, Stuttgart 1973–4
PMG	D. L. Page, *Poetae melici Graeci*, Oxford 1962
RE	A. Pauly, G. Wissowa, W. Kroll, *et al.* (eds.), *Real-Encyclopädie der classischen Altertumswissenschaft*, Stuttgart/Munich 1893–1978
Rhodes–Osborne	P. J. Rhodes and R. Osborne, *Greek historical inscriptions 404–323 BC*, Oxford 2003
Schwyzer	E. Schwyzer, *Griechische Grammatik*, 3 vols., Munich 1939–1953
SH	H. Lloyd-Jones and P. Parsons, *Supplementum Hellenisticum*, Berlin/New York 1983
SLG	D. L. Page, *Supplementum lyricis Graecis*, Oxford 1974
Smyth	H. W. Smyth, *Greek grammar*, Cambridge MA 1920
Thompson, *Birds*	D. W. Thompson, *A glossary of Greek birds*, 2nd edn, London 1936
Thompson, *Fishes*	D. W. Thompson, *A glossary of Greek fishes*, London 1947
Totti	M. Totti, *Ausgewählte Texte der Isis- und Sarapis-Religion*, Hildesheim 1985

MAP

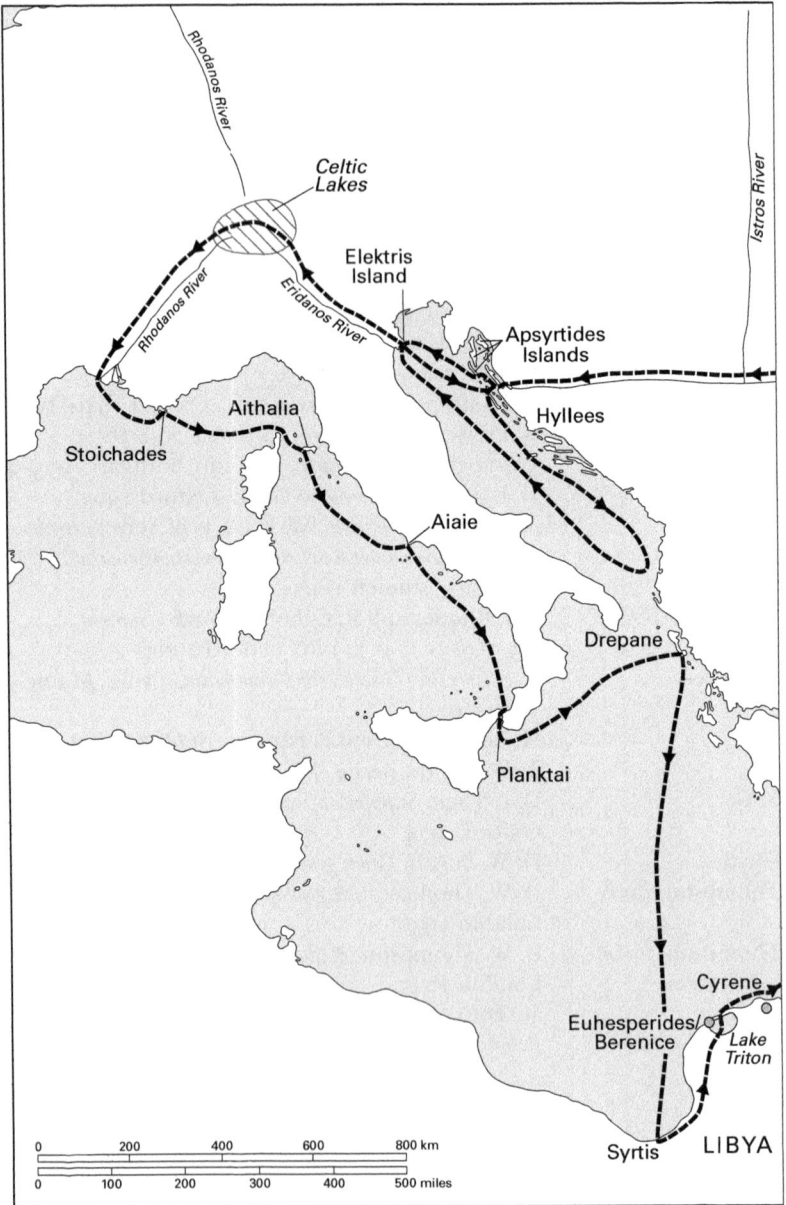

The voyage of the Argonauts

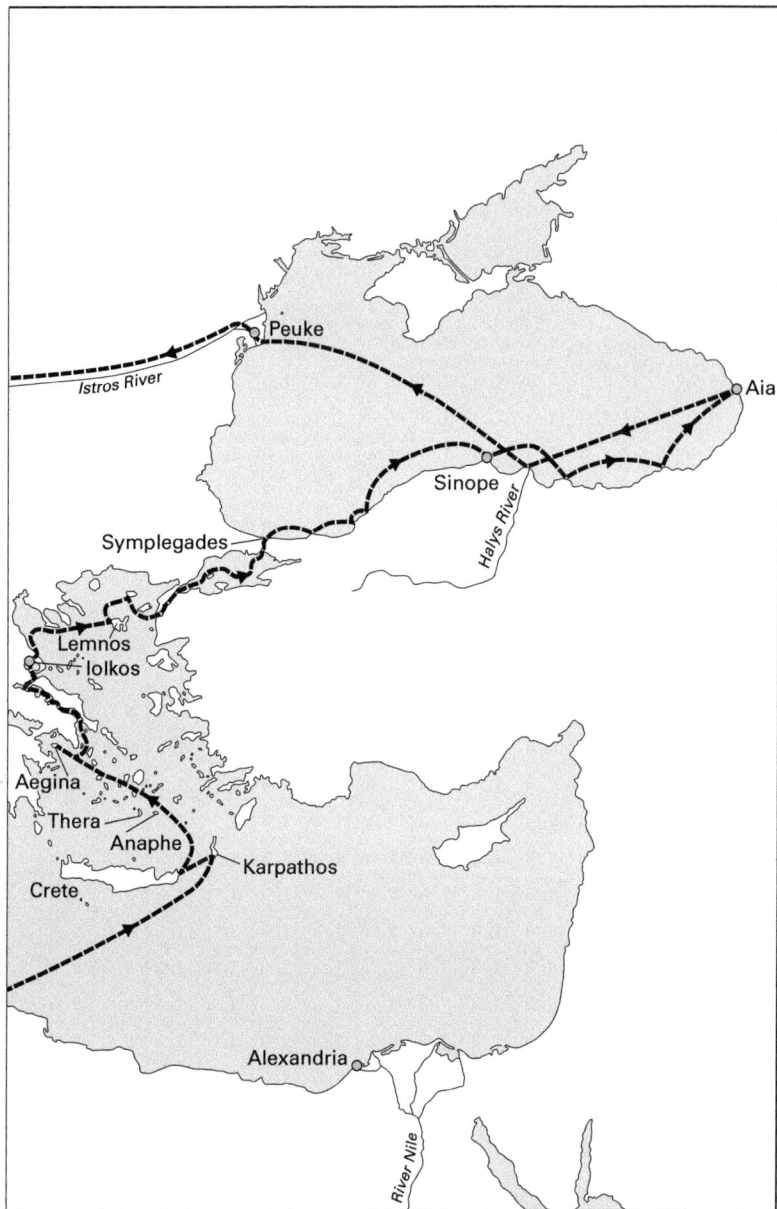

(cont.)

INTRODUCTION

1 APOLLONIUS AND THE ARGONAUTICA

Our principal sources for the life of Apollonius and for the composition of
Arg. are three biographical notices, going back at least to the Roman
imperial period, and what seems to be a list of those who were in charge
of the Royal Library at Alexandria, preserved in a miscellany on a papyrus
of the second century AD; this evidence is, however, riddled with contradiction, anecdote and some obvious errors.[1] A generous reading of these
texts suggests that Ap. served as Librarian at Alexandria in the central
decades of the third century, but poetic and scholarly activity well into the
reign of Ptolemy III Euergetes (246–221 BC) can hardly be ruled out and
may indeed be thought probable. Uncertainty is increased by the fact that
Arg. does not contain explicit references to contemporary events and
personages, and the identification of implicit references, as also the explanation of elements of the narrative in terms of contemporary concerns, is
always a matter for critical judgement and hence potential difference of
opinion;[2] the history of scholarship on *Arg.* clearly illustrates how difficult
it is for agreement to be reached. Similar uncertainties beset attempts to
establish absolute (or even relative) chronologies through the obvious
intertextual relations between *Arg.* and some works of Theocritus and
Callimachus.[3] In particular, the very rich pattern of correspondence
between *Arg.* and Callimachus' *Aitia* has suggested to most of those who
have studied the matter that Ap. is usually the borrower from Callimachus
(which also seems to have been the prevailing view of ancient γραμματικοί),
but that does not take account of the possibility (to put it at its weakest)
that the two poets, working in the same Alexandrian institution, were
engaged in an on-going interchange of poetic ideas. We are, moreover,
hampered by our uncertainty of the process and chronology by which the
four books of the *Aitia* were circulated,[4] and the argument is thus in
constant danger of merely chasing its own tail.

---

[1] Hunter 1989: 1–12 will not be repeated here; translations and fuller discussion
of the ancient evidence may be sought there. See also Rengakos 1992, Green 1997:
1–8, Lefkowitz 2008. Murray 2012 has stressed that we would do well not to assume
that the list of (?) Librarians on *POxy.* 1241 has very good authority, even allowing
for the correction of what look to be a couple of obvious slips.

[2] The rich geographical and cultural material in *Arg.* allows the thought that
much was indeed determined by Ptolemaic and contemporary concerns, but
(again) persuasive 'proof' is very hard to find. For certain aspects of how *Arg.*
reflects a third-century world see Hunter 1995.

[3] See pp. 21–5 below.

[4] There is a helpful summary of views in Harder 2012: 1.2–15.

1

Jackie Murray has recently proposed that a pattern of astronomical indications allows the Argonauts' progress to be mapped precisely against the astronomical calendar of 238 BC, the year in which Ptolemy III seems to have inaugurated a new calendrical era for Egypt.[5] Such a hypothesis can hardly be ruled out on the basis of the ancient biographical notices that have survived, and there is in fact nothing inherently implausible about a date as late as this.[6] What any such reckoning cannot, however, successfully encompass is the length of time (many years?) the composition of a work such as *Arg.* may have taken and the possibility, or even likelihood, that parts at least were constantly being revised; although there are no clear signs of this, we cannot assume that the text we have was considered by Ap. to be fully finished.[7] As for revision, for six places in Book 1, and perhaps also for two in Book 2, the scholia cite variant versions, ranging from one to five verses, which they ascribe to a 'preliminary edition' (προέκδοσις) of the poem; it is clear from the nature of these verses that we are indeed dealing with a different text of the poem, something which cannot be explained as a concentration of the kind of casual variants which inevitably arise in the course of transmission.[8] What lies behind these facts, and to what extent knowledge of this 'preliminary edition' has shaped some of the anecdotal tradition that obviously surrounded Ap. in antiquity, in particular the alleged 'quarrel' with Callimachus, remain fascinating provocations to speculation. The very existence, however, of this προέκδοσις, whatever the term denotes, is a reminder that the search for a date of 'publication' for a poem such as *Arg.* is directed at a very different object than would be the case for a modern literary work.

Many of the principal concerns of *Arg.*, travel, geography and ethnography, cultic and cultural aetiology, female psychology and characterization, the power and effects of *erôs*, magic and the supernatural, are shared not just with other poetry of the third century, but also with what we can reconstruct of Hellenistic literate culture more broadly. It is often observed that the very breadth of the canvas across which the narrative of the epic unfolds is not merely a re-imagining of the spirit of the *Odyssey*, and in particular of the encounters of Odysseus with 'other', often

---

[5] Murray 2014. Murray is to publish a full version of her views in a forthcoming monograph, and a proper judgement about the matter will have to wait until then.

[6] For the view that 1021–2 echo Callimachus' 'Lock of Berenice' (Euergetes' young bride), a poem which cannot have been composed before 245 BC, see n. ad loc. So too, 1629–30 seem related to Callimachus' 'Victoria Berenices', a poem probably of *c.* 240, cf. n. ad loc.

[7] See, e.g., nn. on 945–7, 1601–2.

[8] On these verses of the *proekdosis* cf. Fantuzzi 1988: 87–120.

threatening cultures, but also seems to reflect the broad horizons of the international aspirations of the Ptolemies.

2 THE FOURTH BOOK

The events of Book 4 may be schematically set out as follows:[9]

1–5 Address to the Muse
6–108 Medea's flight from Aietes' palace and reception by the Argonauts
109–82 Medea and Jason take the Fleece
183–293 Flight from Colchis to the Paphlagonian coast
294–337 Argonauts and Colchians sail up the Istros to the Adriatic
338–521 Planning, execution and aftermath of killing of Apsyrtos
522–657 Trip through central Europe to western Mediterranean
658–752 Purification of Jason and Medea by Circe
753–981 Hera and Thetis help the Argonauts pass through the Planktai
982–1222 Stop on Drepane; wedding of Jason and Medea
1223–1392 The Syrtis and the Libyan desert; *Argo* transported to Lake Triton
1393–1619 The Hesperides, deaths of Kanthos and Mopsus, intervention by Triton, gift of clod of earth to Euphemos
1620–88 Voyage to Crete; episode of Talos
1689–1772 Voyage home: Anaphe, Euphemos' dream, Aeginetan *hydrophoria*
1773–81 Farewell to the heroes

Book 3 had concluded with perhaps the most epically 'marked' scene of the whole poem, Jason's overcoming of the fire-breathing bulls and the earthborn warriors. Book 4, by contrast, is characterized by scenes of flight, of despair, and of deception, but also by an eerie other-worldliness (the dragon which guards the Fleece, the ritualized killing of Apsyrtos, Phaethon's smouldering body, Circe's 'Empedoclean' animals, the emptiness of the Syrtis, the Garden of the Hesperides, Triton, Talos etc.) which we have good reason to believe was as experimental when Ap. composed it as it seems to us now. As the Argonauts confront one such τέρας after another, readers too are forced to stretch their own imaginations to encompass the new and the strange: Ap. makes all of us fellow-travellers with the Argonauts. Hera's protection of the Argonauts (cf. 11, 510, 576–80, 640–8, 753–841) lends some pattern to the first parts of the book, but a powerful sense of improvisation and randomness, nowhere more strongly felt than in Jason's formulation to Medea of how he plans to

---

[9] This plan is intended merely as a guide; it does not seek to distinguish the major and minor structural markers which Ap. includes in the text.

deal with the threat from Apsyrtos' pursuit (395–409n.), in the purpose-less 'drift' of the Argonauts past the stench from Phaethon's body and in Hera's intervention to prevent them taking a fatal turn (619–44), lends Book 4 a remarkably unsettling feeling; no more than the Argonauts do we really know where we are.

Book 4 picks up and continues some of the themes of the Greek encounter with foreign cultures adumbrated already in Book 3. Jason had described to Medea the patterns of Greek culture and civilization (3.1085–95), apparently so remote from the barbarian land she inhabits, and she – with what is, for the reader, in the light of Euripides' *Medea*, a savage irony – contrasts Greek respect for agreements with what she knows of her own father;[10] this, on the surface, is a distant eastern land where it is not just burial customs (3.200–9n.) and Medea's practices with drugs and body-parts (51–2) which are surpassingly 'other'. That theme resurfaces strongly in Book 4 after the securing of the Fleece, when Jason presents the success of the Argonauts' expedition as determining whether or not 'Hellas' will win great glory (202–5, with n. ad loc.) and proclaims Medea the benefactor of 'all Achaia' (195–6).[11] In evoking both the Trojan War and the Greek wars against the Persians, Jason casts the present poem within a long tradition of Hellenic struggle. Aietes, conversely, speaks the language of tyrannical threat (231–5n.), so different from the communal values and ὁμόνοια of the Argonauts;[12] the fact that Medea's subsequent actions and those of the two teams of pursuing Colchians are driven by overriding fear of returning to face punishment at Aietes' hands speaks volumes for the difference between cultures. The theme recurs in Arete's arguments to her husband on Drepane, where 'the whole city laughed with pleasure at their arrival – you would say that they rejoiced over their own children' (996–7): Aietes, according to Arete, lives so far away that they know nothing of him, whereas Argos and Thessaly are close at hand. In his reply, Alcinous acknowledges that Aietes could, if he chose, bring war to Hellas (1103), as the barbarian Persians notoriously had done.

It is indeed Medea, the 'foreign body' who accompanies the Argonauts back to Greece, through whom the theme of inter-cultural confrontation is mediated. Much modern discussion has been devoted to the question of Medea's state of mind and attitude to Jason in Book 4,[13] but Ap. uses what may be termed 'mirror passages' between Books 3 and 4 to mark the consequences for Medea of her decision (made with Hera's reinforce-ment, 3.818) to help Jason. Thus, for example, her nocturnal flight in terror from Colchis (41–53) evokes (and reverses) her procession to the

---

[10] Cf. 3.1105n.   [11] For such ideas cf. also, e.g., 1.243, 3.347.
[12] On the importance of ὁμόνοια in *Arg.* see Hunter 1995: 21–4.
[13] The bibliography may be pursued through Hunter 1987 and Dyck 1989.

temple of Hecate to meet Jason in Book 3, just as the simile comparing
Medea in her fear of being handed over to the pursuing Colchians to a
poor working woman (1062–6) forms a pair with the simile depicting the
first awakening of her love for Jason (3.291–7). What is stressed in Book 4
is not, as many critics would have it, any 'extinction' of Medea's *erôs* (far
from it, cf. 445–9, 1168), but rather her fearful isolation now that she has
cut her ties with her family (vividly expressed by Circe at 739–48) and,
particularly, with a father whose penchant for terrible violence and punishment she knows well (e.g. 1043–4); in Book 4, Medea has no alternative
but to follow the consequences of her decision and thus entrust herself
entirely to the protection and promises of Jason and his crew (88–91).
Even in Book 3, Medea had been racked by doubt and guilt almost as soon
as she had handed the φάρμακα over to Jason, an action which she viewed
as a κακὸν ἔργον (3.1157–62), but there is no way back. Arete's defence
of Medea to Alcinous (1080–3), which does not include the killing of
Apsyrtos (of which Arete is ignorant), effectively accepts this view of
Medea's abandonment of Colchis, which is indeed how Medea had presented it to her (1015–19), while glossing Medea's behaviour as the kind
of 'mistake upon mistake' which humans constantly make. Medea's principal actions in Book 4, the taking of the Fleece, the luring of Apsyrtos to
his death and the destruction of Talos, are all aimed at securing a safe and
successful *nostos* for herself and the Argonauts.[14] In fact, however, we know
that her safe arrival in Greece will eventually lead to a very bitter fracturing
of her relationship with Jason, a break most clearly foreshadowed in Book
4 in her speeches of reproach to Jason at 355–90 (where see n.) and to the
Argonauts in turn at 1031–52, which evoke and echo the harsh exchanges
between Jason and Medea in Euripides' *Medea*, thus keeping the events of
that tragedy firmly before our eyes.

   A striking feature of Book 4 is indeed the rich use of tragic models to
mark certain significant moments and narrative patterns.[15] The dominant
tragic pattern in Book 4 is not the foreshadowing of the events of
Euripides' *Medea*, but rather a web of analogies between the killing of
Apsyrtos and tragic versions of the death of Agamemnon and Orestes'
subsequent killing of Clytemnestra. This pattern, by imitating the way in

[14] The poet leaves somewhat unclear why the Argonauts wish to land in Crete
and therefore are threatened by Talos (cf. 1635–6n.), and it is sometimes claimed
that this episode is simply added in an inorganic fashion for the sake of the
description of Medea's magical powers. That Talos is a 'leftover' of the previous
Bronze Race is clearly relevant to the important pattern whereby the Argonauts are
made to confront earlier stages of the cosmos (Hunter 1993: 166–7), but from
Medea's point of view Talos is simply one more obstacle to be removed.
[15] Book 3 also had almost certainly drawn extensively on tragic, very probably
Sophoclean, models, Hunter 1989: 19. On *Arg.* and tragedy more generally cf.
Nishimura-Jensen 1996.

which the paradigm of Orestes' revenge floats in and out of the *Odyssey*, belongs in part with Ap.'s large-scale debt to the Homeric poems (p. 14–21 below); the Homeric model is, morever, elaborated through echoes, including specific verbal allusions, to tragic treatments of the House of Atreus, in particular Aeschylus' *Oresteia*. Both the killing itself and the sacrificial imagery with which it is described, as well as the subsequent mutilation of the body (477–8), all evoke the death of Agamemnon in both epic and tragedy (468n., 477n.), and the explicit place given to the Furies (476, 714) suggests, above all, the aftermath of the death of Clytemnestra in Aeschylus. So too, the purification of Medea and Jason by Circe replays the Delphic purification of Orestes (560n., 693–4n., 705–6n.); Clytemnestra's troubling and prophetic dream is here transferred to Circe herself (663–4n.), as Apsyrtos (like Agamemnon) is not allowed any warning at all of what is to happen. The epic background of much of this material lies not so much in the *Iliad* and the *Odyssey* as in the Cyclic poems, and so these tragic patterns must also be seen within Ap.'s considerable debt to, and *mimesis* of the manner of, the Epic Cycle.[16] There is, then, a rich literary and cultural history written into the epic, which produces an effect of deep layering.

One result of this layering is a sense of successive generic stages in an attempt to encompass and describe a now very past world. What, for example, did Ap.'s contemporaries know of *maschalismos* as a 'real' practice (cf. 477n.)? When the poet says that spitting out the blood of the murdered man 'three times' is θέμις for murderers (479), we may ask what kind of imaginative act we have to perform in order to think ourselves into the past. If early epic and tragedy are two genres which offer models of such imaginative recreation, then Ap. also uses Presocratic science and speculation as a third. Circe is accompanied by creatures which resemble Empedocles' weird forms which first emerged at the beginning of time (672–5n., 676–81n.); Empedoclean cosmogony is thus another cultural model for imagining the past. Parmenides too is evoked in the 'gates and halls of Night' from where the Rhodanos is said to rise (629–30n.), thus 'familiarizing' an extraordinary geography but also – given the context of Parmenides' proem – emphasizing the inspired strangeness of the whole. So too, Medea's powers of 'the evil eye' by which she bewitches Talos are in part described through an evocation of Presocratic physical theory (cf. 1665–72n.).

This marked use of Presocratic speculation is also a contribution to a debate about the kind of traces of 'history' which poetry preserves; our fullest ancient source for that debate is the discussion of Homer in Book 1 of Strabo's *Geography*, written in the time of Augustus, but we know that it

---

[16] See below p. 140.

was a very active debate in third-century Alexandria. Eratosthenes' *bon mot* that one would be able to follow the path of Odysseus' wanderings 'when the shoemaker who stitched the bag of winds was found' (Strabo 1.2.15) is only the best-known reflection of this concern to establish what, if any, 'reality' was to be expected from poetry. Strabo's answer was that Homer's geography was indeed rooted in reality, however much that reality had been elaborated with pleasure-giving μῦθοι, and he will not have been the first to take this view. Apollonius' 'Odyssean' geography (cf. below) already shows clearly how the Homeric hero's wanderings had been located in a known geography (SW Italy, Sicily, Corcyra), even if one where marvellous *paradoxa* can still happen. The use of Presocratic patterns allows the Argonauts to confront extraordinary material which is, nevertheless, sanctioned by an authority which is beyond the 'scholarly' concerns of the Alexandrian Library; from an Alexandrian perspective, the Presocratics (particularly those who composed in hexameters) were, to oversimplify, poised between μῦθος and λόγος, between poetic myth and rational reflection, and this made them very suitable vehicles through which to express the peculiar nature of the 'truth' of poetry. We may perhaps think of this as an alternative model to allegorization for how poetic material could be presented and/or understood.

3 THE RETURN ITINERARY

At 2.420–2 Phineus tells Jason that, if the Argonauts pass safely through the Clashing Rocks on their voyage to Colchis, 'a god will lead you by another route away from Aia', and the Argonauts remember his words at 4.254–5 when they pause on the south coast of the Black Sea in their escape from the pursuing Colchians. Ap.'s readers will have been tantalized by Phineus' riddling lack of detail, which stands in sharp contrast to the pedantic precision of his instructions for the outward voyage, as both poetic and geographical tradition had bequeathed to Ap. a variety of possible return routes for the Argonauts.[17] One possibility was in fact to return by the same (direct) route as that of the outward voyage, as the Clashing Rocks were now fixed immobile and no longer posed an almost insurmountable obstacle (2.604–6); the scholia tell us that Sophocles (in the *Skythai*, fr. 547R), Herodorus of Heraclea (*FGrHist* 31 F10) and Callimachus (fr. 9) were among those who had exploited that possibility.[18] Ap.'s Argonauts do not know (cf. 1252–5, 2.1190–1) that this will be one

[17] Helpful surveys in Delage 1930: ch. 3, Vian III 11–20, Vian 1987, Dufner 1988: 128–33.
[18] Fraser 1972: II 628–9, Harder 2012: 2.162–3. It remains a puzzle how Callimachus combined a return through the Bosporus with episodes clearly set in the west (e.g. on Corcyra).

consequence of their success in traversing the Rocks (this information was perhaps one of the things which Phineus did not believe it was *themis* for them to know, 2.311–13), but little is made of the potential narrative ironies that such a situation lays open. Rather, Ap. adopts a return route which is not only as ἕτερος, 'different', as possible in certain respects from the outward voyage, a difference in fact neatly symbolized by the contrast between the passage through the Clashing Rocks and that through the Planktai, but one which allows him to encompass the whole tradition of Argonautic voyaging to which he was heir. By claiming authority for this route in the primeval knowledge of Egyptian priests and the travels of a now nameless conqueror and civilizer, whose records survive at Aia (259–81, cf. 272–6n.), Ap. not only creates a marked difference from Phineus' dry and precise *periegesis* (cf. 257–93n.), but appeals to a secret wisdom befitting the extraordinary journey which the Argonauts are to undertake, a journey which will, in some senses, take them too back to the beginning of time.

From an early date the Argonauts were brought back to Greece by circuitous and fantastic routes. Hesiod (fr. 241)[19] apparently took them from Aia up the Phasis, and from there into the stream of Ocean in the extreme north, from where they voyaged west and south around the imagined land mass to Africa, where they then carried the *Argo* across the desert to the Mediterranean; this was in principle the route adopted also by Pindar in *Pythian* 4 and, so the scholia inform us, by Antimachus in the *Lyde* (fr. 76 Matthews). Libya, which plays such an important role in *Arg.* 4, had a very firm place in the Argonautic saga. Herodotus 4.179 reports a *logos* which is very reminiscent of *Arg.*, and almost certainly echoed in it,[20] but also very different. Before the expedition, the story goes, Jason wanted to make dedications at Delphi, including a bronze tripod; as he was sailing around the Peloponnese, he was blown off course at Cape Malea southwards to Libya and was caught in the shallows of Lake Triton,[21] where the eponymous god appeared to him and told him to give him the tripod; in return for this, Triton showed Jason and his crew how to leave the lake. The god placed the tripod in his own temple and told the crew that when one of their descendants carried off the tripod, 'one hundred Greek cities would be established around Lake Triton'; as a result of this, the local inhabitants hid the tripod. Herodotus places these events much further west than is Ap.'s 'Lake Triton' (cf. 1311n.), but Ap.'s narrative at 1537–1619 clearly follows the Herodotean pattern very

---

[19] It is debated in which poem or poems (the *Catalogue*, the *Megalai Ehoiai?*) Hesiod told of the Argonauts' return; see Hirschberger 2004: 452–4, D'Alessio 2005: 195–9.

[20] Cf. 1570n., 1581–2n., 1731–64n.

[21] With Jason's ἀπορία of Hdt. 4.179.2 cf. 1539–40.

closely.[22] Herodotus' account also reminds us how deep and early is the fusion of the adventures of Odysseus, who was also blown off course at Cape Malea, with those of the Argonauts; Ap.'s Argonauts will both lead and follow where Odysseus travelled.[23]

Two prose writers nearer in time to Ap. opened new geographical possibilities which he was to exploit. Probably in the first half of the fourth century, in a work *On Harbours*, Timagetos described the Istros (Danube) as rising in the 'Celtic mountains' and splitting into two branches, one emptying into the Black Sea (presumably) on the NW coast, the other into the Mediterranean, though exactly where is uncertain (Σ 257–62b, 282–91a = *FHG* IV 519);[24] the scholia report that Timagetos brought the Argonauts into the Mediterranean through these two branches and claim that Ap. 'follows' him in this. Scholiasts, like modern scholars, are fond of identifying a direct connection between texts which happen to survive, but we do not in fact know whether Timagetos was the first to propose such a river system, nor to what extent he was directly influential upon Ap. What is certain, however, is that by the end of the fourth century it was a common idea that the Istros had a branch which emptied, not west of Italy, but rather on the north coast of the Adriatic;[25] the existence of the Istroi tribe on the northern Adriatic coast and another (small) river there named Istros no doubt helped to facilitate this misconception (cf. Strabo 1.3.15, Diod. Sic. 4.56.8).

Diodorus Siculus 4.56.3–6 reports that 'not a few both of the ancient historians and of those who came after, including Timaeus (*FGrHist* 566 F85)' reported that the Argonauts sailed up the Tanais (Don) to its source and then dragged the *Argo* over land to another river which flowed into Ocean; they then sailed anticlockwise round Ocean and into the Mediterranean through the Pillars of Heracles at its western end.[26] This itinerary allowed such writers to explain 'visible signs' of the Argonauts'

[22] Herodotus notes that Jason was caught 'in the shallows of Lake Triton, before sighting land'; Ap. (and perhaps others before him) redistributed this motif into two parts – the Argonauts are indeed trapped in Lake Triton, but the unforeseen shallows seem to correspond to the Syrtis of 1237–49.
[23] See below pp. 14–17.   [24] Cf. further *RE* 6A.1071–3.
[25] Cf. 282–3n., Ps.-Scylax 20 (with Shipley 2011: 105), Theopompus, *FGrHist* 115 F129, Arist. *HA* 7.598b15–17. The geography of the northern Adriatic, as it appears in *Arg.* 4, is very inexact and impressionistic. Strabo 1.2.39, immediately after citing Callimachus fr. 11 on the Colchian foundations in Illyria (cf. below p. 22), reports that 'some say that Jason's crew sailed a great distance up the Istros, and others say that he reached the Adriatic'. It is unclear to whom Strabo is referring (cf. n. 47 below), but the juxtaposition of that notice to an extensive quotation from Callimachus is at least suggestive.
[26] Σ 282–91b ascribes this Argonautic route to Scymnus of Chios (fr. 5 Gisinger); on this periegetic writer of (probably) the late third – early second century BC cf. *RE* 3A.661–72.

presence in the western Mediterranean, such as on Aethalia (Elba, cf.
654–8), and this would have been particularly important for Timaeus,
the great historian of the Greek west, who was clearly an important source
for Ap.[27] It also allowed the Argonauts to come into close contact with sites
associated with Odysseus' travels by those who placed a major part of them
in the west, rather than removing them to the outer reaches of Ocean, the
so-called ἐξωκεανισμός (cf. Strabo 1.2.37); this too was to prove very important for Ap. After the voyage eastwards (at least as far as the west coast of
Italy), the Argonauts were blown by winds to the Libyan Syrtis, where they
were guided to safety by Triton, 'who ruled Libya at that time', and in
return they gave him 'a bronze tripod inscribed with ancient characters',
which remained 'until recent times' among the people of Euhesperides.
Diodorus proceeds to criticize unnamed others who took the Argonauts
up the Istros to its source and then down a branch of the same river which
allegedly flowed into the Adriatic; 'time has demonstrated them wrong'
(cf. Strabo 1.2.39).

From these various poetic, historiographical and geographical traditions, Ap. constructed (or adopted) a route which allowed his Argonauts
to visit most of the places previously associated with them, except for
Ocean and the far west of the Mediterranean.[28] In his scheme (see the
map at the beginning of the book which shows the route as envisaged by
Ap., including his geography of rivers, imposed on a modern map of the
Mediterranean), the Argonauts (and one group of pursuing Colchians)
sail NE across the Black Sea, and then directly to the Adriatic, by means of
the Istros, which is imagined to flow from the far north before splitting
into branches which flowed into the Black Sea and the Adriatic.[29] After
their Adriatic adventures, including the murder of Apsyrtos, the
Argonauts enter the Eridanos (Po, cf. 505–6n.) and proceed NW until,
thanks to Hera's intervention, they turn south down the Rhodanos
(Rhone), which was imagined to flow from the 'Celtic Lakes' both north
into Ocean and south to the Mediterranean. From there the Argonauts'
route home encompasses the west coast of Italy, the Straits of Messina, with
Scylla, Charybdis and the Wandering Rocks, Corcyra ('Drepane', the
Homeric Scherie), Libya, and finally Crete and the Aegean islands. The
two major 'joins' in the narrative are both clearly signalled, and in such a

[27] Interest in an Ocean route for the Argonauts may have been increased by the
publication near the end of the fourth century of Pytheas' *On Ocean*, an account of
his travels in the northern Atlantic, cf. Cunliffe 2001, Roller 2006: 57–91; the date
of this work remains, however, fiercely debated.
[28] We cannot say whether Ap.'s route was, in its complex comprehensiveness,
original to him, but it seems not unlikely; see Dufner 1988: 145–6.
[29] Callimachus too (frr. 9–11) used this route for the pursuing Colchians, but
not apparently for his Argonauts; see p. 22 below.

way that the 'composite' nature of the route, and hence of the poet's choices, is advertised:[30] a question to the Muses at 552–6 marks the end of the Adriatic adventures and a shift to the voyage to the western Mediterranean, and at 1225–7 the Libyan adventures are 'fated', 'proper', αἴσιμον, and the north winds which carry the Argonauts off (1232–6) come with greater suddenness than usual.

The 'all-inclusive' itinerary of Ap.'s Argonauts, which embraces, on the outward voyage, the northern Aegean, the Hellespont and the south coast of the Black Sea, and, on the return, most of central Europe, the Adriatic, the western Mediterranean, North Africa and the southern Aegean, gives *Arg.* something of the flavour of a *periplous*, or account of the coasts of the known world (or part of it); this sense of a geographical 'tour' is emphasized by ἀκτὰς Παγασηίδας in the final verse, which brings the Argonauts back to exactly where they set off and to a geographical designation which has not been mentioned since their departure. Such a linear (or circular)[31] structure is set in pointed opposition to the *Odyssey*, in which Odysseus' departure for Troy is only briefly alluded to (*Od.* 18.257–71) and he is not even allowed to recognize Ithaca on his return (13.187–216). By the third century there was a rich tradition of geographical 'tours', in both poetry and prose, as well as passages included within other kinds of literature which are clearly related to what was to become a flourishing independent genre (cf., e.g., Hes. frr. 150–6 (pursuit of the Harpies by the Boreads), Aesch., *PV* 707–877).[32] Most such works available to Ap. have not survived, but the so-called '*Periplous* of Pseudo-Scylax', which probably dates in essence from the time of Alexander, 'describes the coasts of the Mediterranean and Black Sea, beginning at Gibraltar and proceeding clockwise to return to the same place (and a little way into the Atlantic)';[33] the style is for the most part very dry and factual, but the significant number of places where it sheds light on Ap.'s geography is suggestive for the extent of the poet's debt to these prose traditions. Phineus' foretelling in Book 2 of the journey along the south coast of the Black Sea clearly evokes the dry style of one kind of *periplous* or *periegesis*, with its admixture of ethnography and mythology,[34] but in Book 4 the emphasis, as we have seen, rather lies on the encounter with the mysterious and the uncanny. Ap.'s Argonauts both follow and pave the

---

[30] See Hunter 2008b: 138–40.
[31] For *Arg.* as a 'cyclic' poem cf. below pp. 19–20, 421–521n.
[32] The best introduction to the richness of this tradition is Marcianus of Heraclea (perhaps 6th cent. AD), *GGM* 1 564–7, who divides such works into *periploi* of a particular region, of the entire Mediterranean, and of Ocean ('the external sea'); for modern accounts see Marcotte 2000: xxiv-lxxii, Janni 1984.
[33] Shipley 2011: 1; on Pseudo-Scylax see Peretti 1979, 1983, Shipley 2011.
[34] Pearson 1938, Hunter 1993: 94–5.

way for Odysseus (see section 4 below), but they also subsume the *Odyssey* into what is, from one perspective, a poetic history of Greek knowledge of the world, a history in which Homer, Herodotus, and Hellenistic science all play significant roles.[35]

It is in the Libyan adventures where Book 4 might be thought at its most experimental.[36] The opening description of the Syrtis (1235–49, cf. 1235n.), a place from where *nostos* is no longer possible (1235–6, 1272–6), replaces the landscapes of the *Odyssey* with a vision of nothingness which evokes the topographies of geographical and paradoxographical writing. The dramatic shift is pointed by the very Odyssean wind which drives the Argonauts south to Libya (cf. 1228–31, 1232–4nn.), but what awaits them is something quite unlike the perils faced by Odysseus. The description of the Syrtis evokes by reversal the famous description of an island lying off the coast of the land of the Cyclopes (*Od.* 9.116–51).[37] Both spaces are uninhabited and neither supports any form of pastoralism; whereas, however, the Syrtis cannot support human life (there is, for example, no drinking water (1247)), the Homeric island would, if exploited, support a flourishing population of traders: it has excellent agricultural land, fresh water, and wonderful harbours, and even offers Odysseus and his men, in the absence of any inhabitants, a very rich supply of food in the form of wild goats ('we sat feasting on limitless meat and sweet wine all day until the sun went down', *Od.* 9.161–2). The Syrtis, by contrast, is a negative space caught between land and sea, a place where ships and the art of navigation are worthless (1261–76) and the most that any man trapped there can expect is 'a most piteous death' by hunger (1295–6), a death that will erase all trace that such a man ever existed (1305–7). The inversion of 'nature' represented by the Syrtis is pointed by the extraordinary comparison of the Argonauts to men whose grim fate has been foreshadowed by prodigies and reversals of the cosmic order (cf. 1280–9n.).

In the Libyan Syrtis the most Greek of all crafts, navigation, is useless, and the steersman Ankaios abandons himself to despair (1259–60). In this 'no-man's land' (cf. esp. 1239–40, 1247–9) of dream-like mirages, of absence, emptiness and negativity, a sea which is no sea, a ἅλμη ἄπλοος (1270–1), Greek knowledge is so powerless that the *Argo* must be transported over land. Here even Heracles' 'traces' are wiped out by blowing sand (4.1463–4), and there are no directional signs, almost quite literally no geography, and certainly no γεωγραφία.[38] It is more than a sense of

---

[35] Meyer 2008 offers an introduction to some of the important issues.

[36] Livrea 1987 offers an account of the Libyan adventures as a whole.

[37] For verbal similarities between the two passages cf. 1247–9n.

[38] Cf., e.g., Clare 2002: 151–2, Thalmann 2011: 78–80. Thalmann's whole discussion (78–91) may be consulted for the growing interest in (and bibliography on) the Libyan episode as a paradigm for the colonization of space.

direction which has been lost (cf. *Odyssey* 10.190–3). The Argonauts are finally led to safety by the signing tracks (4.1378–9) left by a horse of Poseidon, by the ability of Peleus to read oracular images, and then by the offering of a tripod to another watery divinity, Triton. As Odysseus at the end of his journey planted in the earth a visible sign, a 'trace', of his passage – the oar which looked like a winnowing-fan – so the Argonauts' final escape from Libya is marked by a return, not just of man-made signs and ritual spaces, but also of a geography based in the imposition of names and an aetiological practice which is itself a marker of Greek culture (1620–2).

The Argonauts survive in Libya, both in the Syrtis and in the area near Lake Triton, thanks to the intervention of minor divinities (the 'heroines', the Hesperides, Triton), the fact that Heracles had preceded them into this dreadful landscape and created a spring of drinking water (1441–9), and through their own epic heroism (1384) in carrying the *Argo* for twelve days and nights across the desert. Even here, however, not everything is as it seems, or rather perceptions no longer erase doubt. Are these epiphanies only mirages created by extreme conditions (cf. 1312–14n., 1408–9n.)? Even the far-sighted Lynceus only 'thinks' he caught a glimpse of Heracles across the desert wastes (1477–82), and the Argonauts' feat is so extraordinary that the poet must stress that this is a Μουσάων ... μῦθος (1381). The Libyan desert, which many critics have seen as Ap.'s version of the Underworld, is a place where all certainties break down; even epic techniques, such as that of the simile, come under strain (cf. 1338–43n.). If Pindar and Herodotus are the main points of reference here (particularly for Triton and the foundation of Thera), Ap. no doubt drew on many other sources also for individual episodes in the desert.[39] Nevertheless, it seems very likely that the Libyan section shows the poet's own combinatory narrative power as clearly as anywhere in *Arg.* Juxtaposed to the very human events on Drepane/Corcyra and the pleasures of navigation on the open sea (1622–36), Libya stands out as a markedly 'foreign' environment (Triton is a τέρας αἰνόν, 1619), where snakes born from the Gorgon's blood (1513–17) are more at home than men. Three centuries later, in Book 9 of the *Bellum ciuile*, Lucan was to make Cato's soldiers acknowledge that human beings are an intrusion in this hostile environment and thus justly punished (*BC* 9.854–62). Triton here serves as a mediating figure, who belongs to this strange world but also offers the Argonauts a guest-gift (1551–63) which is to prove truly valuable (cf. above), and uses his knowledge of navigation and the pathways of the sea to get them back into Greek waters (1573–85). For Ap.'s Alexandrian readers, many of whom will have had some acquaintance at least with the land between Cyrene and

---

[39] Vian III 58–64.

Alexandria and/or with the desert west of the Nile, this narrative of Greek heroic intrusion into such an unforgiving environment must have had a dislocating effect. This was their story which was being told.

Almost the final event of Book 4 is the foreshadowing of the creation of Thera from the clod of earth which Triton presented to Euphemos and the story of how the island was settled by colonists from Sparta who included Lemnian descendants of the Argonaut (cf. 1731–64n.). The story was a traditional part of Argonautic legend, and Ap.'s readers will have been very aware that it was from Thera that Libya was then colonized and Cyrene founded. As the Argonauts leave Libya behind, they carry with them Triton's gift which will lead eventually to Greek domination in Cyrenaica. The poem thus ends not just with the *aition* of an amusing running-race on Aegina (1766–72), but with what amounts to a large-scale *aition* for the creation of Greek islands and for the Greek presence in North Africa. The Argonautic expedition thus assumes a significance of scale which might otherwise seem to have been lacking. Jason had proclaimed that the glory of Hellas depended upon the success of their mission (204–5), and we see at the end just what this actually meant.

4 *ODYSSEY* AND ARGONAUTICA

One consequence of and (presumably) motive for moving the Argonauts from the Adriatic to the western Mediterranean was to make it possible for them to visit sites that Odysseus was to visit after them, but where of course he had already been, and Zeus's anger at the killing of Apsyrtos here functions as the narrative analogy to the anger of Poseidon and Helios in *Od.*[40] Circe, the Sirens, Scylla and Charybdis, the Planktai and Scherie/Drepane/Corcyra are the most prominent episodes shared by the two epic voyages.[41] For any educated Greek of the third century the starting point for the relationship between the two voyages was Circe's famous warning to Odysseus to avoid the Πλαγκταί, where 'waves and blasts of destructive fire' threaten destruction:

οἴη δὴ κείνηι γε παρέπλω ποντοπόρος νηῦς
Ἀργὼ πασιμέλουσα, παρ' Αἰήταο πλέουσα·
καί νύ κε τὴν ἔνθ' ὦκα βάλεν μεγάλας ποτὶ πέτρας,
ἀλλ' Ἥρη παρέπεμψεν, ἐπεὶ φίλος ἦεν Ἰήσων.

Homer, *Odyssey* 12.69–72

----

[40] The fullest account of how *Od.* is incorporated into *Arg.* 4 is Dufner 1988, and cf. also Knight 1995: 152–266; a briefer survey in Hutchinson 1988: 101–4.

[41] Other Odyssean scenes, of course, provide models for episodes earlier in *Arg.*; thus, for example, the unexpected return of the sons of Phrixos to Colchis evokes the unexpected return of Odysseus and his men to Aeolus, cf. 3.299–438.

Only one sea-going ship has sailed past that way, the *Argo* of which all men know, as it was sailing back from Aietes. It too would have been dashed against the great rocks, but Hera escorted it through, because Jason was dear to her.[42]

Circe speaks with the authority not just of a goddess, but of Aietes' own sister (*Od.* 10.135–9, Hes. *Theog.* 957); Circe herself, then, is already a figure of Argonautic myth, and in Book 12 she seems to evoke not just a story from the past, but a story known through epic song. The similarities between the Argonautic voyage and that of Odysseus were well known to ancient scholars (see below), and many modern students of the *Odyssey* accept that some of Odysseus' most famous adventures were indeed transposed to Homer's epic from an original Argonautic epic setting,[43] though there is no good reason to believe that any very early epic 'Argonautica', as opposed to Argonautic episodes in the Hesiodic corpus[44] or in poems such as the *Naupactia* and Eumelos' *Korinthiaka*,[45] survived to be available to poets of the classical and Hellenistic period. In Book 4 at least, it would seem that, after Homer and Pindar, Ap.'s principal sources are to be sought in prose writing, both earlier annalists such as Pherecydes of Athens and Herodorus of Heraclea[46] and historians nearer in time to Ap. himself, such as Timaeus.

Alexandrian and later scholars were clearly very conscious of a relationship between the two epic stories of Odysseus and Jason; in his discussion of Homer's geography, Strabo lays considerable emphasis upon the fact that Homer knew the Argonautic story in some detail and modelled some features of his *Odyssey* upon this (1.2.10, 38–40 etc.). Strabo has his own particular agenda to pursue – for him the Argonautic story is as rooted in real fact as is the story of Odysseus' wanderings – but there can be little doubt that a long tradition of comparative interpretation of the two adventures lies behind him.[47] It seems likely enough, for example, that

---

[42] On the causes of Hera's devotion to Jason cf. 3.66–75n.

[43] The arguments and bibliography may be traced through Meuli 1921 and West 2005.

[44] See, e.g., Braswell 1988: 8–10, D'Alessio 2005: 195–9.

[45] Cf. 6–10n., Hunter 1989: 15–16. *POxy* 3698 preserves the beginnings of some 35 hexameters of a first-person narration on an Argonautic theme: Orpheus, Jason, Mopsus, Aietes and probably Medea are all mentioned. The editor, Michael Haslam, notes that 'the likeliest supposition' is that the verses are archaic; Debiasi 2003 suggests ascription to Eumelos' *Korinthiaka*, noting that the apparent subject would suit the scenes on Drepane, cf. 1159–64n.

[46] Fowler 2013: 195–228 is a very rich collection of Argonautic material in early mythography; for Pherecydes see also (more briefly) Braswell 1988: 16–19.

[47] Of particular interest is Strabo's claim that the Homeric Circe was modelled on Medea, who was (for Strabo) an historical figure; an impartial reading of the opening of 1.2.10 might lead one to understand that Homer had had almost as

Timaeus at least had taken the Argonauts to some Odyssean sites before Ap. did the same. In choosing to write an epic *Argonautica*, a subject which Homer himself seems to oppose to his own *Odyssey*, Ap. very deliberately set himself both alongside and 'against' Homer.

The Argonauts' 'Odyssey' takes them first to Circe's home on the south-west coast of Italy, and then down past the Sirens (cf. 891–2n.), the treble threat of the Strait of Messina, Scylla–Charybdis and the Planktai (cf. 761–2, 922–4nn.), the meadow of the Cattle of the Sun (cf. 964–5n.), and then finally eastwards to Drepane/Corcyra, the Homeric Scherie. It has long been noted that this part of the return voyage is not marked by *aitia* and visible signs of the Argonauts' passage; after the 'Harbour of the *Argo*' on Aithalie/Elba (667–8), the next visible trace is the 'Cave of Medea' on Drepane where her marriage to Jason took place (1153–4). On one hand, this is imitation of Odyssean technique. Although Odysseus' travels effect radical change in more than one of the places he visits – the Cyclops is blinded, the Cattle of the Sun killed, the Phaeacian ship turned to stone – there is very little sign in Books 9–12 (or indeed elsewhere) of a concern to explain real or alleged features of the world of Homer's audience; the *Odyssey*, even more starkly perhaps than the *Iliad*, shows little interest in aetiology or the archaeology of the past. From another perspective, however, the Argonauts do not leave traces in this landscape because it is not theirs: these are sites which Odysseus will visit and claim as his own, sites known only because of the *Odyssey*; even the 'Cave of Medea' is in the countryside, away from the palace of Alcinous where Odysseus will be entertained.

The sites and their narratives themselves reflect this almost suspended state of being both before and after Odysseus. Circe's strange animals resemble creatures from a time long before the *Odyssey*, from the very beginning of time in fact; they are, however, described in the language of Empedoclean cosmogony, with an intellectual frame that is certainly

much to say about Medea as about Circe. In fact, of course, Homer never mentions Medea: at *Odyssey* 10.137, Circe is 'very sister to dread-minded Aietes', and when Strabo cites this verse at 1.2.40 he notes that Homer gave Circe magical powers 'on the model of Medea' (παρὰ τὴν Μήδειαν). In other words, Medea was so notorious that Homer must have known about her. There is, however, no clear sign in the relevant chapters that Strabo has *Arg.* in mind, even in 1.2.10 where he lists places in the Mediterranean which bear Argonautic traces, virtually all of which appear in *Arg.*, or in 1.2.39 where he criticizes those who took the Argonauts to the Adriatic via the Istros; Strabo in fact never explicitly cites *Arg.* and only mentions Ap. at 14.2.13 as a prominent Rhodian literary figure, though in reality an Alexandrian. In 1.2.10 he cites rather the Callimachean 'Argonautica' (fr. 7.23, 25–6, fr. 11, cf. below pp. 21–5) as evidence for the τεκμήρια of the Argonautic expedition. This will, in part, be due to Strabo's admiration for Callimachus, whom he sees as a learned scholar (not entirely unlike himself) and whom he cites on a number of occasions, and to the very high standing of the *Aitia*.

post-Homeric.[48] Just as increasing geographical knowledge led to an increasing specificity as to where the travels of both Odysseus and Jason were located, so mythic material itself was subject (at need) to transposition into more 'modern' models of interpretation. The Sirens are overcome by a virtuoso performance from Orpheus (cf. 907–9n.), one much more suggestive of contemporary instrumental performance than of archaic 'simplicity', and the description of the Cattle of the Sun seems at least to reflect some of the interpretative interest which the corresponding Homeric passage had aroused (cf. 977–8n.). Scylla and Charybdis are given relatively little attention (825–31), presumably because Homer's detailed account served once for all, whereas the passage through the Planktai, where Ap. had the opportunity to describe an event to which Homer had merely referred (*Od.* 12.69–72, above), is described at length and with considerable ecphrastic decoration. The *Argo* is transported past the Rocks by the Nereids who pass the ship from one to another like girls playing with a ball, or – more specifically – like Nausicaa and her friends on the beach at Scherie (cf. 948–55n.); here too, then, Ap. both writes a prequel to the *Odyssey* and also makes clear 'post-Homeric' allusion to it. So too, events on Drepane show how and why Arete occupied such a position of influence over her husband, as the *Odyssey* had suggested (esp. 7.66–77) but never really demonstrated; they also show a king and a people, far from wishing to avoid contact with outsiders and keep themselves hidden, in fact making decisions based on considerations of *Realpolitik* and international strategy (1074–7, 1098–1109), more like a Hellenistic court than a mythical land of wonders.[49] Drepane becomes the place where the poem's 'Nausicaa' marries the poem's 'Odysseus', but all of Ap.'s readers know that the ideal of ὁμοφροσύνη (*Od.* 6.181–5) will never travel with this couple.

The debt to the *Odyssey*, as indeed to Homer more generally, is not limited to the tour of Odyssean sites. At every level of motif and language, *Arg.* is saturated with the Homeric heritage and with the reworkings of and scholarship upon that heritage from the centuries before Ap. It is very clear, for example, that at the level of poetic diction the text of *Arg.* reflects in literally hundreds of places contemporary and earlier attempts to understand Homeric diction;[50] very frequently we find Homeric words of disputed meaning used in ways that we know were current in the glossographical and scholarly traditions. Homeric 'problems', including

[48] Cf. above pp. 6–7.
[49] Ap. has greatly reduced the Homeric element of the marvellous in his description of the domain of Alcinous and Arete; thus, for example, the wonders of Alcinous' palace (*Od.* 7.81–132) had already been rewritten in the description of Aietes' eastern palace (3.210–37).
[50] See esp. Rengakos 1994.

textual problems, are also regularly evoked in the texture of Ap.'s language. These features, which are shared with the poetry of Callimachus,[51] do not – as often used to be claimed – turn Alexandrian poetry into nothing more than a scholarly *ludus*. Central to the poetic meaning of *Arg.*, in Book 4 more prominently than anywhere else, is the mixing of temporal levels, so that the present constantly intrudes on a narrative of the past, sometimes – as in the description of Circe's animals or of Talos, the remnant of the Bronze Age – the very distant past; one of the earliest readers known to have appreciated this aspect of *Arg.* was Virgil, who developed this technique in his own directions in the *Aeneid*.

Appreciation of the linguistic texture of *Arg.*, archaizing and (as Aristotle would have put it) ξένον, but also constantly drawing attention to itself precisely by the evocation of contemporary and earlier discussion of Homer's linguistic texture, is an important element of the experience of reading *Arg.*; how that experience is both similar to and different from reading Homer is fundamental to Ap.'s poetic enterprise.[52] When reading Homer, whether today or in antiquity, we are pulled up from time to time by words of uncertain meaning, often what the ancients called 'glosses', i.e. archaic words or words from a dialect not our own which require explanation, which delay our progress through the text. If this concern with understanding at the micro-level is carried to extremes, as it is in the scholarship preserved for us in the Homeric scholia, then it may be that the experience of reading Homer is (for a scholar) not so different from the experience of reading *Arg.* On the other hand, the language of Homer becomes so familiar, and is in any case so marked by repetition, that it is 'naturalized', both in the sense that it seems natural for the epic task it performs and in the sense that we are able to read it in a steady forward flow, without constant interruption. The language of *Arg.*, by contrast, constantly holds us up, both by its own difficulties and by its insistent allusion at the micro-level to the language of Homer; reading *Arg.* is a much more fragmented experience than is reading Homer. As we progress through the text, we are always aware of the 'business of reading', and indeed – through Ap.'s intrusions into the text – of the 'business of composition', because of the nature of this Hellenistic epic language. Here, too, Virgil learned from Apollonius.

Even where Ap. seems most remote from the Odyssean pattern, as for example in the Libyan adventures, resonances of Homer's poem are never

---

[51] There are significant differences between the 'scholarly' texture of Callimachus' poetry and that of Ap., but for present purposes it is the similarities which are more significant.

[52] The distinction drawn here is very broad and unnuanced, but also very important to the history of literary self-consciousness.

far away.[53] No epic of travel could fail to be at some level an 'Odyssey', and Book 4 evokes the Homeric poem in its opening verse;[54] nevertheless, after securing the Fleece, the Argonauts are almost constantly on the move, whereas the second half of *Od.* is rooted in Ithacan locations and much of the dynamic of change is psychological rather than physical. *Arg.* is in fact markedly, even strangely, anti-Odyssean in that three of the four books are devoted to travel, whereas it is only in Book 3 where the pattern, which dominates the second half of the *Odyssey*, of intrigue and plotting in a particular setting is replicated. Whereas, moreover, the bulk of Odysseus' travels are recounted by the hero himself in Books 9–12, time in *Arg.* moves relentlessly forward and the narration of the expedition is indeed just that, a narration in the poetic voice of the narrator. This simple narrative ordering of *Arg.*, together with many aspects of its subject matter, has been thought to resemble a Hellenistic version of 'cyclic' or 'continuous' (διηνεκές, συνεχές) poetry,[55] which ancient critical tradition associated with epic poets other than Homer. Two aspects of composition are particularly relevant here.

In chapter 23 of the *Poetics*, Aristotle demands of epic that, as in tragedy, plots (μῦθοι) should concern 'one action (πρᾶξις) which is whole and complete, with a beginning, middle and end' (1459a16–19); if Homer had tried to narrate the entire Trojan War, the *muthos* would have been 'either too large and sprawling (οὐκ εὐσύνοπτος) or reasonable in length but over-complex in its variety' (1459a32–4). Homer showed the right path by choosing a single part with its own internal unity (ἓν μέρος, presumably the wrath of Achilles and its consequences) and including other parts, such as the 'Catalogue of Ships' as episodes.[56] Homer's success may be judged from the fact that from the *Iliad* or the *Odyssey* one could make only 'one or two' tragedies, whereas one could make many from 'Cyclic' epics such as the *Cypria* (cf. 1451a24–9); it is as important in epic as in tragedy that events should follow each other 'by necessity or probability', for it is this internal dynamic which gives unity to the plot. The story of the expedition of the Argonauts is indeed, when viewed from one perspective, 'one action (πρᾶξις) which is whole and complete, with a beginning, middle and end'; it is the story of the Argonautic expedition to bring the

[53] Dufner 1988: 189–95 discusses links between the Libyan adventures and Menelaos' narrative in *Od.* 4 of how he and his crew were stranded on Pharos off the North African coast. The Libyan 'heroines' speak to Jason with echoes of the Homeric Sirens (1319–21n.).
[54] For the possibility that the final verse alludes to *Od.* cf. 1781n.
[55] Cf. 421–521n., 869–79n., Fantuzzi–Hunter 2004: 95–7, Hunter 2008b: 144–5, Rengakos 2004.
[56] See Hunter 1989: 33–4, Hunter 1993: 190–5, citing earlier bibliography. In view of those discussions, the present consideration of the matter is kept brief and largely focused on Book 4.

Golden Fleece back to Greece, and antecedent events, such as what led Pelias to demand the expedition (cf. 1.5–17, 3. 333–9), are only briefly adumbrated in the course of the poem. On the other hand, structuring the whole poem as a voyage emphasizes its episodic nature: there is no inevitable 'necessity or probability' which determines where the *Argo* stops, and what those stops contribute to the successful return of the Fleece. The whole return route is made to seem 'necessary' only because Phineus, who understood divine intention, muttered darkly about 'a different route' (2.421–2); the Argonauts travel in ignorance of the fact that the Symplegades no longer pose a threat. The mere fact that Ap. combined several potential routes for the return journey, while rejecting others (cf. above), adds to the sense that this πρᾶξις is different in kind from those which Aristotle demands; so too does the marking off of individual episodes by a kind of simple 'ring-composition' (the 'Apsyrtos', the 'Circe', 'Drepane'),[57] a device which works towards fragmentation rather than unity. In the final section of the book, after the four hundred verses in Libya, the episodic sense seems to gather pace (Talos, Anaphe, Euphemos and the clod, the Aeginetan 'hydrophoria'), as the Argonauts too hurry home. From our perspective, rather than Aristotle's, this difference in technique between Homer and Ap. must not be blown out of proportion – Aristotelian 'necessity or probability' hardly govern the whole sequence of Odysseus' adventures – but a further (related) difference between *Arg.* and the Homeric poems seems to reinforce the purely linear, non-Homeric structure of the former.

   The two Homeric poems are characterized by remarkable (and differing) narrative techniques. As was noted already in antiquity, the *Iliad* focuses on a set of events near the end of the war, though stopping short of that ending, but encompasses much that seems to belong to, or at least suggest, earlier events (the 'Catalogue', the *teikhoskopia*, the duel of Menelaos and Helen etc.) or to foreshadow those that lie in the future (the fall of Troy, the death of Achilles, the killing of Astyanax etc.); in *Arg.*, it is the events of Euripides' *Medea* which are, above all, foreshadowed at various points.[58] As for the *Odyssey*, it is famously marked by radical dislocations of narrative sequence in its first half: the Telemachy, then the story of Odysseus' voyage from Calypso to Scherie, then the telling of the antecedent adventures. Callimachus' treatment of certain Argonautic events in the *Aitia* seems to have picked up these Homeric dislocations (see section 5 below). In *Arg.*, however, the only interruptions to the straightforward, on-going sequence – from catalogue to launch to voyage out to events at Colchis to the return voyage – are occasional 'mythological' analepses, such as the story of Hyllos at 537–51; the poem moves from

----

[57] Cf. 450–1n., 661–2n., 982–1223n.   [58] Cf. 1108–9, Hunter 1989: 18–19.

episode to episode, as the *Argo* progresses from station to station (cf. 451). At its heart, of course, are the events at Colchis of Book 3 and the first part of Book 4; one wonders if an 'Aristotelian poet' would have written not an 'Argonautica', but rather a 'Colchiad' (*uel sim.*), set in Aietes' city but embracing through inset tales and foreshadowing both the past and the future. To what extent *Arg.* is in fact composed 'against' Aristotelian prescriptions, as well as Homeric practice, has been extensively debated; it may be that the Aristotelian perspective is more hermeneutically useful, in focusing our attention on features of *Arg.*'s narrative ordering, than actually relevant to the poem's compositional context, but the importance of Aristotelian ideas within Alexandrian scholarship is now well established, and – on purely general grounds – we would have expected *Arg.* to reflect critical discussion of narrative technique, just as much as, for example, Homeric lexical scholarship. The balance of probabilities very strongly suggests that it does.

5 APOLLONIUS AND CALLIMACHUS

Arg. is replete with passages, phrases, and even single words which suggest an intertextual relationship with the poetry of Callimachus, who was resident and working in Alexandria at broadly the same period as Ap.[59] The most important Callimachean poem in this regard is the *Aitia*, although the relationship clearly extends well beyond that poem; the *Hymns, Hecale* and *Iambi* all find significant resonance in more than one passage of *Arg.*[60] Since the revolution in our knowledge of the *Aitia*, however, it has been that poem which has dominated discussion, and this is hardly surprising, given the importance of the *Aitia* in antiquity and the importance of aetiology in *Arg.* The majority view, whose most significant proponent was Rudolf Pfeiffer,[61] has always been that Apollonius is almost always imitating or reworking the *Aitia*, rather than *vice versa*; this view continues to hold the field, though significant voices now propose a kind of continuous poetic dialogue between two poets working in very close proximity to each other and (presumably) able constantly to revise their work to respond to the poetry of the other.[62] It is generally agreed that arguments from absolute and relative chronology are too uncertain to be decisive,[63] and so we are forced back to internal,

[59] See further Hunter 1989: 6–9, 34–8.
[60] For the *Hecale* cf., e.g., 110–11n.; for the *Iambi* cf. below on the Aeginetan 'Hydrophoria'.
[61] Pfeiffer II xli-ii.
[62] See, e.g., Harder 2012: 1.4, 32. Stephens 2011: 205–6 sketches an argument for Apollonian priority.
[63] For what we can say about the chronology of *Arg.* cf. above pp. 1–2.

poetic arguments, where disagreement between readers is almost inevitable.

Book 4 has always been central to these discussions because the *aition* for the ribald cult of Apollo Aigletes on Anaphe (1719–30) was extensively narrated in Book 1 of the *Aitia*, and in a manner which puts an intertextual relation with *Arg.* beyond any doubt. Moreover, Argonautic *aitia* seem to occupy significant structural positions in the *Aitia.* The Anaphe-*aition* follows immediately on the first principal *aition* of the poem, the cult of the Graces on Paros, which is still to some extent proemial, as it includes (fr. 7.13–14) a prayer to the goddesses for the success and the longevity of the poet's elegies; so too, the penultimate *aition* of Book 4 (frr. 108–9), immediately before the 'Coma Berenices', was the story of how the Argonauts left behind at Cyzicus an anchor-stone which was too light and how this was later dedicated to Athena, a story which Ap. tells briefly at 1.955–60. Of itself, such parallelism may simply be one of the many devices by which Callimachus gave shape to his poem, but the coincidence (if that is what it is) of reversed correspondences between Books 1 and 4 of both poems, together with the nature of Callimachus' Anaphe-*aition*, prompts closer inspection.

In fr. 7 of the *Aitia* the tirelessly eager poet asks the Muses about two cults involving ritual abuse, the cult of Apollo on Anaphe and the cult of Heracles at Lindos, and in response Calliope offers a relatively extended version of the Argonautic story which culminates in what seems to be very much the same *aition* as that in *Arg.* The narrative begins with an angry and threatening speech by Aietes (cf. 212–35); much is lost after that, but Calliope seems at least to have mentioned the death of Apsyrtos (in Colchis), the return route of the Argonauts with the Colchians in pursuit (p. 10 above), some events on Corcyra and the fate of the pursuing Colchians and their foundations in Illyria (frr. 11–12), before coming to the darkness which threatened the Argonauts and from which they were saved by Apollo's revelation of Anaphe, to be followed by the *aition* for the cult of Apollo Aigletes. There are close (sometimes very close) verbal correspondences throughout this sequence with the parallel events in *Arg.* 4, and these are recorded as appropriate in the commentary;[64] these similarities far outweigh visible differences of plot or treatment.[65]

[64] It is suggestive of how much we might be missing that a new Michigan papyrus has added another very close parallel between the Callimachean and Apollonian accounts of the ritual at Anaphe (Call. fr. 21.11 Harder ~ 1727). For discussion of *Arg.* and the Callimachean 'Argonautica' cf. Eichgrün 1961: 125–33, Hutchinson 1988: 87–93, Albis 1996: 125–9, Harder 2002: 217–23.

[65] Perhaps the most interesting of these is that Callimachus appears to have Tiphys still steering the boat in the Anaphe-episode (cf. fr. 17.9 Harder), whereas in *Arg.* he dies on the outward journey. The tradition knew different accounts of

It is also clear that Callimachus' narrative was able to embrace some events from the very beginning of the Argonautic expedition (cf. fr. 18.9–13), and here again there are striking similarities to Ap.'s narrative.

The opening of Calliope's response in the *Aitia* is preserved:

"Αἰγλήτην Ἀνάφην τε, Λακωνίδι γείτονα Θήρηι,
    πρῶτον ἐνὶ μνήμηι κάτθεο καὶ Μινύας,
ἀρχμενος ὡς ἥρωες ἀπ' Αἰήταο Κυταίου
    αὖτις ἐς ἀρχαίην ἔπλεον Αἱμονίην ...

Callimachus fr. 7.23–6

"The Gleamer and Anaphe, neighbour to Laconian Thera, first commit to your memory, and the Minyans, taking your start from how the heroes were sailing back from Cytaean Aietes to ancient Haimonie ... "

Calliope's response plays with techniques of epic opening, as is appropriate to the Muse of epic herself.[66] Her opening couplet functions like the poet's announcement of his theme or his request to the Muse(s) for a particular theme ('wrath', 'the man'), except that now it is the 'audience' which is to exercise its memory; ἐνὶ μνήμηι κάτθεο functions both as an instruction to an audience and as a version of the standard μνήσομαι with which poets, including Apollonius (1.2), announce their theme. This play with epic narrative is emphasized by the fact that the poet has, immediately before, asked about the behaviour of 'the man of Anaphe', and so it is surprising that the Muse should begin by telling him to turn his mind to Anaphe, but this apparent lack of connection between Muse and poet calls attention to the marked 'epic technique'. The second couplet then specifies the point at which the tale is to begin (cf., e.g., *Od.* 1.10, 8.500),[67] but this beginning is situated when the main deed of the heroic expedition (the acquisition of the Golden Fleece) is already over (it is in fact never mentioned in what survives to us of the text), and we are hurled *in medias res* in such a way as to impose serious demands on our knowledge of the story: very few details of Medea's ἔργα (cf. 213n.) can have been given in the lacunae in vv. 27–8. This then is 'epic' as a λεπταλέη Μοῦσα would

---

when he died (cf. Σ 2.854), but one might conclude that, in Callimachus at least (and cf. Lyc. *Alex.* 890), he survived the expedition. It is hard to see why Callimachus would have used a different version if he was, in the main, following *Arg.*, whereas it would be easy enough to explain Ap.'s choice, given that in *Arg.* Tiphys' death is one of a pair on the outward journey, matched by the deaths of Kanthos and Mopsus in Libya (1485–1536), and this is clearly part of a large-scale structure shaping the epic.

[66] Harder 2012: 2.150–1. On the possible significance of the reference to Thera cf. below p. 25 n. 72.

[67] For a very similar sequence cf. Call. *h.* 3.1–4.

perform it in elegiacs. Moreover, the ordering of Calliope's narrative seems to play with one of the most admired characteristics of Homeric narrative, namely the way in which he began 'at the end', but in such a way as to embrace the whole, a technique which belonged to ἀρετὴ ποιητική, as the exegetical scholia on the opening verse of the *Iliad* put it.[68] The contrast with the linearity of *Arg.*, which 'begins at the beginning' and 'ends at the end' and which looks to events outside itself in only very limited ways, could hardly be greater;[69] everything we can reasonably infer about Callimachus' 'Argonautica' suggests that its manner was utterly different. This, however, need not mean that this sequence of the *Aitia* was written in reaction to *Arg.*

The epic colouring of Callimachus' 'Argonautica' might simply be owed to the epic nature of the theme, one of the manifestations of which is the 'epic' length at which Pindar too had narrated the story in *Pythian* 4. Why Callimachus chose to give such prominence to an Argonautic narrative we can only guess, but progress in understanding the intertextual relationship between the poets might well be made, if – discounting for the moment the probability of borrowing between them – we knew more about their sources for the Anaphe-narrative. It seems clear from later mythographic sources that there were indeed other narratives of this part of the Argonautic voyage that are now lost to us. In Apollodorus, *Bibl.* the Argonauts encounter a violent storm, rather than impenetrable darkness, after leaving Corcyra, and it is from this which Apollo saves them, leading to their discovery of Anaphe and the *aition* for the cult (1.9.26); it is after this that the episode of Talos on Crete is placed by Apollodorus, although it is not explained why the Argonauts turned south when they would have wanted to get home (unless Apollodorus has simply jumbled the order of events).[70] In the Augustan mythographer Conon (cf. 1701n.), Apollo's saving intervention causes an island to rise from the seabed, rather than simply become visible, and the mutual ribaldry between Medea's maids and the Argonauts is the result of good spirits after alcoholic celebration, not of impoverished circumstances. How much of these differences from Ap.'s version is owed to Callimachus' narrative itself is uncertain,[71] but it does seems highly likely that there were other narratives of this part of the Argonautic voyage available to Ap. and Callimachus. We might, for example, have expected Callimachus (and Ap.) to draw on local historiography or antiquarian research, as the Florentine scholia claim that Callimachus drew on the

---

[68] On this scholion see Nünlist 2009: 88 n.51.   [69] Cf. above p. 20.

[70] Callimachus also seems to have taken his Argonauts directly from Corcyra to Anaphe, and there is no obvious trace of a stop in either Libya or Crete in his narrative.

[71] Pfeiffer I 17.

Argive historians Agias and Derkylos for the preceding *aition* of the Parian
cult of the Graces. We also know nothing of the sources either poet used
for the *aition* of the Aeginetan festival of the 'Hydrophoria', the final *aition*
of *Arg.* (cf. 1765–72n.), which Callimachus narrated in *Iambus* 8.

While there is obviously a close relationship to *Arg.* in this prominent
and extended narrative near the beginning of *Aitia* 1, there is also, when
viewed from the other perspective, a very thick 'Callimachean flavour' as
Arg. draws to an end: Apollo Aigletes, Anaphe, the foundation legends of
Thera and Cyrene (cf. 1731–64n.),[72] and the Aeginetan 'Hydrophoria' all
contribute to this effect. Unless we take the view of an on-going poetic
exchange which almost rules out of court questions of 'priority', perhaps
the strongest argument remains the fact that the same passages of
Callimachus seem to be paralleled in more than one place in *Arg.* A very
striking instance are the multiple parallels in *Arg.* for Call. fr. 18, Jason's
prayers to Apollo to save them at Anaphe, together with (apparently) a
flashback to the launching of the expedition and the building of an altar to
Apollo Ἐμβάσιος, cf. *Arg.* 1.402–24, 4.1701–06 (with 1701–5n.). So too,
one verse of the Callimachean 'Argonautica', καὶ τὰ μὲν ὡς ἤμελλε μετὰ
χρόνον ἐκτελέεσθαι (fr. 12.6), is found once in *Arg.* in this very form
(1.1309) and once (4.1216, where see n.) in the same context but with
verbal variation and clear signposting to the original verbal form. At the
very least, such textual phenomena suggest that the burden of proof lies
with those who see Callimachus as the borrower.

6 THE HEXAMETER

Arg. shares the same general trends for the hexameter[73] as witnessed in
Callimachus[74] and Theocritus,[75] namely a greater prominence of dactyls
over spondees than in Homer,[76] and also a narrowing of the range of

---

[72] To describe Anaphe as Λακωνίδι γείτονα Θήρηι, 'neighbour to Laconian Thera',
a description which evokes the foundation of Thera and hence of Callimachus'
home-city of Cyrene, and one of considerable interest to an Alexandrian audience,
Callimachus required no external stimulus, such as the fact that Pindar's narrative in
Pythian 4 begins on Thera; it is nevertheless noteworthy (see, e.g., Harder 2012: II
152) that in *Arg.* the Anaphe-episode is immediately followed by (i.e. 'is neighbour
to') Euphemos' dream and the foundation-legends of Thera, colonized from Sparta
(note the emphatic repetition in 1761–2). Arguments for priority based on this
similarity could, however, cut both ways.

[73] For a fuller account cf. Mooney 1912: 411–28; the present brief note essentially repeats Hunter 1989: 41–2. West 1982: 152–7 surveys the general differences
between Hellenistic literary hexameters and those of the archaic and classical
periods. On hiatus in *Arg.*, a very common prosodic feature, see Campbell 1995.

[74] Helpful survey in Hopkinson 1984: 51–5.   [75] Hunter 1999: 17–21.

[76] 67.4% of the hexameters in *Arg.* have at most one spondee, against 61.3% for
Il. and 58.9% for *Od.*; the three most common shapes of the hexameter (*ddddd*,

verse-patterns which are at all prominent; two significant aspects of this
general trend towards greater standardization are an increasing reliance
on the 'feminine' caesura, i.e. word-break after the first short of a third-
foot dactyl (67% v. 57% in Homer), and an extension of the regularity of
'bucolic diaeresis', i.e. word-break after a fourth-foot dactyl (57% v. 47%
in Homer). Conversely, verses with a spondaic fifth foot, so-called *spondeiazontes*, became something of a Hellenistic mannerism (8% in *Arg.* v. 5%
for Homer), which was then picked up and imitated by the Roman 'neo-
terics'; such verses often appear in pairs, and this distinctive rhythm can be
used to produce expressive effects.[77]

Ap.'s written epic allows the building of more complex blocks of meaning across several verses than is normal in Homer, where the basic unit of
composition and meaning is the single hexameter, and features such as
verbal hyperbaton across verses are comparatively rare. *Arg.* has moved a
considerable distance from the Homeric norm: 'necessary enjambment',
that is when syntax forbids any strong break at the end of a verse, is a
feature of nearly one half of *Arg.*, whereas the Homeric figure is around
30%.[78] Such statistics do not, of course, tell the whole story, but the greater
freedom of the written epic offered the poet further opportunities to
reinforce meaning through the rhythm and structure of his verses.[79] So
too, the changes in the conditions of poetic composition and reception
allowed Ap. (and other poets) to move decisively away from repetition as a
fundamental tool of composition, particularly in regard to repeated
scenes, messenger-speeches, and reports from one character to another
of events previously recounted by the narrator.[80] At the micro-level of
language, Ap. constantly exploits and varies the Homeric heritage through
analogy and the riches of post-Homeric poetic diction, but he also stays
within epic generic conventions by creating a 'para-formulaic' style, which
avoids the constant verbal repetitiveness which is the most striking feature
of Homeric style but also gestures to that authorizing heritage through
phrasing and word-combinations which become familiar as our reading
progresses.[81] As with every aspect of Ap.'s poetic creation, the linguistic
patterns of the hexameters are unthinkable without Homer: we are meant
to recognize their origins and also recognize what Ap. has done with that
heritage.

sdddd, and *dsddd*) account for 52.7% of *Arg.*, 47.5% of *Il.*, and 45.5% of *Od.* These
figures are derived from La Roche 1899 and Groningen 1953: 202.
   [77] See, e.g., nn. on 192, 663–4, 893, 944.   [78] Janko 1982: 32.
   [79] Cf., e.g., 355–90n., 3.649–53n.
   [80] See Hunter 1993: 142–3. Jason's report to his comrades at 1347–62 of the
epiphany of the 'heroines' is a very good example.
   [81] See esp. Fantuzzi–Hunter 2004: 266–82, and above p. 18 on how the 'reading
experience' for the two poets differs.

7 THE TEXT

The text and apparatus in this edition are based on Vian III, from which all information about readings, except for those of papyri not known to Vian, is taken. The apparatus is extremely selective, and silence should never be interpreted to indicate that the tradition is unanimous. Anyone seeking fuller information about the transmission should, in the first instance, consult Vian's apparatus.

There are some 55 medieval and later MSS of *Arg.*, which all probably go back to a common source, here designated by Ω, though whether sources other than Ω also lie behind some of the variants in the tradition is disputed. The MSS fall broadly into two classes, here designated as *m* and *w*.[82] The two independent witnesses to *m* are L and A.[83] Vian has argued that, at least in Book 4, L was originally copied from a manuscript with a text different from that of Ω and then subsequently corrected from the Ω text; this will explain a number of good readings preserved only in L, often subsequently replaced by correction. Be that as it may, L also contains a rich body of scholia, certainly copied in from a text other than that from which L was copied, and often preserving important variant readings. Class *m* also contains an important 'Cretan' sub-family, of which the principal witness is E. For *w* we rely on S, a manuscript prepared for Maximus Planudes, and G. In addition to the medieval tradition, there is a rich body of papyri from the Roman period,[84] which attests to the popularity of *Arg.* in later antiquity, and an extensive indirect tradition, largely preserved in ancient lexica and scholia; both the papyri and the indirect tradition attest to many ancient variants, often offering an improved text, which have been lost to the medieval tradition. The text of *Arg.* remains in fact doubtful in many places, and new papyri regularly warn against over-confidence.

---

[82] On the textual transmission of *Arg.* see esp. Fränkel 1961: viii-xvi, Fränkel 1964, Haslam 1978, Vian I xl-lxvii, II ix-xi, Schade-Eleuteri 2008.

[83] For the designations of individual MSS see 'Sigla', below p. 28.

[84] Haslam 1978, Schade-Eleuteri 2008: 35–41.

SIGLA

1 PAPYRI

Π^1 *P. Oxy.* 2694 (saec. II)
Π^2 *P. Oxy.* 2691 (saec. I ex.)
Π^3 *P. Berol.* 17011 (saec. IV-V), cf. Müller 1968: 126
Π^4 *P. Columbia inv.* 437 (saec. III), cf. Keyes 1929: 263–5
Π^5 *P. Oxy.* 692 (saec. II)
Π^6 *P. Oxy.* 5030 (saec. II in.)
Π^7 *P. Bodl.* I 164 (saec. VII in.), cf. Luiselli 2003

2 MANUSCRIPTS

codd.	consensus codicum omnium
Ω	archetypus codicum omnium
Σ	scholiasta, scholia
d	consensus codicum CDQR
m	codex deperditus e quo LA descripti sunt
w	codex deperditus e quo SG descripti sunt
A	Ambrosianus gr. 120 (saec. XV in.)
B	Bruxellensis 18170–73 (AD 1489)
C	Casanatensis gr. 408 (saec. XV ex. – XVI in.)
D	Parisinus gr. 2729 (saec. XV ex. – XVI in.)
E	Scorialensis gr. Σ III 3 (saec. XV ex.)
G	Guelferbytanus Aug. 4° 10.2 (saec. XIV)
I	Matritensis gr. 4691 (AD 1465)
L	Laurentianus gr. 32, 9 (AD 960–80)
Q	Vaticanus gr. 37 (saec. XV ex. – XVI in.)
R	Vaticanus gr. 1358 (saec. XVI in.)
S	Laurentianus gr. 32, 16 (AD 1280)
U	Urbinas gr. 146 (saec. XV)
V	Vaticanus Pal. Gr. 186 (saec. XV)
W	Vratislavensis Rehdigeranus 35 (AD 1488)
Y	Vaticanus gr. 36 (saec. XV)
Flor.	*editio princeps*, J. Lascaris, Florence 1496

3 ABBREVIATIONS

L^2	manus secunda in L
L^{yp} uel $L^{v.l.}$	uaria lectio in L
L^{ac}	L ante correctionem
L^{pc}	L post correctionem
L^{mg}	L in margine
L^{sl}	L supra lineam

ΑΠΟΛΛΩΝΙΟΥ ΡΟΔΙΟΥ
ΑΡΓΟΝΑΥΤΙΚΩΝ Δ

αὐτὴ νῦν κάματόν γε, θεά, καὶ δήνεα κούρης
Κολχίδος ἔννεπε, Μοῦσα, Διὸς τέκος· ἦ γὰρ ἔμοιγε
ἀμφασίηι νόος ἔνδον ἑλίσσεται, ὁρμαίνοντι
ἠέ μιν ἄτης πῆμα δυσίμερον ἦ τό γ᾽ ἐνίσπω
φύζαν ἀεικελίην ἧι κάλλιπεν ἔθνεα Κόλχων.   5
ἤτοι ὁ μὲν δήμοιο μετ᾽ ἀνδράσιν ὅσσοι ἄριστοι
παννύχιος δόλον αἰπὺν ἐπὶ σφίσι μητιάασκεν
οἷσιν ἐνὶ μεγάροις, στυγερῶι ἐπὶ θυμὸν ἀέθλωι
Αἰήτης ἄμοτον κεχολωμένος, οὐδ᾽ ὅ γε πάμπαν
θυγατέρων τάδε νόσφιν ἑῶν τετελέσθαι ἐώλπει.   10
τῆι δ᾽ ἀλεγεινότατον κραδίηι φόβον ἔμβαλεν Ἥρη,
τρέσσεν δ᾽ ἠύτε τις κούφη κεμὰς ἥν τε βαθείης
τάρφεσιν ἐν ξυλόχοιο κυνῶν ἐφόβησεν ὁμοκλή.
αὐτίκα γὰρ νημερτὲς ὀίσσατο μή μιν ἀρωγήν
λαθέμεν, αἶψα δὲ πᾶσαν ἀναπλήσειν κακότητα·   15
τάρβει δ᾽ ἀμφιπόλους ἐπιίστορας. ἐν δέ οἱ ὄσσε
πλῆτο πυρός, δεινὸν δὲ περιβρομέεσκον ἀκουαί·
πυκνὰ δὲ λαυκανίης ἐπεμάσσετο, πυκνὰ δὲ κουρὶξ
ἑλκομένη πλοκάμους γοερῆι βρυχήσατ᾽ ἀνίηι.
καὶ νύ κεν αὐτοῦ τῆμος ὑπὲρ μόρον ὤλετο κούρη   20
φάρμακα πασσαμένη, Ἥρης δ᾽ ἁλίωσε μενοινάς,
εἰ μή μιν Φρίξοιο θεὰ σὺν παισὶ φέβεσθαι
ὦρσεν ἀτυζομένην. πτερόεις δέ οἱ ἐν φρεσὶ θυμός
ἰάνθη, μετὰ δ᾽ ἥ γε παλίσσυτος ἀθρόα κόλπωι
φάρμακα πάντ᾽ ἄμυδις κατεχεύατο φωριαμοῖο.   25
κύσσε δ᾽ ἑόν τε λέχος καὶ δικλίδας ἀμφοτέρωθεν
σταθμοὺς καὶ τοίχων ἐπαφήσατο· χερσί τε μακρόν
τμηξαμένη πλόκαμον, θαλάμωι μνημήια μητρί
κάλλιπε παρθενίης, ἀδινῆι δ᾽ ὀλοφύρατο φωνῆι·
"τόνδε τοι ἀντ᾽ ἐμέθεν ταναὸν πλόκον εἶμι λιποῦσα, 30
μῆτερ ἐμή· χαίροις δὲ καὶ ἄνδιχα πολλὸν ἰούσηι·
χαίροις Χαλκιόπη καὶ πᾶς δόμος. αἴθε σε πόντος,
ξεῖνε, διέρραισεν πρὶν Κολχίδα γαῖαν ἱκέσθαι."
ὣς ἄρ᾽ ἔφη, βλεφάρων δὲ κατ᾽ ἀθρόα δάκρυα χεῦεν.

10 τετελέσθαι Naber: τελέεσθαι Ω   13 ξυλόχοιο Stephanus: ξυλόχοισι Ω   24 κόλπωι
Platt: κόλπων Ω   28 τμηξαμένη Maas: ῥηξαμένη Ω

οἵη δ᾽ ἀφνειοῖο †διειλυσθεῖσα δόμοιο   35
ληιάς, ἥν τε νέον πάτρης ἀπενόσφισεν αἶσα,
οὐδέ νύ πω μογεροῖο πεπείρηται καμάτοιο,
ἀλλ᾽ ἔτ᾽ ἀηθέσσουσα δύην καὶ δούλια ἔργα
εἶσιν ἀτυζομένη χαλεπὰς ὑπὸ χεῖρας ἀνάσσης·
τοίη ἄρ᾽ ἱμερόεσσα δόμων ἐξέσσυτο κούρη.   40
τῆι δὲ καὶ αὐτόματοι θυρέων ὑπόειξαν ὀχῆες,
ὠκείαις ἄψορροι ἀναθρώισκοντες ἀοιδαῖς.
γυμνοῖσιν δὲ πόδεσσιν ἀνὰ στεινὰς θέεν οἴμους,
λαιῆι μὲν χερὶ πέπλον ἐπ᾽ ὀφρύσιν ἀμφὶ μέτωπα
στειλαμένη καὶ καλὰ παρήια, δεξιτερῆι δὲ   45
ἄκρην ὑψόθι πέζαν ἀερτάζουσα χιτῶνος.
καρπαλίμως δ᾽ ἀίδηλον ἀνὰ στίβον ἔκτοθι πύργων
ἄστεος εὐρυχόροιο φόβωι ἵκετ᾽, οὐδέ τις ἔγνω
τήνδε φυλακτήρων, λάθε δέ σφεας ὁρμηθεῖσα.
ἔνθεν ἴμεν νειόνδε μάλ᾽ ἐφράσατ᾽· οὐ γὰρ ἄιδρις   50
ἦεν ὁδῶν, θαμὰ καὶ πρὶν ἀλωμένη ἀμφί τε νεκρούς
ἀμφί τε δυσπαλέας ῥίζας χθονός, οἷα γυναῖκες
φαρμακίδες· τρομερῶι δ᾽ ὑπὸ δείματι πάλλετο θυμός.
τὴν δὲ νέον Τιτηνὶς ἀνερχομένη περάτηθεν
φοιταλέην ἐσιδοῦσα θεὰ ἐπεχήρατο Μήνη   55
ἁρπαλέως, καὶ τοῖα μετὰ φρεσὶν ἧισιν ἔειπεν·
"οὐκ ἄρ᾽ ἐγὼ μούνη μετὰ Λάτμιον ἄντρον ἀλύσκω,
οὐδ᾽ οἴη καλῶι περιδαίομαι Ἐνδυμίωνι.
ἦ θαμὰ δὴ καὶ σεῖο, κύον, δολίηισιν ἀοιδαῖς
⟨   ⟩
μνησαμένη φιλότητος, ἵνα σκοτίηι ἐνὶ νυκτί   60
φαρμάσσηις εὔκηλος, ἅ τοι φίλα ἔργα τέτυκται.
νῦν δὲ καὶ αὐτὴ δῆθεν ὁμοίης ἔμμορες ἄτης,
δῶκε δ᾽ ἀνιηρόν τοι Ἰήσονα πῆμα γενέσθαι
δαίμων ἀλγινόεις. ἀλλ᾽ ἔρχεο, τέτλαθι δ᾽ ἔμπης,
καὶ πινυτή περ ἐοῦσα, πολύστονον ἄλγος ἀείρειν."   65
    ὣς ἄρ᾽ ἔφη· τὴν δ᾽ αἶψα πόδες φέρον ἐγκονέουσαν.
ἀσπασίως δ᾽ ὄχθηισιν ἐπηέρθη ποταμοῖο,
ἀντιπέρην λεύσσουσα πυρὸς σέλας ὅ ῥά τ᾽ ἀέθλου

35 διειλυσθεῖσα Ω: διελκυσθεῖσα Ardizzoni (διειλκυσ- iam Fränkel)   38 δύην Huet:
δύης Ω   44 χερὶ E: χειρὶ Ω   ἐπ᾽ *mG*: ὑπ᾽ SD   50 ἔνθεν ἴμεν Hartung: ἐν θ᾽ ἔνι μὲν Ω
νειόνδε Fränkel: νηόνδε Ω: νειὸν μὲν E   59 post h. v. lacunam posuit Campbell
κύον Ω: κίον B²: κλύον Fantuzzi   δολίηισιν W: δολίαισιν Ω

παννύχιοι ἥρωες ἐυφροσύνῃσιν ἔδαιον.
ὀξείῃ δῆπειτα διὰ κνέφας ὄρθια φωνῇ   70
ὁπλότατον Φρίξοιο περαιόθεν ἧπυε παίδων,
Φρόντιν. ὁ δὲ ξὺν ἑοῖσι κασιγνήτοις ὄπα κούρης
αὐτῶι τ' Αἰσονίδῃ τεκμαίρετο· σῖγα δ' ἑταῖροι
θάμβεον, εὖτ' ἐνόησαν ὃ δὴ καὶ ἐτήτυμον ἦεν.
τρὶς μὲν ἀνήυσεν, τρὶς δ' ὀτρύνοντος ὁμίλου   75
Φρόντις ἀμοιβήδην ἀντίαχεν· οἱ δ' ἄρα τείως
ἥρωες μετὰ τήν γε θοοῖς ἐλάασκον ἐρετμοῖς.
οὔ πω πείσματα νηὸς ἐπ' ἠπείροιο περαίης
βάλλον, ὁ δὲ κραιπνοὺς χέρσωι πόδας ἧκεν Ἰήσων
ὑψοῦ ἀπ' ἰκριόφιν· μετὰ δὲ Φρόντις τε καὶ Ἄργος,   80
υἷε δύω Φρίξου, χαμάδις θόρον. ἡ δ' ἄρα τούς γε
γούνων ἀμφοτέρῃσι περισχομένη προσέειπεν·
"ἔκ με, φίλοι, ρύσασθε δυσάμμορον, ὣς δὲ καὶ αὐτούς
ὑμέας, Αἰήταο· πρὸ γάρ τ' ἀναφανδὰ τέτυκται
πάντα μάλ', οὐδέ τι μῆχος ἱκάνεται. ἀλλ' ἐπὶ νηί   85
φεύγωμεν, πρὶν τόν γε θοῶν ἐπιβήμεναι ἵππων.
δώσω δὲ χρύσειον ἐγὼ δέρος, εὐνήσασα
φρουρὸν ὄφιν· τύνη δὲ θεοὺς ἐνὶ σοῖσιν ἑταίροις,
ξεῖνε, τεῶν μύθων ἐπιίστορας, οὕς μοι ὑπέστης,
ποίησαι, μηδ' ἔνθεν ἑκαστέρω ὁρμηθεῖσαν   90
χήτεϊ κηδεμόνων ὀνοτὴν καὶ ἀεικέα θείης."
    ἴσκεν ἀκηχεμένη· μέγα δὲ φρένες Αἰσονίδαο
γήθεον. αἶψα δέ μιν περὶ γούνασι πεπτηυῖαν
ἧκ' ἀναειρόμενος προσπτύξατο θάρσυνέν τε·
"δαιμονίη, Ζεὺς αὐτὸς Ὀλύμπιος ὅρκιος ἔστω   95
Ἥρη τε Ζυγίη, Διὸς εὐνέτις, ἦ μὲν ἐμοῖσιν
κουριδίην σε δόμοισιν ἐνιστήσεσθαι ἄκοιτιν,
εὖτ' ἂν ἐς Ἑλλάδα γαῖαν ἱκώμεθα νοστήσαντες."
    ὣς ηὔδα, καὶ χεῖρα παρασχεδὸν ἥραρε χειρί
δεξιτερήν. ἡ δέ σφιν ἐς ἱερὸν ἄλσος ἀνώγει   100
νῆα θοὴν ἐλάαν αὐτοσχεδόν, ὄφρ' ἔτι νύκτωρ
κῶας ἑλόντες ἄγοιντο παρὲκ νόον Αἰήταο.
ἔνθ' ἔπος ἠδὲ καὶ ἔργον ὁμοῦ πέλεν ἐσσυμένοισιν·
εἰς γάρ μιν βήσαντες, ἀπὸ χθονὸς αὐτίκ' ἔωσαν

80 ἀπ' w: ἐπ' Π⁵m   Φρόντις τε Ω: de Π⁶ non liquet   83 ὣς δὲ Ω: ἐκ δὲ Π⁶   85 ἐπὶ
Ω: de Π⁶ non liquet: ἐνὶ Brunck   86 τόν γε Π⁵ (ut vid.): τόνδε vel τῶνδε Ω   91 θείης
Ω: θείῃς Platt   94 θάρσυνεν Ω: φώνησεν D

νῆα· πολὺς δ᾽ ὀρυμαγδὸς ἐπειγομένων ἐλάτῃσιν   105
ἦεν ἀριστήων. ἡ δ᾽ ἔμπαλιν ἀίσσουσα
γαίῃ χεῖρας ἔτεινεν, ἀμήχανος· αὐτὰρ Ἰήσων
θάρσυνέν τ᾽ ἐπέεσσι καὶ ἴσχανεν ἀσχαλόωσαν.
ἦμος δ᾽ ἀνέρες ὕπνον ἀπ᾽ ὀφθαλμῶν ἐβάλοντο
ἀγρόται, οἵ τε κύνεσσι πεποιθότες οὔ ποτε νύκτα   110
ἄγχαυρον κνώσσουσιν, ἀλευάμενοι φάος ἠοῦς,
μὴ πρὶν ἀμαλδύνῃ θηρῶν στίβον ἠδὲ καὶ ὀδμήν
θηρείην λευκῇσιν ἐνισκίμψασα βολῇσι,
τῆμος ἄρ᾽ Αἰσονίδης κούρη τ᾽ ἀπὸ νηὸς ἔβησαν
ποιήεντ᾽ ἀνὰ χῶρον ἵνα Κριοῦ καλέονται   115
Εὐναί, ὅθι πρῶτον κεκμηότα γούνατ᾽ ἔκαμψε,
νώτοισιν φορέων Μινυήιον υἷ᾽ Ἀθάμαντος.
ἐγγύθι δ᾽ αἰθαλόεντα πέλεν βωμοῖο θέμεθλα,
ὅν ῥά ποτ᾽ Αἰολίδης Διὶ Φυξίωι εἵσατο Φρίξος,
ῥέζων κεῖνο τέρας παγχρύσεον, ὥς οἱ ἔειπεν   120
Ἑρμείας πρόφρων ξυμβλήμενος. ἔνθ᾽ ἄρα τούς γε
Ἄργου φραδμοσύνῃσιν ἀριστῆες μεθέηκαν.
τὼ δὲ δι᾽ ἀτραπιτοῖο μεθ᾽ ἱερὸν ἄλσος ἵκοντο,
φηγὸν ἀπειρεσίην διζημένω ἧι ἔπι κῶας
βέβλητο, νεφέλῃ ἐναλίγκιον ἥ τ᾽ ἀνιόντος   125
ἠελίου φλογερῇσιν ἐρεύθεται ἀκτίνεσσιν.
αὐτὰρ ὁ ἀντικρὺ περιμήκεα τείνετο δειρήν
ὀξὺς ἀύπνοισι προϊδὼν ὄφις ὀφθαλμοῖσι
νισσομένους· ῥοίζει δὲ πελώριον, ἀμφὶ δὲ μακραί
ἠιόνες ποταμοῖο καὶ ἄσπετον ἴαχεν ἄλσος.   130
ἔκλυον οἵ καὶ πολλὸν ἑκὰς Τιτηνίδος Αἴης
Κολχίδα γῆν ἐνέμοντο παρὰ προχοῇσι Λύκοιο,
ὅς τ᾽ ἀποκιδνάμενος ποταμοῦ κελάδοντος Ἀράξεω
Φάσιδι συμφέρεται ἱερὸν ῥόον, οἱ δὲ συνάμφω
Καυκασίην ἅλαδ᾽ εἰς ἕν ἐλαυνόμενοι προρέουσι·   135
δείματι δ᾽ ἐξέγροντο λεχωίδες, ἀμφὶ δὲ παισί
νηπιάχοις, οἵ τέ σφιν ὑπ᾽ ἀγκαλίδεσσιν ἴαυον,
ῥοίζωι παλλομένοις χεῖρας βάλον ἀσχαλόωσαι.
ὡς δ᾽ ὅτε τυφομένης ὕλης ὕπερ αἰθαλόεσσαι
καπνοῖο στροφάλιγγες ἀπείριτοι εἰλίσσονται,   140
ἄλλη δ᾽ αἶψ᾽ ἑτέρῃ ἐπιτέλλεται αἰὲν ἐπιπρό

112 θηρῶν Ω: θερμὸν Fränkel   135 προρέουσι Fränkel: προχέουσι Ω

νειόθεν εἰλίγγοισιν ἐπήορος ἀίσσουσα·
ὡς τότε κεῖνο πέλωρον ἀπειρεσίας ἐλέλιζε
ῥυμβόνας, ἀζαλέηισιν ἐπηρεφέας φολίδεσσι.
τοῖο δ' ἑλισσομένοιο †κατόμματον εἴσετο† κούρη,   145
Ὕπνον ἀοσσητῆρα, θεῶν ὕπατον, καλέουσα
ἥδείηι ἐνοπῆι θέλξαι τέρας, αὖε δ' ἄνασσαν
νυκτιπόλον χθονίην εὐαντέα δοῦναι ἐφορμήν.
εἵπετο δ' Αἰσονίδης πεφοβημένος· αὐτὰρ ὅ γ' ἤδη
οἴμηι θελγόμενος δολιχὴν ἀνελύετ' ἄκανθαν   150
γηγενέος σπείρης, μήκυνε δὲ μυρία κύκλα,
οἷον ὅτε βληχροῖσι κυλινδόμενον πελάγεσσιν
κῦμα μέλαν κωφόν τε καὶ ἄβρομον· ἀλλὰ καὶ ἔμπης
ὑψοῦ σμερδαλέην κεφαλὴν μενέαινεν ἀείρας
ἀμφοτέρους ὀλοῆισι περιπτύξαι γενύεσσιν.   155
ἡ δέ μιν ἀρκεύθοιο νέον τετμηότι θαλλῶι
βάπτουσ' ἐκ κυκεῶνος ἀκήρατα φάρμακ' ἀοιδαῖς
ῥαῖνε κατ' ὀφθαλμῶν, περί τ' ἀμφί τε νήριτος ὀδμή
φαρμάκου ὕπνον ἔβαλλε. γένυν δ' αὐτῆι ἐνὶ χώρηι
θῆκεν ἐρεισάμενος, τὰ δ' ἀπείρονα πολλὸν ὀπίσσω   160
κύκλα πολυπρέμνοιο διὲξ ὕλης τετάνυστο.
    ἔνθα δ' ὁ μὲν χρύσειον ἀπὸ δρυὸς αἴνυτο κῶας,
κούρης κεκλομένης· ἡ δ' ἔμπεδον ἑστηυῖα
φαρμάκωι ἔψηχεν θηρὸς κάρη, εἰσόκε δή μιν
αὐτὸς ἑὴν ἐπὶ νῆα παλιντροπάασθαι Ἰήσων   165
ἤνωγεν· λεῖπον δὲ πολύσκιον ἄλσος Ἄρηος.
ὡς δὲ σεληναίης διχομήνιδα παρθένος αἴγλην
ὑψόθεν ἐξανέχουσαν ὑπωροφίου θαλάμοιο
λεπταλέωι ἑανῶι ὑποΐσχεται, ἐν δέ οἱ ἦτορ
χαίρει δερκομένης καλὸν σέλας· ὡς τότ' Ἰήσων   170
γηθόσυνος μέγα κῶας ἑαῖς ἀναείρετο χερσί,
καί οἱ ἐπὶ ξανθῆισι παρηίσιν ἠδὲ μετώπωι
μαρμαρυγῆι ληνέων φλογὶ εἴκελον ἷζεν ἔρευθος.
ὅσση δὲ ῥινὸς βοὸς ἤνιος ἢ ἐλάφοιο
γίνεται, ἥν τ' ἀγρῶσται ἀχαιινέην καλέουσι,   175

τόσσον ἔην, πάντηι χρύσεον, ἐφύπερθε δ᾽ ἄωτον
βεβρίθει λήνεσσιν ἐπηρεφές· ἤλιθα δὲ χθών
αἰὲν ὑποπρὸ ποδῶν ἀμαρύσσετο νισσομένοιο.
ἤιε δ᾽ ἄλλοτε μὲν λαιῶι ἐπιειμένος ὤμωι
αὐχένος ἐξ ὑπάτοιο ποδηνεκές, ἄλλοτε δ᾽ αὖτε   180
εἴλει ἀφασσόμενος· περὶ γὰρ δίεν ὄφρα ἑ μή τις
ἀνδρῶν ἠὲ θεῶν νοσφίσσεται ἀντιβολήσας.
ἠὼς μέν ῥ᾽ ἐπὶ γαῖαν ἐκίδνατο, τοὶ δ᾽ ἐς ὅμιλον
ἷξον. θάμβησαν δὲ νέοι μέγα κῶας ἰδόντες
λαμπόμενον στεροπῆι ἴκελον Διός· ὦρτο δ᾽ ἕκαστος   185
ψαῦσαι ἐελδόμενος δέχθαι τ᾽ ἐνὶ χερσὶν ἑῆισιν·
Αἰσονίδης δ᾽ ἄλλους μὲν ἐρήτυε, τῶι δ᾽ ἐπὶ φᾶρος
κάββαλε νηγάτεον. πρύμνηι δ᾽ ἐνεείσατο κούρην
ἀνθέμενος, καὶ τοῖον ἔπος μετὰ πᾶσιν ἔειπε·
"μηκέτι νῦν χάζεσθε, φίλοι, πάτρηνδε νέεσθαι·   190
ἤδη γὰρ χρειὼ τῆς εἵνεκα τήνδ᾽ ἀλεγεινήν
ναυτιλίην ἔτλημεν, ὀιζύι μοχθίζοντες,
εὐπαλέως κούρης ὑπὸ δήνεσι κεκράανται.
τὴν μὲν ἐγὼν ἐθέλουσαν ἀνάξομαι οἴκαδ᾽ ἄκοιτιν
κουριδίην· ἀτὰρ ὔμμες, Ἀχαιίδος οἷά τε πάσης   195
αὐτῶν θ᾽ ὑμείων ἐσθλὴν ἐπαρωγὸν ἐοῦσαν,
σώετε· δὴ γὰρ που μάλ᾽, ὀίομαι, εἶσιν ἐρύξων
Αἰήτης ὁμάδωι πόντονδ᾽ ἵμεν ἐκ ποταμοῖο.
ἀλλ᾽ οἱ μὲν διὰ νηὸς ἀμοιβαδὶς ἀνέρος ἀνήρ
ἑζόμενος πηδοῖσιν ἐρέσσετε, τοὶ δὲ βοείας   200
ἀσπίδας ἡμίσεες δηίων θοὸν ἔχμα βολάων
προσχόμενοι νόστωι ἐπαμύνετε. νῦν δ᾽ ἐνὶ χερσίν
παῖδας ἑοὺς πάτρην τε φίλην γεραρούς τε τοκῆας
ἴσχομεν· ἡμετέρηι δ᾽ ἐπερείδεται Ἑλλὰς ἐφορμῆι
ἠὲ κατηφείην ἢ καὶ μέγα κῦδος ἀρέσθαι."   205
ὣς φάτο, δῦνε δὲ τεύχε᾽ ἀρήια· τοὶ δ᾽ ἰάχησαν
θεσπέσιον μεμαῶτες. ὁ δὲ ξίφος ἐκ κολεοῖο
σπασσάμενος πρυμναῖα νεὼς ἀπὸ πείσματ᾽ ἔκοψεν·
ἄγχι δὲ παρθενικῆς κεκορυθμένος ἰθυντῆρι
Ἀγκαίωι παρέβασκεν· ἐπείγετο δ᾽ εἰρεσίηι νηῦς   210
σπερχομένων ἄμοτον ποταμοῦ ἄφαρ ἐκτὸς ἐλάσσαι.
ἤδη δ᾽ Αἰήτηι ὑπερήνορι πᾶσί τε Κόλχοις

176 ἐφύπερθε δ᾽ nescioquis: ἐφύπερθεν Ω   182 ἠὲ D: ἠδὲ Ω   202 δ᾽ ἐνὶ codd. : ἐνὶ
Brunck

Μηδείης περίπυστος ἔρως καὶ ἔργ᾽ ἐτέτυκτο·
ἐς δ᾽ ἀγορὴν ἀγέροντ᾽ ἐνὶ τεύχεσιν, ὅσσα τε πόντου
κύματα χειμερίοιο κορύσσεται ἐξ ἀνέμοιο   215
ἢ ὅσα φύλλα χαμᾶζε περικλαδέος πέσεν ὕλης
φυλλοχόωι ἐνὶ μηνί (τίς ἂν τάδε τεκμήραιτο;)·
ὣς οἱ ἀπειρέσιοι ποταμοῦ παρεμέτρεον ὄχθας,
κλαγγῆι μαιμώοντες. ὁ δ᾽ εὐτύκτωι ἐνὶ δίφρωι
Αἰήτης ἵπποισι μετέπρεπεν οὕς οἱ ὄπασσεν   220
Ἥλιος πνοιῆισιν ἐειδομένους ἀνέμοιο,
σκαιῆι μέν ῥ᾽ ἐνὶ χειρὶ σάκος δινωτὸν ἀείρων,
τῆι δ᾽ ἑτέρηι πεύκην περιμήκεα, πὰρ δέ οἱ ἔγχος
ἀντικρὺ τετάνυστο πελώριον· ἡνία δ᾽ ἵππων
γέντο χεροῖν Ἄψυρτος. ὑπεκπρὸ δὲ πόντον ἔταμνε   225
νηῦς ἤδη, κρατεροῖσιν ἐπειγομένη ἐρέτηισιν
καὶ μεγάλου ποταμοῖο καταβλώσκοντι ῥεέθρωι·
αὐτὰρ ἄναξ ἄτηι πολυπήμονι χεῖρας ἀείρας
Ἥλιον καὶ Ζῆνα κακῶν ἐπιμάρτυρας ἔργων
κέκλετο, δεινὰ δὲ παντὶ παρασχεδὸν ἤπυε λαῶι·   230
εἰ μή οἱ κούρην αὐτάγρετον ἢ ἀνὰ γαῖαν
ἢ πλωτῆς εὑρόντες ἔτ᾽ εἰν ἁλὸς οἴδματι νῆα
ἄξουσιν καὶ θυμὸν ἐνιπλήσει μενεαίνων
τείσασθαι τάδε πάντα, δαήσονται κεφαλῆισιν
πάντα χόλον καὶ πᾶσαν ἑὴν ὑποδέγμενοι ἄτην.   235
    ὣς ἔφατ᾽ Αἰήτης. αὐτῶι δ᾽ ἐνὶ ἤματι Κόλχοι
νῆάς τ᾽ εἰρύσσαντο καὶ ἄρμενα νηυσὶ βάλοντο,
αὐτῶι δ᾽ ἤματι πόντον ἀνήιον· οὐδέ κε φαίης
τόσσον νηίτην στόλον ἔμμεναι, ἀλλ᾽ οἰωνῶν
ἰλαδὸν ἄσπετον ἔθνος ἐπιβρομέειν πελάγεσσιν.   240
    οἱ δ᾽, ἀνέμου λαιψηρὰ θεῆς βουλῆισιν ἀέντος
Ἥρης, ὄφρ᾽ ὤκιστα κακὸν Πελίαο δόμοισιν
Αἰαίη Μήδεια Πελασγίδα γαῖαν ἵκηται,
ἠοῖ ἐνὶ τριτάτηι πρυμνήσια νηὸς ἔδησαν
Παφλαγόνων ἀκτῆισι, πάροιθ᾽ Ἅλυος ποταμοῖο·   245
ἡ γάρ σφ᾽ ἐξαποβάντας ἀρέσσασθαι θυέεσσιν
ἠνώγει Ἑκάτην. καὶ δὴ τὰ μὲν ὅσσα θυηλὴν
κούρη πορσανέουσα τιτύσκετο (μήτε τις ἴστωρ
εἴη μήτ᾽ ἐμὲ θυμὸς ἐποτρύνειεν ἀείδειν)

232 πλωτὴν Campbell   247 θυηλὴν d : θυηλῆι Ω

ἅζομαι αὐδῆσαι· τό γε μὴν ἕδος ἐξέτι κείνου,
ὅ ρα θεᾶι ἥρωες ἐπὶ ῥηγμῖσιν ἔδειμαν,
ἀνδράσιν ὀψιγόνοισι μένει καὶ τῆμος ἰδέσθαι.
αὐτίκα δ᾽ Αἰσονίδης ἐμνήσατο, σὺν δὲ καὶ ὤλλοι
ἥρωες, Φινῆος ὃ δὴ πλόον ἄλλον ἔειπεν
ἐξ Αἴης ἔσσεσθαι· ἀνώιστος δ᾽ ἐτέτυκτο
πᾶσιν ὁμῶς. Ἄργος δὲ λιλαιομένοις ἀγόρευσεν·
"νισόμεθ᾽ Ὀρχομενόν, τὴν ἔχραεν ὔμμι περῆσαι
νημερτὴς ὅδε μάντις ὅτωι ξυνέβητε πάροιθεν.
ἔστιν γὰρ πλόος ἄλλος, ὃν ἀθανάτων ἱερῆες
πέφραδον οἳ Θήβης Τριτωνίδος ἐκγεγάασιν.
οὔπω τείρεα πάντα τά τ᾽ οὐρανῶι εἱλίσσονται,
οὐδέ τί πω Δαναῶν ἱερὸν γένος ἦεν ἀκοῦσαι
πευθομένοις· οἶοι δ᾽ ἔσαν Ἀρκάδες Ἀπιδανῆες,
Ἀρκάδες, οἳ καὶ πρόσθε σεληναίης ὑδέονται
ζώειν, φηγὸν ἔδοντες ἐν οὔρεσιν· οὐδὲ Πελασγίς
χθὼν τότε κυδαλίμοισιν ἀνάσσετο Δευκαλίδηισιν,
ἦμος ὅτ᾽ Ἠερίη πολυλήιος ἐκλήιστο
μήτηρ Αἴγυπτος προτερηγενέων αἰζηῶν,
καὶ ποταμὸς Τρίτων εὐρύρροος ὧι ὕπο πᾶσα
ἄρδεται Ἠερίη — Διόθεν δέ μιν οὔποτε δεύει
ὄμβρος ἅλις — προχοῆισι δ᾽ ἀνασταχύουσιν ἄρουραι.
ἔνθεν δή τινά φασι πέριξ διὰ πᾶσαν ὁδεῦσαι
Εὐρώπην Ἀσίην τε, βίηι καὶ κάρτεϊ λαῶν
σφωιτέρων θάρσει τε πεποιθότα· μυρία δ᾽ ἄστη
νάσσατ᾽ ἐποιχόμενος, τὰ μὲν ἤ ποθι ναιετάουσιν
ἠὲ καὶ οὔ· πουλὺς γὰρ ἄδην ἐπενήνοθεν αἰών.
Αἶά γε μὴν ἔτι νῦν μένει ἔμπεδον υἱωνοί τε
τῶνδ᾽ ἀνδρῶν οὓς †ὅγε καθίσσατο ναιέμεν Αἶαν·
οἳ δή τοι γραπτῦς πατέρων ἔθεν εἰρύονται,
κύρβιας οἷς ἔνι πᾶσαι ὁδοὶ καὶ πείρατ᾽ ἔασιν
ὑγρῆς τε τραφερῆς τε πέριξ ἐπινισομένοισιν.
ἔστι δέ τις ποταμός, ὕπατον κέρας Ὠκεανοῖο,
εὐρύς τε προβαθής τε καὶ ὁλκάδι νηὶ περῆσαι·
Ἴστρον μιν καλέοντες ἑκὰς διετεκμήραντο·

250

255

260

265

270

275

280

257 ante h. v. lacunam posuit Fränkel νισόμεθ᾽ S : νεισόμεθ᾽ ἐς ΛΑΣ : νεύμεθ᾽ ἐς Ε
269 εὐρύρροος Meineke : εὐρ(ρ)οος Ω   271 προχοῆισι δ᾽ Q : –οαῖσι δ᾽ vel –οαῖς ἰδ᾽
vel –οήισιν cett.   274 σφωιτέρων m : –ρωι wD   275 ἤ SE : οὐ cett.   278 ὅγε codd: ὅς
γε Hölzlin   283 προβαθής LAS : προβαθύς wE

ὃς δ᾽ ἤτοι τείως μὲν ἀπείρονα τέμνετ᾽ ἄρουραν   285
εἷς οἶος, πηγαὶ γὰρ ὑπὲρ πνοιῆς βορέαο
Ῥιπαίοις ἐν ὄρεσσιν ἀπόπροθι μορμύρουσιν·
ἀλλ᾽ ὁπόταν Θρηικῶν Σκυθέων τ᾽ ἐπιβήσεται οὔρους,
ἔνθα διχῆι, τὸ μὲν ἔνθα μετ᾽ ἠοίην ἅλα βάλλει
τῆιδ᾽ ὕδωρ, τὸ δ᾽ ὄπισθε βαθὺν διὰ κόλπον ἵησι   290
σχιζόμενος πόντου Τρινακρίου εἰσανέχοντα,
γαίηι ὃς ὑμετέρηι παρακέκλιται, εἰ ἐτεὸν δή
ὑμετέρης γαίης Ἀχελώιος ἐξανίησιν."
    ὣς ἄρ᾽ ἔφη. τοῖσιν δὲ θεὰ τέρας ἐγγυάλιξεν
αἴσιον, ὧι καὶ πάντες ἐπευφήμησαν ἰδόντες   295
στέλλεσθαι τήνδ᾽ οἶμον· ἐπιπρὸ γὰρ ὁλκὸς ἐτύχθη
οὐρανίης ἀκτῖνος, ὅπηι καὶ ἀμεύσιμον ἦεν.
γηθόσυνοι δέ, Λύκοιο καταυτόθι παῖδα λιπόντες,
λαίφεσι πεπταμένοισιν ὑπεὶρ ἅλα ναυτίλλοντο
οὔρεα Παφλαγόνων θηεύμενοι· οὐδὲ Κάραμβιν   300
γνάμψαν, ἐπεὶ πνοιαί τε καὶ οὐρανίου πυρὸς αἴγλη
μίμνεν ἕως Ἴστροιο μέγαν ῥόον εἰσαφίκοντο.
    Κόλχοι δ᾽ αὖτ᾽, ἄλλοι μὲν ἐτώσια μαστεύοντες
Κυανέας Πόντοιο διὲκ πέτρας ἐπέρησαν,
ἄλλοι δ᾽ αὖ ποταμὸν μετεκίαθον, οἷσιν ἄνασσεν   305
Ἄψυρτος, Καλὸν δὲ διὰ στόμα πεῖρε λιασθείς·
τῶ καὶ ὑπέφθη τούς γε βαλὼν ὕπερ αὐχένα γαίης
κόλπον ἔσω πόντοιο πανέσχατον Ἰονίοιο.
Ἴστρωι γάρ τις νῆσος ἐέργεται οὔνομα Πεύκη
τριγλώχιν, εὖρος μὲν ἐς αἰγιαλοὺς ἀνέχουσα,   310
στεινὸν δ᾽ αὖτ᾽ ἀγκῶνα ποτὶ ῥόον· ἀμφὶ δὲ δοιαί
σχίζονται προχοαί· τὴν μὲν καλέουσι Νάρηκος,
τὴν δ᾽ ὑπὸ τῆι νεάτηι Καλὸν στόμα· τῆιδε διαπρό
Ἄψυρτος Κόλχοι τε θοώτερον ὡρμήθησαν,
οἱ δ᾽ ὑψοῦ νήσοιο κατ᾽ ἀκροτάτης ἐνέοντο   315
τηλόθεν. εἰαμενῆισι δ᾽ ἐν ἄσπετα πώεα λεῖπον
ποιμένες ἄγραυλοι νηῶν φόβωι, οἷά τε θῆρας
ὀσσόμενοι πόντου μεγακήτεος ἐξανιόντας.
οὐ γάρ πω ἁλίας γε πάρος ποθὶ νῆας ἴδοντο

285 τέμνει Fränkel   288 ἐπιβήσεται E : ἐνι- Ω   289 ἠοίην Guyet : ἰονίην Ω : ἡμετέρην
Wilamowitz   292 ὑμετέρηι SEΞ : ἠμ- LAGDΣ   297 ἀμεύσιμον Etym. Gen.: μόρσιμον Ω
302 μίμνεν wΣ : μεῖνεν m   313 τῆιδε vel τῆι δὲ codd.: τῆσδε Livrea   διαπρό codd.:
ἐπιπρό Π⁷

οὔτ' οὖν Θρήϊξι μιγάδες Σκύθαι οὐδὲ Σίγυννοι,   320
οὔτ' οὖν Τραυκένιοι, οὔθ' οἱ περὶ Λαύριον ἤδη
Σίνδοι ἐρημαῖον πεδίον μέγα ναιετάοντες.
αὐτὰρ ἐπεί τ' Ἄγγουρον ὄρος καὶ ἄπωθεν ἐόντα
Ἀγγούρου ὄρεος σκόπελον παρὰ Καυλιακοῖο,
ὧι πέρι δὴ σχίζων Ἴστρος ῥόον ἔνθα καὶ ἔνθα   325
βάλλει ἁλός, πεδίον τε τὸ Λαύριον ἠμείψαντο,
δή ῥα τότε Κρονίην Κόλχοι ἄλαδ' ἐκπρομολόντες,
πάντηι, μή σφε λάθοιεν, ὑπετμήξαντο κελεύθους.
οἱ δ' ὄπιθεν ποταμοῖο κατήλυθον, ἐκ δ' ἐπέρησαν
δοιὰς Ἀρτέμιδος Βρυγηΐδας ἀγχόθι νήσους.   330
τῶν δ' ἤτοι ἑτέρηι μὲν ἐν ἱερὸν ἔσκεν ἔδεθλον·
ἐν δ' ἑτέρηι, πληθὺν πεφυλαγμένοι Ἀψύρτοιο,
βαῖνον· ἐπεὶ †κείνας πολέων λίπον ἔνδοθι νήσους†
αὔτως, ἁζόμενοι κούρην Διός, αἱ δὲ δὴ ἄλλαι
στεινόμεναι Κόλχοισι πόρους εἴρυντο θαλάσσης.   335
ὣς δὲ καὶ εἰς ἀκτὰς πληθὺν λίπεν ἀγχόθι νήσων
μέσφα Σαλαγγῶνος ποταμοῦ καὶ Νέστιδος αἴης.
   ἔνθα κε λευγαλέηι Μινύαι τότε δηιοτῆτι
παυρότεροι πλεόνεσσιν ὑπείκαθον· ἀλλὰ πάροιθεν
συνθεσίην, μέγα νεῖκος ἀλευάμενοι, ἐτάμοντο·   340
κῶας μὲν χρύσειον, ἐπεί σφισιν αὐτὸς ὑπέστη
Αἰήτης, εἴ κέν οἱ ἀναπλήσειαν ἀέθλους,
ἔμπεδον εὐδικίηι σφέας ἕξέμεν, εἴτε δόλοισιν
εἴτε καὶ ἀμφαδίην αὔτως ἀέκοντος ἀπηύρων·
αὐτὰρ Μήδειαν — τόδε γὰρ πέλεν ἀμφήριστον —   345
παρθέσθαι κούρηι Λητωΐδι νόσφιν ὁμίλου,
εἰσόκε τις δικάσηισι θεμιστούχων βασιλήων
εἴτε μιν εἰς πατρὸς χρειὼ δόμον αὖτις ἱκάνειν
[εἴτε μετ' ἀφνειὴν θείου πόλιν Ὀρχομενοῖο]   348a
εἴτε μεθ' Ἑλλάδα γαῖαν ἀριστήεσσιν ἕπεσθαι.
   ἔνθα δ' ἐπεὶ τὰ ἕκαστα νόωι πεμπάσσατο κούρη,   350
δή ῥά μιν ὀξεῖαι κραδίην ἐλέλιξαν ἀνῖαι

320 Θρήιξιν L^{ac}S   321 οὔτ' οὖν Ω (]ν Π¹): οὔτ' αὖ Ε   Τραυκένιοι Kassel: Γρ- Π¹
codd.   323 ἐπεί τ' S: ἔπειτ' Ω   330 Βρυγηΐδας Σ1002–3: Βρυτ- Ω   331 τῶν ἤτοι Ε
333 λίπεν Fränkel νήσων Livrea   334 ἁζόμενος Fränkel   336 ἀκτὰς L^{pc}:
αὐτὰς L^{ac}: ἄλλας cett.   λίπον Ε   νήσων W^{mg}V^{2sl}: νήσους Ω   340 συνθεσίην
Schneider: –ίηι Ω: –ίας Ε   342 κέν οἱ Fränkel: κεῖνοι Ω   345 τόδε RQ: τὸ Ω: τόγε S
348a (=2.1186) del. Ruhnken (ignorat Σ; de Π^x non liquet) ἀφνειὴν Bigot: ἀφνειοῖο Ω
349 εἴτε Ω: καί τε Ε (de Π^x non liquet)

νωλεμές. αἶψα δὲ νόσφιν Ἰήσονα μοῦνον ἑταίρων
ἐκπροκαλεσσαμένη ἄγεν ἄλλυδις, ὄφρ' ἐλίασθεν
πολλὸν ἑκάς, στονόεντα δ' ἐνωπαδὶς ἔκφατο μῦθον·
"Αἰσονίδη, τίνα τήνδε συναρτύνασθε μενοινήν   355
ἀμφ' ἐμοί; ἦέ σε πάγχυ λαθιφροσύναις ἐνέηκαν
ἀγλαΐαι, τῶν δ' οὔ τι μετατρέπηι ὅσσ' ἀγόρευες
χρειοῖ ἐνισχόμενος; ποῦ τοι Διὸς Ἱκεσίοιο
ὅρκια, ποῦ δὲ μελιχραὶ ὑποσχεσίαι βεβάασιν;
ἧις ἐγὼ οὐ κατὰ κόσμον ἀναιδήτωι ἰότητι   360
πάτρην τε κλέα τε μεγάρων αὐτούς τε τοκῆας
νοσφισάμην, τά μοι ἦεν ὑπέρτατα, τηλόθι δ' οἴη
λυγρῆισιν κατὰ πόντον ἅμ' ἀλκυόνεσσι φορεῦμαι,
σῶν ἕνεκεν καμάτων, ἵνα μοι σόος ἀμφί τε βουσίν
ἀμφί τε γηγενέεσσιν ἀναπλήσειας ἀέθλους·   365
ὕστατον αὖ καὶ κῶας, ἐπεί τ' ἐπάιστον ἐτύχθη,
εἷλες ἐμῆι ματίηι, κατὰ δ' οὐλοὸν αἶσχος ἔχευα
θηλυτέραις. τῶ φημὶ τεὴ κούρη τε δάμαρ τε
αὐτοκασιγνήτη τε μεθ' Ἑλλάδα γαῖαν ἕπεσθαι.
πάντηι νυν πρόφρων ὑπερίστασο, μηδέ με μούνην   370
σεῖο λίπηις ἀπάνευθεν, ἐποιχόμενος βασιλῆας,
ἀλλ' αὔτως εἴρυσο· δίκη δέ τοι ἔμπεδος ἔστω
καὶ θέμις ἣν ἄμφω συναρέσσαμεν· ἢ σύ γ' ἔπειτα
φασγάνωι αὐτίκα τόνδε μέσον διὰ λαιμὸν ἀμῆσαι,
ὄφρ' ἐπίηρα φέρωμαι ἐοικότα μαργοσύνηισιν.   375
σχέτλιε· εἴ †κέν μετ† κασιγνήτοιο δικάσσηι
ἔμμεναι οὗτος ἄναξ τῶι ἐπίσχετε τάσδ' ἀλεγεινάς
ἄμφω συνθεσίας, πῶς ἵξομαι ὄμματα πατρός;
ἦ μάλ' ἐυκλειής. τίνα δ' οὐ τίσιν ἠὲ βαρεῖαν
ἄτην οὐ σμυγερῶς δεινῶν ὕπερ οἷα ἔοργα   380
ὀτλήσω; σὺ δέ κεν θυμηδέα νόστον ἕλοιο.
μὴ τό γε παμβασίλεια Διὸς τελέσειεν ἄκοιτις,
ἧι ἔπι κυδιάεις· μνήσαιο δὲ καί ποτ' ἐμεῖο
στρευγόμενος καμάτοισι, δέρος δέ τοι ἶσον ὀνείρωι
οἴχοιτ' εἰς ἔρεβος μεταμώνιον· ἐκ δέ σε πάτρης   385
αὐτίκ' ἐμαί σ' ἐλάσειαν Ἐρινύες, οἷα καὶ αὐτή

---

366 ἐπεί τ' ἐπάιστον ἐτύχθη Mooney: ἐπεί τε παιστὸν ἐτύχθη LA: ἐπείτ' ἐπάιστος ἐτύχθην
w: ἐφ' ὧι πλόος ὕμμιν ἐτύχθη E   370 πρόφρων Bᵛˡ: προφέρων Ω   371 βασιλῆας E:
–ῆος Ω   376 κεν με LA: με G: κεν δή με E: εἰ γάρ κέν με Wilamowitz: εἰ μέν κέν με Campbell
379 ἦ μάλ' ἐυκλειής nescioquis: ἠὲ μάλ' εὐκλ- Ω   380 οἷα E: οἷά τ' w: οἷά θ' LA   381 σὺ
δέ κεν Wellauer, Brunck: οὐδέ κε LA: οὐ δή κε G: οὔ κεν SE   384 ὀνείρωι Miller: –ροις Ω

σῇι πάθον ἀτροπίηι· τὰ μὲν οὐ θέμις ἀκράαντα
ἐν γαίηι πεσέειν, μάλα γὰρ μέγαν ἤλιτες ὅρκον,
νηλεές· ἀλλ' οὐ θήν μοι ἐπιλλίζοντες ὀπίσσω
δὴν ἔσσεσθ' εὔκηλοι ἔκητί γε συνθεσιάων."   390
ὣς φάτ' ἀναζείουσα βαρὺν χόλον· ἵετο δ' ἥ γε
νῆα καταφλέξαι διά τ' †ἔμπεδα πάντα κεάσσαι,
ἐν δὲ πεσεῖν αὐτὴ μαλερῶι πυρί. τοῖα δ' Ἰήσων
μειλιχίοις ἐπέεσσιν ὑποδδείσας προσέειπεν·
"ἴσχεο, δαιμονίη· τὰ μὲν ἀνδάνει οὐδ' ἐμοὶ αὐτῶι,   395
ἀλλά τιν' ἀμβολίην διζήμεθα δηιοτῆτος,
ὅσσον δυσμενέων ἀνδρῶν νέφος ἀμφιδέδηεν
εἵνεκα σεῦ. πάντες γὰρ ὅσοι χθόνα τήνδε νέμονται
Ἀψύρτωι μεμάασιν ἀμυνέμεν, ὄφρα σε πατρί,
οἷά τε ληισθεῖσαν, ὑπότροπον οἴκαδ' ἄγοιτο·   400
αὐτοὶ δὲ στυγερῶι κεν ὀλοίμεθα πάντες ὀλέθρωι,
μείξαντες δαῒ χεῖρας· ὅ τοι καὶ ῥίγιον ἄλγος
ἔσσεται, εἴ σε θανόντες ἕλωρ κείνοισι λίποιμεν.
ἥδε δὲ συνθεσίη κρανέει δόλον ὧι μιν ἐς ἄτην
βήσομεν· οὐδ' ἂν ὁμῶς περιναιέται ἀντιόωσι   405
Κόλχοις ἦρα φέροντες ὑπὲρ σέο, νόσφιν ἄνακτος
ὅς τοι ἀοσσητήρ τε κασίγνητός τε τέτυκται·
οὐδ' ἂν ἐγὼ Κόλχοισιν †ὑπείξομαι πτολεμίζειν
ἀντιβίην, ὅτε μή με διὲξ εἰῶσι νέεσθαι."
ἴσκεν ὑποσσαίνων· ἡ δ' οὐλοὸν ἔκφατο μῦθον·   410
"φράζεο νῦν· χρειὼ γὰρ ἀεικελίοισιν ἐπ' ἔργοις
καὶ τόδε μητίσασθαι, ἐπεὶ τὸ πρῶτον ἀάσθην
ἀμπλακίηι, θεόθεν δὲ κακὰς ἤνυσσα μενοινάς·
τύνη μὲν κατὰ μῶλον ἀλέξεο δούρατα Κόλχων,
αὐτὰρ ἐγὼ κεῖνόν γε τεὰς ἐς χεῖρας ἱκέσθαι   415
μειλίξω· σὺ δέ μιν φαιδροῖς ἀγαπάζεο δώροις,
εἴ κέν πως †κήρυκας ἀπερχομένους† πεπίθοιμι
οἰόθεν οἶον ἐμοῖσι συναρθμῆσαι ἐπέεσσιν.
ἔνθ' εἴ τοι τόδε ἔργον ἐφανδάνει, οὔ τι μεγαίρω,
κτεῖνέ τε καὶ Κόλχοισιν ἀείρεο δηιοτῆτα."   420
ὣς τώ γε ξυμβάντε μέγαν δόλον ἠρτύναντο

---

391 ἀναζείουσα Ruhnken: ἀνιάζουσα Ω   400 ἄγοιτο D: ἄγοιντο Ω   405 ἀντιόωσι w:
ἀντιόωντες m: εἰσαῖοντες D: ἀντιόωιντο Diels   406 φέροντες Ω: –οιεν E   408 ὑπείξομαι
Ω: –ωμαι G: ὑπείξαιμι Brunck: ὑπείξω μὴ Gerhard   πτολεμίζειν wE: –ίξειν LA: –ίζων
Platt   409 διὲξ εἰῶσι Gerhard: διεξίωσι Ω   417 ἀπερχομένη G

Ἀψύρτωι, καὶ πολλὰ πόρον ξεινήια δῶρα·
οἷς μέτα καὶ πέπλον δόσαν ἱερὸν Ὑψιπυλείης
πορφύρεον. τὸν μέν ῥα Διωνύσωι κάμον αὐταί
Δίηι ἐν ἀμφιάλωι Χάριτες θεαί, αὐτὰρ ὁ παιδί   425
δῶκε Θόαντι μεταῦτις, ὁ δ᾿ αὖ λίπεν Ὑψιπυλείηι,
ἡ δ᾿ ἔπορ᾿ Αἰσονίδηι πολέσιν μετὰ καὶ τὸ φέρεσθαι
γλήνεσιν εὐεργὲς ξεινήιον. οὔ μιν ἀφάσσων
οὔτε κεν εἰσορόων γλυκὺν ἵμερον ἐμπλήσειας·
τοῦ δὲ καὶ ἀμβροσίη ὀδμὴ ἄεν ἐξέτι κείνου   430
ἐξ οὗ ἄναξ αὐτὸς Νυσήιος ἐγκατέλεκτο
ἀκροχάλιξ οἴνωι καὶ νέκταρι, καλὰ μεμαρπώς
στήθεα παρθενικῆς Μινωίδος, ἥν ποτε Θησεύς
Κνωσσόθεν ἑσπομένην Δίηι ἔνι κάλλιπε νήσωι.
ἡ δ᾿ ὅτε κηρύκεσσιν ἐπεξυνώσατο μύθους   435
θελγέμεν, εὖτ᾿ ἂν πρῶτα θεᾶς μετὰ νηὸν ἵκηται
συνθεσίηι νυκτός τε μέλαν κνέφας ἀμφιβάλησιν,
ἐλθέμεν, ὄφρα δόλον συμφράσσεται ὧι κεν ἑλοῦσα
χρύσειον μέγα κῶας ὑπότροπος αὖτις ὀπίσσω
βαίη ἐς Αἰήταο δόμους· πέρι γάρ μιν ἀνάγκηι   440
υἱῆες Φρίξοιο δόσαν ξείνοισιν ἄγεσθαι –
τοῖα παραιφαμένη, θελκτήρια φάρμακ᾿ ἔπασσεν
αἰθέρι καὶ πνοιῆισι, τά κεν καὶ ἄπωθεν ἐόντα
ἄγριον ἠλιβάτοιο κατ᾿ οὔρεος ἤγαγε θῆρα.
    σχέτλι᾿ Ἔρως, μέγα πῆμα, μέγα στύγος ἀνθρώποισιν,   445
ἐκ σέθεν οὐλόμεναί τ᾿ ἔριδες στοναχαί τε πόνοι τε,
ἄλγεά τ᾿ ἄλλ᾿ ἐπὶ τοῖσιν ἀπείρονα τετρήχασι·
δυσμενέων ἐπὶ παισὶ κορύσσεο, δαῖμον, ἀερθείς
οἷος Μηδείηι στυγερὴν φρεσὶν ἔμβαλες ἄτην.
    πῶς γὰρ δὴ μετιόντα κακῶι ἐδάμασσεν ὀλέθρωι   450
Ἄψυρτον; τὸ γὰρ ἧμιν ἐπισχερὼ ἦεν ἀοιδῆς.
    ἦμος ὅτ᾿ Ἀρτέμιδος νήσωι ἔνι τήν γε λίποντο
συνθεσίηι, τοὶ μέν ῥα διάνδιχα νηυσὶν ἔκελσαν
σφωιτέραις κρινθέντες· ὁ δ᾿ ἐς λόχον ἦιεν Ἰήσων,
δέγμενος Ἄψυρτόν τε καὶ οὓς ἐξαῦτις ἑταίρους.   455
αὐτὰρ ὅ γ᾿, αἰνοτάτηισιν ὑποσχεσίηισι δολωθείς,
καρπαλίμως ἧι νηὶ διὲξ ἁλὸς οἶδμα περήσας,

---

430 α[]ν Π¹ teste Haslam: πέλεν Ω   436 μετ[ὰ Π¹: περὶ Ω   438 δόλον Ω:]ρ fortasse
Π¹   ὥ]ι Π¹: ὥς Ω   446 οὐλόμεναί ἔριδες Π¹   πόνοι Π¹: γόοι Ω   450 εδαμ[ασ]σας
Π¹   452 νηῶι Fränkel   454 ἦιεν Brunck: ἦεν Ω

νύχθ' ὕπο λυγαίην ἱερῆς ἐπεβήσετο νήσου·
οἰόθι δ' ἀντικρὺ μετιών, πειρήσατο μύθοις
εἷο κασιγνήτης, ἀταλὸς πάις οἷα χαράδρης   460
χειμερίης ἣν οὐδὲ δι' αἴζηοὶ περόωσιν,
εἴ κε δόλον ξείνοισιν ἐπ' ἀνδράσι τεχνήσαιτο.
καὶ τώ μὲν τὰ ἕκαστα συνήινεον ἀλλήλοισιν·
αὐτίκα δ' Αἰσονίδης πυκινοῦ ἐξᾶλτο λόχοιο
γυμνὸν ἀνασχόμενος παλάμηι ξίφος. αἶψα δὲ κούρη   465
ἔμπαλιν ὄμματ' ἔνεικε, καλυψαμένη ὀθόνηισι,
μὴ φόνον ἀθρήσειε κασιγνήτοιο τυπέντος·
τὸν δ' ὅ γε, βουτύπος ὥστε μέγαν κερεαλκέα ταῦρον,
πλῆξεν ὀπιπεύσας νηοῦ σχεδὸν ὅν ποτ' ἔδειμαν
Ἀρτέμιδι Βρυγοὶ περιναιέται ἀντιπέρηθεν.   470
τοῦ ὅ γ' ἐνὶ προδόμωι γνὺξ ἤριπε· λοίσθια δ' ἥρως
θυμὸν ἀποπνείων χερσὶν μέλαν ἀμφοτέρηισιν
αἷμα κατ' ὠτειλὴν ὑποῖσχετο· τῆς δὲ καλύπτρην
ἀργυφέην καὶ πέπλον ἀλευομένης ἐρύθηνεν.
ὀξὺ δὲ πανδαμάτωρ λοξῶι ἴδεν οἷον ἔρεξαν   475
ὄμματι νηλειὴς ὀλοφώιον ἔργον Ἐρινύς.
ἥρως δ' Αἰσονίδης ἐξάργματα τάμνε θανόντος,
τρὶς δ' ἀπέλειξε φόνου, τρὶς δ' ἐξ ἄγος ἔπτυσ' ὀδόντων,
ἧ θέμις αὐθέντηισι δολοκτασίας ἱλάεσθαι.
ὑγρὸν δ' ἐν γαίηι κρύψεν νέκυν, ἔνθ' ἔτι νῦν περ   480
κείαται ὀστέα κεῖνα μετ' ἀνδράσιν Ἀψυρτεῦσιν.
   οἱ δ' ἄμυδις πυρσοῖο σέλας προπάροιθεν ἰδόντες
τό σφιν παρθενικὴ τέκμαρ μετιοῦσιν ἄειρε,
Κολχίδος ἀγχόθι νηὸς ἑὴν παρὰ νῆα βάλοντο
ἥρωες· Κόλχον δ' ὄλεκον στόλον, ἠύτε κίρκοι   485
φῦλα πελειάων ἠὲ μέγα πῶϋ λέοντες
ἀγρότεροι κλονέουσιν ἐνὶ σταθμοῖσι θορόντες.
οὐδ' ἄρα τις κείνων θάνατον φύγε, πάντα δ' ὅμιλον
πῦρ ἅτε δηιόωντες ἐπέδραμον. ὀψὲ δ' Ἰήσων
ἤντησεν, μεμαὼς ἐπαμυνέμεν οὐ μάλ' ἀρωγῆς   490
δευομένοις, ἤδη δὲ καὶ ἀμφ' αὐτοῖο μέλοντο.
   ἔνθα δὲ ναυτιλίης πυκινὴν πέρι μητιάασκον
ἑζόμενοι βουλήν, ἐπὶ δέ σφισιν ἤλυθε κούρη

---

458 ἐπεβήσετο *m*: −σατο *w*   464 ἐξᾶλτο Hölzlin : ἐπᾶλτο Ω   468 κερεαλκέα LA:
κεραελκέα *w*   472 ἀποπν[είων Π¹: ἀνα- Ω   481 ὀστέα γυμνά Etym. Gen.ᴮ   485
Κόλχον *m*: −ων *w*   492 πυκινὴν *w*: πυκινῆς LA*d*

φραζομένοις. Πηλεὺς δὲ παροίτατος ἔκφατο μῦθον·
"ἤδη νῦν κέλομαι νύκτωρ ἔτι νῆ' ἐπιβάντας   495
εἰρεσίῃ περάαν πλόον ἀντίον ὧι ἐπέχουσι
δήιοι. ἠῶθεν γὰρ ἐπαθρήσαντας ἕκαστα
ἔλπομαι οὐχ ἕνα μῦθον, ὅ τις προτέρωσε δίεσθαι
ἡμέας ὀτρυνέει, τοὺς πεισέμεν· οἶά δ' ἄνακτος
εὔνιδες ἀργαλέῃσι διχοστασίῃς κεδόωνται·   500
ῥηιδίη δέ κεν ἄμμι, κεδασθέντων δίχα λαῶν,
ἤδ' εἴη μετέπειτα κατερχομένοισι κέλευθος."
ὣς ἔφατ'· ᾔνησαν δὲ νέοι ἔπος Αἰακίδαο.
ῥίμφα δὲ νῆ' ἐπιβάντες ἐπερρώοντ' ἐλάτῃσι
νωλεμές, ὄφρ' ἱερὴν Ἠλεκτρίδα νῆσον ἵκοντο,   505
ἀλλάων ὑπάτην, ποταμοῦ σχεδὸν Ἠριδανοῖο.
Κόλχοι δ' ὁππότ' ὄλεθρον ἐπεφράσθησαν ἄνακτος,
ἤτοι μὲν δίζεσθαι ἐπέχραον ἔνδοθι πάσης
Ἀργὼ καὶ Μινύας Κρονίης ἁλός, ἀλλ' ἀπέρυκεν
Ἥρη σμερδαλέῃσι κατ' αἰθέρος ἀστεροπῇσιν.   510
ὕστατον αὖ – δὴ γάρ τε Κυταιίδος ἤθεα γαίης
στύξαν, ἀτυζόμενοι χόλον ἄγριον Αἰήταο –
ἔμπεδον ἄλλυδις ἄλλοι ἀφορμηθέντες ἔνασθεν.
οἱ μὲν ἐπ' αὐτάων νήσων ἔβαν ᾗσιν ἐπέσχον
ἥρωες, ναίουσι δ' ἐπώνυμοι Ἀψύρτοιο·   515
οἱ δ' ἄρ' ἐπ' Ἰλλυρικοῖο μελαμβαθέος ποταμοῖο,
τύμβος ἵν' Ἁρμονίης Κάδμοιό τε, πύργον ἔδειμαν,
ἀνδράσιν Ἐγχελέεσσιν ἐφέστιοι· οἱ δ' ἐν ὄρεσσιν
ἐνναίουσιν ἅ περ τε Κεραύνια κικλήσκονται
ἐκ τόθεν ἐξότε τούς γε Διὸς Κρονίδαο κεραυνοί   520
νῆσον ἐς ἀντιπέραιαν ἀπέτραπον ὁρμηθῆναι.
ἥρωες δ', ὅτε δή σφιν ἐείσατο νόστος ἀπήμων,
δή ῥα τότε προμολόντες ἐπὶ χθονὶ πείσματ' ἔδησαν
Ὑλλήων· νῆσοι γὰρ ἐπιπρούχοντο θαμειαί
ἀργαλέην πλώουσιν ὁδὸν μεσσηγὺς ἔχουσαι.   525
οὐδέ σφιν, ὡς καὶ πρίν, ἀνάρσια μητιάασκον
Ὑλλῆες· πρὸς δ' αὐτοὶ ἐμηχανόωντο κέλευθον,
μισθὸν ἀειρόμενοι τρίποδα μέγαν Ἀπόλλωνος.
δοιοὺς γὰρ τρίποδας τηλοῦ πόρε Φοῖβος ἄγεσθαι
Αἰσονίδῃ περόωντι κατὰ χρέος, ὁππότε Πυθώ   530

505 νω[λε]με[[ω]]ς.. ε[Π¹   511 αὖ – δὴ γάρ τε Merkel: δὴ γάρ τε Etym. Gen., Mag.:
αὐτοὶ δ' αὖτε Ω   528 ἀειράμενοι E

ἱρὴν πευσόμενος μετεκίαθε τῆσδ᾽ ὑπὲρ αὐτῆς
ναυτιλίης· πέπρωτο δ᾽, ὅπῃ χθονὸς ἱδρυθεῖεν,
μήποτε τὴν δήιοισιν ἀναστήσεσθαι ἰοῦσι.
τούνεκεν εἰσέτι νῦν κείνῃ ὅδε κεύθεται αἴῃ
ἀμφὶ πόλιν ἀγανὴν Ὑλληίδα, πολλὸν ἔνερθεν　　535
οὔδεος, ὥς κεν ἄφαντος ἀεὶ μερόπεσσι πέλοιτο.
οὐ μὲν ἔτι ζώοντα καταυτόθι τέτμον ἄνακτα
Ὕλλον, ὃν εὐειδὴς Μελίτη τέκεν Ἡρακλῆι
δήμωι Φαιήκων· ὁ γὰρ οἰκία Ναυσιθόοιο
[τυτθὸς ἐὼν ποτ᾽ ἔναιεν· ἀτὰρ λίπε νῆσον ἔπειτα]　　539a
Μάκριν τ᾽ εἰσαφίκανε, Διωνύσοιο τιθήνην,　　540
νιψόμενος παίδων ὀλοὸν φόνον· ἔνθ᾽ ὅ γε κούρην
Αἰγαίου ἐδάμασσεν ἐρασσάμενος ποταμοῖο,
νηιάδα Μελίτην· ἡ δὲ σθεναρὸν τέκεν Ὕλλον.　　543
οὐδ᾽ ἄρ᾽ ὅ γ᾽ ἡβήσας αὐτῇ ἐνὶ ἔλδετο νήσωι　　546
ναίειν κοιρανέοντος ὑπ᾽ ὀφρύσι Ναυσιθόοιο·
βῆ δ᾽ ἅλαδε Κρονίην, αὐτόχθονα λαὸν ἀγείρας
Φαιήκων, σὺν γάρ οἱ ἄναξ πόρσυνε κέλευθον
ἥρως Ναυσίθοος· τόθι δ᾽ εἵσατο· καί μιν ἔπεφνον　　550
Μέντορες, ἀγραύλοισιν ἀλεξόμενοι περὶ βουσίν.
　　ἀλλά, θεαί, πῶς τῆσδε παρὲξ ἁλὸς ἀμφί τε γαῖαν
Αὐσονίην νήσους τε Λιγυστίδας, αἳ καλέονται
Στοιχάδες, Ἀργώιης περιώσια σήματα νηός
νημερτὲς πέφαται; τίς ἀπόπροθι τόσσον ἀνάγκη　　555
καὶ χρειώ σφ᾽ ἐκόμισσε; τίνες σφέας ἤγαγον αὖραι;
　　αὐτόν που μεγαλωστὶ δεδουπότος Ἀψύρτοιο
Ζῆνα θεῶν βασιλῆα χόλος λάβεν οἷον ἔρεξαν·
Αἰαίης δ᾽ ὀλοὸν τεκμήρατο δήνεσι Κίρκης
αἷμ᾽ ἀπονιψαμένους πρό τε μυρία πημανθέντας　　560
νοστήσειν. τὸ μὲν οὔ τις ἀριστήων ἐνόησεν·
ἀλλ᾽ ἔθεον γαίης Ὑλληίδος ἐξανιόντες
τηλόθι· τὰς δ᾽ ἀπέλειπον ὅσαι Κόλχοισι πάροιθεν
ἑξείης πλήθοντο Λιβυρνίδες εἰν ἁλὶ νῆσοι,
Ἴσσα τε Δυσκέλαδός τε καὶ ἱμερτὴ Πιτύεια.　　565
αὐτὰρ ἔπειτ᾽ ἐπὶ τῇσι παραὶ Κέρκυραν ἵκοντο,
ἔνθα Ποσειδάων Ἀσωπίδα νάσσατο κούρην,

539a habent LAw: om. E, ignorat Σ　546 ἐνὶ ἔλδετο Facius: ἐν ἐέλδ- vel ἐνεέλδ- Ω
547 ὑπ᾽ L² w. ἐπ᾽ mΣ　551 ἀλεξόμενοι Castiglioni: –μενον Ω: –μενος S　563 ὅσαι I²E:
ὅσοι Ω　564 Λιβυρνίδες S: Λιγυστίδες LA: Λιγυρνίδες L²GEΣ

ἠύκομον Κέρκυραν, ἑκὰς Φλειουντίδος αἴης,
ἁρπάξας ὑπ' ἔρωτι· μελαινομένην δέ μιν ἄνδρες
ναυτίλοι ἐκ πόντοιο κελαινῆι πάντοθεν ὕληι   570
δερκόμενοι, Κέρκυραν ἐπικλείουσι Μέλαιναν.
τῆι δ' ἐπὶ καὶ Μελίτην, λιαρῶι περιγηθέες οὔρωι,
αἰπεινήν τε Κερωσσόν, ὕπερθε δὲ πολλὸν ἐοῦσαν
Νυμφαίην παράμειβον, ἵνα κρείουσα Καλυψὼ
Ἀτλαντὶς ναίεσκε· τὰ δ' ἠεροειδέα λεύσσειν   575
οὔρεα δοιάζοντο Κεραύνια. καὶ τότε βουλὰς
ἀμφ' αὐτοῖς Ζηνός τε μέγαν χόλον ἐφράσαθ' Ἥρη.
μηδομένη δ' ἄνυσιν τοῖο πλόου, ὦρσεν ἀέλλας
ἀντικρύ, ταῖς αὖτις ἀναρπάγδην φορέοντο
νήσου ἐπὶ κραναῆς Ἠλεκτρίδος. αὐτίκα δ' ἄφνω   580
ἴαχεν ἀνδρομέηι ἐνοπῆι μεσσηγὺ θεόντων
αὐδῆεν γλαφυρῆς νηὸς δόρυ, τό ῥ' ἀνὰ μέσσην
στεῖραν Ἀθηναίη Δωδωνίδος ἥρμοσε φηγοῦ.
τοὺς δ' ὀλοὸν μεσσηγὺ δέος λάβεν εἰσαΐοντας
φθογγήν τε Ζηνός τε βαρὺν χόλον. οὐ γὰρ ἀλύξειν   585
ἔννεπεν οὔτε πόνους δολιχῆς ἁλὸς οὔτε θυέλλας
ἀργαλέας, ὅτε μὴ Κίρκη φόνον Ἀψύρτοιο
νηλέα νίψειεν· Πολυδεύκεα δ' εὐχετάασθαι
Κάστορά τ' ἀθανάτοισι θεοῖς ἤνωγε κελεύθους
Αὐσονίης ἔντοσθε πορεῖν ἁλός, ἧι ἔνι Κίρκην   590
δήουσιν, Πέρσης τε καὶ Ἠελίοιο θύγατρα.
    ὣς Ἀργὼ ἰάχησεν ὑπὸ κνέφας. οἱ δ' ἀνόρουσαν
Τυνδαρίδαι καὶ χεῖρας ἀνέσχεθον ἀθανάτοισιν
εὐχόμενοι τὰ ἕκαστα· κατηφείη δ' ἔχεν ἄλλους
ἥρωας Μινύας. ἡ δ' ἔσσυτο πολλὸν ἐπιπρὸ   595
λαίφεσιν· ἐς δ' ἔβαλον μύχατον ῥόον Ἠριδανοῖο,
ἔνθα ποτ' αἰθαλόεντι τυπεὶς πρὸς στέρνα κεραυνῶι
ἡμιδαὴς Φαέθων πέσεν ἅρματος Ἠελίοιο
λίμνης ἐς προχοὰς πολυβενθέος· ἡ δ' ἔτι νῦν περ
τραύματος αἰθομένοιο βαρὺν ἀνακηκίει ἀτμόν,   600
οὐδέ τις ὕδωρ κεῖνο διὰ πτερὰ κοῦφα τανύσσας
οἰωνὸς δύναται βαλέειν ὕπερ, ἀλλὰ μεσηγὺς
φλογμῶι ἐνιθρώισκει πεποτημένος. ἀμφὶ δὲ κοῦραι

577 μέγαν m: βαρὺν w   578 τοῖο m: τοίου L^{pc}w   579 ταῖς m: τοὶ δ' L^{2} w   586 πόνους
m: πόρους L^{pc}V^{2}wd   600 ἀνακηκίει w: ἀνεκήκιεν m   603 ἐνιθρώισκει Damsté: ἐπι- Ω

Ἡλιάδες ταναῇσιν †ἀείμεναι αἰγείροισι
μύρονται κινυρὸν μέλεαι γόον· ἐκ δὲ φαεινάς 605
ἠλέκτρου λιβάδας βλεφάρων προχέουσιν ἔραζε·
αἱ μέν τ' ἠελίωι ψαμάθοις ἔπι τερσαίνονται,
εὖτ' ἂν δὲ κλύζηισι κελαινῆς ὕδατα λίμνης
ἠιόνας πνοιῆι πολυηχέος ἐξ ἀνέμοιο,
δὴ τότ' ἐς Ἠριδανὸν προκυλίνδεται ἀθρόα πάντα 610
κυμαίνοντι ῥόωι. Κελτοὶ δ' ἐπὶ βάξιν ἔθεντο
ὡς ἄρ' Ἀπόλλωνος τάδε δάκρυα Λητοΐδαο
ἐμφέρεται δίναις, ἅ τε μυρία χεῦε πάροιθεν,
ἦμος Ὑπερβορέων ἱερὸν γένος εἰσαφίκανεν,
οὐρανὸν αἰγλήεντα λιπὼν ἐκ πατρὸς ἐνιπῆς, 615
χωόμενος περὶ παιδί, τὸν ἐν λιπαρῆι Λακερείηι
δῖα Κορωνὶς ἔτικτεν ἐπὶ προχοῆις Ἀμύροιο.
καὶ τὰ μὲν ὣς κείνοισι μετ' ἀνδράσι κεκλήϊσται.
τοὺς δ' οὔτε βρώμης ᾕρει πόθος οὔτε ποτοῖο,
οὔτ' ἐπὶ γηθοσύνας νόος ἐτράπετ'· ἀλλ' ἄρα τοί γε 620
ἤματα μὲν στρεύγοντο περιβληχρὸν βαρύθοντες
ὀδμῆι λευγαλέηι τήν ῥ' ἄσχετον ἐξανίεσκον
τυφομένου Φαέθοντος ἐπιρροαὶ Ἠριδανοῖο,
νύκτας δ' αὖ γόον ὀξὺν ὀδυρομένων ἐσάκουον
Ἡλιάδων λιγέως· τὰ δὲ δάκρυα μυρομένηισιν 625
οἷον ἐλαιηραὶ στάγες ὕδασιν ἐμφορέοντο.
ἐκ δὲ τόθεν Ῥοδανοῖο βαθὺν ῥόον εἰσεπέρησαν,
ὅς τ' εἰς Ἠριδανὸν μετανίσσεται, ἄμμιγα δ' ὕδωρ
ἐν ξυνοχῆι βέβρυχε κυκώμενον. αὐτὰρ ὁ γαίης
ἐκ μυχάτης, ἵνα τ' εἰσὶ πύλαι καὶ ἐδέθλια Νυκτός, 630
ἔνθεν ἀπορνύμενος, τῆι μέν τ' ἐπερεύγεται ἀκτάς
Ὠκεανοῦ, τῆι δ' αὖτε μετ' Ἰονίην ἅλα βάλλει,
τῆι δ' ἐπὶ Σαρδόνιον πέλαγος καὶ ἀπείρονα κόλπον
ἑπτὰ διὰ στομάτων ἱεὶς ῥόον. ἐκ δ' ἄρα τοῖο
λίμνας εἰσέλασαν δυσχείμονας, αἵ τ' ἀνὰ Κελτῶν 635
ἤπειρον πέπτανται ἀθέσφατον. ἔνθα κεν οἵ γε
ἄτηι ἀεικελίηι πέλασαν· φέρε γάρ τις ἀπορρὼξ
κόλπον ἐς Ὠκεανοῖο, τὸν οὐ προδαέντες ἔμελλον

604 ἀείμεναι L: ἀειμέναι AE: ἐφήμεναι L²Aˢˡ w̄: ἐελμέναι Gerhard 608 δὲ Ω: δὴ Π³ 620 νόος ἐτράπετ' Hermann: τράπετο νόος m: τρέπετο νοός S: τέρπε νόος G 624 νύκτας L w̄: νυκτός AE 627 εἰσεπέρησαν wΣDion. Perieg. 289: ἔξεπ- D: εἰσαπέβησαν m 633 κόλπον m: πόντον L² w 634 ἱεὶς Lᵃᶜ w̄: ἵει L²AE 636 ἀθέσφατον Ω: –ται E: –τοι RQ

εἰσβαλέειν, τόθεν οὔ κεν ὑπότροποι ἐξεσάωθεν.
ἀλλ' Ἥρη σκοπέλοιο καθ' Ἑρκυνίου ἰάχησεν   640
οὐρανόθεν προθοροῦσα, φόβωι δ' ἐτίναχθεν αὐτῆς
πάντες ὁμῶς· δεινὸν γὰρ ἐπὶ μέγας ἔβραχεν αἰθήρ.
ἂψ δὲ παλιντροπόωντο θεᾶς ὕπο, καί ῥ' ἐνόησαν
τὴν οἶμον τῆι πέρ τε καὶ ἔπλετο νόστος ἰοῦσι.
δηναιοὶ δ' ἀκτὰς ἁλιμυρέας εἰσαφίκοντο,   645
Ἥρης ἐννεσίηισι δι' ἔθνεα μυρία Κελτῶν
καὶ Λιγύων περόωντες ἀδήϊοι· ἀμφὶ γὰρ αἰνήν
ἠέρα χεῦε θεὰ πάντ' ἤματα νισσομένοισι.
μεσσότατον δ' ἄρα τοί γε διὰ στόμα νηὶ βαλόντες,
Στοιχάδας εἰσαπέβαν νήσους, σόοι εἵνεκα κούρων   650
Ζηνός· ὃ δὴ βωμοί τε καὶ ἱερὰ τοῖσι τέτυκται
ἔμπεδον· οὐδ' οἷον κείνης ἐπίουροι ἕποντο
ναυτιλίης, Ζεὺς δέ σφι καὶ ὀψιγόνων πόρε νῆας.
Στοιχάδας αὖτε λιπόντες ἐς Αἰθαλίην ἐπέρησαν
νῆσον, ἵνα ψηφῖσιν ἀπωμόρξαντο καμόντες   655
ἱδρῶ ἅλις· χροιῆι δὲ κατ' αἰγιαλοῖο κέχυνται
εἴκελοι ⟨
  ⟩ ἐν δὲ σόλοι καὶ †τρύχεα θέσκελα κείνων,   657
ἔνθα λιμὴν Ἀργῶιος ἐπωνυμίην πεφάτισται.
  καρπαλίμως δ' ἐνθένδε διὲξ ἁλὸς οἶδμα νέοντο
Αὐσονίης, ἀκτὰς Τυρσηνίδας εἰσορόωντες·   660
ἷξον δ' Αἰαίης λιμένα κλυτόν, ἐκ δ' ἄρα νηός
πείσματ' ἐπ' ἠιόνων σχεδόθεν βάλον. ἔνθα δὲ Κίρκην
εὗρον ἁλὸς νοτίδεσσι κάρη ἐπιφαιδρύνουσαν·
τοῖον γὰρ νυχίοισιν ὀνείρασιν ἐπτοίητο.
αἵματί οἱ θάλαμοί τε καὶ ἕρκεα πάντα δόμοιο   665
μύρεσθαι δόκεον, φλὸξ δ' ἀθρόα φάρμακ' ἔδαπτεν
οἷσι πάρος ξείνους θέλγ' ἀνέρας ὅστις ἵκοιτο·
τὴν δ' αὐτὴ φονίωι σβέσεν αἵματι πορφύρουσαν,
χερσὶν ἀφυσσαμένη, λῆξεν δ' ὀλοοῖο φόβοιο.
τῶ καὶ ἐπιπλομένης ἠοῦς νοτίδεσσι θαλάσσης   670
ἐγρομένη πλοκάμους τε καὶ εἵματα φαιδρύνεσκε.
θῆρες δ', οὐ θήρεσσιν ἐοικότες ὠμηστῆισιν

---

641 αὐτῆς *w*E: αὐτῆι LA   644 τὴν οἶμον LE: τήνδ' οἶμον L²AG: τὴν δ' οἶμον S   652 ἐπίουροι *w*: ἐπίκουροι *m*   657 εἴκελοι vel ἴκ- Ω: εἴκελαι Brunck   lacunam stat. Fränkel   τρύχεα L²S: τεύχεα *m*G   658 ἔνθα Beck: ἐν δὲ Ω   663 ἐπιφαιδρύνουσαν *m*: περι- *w*

οὐδὲ μὲν οὐδ᾽ ἄνδρεσσιν ὅλον δέμας, ἄλλο δ᾽ ἀπ᾽ ἄλλων
συμμιγέες μελέων, κίον ἀθρόοι, ἠΰτε μῆλα
ἐκ σταθμῶν ἅλις εἶσιν ὀπηδεύοντα νομῆι.   675
τοίους καὶ προτέρους ἐξ ἰλύος ἐβλάστησε
χθὼν αὐτὴ μικτοῖσιν ἀρηρεμένους μελέεσσιν,
οὔπω διψαλέωι μάλ᾽ ὑπ᾽ ἠέρι πιληθεῖσα
οὐδέ πω ἀζαλέοιο βολαῖς τόσον ἠελίοιο
ἰκμάδας αἰνυμένη· τὰ δ᾽ ἐπὶ στίχας ἤγαγεν αἰών   680
συγκρίνας. τὼς οἵ γε φυὴν ἀΐδηλοι ἕποντο,
ἥρωας δ᾽ ἕλε θάμβος ἀπείριτον. αἶψα δ᾽ ἕκαστος,
Κίρκης εἴς τε φυὴν εἴς τ᾽ ὄμματα παπταίνοντες,
ῥεῖα κασιγνήτην φάσαν ἔμμεναι Αἰήταο.
   ἡ δ᾽ ὅτε δὴ νυχίων ἀπὸ δείματα πέμψεν ὀνείρων,   685
αὐτίκ᾽ ἔπειτ᾽ ἄψορρον ἀπέστιχε· τοὺς δ᾽ ἅμ᾽ ἕπεσθαι
χειρὶ καταρρέξασα δολοφροσύνηισιν ἄνωγεν.
ἔνθ᾽ ἤτοι πληθὺς μὲν ἐφετμαῖς Αἰσονίδαο
μίμνεν ἀπηλεγέως, ὁ δ᾽ ἐρύσσατο Κολχίδα κούρην.
ἄμφω δ᾽ ἑσπέσθην αὐτὴν ὁδόν, ἔστ᾽ ἀφίκοντο   690
Κίρκης ἐς μέγαρον. τοὺς δ᾽ ἐν λιπαροῖσι κέλευεν
ἥ γε θρόνοις ἕζεσθαι, ἀμηχανέουσα κιόντων·
τὼ δ᾽ ἄνεωι καὶ ἄναυδοι ἐφ᾽ ἑστίηι ἀΐξαντε
ἵζανον, ἥ τε δίκη λυγροῖς ἱκέτηισι τέτυκται,
ἡ μὲν ἐπ᾽ ἀμφοτέραις θεμένη χείρεσσι μέτωπα,   695
αὐτὰρ ὁ κωπῆεν μέγα φάσγανον ἐν χθονὶ πήξας
ὧι πέρ τ᾽ Αἰήταο πάϊν κτάνεν· οὐδέ ποτ᾽ ὄσσε
ἰθὺς ἐνὶ βλεφάροισιν ἀνέσχεθον. αὐτίκα δ᾽ ἔγνω
Κίρκη φύξιον οἶτον ἀλιτροσύνας τε φόνοιο.
τῶ καὶ ὀπιζομένη Ζηνὸς θέμιν Ἱκεσίοιο,   700
ὃς μέγα μὲν κοτέει, μέγα δ᾽ ἀνδροφόνοισιν ἀρήγει,
ῥέζε θυηπολίην οἵηι τ᾽ ἀπολυμαίνονται
†νηλεῖς† ἱκέται, ὅτ᾽ ἐφέστιοι ἀντιόωσι.
πρῶτα μὲν ἀτρέπτοιο λυτήριον ἥ γε φόνοιο
τειναμένη καθύπερθε συὸς τέκος, ἧς ἔτι μαζοὶ   705
πλήμυρον λοχίης ἐκ νηδύος, αἵματι χεῖρας
τέγγεν, ἐπιτμήγουσα δέρην· αὖτις δὲ καὶ ἄλλοις
μείλισσεν χύτλοισι Καθάρσιον ἀγκαλέουσα

---

673 ὅλον *w*. ὁμὸν *m*   676 προτέρους L² *w*: –ρης *m*   680 αἰνυμένου Wilamowitz   685 πέμψεν *m*: πέμπεν *w*   689 μίμνεν Ω: μίμνον E   693 ἀΐξαντε] fortasse Π⁴   700 θέμιν *m*: χόλον *w*   703 νηλεῖς LAD: νηλειεῖς *w*E: νηλητεῖς vel νηλιτεῖς Hölzlin

Ζῆνα παλαμναίων τιμήορον ἱκεσιάων.

καὶ τὰ μὲν ἀθρόα πάντα δόμων ἐκ λύματ' ἔνεικαν   710
νηιάδες πρόπολοι, ταί οἱ πόρσυνον ἕκαστα·
ἡ δ' εἴσω πελανούς μείλικτρά τε νηφαλίηισι
καῖεν ἐπ' εὐχωλῆισι παρέστιος, ὄφρα χόλοιο
σμερδαλέας παύσειεν Ἐρινύας ἠδὲ καὶ αὐτός
εὐμειδής τε πέλοιτο καὶ ἤπιος ἀμφοτέροισιν,   715
εἴ τ' οὖν ὀθνείωι μεμιασμένοι αἵματι χεῖρας
εἴ τε καὶ ἐμφύλωι προσκηδέες ἀντιόωσιν.
   αὐτὰρ ἐπεὶ μάλα πάντα πονήσατο, δὴ τότ' ἔπειτα
εἷσεν ἐπὶ ξεστοῖσιν ἀναστήσασα θρόνοισι,
καὶ δ' αὐτὴ πέλας ἷζεν ἐνωπαδίς. αἶψα δὲ μύθωι   720
χρειὼ ναυτιλίην τε διακριδὸν ἐξερέεινεν,
ἠδ' ὁπόθεν μετὰ γαῖαν ἑὴν καὶ δώματ' ἰόντες
αὕτως ἱδρύθησαν ἐφέστιοι. ἦ γὰρ ὀνείρων
μνῆστις ἀεικελίη δῦνεν φρένας ὁρμαίνουσαν·
ἵετο δ' αὖ κούρης ἐμφύλιον ἴδμεναι ὀμφήν,   725
αὐτίχ' ὅπως ἐνόησεν ἀπ' οὔδεος ὄσσε λαβοῦσαν.
πᾶσα γὰρ Ἡελίου γενεὴ ἀρίδηλος ἰδέσθαι
ἦεν, ἐπεὶ βλεφάρων ἀποτηλόθι μαρμαρυγῆισιν
οἷόν τε χρυσέην ἀντώπιον ἵεσαν αἴγλην.
ἡ δ' ἄρα τῆι τὰ ἕκαστα διειρομένηι κατέλεξε,   730
Κολχίδα γῆρυν ἱεῖσα, βαρύφρονος Αἰήταο
κούρη μειλιχίως, ἠμὲν στόλον ἠδὲ κελεύθους
ἡρώων, ὅσα τ' ἀμφὶ θοοῖς ἐμόγησαν ἀέθλοις,
ὥς τε κασιγνήτης πολυκηδέος ἤλιτε βουλαῖς,
ὥς τ' ἀπονόσφιν ἄλυξεν ὑπέρβια δείματα πατρός   735
σὺν παισὶ Φρίξοιο. φόνον δ' ἀλέεινεν ἐνισπεῖν
Ἀψύρτου, τὴν δ' οὔ τι νόωι λάθεν· ἀλλὰ καὶ ἔμπης
μυρομένην ἐλέαιρεν, ἔπος δ' ἐπὶ τοῖον ἔειπεν·
"σχετλίη, ἦ ῥα κακὸν καὶ ἀεικέα μήσαο νόστον.
ἔλπομαι οὐκ ἐπὶ δήν σε βαρὺν χόλον Αἰήταο   740
ἐκφυγέειν· τάχα δ' εἶσι καὶ Ἑλλάδος ἤθεα γαίης
τεισόμενος φόνον υἱός, ὅτ' ἄσχετα ἔργα τέλεσσας.
ἀλλ' ἐπεὶ οὖν ἱκέτις καὶ ὁμόγνιος ἔπλευ ἐμεῖο,

709 παλαμναίων LASE²: –αῖον I^{sl}GE^{ac}d: utrumque nouerunt scholia   ἱκεσιάων m: ἱκεσίηισι L² w: utrumque nouerunt scholia   710 λύματ' m: δείματ' w   717 ἐμφύλωι Hölzlin: ἐμφύλωι Ω   720 μύθωι m: μύθοις w   724 ὁρμαίνουσαν w. –σα m   726 ἀπ' οὔδεος Ω: ἐπ' οὔδεος Fränkel: de Π⁴ non liquet   λαβοῦσαν Fränkel: βαλοῦσαν Ω   736 παισὶ Π⁴ Ω: παισίν L

ἄλλο μὲν οὔ τι κακὸν μητίσομαι ἐνθάδ᾽ ἰούσηι·
ἔρχεο δ᾽ ἐκ μεγάρων ξείνωι συνοπηδὸς ἐοῦσα 745
ὅν τινα τοῦτον ἄιστον ἀείραο πατρὸς ἄνευθεν.
μηδέ με γουνάσσηαι ἐφέστιος· οὐ γὰρ ἔγωγε
αἰνήσω βουλάς τε σέθεν καὶ ἀεικέα φύξιν."
  ὣς φάτο· τὴν δ᾽ ἀμέγαρτον ἄχος λάβεν· ἀμφὶ δὲ πέπλον
ὀφθαλμοῖσι βαλοῦσα γόον χέεν, ὄφρα μιν ἥρως 750
χειρὸς ἐπισχόμενος μεγάρων ἐξῆγε θύραζε
δείματι παλλομένην· λεῖπον δ᾽ ἀπὸ δώματα Κίρκης.
  οὐδ᾽ ἄλοχον Κρονίδαο Διὸς λάθον· ἀλλά οἱ Ἶρις
πέφραδεν, εὖτ᾽ ἐνόησεν ἀπὸ μεγάροιο κιόντας·
αὐτὴ γάρ μιν ἄνωγε δοκευέμεν ὁππότε νῆα 755
στείχοιεν. τὸ καὶ αὖτις ἐποτρύνουσ᾽ ἀγόρευεν·
"Ἶρι φίλη, νῦν, εἴ ποτ᾽ ἐμὰς ἐτέλεσσας ἐφετμάς,
εἰ δ᾽ ἄγε λαιψηρῆισι μετοιχομένη πτερύγεσσι
δεῦρο Θέτιν μοι ἄνωχθι μολεῖν ἁλὸς ἐξανιοῦσαν·
κείνης γὰρ χρειώ με κιχάνεται. αὐτὰρ ἔπειτα 760
ἐλθεῖν εἰς ἀκτὰς ὅθι τ᾽ ἄκμονες Ἡφαίστοιο
χάλκειοι στιβαρῆισιν ἀράσσονται τυπίδεσσιν·
εἰπὲ δὲ κοιμῆσαι φύσας πυρός, εἰσόκεν Ἀργὼ
τάς γε παρεξελάσηισιν. ἀτὰρ καὶ ἐς Αἴολον ἐλθεῖν,
Αἴολον ὅς τ᾽ ἀνέμοις αἰθρηγενέεσσιν ἀνάσσει· 765
καὶ δὲ τῶι εἰπέμεναι τὸν ἐμὸν νόον, ὡς κεν ἀήτας
πάντας ἀπολλήξειεν ὑπ᾽ ἠέρι, μηδέ τις αὔρη
τρηχύνοι πέλαγος· Ζεφύρου γε μὲν οὖρος ἀήτω,
ὄφρ᾽ οἵ γ᾽ Ἀλκινόου Φαιηκίδα νῆσον ἵκωνται."
  ὣς ἔφατ᾽· αὐτίκα δ᾽ Ἶρις ἀπ᾽ Οὐλύμποιο θοροῦσα 770
τέμνε, τανυσσαμένη κοῦφα πτερά. δῦ δ᾽ ἐνὶ πόντωι
Αἰγαίωι, τόθι πέρ τε δόμοι Νηρῆος ἔασι·
πρώτην δ᾽ εἰσαφίκανε Θέτιν καὶ ἐπέφραδε μῦθον
Ἥρης ἐννεσίηις ὦρσέν τέ μιν εἰς ἓ νέεσθαι·
δεύτερα δ᾽ εἰς Ἥφαιστον ἐβήσατο, παῦσε δὲ τόν γε 775
ρίμφα σιδηρείων τυπίδων, ἔσχοντο δ᾽ ἀυτμῆς
αἰθαλέοι πρηστῆρες. ἀτὰρ τρίτον εἰσαφίκανεν
Αἴολον Ἱππότεω παῖδα κλυτόν. ὄφρα δὲ καὶ τῶι
ἀγγελίην φαμένη θοὰ γούνατα παῦεν ὁδοῖο,
τόφρα Θέτις, Νηρῆα κασιγνήτας τε λιποῦσα, 780

746 ἀείραο LSE: ἀνείραο L²AG 747 γουνάσσηαι Wellauer: –άσηαι w. –άση m 749
πέπλον m: –ους w 779 παῦεν Platt: παῦσεν Ω

ἐξ ἁλὸς Οὔλυμπόνδε θεὰν μετεκίαθεν Ἥρην.
ἡ δέ μιν ἆσσον ἑοῖο παρεῖσέ τε φαῖνέ τε μῦθον·
"κέκλυθι νῦν, Θέτι δῖα, τά τοι ἐπιέλδομ' ἐνισπεῖν.
οἶσθα μὲν ὅσσον ἐμῇσιν ἐνὶ φρεσὶ τίεται ἥρως
Αἰσονίδης ἠδ' ἄλλοι ἀοσσητῆρες ἀέθλου,   785
†οἵη τέ σφ' ἐσάωσα† ⟨
                      ⟩ διὰ Πλαγκτὰς περόωντας
πέτρας, ἔνθα πυρὸς δειναὶ βρομέουσι θύελλαι,
κύματά τε σκληρῇσι περιβλύει σπιλάδεσσι.
νῦν δὲ παρὰ Σκύλλης σκόπελον μέγαν ἠδὲ Χάρυβδιν
δεινὸν ἐρευγομένην δέχεται ὁδός. ἀλλὰ – σὲ γὰρ δή   790
ἐξέτι νηπυτίης αὐτὴ τρέφον ἠδ' ἀγάπησα
ἔξοχον ἀλλάων αἵ τ' εἰν ἁλὶ ναιετάουσιν·
οὕνεκεν οὐκ ἔτλης εὐνῇ Διὸς ἱεμένοιο
λέξασθαι – κεῖνοι γὰρ ἀεὶ τάδε ἔργα μέμηλεν,
ἠὲ σὺν ἀθανάταις ἠὲ θνητῇσιν ἰαύειν –   795
ἀλλ' ἐμέ τ' αἰδομένη καὶ ἐνὶ φρεσὶ δειμαίνουσα
ἠλεύω· ὁ δ' ἔπειτα πελώριον ὅρκον ὄμοσσε,
μή ποτέ σ' ἀθανάτοιο θεοῦ καλέεσθαι ἄκοιτιν.
ἔμπης δ' οὐ μεθίεσκεν ὀπιπεύων ἀέκουσαν,
εἰσότε οἱ πρέσβειρα Θέμις κατέλεξεν ἕκαστα,   800
ὡς δή τοι πέπρωται ἀμείνονα πατρὸς ἑοῖο
παῖδα τεκεῖν· τῶ καί σε λιλαιόμενος μεθέηκε
δείματι, μή τις ἑοῦ ἀντάξιος ἄλλος ἀνάσσοι
ἀθανάτων, ἀλλ' αἰὲν ἑὸν κράτος εἰρύοιτο.
αὐτὰρ ἐγὼ τὸν ἄριστον ἐπιχθονίων πόσιν εἶναι   805
δῶκά τοι, ὄφρα γάμου θυμηδέος ἀντιάσειας
τέκνα τε φιτύσαιο· θεοὺς δ' εἰς δαῖτα κάλεσσα
πάντας ὁμῶς, αὐτὴ δὲ σέλας χείρεσσιν ἀνέσχον
νυμφίδιον, κείνης ἀγανόφρονος εἵνεκα τιμῆς.
ἀλλ' ἄγε καί τινά τοι νημερτέα μῦθον ἐνίψω.   810
εὖτ' ἂν ἐς Ἠλύσιον πεδίον τεὸς υἱὸς ἵκηται,
ὃν δὴ νῦν Χείρωνος ἐν ἤθεσι Κενταύροιο
Νηιάδες κομέουσι τεοῦ λίπτοντα γάλακτος,
χρειὼ μιν κούρης πόσιν ἔμμεναι Αἰήταο
Μηδείης· σὺ δ' ἄρηγε νυῷ ἑκυρή περ ἐοῦσα,   815
ἠδ' αὐτῷ Πηλῆι. τί τοι χόλος ἐστήρικται;

786 οἵη m: οἵως w   lacunam stat. Seaton   800 ἕκαστα w: ἅπαντα m   810
νημερτέα m: θυμηδέα L² w

ἀάσθη· καὶ γάρ τε θεοὺς ἐπινίσεται ἄτη.
ναὶ μὲν ἐφημοσύνῃσιν ἐμαῖς Ἥφαιστον ὀίω
λωφήσειν πρήσσοντα πυρὸς μένος, Ἱπποτάδην δέ
Αἴολον ὠκείας ἀνέμων ἄικας ἐρύξειν   820
νόσφιν ἐυσταθέος Ζεφύρου, τείως κεν ἵκωνται
Φαιήκων λιμένας. σὺ δ᾽ ἀκηδέα μήδεο νόστον·
δεῖμα δέ τοι πέτραι καὶ ὑπέρβια κύματ᾽ ἔασι
μοῦνον, ἅ κεν τρέψαιο κασιγνήτῃσι σὺν ἄλλαις.
μηδὲ σύ γ᾽ ἠὲ Χάρυβδιν ἀμηχανέοντας ἐάσῃς   825
εἰσβαλέειν, μὴ πάντας ἀναβρόξασα φέρῃσιν,
ἠὲ παρὰ Σκύλλης στυγερὸν κευθμῶνα νέεσθαι –
Σκύλλης Αὐσονίης ὀλοόφρονος, ἣν τέκε Φόρκωι
νυκτιπόλος Ἑκάτη, τήν τε κλείουσι Κράταιιν –,
μή πως σμερδαλέῃσιν ἐπαΐξασα γένυσσι   830
λεκτοὺς ἡρώων δηλήσεται· ἀλλ᾽ ἔχε νῆα
κεῖσ᾽ ὅθι περ τυτθή γε παραίβασις ἔσσετ᾽ ὀλέθρου."
    ὣς φάτο· τὴν δὲ Θέτις τοίωι προσελέξατο μύθωι·
"εἰ μὲν δὴ μαλεροῖο πυρὸς μένος ἠδὲ θύελλαι
ζαχρηεῖς λήξουσιν ἐτήτυμον, ἦ τ᾽ ἂν ἔγωγε   835
θαρσαλέη φαίην καὶ κύματος ἀντιόωντος
νῆα σαωσέμεναι, Ζεφύρου λίγα κινυμένοιο.
ἀλλ᾽ ὥρη δολιχήν τε καὶ ἄσπετον οἶμον ὁδεύειν,
ὄφρα κασιγνήτας μετελεύσομαι αἵ μοι ἀρωγοί
ἔσσονται, καὶ νηὸς ὅθι πρυμνῆσι᾽ ἀνῆπται,   840
ὥς κεν ὑπηῶιοι μνησαίατο νόστον ἑλέσθαι."
    ἦ, καὶ ἀναΐξασα κατ᾽ αἰθέρος ἔμπεσε δίναις
κυανέου πόντοιο. κάλει δ᾽ ἐπαμυνέμεν ἄλλας
αὐτοκασιγνήτας Νηρηίδας· αἱ δ᾽ ἀίουσαι
ἤντεον ἀλλήλῃσι· Θέτις δ᾽ ἀγόρευεν ἐφετμάς   845
Ἥρης, αἶψα δ᾽ ἴαλλε μετ᾽ Αὐσονίην ἅλα πάσας.
αὐτὴ δ᾽ ὠκυτέρη ἀμαρύγματος ἠὲ βολάων
ἠελίου, ὅτ᾽ ἄνεισι περαίης ὑψόθι γαίης,
σεύατ᾽ ἴμεν λαιψηρὰ δι᾽ ὕδατος, ἔστ᾽ ἀφίκανεν
ἀκτὴν Αἰαίην Τυρσηνίδος ἠπείροιο.   850
τοὺς δ᾽ εὗρεν παρὰ νηὶ σόλωι ῥιπῇσί τ᾽ ὀιστῶν
τερπομένους· στῆ δ᾽ ἄσσον ὀρεξαμένη χερὸς ἄκρης
Αἰακίδεω Πηλῆος – ὁ γάρ ῥά οἱ ἦεν ἀκοίτης·

819 πρήσσοντα LAS: πρήσοντα GE: πρήθ-Brunck   826 ἀναβρόξασα w: ἀναβρώξασα m
834 ἠδὲ L^{ac}E: ἠὲ L²AwD   850 Αἰαίην Ω: Αἰαίης S   852 στῆ Fränkel: ἡ Ω

οὐδέ τις εἰσιδέειν δύνατ᾽ ἔμπεδον, ἀλλ᾽ ἄρα τῶι γε
οἵωι ἐν ὀφθαλμοῖσιν ἐείσατο φώνησέν τε·   855
"μηκέτι νῦν ἀκταῖς Τυρσηνίσιν ἦσθε μένοντες·
ἠῶθεν δὲ θοῆς πρυμνήσια λύετε νηός,
Ἥρηι πειθόμενοι ἐπαρηγόνι. τῆς γὰρ ἐφετμῆις
πασσυδίηι κοῦραι Νηρηίδες ἀντιόωσι,
νῆα διὲκ πέτρας αἵ τε Πλαγκταὶ καλέονται   860
ῥυσόμεναι· κείνη γὰρ ἐναίσιμος ὔμμι κέλευθος.
ἀλλὰ σὺ μή τωι ἐμὸν δείξηις δέμας, εὖτ᾽ ἂν ἴδηαι
ἀντομένην σὺν τῆισι· νόωι δ᾽ ἔχε, μή με χολώσηις
πλεῖον ἔτ᾽ ἢ τὸ πάροιθεν ἀπηλεγέως ἐχόλωσας."
ἦ, καὶ ἔπειτ᾽ ἀίδηλος ἐδύσατο βένθεα πόντου.   865
τὸν δ᾽ ἄχος αἰνὸν ἔτυψεν, ἐπεὶ πάρος οὐκέτ᾽ ἰοῦσαν
ἔδρακεν, ἐξότε πρῶτα λίπεν θάλαμόν τε καὶ εὐνήν,
χωσαμένη Ἀχιλῆος ἀγαυοῦ νηπιάχοντος.
ἡ μὲν γὰρ βροτέας αἰεὶ περὶ σάρκας ἔδαιε
νύκτα διὰ μέσσην φλογμῶι πυρός· ἤματα δ᾽ αὖτε   870
ἀμβροσίηι χρίεσκε τέρεν δέμας, ὄφρα πέλοιτο
ἀθάνατος καί οἱ στυγερὸν χροΐ γῆρας ἀλάλκοι·
αὐτὰρ ὅ γ᾽ ἐξ εὐνῆς ἀναπάλμενος εἰσενόησε
παῖδα φίλον σπαίροντα διὰ φλογός· ἧκε δ᾽ ἀυτήν
σμερδαλέην ἐσιδών, μέγα νήπιος. ἡ δ᾽ ἀίουσα,   875
τὸν μὲν ἄρ᾽ ἁρπάγδην χαμάδις βάλε κεκληγῶτα,
αὐτὴ δὲ, πνοιῆι ἰκέλη δέμας, ἠύτ᾽ ὄνειρος,
βῆ ῥ᾽ ἴμεν ἐκ μεγάροιο θοῶς καὶ ἐσήλατο πόντον
χωσαμένη· μετὰ δ᾽ οὔ τι παλίσσυτος ἵκετ᾽ ὀπίσσω.
τῶ μιν ἀμηχανίη δῆσεν φρένας· ἀλλὰ καὶ ἔμπης   880
πᾶσαν ἐφημοσύνην Θέτιδος μετέειπεν ἑταίροις.
οἱ δ᾽ ἄρα μεσσηγὺς λῆξαν καὶ ἔπαυσαν ἀέθλους
ἐσσυμένως, δόρπον τε χαμεύνας τ᾽ ἀμφεπένοντο,
τῆις ἔνι δαισάμενοι νύκτ᾽ ἄεσαν ὡς τὸ πάροιθεν.
ἦμος δ᾽ ἄκρον ἔβαλλε φαεσφόρος οὐρανὸν ἠώς,   885
δὴ τότε λαιψηροῖο κατηλυσίηι Ζεφύροιο
βαῖνον ἐπὶ κληῖδας ἀπὸ χθονός· ἐκ δὲ βυθοῖο
εὐναίας εἷλκον περιγηθέες ἄλλα τε πάντα
ἄρμενα μηρύοντο κατὰ χρέος· ὕψι δὲ λαῖφος
εἴρυσσαν τανύσαντες ἐν ἱμάντεσσι κεραίης.   890

866 οὐκέτ᾽ Ω: οὔποτ᾽ Lloyd-Jones   873 ὅγ᾽ SE: ὅτ᾽ LAG: ὁ Wellauer

νῆα δ' εὐκραὴς ἄνεμος φέρεν· αἶψα δὲ νῆσον
καλὴν Ἀνθεμόεσσαν ἐσέδρακον, ἔνθα λίγειαι
Σειρῆνες σίνοντ' Ἀχελωίδες ἡδείῃσι
θέλγουσαι μολπῇσιν ὅ τις παρὰ πεῖσμα βάλοιτο.
τὰς μὲν ἄρ' εὐειδὴς Ἀχελωίωι εὐνηθεῖσα   895
γείνατο Τερψιχόρη, Μουσέων μία· καί ποτε Δηοῦς
θυγατέρ' ἰφθίμην, ἀδμῆτ' ἔτι, πορσαίνεσκον
ἄμμιγα μελπόμεναι· τότε δ' ἄλλο μὲν οἰωνοῖσιν
ἄλλο δὲ παρθενικῇς ἐναλίγκιαι ἔσκον ἰδέσθαι.
αἰεὶ δ' εὐόρμου δεδοκημέναι ἐκ περιωπῆς   900
ἢ θαμὰ δὴ πολέων μελιηδέα νόστον ἕλοντο,
τηκεδόνι φθινύθουσαι. ἀπηλεγέως δ' ἄρα καὶ τοῖς
ἵεσαν ἐκ στομάτων ὄπα λείριον· οἱ δ' ἀπὸ νηός
ἤδη πείσματ' ἔμελλον ἐπ' ἠιόνεσσι βαλέσθαι,
εἰ μὴ ἄρ' Οἰάγροιο πάις Θρηίκιος Ὀρφεύς,   905
Βιστονίην ἐνὶ χερσὶν ἑαῖς φόρμιγγα τανύσσας,
κραιπνὸν εὐτροχάλοιο μέλος κανάχησεν ἀοιδῆς,
ὄφρ' ἄμυδις κλονέοντος ἐπιβρομέωνται ἀκουαί
κρεγμῶι· παρθενίην δ' ἐνοπὴν ἐβιήσατο φόρμιγξ.
νῆα δ' ὁμοῦ Ζέφυρός τε καὶ ἠχῆεν φέρε κῦμα   910
πρυμνόθεν ὀρνύμενον· ταὶ δ' ἄκριτον ἵεσαν αὐδήν.
ἀλλὰ καὶ ὧς Τελέοντος ἐὺς πάις οἶος ἑταίρων
προφθάμενος ξεστοῖο κατὰ ζυγοῦ ἔνθορε πόντωι
Βούτης, Σειρήνων λιγυρῇι ὀπὶ θυμὸν ἰανθείς·
νῆχε δὲ πορφυρέοιο δι' οἴδματος, ὄφρ' ἐπιβαίη,   915
σχέτλιος· ἦ τέ οἱ αἶψα καταυτόθι νόστον ἀπηύρων,
ἀλλά μιν οἰκτείρασα θεὰ Ἔρυκος μεδέουσα
Κύπρις ἔτ' ἐν δίναις ἀνερέψατο καί ῥ' ἐσάωσε
πρόφρων ἀντομένη, Λιλυβηίδα ναιέμεν ἄκρην.
οἱ δ' ἀχεῖ σχόμενοι τὰς μὲν λίπον, ἄλλα δ' ὄπαζον   920
κύντερα μιξοδίῃσιν ἁλὸς ῥαιστήρια νηῶν.
τῆι μὲν γὰρ Σκύλλης λισσὴ προυφαίνετο πέτρη,
τῆι δ' ἄμοτον βοάασκεν ἀναβλύζουσα Χάρυβδις.
ἄλλοθι δὲ Πλαγκταὶ μεγάλωι ὑπὸ κύματι πέτραι
ῥόχθεον, ᾗχι πάροιθεν ἀπέπτυεν αἰθομένη φλόξ   925
ἄκρων ἐκ σκοπέλων πυριθαλπέος ὑψόθι πέτρης,
καπνῶι δ' ἀχλυόεις αἰθὴρ πέλεν οὐδέ κεν αὐγάς

925 ἀνέπτυεν Fränkel   926 πυριθαλπέος ... πέτρης Ω: πυριθαλπέας ... πέτρας Wˢˡ

ἔδρακες ἠελίοιο. τότ' αὖ, λήξαντος ἀπ' ἔργων
Ἡφαίστου, θερμὴν ἔτι κήκιε πόντος ἀυτμήν.
ἔνθα σφιν κοῦραι Νηρηίδες ἄλλοθεν ἄλλαι   930
ἤντεον· ἡ δ' ὄπιθεν πτέρυγος θίγε πηδαλίοιο
δῖα Θέτις, Πλαγκτῆισιν ἐνὶ σπιλάδεσσιν ἔρυσθαι.
ὡς δ' ὁπότ' ἂν δελφῖνες ὑπὲξ ἁλὸς εὐδιόωντες
σπερχομένην ἀγεληδὸν ἑλίσσωνται περὶ νῆα,
ἄλλοτε μὲν προπάροιθεν ὁρώμενοι, ἄλλοτ' ὄπισθεν,   935
ἄλλοτε παρβολάδην, ναύτηισι δὲ χάρμα τέτυκται·
ὣς αἱ ὑπεκπροθέουσαι ἐπήτριμοι εἱλίσσοντο
Ἀργώιηι περὶ νηί· Θέτις δ' ἴθυνε κέλευθον.
καὶ ῥ' ὅτε δὴ Πλαγκτῆισιν ἐνιχρίμψεσθαι ἔμελλον,
αὐτίκ' ἀνασχόμεναι λευκοῖς ἐπὶ γούνασι πέζας,   940
ὑψοῦ ἐπ' αὐτάων σπιλάδων καὶ κύματος ἀγῆς
ῥώοντ' ἔνθα καὶ ἔνθα διασταδὸν ἀλλήληισι.
τὴν δὲ παρηορίην κόπτεν ῥόος· ἀμφὶ δὲ κῦμα
λάβρον ἀειρόμενον πέτραις ἐπικαχλάζεσκεν·
αἱ δ' ὁτὲ μὲν κρημνοῖς ἐναλίγκιαι ἠέρι κῦρον,   945
ἄλλοτε δὲ βρύχιαι νεάτωι ὑπὸ πυθμένι πόντου
ἠρήρειν, τὸ δὲ πολλὸν ὑπείρεχεν ἄγριον οἶδμα.
αἱ δ', ὥς τ' ἠμαθόεντος ἐπισχεδὸν αἰγιαλοῖο
παρθενικαὶ δίχα κόλπον ἐπ' ἰξύας εἱλίξασαι,
σφαίρηι ἀθύρουσιν περιηγέι· τῆ μὲν ἔπειτα†   950
ἄλλη ὑπ' ἐξ ἄλλης δέχεται καὶ ἐς ἠέρα πέμπει
ὕψι μεταχρονίην, ἡ δ' οὔ ποτε πίλναται οὔδει·
ὣς αἱ νῆα θέουσαν ἀμοιβαδὶς ἄλλοθεν ἄλλη
πέμπε διηερίην ἐπὶ κύμασιν, αἰὲν ἄπωθεν
πετράων· περὶ δέ σφιν ἐρευγόμενον ζέεν ὕδωρ.   955
τὰς δὲ καὶ αὐτὸς ἄναξ κορυφῆς ἐπὶ λισσάδος ἄκρης
ὀρθός, ἐπὶ στελεῆι τυπίδος βαρὺν ὦμον ἐρείσας,
Ἥφαιστος θηεῖτο, καὶ αἰγλήεντος ὕπερθεν
οὐρανοῦ ἑστηυῖα Διὸς δάμαρ, ἀμφὶ δ' Ἀθήνηι
βάλλε χέρας, τοῖόν μιν ἔχεν δέος εἰσορόωσαν.   960
ὅσση δ' εἰαρινοῦ μηκύνεται ἤματος αἶσα,
τοσσάτιον μογέεσκον ἐπὶ χρόνον, ὀχλίζουσαι

932 ἔρυσθαι Fränkel: ἐρύσσαι Ω   939 ἐνιχρίμψεσθαι L¹AS: –ασθαι G: –μπτεσθαι E
943 ῥόος L⁴ˢˡSˢˡE: ῥόον Ω   947 ἠρήρειν, τὸ δὲ UY: ἠρήρειντο δὲ Ω: ἠρήρεινθ' ὅτι E
950 ἡ Ω: τὴν E: αἱ Flor.   955 ζέεν Facius: θέεν Ω   956 κορυφῆς L¹AωE: κορυφῆι L
961 ὅσση Ω: ὅσσον Iˢˡ: ὅσσωι Fränkel

νῆα διὲκ πέτρας πολυηχέας. οἱ δ᾽ ἀνέμοιο
αὖτις ἐπαυρόμενοι προτέρω θέον· ὦκα δ᾽ ἄμειβον
Θρινακίης λειμῶνα, βοῶν τροφὸν Ἠελίοιο.   965
ἔνθ᾽ αἱ μὲν κατὰ βένθος ἀλίγκιαι αἰθυίῃσι
δῦνον, ἐπεί ῥ᾽ ἀλόχοιο Διὸς πόρσυνον ἐφετμάς·
τοὺς δ᾽ ἄμυδις βληχῇ τε δι᾽ ἠέρος ἵκετο μήλων
μυκηθμός τε βοῶν αὐτοσχεδὸν οὔατ᾽ ἔβαλλεν.
καὶ τὰ μὲν ἑρσήεντα κατὰ δρία ποιμαίνεσκεν   970
ὁπλοτέρη Φαέθουσα θυγατρῶν Ἠελίοιο,
ἀργύρεον χάϊον παλάμῃ ἔνι πηχύνουσα·
Λαμπετίη δ᾽ ἐπὶ βουσὶν ὀρειχάλκοιο φαεινοῦ
πάλλεν ὀπηδεύουσα καλαύροπα. τὰς δὲ καὶ αὐτοὶ
βοσκομένας ποταμοῖο παρ᾽ ὕδασιν εἰσορόωντο   975
ἂμ πεδίον καὶ ἕλος λειμώνιον· οὐδέ τις ἦεν
κυανέη μετὰ τῇσι δέμας, πᾶσαι δὲ γάλακτι
εἰδόμεναι χρυσέοισι κεράασι κυδιάασκον.
καὶ μὲν τὰς παράμειβον ἐπ᾽ ἤματι· νυκτὶ δ᾽ ἰούσῃ
πεῖρον ἁλὸς μέγα λαῖτμα κεχαρμένοι, ὄφρα καὶ αὖτις   980
ἠὼς ἠριγενὴς φέγγος βάλε νισομένοισιν.
     ἔστι δέ τις πορθμοῖο παροιτέρη Ἰονίοιο
ἀμφιλαφὴς πίειρα Κεραυνίῃ εἰν ἁλὶ νῆσος,
ᾗ ὕπο δὴ κεῖσθαι δρέπανον φάτις — ἵλατε Μοῦσαι,
οὐκ ἐθέλων ἐνέπω προτέρων ἔπος — ᾧ ἀπὸ πατρός   985
μήδεα νηλειῶς ἔταμε Κρόνος· — οἱ δέ ἑ Δηοῦς
κλείουσι χθονίης καλαμητόμον ἔμμεναι ἅρπην·
Δηὼ γὰρ κείνῃ ἐνὶ δή ποτε νάσσατο γαίῃ,
Τιτῆνας δ᾽ ἔδαεν στάχυν ὄμπνιον ἀμήσασθαι,
Μάκριδα φιλαμένη —· Δρεπάνη τόθεν ἐκλήϊσται   990
οὔνομα Φαιήκων ἱερὴ τροφός· ὣς δὲ καὶ αὐτοὶ
αἵματος Οὐρανίοιο γένος Φαίηκες ἔασι.
τοὺς Ἀργὼ πολέεσσιν ἐνισχομένη καμάτοισιν
Θρινακίης αὔρῃς ἵκετ᾽ ἐξ ἁλός. οἱ δ᾽ ἀγανῇσιν
Ἀλκίνοος λαοί τε θυηπολίῃσιν ἰόντας   985... 995
δειδέχατ᾽ ἀσπασίως, ἐπὶ δέ σφισι καγχαλάασκε
πᾶσα πόλις· φαίης κεν ἑοῖς ἐπὶ παισὶ γάνυσθαι.
καὶ δ᾽ αὐτοὶ ἥρωες ἀνὰ πληθὺν κεχάροντο,
τῷ ἴκελοι οἷόν τε μεσαιτάτῃ ἐμβεβαῶτες

978 κεράασι S: κεράεσσι Ω   979 μέν τὰς m: τὰς μὲν wd   997 ἐπὶ m: περὶ w   999
ἴκελοι m: ἴκελον w

Αἱμονίηι. μέλλον δὲ βοῆι ἔπι θωρήξεσθαι·   1000
ὧδε μάλ' ἀγχίμολον στρατὸς ἄσπετος ἐξεφαάνθη
Κόλχων, οἳ Πόντοιο κατὰ στόμα καὶ διὰ πέτρας
Κυανέας μαστῆρες ἀριστήων ἐπέρησαν·
Μήδειαν δ' ἔξαιτον ἑοῦ ἐς πατρὸς ἄγεσθαι
ἵεντ' ἀπροφάτως, ἠὲ στονόεσσαν ἀυτήν   1005
νωμήσειν χαλεπῆισιν ὁμόκλεον ἀτροπίηισιν
αὖθί τε καὶ μετέπειτα σὺν Αἰήταο κελεύθωι.
ἀλλά σφεας κατέρυκεν ἐπειγομένους πολέμοιο
κρείων Ἀλκίνοος· λελίητο γὰρ ἀμφοτέροισιν
δηιοτῆτος ἄνευθεν ὑπέρβια νείκεα λῦσαι.   1010
   κούρη δ' οὐλομένωι ὑπὸ δείματι πολλὰ μὲν αὐτούς
Αἰσονίδεω ἑτάρους μειλίσσετο, πολλὰ δὲ χερσίν
Ἀρήτης γούνων ἀλόχου θίγεν Ἀλκινόοιο·
"γουνοῦμαι, βασίλεια· σὺ δ' ἵλαθι, μηδέ με Κόλχοις
ἐκδώηις ὧι πατρὶ κομιζέμεν, εἰ νυ καὶ αὐτή   1015
ἀνθρώπων γενεῆς μία φέρβεαι, οἷσιν ἐς ἄτην
ὠκύτατος κούφηισι θέει νόος ἀμπλακίηισιν,
ὡς ἐμοὶ ἐκ πυκιναὶ ἔπεσον φρένες — οὐ μὲν ἕκητι
μαργοσύνης. ἴστω ἱερὸν φάος Ἠελίοιο,
ἴστω νυκτιπόλου Περσηίδος ὄργια κούρης,   1020
μὴ μὲν ἐγὼν ἐθέλουσα σὺν ἀνδράσιν ἀλλοδαποῖσι
κεῖθεν ἀφωρμήθην· στυγερὸν δέ με τάρβος ἔπεισεν
τῆσδε φυγῆς μνήσασθαι, ὅτ' ἤλιτον οὐδέ τις ἄλλη
μῆτις ἔην. ἔτι μοι μίτρη μένει, ὡς ἐνὶ πατρός
δώμασιν, ἄχραντος καὶ ἀκήρατος. ἀλλ' ἐλέαιρε,   1025
πότνα, τεόν τε πόσιν μειλίσσεο· σοὶ δ' ὀπάσειαν
ἀθάνατοι βίοτόν τε τελεσφόρον ἀγλαΐην τε
καὶ παῖδας καὶ κῦδος ἀπορθήτοιο πόληος."
   τοῖα μὲν Ἀρήτην γουνάζετο δάκρυ χέουσα·
τοῖα δ' ἀριστήων ἐναμοιβαδὶς ἄνδρα ἕκαστον·   1030
"ὑμέων, ὦ πέρι δή μέγα φέρτατοι, ἀμφί τ' ἀέθλοις
†τοὔνεκεν† ὑμετέροισιν ἀτύζομαι· ἧς ἰότητι
ταύρους τ' ἐζεύξασθε καὶ ἐκ θέρος οὐλοὸν ἀνδρῶν
κείρατε γηγενέων, ἧς εἵνεκεν Αἱμονίηνδε
χρύσεον αὐτίκα κῶας ἀνάξετε νοστήσαντες.   1035

1000 ἔπι Hölzlin: ἔνι Ω   θωρήξεσθαι m: –ασθαι L² w   1019 ἴστω w: ἴστω δ' m
1026 τε m: δὲ w   1030 ἐναμοιβαδὶς Brunck: ἐν' ἀμ– L² w: ἀμ– L: ἔτ' ἀμ– A: ἐπαμ– E
1031 ὑμέων ὦ Ω: ὑμείων ὦ d: ὑμείων Fränkel

ἥδ' ἐγὼ ἢ πάτρην τε καὶ οὓς ὤλεσσα τοκῆας,
ἢ δόμον, ἢ σύμπασαν ἐυφροσύνην βιότοιο,
ὔμμι δὲ καὶ πάτρην καὶ δώματα ναιέμεν αὖτις
ἤνυσα, καὶ γλυκεροῖσ̣ν ἔτ' εἰσόψεσθε τοκῆας
ὄμμασιν· αὐτὰρ ἐμοὶ ἀπὸ δὴ βαρὺς εἵλετο δαίμων   1040
ἀγλαΐας, στυγερῇ δὲ σὺν ὀθνείοις ἀλάλημαι.
δείσατε συνθεσίας τε καὶ ὅρκια, δείσατ' Ἐρινύν
Ἱκεσίην νέμεσίν τε θεῶν, εἰς χεῖρας ἰούσης
Αἰήτεω λώβῃ πολυπήμονι δηιωθῆναι.
οὐ νηούς, οὐ πύργον ἐπίρροθον, οὐκ ἀλεωρήν   1045
ἄλλην, οἰόθι δὲ προτιβάλλομαι ὑμέας αὐτούς.
σχέτλιοι ἀτροπίης καὶ ἀνηλέες, οὐδ' ἐνὶ θυμῶι
αἰδεῖσθε ξείνης μ' ἐπὶ γούνασι χεῖρας ἀνάσσης
δερκόμενοι τείνουσαν ἀμήχανον· ἀλλά κε πᾶσι,
κῶας ἑλεῖν μεμαῶτες, ἐμίξατε δούρατα Κόλχοις   1050
αὐτῶι τ' Αἰήτῃ ὑπερήνορι· νῦν δὲ λάθεσθε
ἠνορέης, ὅτε μοῦνοι ἀποτμηγέντες ἔασιν."
     ὣς φάτο λισσομένη· τῶν δ' ὅν τινα γουνάζοιτο,
ὅς μιν θαρσύνεσκεν ἐρητύων ἀχέουσαν·
σεῖον δ' ἐγχείας εὐήκεας ἐν παλάμῃσι   1055
φάσγανά τ' ἐκ κολεῶν, οὐδὲ σχήσεσθαι ἀρωγῆς
ἔννεπον, εἴ κε δίκης ἀλιτήμονος ἀντιάσειεν.
στρευγομένης δ' ἀν' ὅμιλον ἐπήλυθεν εὐνήτειρα
νὺξ ἔργων ἀνδρεσσι, κατευκήλησε δὲ πᾶσαν
γαῖαν ὁμῶς. τὴν δ' οὔ τι μίνυνθά περ εὔνασεν ὕπνος,   1060
ἀλλά οἱ ἐν στέρνοις ἀχέων εἱλίσσετο θυμός,
οἷον ὅτε κλωστῆρα γυνὴ ταλαεργὸς ἑλίσσει
ἐννυχίη, τῇ δ' ἀμφὶ κινύρεται ὀρφανὰ τέκνα,
χηροσύνῃ πόσιος· σταλάει δ' ἐπὶ δάκρυ παρειάς
μυρομένης οἵη μιν ἐπισμυγερὴ λάβεν αἶσα·   1065
ὣς τῆς ἰκμαίνοντο παρηίδες, ἐν δέ οἱ ἦτορ
ὀξείῃς εἱλεῖτο πεπαρμένον ἀμφ' ὀδύνῃσι.
     τὼ δ' ἔντοσθε δόμοιο κατὰ πτόλιν, ὡς τὸ πάροιθεν,
κρείων Ἀλκίνοος πολυπότνιά τ' Ἀλκινόοιο
Ἀρήτη ἄλοχος κούρης πέρι μητιάασκον   1070
οἷσιν ἐνὶ λεχέεσσι διὰ κνέφας· οἷα δ' ἀκοίτην

1038 ὔμμε Campbell   1043 ἰούσης Wilamowitz: ἰοῦσαν Ω   1049 κε Sᴾᶜ: καὶ Ω
1057 ἀντιάσειεν L² w. –ειαν m   1058 στρευγομένης Wifstrand: –νοις Ω: –νων S: –νη
Etym.Gen./Mag.   1064 ἐπὶ Schneider: ὑπὸ Ω   1065 μυρομένης m: μνωομένης L²wd

κουρίδιον θαλεροῖσι δάμαρ προσπτύσσετο μύθοις·
"ναὶ φίλος, εἰ δ' ἄγε μοι πολυκηδέα ῥύεο Κόλχων
παρθενικήν, Μινύαισι φέρων χάριν. ἐγγύθι δ' Ἄργος
ἡμετέρης νήσοιο καὶ ἀνέρες Αἱμονιῆες·   1075
Αἰήτης δ' οὔτ' ἄρ ναίει σχεδόν, οὐδέ τι ἴδμεν
Αἰήτην, ἀλλ' οἷον ἀκούομεν. ἥδε δὲ κούρη
αἰνοπαθὴς κατά μοι νόον ἔκλασεν ἀντιόωσα·
μή μιν ἄναξ Κόλχοισι πόροις ἐς πατρὸς ἄγεσθαι.
ἀάσθη, ὅτε πρῶτα βοῶν θελκτήρια δῶκε   1080
φάρμακά οἱ· σχεδόθεν δὲ κακῶι κακόν, οἷά τε πολλά
ῥέζομεν ἀμπλακίηισιν, ἀκειομένη ὑπάλυξε
πατρὸς ὑπερφιάλοιο βαρὺν χόλον. αὐτὰρ Ἰήσων,
ὡς ἀίω, μεγάλοισιν ἐνίσχεται ἐξ ἕθεν ὅρκοις
κουριδίην θήσεσθαι ἐνὶ μεγάροισιν ἄκοιτιν·   1085
τῶ, φίλε, μήτ' οὖν αὐτὸς ἑκὼν ἐπίορκον ὀμόσσαι
θείης Αἰσονίδην, μήτ' ἄσχετα σεῖο ἕκητι
παῖδα πατὴρ θυμῶι κεκοτηότι δηλήσαιτο.
λίην γὰρ δύσζηλοι ἑαῖς ἐπὶ παισὶ τοκῆες·
οἷα μὲν Ἀντιόπην εὐώπιδα μήσατο Νυκτεύς,   1090
οἷα δὲ καὶ Δανάη πόντωι ἔνι πήματ' ἀνέτλη
πατρὸς ἀτασθαλίηισι· νέον γε μέν, οὐδ' ἀποτηλοῦ,
ὑβριστὴς Ἔχετος γλήναις ἔνι χάλκεα κέντρα
πῆξε θυγατρὸς ἑῆς, στονόεντι δὲ κάρφεται οἴτωι,
ὀρφναίηι ἐνὶ χαλκὸν ἀλετρεύουσα καλιῆι."   1095
   ὣς ἔφατ' ἀντομένη· τοῦ δὲ φρένες ἰαίνοντο
ἧς ἀλόχου μύθοισιν, ἔπος δ' ἐπὶ τοῖον ἔειπεν·
" Ἀρήτη, καί κεν σὺν τεύχεσιν ἐξελάσαιμι
Κόλχους, ἡρώεσσι φέρων χάριν, εἵνεκα κούρης.
ἀλλὰ Διὸς δείδοικα δίκην ἰθεῖαν ἀτίσσαι·   1100
οὐδὲ μὲν Αἰήτην ἀθεριζέμεν, ὡς ἀγορεύεις,
λώιον· οὐ γάρ τις βασιλεύτερος Αἰήταο,
καί κ' ἐθέλων ἑκάθέν περ ἐφ' Ἑλλάδι νεῖκος ἄγοιτο.
τῶ μ' ἐπέοικε δίκην, ἥ τις μετὰ πᾶσιν ἀρίστη
ἔσσεται ἀνθρώποισι, δικαζέμεν. οὐδέ σε κεύσω·   1105
παρθενικὴν μὲν ἐοῦσαν ἑῶι ἀπὸ πατρὶ κομίσσαι
ἰθύνω· λέκτρον δὲ σὺν ἀνέρι πορσαίνουσαν,
οὔ μιν ἑοῦ πόσιος νοσφίσσομαι, οὐδὲ γενέθλην

1072 κουρίδιον *m*: κουρίδιη *w*   1076 οὐδέ *m*: οὔτέ *wd*   1086 αὐτὸς Brunck: αὐτὸν Ω
1089 ἐπὶ *m*: περὶ *w*   1103 ἄγοιτο Ω: ἄροιτο E

εἴ τιν᾿ ὑπὸ σπλάγχνοισι φέρει δηίοισιν ὀπάσσω."
ὣς ἄρ᾿ ἔφη· καὶ τὸν μὲν ἐπισχεδὸν εὔνασεν ὕπνος.   1110
ἡ δ᾿ ἔπος ἐν θυμῶι πυκινὸν βάλετ᾿· αὐτίκα δ᾿ ὦρτο
ἐκ λεχέων ἀνὰ δῶμα, συνήιξαν δὲ γυναῖκες
ἀμφίπολοι, δέσποιναν ἑὴν μέτα ποιπνύουσαι.
σῖγα δ᾿ ἑὸν κήρυκα καλεσσαμένη προσέειπεν
ᾗσιν ἐπιφροσύνηισιν ἐποτρυνέουσα μιγῆναι   1115
Αἰσονίδην κούρηι, μηδ᾿ Ἀλκίνοον βασιλῆα
λίσσεσθαι· τὸ γὰρ αὐτὸς ἰὼν Κόλχοισι δικάσσει,
παρθενικὴν μὲν ἐοῦσαν ἑοῦ ποτὶ δώματα πατρός
ἐκδώσειν, λέκτρον δὲ σὺν ἀνέρι πορσαίνουσαν
οὐκέτι κουριδίης μιν ἀποτμήξειν φιλότητος.   1120
ὣς ἄρ᾿ ἔφη· τὸν δ᾿ αἶψα πόδες φέρον ἐκ μεγάροιο,
ὥς κεν Ἰήσονι μῦθον ἐναίσιμον ἀγγείλειεν
Ἀρήτης βουλάς τε θεουδέος Ἀλκινόοιο.
τοὺς δ᾿ εὗρεν παρὰ νηὶ σὺν ἔντεσιν ἐγρήσσοντας
Ὑλλικῶι ἐν λιμένι σχεδὸν ἄστεος· ἐκ δ᾿ ἄρα πᾶσαν   1125
πέφραδεν ἀγγελίην· γήθησε δὲ θυμὸς ἑκάστου
ἡρώων, μάλα γάρ σφιν ἑαδότα μῦθον ἔειπεν.
αὐτίκα δὲ κρητῆρα κερασσάμενοι μακάρεσσιν,
ἡ θέμις, εὐαγέως τ᾿ ἐπιβώμια μῆλ᾿ ἐρύσαντες,
αὐτονυχὶ κούρηι θαλαμήιον ἔντυον εὐνήν   1130
ἄντρωι ἐνὶ ζαθέωι, τόθι δή ποτε Μάκρις ἔναιε
κούρη Ἀρισταίοιο περίφρονος, ὅς ῥα μελισσέων
ἔργα πολυκμήτοιό τ᾿ ἀνεύρατο πῖαρ ἐλαίης.
κείνη δὴ πάμπρωτα Διὸς Νυσήιον υἷα
Εὐβοίης ἔντοσθεν Ἀβαντίδος ὧι ἐνὶ κόλπωι   1135
δέξατο καὶ μέλιτι ξηρὸν περὶ χεῖλος ἔδευσεν,
εὖτέ μιν Ἑρμείης φέρεν ἐκ πυρός· ἔδρακε δ᾿ Ἥρη,
καί ἑ χολωσαμένη πάσης ἐξήλασε νήσου·
ἡ δ᾿ ἄρα Φαιήκων ἱερῶι ἐνὶ τηλόθεν ἄντρωι
νάσσατο, καὶ πόρεν ὄλβον ἀθέσφατον ἐνναέτηισιν.   1140
ἔνθα τότ᾿ ἐστόρεσαν λέκτρον μέγα· τοῖο δ᾿ ὕπερθεν
χρύσεον αἰγλῆεν κῶας βάλον, ὄφρα πέλοιτο
τιμήεις τε γάμος καὶ ἀοίδιμος. ἄνθεα δέ σφι
νύμφαι ἀμεργόμεναι λευκοῖς ἐνὶ ποικίλα κόλποις
ἐσφόρεον. πάσας δὲ πυρὸς ὣς ἄμφεπεν αἴγλη,   1145

1115 ἐπιφροσύνηισιν m: ἐφημοσ- L² w   1129 τ᾿ Π²: om. Ω   1131 ἐνὶ ζαθέωι Π²: ἐν
ἠγαθέωι Ω   1132 περίφρονος L: πε[Π²: μελίφρονος L¹AwE

τοῖον ἀπὸ χρυσέων θυσάνων ἀμαρύσσετο φέγγος.
δαῖε δ᾽ ἐν ὀφθαλμοῖς γλυκερὸν πόθον· ἴσχε δ᾽ ἑκάστην
αἰδὼς ἱεμένην περ ὅμως ἐπὶ χεῖρα βαλέσθαι.
αἱ μέν τ᾽ Αἰγαίου ποταμοῦ καλέοντο θύγατρες,
αἱ δ᾽ ὄρεος κορυφὰς Μελιτηίου ἀμφενέμοντο,   1150
αἱ δ᾽ ἔσαν ἐκ πεδίων ἀλσηίδες· ὦρσε γὰρ αὐτή
Ἥρη Ζηνὸς ἄκοιτις, Ἰήσονα κυδαίνουσα.
κεῖνο καὶ εἰσέτι νῦν ἱερὸν κληίζεται Ἄντρον
Μηδείης, ὅθι τούς γε σὺν ἀλλήλοισιν ἔμιξαν,
τεινάμεναι ἑανοὺς εὐώδεας. οἱ δ᾽ ἐνὶ χερσί   1155
δούρατα νωμήσαντες ἀρήια, μὴ πρὶν ἐς ἀλκήν
δυσμενέων ἀίδηλος ἐπιβρίσειεν ὅμιλος,
κράατα δ᾽ εὐφύλλοις ἐστεμμένοι ἀκρεμόνεσσιν,
ἐμμελέως Ὀρφῆος ὑπαὶ λίγα φορμίζοντος
νυμφιδίαις ὑμέναιον ἐπὶ προμολῇσιν ἄειδον.   1160
οὐ μὲν ἐν Ἀλκινόοιο γάμον μενέαινε τελέσσαι
ἥρως Αἰσονίδης, μεγάροις δ᾽ ἐνὶ πατρὸς ἑοῖο
νοστήσας ἐς Ἰωλκὸν ὑπότροπος, ὣς δὲ καὶ αὐτή
Μήδεια φρονέεσκε· τότ᾽ αὖ χρεὼ ἦγε μιγῆναι.
ἀλλὰ γὰρ οὔ ποτε φῦλα δυηπαθέων ἀνθρώπων   1165
τερπωλῆς ἐπέβημεν ὅλωι ποδί· σὺν δέ τις αἰεί
πικρὴ παρμέμβλωκεν ἐυφροσύνηισιν ἀνίη.
τῶι καὶ τούς, γλυκερῆι περ ἰαινομένους φιλότητι,
δεῖμ᾽ ἔχεν, εἰ τελέοιτο διάκρισις Ἀλκινόοιο.
   ἠὼς δ᾽ ἀμβροσίοισιν ἀνερχομένη φαέεσσι   1170
λῦε κελαινὴν νύκτα δι᾽ ἠέρος· αἱ δ᾽ ἐγέλασσαν
ἠιόνες νήσοιο καὶ ἑρσήεσσαι ἄπωθεν
ἀτραπιτοὶ πεδίων· ἐν δὲ θρόος ἔσκεν ἀγυιαῖς·
κίνυντ᾽ ἐνναέται μὲν ἀνὰ πτόλιν, οἱ δ᾽ ἀποτηλοῦ
Κόλχοι Μακριδίης ἐπὶ πείρασι χερνήσοιο.   1175
αὐτίκα δ᾽ Ἀλκίνοος μετεβήσετο συνθεσίηισιν
ὃν νόον ἐξερέων κούρης ὕπερ· ἐν δ᾽ ὅ γε χειρί
σκῆπτρον ἔχεν χρυσοῖο δικασπόλον, ὧι ὕπο λαοί
ἰθείας ἀνὰ ἄστυ διεκρίνοντο θέμιστας.
τῶι δὲ καὶ ἑξείης πολεμήια τεύχεα δύντες   1180
Φαιήκων οἱ ἄριστοι ὁμιλαδὸν ἐστιχόωντο.
ἥρωας δὲ γυναῖκες ἀολλέες ἔκτοθι πύργων

1178 λαοί Flor. : πολλοί Ω

βαῖνον ἐποψόμεναι, σὺν δ᾽ ἀνέρες ἀγροιῶται
ἤντεον εἰσαΐοντες, ἐπεὶ νημερτέα βάξιν
Ἥρη ἐπιπροέηκεν. ἄγεν δ᾽ ὁ μὲν ἔκκριτον ἄλλων   1185
ἀρνειὸν μήλων, ὁ δ᾽ ἀεργηλὴν ἔτι πόρτιν·
ἄλλοι δ᾽ ἀμφιφορῆας ἐπισχεδὸν ἵστασαν οἴνου
κίρνασθαι· θυέων δ᾽ ἀπὸ τηλόθι κήκιε λιγνύς.
αἱ δὲ πολυκμήτους ἑανοὺς φέρον, οἷα γυναῖκες,
μείλιά τε χρυσοῖο καὶ ἀλλοίην ἐπὶ τοῖσιν   1190
ἀγλαΐην, οἵην τε νεόζυγες ἐντύνονται.
θάμβευν δ᾽ εἰσορόωσαι ἀριπρεπέων ἡρώων
εἴδεα καὶ μορφάς, ἐν δέ σφισιν Οἰάγροιο
υἱὸν ὑπαὶ φόρμιγγος ἐυκρέκτου καὶ ἀοιδῆς
ταρφέα σιγαλόεντι πέδον κρούοντα πεδίλωι.   1195
νύμφαι δ᾽ ἄμμιγα πᾶσαι, ὅτε μνήσαιτο γάμοιο,
ἱμερόενθ᾽ ὑμέναιον ἀνήπυον· ἄλλοτε δ᾽ αὖτε
οἰόθεν οἶαι ἄειδον ἑλισσόμεναι περὶ κύκλον,
Ἥρη, σεῖο ἕκητι· σὺ γὰρ καὶ ἐπὶ φρεσὶ θῆκας
Ἀρήτηι πυκινὸν φάσθαι ἔπος Ἀλκινόοιο.   1200
   αὐτὰρ ὅ γ᾽, ὡς τὰ πρῶτα δίκης ἀνὰ πείρατ᾽ ἔειπεν
ἰθείης, ἤδη δὲ γάμου τέλος ἐκλήιστο,
ἔμπεδον ὣς ἀλέγυνε διαμπερές, οὐδέ ἑ τάρβος
οὐλοὸν οὐδὲ βαρεῖαι ἐπήλυθον Αἰήταο
μήνιες· ἀρρήκτοισι δ᾽ ἐνιζεύξας ἔχεν ὅρκοις.   1205
τῶ καὶ ὅτ᾽ ἠλεμάτως Κόλχοι μάθον ἀντιόωντες,
καί σφεας ἠὲ θέμιστας ἑὰς εἴρυσθαι ἄνωγεν
ἢ λιμένων γαίης τ᾽ ἀπὸ τηλόθι νῆας ἐέργειν,
δὴ τότε μιν, βασιλῆος ἑοῦ τρομέοντες ἐνιπάς,
δέχθαι μειλίξαντο συνήμονας. αὖθι δὲ νήσωι   1210
δὴν μάλα Φαιήκεσσι μετ᾽ ἀνδράσι ναιετάασκον,
εἰσότε Βακχιάδαι γενεὴν Ἐφύρηθεν ἐόντες
ἀνέρες ἐννάσσαντο μετὰ χρόνον, οἱ δὲ περαίην
νήσου ἔβαν· κεῖθεν δὲ Κεραύνια μέλλον Ἀμάντων
οὔρεα Νεσταίους τε καὶ Ὥρικον εἰσαφικέσθαι.   1215
ἀλλὰ τὰ μὲν στείχοντος ἄδην αἰῶνος ἐτύχθη·
Μοιράων δ᾽ ἔτι κεῖσε θύη ἐπέτεια δέχονται
καὶ Νυμφέων Νομίοιο καθ᾽ ἱερὸν Ἀπόλλωνος

1193 ἐν m: σὺν w   1195 κρούοντα Lac Vac: κροτέοντα L4AwE   1196 μνήσαιτο Brunck: μνήσαιντο Ω   1200 Ἀρήτηι w: Ἀρήτης m   1204 ὑπήλυθον Madvig   1209 μιν w: δή m   1214 νήσου Pfeiffer: νῆσον Ω   Ἀμάντων Etym. Gen.: Ἀβάντων Ω

βωμοὶ τοὺς Μήδεια καθίσσατο. πολλὰ δ' ἰοῦσιν
Ἀλκίνοος Μινύαις ξεινήια, πολλὰ δ' ὄπασσεν   1220
Ἀρήτη, μετὰ δ' αὖτε δυώδεκα δῶκεν ἕπεσθαι
Μηδείηι δμωὰς Φαιηκίδας ἐκ μεγάροιο.
    ἤματι δ' ἑβδομάτωι Δρεπάνην λίπον· ἤλυθε δ' οὖρος
ἀκραὴς ἠῶθεν ὑπεύδιος, οἱ δ' ἀνέμοιο
πνοιῆι ἐπειγόμενοι προτέρω θέον. ἀλλὰ γὰρ οὔπω   1225
αἴσιμον ἦν ἐπιβῆναι Ἀχαιίδος ἡρώεσσιν,
ὄφρ' ἔτι καὶ Λιβύης ἐπὶ πείρασιν ὀτλήσειαν.
    ἤδη μὲν †ποτὶ κόλπον ἐπώνυμον Ἀμβρακιήων,
ἤδη Κουρῆτιν ἔλιπον χθόνα πεπταμένοισι
λαίφεσι καὶ στεινὰς αὐταῖς σὺν Ἐχινάσι νήσους   1230
ἑξείης, Πέλοπος δὲ νέον κατεφαίνετο γαῖα·
καὶ τότ' ἀναρπάγδην ὀλοὴ Βορέαο θύελλα
μεσσηγὺς πελαγόσδε Λιβυστικὸν ἐννέα πάσας
νύκτας ὁμῶς καὶ τόσσα φέρ' ἤματα, μέχρις ἵκοντο
προπρὸ μάλ' ἔνδοθι Σύρτιν, ἵν' οὐκέτι νόστος ὀπίσσω   1235
νηυσὶ πέλει, ὅτε τόνδε βιώιατο κόλπον ἱκέσθαι·
πάντηι γὰρ τέναγος, πάντηι μνιόεντα βυθοῖο
τάρφεα, κωφὴ δέ σφιν ἐπιβλύει ὕδατος ἄχνη·
ἠερίη δ' ἄμαθος παρακέκλιται, οὐδέ τι κεῖσε
ἑρπετὸν οὐδὲ ποτητὸν ἀείρεται. ἔνθ' ἄρα τούς γε   1240
πλημυρίς (καὶ γάρ τ' ἀναχάζεται ἠπείροιο
ἢ θαμὰ δὴ τόδε χεῦμα, καὶ ἂψ ἐπερεύγεται ἀκτάς
λάβρον ἐποιχόμενον) μυχάτηι ἐνέωσε τάχιστα
ἠιόνι, τρόπιος δὲ μάλ' ὕδασι παῦρον ἔλειπτο.
    οἱ δ' ἀπὸ νηὸς ὄρουσαν, ἄχος δ' ἕλεν εἰσορόωντας   1245
ἠέρα καὶ μεγάλης νῶτα χθονὸς ἠέρι ἶσα
τηλοῦ ὑπερτείνοντα διηνεκές· οὐδέ τιν' ἀρδμόν,
οὐ πάτον, οὐκ ἀπάνευθε κατηυγάσσαντο βοτήρων
αὔλιον, εὐκήλωι δὲ κατείχετο πάντα γαλήνηι.
    ἄλλος δ' αὖτ' ἄλλον τετιημένος ἐξερέεινε·   1250
"τίς χθὼν εὔχεται ἥδε; πόθι ξυνέωσαν ἄελλαι
ἡμέας; αἴθ' ἔτλημεν, ἀφειδέες οὐλομένοιο
δείματος, αὐτὰ κέλευθα διαμπερὲς ὁρμηθῆναι
πετράων· ἢ τ' ἂν καὶ ὑπὲρ Διὸς αἶσαν ἰοῦσι
βέλτερον ἦν μέγα δή τι μενοινώοντας ὀλέσθαι.   1255

1228 ποτὶ Ω: παρά Campbell   1229 Κουρῆτιν m: –ρήτων w   1236 τόνδε Fränkel:
τόνγε Ω   1243 ἐνέωσε τάχιστα m: –σεν ἄγεσθαι w   1246 ἠέρι Buttmann: ἠέρι δ' Ω

νῦν δὲ τί κεν ῥέξαιμεν, ἐρυκόμενοι ἀνέμοισιν
αὖθι μένειν τυτθόν περ ἐπὶ χρόνον; οἷον ἐρήμη
πέζα διωλυγίης ἀναπέπταται ἠπείροιο. "

ὣς ἄρ' ἔφη· μετὰ δ' αὐτὸς ἀμηχανίηι κακότητος
ἰθυντὴρ Ἀγκαῖος ἀκηχεμένοις ἀγόρευσεν·   1260
"ὠλόμεθ' αἰνότατον δῆθεν μόρον, οὐδ' ὑπάλυξις
ἔστ' ἄτης· πάρα δ' ἄμμι τὰ κύντατα πημανθῆναι
τῆιδ' ὑπ' ἐρημαίηι πεπτηότας, εἰ καὶ ἄηται
χερσόθεν ἀμπνεύσειαν· ἐπεὶ τεναγώδεα λεύσσω
τῆλε περισκοπέων ἅλα πάντοθεν, ἤλιθα δ' ὕδωρ   1265
ξαινόμενον πολιῆισιν ἐπιτροχάει ψαμάθοισι.
καί κεν ἐπισμυγερῶς διὰ δὴ πάλαι ἥδε κεάσθη
νηῦς ἱερὴ χέρσου πολλὸν πρόσω, ἀλλά μιν αὐτή
πλημυρὶς ἐκ πόντοιο μεταχρονίην ἐκόμισσε.
νῦν δ' ἡ μὲν πελαγόσδε μετέσσυται, οἰόθι δ' ἄλμη   1270
ἄπλοος εἰλεῖται, γαίης ὕπερ ὅσσον ἔχουσα.
τούνεκ' ἐγὼ πᾶσαν μὲν ἀπ' ἐλπίδα φημὶ κεκόφθαι
ναυτιλίης νόστου τε· δαημοσύνην δέ τις ἄλλος
φαίνοι ἑήν· πάρα γάρ οἱ ἐπ' οἰήκεσσι θαάσσειν
μαιομένωι κομιδῆς· ἀλλ' οὐ μάλα νόστιμον ἦμαρ   1275
Ζεὺς ἐθέλει καμάτοισιν ἐφ' ἡμετέροισι τελέσσαι. "

ὣς φάτο δακρυόεις, σὺν δ' ἔννεπον ἀσχαλόωντι
ὅσσοι ἔσαν νηῶν δεδαημένοι. ἐν δ' ἄρα πᾶσι
παχνώθη κραδίη, χύτο δὲ χλόος ἀμφὶ παρειάς.
οἷον δ' ἀψύχοισιν ἐοικότες εἰδώλοισιν   1280
ἀνέρες εἰλίσσονται ἀνὰ πτόλιν, ἢ πολέμοιο
ἢ λοιμοῖο τέλος ποτιδέγμενοι ἠέ τιν' ὄμβρον
ἄσπετον, ὅς τε βοῶν κατὰ μυρία ἔκλυσεν ἔργα,
ἢ ὅταν αὐτόματα ξόανα ῥέηι ἱδρώοντα
αἵματι καὶ μυκαὶ σηκοῖς ἔνι φαντάζωνται,   1285
ἠὲ καὶ ἥλιος μέσωι ἤματι νύκτ' ἐπάγηισιν
οὐρανόθεν, τὰ δὲ λαμπρὰ δι' ἠέρος ἄστρα φαείνει·
ὣς τότ' ἀριστῆες δολιχοῦ πρόπαρ αἰγιαλοῖο
ἤλυον ἑρπύζοντες. ἐπήλυθε δ' αὐτίκ' ἐρεμνή
ἕσπερος· οἱ δ' ἐλεεινὰ χεροῖν σφέας ἀμφιβαλόντες   1290

1263 καὶ L^{ac}: κεν L²AwE   1274 φαίνοι ἑήν Madvig: φαίνοι ... L^{ac}: φαίνοιεν L²Aw.
φήνειεν E   1277 ἀσχαλόωντι m: ἀσχαλόωντες w   1284 ἢ ὅταν Ω: ὁππότ' ἂν
Wilamowitz   1285 φαντάζωνται S^{pc}GΣ: –ονται mS^{ac}   1287 φαείνει wE: –νοι LA:
–νηι Stephanus   1289 ἤλυον Brunck: ἤλυθον Ω

δακρυόειν ἀγάπαζον, ἵν᾽ ἄνδιχα δῆθεν ἕκαστος
θυμὸν ἀποφθείσειαν ἐνὶ ψαμάθοισι πεσόντες.
βὰν δ᾽ ἴμεν ἄλλυδις ἄλλος, ἑκαστέρω αὖλιν ἑλέσθαι·
ἐν δὲ κάρη πέπλοισι καλυψάμενοι σφετέροισιν,
ἄκμηνοι καὶ ἄπαστοι ἐκείατο νύκτ᾽ ἔπι πᾶσαν   1295
καὶ φάος, οἰκτίστωι θανάτωι ἔπι. νόσφι δὲ κοῦραι
ἀθρόαι Αἰήταο παρεστενάχοντο θυγατρί.
ὡς δ᾽ ὅτ᾽ ἐρημαῖοι, πεπτηότες ἔκτοθι πέτρης
χηραμοῦ, ἀπτῆνες λιγέα κλάζουσι νεοσσοί,
ἢ ὅτε καλὰ νάοντος ἐπ᾽ ὀφρύσι Πακτωλοῖο   1300
κύκνοι κινήσωσιν ἑὸν μέλος, ἀμφὶ δὲ λειμών
ἑρσήεις βρέμεται ποταμοῖό τε καλὰ ῥέεθρα·
ὣς αἱ ἐπὶ ξανθὰς θέμεναι κονίηισιν ἐθείρας
παννύχιαι ἐλεεινὸν ἰήλεμον ὠδύροντο.
    καί νύ κεν αὐτοῦ πάντες ἀπὸ ζωῆς ἐλίασθεν   1305
νώνυμνοι καὶ ἄφαντοι ἐπιχθονίοισι δαῆναι
ἡρώων οἱ ἄριστοι ἀνηνύστωι ἐπ᾽ ἀέθλωι,
ἀλλά σφεας ἐλέηραν ἀμηχανίηι μινύθοντας
ἡρῶσσαι Λιβύης τιμήοροι, αἵ ποτ᾽ Ἀθήνην,
ἦμος ὅτ᾽ ἐκ πατρὸς κεφαλῆς θόρε παμφαίνουσα,   1310
ἀντόμεναι Τρίτωνος ἐφ᾽ ὕδασι χυτλώσαντο.
ἔνδιον ἦμαρ ἔην, περὶ δ᾽ ὀξύταται θέρον αὐγαί
ἠελίου Λιβύην· αἱ δὲ σχεδὸν Αἰσονίδαο
ἔσταν, ἕλον δ᾽ ἀπὸ χερσὶ καρήατος ἠρέμα πέπλον.
αὐτὰρ ὅ γ᾽ εἰς ἑτέρωσε παλιμπετὲς ὄμματ᾽ ἔνεικε,   1315
δαίμονας αἰδεσθείς· αὐτὸν δέ μιν ἀμφαδὸν οἶον
μειλιχίοις ἐπέεσσιν ἀτυζόμενον προσέειπον·
"κάμμορε, τίπτ᾽ ἐπὶ τόσσον ἀμηχανίηι βεβόλησαι;
ἴδμεν ἐποιχομένους χρύσεον δέρος, ἴδμεν ἕκαστα
ὑμετέρων καμάτων ὅσ᾽ ἐπὶ χθονὸς ὅσσα τ᾽ ἐφ᾽ ὑγρήν   1320
πλαζόμενοι κατὰ πόντον ὑπέρβια ἔργα κάμεσθε.
οἰοπόλοι δ᾽ εἰμὲν χθόνιαι θεαὶ αὐδήεσσαι,
ἡρῶσσαι Λιβύης τιμήοροι ἠδὲ θύγατρες.
ἀλλ᾽ ἄνα, μηδ᾽ ἔτι τοῖον ὀιζύων ἀκάχησο,
ἄνστησον δ᾽ ἑτάρους· εὖτ᾽ ἂν δέ τοι Ἀμφιτρίτη   1325
ἅρμα Ποσειδάωνος ἐύτροχον αὐτίκα λύσηι,
δή ῥα τότε σφετέρηι ἀπὸ μητέρι τίνετ᾽ ἀμοιβήν

1301 κινήσωσιν *w*D: –σουσιν *m*   1308 ἐλέηραν *m*: ἐλέαιρον *w*   1312 ὀξύταται S*d*:
–τατοι LAG   1318 ἐπὶ Spitzner: ἔτι vel (τίπτ)ε τι Ω

ὧν ἔκαμεν δηρὸν κατὰ νηδύος ὔμμε φέρουσα·
καί κεν ἔτ' ἠγαθέην ἐς Ἀχαιίδα νοστήσαιτε."
   ὣς ἄρ' ἔφαν, καὶ ἄφαντοι, ἵν' ἔσταθεν, ἔνθ' ἄρα ταί γε   1330
φθογγῆι ὁμοῦ ἐγένοντο παρασχεδόν. αὐτὰρ Ἰήσων
παπτήνας ἀν' ἄρ' ἕζετ' ἐπὶ χθονός, ὧδέ τ' ἔειπεν·
"Ἵλατ', ἐρημονόμοι κυδραὶ θεαί. ἀμφὶ δὲ νόστωι
οὔ τι μάλ' ἀντικρὺ νοέω φάτιν· ἢ μὲν ἑταίρους
εἰς ἓν ἀγειράμενος μυθήσομαι, εἴ νύ τι τέκμωρ   1335
δήωμεν κομιδῆς· πολέων δέ τε μῆτις ἀρείων."
   ἦ, καὶ ἀναΐξας ἑτάρους ἐπὶ μακρὸν ἀύτει
αὐσταλέος κονίηισι, λέων ὥς, ὅς ῥά τ' ἀν' ὕλην
σύννομον ἦν μεθέπων ὠρύεται· αἱ δὲ βαρείηι
φθογγῆι ὑποβρομέουσιν ἀν' οὔρεα τηλόθι βῆσσαι·   1340
δείματι δ' ἄγραυλοί τε βόες μέγα πεφρίκασι
βουπελάται τε βοῶν. τοῖς δ' οὔ νύ τι γῆρυς ἐτύχθη
ῥιγεδανὴ ἑτάροιο φίλοις ἐπικεκλομένοιο·
ἀγχοῦ δ' ἠγερέθοντο κατηφέες. αὐτὰρ ὁ τούς γε
ἀχνυμένους ὅρμοιο πέλας μίγα θηλυτέρηισιν   1345
ἱδρύσας, μυθεῖτο πιφαυσκόμενος τὰ ἕκαστα·
"κλῦτε φίλοι· τρεῖς γάρ μοι ἀνιάζοντι θεάων,
στέρφεσιν αἰγείοις ἐζωσμέναι ἐξ ὑπάτοιο
αὐχένος ἀμφί τε νῶτα καὶ ἰξύας, ἠύτε κοῦραι,
ἔσταν ὑπὲρ κεφαλῆς μάλ' ἐπισχεδόν· ἂν δ' ἐκάλυψαν   1350
πέπλον ἐρυσσάμεναι κούφηι χερί, καί μ' ἐκέλοντο
αὐτόν τ' ἔγρεσθαι ἀνά θ' ὑμέας ὄρσαι ἰόντα·
μητέρι δὲ σφετέρηι μενοεικέα τῖσαι ἀμοιβήν
ὧν ἔκαμεν δηρὸν κατὰ νηδύος ἄμμε φέρουσα,
ὁππότε κεν λύσηισιν ἐύτροχον Ἀμφιτρίτη   1355
ἅρμα Ποσειδάωνος· ἐγὼ δ' οὐ πάγχυ νοῆσαι
τῆσδε θεοπροπίης ἴσχω πέρι. φάν γε μὲν εἶναι
ἡρῶσσαι Λιβύης τιμήοροι ἠδὲ θύγατρες·
καὶ δ' ὁπόσ' αὐτοὶ πρόσθεν ἐπὶ χθονὸς ἠδ' ὅσ' ἐφ' ὑγρήν
ἔτλημεν, τὰ ἕκαστα διίδμεναι εὐχετόωντο.   1360
οὐδ' ἔτι τάσδ' ἀνὰ χῶρον ἐσέδρακον, ἀλλά τις ἀχλὺς
ἠὲ νέφος μεσσηγὺ φαεινομένας ἐκάλυψεν."

1336 ἀρείων m: ἀρίστη w   1339 δὲ βαρείηι Wellauer: –είαι vel –εῖαν vel –εία vel –εῖα·
codd.   1340 ὑποβρομέουσιν L^{ac}: ὑποτρομ- L²AwE   1343 φίλοις m: φίλους L² w
1350 ἂν L in ras. AwE: ἐκ D   1359 ὑγρήν m: ὑγρῆς w

ὣς ἔφαθ'· οἱ δ' ἄρα πάντες ἐθάμβεον εἰσαΐοντες.
ἔνθα τὸ μήκιστον τεράων Μινύαισιν ἐτύχθη.
ἐξ ἁλὸς ἠπειρόνδε πελώριος ἔκθορεν ἵππος,   1365
ἀμφιλαφὴς χρυσέῃσι μετήορος αὐχένα χαίταις·
ῥίμφα δὲ σεισάμενος γυίων ἄπο νήχυτον ἅλμην
ὦρτο θέειν πνοιῇ ἴκελος πόδας. αἶψα δὲ Πηλεύς
γηθήσας ἑτάροισιν ὁμηγερέεσσι μετηύδα·
"ἅρματα μὲν δή φημι Ποσειδάωνος ἔγωγε   1370
ἤδη νῦν ἀλόχοιο φίλης ὑπὸ χερσὶ λελύσθαι·
μητέρα δ' οὐκ ἄλλην προτιόσσομαι ἠέ περ αὐτήν
νῆα πέλειν· ἦ γὰρ κατὰ νηδύος αἰὲν ἔχουσα
ἡμέας ἀργαλέοισιν ὀϊζύει καμάτοισιν.
ἀλλά μιν ἀστεμφεῖ τε βίῃ καὶ ἀτειρέσιν ὤμοις   1375
ὑψόθεν ἀνθέμενοι ψαμαθώδεος ἔνδοθι γαίης
οἴσομεν ἧι προτέρωσε ταχὺς πόδας ἤλασεν ἵππος·
οὐ γὰρ ὅ γε ξηρὴν ὑποδύσεται, ἴχνια δ' ἡμῖν
σημανέειν τιν' ἔολπα μυχὸν καθύπερθε θαλάσσης."
ὣς ηὔδα· πάντεσσι δ' ἐπήβολος ἥνδανε μῆτις.   1380
Μουσάων ὅδε μῦθος, ἐγὼ δ' ὑπακουὸς ἀείδω
Πιερίδων, καὶ τήνδε πανατρεκὲς ἔκλυον ὀμφήν,
ὑμέας, ὦ πέρι δὴ μέγα φέρτατοι υἷες ἀνάκτων,
ἦι βίῃ, ἦι ἀρετῇ Λιβύης ἀνὰ θῖνας ἐρήμους
νῆα μεταχρονίην ὅσα τ' ἔνδοθι νηὸς ἄγεσθε   1385
ἀνθεμένους ὤμοισι φέρειν δυοκαίδεκα πάντα
ἤμαθ' ὁμοῦ νύκτας τε. δύην γε μὲν ἢ καὶ ὀϊζύν
τίς κ' ἐνέποι, τὴν κεῖνοι ἀνέπλησαν μογέοντες;
ἔμπεδον ἀθανάτων ἔσαν αἵματος, οἷον ὑπέσταν
ἔργον ἀναγκαίῃ βεβιημένοι. αὐτὰρ ἐπιπρό   1390
τῆλε μάλ' ἀσπασίως Τριτωνίδος ὕδασι λίμνης
ὣς φέρον, ὣς εἰσβάντες ἀπὸ στιβαρῶν θέσαν ὤμων.
λυσσαλέοις δήπειτ' ἴκελοι κυσὶν ἀΐσσοντες
πίδακα μαστεύεσκον· ἐπὶ ξηρῇ γὰρ ἔκειτο
δίψα δυηπαθίῃ τε καὶ ἄλγεσιν. οὐδ' ἐμάτησαν   1395
πλαζόμενοι· ἷξον δ' ἱερὸν πέδον, ὧι ἔνι Λάδων
εἰσέτι που χθιζὸν παγχρύσεα ῥύετο μῆλα
χώρωι ἐν Ἄτλαντος, χθόνιος ὄφις· ἀμφὶ δὲ νύμφαι
Ἑσπερίδες ποίπνυον ἐφίμερον ἀείδουσαι.

1365 ἔκθορεν LAD: ἀν- *w.* ἐν- E   1373 αἰὲν ἔχουσα *w.* ἄμμε φέρουσα *m*   1374 ἡμέας Ω:
νωλεμὲς E   1385 ἄγεσθε Flor.: ἄγεσθαι Ω

δὴ τότε γ᾿ ἤδη κεῖνος ὑφ᾿ Ἡρακλῆϊ δαϊχθείς   1400
μήλειον βέβλητο ποτὶ στύπος, οἰόθι δ᾿ ἄκρη
οὐρὴ ἔτι σπαίρεσκεν, ἀπὸ κρατὸς δὲ κελαινήν
ἄχρις ἐπ᾿ ἄκνηστιν κεῖτ᾿ ἄπνοος· ἐν δὲ λιπόντων
ὕδρης Λερναίης χόλον αἵματι πικρὸν ὀιστῶν,
μυῖαι πυθομένοισιν ἐφ᾿ ἕλκεσι τερσαίνοντο.   1405
ἀγχοῦ δ᾿ Ἑσπερίδες, κεφαλαῖς ἔπι χεῖρας ἔχουσαι
ἀργυφέας ξανθῇσι, λίγ᾿ ἔστενον. οἱ δ᾿ ἐπέλασσαν
ἄφνω ὁμοῦ· ταὶ δ᾿ αἶψα κόνις καὶ γαῖα, κιόντων
ἐσσυμένως, ἐγένοντο καταυτόθι. νώσατο δ᾿ Ὀρφεύς
θεῖα τέρα, †τὰς δέ σφι† παρηγορέεσκε λιτῇσι·   1410
"δαίμονες ὦ καλαὶ καὶ ἐύφρονες, ἵλατ᾿, ἄνασσαι,
εἴ τ᾿ οὖν οὐρανίαις ἐναρίθμιοί ἐστε θεῇσιν
εἴ τε καταχθονίαις, εἴτ᾿ οἰοπόλοι καλέεσθε
νύμφαι· ἴτ᾿, ὦ νύμφαι, ἱερὸν γένος Ὠκεανοῖο,
δείξατ᾿ ἐελδομένοισιν ἐνωπαδὶς ἄμμι φανεῖσαι   1415
ἤ τινα πετραίην χύσιν ὕδατος ἤ τινα γαίης
ἱερὸν ἐκβλύοντα, θεαί, ῥόον, ᾧ ἀπὸ δίψαν
αἰθομένην ἄμοτον λωφήσομεν. εἰ δέ κεν αὖτις
δή ποτ᾿ Ἀχαιίδα γαῖαν ἱκώμεθα ναυτιλίῃσι,
δὴ τότε μυρία δῶρα μετὰ πρώτῃσι θεάων   1420
λοιβάς τ᾿ εἰλαπίνας τε παρέξομεν εὐμενέοντες."
    ὣς φάτο λισσόμενος ἀδινῇ ὀπί· ταὶ δ᾿ ἐλέαιρον
ἐγγύθεν ἀχνυμένους. καὶ δὴ χθονὸς ἐξανέτειλαν
ποίην πάμπρωτον, ποίης γε μὲν ὑψόθι μακροί
βλάστεον ὄρπηκες, μετὰ δ᾿ ἔρνεα τηλεθάοντα   1425
πολλὸν ὑπὲρ γαίης ὀρθοσταδὸν ἠέξοντο·
Ἑσπέρη αἴγειρος, πτελέη δ᾿ Ἐρυθηὶς ἔγεντο,
Αἴγλη δ᾿ ἰτέης ἱερὸν στύπος. ἐκ δέ νυ κείνων
δενδρέων, οἷαι ἔσαν, τοῖαι πάλιν ἔμπεδον αὔτως
ἐξέφανεν, θάμβος περιώσιον. ἔκφατο δ᾿ Αἴγλη   1430
μειλιχίοις ἐπέεσσιν ἀμειβομένη χατέοντας·
"ἦ ἄρα δὴ μέγα πάμπαν ἐφ᾿ ὑμετέροισιν ὄνειαρ
δεῦρ᾿ ἔμολεν καμάτοισιν ὁ κύντατος, ὅστις ἀπούρας
φρουρὸν ὄφιν ζωῆς, παγχρύσεα μῆλα θεάων
οἴχετ᾿ ἀειράμενος· στυγερὸν δ᾿ ἄχος ἄμμι λέλειπται.   1435

1400 δὴ τότε γ᾿ ἤδη κεῖνος *ш.* δὴ τότε δὴ τῆμος *m*   1401–2 ἄκρη | οὐρὴ Ω: ἄκρηι | οὐρῆι Ε
1402 σπαίρεσκεν Brunck: σκαί- Ω   1403 ἐν Seaton: ἐκ Ω   1410 τὰς Ω: στὰς Ε: τὼς
Platt   σφι Ω: σφε Brunck

ἤλυθε γὰρ χθιζός τις ἀνὴρ ὀλοώτατος ὕβριν
καὶ δέμας, ὄσσε δέ οἱ βλοσυρῶι ὑπέλαμπε μετώπωι,
νηλής· ἀμφὶ δὲ δέρμα πελωρίου ἕστο λέοντος
ὠμόν, ἀδέψητον· στιβαρὸν δ' ἔχεν ὄζον ἐλαίης
τόξα τε, τοῖσι πέλωρ τόδ' ἀπέφθισεν ἰοβολήσας.   1440
ἤλυθε δ' οὖν κἀκεῖνος, ἅ τε χθόνα πεζὸς ὁδεύων,
δίψηι καρχαλέος· παίφασσε δὲ τόνδ' ἀνὰ χῶρον,
ὕδωρ ἐξερέων. τὸ μὲν οὔ ποθι μέλλεν ἰδέσθαι·
ἥδε δέ τις πέτρη Τριτωνίδος ἐγγύθι λίμνης·
τὴν ὅ γ', ἐπιφρασθεὶς ἢ καὶ θεοῦ ἐννεσίηισι,   1445
λὰξ ποδὶ τύψεν ἔνερθε· τὸ δ' ἀθρόον ἔβλυσεν ὕδωρ.
αὐτὰρ ὅ γ', ἄμφω χεῖρε πέδωι καὶ στέρνον ἐρείσας,
ῥωγάδος ἐκ πέτρης πίεν ἄσπετον, ὄφρα βαθεῖαν
νηδύν, φορβάδι ἶσος ἐπιπροπεσών, ἐκορέσθη."
    ὣς φάτο· τοὶ δ' ἀσπαστὸν ἵνα σφίσι πέφραδεν Αἴγλη   1450
πίδακα, τῆι θέον αἶψα κεχαρμένοι, ὄφρ' ἐπέκυρσαν.
ὡς δ' ὁπότε στεινὴν περὶ χηραμὸν εἱλίσσονται
γειομόροι μύρμηκες ὁμιλαδόν, ἢ ὅτε μυῖαι
ἀμφ' ὀλίγην μέλιτος γλυκεροῦ λίβα πεπτηυῖαι
ἄπλητον μεμάασιν ἐπήτριμοι· ὣς τότ' ἀολλεῖς   1455
πετραίηι Μινύαι περὶ πίδακι δινεύεσκον.
καὶ πού τις διεροῖς ἐπὶ χείλεσιν εἶπεν ἰανθείς·
"ὢ πόποι, ἦ καὶ νόσφιν ἐὼν ἐσάωσεν ἑταίρους
Ἡρακλέης δίψηι κεκμηότας. ἀλλά μιν εἴ πως
δήοιμεν στείχοντα δι' ἠπείροιο κιόντες."   1460
    ἦ· καὶ ἀμειβομένων οἵ τ' ἄρμενοι ἐς τόδε ἔργον
ἔκριθεν ἄλλυδις ἄλλος ἀναΐξας ἐρεείνειν·
ἴχνια γὰρ νυχίοισιν ἐπηλίνδητ' ἀνέμοισι
κινυμένης ἀμάθου. Βορέαο μὲν ὡρμήθησαν
υἷε δύω πτερύγεσσι πεποιθότε, ποσσὶ δὲ κούφοις   1465
Εὔφημος πίσυνος, Λυγκεύς γε μὲν ὀξέα τηλοῦ
ὄσσε βαλεῖν, πέμπτος δὲ μετὰ σφίσιν ἔσσυτο Κάνθος.
τὸν μὲν ἄρ' αἶσα θεῶν κείνην ὁδὸν ἠνορέη τε
ὦρσεν, ἵν' Ἡρακλῆος ἀπηλεγέως πεπύθοιτο
Εἰλατίδην Πολύφημον ὅπηι λίπε· μέμβλετο γάρ οἱ   1470
οὗ ἕθεν ἀμφ' ἑτάροιο μεταλλῆσαι τὰ ἕκαστα.

1441 ἤλυθε δ' L¹SᵖᶜGE: ἤλυθεν ASᵃᶜ   1450 τοὶ E: τοῖς Ω   1453 γειομόροι *m*Σ:
—οτόμοι Lˢˡ*w*Etym.Gen.   ἢ ὅτε E: ἠύτε Ω Etym.Gen.   1462 ἀναΐξας Campbell:
ἐπαΐξας Ω   1465 πεποιθότε SᵖᶜE: πεποιθότες Ω

ἀλλ᾿ ὁ μὲν οὖν, Μυσοῖσιν ἐπικλεὲς ἄστυ πολίσσας,
νόστου κηδοσύνηισιν ἔβη διζήμενος Ἀργώ
τῆλε δι᾿ ἠπείροιο, τέως ἐξίκετο γαῖαν
ἀγχιάλων Χαλύβων· τόθι μιν καὶ μοῖρ᾿ ἐδάμασσε,   1475
καί οἱ ὑπὸ βλωθρὴν ἀχερωίδα σῆμα τέτυκται
τυτθὸν ἁλὸς προπάροιθεν. ἀτὰρ τότε γ᾿ Ἡρακλῆα
μοῦνον ἀπειρεσίης τηλοῦ χθονὸς εἴσατο Λυγκεύς
τὼς ἰδέειν, ὥς τίς τε νέωι ἐνὶ ἤματι μήνην
ἢ ἴδεν ἢ ἐδόκησεν ἐπαχλύουσαν ἰδέσθαι·   1480
ἐς δ᾿ ἑτάρους ἀνιὼν μυθήσατο μή μιν ἔτ᾿ ἄλλον
μαστῆρα στείχοντα κιχησέμεν. οἱ δὲ καὶ αὐτοί
ἤλυθον Εὔφημός τε πόδας ταχὺς υἷέ τε δοιώ
Θρηικίου Βορέω, μεταμώνια μοχθήσαντες.
    Κάνθε, σὲ δ᾿ οὐλόμεναι Λιβύηι ἔνι Κῆρες ἕλοντο.   1485
πώεσι φερβομένοισι συνήντεες, εἴπετο δ᾿ ἀνήρ
αὐλίτης· ὅ σ᾿ ἑῶν μήλων πέρι, τόφρ᾿ ἑτάροισι
δευομένοις κομίσειας, ἀλεξόμενος κατέπεφνε
λᾶϊ βαλών· ἐπεὶ οὐ μὲν ἀφαυρότερός γ᾿ ἐτέτυκτο,
υἱωνὸς Φοίβοιο Λυκωρείοιο Κάφαυρος   1490
κούρης τ᾿ αἰδοίης Ἀκακαλλίδος, ἥν ποτε Μίνως
ἐς Λιβύην ἀπένασσε θεοῦ βαρὺ κῦμα φέρουσαν,
θυγατέρα σφετέρην· ἡ δ᾿ ἀγλαὸν υἱέα Φοίβωι
τίκτεν, ὃν Ἀμφίθεμιν Γαράμαντά τε κικλήσκουσιν·
Ἀμφίθεμις δ᾿ ἄρ᾿ ἔπειτα μίγη Τριτωνίδι νύμφηι·   1495
ἡ δ᾿ ἄρα οἱ Νασάμωνα τέκε κρατερόν τε Κάφαυρον,
ὃς τότε Κάνθον ἔπεφνεν ἐπὶ ῥήνεσσιν ἑοῖσιν.
οὐδ᾿ ὅ γ᾿ ἀριστήων χαλεπὰς ἠλεύατο χεῖρας,
ὡς μάθον οἷον ἔρεξε. νέκυν δ᾿ ἀνάειραν ὀπίσσω
†πυθόμενοι† Μινύαι, γαίηι δ᾿ ἐνὶ ταρχύσαντο   1500
μυρόμενοι· τὰ δὲ μῆλα μετὰ σφέας οἵ γ᾿ ἐκόμισσαν.
    ἔνθα καὶ Ἀμπυκίδην αὐτῶι ἐνὶ ἤματι Μόψον
νηλειὴς ἕλε πότμος, ἀδευκέα δ᾿ οὐ φύγεν αἶσαν
μαντοσύναις· οὐ γάρ τις ἀποτροπίη θανάτοιο.
κεῖτο δ᾿ ἐνὶ ψαμάθοισι, μεσημβρινὸν ἦμαρ ἀλύσκων,   1505
δεινὸς ὄφις, νωθὴς μὲν ἑκὼν ἀέκοντα χαλέψαι,

1474 τέως Fränkel: τέως δ᾿ Ω   1478 μοῦνον Ω: μοῦνος Ε²   1484 μοχθήσαντες ASE:
μοχθήσαντε L¹ G   1487 ὅ σ᾿ Brunck: ὃς Ω   1489 μεν (sic) Ε: μιν Ω   1490 Κάφαυρος
Ω: Κάφαλος Etym.Gen   1500 πυθόμενοι Ω: πευθ- Ε: πυθόμενον Wifstrand   1501 τὰ
δὲ Hölzlin: δὲ τὰ Ω   1505 ἐνὶ Wifstrand: ἐπὶ Ω

οὐδ᾽ ἂν ὑποτρέσσαντος ἐνωπαδὶς ἀίξειεν·
ἀλλ᾽ ὧι κεν τὰ πρῶτα μελάγχιμον ἰὸν ἐνείη
ζωόντων, ὅσα γαῖα φερέσβιος ἔμπνοα βόσκει,
οὐδ᾽ ὁπόσον πήχυιον ἐς Ἅιδα γίγνεται οἶμος,   1510
οὐδ᾽ εἰ Παιήων — εἴ μοι θέμις ἀμφαδὸν εἰπεῖν —
φαρμάσσοι, ὅτε μοῦνον ἐνιχρίμψηισιν ὀδοῦσιν.
εὖτε γὰρ ἰσόθεος Λιβύην ὑπερέπτατο Περσεύς
Εὐρυμέδων — καὶ γὰρ τὸ κάλεσκέ μιν οὔνομα μήτηρ —
Γοργόνος ἀρτίτομον κεφαλὴν βασιλῆι κομίζων,   1515
ὅσσαι κυανέου στάγες αἵματος οὖδας ἵκοντο,
αἱ πᾶσαι κείνων ὀφίων γένος ἐβλάστησαν.
τῶι δ᾽ ἄκρην ἐπ᾽ ἄκανθαν ἐνεστηρίξατο Μόψος
λαιὸν ἐπιπροφέρων ταρσὸν ποδός· αὐτὰρ ὁ μέσσην
κερκίδα καὶ μυῶνα πέριξ ὀδύνηισιν ἑλιχθεὶς   1520
σάρκα δακὼν ἐχάραξεν. ἀτὰρ Μήδεια καὶ ἄλλαι
ἔτρεσαν ἀμφίπολοι· ὁ δὲ φοίνιον ἕλκος ἄφασσε
θαρσαλέως, ἔνεκ᾽ οὔ μιν ὑπέρβιον ἄλγος ἔτειρε,
σχέτλιος· ἦ τέ οἱ ἤδη ὑπὸ χροῒ δύετο κῶμα
λυσιμελές, πολλὴ δὲ κατ᾽ ὀφθαλμῶν χέετ᾽ ἀχλύς.   1525
αὐτίκα δὲ κλίνας δαπέδωι βεβαρηότα γυῖα
ψύχετ᾽ ἀμηχανίηι· ἕταροι δέ μιν ἀμφαγέροντο
ἥρως τ᾽ Αἰσονίδης, ἀδινῆι περιθαμβέες ἄτηι.
οὐδὲ μὲν οὐδ᾽ ἐπὶ τυτθὸν ἀποφθίμενός περ ἔμελλε
κεῖσθαι ὑπ᾽ ἠελίωι· πύθεσκε γὰρ ἔνδοθι σάρκας   1530
ἰὸς ἄφαρ, μυδόωσα δ᾽ ἀπὸ χροὸς ἔρρεε λάχνη.
αἶψα δὲ χαλκείηισι βαθὺν τάφον ἐξελάχαινον
ἐσσυμένως μακέληισιν· ἐμοιρήσαντο δὲ χαίτας
αὐτοὶ ὁμῶς κοῦραί τε, νέκυν ἐλεεινὰ παθόντα
μυρόμενοι· τρὶς δ᾽ ἀμφὶ σὺν ἔντεσι δινηθέντες   1535
εὖ κτερέων ἴσχοντα, χυτὴν ἐπὶ γαῖαν ἔθεντο.
   ἀλλ᾽ ὅτε δή ῥ᾽ ἐπὶ νηὸς ἔβαν, πρήσσοντος ἀήτεω
ἂμ πέλαγος νοτίοιο, πόρους τ᾽ ἀπετεκμαίροντο
λίμνης ἐκπρομολεῖν Τριτωνίδος, οὔ τινα μῆτιν
δὴν ἔχον, ἀφραδέως δὲ πανημέριοι φορέοντο.   1540
ὡς δὲ δράκων σκολιὴν εἱλιγμένος ἔρχεται οἶμον,
εὖτέ μιν ὀξύτατον θάλπει σέλας ἠελίοιο,

1508 ἀλλ᾽ ὧι κεν Merkel: ἀλλά κεν ὧι Ω   1523 ἄλγος Brunck: ἕλκος Ω   1537
πρήσσοντος L¹AS: πρήσοντος ΕΣ: πρήθ- Brunck   1538 ἀπετεκ- m: ἀποτεκ- w
—μαίροντο Ε: —μήραντο Ω

ῥοίζωι δ᾽ ἔνθα καὶ ἔνθα κάρη στρέφει, ἐν δέ οἱ ὄσσε
σπινθαρύγεσσι πυρὸς ἐναλίγκια μαιμώοντι
λάμπεται, ὄφρα μυχόνδε διὰ ῥωχμοῖο δύηται·   1545
ὡς Ἀργὼ λίμνης στόμα ναύπορον ἐξερέουσα
ἀμφεπόλει δηναιὸν ἐπὶ χρόνον. αὐτίκα δ᾽ Ὀρφεύς
κέκλετ᾽ Ἀπόλλωνος τρίποδα μέγαν ἔκτοθι νηός
δαίμοσιν ἐγγενέταις νόστωι ἔπι μείλια θέσθαι.
καὶ τοὶ μὲν Φοίβου κτέρας ἵδρυον ἐν χθονὶ βάντες·   1550
τοῖσιν δ᾽ αἰζηῶι ἐναλίγκιος ἀντεβόλησε
Τρίτων εὐρυβίης, γαίης δ᾽ ἀνὰ βῶλον ἀείρας
ξείνι᾽ ἀριστήεσσι προΐσχετο, φώνησέν τε·
"δέχθε, φίλοι, ἐπεὶ οὐ περιώσιον ἐγγυαλίξαι
ἐνθάδε νῦν πάρ᾽ ἐμοὶ ξεινήιον ἀντομένοισιν.   1555
εἰ δέ τι τῆσδε πόρους μαίεσθ᾽ ἁλός, οἷά τε πολλά
ἄνθρωποι χατέουσιν ἐπ᾽ ἀλλοδαπῆι περόωντες,
ἐξερέω· δὴ γάρ με πατὴρ ἐπιίστορα πόντου
θῆκε Ποσειδάων τοῦδ᾽ ἔμμεναι· αὐτὰρ ἀνάσσω
παρραλίης, εἰ δή τιν᾽ ἀκούετε νόσφιν ἐόντες   1560
Εὐρύπυλον Λιβύηι θηροτρόφωι ἐγγεγαῶτα."
    ὣς ηὔδα· πρόφρων δ᾽ ὑπόεσχεθε βώλακι χεῖρας
Εὔφημος, καὶ τοῖα παραβλήδην προσέειπεν·
"Ἀπίδα καὶ πέλαγος Μινώιον εἴ νύ που, ἥρως,
ἐξεδάης, νημερτὲς ἀνειρομένοισιν ἔνισπε.   1565
δεῦρο γὰρ οὐκ ἐθέλοντες ἱκάνομεν, ἀλλὰ βορείαις
χρίμψαντες γαίης ἐνὶ πείρασι τῆσδε θυέλλαις,
νῆα μεταχρονίην ἐκομίσσαμεν ἐς τόδε λίμνης
χεῦμα δι᾽ ἠπείρου, βεβαρημένοι· οὐδέ τι ἴδμεν
πῆι πλόος ἐξανάγει Πελοπηίδα γαῖαν ἱκέσθαι."   1570
ὣς ἄρ᾽ ἔφη· ὁ δὲ χεῖρα τανύσσατο, δεῖξε δ᾽ ἄπωθεν
φωνήσας πόντον τε καὶ ἀγχιβαθὲς στόμα λίμνης·
"κείνη μὲν πόντοιο διήλυσις, ἔνθα μάλιστα
βένθος ἀκίνητον μελανεῖ, ἑκάτερθε δὲ λευκαί
ῥηγμῖνες φρίσσουσι διαυγέες· ἡ δὲ μεσηγύ   1575
ῥηγμίνων στεινὴ τελέθει ὁδὸς ἐκτὸς ἐλάσσαι.
κεῖνο δ᾽ ὑπηέριον θείην Πελοπηίδα γαῖαν
εἰσανέχει πέλαγος Κρήτης ὕπερ. ἀλλ᾽ ἐπὶ χειρός

1561 θηροτρόφωι ΩΣ: μηλο- Σ   1562 ὑπόεσχεθε Madvig: ὑπερέσχεθε Ω   1564 Ἀπίδα
ΣΣ: Ἀτθίδα ΩΣ   1566 βορείαις w: βαρείαις m   1567 ἐνὶ m: ἐπὶ w   1570 ἐξανάγει d:
ἐξανέχει Ω: ἐξενάγει Ε

δεξιτερῆς, λίμνηθεν ὅτ' εἰς ἁλὸς οἶδμα βάλητε,
τόφρ' αὐτὴν παρὰ χέρσον ἐεργμένοι ἰθύνεσθε,   1580
ἔστ' ἂν ἄνω τείνηισι· περιρρήδην δ' ἑτέρωσε
κλινομένης χέρσοιο, τότε πλόος ὔμμιν ἀπήμων
ἀγκῶνος τετάνυσται ἀπὸ προύχοντος ἰοῦσιν.
ἀλλ' ἴτε γηθόσυνοι, καμάτοιο δὲ μή τις ἀνίη
γινέσθω, νεότητι κεκασμένα γυῖα μογῆσαι."   1585
   ἴσκεν ἐυφρονέων· οἱ δ' αἶψ' ἐπὶ νηὸς ἔβησαν,
λίμνης ἐκπρομολεῖν λελιημένοι εἰρεσίηισι.
καὶ δὴ ἐπιπρονέοντο μεμαότες· αὐτὰρ ὁ τείως
Τρίτων, ἀνθέμενος τρίποδα μέγαν, εἴσατο λίμνην
εἰσβαίνειν· μετὰ δ' οὔ τις ἐσέδρακεν, οἷον ἄφαντος   1590
αὐτῶι σὺν τρίποδι σχεδὸν ἔπλετο. τοῖσι δ' ἰάνθη
θυμός, ὃ δὴ μακάρων τις ἐναίσιμος ἀντεβόλησε·
καί ῥά οἱ Αἰσονίδην μήλων ὅ τι φέρτατον ἄλλων
ἤνωγον ῥέξαι καὶ ἐπευφημῆσαι ἑλόντα.
αἶψα δ' ὅ γ' ἐσσυμένως ἐκρίνατο, καί μιν ἀείρας   1595
σφάξε κατὰ πρύμνης, ἐπὶ δ' ἔννεπεν εὐχωλῆισι·
"δαῖμον, ὅ τις λίμνης ἐπὶ πείρασι τῆσδε φάνθης,
εἴ τε σύ γε Τρίτων, ἅλιον τέρας, εἴ τέ σε Φόρκυν
ἢ Νηρῆα θύγατρες ἐπικλείουσ' ἁλοσύδναι,
ἵλαθι καὶ νόστοιο τέλος θυμηδὲς ὄπαζε."   1600
   ἦ ῥ', ἅμα δ' εὐχωλῆισιν ἐς ὕδατα λαιμοτομήσας
ἧκε κατὰ πρύμνης. ὁ δὲ βένθεος ἐξεφαάνθη
τοῖος ἐὼν οἷός περ ἐτήτυμος ἦεν ἰδέσθαι·
ὡς δ' ὅτ' ἀνὴρ θοὸν ἵππον ἐς εὐρέα κύκλον ἀγῶνος
στέλληι ὀρεξάμενος λασίης εὐπειθέα χαίτης,   1605
εἶθαρ ἐπιτροχάων, ὁ δ' ἐπ' αὐχένι γαῦρος ἀερθεὶς
ἕσπεται, ἀργινόεντα δ' ἐπὶ στομάτεσσι χαλινὰ
ἀμφὶς ὀδακτάζοντι παραβλήδην κροτέονται·
ὣς ὅ γ' ἐπισχόμενος γλαφυρῆς ὁλκήιον Ἀργοῦς
ἦγ' ἅλαδε προτέρωσε. δέμας δέ οἱ ἐξ ὑπάτοιο   1610
κράτος ἀμφί τε νῶτα καὶ ἰξύας ἔστ' ἐπὶ νηδὺν
ἀντικρὺ μακάρεσσι φυὴν ἔκπαγλον ἔικτο·
αὐτὰρ ὑπαὶ λαγόνων δίκραιρά οἱ ἔνθα καὶ ἔνθα

1583 τετάνυσται Brunck: τετάνυσται ἰθὺς Ω   1595 ἐκρίνατο *m*: ἐκρίνετο *w*   1598 σύ
γε *w*: σε *m*: σέ γε Merkel   Τρίτων L^{pc}*w*E: Τρίτων' L^{ac}A   1601 ἦ ῥ', ἅμα δ' *m*: ἦ ῥα
καὶ *w*: ἦ καὶ ἅμ' Brunck   1603 ἐτήτυμος Ω: –ον Flor.   1607 ἐπὶ *m*: ἐνὶ *w*   1613 ὑπαὶ
*m*SG^{pc}: ὑπὲκ *d*: ὑπὸ G

κήτεος ἀλκαίη μηκύνετο· κόπτε δ᾽ ἀκάνθαις
ἄκρον ὕδωρ, αἵ τε σκολιοῖς ἐπινειόθι κέντροις   1615
μήνης ὡς κεράεσσιν ἐειδόμεναι διχόωντο.
τόφρα δ᾽ ἄγεν, τείως μιν ἐπιπροέηκε θαλάσσηι
νισομένην. δῦ δ᾽ αἶψα μέγαν βυθόν· οἱ δ᾽ ὁμάδησαν
ἥρωες, τέρας αἰνὸν ἐν ὀφθαλμοῖσιν ἰδόντες.
  ἔνθα μὲν Ἀργῷός τε λιμὴν καὶ σήματα νηός   1620
ἠδὲ Ποσειδάωνος ἰδὲ Τρίτωνος ἔασι
βωμοί, ἐπεὶ κεῖν᾽ ἦμαρ ἐπέσχεθον· αὐτὰρ ἐς ἠῶ
λαίφεσι πεπταμένοις, αὐτὴν ἐπὶ δεξί᾽ ἔχοντες
γαῖαν ἐρημαίην, πνοιῆι ζεφύροιο θέεσκον.
ἦρι δ᾽ ἔπειτ᾽ ἀγκῶνά θ᾽ ὁμοῦ μυχάτην τε θάλασσαν   1625
κεκλιμένην ἀγκῶνος ὑπὲρ προύχοντος ἴδοντο.
αὐτίκα δὲ ζέφυρος μὲν ἐλώφεεν, ἦλυθε δ᾽ αὔρη
πρυμνήταο νότου, χήραντο δὲ θυμὸν ἰωῆι.
ἦμος δ᾽ ἠέλιος μὲν ἔδυ. ἀνὰ δ᾽ ἤλυθεν ἀστήρ
αὔλιος, ὅς τ᾽ ἀνέπαυσεν ὀιζυροὺς ἀροτῆρας,   1630
δὴ τότ᾽ ἔπειτ᾽, ἀνέμοιο κελαινῆι νυκτὶ λιπόντος,
ἱστία λυσάμενοι περιμήκεά τε κλίναντες
ἱστόν, ἐυξέστηισιν ἐπερρώοντ᾽ ἐλάτηισι
παννύχιοι καὶ ἐπ᾽ ἦμαρ, ἐπ᾽ ἤματι δ᾽ αὖτις ἰοῦσαν
νύχθ᾽ ἑτέρην· ὑπέδεκτο δ᾽ ἀπόπροθι παιπαλόεσσα   1635
Κάρπαθος. ἔνθεν δ᾽ οἵ γε περαιώσεσθαι ἔμελλον
Κρήτην, ἥ τ᾽ ἄλλων ὑπερέπλετο εἰν ἁλὶ νήσων.
τοὺς δὲ Τάλως χάλκειος, ἀπὸ στιβαροῦ σκοπέλοιο
ῥηγνύμενος πέτρας, εἶργε χθονὶ πείσματ᾽ ἀνάψαι
Δικταίην ὅρμοιο κατερχομένους ἐπιωγήν.   1640
τὸν μέν, χαλκείης μελιηγενέων ἀνθρώπων
ῥίζης λοιπὸν ἐόντα μετ᾽ ἀνδράσιν ἡμιθέοισιν,
Εὐρώπηι Κρονίδης νήσου πόρεν ἔμμεναι οὖρον,
τρὶς περὶ χαλκείοις Κρήτην ποσὶ δινεύοντα·
ἀλλ᾽ ἤτοι τὸ μὲν ἄλλο δέμας καὶ γυῖα τέτυκτο   1645
χάλκεος ἠδ᾽ ἄρρηκτος, ὑπαὶ δέ οἱ ἔσκε τένοντος
σῦριγξ αἱματόεσσα κατὰ σφυρόν· †αὐτὰρ ὁ τήν γε†
λεπτὸς ὑμὴν ζωῆς ἔχε πείρατα καὶ θανάτοιο.
οἱ δέ, δύηι μάλα περ δεδμημένοι, αἶψ᾽ ἀπὸ χέρσου

1614 ἀλκαίη Flor.: ὁλκαίη Ω   1618 μέγαν *m*: μέσον *w*   1628 πρυμνήταο *w*:
ἀργέσταο *m*   1634 ἰοῦσαν E: ἰοῦσι(ν) Ω   1644 Κρήτην ποσὶ Ω: ποσὶν ἤματι Fränkel
1647 αὐτὰρ ὁ τήν γε Ω: ἀμφ᾽ ἄρα τήν γε Fränkel

νῆα περιδδείσαντες ἀνακρούεσκον ἐρετμοῖς.   1650
καί νύ κ' ἐπισμυγερῶς Κρήτης ἑκὰς ἤερθησαν,
ἀμφότερον δίψῃ τε καὶ ἄλγεσι μοχθίζοντες,
εἰ μή σφιν Μήδεια λιαζομένοις ἀγόρευσε·
"κέκλυτέ μευ· μούνη γὰρ ὀίομαι ὔμμι δαμάσσειν
ἄνδρα τὸν ὅς τις ὅδ' ἐστί, καὶ εἰ παγχάλκεον ἴσχει   1655
ὃν δέμας, ὁππότε μή οἱ ἐπ' ἀκάματος πέλοι αἰών.
ἀλλ' ἔχετ' αὐτοῦ νῆα θελήμονες ἐκτὸς ἐρωῆς
πετράων, εἵως κεν ἐμοὶ εἴξειε δαμῆναι."
    ὣς ἄρ' ἔφη· καὶ τοὶ μὲν ὑπὲκ βελέων ἐρύσαντο
νῆ' ἐπ' ἐρετμοῖσιν, δεδοκημένοι ἥν τινα ῥέξει   1660
μῆτιν ἀνωίστως. ἡ δὲ πτύχα πορφυρέοιο
προσχομένη πέπλοιο παρειάων ἑκάτερθεν
βήσατ' ἐπ' ἰκριόφιν· χειρὸς δέ ἑ χειρὶ μεμαρπώς
Αἰσονίδης ἐκόμιζε διὰ κληῖδας ἰοῦσαν.
ἔνθα δ' ἀοιδῇσιν μειλίσσετο, μέλπε δὲ Κῆρας   1665
θυμοβόρους, Ἀίδαο θοὰς κύνας, αἳ περὶ πᾶσαν
ἠέρα δινεύουσαι ἐπὶ ζωοῖσιν ἄγονται.
τὰς γουναζομένη τρὶς μὲν παρακέκλετ' ἀοιδαῖς,
τρὶς δὲ λιταῖς· θεμένη δὲ κακὸν νόον, ἐχθοδοποῖσιν
ὄμμασι χαλκείοιο Τάλω ἐμέγηρεν ὀπωπάς·   1670
λευγαλέον δ' ἐπὶ οἷ πρῖεν χόλον, ἐκ δ' ἀίδηλα
δείκηλα προΐαλλεν, ἐπιζάφελον κοτέουσα.
Ζεῦ πάτερ, ἦ μέγα δή μοι ἐνὶ φρεσὶ θάμβος ἄηται,
εἰ δὴ μὴ νούσοισι τυπῇσί τε μοῦνον ὄλεθρος
ἀντιάει, καὶ δή τις ἀπόπροθεν ἄμμε χαλέπτει,   1675
ὡς ὅ γε, χάλκειός περ ἐών, ὑπόειξε δαμῆναι
Μηδείης βρίμῃ πολυφαρμάκου. ἂν δὲ βαρείας
ὀχλίζων λάιγγας ἐρυκέμεν ὅρμον ἱκέσθαι,
τετραίῳ στόνυχι χρίμψε σφυρόν· ἐκ δέ οἱ ἰχὼρ
τηκομένῳ ἴκελος μολίβῳ ῥέεν. οὐδ' ἔτι δηρόν   1680
ἱστήκει προβλῆτος ἐπεμβεβαὼς σκοπέλοιο·
ἀλλ' ὡς τίς τ' ἐν ὄρεσσι πελωρίη ὑψόθι πεύκη,
ἥν τε θοοῖς πελέκεσσιν ἔθ' ἡμιπλῆγα λιπόντες
ὑλοτόμοι δρυμοῖο κατήλυθον, ἡ δ' ὑπὸ νυκτὶ
ῥιπῇσιν μὲν πρῶτα τινάσσεται, ὕστερον αὖτε   1685

653 λιαζομένοις *m*: λιλαιο- *w*   1659 ἐρύσαντο *m*: ἐρύοντο *w*   1664 κληῖδας Brunck:
λητδος Ω   1665 μέλπε *m*: θέλγε *w*   1669 ἐχθοδοποῖσιν SE: –δαποῖσιν LAG   1673
ἢ φρεσὶ θάμβος *w*: θάμβος ἐνὶ φρεσὶ *m*

πρυμνόθεν ἐξεαγεῖσα κατήριπεν· ὣς ὅ γε ποσσίν
ἀκαμάτοις τείως μὲν ἐπισταδὸν ἠωρεῖτο,
ὕστερον αὖτ' ἀμενηνὸς ἀπείρονι κάππεσε δούπωι.
κεῖνο μὲν οὖν Κρήτηι ἐνὶ δὴ κνέφας ηὐλίζοντο
ἥρωες· μετὰ δ' οἵ γε νέον φαέθουσαν ἐς ἠῶ   1690
ἱρὸν Ἀθηναίης Μινωίδος ἱδρύσαντο,
ὕδωρ τ' εἰσαφύσαντο, καὶ εἰσέβαν, ὥς κεν ἐρετμοῖς
παμπρώτιστα βάλοιεν ὑπὲρ Σαλμωνίδος ἄκρης.
αὐτίκα δὲ Κρηταῖον ὑπὲρ μέγα λαῖτμα θέοντας
νὺξ ἐφόβει, τήν πέρ τε κατουλάδα κικλήσκουσι·   1695
νύκτ' ὀλοὴν οὐκ ἄστρα διίσχανεν, οὐκ ἀμαρυγαί
μήνης, οὐρανόθεν δὲ μέλαν χάος ἠέ τις ἄλλη
ὠρώρει σκοτίη μυχάτων ἀνιοῦσα βερέθρων·
αὐτοὶ δ' εἴ τ' Ἀίδηι εἴ θ' ὕδασιν ἐμφορέοντο
ἠείδειν οὐδ' ὅσσον, ἐπέτρεψαν δὲ θαλάσσηι   1700
νόστον, ἀμηχανέοντες ὅπηι φέροι. αὐτὰρ Ἰήσων
χεῖρας ἀνασχόμενος μεγάληι ὀπὶ Φοῖβον ἀύτει,
ῥύσασθαι καλέων· κατὰ δ' ἔρρεεν ἀσχαλόωντι
δάκρυα. πολλὰ δὲ Πυθοῖ ὑπέσχετο, πολλὰ δ' Ἀμύκλαις,
πολλὰ δ' ἐς Ὀρτυγίην ἀπερείσια δῶρα κομίσσειν.   1705
Λητοΐδη, τύνη δὲ κατ' οὐρανοῦ ἵκεο πέτρας
ῥίμφα Μελαντείους ἀριήκοος, αἵ τ' ἐνὶ πόντωι
ἧνται· δοιάων δὲ μιῆς ἐφύπερθεν ὀρούσας,
δεξιτερῆι χρύσειον ἀνέσχεθες ὑψόθι τόξον,
μαρμαρέην δ' ἀπέλαμψε βιὸς περὶ πάντοθεν αἴγλην.   1710
τοῖσι δέ τις Σποράδων βαιὴ ἀνὰ τόφρ' ἐφαάνθη
νῆσος ἰδεῖν, ὀλίγης Ἱππουρίδος ἀγχόθι νήσου·
ἔνθ' εὐνὰς ἐβάλοντο καὶ ἔσχεθον. αὐτίκα δ' ἠώς
φέγγεν ἀνερχομένη· τοὶ δ' ἀγλαὸν Ἀπόλλωνι
ἄλσει ἐνὶ σκιερῶι τέμενος †σκιόεντά† τε βωμὸν   1715
ποίεον, Αἰγλήτην μὲν εὐσκόπου εἵνεκεν αἴγλης
Φοῖβον κεκλόμενοι· Ἀνάφην δέ τε λισσάδα νῆσον
ἴσκον, ὃ δὴ Φοῖβός μιν ἀτυζομένοις ἀνέφηνεν.
ῥέζον δ' οἷά κεν ἄνδρες ἐρημαίηι ἐνὶ ῥέζειν
ἀκτῆι ἐφοπλίσσειαν· ὃ δή σφεας ὁππότε δαλοῖς   1720
ὕδωρ αἰθομένοισιν ἐπιλλείβοντας ἴδοντο
Μηδείης δμωαὶ Φαιηκίδες, οὐκέτ' ἔπειτα

1696 οὐκ ἀμαρυγαί m: οὐδ' ἀμ- w   1711 ἀνὰ Lᵃᶜ: ἀπὸ L²AwE   1712 ἀγχόθι u
ἀντία m   1718 μιν YSteph.: μὲν Ω   1719 οἷά κεν w: ὅσ(σ)α περ m

ἴσχειν ἐν στήθεσσι γέλω σθένον, οἷα θαμειάς
αἰὲν ἐν Ἀλκινόοιο βοοκτασίας ὁρόωσαι.
τὰς δ᾽ αἰσχροῖς ἥρωες ἐπεστοβέεσκον ἔπεσσι   1725
χλεύηι γηθόσυνοι· γλυκερή δ᾽ ἀνεδαίετο μέσσωι
κερτομίη καὶ νεῖκος ἐπεσβόλον. ἐκ δέ νυ κείνης
μολπῆς ἡρώων νήσωι ἔνι τοῖα γυναῖκες
ἀνδράσι δηριόωνται, ὅτ᾽ Ἀπόλλωνα θυηλαῖς
Αἰγλήτην Ἀνάφης τιμήορον ἱλάσκωνται.   1730
ἀλλ᾽ ὅτε δὴ κἀκεῖθεν ὑπεύδια πείσματ᾽ ἔλυσαν,
μνήσατ᾽ ἔπειτ᾽ Εὔφημος ὀνείρατος ἐννυχίοιο,
ἁζόμενος Μαίης υἷα κλυτόν. εἴσατο γάρ οἱ
δαιμονίη βῶλαξ ἐπιμάστιος ὧι ἐν ἀγοστῶι
ἄρδεσθαι λευκῆισιν ὑπὸ λιβάδεσσι γάλακτος,   1735
ἐκ δὲ γυνὴ βώλοιο πέλειν ὀλίγης περ ἐούσης
παρθενικῆι ἰκέλη· μίχθη δέ οἱ ἐν φιλότητι
ἄσχετον ἱμερθείς· ὀλοφύρετο δ᾽ ἠΰτε κούρην
ζευξάμενος, τὴν αὐτὸς ἑῶι ἀτίταλλε γάλακτι·
ἡ δέ ἑ μειλιχίοισι παρηγορέεσκεν ἔπεσσι·   1740
"Τρίτωνος γένος εἰμί, τεῶν τροφός, ὦ φίλε, παίδων,
οὐ κούρη· Τρίτων γὰρ ἐμοὶ Λιβύη τε τοκῆες.
ἀλλά με Νηρῆος παρακάτθεο παρθενικῆισιν
ἂμ πέλαγος ναίειν Ἀνάφης σχεδόν· εἶμι δ᾽ ἐς αὐγάς
ἠελίου μετόπισθε τεοῖς νεπόδεσσιν ἑτοίμη."   1745
τῶν ἄρ᾽ ἐπὶ μνῆστιν κραδίηι βάλεν, ἔκ τ᾽ ὀνόμηνεν
Αἰσονίδηι· ὁ δ᾽ ἔπειτα, θεοπροπίας Ἑκάτοιο
θυμῶι πεμπάζων, ἀνενείκατο φώνησέν τε·
"ὦ πέπον, ἦ μέγα δή σε καὶ ἀγλαὸν ἔμμορε κῦδος.
βώλακα γὰρ τεύξουσι θεοὶ πόντονδε βαλόντι   1750
νῆσον, ἵν᾽ ὁπλότεροι παίδων σέθεν ἐννάσσονται
παῖδες, ἐπεὶ Τρίτων ξεινήιον ἐγγυάλιξε
τήνδε τοι ἠπείροιο Λιβυστίδος· οὔ νύ τις ἄλλος
ἀθανάτων ἢ κεῖνος, ὅ μιν πόρεν ἀντιβολήσας."
ὣς ἔφατ᾽· οὐδ᾽ ἁλίωσεν ὑπόκρισιν Αἰσονίδαο   1755
Εὔφημος, βῶλον δὲ θεοπροπίηισιν ἰανθεὶς
ἧκεν ὑποβρυχίην. τῆς δ᾽ ἔκτοθι νῆσος ἀέρθη

1723 γέλω *wd*: γέλων ΑΕ   1726 μέσσωι L² *w*: τοῖσι(ν) *m*   1730 ἱλάσκωνται LA:
ἱλάσκονται *w*Ε   1735 ὑπὸ Ε: ὑπαὶ Ω   1738 ὀλοφύρετο   *m*: –ρατο *w*   1743
παρακάτθεο Flor.: –θετο Ω   1746 τῶν L^{ac}: τῶι δ᾽ L²Α*w*Ε   κραδίηι *m*: κραδίη *w*D
1749 πέπον *w*: πόποι *m*   1753 οὔ νύ *m*: οὐδέ *w*

Καλλίστη, παίδων ἱερὴ τροφὸς Εὐφήμοιο·
οἳ πρὶν μέν ποτε δὴ Σιντηίδα Λῆμνον ἔναιον,
Λήμνου τ' ἐξελαθέντες ὑπ' ἀνδράσι Τυρσηνοῖσι   1760
Σπάρτην εἰσαφίκανον ἐφέστιοι· ἐκ δὲ λιπόντας
Σπάρτην Αὐτεσίωνος ἐὺς πάις ἤγαγε Θήρας
Καλλίστην ἐπὶ νῆσον, ἀμείψατο δ' οὔνομα, Θήρα,
ἐκ σέθεν. ἀλλὰ τὰ μὲν μετόπιν γένετ' Εὐφήμοιο.
  κεῖθεν δ' ἀπτερέως διὰ μυρίον οἶδμα ταμόντες   1765
Αἰγίνης ἀκτῆισιν ἐπέσχεθον. αἶψα δὲ τοί γε
ὑδρείης πέρι δῆριν ἀμεμφέα δηρίσαντο,
ὅς κεν ἀφυσσάμενος φθαίη μετὰ νῆάδ' ἱκέσθαι·
ἄμφω γὰρ χρειώ τε καὶ ἄσπετος οὖρος ἔπειγεν.
  ἔνθ' ἔτι νῦν, πλήθοντας ἐπωμαδὸν ἀμφιφορῆας   1770
ἀνθέμενοι, κούφοισιν ἄφαρ κατ' ἀγῶνα πόδεσσι
κοῦροι Μυρμιδόνων νίκης πέρι δηριόωνται.
  ἵλατ', ἀριστῆες, μακάρων γένος, αἵδε δ' ἀοιδαί
εἰς ἔτος ἐξ ἔτεος γλυκερώτεραι εἶεν ἀείδειν
ἀνθρώποις. ἤδη γὰρ ἐπὶ κλυτὰ πείραθ' ἱκάνω   1775
ὑμετέρων καμάτων, ἐπεὶ οὔ νύ τις ὕμμιν ἄεθλος
αὖτις ἀπ' Αἰγίνηθεν ἀνερχομένοισιν ἐτύχθη,
οὔτ' ἀνέμων ἐριῶλαι ἐνέσταθεν, ἀλλὰ ἔκηλοι
γαῖαν Κεκροπίην παρά τ' Αὐλίδα μετρήσαντες
Εὐβοίης ἔντοσθεν Ὀπούντιά τ' ἄστεα Λοκρῶν,   1780
ἀσπασίως ἀκτὰς Παγασηίδας εἰσαπέβητε.

1759 Σιντηίδα Brunck: Σιντιάδα Ω   1763 om. w   Θήρα Fränkel: Θήρης m   1764
ἐκ σέθεν Wendel: ἐξ ἔθεν Ω   1765 ταμόντες Maas: λιπόντες Ω: θαλάσσης Et. Gen., Et.
Mag.   1767 δηρίσαντο m: –ιόωντο w   1771 ἀνθέμενοι Brunck: ἐνθ- Ω   1773
ἀριστῆες Fränkel: ἀριστήων Ω   1778 οὔτ' Ω: οὐδ' Platt   ἐνέσταθεν LA: ἀνέ- wE

COMMENTARY

1–5 *Invocation of the Muse.* Like Book 3, Book 4 begins with a 5-verse invocation of a Muse, and we will naturally infer that this is the same Muse who was invoked in Book 3, namely Erato: she 'herself' is now to take over the tale, whereas in Book 3 she was asked to 'stand beside' the poet and tell him the story; 3.1–5 clearly introduce the whole second half of the poem, not just Book 3, and this too suggests continuity here. Erato remains an appropriate Muse to tell of the sufferings of Medea (cf. δυσίμερον in 4), just as in Book 3 she had been asked to tell how Jason's success depended upon Medea's *erôs*, but the fact that the Muse's name is not repeated lessens the special emphasis upon *erôs*, and assimilates the invoked Muse more to the traditional Muse of epic poetry (1–2n.). Acosta-Hughes 2010: 43–7 argues that the anonymity points to the poet's generic uncertainty as to whether a 'lyric' or an 'epic' voice is now to predominate, and Payne 2013: 305–6 associates the poet's abandonment of his narrative to the Muse with the fact that Medea's departure 'maps exactly onto the moment at which the poet must surrender his fictional Medea to the bigger story to which she belongs as a character of myth'.

The poet asks the Muse herself to take over because he cannot decide which motive for Medea's flight to privilege (4–5n., Hunter 1987: 134–9). He thus puts the poet's dependence upon the Muse to a new use: like a historian, the poet is presented with traditional 'facts' which are incontrovertible but which require interpretation, and here he can only turn to the Muse for help. At the opening of *Od.*, by contrast, Homer had had no doubt at all what caused the death of the suitors; Ap. is now a much less confident narrator than the poet of the proem to Book 1; see, e.g., Feeney 1991: 90–1. Such puzzles of motivation were, however, not restricted to historians. In *Pythian* 11, Pindar raises two possibilities (the killing of Iphigeneia and sexual desire for Aegisthus) as to why Clytemnestra killed Agamemnon and Cassandra (vv. 22–5); there – as here – the second of the two possibilities is subsequently given greater prominence, and there – as here – the male poet is apparently confronted with the inexplicable deeds of a female. If the literary tradition, represented for us by Pind. *Pyth.* 4 and Eur. *Med.*, had largely had little doubt that it was indeed desire which caused Medea to flee, in Helen, however, there was another figure of literature and myth who had abandoned her home with a foreign man and who had proved the source of enormous suffering; tragedy (e.g. Eur. *Tr.*) and rhetoric (Gorgias, Isocrates) had long made Helen's motives a subject for enquiry and puzzlement, and Helen is a very important model for Ap.'s Medea throughout the second half of the poem (Hunter 1989: 29).

1 In asking the Muse to tell him about the κάματον ... καὶ δήνεα κούρης, the
poet strikingly varies Homer's requests to the Muse to tell of μῆνιν ...
Ἀχιλῆος (Il. 1.1) and ἄνδρα ... πολύτροπον (Od. 1.1); the female is very
much at the centre of this epic.   κάματον 'emotional torment', cf.
3.961, where Jason's appearance causes κάματον ... δυσίμερον.   δήνεα
is glossed by Σ as τὰς βουλάς (cf. also the D-scholia on Il. 4.361), and 'plans,
intentions, counsels, skills' is indeed a common semantic field for this
noun, cf. 193, 3.1168 (δήνεα κούρης again), Od. 10.289 δήνεα Κίρκης, though
elsewhere a rather vaguer 'qualities' seems intended (3.661n.).
'Intentions' is perhaps most appropriate here, though much depends
on whether the Muse is being asked to tell merely of Medea's immediate
reaction to her predicament (note γάρ in v. 2) or of a good part of
Book 4.   θεά is placed at a different point in the verse than in Il. 1.1
and Od. 1.10.

2 ἔννεπε, Μοῦσα: cf. Od.1.1 (same verse-position).   Διὸς τέκος: cf. Hom.
Hymn 31.1, Διὸς τέκος ἄρχεο Μοῦσα, Od. 1.10 θεά, θύγατερ Διός.

3–5 recall Zeus's dilemma at Il. 16.435–8 as to whether he should save
Sarpedon, διχθὰ δέ μοι κραδίη μέμονε φρεσὶν ὁρμαίνοντι, | ἤ μιν ζωὸν ἐόντα μάχης
ἄπο δακρυοέσσης | θείω ἀναρπάξας Λυκίης ἐν πίονι δήμωι, | ἤ' ἤδη ὑπὸ χερσὶ
Μενοιτιάδαο δαμάσσω. There too the uncertainty is apparently then settled
by a decisive intervention from Hera. The transference of such uncertainties from a (divine) character in Homer to the poet himself is a good
illustration of the much greater prominence given to 'the poetic voice' in
Hellenistic poetry (Hunter 1993: ch. 5); just as Zeus's dilemma was in
essence about the direction in which the narrative was to proceed, so is the
poet's here.

3 ἀμφασίηι 'speechless amazement'; the literal sense is particularly felt
here as the poet can no longer utter, cf. 2.409, 3.811, Campbell on 3.284.

4–5 'whether I am to call it the wearying torment of mad desire or
[whether I am to call] it terrible panic, which caused her to leave ... '.
The poet cannot decide on Medea's motivation, although, as often, γε
marks the alternative to which greater prominence is to be given (K–G II
173); the two motives, of course, co-exist (Fusillo 1985: 368, Natzel 1992:
85–8).   μιν: neuter, varying Il. 16.436 (above). The text seems rather
awkward, however, and corruption has often been suspected. Hutchinson
1988: 122 adopts Maas's μέν for μιν, with the poet's dilemma being not
about Medea's motivation, but rather whether he should tell of 'her
anguish or her flight'; it is hard, however, to understand what such a
choice might mean.   ἄτης πῆμα δυσίμερον picks up the language of
Medea's suffering in the previous book, cf. 3.798, 961, 973 etc. It will recur
at significant moments of Book 4, cf. 62, 449, 1016, 1080.   ἐνίσπω: aor.

subj. of ἐν(ν)έπω; the use of the same verb as in line 2 reinforces the poet's yielding to the Muse. **ἀεικελίην**, particularly in the mouth of the narrator, need not carry moral reproof, i.e. 'shameful', cf. 637, 724, but the present instance is finely balanced. For a daughter to flee her father's house in the company of strangers is indeed 'shameful' by ordinary standards, but Σ gloss this second alternative as a flight from maltreatment (κάκωσις), and Medea's fear of her father, already a theme at 3.614, is certainly justified (cf. 15, 234–5, 379–81). In her later fury Medea pours scorn on her own lack of αἰδώς (360), and Circe is in no doubt that her flight is ἀεικής (739, 748).

6–10 At the end of Book 3 Aietes was already plotting (3.1406), and here he holds a nocturnal council to decide how to deal with the Argonauts. In an early epic poem usually cited as *Naupactia*, Aietes apparently invited the Argonauts to a dinner in order to kill them, but was distracted by Aphrodite who filled him with desire to go to bed with his wife instead (frr. 6–8 Davies). Idmon realized the danger and the Argonauts made good their escape; Medea went with them, 'on hearing the noise of their feet', bringing the Fleece with her (Huxley 1969: 68–73, West 2003: 33). Ap.'s presentation of the aftermath of Jason's successful completion of the challenge will have drawn on a rich literary heritage, most of which is now lost to us.

6 ἤτοι marks the resumption of the narrative after the proemial expression of uncertainty (Sens 2000: 187–9).

7 παννύχιος: Jason's contest with the bulls and the sown warriors had ended at sundown (3.1407). English would naturally use an adverb, 'all night long', but Greek regularly uses instead the adjective in agreement with the subject, cf. 69, 1.929, where adverbial ἦρι 'in the morning' is set against ἐννύχιοι, *Il.* 2.2.   **δόλον αἰπύν** is a familiar combination (cf. Hes. *Theog.* 589, *WD* 83 (both of Pandora), *HHHerm.* 66), but the adjective was very variously glossed, either as purely intensifying, 'great', 'perfect', or as 'difficult, dangerous' (*LfgrE* s.v.). The sense here is probably 'impossible to escape', a sense reinforced by ἀμήχανον, which accompanies the phrase in both Hesiodic passages.

8–10 In Book 3 the angry (3.607) Aietes had seen the coming of the Argonauts as part of a plot hatched by the sons of Phrixos, and he had 'little fear lest his daughters make some hateful (στυγερήν) plan' (3.602–5); here he realizes that that confidence was misplaced.   **στυγερῶι:** at the end of Book 3 Aietes felt βαρεῖαι ἀνῖαι at the outcome of the contest (3.1404).   **τάδε ... τετελέσθαι:** cf. 3.605 (Aietes' thoughts) ἀλλ' ἐνὶ Χαλκιόπης γενεῆι τάδε λυγρὰ τετύχθαι. The transmitted τελέεσθαι is not impossible – Aietes sees ongoing plots all around

him – but suits τάδε (i.e. the successful completion of the challenge) much
less well.

11–25 Medea's panic and thoughts of suicide replay her night of torment
from Book 3 (πῆμα 3.773, πολυκλαύτους ... ἀνίας 3.777, cf. 19). There,
suicide is at first mixed in with other possible options as her resolution
fluctuates wildly (3.766–9); she wonders how she could offer Jason help
(ἀρωγή) without her parents noticing (3.779–81 ~ 14–15), and then again
considers immediate suicide, by hanging herself or swallowing poisons
(3.787–801 ~ 20–1). The temptation of suicide is there rejected in
detailed human terms (the fear of death, the delights of life, 3.809–16),
and Hera is introduced only at the end (3.818n.); here, the human
motivation for her fear and then flight is still explained (14–16), but
the rejection of suicide is Hera's doing alone, not just to avoid repetition, but
because Medea's situation is now even more perilous.

11 For the common double dative, 'her ... her heart', cf. 449, and for the
related double accusative cf. 351n.

12–13 Medea's panic is compared to that of a young deer, a simile which
stresses her female vulnerability and continues to break down any clear
opposition between erotic and 'epic' motivation (Hunter 1987: 136). At *Il.*
10.360–2 Odysseus and Diomedes are compared to hunting-dogs pursuing 'a deer (κεμάδ᾽) or a hare', but the primary model is *Il.* 11.544–6 where
Zeus induces φόβος in Ajax who then 'flees' (τρέσσε). Deer commonly
appear as timid, frightened creatures in simile, cf. *Il.* 22.1 πεφυζότες ἠύτε
νεβροί.   **τρέσσεν** 'she panicked, was terrified'(*LfgrE* s.v. B I 1a). The
standard sense is 'fled' (cf. 1507, 1522, Lehrs 1882, Nelis 1991), but
the structure of the narrative, with 'flight' picked up in 21–2, would then
be at least awkward, though not impossible, and may perhaps indeed
be thought to be supported by the use of the aorist. Many translators
offer 'she trembled', which would make excellent sense (cf. Sappho
fr. 31.13–14 V), but there is no good evidence for this sense for τρεῖν or
for such an interpretation in antiquity.   **κεμάς**: grammarians were
uncertain as to what kind of young deer was referred to at *Il.* 10.361
(above); see Rengakos 1994: 102–3. Ap. uses the term also at 2.696 and
3.879. Aristophanes of Byzantium identified it as a deer just beyond the
'fawn stage' (181–5 Slater).   **ὁμοκλή** 'loud noise', i.e. (here) barking;
the other sense of the noun which ancient scholarship recognized, 'threat,
challenge', is used at 2.20; Rengakos 1994: 120–1.

14–15 'For at once she correctly suspected that her father was not unaware
of her help, and that she would soon suffer the full measure of wretched-
ness.' The passage strikingly reworks *Od.* 19.390–1, 'for at once [Odysseus]
was concerned (ὀίσατο) in his heart, lest [Eurycleia] recognize the scar

and everything would be revealed (ἀμφαδά, cf. 84)'. Eurycleia was indeed an ἀμφίπολος ἐπιίστωρ (cf. 16).   ὀίσσατο 'suspected, foreboded'. The construction with μή and an infinitive is that of a verb of fearing (Smyth §2238).   ἀναπλήσειν: for this use cf. Il. 15.132, Od. 5.302.

16 ἀμφιπόλους ἐπιίστορας 'her maids who were in the know'. These are the maids who accompanied Medea to her meeting with Jason (3.838–43, 872–912); Medea's deceit now comes home to roost.

16–17 τάρβει: unaugmented imperfect.   **ἐν δέ οἱ ὄσσε**: the verse-end recurs at 1543, but the Homeric model is the terrified Eurylochos returning to tell his comrades of what Circe has done, Od. 10.246–8; in his anguish, Eurylochos cannot speak, his eyes are full of tears and 'his heart foresaw lamentation' (cf. 19). The echo is particularly powerful, given that Circe is Medea's aunt and her principal model as 'magician', but Ap. may also be drawing a link between that Homeric passage and Sappho fr. 31 V, by a kind of 'window allusion'.   **πλῆτο**: Ap. follows Homer in using a singular verb with a dual subject, cf. 1437, 1545. Fire in the eyes is in epic a marker of very intense emotion of various kinds, cf. 1.1296–7, Graz 1965: 240–7.   **δεινὸν δὲ περιβρομέεσκον ἀκουαί**: cf. Sappho fr. 31.11–12 V ἐπιρρόμ- | βεισι δ᾽ ἄκουαι, echoed also at 908. Sappho's famous poem had already been evoked to describe Medea's experience of 'love at first sight' (3.284–90), and its use here, as at Theocr. 2.106–10, to describe symptoms of panic perhaps reflects two different ancient interpretations of that poem, both of which have resurfaced in modern criticism, cf. Hunter forthcoming.

18–19 ἐπεμάσσετο 'clutched at', a 'mixed' aorist of ἐπιμαίομαι, cf. 458n. This may be merely a gesture of despair, or it may hint at the possibility of suicide by hanging, cf. 3.789–90.   **κουρίξ** occurs at Od. 22.188, where later grammarians were divided between 'by the hair' (cf. Call. fr. 722) and 'strongly, violently' (νεανικῶς), cf. Hesych. κ3857; Livrea 1972: 237–8 suggests that Ap. alludes to both senses here, with 19 essentially glossing the adverb. Ap. may, however, have intended 'by the roots', i.e. προθελύμνους or προρρίζους, cf. Il. 10.15–16, Agamemnon in distress pulling out (εἵλκετο) his hair by the roots and groaning loudly, 22.77–8 (Priam). Medea is tearing her hair in lamentation for herself.   **βρυχήσατ᾽**: Homer uses this verb of the groans of dying warriors (Il. 13.393, 16.486), but cf. also Soph. Tr. 904 (Deianeira before her suicide).

20–3 Cf. 636–42n. Hera's overall plan to use Medea as a weapon of punishment for Pelias was last mentioned at 3.1133–6.   **αὐτοῦ τῆμος**, 'there at that time', corresponds to τῆιδ᾽ αὐτῆι ἐν νυκτί in the corresponding scene at 3.799.   **ὑπὲρ μόρον**, 'prematurely', lit. 'contrary to what was fated', is used, like ὑπὲρ αἶσαν (1254), to mark moments of high narrative tension, even when we know that gods are directing events; see S. West on *Od.* 1.34–5, Edwards on *Il.* 17.321.   **φάρμακα πασσαμένη**: cf. 3.790n.   **Φρίξοιο . . . σὺν παισί**: Hera thus allows Medea to retain some 'shame', cf. 736–7: she is fleeing not with a lover but with her nephews, with whom she had grown up (3.730–5).   **φέβεσθαι | ὦρσεν ἀτυζομένην** again evokes the rout of Iliadic warriors, cf., e.g., *Il.* 6.41, 21.4. **πτερόεις**, 'fluttering', suggests Medea's irresolute uncertainty before Hera's intervention; cf. the simile of the dancing light-beam at 3.755–60. Alternatively, it may be taken very closely with ἰάνθη, 'was warmed and took wing'; cf. 3.724 τῆι δ' ἔντοσθεν ἀνέπτατο χάρματι θυμός.

24–5 παλίσσυτος 'changing her mind'; elsewhere, e.g., 879, the 'return' implied by the adjective (from πάλιν – σεύω) is one of physical movement: here it is an emotional change.   **κόλπωι**: Medea's drugs are normally kept in a casket (φωριαμός), cf. 3.802–4, and we are perhaps here to imagine that, as in Book 3, the casket is already on her lap preparatory to suicide. When the hurried change of mind comes, she empties 'absolutely all the drugs in a jumble' into the folds of her dress, in order to take them with her. Valerius Flaccus follows this scenario exactly (8.16–19, with *uirgineosque sinus* ~ κόλπωι). The transmitted κόλπων would have her pouring the drugs 'from' her lap 'down into' the chest and then, presumably, taking the casket with her; most (but not all) vase-paintings of Medea's confrontation with the dragon do show her with the casket (cf. *LIMC* s.v. Iason, nos. 37–42), but there is no further sign of it in *Arg.*, unless 155–7 presuppose its presence (cf. 156n.). Why she should have had 'all' of her drugs out of the casket would remain mysterious. The narrative here is very compressed, and so the fact that both her hands are otherwise engaged during her flight (44–6) is perhaps not decisive as to the reading and interpretation here.

26–33 Medea's farewell to her virginal life concludes a fraught process begun at 3.645–55. The farewell evokes that of tragic heroines before suicide or death (cf. esp. Soph. *Tr.* 900–11, Eur. *Alc.* 175–88), and Medea's departure is indeed for her a kind of death. Virgil exploited these resonances in using this passage for his description of Dido's suicide at *Aen.* 4.648–705, where the motif of the cut lock is put to a new use (lines 704–5), cf. Nelis 2001: 169–72.

26–7 δικλίδας . . . | σταθμούς 'the posts of the double-doors', lit. 'double door-posts'. In Homer δικλίδες is used with θύραι (*Od.* 17.268, cf. *Arg.* 1.786–7), σάνιδες (*Od.* 2.345) and πύλαι (*Il.* 12.455), and Ap. uses δικλίδες as a noun at 3.236; the present usage is at least awkward, and δικλίδος (Campbell 1971: 418) is worth considering.

28–9 Medea leaves behind a lock of hair for her mother, a gesture which evokes both a familiar pre-nuptial rite of young women (Call. *h.* 4.296–9, Hesych. γ 133, Oakley–Sinos 1993: 14) and a funerary practice best attested at Eur. *IT* 820–1 (Iphigeneia before her sacrifice). For a similar mixture cf. Eur. *Hipp.* 1425–7 (with Barrett 1964: 3–4), Paus. 2.32.1.   **τμηξαμένη**: Medea cuts a lock for her mother in pointed contrast with the violent hair 'tearing' of 18–19; χερσί thus indicates not what she used to cut her hair, which was presumably sharp metal (as in Call.'s 'Coma Berenices'), but the care she took over the action (cf. Virg. *Aen.* 4.704 *dextra crinem secat*). The transmitted ῥηξαμένη suits χερσί rather better, but 'tearing off' a long lock to leave for her mother seems out of keeping with such a deliberate act (though cf. Heliodorus 6.8.6, ἔτιλλε).   **ἀδινῆι** 'plaintive, sad', cf. 1422n.

30 ταναόν: such 'long' tresses are one of the things which distinguish female from male hair, cf. Eur. *Ba.* 455, 831.

31 'May you fare well – this is my wish though I go far away from you'; μοι is understood with ἰούσηι, cf. *Il.* 23.19 χαῖρέ μοι, ὦ Πάτροκλε, καὶ εἰν Ἀίδαο δόμοισιν, and the ellipse is aided by ἐμή.

32–3 Cf. 3.775–6n. The most famous expression of the wish that Jason had never reached Colchis is the opening of Eur. *Medea.*   **διέρραισεν** 'dashed to pieces'.

34 κατ' ... **χεῦεν**: tmesis.

35–40 Medea's departure is like that of a young girl captured in war and cast into slavery, who must now get used to physical and emotional suffering and a brutal mistress; the striking dissonance between the unhappiness and obvious reluctance of the slave-girl and the speed of Medea's departure (40) marks the terrible anomalies of the new situation facing the Colchian princess and foreshadows the marginal position she will finally be asked to assume in Greece; see further Hunter 1987: 136–7, Asper 2008: 183. The simile was perhaps suggested by the Euripidean Medea's claim that she was 'plundered (λεληισμένη) from a barbarian land' (256) and is now utterly without family to help her; cf. also Jason's words at 400. We may recall the chorus of Eur. *Tr.* who speculate about the drudgery which awaits them in a foreign land (lines 197–213, 1081–99, 1311 Εκ. δούλειον ὑπὸ μέλαθρον. Χο. ἐκ πάτρας γ' ἐμᾶς.). With a particular interpretation of 35, the simile is sometimes taken rather to describe a slave-girl escaping *from* her new masters' house; elements of this interpretation are attractive, but it is very difficult then to reconcile 38–9.

35 †διειλυσθεῖσα: no reasonable sense can be made of this participle. Σ gloss as 'passing secretly out through the house, running away, fleeing', but the slow movement implied by εἰλύομαι, 'crawl' (cf. Soph. *Phil.* 291, LSJ s.v. εἰλύω II 1), seems rather different from that; this compound is not otherwise attested. ἕλκειν is a standard verb for carrying off captives in war, but διέλκειν is not so used, and the only sense which could be given to διελκυσθεῖσα, which is commonly read, is 'dragged through her rich home', that is, through her new home, not that of her fatherland.

38 δύην καὶ δούλια ἔργα are objects of ἀηθέσσουσα, 'not being accustomed to'. Homer uses this verb with the genitive (*Il.* 10.493), and if the transmitted δύης is retained, there will be a marked chiasmus, with δούλια ἔργα governed by ἀτυζομένη in 39; there is, however, a natural tendency to take δύην καὶ δούλια ἔργα together, as expressing a single idea. The doublet occurs at Semonides fr. 7.58 West in the description of an idle and pampered wife who will not work; the echo may thus be a deliberate one.

39 'terrorised, she passes into the grim control of a mistress'; for this use of ὑπό see LSJ s.v. C II, Hopkinson on Call. *h.* 6.62.   χεῖρας suggests not just power, but also physical threat.   ἀνάσσης 'mistress (of a house)', LSJ s.v. ἄναξ III.

40 ἱμερόεσσα ... κούρη forms a pointed contrast to ληϊάς.

41–53 The manner of Medea's furtive and lonely flight stands in sharp contrast to her previous, very public trip in Book 3, in the manner befitting a princess, to meet Jason at the temple; see Rose 1985: 37, Hunter 1993: 65.

41 'The bolts of the doors gave way by themselves to her', though 'the bolts gave way from the doors ... ' is also possible, cf. *Od.* 21. 47 (Penelope) θυρέων δ' ἀνέκοπτεν ὀχῆας.   αὐτόματοι: doors open 'by themselves' at the approach of gods, cf. *Il.* 5.749, Call. *h.* 2.6–7, and expert magicians may also have this power; see Weinreich 1929, McKay 1967. Spells for opening doors are preserved (*PGM* XIII 1064–74, XXXVI 312–20 (= Betz 1992: 195, 277), Weinreich 1929: 343–51); the instruction for open doors delivered by a female magician at Sophron fr. 4.10–12K-A/Hordern may be 'magical', rather than a command to her servants.

42 ὠκείαις: no current explanation of this epithet for Medea's incantations ('uttered swiftly', 'swiftly working'), is satisfactory; Spitzner conjectured ὀξείαις. Grammarians recognized places in Homer where an adjective took the place of an adverb, e.g. *Il.* 23.880 ὠκὺς δ' ἐκ μελέων θυμὸς πτάτο, Erbse on Σ *Il.* 4.182, and in the model scene in *Od.* (above, 41n.), the doors open ὦκα (21.50), but with that trope 'swift' should here be used of the bolts or the doors, rather than the spells. Campbell 1969: 282 suggests that 'ὠκείαις governs not ἀοιδαῖς exclusively ... but the sentence in general'.

43 γυμνοῖσιν δὲ πόδεσσιν: principally in order to make as little noise as possible, but perhaps also a mark of the hurry in which she left (cf. 3.646). Later evidence (Virg. *Aen.* 4.518, Plin. *HN* 23.110, 24.103) shows that some magical practices were believed to be carried out barefoot, and Ovid, *Met.* 7.183, in a passage heavily indebted to *Arg.*, depicts a barefooted Medea gathering herbs by night (see Kenney ad loc.). If such lore was familiar to Ap.'s audience, then this may be a further way (cf. 50–3) in which this nocturnal expedition of Medea both resembles her previous activities (as the Moon mockingly notes) and is also utterly different; in Sophocles' Ῥιζοτόμοι (cf. 51–2n.), Medea is described gathering herbs 'naked' (fr. 534.7R). **στεινάς ... οἴμους:** in Book 3 she had travelled 'along the broad wagon-way' (3.874).

44–5 Medea seeks (successfully, cf. 48–9) to conceal her identity, whereas in Book 3 it was the ordinary people who looked away as she passed, 3.885–6.

46 Cf. 94on. In Book 3 it was her maids who lifted up their dresses as they ran along behind Medea's cart, 3.874–5.

47 ἀίδηλον ἀνὰ στίβον 'along an unknown/hidden path'. ἀίδηλος is used in a variety of pejorative senses (cf. 681, 1157, 3.1132, Rengakos 1994: 40–1), but here the idea of ἀ – δῆλον is uppermost, cf. 865n., and ἄδηλον is one of the standard grammatical glosses for this term (*LfgrE* s.v.).

48 εὐρυχόροιο: the contrast with στεινάς in 43 points to Medea's terrible diminution in status.

49 ὁρμηθεῖσα 'as she hastened', cf. LSJ s.v. ὁρμάω B 3b.

50 νειόνδε 'to the ploughing-field (of Ares)', where Medea knew she would find the Argonauts, who had moored there for the contest (3.1270–7n.). The transmitted 'to the temple' will not do, as the Argonauts are not there, and it would be pointless to add that Medea was 'not ignorant' of the paths to the temple where she went every day; ἀσπασίως in 67 indicates that she reaches a destination that was intended. The field is on the opposite side of the river to the city and to where Medea now is (2.1266–9), but she gets as close as she can and within shouting-distance. An alternative to νειόνδε would be νηῦνδε (Maas), 'to the ship', cf. Σ 86 'Apollonius says that Medea fled at night to the ship ... '; this form of the accusative is, however, normally scanned as a single syllable. **μάλ' ἐφράσατ'** 'she was fully minded to ... '; the phrase is normally understood as 'she gave close thought as to how to ... ', but the idea of Medea carefully 'planning her route' seems out of keeping with the haste of the narrative.

51–2 Medea belongs to those magicians whom Heliodorus' Kalasiris dismisses as 'skulking around dead bodies, addicted to herbs and magic spells' (*Aith.* 3.16.3). Medea's nocturnal activities were described in Sophocles, Ῥιζοτόμοι (fr. 534); here, as elsewhere (cf. 3.845, 865nn.), Ap. may be indebted to that play. Medea's goddess, Hecate, is often said to roam 'through tombs', cf. Theocr. 2.13, Heitsch LIV 5 ἐν νέκυσιν στείχουσα κατ᾽ ἠρία τεθνηώτων. Colchian burial practices had been described at 3.200–9. ἀμφί . . . ἀμφί 'in search of', LSJ s.v. C 5. νεκρούς: perhaps either for necromancy (e.g. Heliod. *Aith.* 6.14–15) or to collect body-parts, cf. Ov. *Her.* 6.89–90 (Medea), *PGM* IV 2578–80 [= Betz 1992: 95]. δυσπαλέας 'maleficent', glossed by Σ as χαλεπὰς καὶ κακάς, cf. Ov. *Her.* 6.84 *diraque cantata pabula falce metit* (sc. Medea). This seems a more likely interpretation than 'difficult to find'.

53 δ᾽ is here adversative: despite her knowledge, Medea was terrified.

54–65 Medea is mocked by the Moon goddess, exulting in Medea's distress. In the past, Medea had 'drawn down the moon', i.e. produced the total darkness she needed to work her magic, by urging the Moon to visit her lover Endymion, instead of shining in the heavens; now Medea too has her 'Endymion', as well as a future full of grief. For the traditional motif of magicians 'drawing down the moon' cf. 3.531–3n., Ar. *Clouds* 749–50, Pl. *Gorg.* 513a5–6, Mugler 1959. On this scene see esp. Fantuzzi 2007, 2008b: 301–10.

54 Τιτηνίς: Selene's parents were the Titan Hyperion and Theia (Hes. *Theog.* 371–4). The collocation νέον Τιτηνὶς . . . Μήνη evokes νουμηνία, 'new moon'; Murray 2014: 264 identifies 29 September as the date of such a new moon in the year of performance (Introduction, p. 2). περάτηθεν 'from the horizon', cf. 1.1281–2, Arat. *Phain.* 821.

55 φοιταλέην combines the ideas of hurried movement and mental distress, cf. Moschus, *Eur.* 46 (Io), Antipater, *AP* 9.603.7 (= *HE* 598, maenads); the same combination is suggested by the verb φοιτᾶν at 1.1249. ἐπεχήρατο 'exulted', cf. 1628.

56 ἁρπαλέως: a strong intensive, 'very greatly', which is often found with verbs expressing pleasure; see Rengakos 1994: 58–9.

57–8 Endymion was the subject of a very rich mythological tradition, going back for us to Hesiod (frr. 10a.60–2, 245), Sappho (fr. 199 V) and Epimenides (*FGrHist* 457 F10), and perhaps combining stories about more than one character. The sleeping Endymion loved by the Moon is, however, always identified as a Carian shepherd or hunter, and his cave, where a cult in his honour was established (Strabo 14.1.8), is in the Latmos mountains near Heraclea-under-Latmos (Barrington 61 F2), Williams

1991: 104–5; in some versions, Endymion's sleep was a gift which he himself chose from Zeus (cf. Apollod. *Bibl.* 1.7.5). The principal sources for this figure are gathered by Σ here and on Theocr. 3.49–51.

The opening of Theocr. 13 (1–4) is very similar to 57–8, and there too the same idea is essentially repeated twice; that poem, on the story of Hylas, has a close (though disputed) intertextual relationship with *Arg.*, Fantuzzi 2008b: 304–5. The Moon does not of course mean 'I am not the only one in love with Endymion', but rather 'I am not the only one who has felt (a shameful) love'.   ἄρ' marks a conclusion just reached on the basis of evidence and/or inference (Denniston 36–7).   ἀλύσκω 'slink off to'; the normal sense is 'flee, avoid' (cf. 585, 1505), but here the verb has attracted something of the flavour of ἀλυσκάζω (*Il.* 5.253, 6.443).   περιδαίομαι, 'burn for', carries a particular charge when used of the moon. Σ Theocr. 2.10c suggests that one explanation why lovesick women call on Selene is that 'the goddess is fiery (διάπυρος), and so is this emotion (i.e. love)'.

59–60 The transmitted text lacks a main verb, and the participle can hardly be made to depend upon περιδαίομαι. The solution adopted here (Campbell 1971: 418) is to assume that a verse has fallen out; the Moon would make clear how she left the sky at Medea's behest. The alternative approach has been to replace the sarcastic address κύον with a verb. κίον 'I went, came', is just the wrong verb; Fränkel proposed κύθον, 'I lay hidden', an intransitive aorist of κεύθω which is attested in tragedy, and Fantuzzi κλύον, 'I heard, obeyed', which would probably govern the following dative (LSJ s.v. II), rather than the preceding genitive. κλύον, which would pick up the standard prayer to a god to 'hear', would however entail a rare instance (cf. 2.73) of initial κλ- failing to lengthen a preceding short syllable.   **κύον**: with bitter humour, the Moon mocks Medea's shamelessness, not only, like Helen (also 'dog-like' at *Il.* 3.180, 6.344, *Od.* 4.145), in abandoning her home contrary to all decency, but also in practising her magic contrary to natural law. It is very unlikely that the close association of Selene-Hecate with dogs (3.749n.) is relevant here.   **μνησαμένη φιλότητος** 'with my mind set on love-making'. Σ Theocr. 2.10c (cf. 57–8) suggests that lovesick women call on Selene because the goddess herself knew what it was to be in love and therefore was willing to help.

61 εὔκηλος 'without being disturbed'.

62–3 recall the language of 4, just as this language is to recur in 445–9: the Moon almost mocks Medea with the language of the prooemial quandary.   **δῆθεν**, 'as it seems', lays the irony on thick.   **ὁμοίης**: some ancient interpreters ('the glossographers', cf. Dyck 1987: 152–3, Rengakos 1994: 119–20) took ὁμοῖος in Homer as a synonym of κακός, and

Ap. may here allow both 'wretched' and 'equal (to mine)' to resonate. The Moon herself plays with language like an Alexandrian scholar.   ἀνιηρόν τοι Ἰήσονα πῆμα: the assonance perhaps adds to the mockery.

64 δαίμων ἀλγινόεις: the responsible δαίμων is of course Hera, but the Moon's language also suggests that it is Medea's personal 'fate' which is in play here, cf. 3.388–90n.

65 πινυτή: Medea's 'cleverness' consists in her mastery of magic. **πολύστονον ἄλγος**: the repetition after ἀλγινόεις is emphatic. ἀείρειν 'pick up and carry/endure', cf. [Theocr.] 27.21 σὺ δὲ ζυγὸν αἰὲν ἀείραις. Somewhat similar is the conclusion of Theocr. 2 (Simaitha to the moon) ἐγὼ δ' οἰσῶ τὸν ἐμὸν πόθον ὥσπερ ὑπέσταν.

67 ἐπηέρθη 'she climbed up on', lit. 'she was raised on', aorist passive ἐπαείρω.

68 ἀέθλου depends upon ἐυφροσύνῃσιν, 'in delight at (the outcome of) the contest'.

69 The Argonauts were celebrating both Jason's survival and – as they thought – the successful acquisition of the Fleece. At 3.419 Aietes had said that, if Jason successfully completed the challenge, 'on that very day' he could carry off the Fleece.   **παννύχιοι**: cf. 7n.

70 ὀξείῃ 'clear, sharp', particularly suited to male perceptions of the female voice.   **ὄρθια**: adverbial, 'loudly'.

71–2 Cf. 20–3n. Phrontis has otherwise been named only at 2.1155 and we were not told there that he was the youngest. Ap. may be making a mythological point. Argos seems always to have been regarded as the oldest, but otherwise the order in surviving lists varies (cf. Σ 2.1122a, *RE* 20.771); lists need not of course be chronologically ordered, and Argos presents Phrontis second at 2.1155.   **περαιόθεν** 'from the opposite bank'.

73 Αἰσονίδῃ: Jason was the only Argonaut who had heard Medea's voice before.   **τεκμαίρετο**: lit. 'judged by signs', i.e. deduced from the voice that it was Medea who was calling; the standard translation 'recognized' obscures the force of the verb. The verb catches the surprise and hesitation of the men, until the truth dawns on them.

74 ἐνόησαν 'understood' (from what Jason and the sons of Phrixos told them).

75 Three is a common number in such situations, cf. *Il.* 11.462–3 (Odysseus calling for help), Theocr. 13.58–9 (Hylas), but whereas in those passages τρίς ... τρίς is spread over two hexameters, here (as at *Il.*

23.817) it is speed and compression which are stressed. The narrative is now moving very fast.

78 ἐπ' ἠπείροιο περαίης 'on to the bank opposite'.

83 ἔκ ... ῥύσασθε: tmesis.   **φίλοι** 'stresses their obligations towards her' (Plantinga 2000: 116).   **ὡς δὲ καί**: ἐκ δὲ καί (Π⁶) would give an emotive anaphora and may be correct.

84 πρό is usually analysed as in tmesis with τέτυκται (in Homer the compound verb means 'happen beforehand', *Il.* 16.60, 18.112), but its function is to reinforce the adjectival ἀναφανδά, 'in full and open view'. The terrible scenario of 3.615 has now become a reality.

85 ἐπὶ νηΐ: Brunck's ἐνὶ νηΐ or Fränkel's ἐπὶ νηός may be correct, as Ap. normally uses these forms.

86 Given Aietes' close association with the sun (cf. esp. 3.1228–30), there is a suggestion here of 'before sunrise' (cf. 101), as well as 'before Aietes mounts his horses'; Helios' horses were the god's most familiar attributes, cf. 220–1n.

87–91 Medea offers herself in marriage with the Fleece as dowry, and calls on Jason to show reciprocity (ἐγώ ... τύνη). Medea has no male κύριος (91n.) and therefore must act on her own initiative, as was presumably very common in the Hellenistic world, even in royal families (Vatin 1970: 70). Σ report that in the *Naupactia* (fr. 8 Davies, cf. 6–10n.) Medea brought the Fleece with her, as it had been kept in Aietes' palace.

89 Medea recalls Jason's promises at 3.1122–30 that she would find great honour and be his lawful wife, 'if ever she were to come to Greece'. **ξεῖνε** shows the depth of Medea's misery and loneliness. **ἐπιίστορας** '(formal) witnesses' (cf. 229), a sense occasionally found for the simple ἴστωρ/ἵστωρ, cf. Hippocr. *Oath* Proem, *IG* VII 1779 (Thespiae); the lexical rarity adds solemnity to Medea's request. Some grammarians claimed to find this sense of the compound noun at *Il.* 18.501 (the legal case depicted on the Shield), cf. Hesych. ε 4761. For other senses of ἐπιίστωρ cf. 16, 1558.

90 ἑκαστέρω: the comparative 'further away' (cf. 1293) is here used as a strong form of the simple, 'far away'.

91 κηδεμόνων 'guardians, protectors'. At 3.732 Medea had called Phrixos' sons her κηδεμόνες τε φίλοι καὶ ὁμήλικες, but the rhetorical situation is now very different: as a foreign, unmarried woman in Greece, Medea's position will be precarious indeed. The context perhaps also allows the link between κηδεμών and κῆδος, κηδεστής etc. to resonate (cf. Eur. *Med.* 990);

if Jason does not keep his promises, Medea will have no 'protectors' and
no 'relations by marriage' to fulfil that role.   ὀνοτήν 'an object of
blame'.   θείης: Platt's θείῃς, subjunctive instead of optative, may be
correct.

92 ἴσκεν: cf. 410n.

93–4 The solemnity of the moment is perhaps marked by a pair of spondaic
verses.   πεπτηυῖαν: perfect participle from πίπτω.   προσπτύξατο
'spoke affectionately', cf. LSJ s.v. B II 2.   θάρσυνεν is not inappropriate,
though it seems more natural in 108, and D's φώνησεν would echo a pattern
found at *Il.* 24.193–4 (Priam to Hecuba).

95–8 In response to Medea's request to him to repeat his earlier promises,
Jason's speech is indeed marked by 'fragments' of 3.1120–30 (δαιμονίη,
κουριδίην ... ἄκοιτιν, Ἑλλάδα γαῖαν); cf. also 194–5, 1084–5. The future,
as represented above all in Eur. *Med.*, hangs very heavy here.   δαιμονίη
marks, as at 3.1120, the unnecessary or mistaken nature of what Medea
has just said; cf. 395.   ὅρκιος 'witness to the oath', but also evoking a
familiar epithet or cult-title of Zeus.   Ἥρη τε Ζυγίη, Διὸς εὐνέτις lays
great emphasis upon the notion of marriage. This is the earliest appearance of this title of Hera, and it remains a largely isolated example until
much later antiquity, where the influence of the Roman Juno *iugalis* or
iuga may be felt. The rarity may be a further marker of solemnity, but the
epithet may have carried a resonance for Ap.'s readers which we can no
longer recover.   ἦ μέν introduces, as commonly, the terms of an oath
(Smyth §2865).   δόμοισιν: Jason envisages a formal wedding back in
Greece, which would include the ritual transference of the bride to the
groom's house, but events were to prove different (1161–4).

99–100 Jason offers his hand in pledge of (a future) marriage, just as,
under different circumstances, a bride's father would shake the hand of
his future son-in-law (Oakley-Sinos 1993: 9). The gesture replays Medea's
own at 3.1067–8, when she thought that she was seeing Jason for the last
time.   παρασχεδόν 'immediately'.

101 νῆα θοήν evokes, as elsewhere (857n.), an etymology of Ἀργώ as the
'swift ship'. For νῆα θοήν as an Apollonian 'formula' see Fantuzzi–Hunter
2004: 267–8.   αὐτοσχεδόν 'there and then, at once'.

102 κῶας ἑλόντες ἄγοιντο 'take the Fleece and carry it away'.

103 'Then word and deed were simultaneous for them in their haste', i.e.
'no sooner said than done'. The most common form of this proverbial
saying was ἅμα ἔπος ἅμα ἔργον (e.g. Suda α 1462, Zenobius 1.77), but it
turns up in various forms in literary texts, cf. *HHHerm.* 46, Hdt. 3.135.1,

and already in epic form at *Il.* 19.242 αὐτίκ' ἔπειθ' ἅμα μῦθος ἔην, τετέλεστο δὲ ἔργον.

104 εἰς γάρ μιν βήσαντες 'putting her (Medea) on board ... '.

106–8 Medea's gesture of despair evokes (and reverses) that of Jason himself who, at departure from Iolcos, 'turned his eyes, full of tears, away from his homeland' (1.534–5). **ἔμπαλιν** 'back', i.e. to the stern of the ship, which would have been closest to the land. **ἀμήχανος** 'in helpless despair'. **ἴσχανεν** 'held her back', i.e. from jumping overboard.

109–13 An elaborate time-description (cf., e.g., 1.1172–6, 2.164–5, 3.1340–4) has, as often, some of the functions of a simile: Medea and Jason are indeed like hunters eager to secure their prey before the sun comes up. The verses well capture the stealth and necessary caution of the current situation; see further Fantuzzi 1988: 151–2.

109 ἐβάλοντο: the aorist is generalizing, like aorists of repeated action in similes, cf. 1.1174, Smyth §1935.

110–11 ἀγρόται 'hunters', a sense which some grammarians found at *Od.* 16.218 (cf. Ap. Soph. 7.29 Bekker), but which makes its first certain appearance in *Arg.*, cf. 2.509 (ἀγρότιν of Cyrene), Rengakos 1994: 32–3. Some grammatical lore saw this as an Attic usage (Σ *Il.* 15.272). See further 175n.

νύκτα | ἄγχαυρον 'the last part of the night', 'the period just before dawn'; ancient scholarship etymologized ἄγχαυρος as the period 'near the breezes' (ἄγχι, αὖραι), citing *Od.* 5.469, αὔρη δ' ἐκ ποταμοῦ ψυχρή πνέει ἠῶθι πρό. Hesych. α 292 has ἀγχοῦρος (*sic*) as a Cypriot gloss for the earliest dawn. Here this rare term functions as an adjective, cf. ἀμφιλύκη νύξ at *Il.* 7.433, but simple ἀμφιλύκη at *Arg.* 2.671. Its only other appearance in literature is as a noun in another 'time description' at Call. *Hecale* fr. 74.21–7 H (= fr. 260.62–8 Pf.), the conversation of two birds: 'Sleep took hold of her who had spoken thus and the other who was listening. They did not sleep for long, for quickly arrived the frosty pre-dawn (στιβήεις ἄγχαυρος [Pfeiffer: αγχουρος]), when the hands of thieves no longer seek booty (ἔπαγροι). Already there was the gleam of morning lights ... '. The two time-descriptions are clearly connected, and not merely by the theme of sleep and waking and the gloss ἄγχαυρος; ἀγρόται ~ ἔπαγροι and στίβον ~ στιβήεις (two quite different words) reinforce the connection. The fact that Call.'s στιβήεις itself points to the etymology of ἄγχαυρος (cf. *Od.* 5.469 above) may be thought to favour Callimachean priority.

112–13 In the *Cynegetica* Xenophon has much to say about the effect of the season and the weather on the tracks and scents left by game, cf. esp. *Cyn.* 5.1–6; in general, an early start is advised (6.4), as scent will never last all day, but in summer, in particular, one will want to make a very early start before the heat of the sun dissipates scents (5.5, cf. [Oppian], *Cyn.* 135 πρώτηι ὑπ' ἀμφιλύκηι). **θηρῶν ... θηρείην**: a remarkable repetition and chiasmus. Fränkel proposed θερμόν, 'fresh', in 112, cf. Theocr. 17.121–2 ἔτι θερμά ... ἴχνη, Erinna, *SH* 401.20, *AP* 9.371.2 (= *FGE* 2057, a dog chasing a hare) θερμοῖς ἴχνεσιν. Xenophon discusses τὸ θερμόν of a hare's ἴχνη, specifically in the context of the hot ground dissipating it in summer (*Cyn.* 5.5), but the reference there, as principally throughout those chapters, is to 'scent' rather than physical tracks. Ap. here draws a distinction between the physically marked 'path' or 'track' of animals (for στίβος in this sense cf. *HHHerm.* 353) and the scent (ὀδμή) they leave, but θερμόν remains an attractive emendation. **ἐνισκίμψασα** 'pressing upon (them) with ... '.

115–16 lit. 'in a grassy spot where the Ram's Bed is called', i.e. 'in a grassy spot called the Ram's Bed'; for such compressed expressions cf. 1.215–16, 237–8, *Il.* 11.757–8, K–G II 437–8. This is where Phrixos and the Ram first landed on Colchian soil.

117 Μινυήιον υἷ' Ἀθάμαντος: i.e. Phrixos, who originated in 'Minyan' Orchomenos in Boeotia, cf. 1.763, 3.265–7n., 3.1093–5.

118 βωμοῖο θέμεθλα 'foundations of an altar' is a poetically elaborate expression for 'altar'.

119 Cf. 2.1141–7. **Αἰολίδης**: Phrixos' grandfather was Aeolus. **Φυξίωι**: Σ 2.1147 claim that this title of Zeus, here understood as the god who granted successful escape from persecution (so also Lyc. *Alex.* 288), is especially Thessalian, which would be appropriate to Phrixos. *Arg.* offers the earliest attestations of this title, cf. 699n. **εἴσατο** 'established', aorist middle of ἵζω, LSJ s.v. I 2.

121 The poet evokes a scene such as Hermes meeting Odysseus on his way to Circe in *Od.* 10 or Priam on his way to Achilles in *Il.* 24. Hermes ὅδιος is the most familiar god for travellers to encounter, and here, as regularly, we may imagine that he was acting on Zeus's instructions. At 2.1146 (and cf. 1.763–4) the text rather seems to suggest that the ram itself told Phrixos to sacrifice it (cf. Vian I 283), but the inconsistency is not disturbing. Hermes appears at several points in stories of the background to the expedition: at 2.1144–5 we are told that he 'made the ram golden', and at 3.587–8 Aietes claims that Hermes told him to receive Phrixos hospitably. Apollod. 1.9.1 reports that Hermes originally gave the golden ram to Nephele.

122 Argos is the oldest brother (71–2n.) and knows the territory; he also acted as guide at 2.1260–1, 1281–2.

124 φηγόν: Ap. uses φηγός (2.405) and δρῦς (162, 2.1270) interchangeably for the tree on which the Fleece hangs.

125–6 Cf. 3.162–3. The Fleece gleams like the sun rising after the pre-dawn of 109–13, and this is one of a number of similarities between the Fleece and Jason's marvellous cloak in Book 1, cf. 167–70, 725–6. Virgil used these verses for his description of Aeneas' breastplate at *Aen.* 8.622–3.   **βέβλητο:** the final syllable is lengthened in arsis before initial ν, cf. 620, 3.1384; Homer has an example of such lengthening before νεφέλην (*Il.* 14.350).

127 ἀντικρύ 'straight in front of them'.   **περιμήκεα . . . δειρήν:** a memory of Scylla, who had six δειραὶ περιμήκεες (*Od.* 12.90), cf. 154n.

128 ὀξύς 'sharp-sighted', LSJ s.v. II 2. A connection between δράκων and δέρκομαι was familiar in antiquity; *Et. Mag.* 286.7–8 explains that a δράκων is ὀξυδερκές. So too, the collocation ὄφις ὀφθαλμοῖσι suggests an etymological connection, such as is certainly attested later; *Et. Mag.* 644.6–7 derives ὄφις from ὄπτω (explained as βλέπω) and notes that snakes sleep with their eyes open. Similar etymological patterns are involved in the description of the dragon at 2.405–7.   **ἀύπνοισι . . . ὀφθαλμοῖσι:** cf. 2.406–7, Ov. *Met.* 7.155, *somnus in ignotos oculos* † *ubi uenit* †.

129 νισσομένους '(them) approaching', the object of προϊδών. **ῥοίζει** is also used of a (smaller) snake's hiss at 1543, but Ap. has in mind Hes. *Theog.* 835 (Typhoeus) ἄλλοτε δ' αὖ ῥοίζεσχ', ὑπὸ δ' ἤχεεν οὔρεα μακρά. Although the sound is there not specified, it is reasonable to think of the monster's snaky heads (West ad loc.), and the Colchian snake is in fact related to the Hesiodic monster (2.1209–13); Typhoeus thus joins Scylla (127n.) among the epic predecessors of this dragon.   **πελώριον,** 'very loudly', is also appropriate to a monster (πέλωρ) of an unearthly kind, cf. 143, Fränkel 1968: 284–5.   **ἀμφί** is best analysed as adverbial, rather than in tmesis with ἴαχεν.

131–8 Ap. conjures up the vastness of the geography in which the Argonauts are trapped and which is almost unimaginable to Greeks, as well as the terrifying power of the dragon's hiss. Virgil reworked this passage to describe Allecto's call to war at *Aen.* 7.511–18; Nelis 2001: 296–8.

131 Τιτηνίδος: Aietes' grandfather and Helios' father was the Titan Hyperion (Hes. *Theog.* 371). Σ however explain the adjective as referring to a river called Titan 'which was mentioned by Eratosthenes' (III B76 Berger); there is no other record of such a river.

132 παρὰ προχοῇσι Λύκοιο 'beside the streams of the Lycus'; for this sense of προχοαί cf. 271, 617, 3.67n., Bühler 1960: 79–81. Strabo 11.14.7 mentions a local river Lycus which, like the Phasis, empties into the Black Sea, but the identity of Ap.'s tributary of the Araxes (mod. Aras), the great river (Hdt. 1.202) which separates Armenia from Georgia and which joins the Kura shortly before it flows into the Caspian, is unknown. Ap. may have been thinking of a river of this name which, according to Strabo 12.3.15, rises in Armenia and then joins the Iris, which flows into the Black Sea at Themiskyra; Delage 1930: 182–3.

133 κελάδοντος may be applied to any large river, but it is not inappropriate to the Araxes which Strabo 11.4.2 calls τραχύς, just as the Phasis is τραχὺς καὶ βίαιος at 11.3.4. 'Araxes' was variously etymologized from ἀράσσειν and ῥήγνυμι (Strabo 11.14.13, Et. Mag. 134.39–40, Σ Aesch. Pers. 716) and either or both of ἀποκιδνάμενος and κελάδοντος may allude to one of these etymologies.

135 Καυκασίην ἅλαδ': the marker of motion towards is here attached to the second element of a compound geographical phrase (contrast 548, 1233), and this appears to be an innovation by Ap. in the epic language; Wackernagel 1920: 200 (= 2009: 650). The 'Caucasian sea' must be the eastern end of the Black Sea; Ap. makes a close connection between Aietes' city and the Caucasus, cf. 2.1267.   **προρέουσι:** the transmitted προχέουσι would require ῥόον to be understood from 134, and that seems very awkward.

136 λεχωίδες 'women who have just given birth', a variant of λεχώ which first appears here and in Call. (h. 3.127, 4.56, 124). We are perhaps to understand that it was popularly believed that the dragon snatched and ate babies.

139–44 The movement of the dragon's coils is compared to the endless spirals of smoke which rise from a smouldering forest fire; as Jason and Medea find themselves in a 'boundless grove' (130) lit by the gleam of the Fleece, the simile is evocative and appropriate.

141–2 'and one (spiral) swiftly rises up after another, ever coming forward, lifted up from below in swirls'.   **ἐπιτέλλεται** 'rises up after', an unusual role for the prefix in this compound.   **ἐπιπρό:** cf. 595, 1390.   **ἐπήορος:** a synonym of μετέωρος found only in Arg. (cf. also 3.856) before Nonnus.   **ἀίσσουσα:** the better attested ἐξανιοῦσα is certainly possible, but ἀίσσουσα has excellent parallels at 1.438 and 2.133–4 (both of smoke), and cf. 3.759.

143 ἀπειρεσίας picks up ἀπείριτοι, as ἑλισσομένοιο in 145 picks up εἱλίσσονται … εἱλίγγοισιν in the simile. Virgil may have remembered this description at *G.* 2.153–4.   ἐλέλιζε 'rolled'. The transitive use is unusual; the medio-passive is standardly used of snakes moving in coils.

144 ῥυμβόνας 'coils', a word occurring only here, though ῥύμβος exists alongside ῥόμβος to mark anything circular. The lexical rarity adds to the eeriness of the whole scene.   ἀζαλέηισιν ἐπηρεφέας φολίδεσσι 'covered with dry scales'; similar phrases at Nic. *Ther.* 157 and 221 may be indebted to *Arg.*, rather than to a common source in Noumenios' *Theriakon* (*SH* 589–94), as Morel 1928: 364 claims, cf. 1505–31n.

145–66 Medea lulls the dragon to sleep and Jason grabs the Fleece from the tree. Σ 156–66 note that this is the version used by Antimachus (fr. 63W = 73M, in the *Lyde*), whereas in Pherecydes (*FGrHist* 3 F31) and Herodorus (*FGrHist* 31 F52) Jason killed the dragon; it is, however, unlikely that Antimachus was Ap.'s only predecessor. At *Pyth.* 4.249 Pindar reports that Jason killed the snake τέχναις, and the ancient scholiasts at least understood these to be Medea's τέχναι (II 158 Drachmann); at Eur. *Med.* 482 Medea claims (to Jason) to have killed the dragon (see Mastronarde 2002: 47). On the various versions see Ogden 2013a: 58–63. The scene is illustrated on many surviving vases, which could be adduced to support almost any attested version; cf. further 156, 157nn. In Valerius Flaccus 8.59–120, Medea has clearly been to the dragon before and it is a kind of pet for her; there is no sign (*pace* Ogden 2013b: 128) that we are to understand that scenario here.

145 †κατόμματον εἴσετο†: no explanation or emendation is convincing. Σ glosses the verb as ὥρμησεν, which has led some to take εἴσατο, which in *Arg.* is normally from εἴδομαι, as an epic aorist of ἵεμαι, but – morphology aside – 'rushed to look it in the eye' (Race) seems a very improbable action; that Medea 'drew near' to the dragon is, however, what we might have expected the text to say. κατόμματον occurs nowhere else, and would be a very singular formation. Attempted solutions include κατ' ὄμματα νίσετο (Merkel) and κατ' ὄμματ' ἀείσατο (Livrea).

146–8 As commonly (cf. 709n., 1665–6, 3.862n.), the lists of titles which we are to imagine Medea used in her invocation are here transposed into narrative. Such lists are very common in texts such as magical papyri and the Orphic Hymns; at *PGM* iv 2851 (= Betz 1992: 92) Selene/Hecate is invoked to 'give heed to your titles (ἐπωνυμίαι)'.

146 ἀοσσητῆρα, 'helper', cf. Call. fr. 18.4 (the Anaphe episode).   θεῶν ὕπατον: Ap. has in mind Hera's plea to Sleep for his help at *Il.* 14.233, Ὕπνε, ἄναξ πάντων τε θεῶν πάντων τ' ἀνθρώπων.

147 ἠδείηι 'gentle, calming'.   τέρας: cf. 2.405 (the dragon) τέρας αἰνὸν ἰδέσθαι.   ἄνασσαν: Hecate, cf. *HHDem.* 440, 3.862 Βριμὼ νυκτιπόλον χθονίην ἐνέροισιν ἄνασσαν, with n. ad loc.. One of Hecate's most familiar manifestations, particularly in the context of magic, is as Selene, the moon-goddess, but there is no sense of irony here, despite the Moon's speech at 55–65; this is a good example of how poets do not activate all of our knowledge all of the time.

148 νυκτιπόλον: cf. 829, 1020, 3.862n.   εὐαντέα, 'gracious, kindly', may be euphemistic when applied to Hecate (εὐάντητος is a more common form in prayers and related texts, and cf. 1.1141 ἀνταίη δαίμων); ἐφορμήν will then mean 'a successful means to approach', and this interpretation is perhaps supported by the parallelism of θέλξαι τέρας and δοῦναι ἐφορμήν. It is possible, however, that we are to understand εὐαντέα with ἐφορμήν, 'to grant a favourable enterprise' (cf. 204n.), and the rhythm of the verse perhaps favours this interpretation.

149 Jason's 'natural' fear, like that of the mothers of young babies (136–8), accentuates Medea's supernatural powers and her protection of him.

150–1 Cf. Virg. *Aen.* 6.422–3 (Cerberus, after eating the drugged cake) *immania terga resoluit | fusus humi totoque ingens extenditur antro.* Virgil draws extensively on this scene of *Arg.* in his Underworld book (Golden Fleece ~ Golden Bough etc.); Hunter 1993: 185, Nelis 2001: 240–51.   οἴμηι 'by her song'.   δολιχὴν ... | γηγενέος σπείρης 'was relaxing the long spine of his earthborn coils'. English would naturally use the plural 'coils' (cf. Eur. *Med.* 481), but for the singular cf. Arat. *Phain.* 47, 89, Nic. *Ther.* 156. The dragon sprang from the Earth where drops of Typhaon's blood had fallen (2.1209–13).   μυρία κύκλα varies ἀπειρεσίας ... ῥυμβόνας in 143–4.

152–3 'As when a dark wave rolls silently and noiselessly over sluggish seas ... ', a marvellous comparison of the relaxing coils to a slow swell coming in over calm waters. The principal model (Campbell 1969: 283–4) is a simile at *Il.* 14.16–19, ὡς δ' ὅτε πορφύρηι πέλαγος μέγα κύματι κωφῶι κτλ. (with προκυλίνδεται in line 18), where Σ note that the sea does indeed grow dark in such conditions when there is a wave (κῦμα κωφόν) which does not break; such a swell was sometimes called κολόκυμα or σκῶληξ ('worm'), Hesych. κ 3368. The ellipse of a finite verb in similes after ὅτε is not uncommon (although μέλαν has here been emended to πέλει or πέλεν), and the idea of μηκύνεσθαι will here be carried over from 151. Valerius Flaccus turns this passage into an image of great rivers receding (8.90–1).   βληχροῖσι 'sluggish, weak', a secondary formation from ἀβληχρός (cf. 2.205).   κωφόν τε καὶ ἄβρομον may be taken either adverbially with κυλινδόμενον, or as adjectives modifying the single idea κῦμα μέλαν; the former seems preferable. ἄβρομος occurs in Homer only at *Il.* 13.41, where later grammarians differed as to whether the α– should be understood as privative or intensive, i.e. 'noiseless' or 'very noisy' (Rengakos 1994: 29). Ap. uses it here in the former sense.

154 σμερδαλέην κεφαλήν: another (cf. 127n.) memory of Scylla, cf. *Od.* 12.90–2 (the whole passage is evoked here), 'on each of her six necks was a terrible head (σμερδαλέη κεφαλή), with three rows of teeth, close-set and numerous, full of black death'.

155 Cf. Pind. *Pyth.* 4.244 λαβροτατᾶν γενύων. A famous red-figure vase of *c.* 475 BC (*LIMC* s.v. Iason 32) shows a (possibly unconscious) Jason in the mouth of the huge dragon (the teeth – see 154n. – are very prominent); Athena stands next to the scene, watching. If the painter was depicting a known version of the story, we do not know what that was (see, e.g., Gantz 1993: 359–60), but the painting makes clear that Jason's fear (149) was entirely understandable.

156–9 Later reworkings of these verses include Virg. *Aen.* 5.854–6 (Palinurus) and Ov. *Met.* 7.152–5 (Medea and the dragon).

156 ἀρκεύθοιο νέον τετμηότι θαλλῶι 'with a newly-cut sprig of juniper'. We are not told whether Medea brought this with her, nor from where she produced the potion of 157, cf. 24–5n.; these ellipses have led some to assume that Ap. is here using a fuller narrative which his readers knew, cf. Wilamowitz 1924: II 231 (suggesting Antimachus). Some vase-paintings show Medea with a sprig or leaf in her hand, cf. *LIMC* s.v. Argonautai 21, Iason 41.   **ἀρκεύθοιο:** juniper was thought to keep snakes away (Plin. *HN* 24.54, *Et. Mag.* 144.38–41) or to be an antidote to their poison (Nic. *Ther.* 584), but juniper-wood is specified for use in rites on several occasions in the magical papyri, and its use here may evoke further magical associations.   **τετμηότι:** in form, this is a perfect active participle of τέμνω, but it is here used with passive force.

157 κυκεῶνος: the nature of this 'potion' is not further specified, but we naturally think of Circe's κυκεών, laced with φάρμακα λυγρά and consisting of cheese, grain, honey and wine (*Od.* 10.234–6, 290, 316–17), cf. further *Il.* 11.638–41, Richardson 1974: 344–8. A number of vase-paintings show Medea offering the dragon something to eat or drink out of a bowl (e.g. *LIMC* s.v. Iason 42), and this 'potion' may also reflect such versions.   **ἀκήρατα:** the meaning is quite uncertain. 'Pure' or 'undamaged' drugs are presumably 'powerful', but the semantics of the adjective are unclear; the sense of ἀκήρατα … φάρμακα at *Orph. Lith.* 663–4 is similarly uncertain.   **ἀοιδαῖς** 'to the accompaniment of incantations'.

158 νήριτος is glossed by Σ as πολλή, cf. Hes. *WD* 511 νήριτος ὕλη, and it is found elsewhere as a strong intensive; so here 'powerful' or the like. Cf. further 3.1288n., Leumann 1950: 243–7.

159–60 Lit. 'It laid its jaw just where it was, pressing it down', i.e. 'it let its jaw fall to the ground just where it was'.

161 πολυπρέμνοιο ... ὕλης 'the wood with many tree-trunks' varies ἄσπετον ... ἄλσος (130); the adjective appears only here before late antiquity.

162–3 This moment, when the Fleece is finally taken from the tree, is shown on several vase-paintings.   κούρης κεκλομένης opens a hexameter at *HHDem.* 27, where the participle means 'calling upon', rather than, as here, 'giving instructions'; the contrast between the rape of a powerless Persephone and Medea's calm control is a powerful effect. Hellenistic and later poets created κέκλομαι as a new present form with the range of meanings of κέλομαι, perhaps through interpretation of the Homeric aorist ἐκέκλετο as an imperfect.   ἔμπεδον 'fixedly, without moving', cf. *Od.* 17.463–4 ὁ δ᾽ ἐστάθη ἠΰτε πέτρη | ἔμπεδον.

166 ἤνωγεν, coming so soon after κεκλομένης, marks Jason's reassertion of 'masculine leadership', now that he has what he wanted. He is, however, about to be compared to a παρθένος.   λεῖπον: the transmitted singular leaves Medea stranded; cf. the similar sequence at 750–2.

167–70 Jason's pleasure in the gleaming Fleece is compared to that of a young girl who catches the moonlight in the fine texture of her dress. The simile is strikingly original, though it takes off from Homeric similes in which heroes are compared to females (note esp. *Il.* 16.7–10, Patroclus crying). The simile is closely related to 1.774–80, the effect of Jason's cloak compared to women watching a star, and this reinforces the connection between the two marvellous objects, cf. 125–6n.; we are also reminded of the erotically charged blush which the moon brought to Hylas' face (1.1228–33). Some critics have argued that we naturally understand the girl to be 'like' Medea in her pleasure at the Fleece, only to be surprised when we learn that it is in fact Jason; there is, however, no reason to imagine that 'joy' is one of the emotions which Medea is feeling (far from it). On this passage see esp. Bremer 1987, Knight 1991.

167 σεληναίης διχομήνιδα ... αἴγλην 'the month-dividing gleam of the moon' is the gleam of a full moon, cf. 1.1231. There is some evidence (e.g. Eur. *IA* 716–17, see Bremer 1987) that the full moon was considered a propitious time for weddings, and this may give a particularly erotic charge to the maiden's pleasure, just as the gleam of Jason's cloak induces a maiden to think of her future bridegroom at 1.778–80.

168 'rising high above her bed-chamber under the roof'. The text is however uncertain.   ἐξανέχουσαν is presumably an emendation in E, but it gives a reasonable sense (cf. 2.369–70, Theocr. 22.207 for this intransitive use) and is close to the transmission. Σ offer the gloss εἰσβάλλουσαν, perhaps 'striking into', but we do not know what text was being glossed; Livrea proposed ἀντέλλουσαν (cf. 1.776). The truth is perhaps yet to be found. **ὑπωροφίου**: in Homer women's quarters are upstairs (the ὑπερῷον), cf., e.g., *Il.* 2.514, *Od.* 1.362. Moschus presumably remembers this passage when his Europa sleeps ὑπωροφίοισιν ἐνὶ ... δόμοισι (*Eur.* 6).

169 λεπταλέωι ἑανῶι ὑποΐσχεται 'catches on her fine dress'; for the verb cf. 473.

170 δερκομένης: as commonly, the participle is in the genitive though the pronoun (οἱ) is dative, cf. 3.371n., Chantraine II 322–3.

171 ἀναείρετο 'lifted and carried'; this verb is used in *Il.* 23 of 'carrying off' prizes in the athletic contests (e.g. 614, 778, 856 (middle)), and there may be something of that resonance here. The alternative compound ἐναείρειν is otherwise unattested.

173 'a red blush like fire settled from the gleam of the wool', cf. 125, 3.163. Others understand ἷζεν as transitive with μαρμαρυγή as the subject, but the intransitive use seems more natural here. Rose 1985: 38–9 discusses the thematic use of ἔρευθος and related words through the poem.   **ληνέων** is scanned as two long syllables with synizesis. λῆνη are tufts or clumps of wool (cf. 177), but here simply 'wool' or 'fleece', cf. Pfeiffer on Call. fr. 722.

174–5 The size of the Fleece is given through a comparison to the skin of two animals, both characterized by rare linguistic glosses. Some modern taste finds this display of 'learning' intrusive and destructive at a major narrative moment, but the very precision of the specification of size, combined with a focus, not just on the Fleece as a whole, but on the individual clumps of wool (175), creates a powerful ecphrastic effect. Even readers who are puzzled by the glosses of 174–5 are pushed towards a very precise image of this extraordinary (mythical) artefact.   **ἤνιος**: perhaps 'one year old', cf. 1185–6n., *LfgrE* s.v. ἦνις.   **ἀγρῶσται** is explained by Σ as 'hunters', from a supposed derivation from ἀγρώσσω (cf. 110–11n.), cf. Hesych. α844. Elsewhere in literature the word means 'country-people' or 'rustic' (Soph. fr. 94R, Eur. *HF* 376, *Rhes.* 287, Call. *Hecale* fr. 69.13 H), and either sense is possible here; the linguistic context does, however, suggest 'hunters'.   **ἀχαιινέην**: Aristotle mentions this type of deer in two uninformative notices (*HA* 2.506a24, 611b18), and Eratosthenes too seems not to have been able to give a close identification (181–5 Slater); Eustathius observes that the term 'gives interpreters a great deal of trouble' (*Hom.* 711.44). Most likely, the word designates a deer at a particular stage of growth; Σ associates it with a Cretan town called Achaia.

176–7 As transmitted, there are two finite verbs in asyndeton; ἐφύπερθε δ᾽ allows both to be retained with minimal change, but some uncertainty remains. Other suggested solutions involve turning one of the finite verbs into a participle (ἐὸν Chretien, βεβριθός Erbse).   **ἐφύπερθε δ᾽ ... ἐπηρεφές** 'and on the top the fleece was heavy with its covering of woollen tufts'. ἐπηρεφές is almost pleonastic, as βρίθειν is regularly constructed with the dative.   **ἄωτον** 'the fleece', cf. *Od.* 1.443, 9.434. This noun was much discussed by grammarians (cf. Σ on the *Od.* passages just cited), and Σ on *Il.* 13.599 note the word's polyvalence, cf. Raman 1975.   **λήνεσσιν** 'clumps/tufts of wool', cf. 173, Val. Flacc. 8.122–3 *uillisque comantem ... pellem.*   **ἤλιθα** 'very much, with great intensity', a strong intensive adverb which ancient grammarians connected with ἅλις, cf. 3.342 (with Campbell's n.), Apoll. Soph. 83.26 Bekker. For the meaning 'in vain' cf. 1265n.

178 αἰέν 'with every step'.   **ὑποπρό** occurs only here; the force of the compound preposition is presumably 'under and in front of'.

179–82 Valerius Flaccus compares Jason at this moment to Heracles putting the lionskin over his shoulders for the first time (8.125–6), and some modern critics have found Heracles evoked in the present passage also and drawn harsh conclusions for the presentation of Jason (e.g. Natzel 1992: 95). There is, however, no clear textual signal that we are to think of Heracles at this point (and Valerius' hero is a very different figure).

179 ἐπιειμένος 'letting it fall over', i.e. 'draping it over', a perfect middle participle of ἐφίημι, cf. 3.45. The form could also be from ἐπιέννυμι, i.e. 'dressed in' (cf. *Il.* 15.308), and in this context Ap. may be playing with the ambiguity.

180 Cf. 1348–9.   **ποδηνεκές**: sc. ἄωτον or κῶας, the Fleece.

181 εἷλει 'rolled it up (and carried it)'.   **ἀφασσόμενος**: cf. 184–6. Jason 'strokes' the Fleece, not just because of its powerful attraction, but also because (γάρ) he needs constant tactile reassurance that he really does finally have it and that it has not been stolen.   **ὄφρα ... μή**, rather than simple μή, after a verb of fearing is almost unparalleled, though many purpose clauses themselves imply a sense of fear or precaution, cf., e.g., 1.1293, 3.64.

182 νοσφίσσεται is best understood as a vivid future (Smyth §2229), rather than an aorist subjunctive with short vowel.

183 The typically Hellenistic restriction of the time-indication to less a than full verse (contrast, e.g., *Il.* 8.1, 19.1–2, 24.695) perhaps indicates also the speed of their arrival back at the ship. The coming of dawn shows that the 'hunters' have successfully caught their prey, cf. 109–13n.   ὅμιλον: often used of the crew of Argonauts without a defining genitive, cf. 346, 1.48, 1207 etc.

184–6 The Argonauts' θαῦμα enhances the sense of the Fleece as a marvellous work of art, cf., e.g., *Il.* 18.377, 549 (the shield of Achilles), Theocr. 1.56, Virg. *Aen.* 8.619, 730 (*miratur* frames the description of Aeneas' shield); so too does their desire to touch it, cf. 181, 428–9, 1145–8, Moschus, *Europa* 90–1 (perhaps indebted to this passage), Virg. *Aen.* 8.617–19. Virgil clearly used this passage, as well as Jason's cloak from Book 1, in his description of the shield of Aeneas, cf. 202–5n., Hunter 1993: 187–8, Nelis 2001: 356–9.   στεροπῆι ἴκελον: the hiatus (cf. 1.1027 etc.) imitates archaic practice in which the initial digamma of ἴκελος was still sometimes felt. In Homer such a gleam usually comes from armour and causes fear, cf. *Il.* 10.153–4, 13.339–44, 20.44–6, and the transference from such situations to the erotic and pleasurable gleam of the Fleece is a 'not quite sublime' effect characteristic of Ap.; Hunter 2009: 149–54. Works of art also gleam radiantly, cf. *Il.* 18.492, 510, Virg. *Aen.* 8. 622–3 etc.

187–9 τῶι δ' ἐπί 'over the Fleece'; the preposition follows in 'anastrophe', as frequently in poetry.   κάββαλε: i.e. κατέβαλε (a form impossible in hexameters) with omission ('apocope') of the second syllable of the prefix (cf. ἀνθέμενος immediately below) and subsequent assimilation of consonants; this is a familiar feature of poetic language, cf. 1.1239, 3.1308, K–B I 176–8.   νηγάτεον: almost certainly to be understood as 'new' (cf. 1.775), though sense and etymology in Homer, where it is only used of textiles (*Il.* 2.43, 14.185, *HHAp.* 122 (a φᾶρος)), are uncertain.   ἐνεείσατο 'placed upon', probably an aorist middle of ἐνίζω, or perhaps of transitive ἐνέζω, cf. 3.1186, *Od.* 14.295.   ἀνθέμενος 'lifting [her] on board', LSJ s.v. 1 1b.

190 χάζεσθε: in *Il.* this verb is standardly used of withdrawing or slinking away from the fighting: Jason thus begins (and then continues) as if exhorting his men to combat, rather than to a 'hasty getaway'; the unparalleled use of χάζεσθαι with an infinitive is a syntactic marker of the paradoxical surprise of πάτρηνδε νέεσθαι, which may make us think of speeches such as Agamemnon's deception-speech urging retreat (*Il.* 2.137–41). Ap. and his readers almost certainly knew versions in which the Colchians and the Argonauts did indeed engage in armed fighting before the Greeks made their getaway, cf. Dionys. Scyt. *FGrHist* 32 F10.

191 χρειώ 'object, purpose'.   ἀλεγεινήν 'difficult', 'which has involved ἄλγη'.

192 μοχθίζοντες: the spondaic ending imitates the Argonauts' labourings, cf. 1652, Hunter on Theocr. 1.38. At 1484, μεταμώνια μοχθήσαντες of the Boreads, there is an almost oxymoronic effect ('airy labouring'); see n. ad loc.

193 A second successive *spondeiazon*. **εὐπαλέως** 'successfully', cf. 2.617–18; the adverb is in pointed contrast to the 'laboured' conclusion of the preceding verse. **δήνεσι**: cf. 1n., 3.661n. **κεκράανται**: 3rd sing. perf. pass. from κραίνω 'accomplish'; the lengthening from –ανται to –άανται is borrowed from Homer (*Od.* 4.132, 616).

194 Jason's declaration is echoed, with (for us) a savage irony, by Medea at 1021 (see 1021–2n.). The Homeric model is *Od.* 3.272 (Aegisthus and Clytemnestra), τὴν δ' ἐθέλων ἐθέλουσαν ἀνήγαγεν ὅνδε δόμονδε – not a good omen under which to travel. In a lawful and 'ordinary' Greek marriage, the bride's 'will' would be largely irrelevant, as the marriage would be arranged by her father or other male κύριος, but this is hardly the case here, cf. 87–91n. Moreover, we are invited (long before 1021) to wonder whether Medea could really be described as 'willing', any more than Ariadne had been cf. 1–5, 32–3, 3.997–1004n., Hunter 1987. Whether a woman acting under the power of ἔρως is really responsible for her actions was one of the questions raised by Gorgias in his *Encomium of Helen*. At *Pyth.* 4.250 Pindar says that Jason 'stole' Medea σὺν αὐτᾶι, which the scholia (II 158 Drachmann) gloss as ἑκοῦσαν.

195–6 Just as Medea is the benefactor of 'all Achaea', so soon Jason will declare the fate of 'Hellas' to hang upon the successful completion of their expedition (204–5n., Introduction p. 4). **οἵά τε** 'in as much as [she is the benefactor . . .]'.

197 δὴ γάρ που μάλ' 'For, no doubt . . .' cf. *Il.* 9.40, 21.583, Denniston 257.

198 ὁμάδωι 'with a throng of men'. The basic sense of the noun is 'din, loud inarticulate noise' (cf. 2.1077), and thus it prepares for the comparison of the Colchians to Homer's noisy Trojan masses, cf. 238–40n. Such a suggestion is very appropriate to Jason's patriotic appeal to shared Greek identity.

199–202 'Through the length of the ship half of you – each alternate man – sit and row with your oars, and the other half protect our return by holding out your ox-hide shields as a ready barrier against enemy missiles.' The syntax seems broken ('anacoluthon'), but the sense is clear, and the Argonauts adopt a very similar strategy (in similar language) at 2.1061–72; for a similar syntactic break cf. 1.394–6 and in general K–G II 107. At *Il.*3.211 Zenodotus objected to the 'nominative absolute' ἄμφω δ' ἑζομένω, and there may here be an allusion to that passage; Rengakos 1993:

68–9.   ἀμοιβαδὶς ἀνέρος ἀνήρ 'man alternating with man'. Jason's
stirring polyptoton, ἀνέρος ἀνήρ, again evokes Iliadic combat, cf. *Il.*
13.131 = 16.215.   πηδοῖσιν 'oar blades', a choice alternative for
ἐρετμόν, used only here in *Arg.* and twice in Homer (*Od.* 7.328,
13.78).   δηίων: probably to be understood as the epic trisyllabic form,
but scanned as two long syllables through synizesis of –ιων.   θοόν:
perhaps 'easy to handle, mobile', cf. 1.743 θοὸν σάκος (Aphrodite and
Ares' shield) which Σ gloss as εὐκίνητον καὶ εὐμετάφορον. If Ap. has in
mind *Il.* 14.410 θοάων ἔχματα νηῶν of stones used to prop up ships, then
there is a striking redirection of language.

202–5 Jason's appeal to a shared 'Hellenic' identity is anachronistic (see,
e.g., Thalmann 2011: 122–3), but has been prepared by 195, and contributes to the assimilation of the Argonautic expedition both to the
Greeks' campaign at Troy (cf. Hdt. 1.1.2–3) and to the historical struggles
of Greeks against 'barbarians', notably Persians, for which the Trojan War
had been subsequently shaped as the paradigmatic model (Introduction,
p. 4). As Medea (or her son) had, in some traditions, given their name to
the Medes (Hdt. 7.62.1, Diod. Sic. 4.55.5–7) and both Perse (Circe's
mother) and Perses (Aietes' brother, Diod. Sic. 4.56.1) were prominent
names in her family, the assimilation of the Argonauts' escape with Medea
to the struggle between Greece and Persia is at least tonally complex; see
further Clauss 2000: 27–8. The verses have several Homeric analogues
(cf. *Il.* 15.661–4), but are particularly reminiscent of the report of the
Greek cry at Salamis in Aeschylus' *Persians*, ὦ παῖδες Ἑλλήνων, ἴτε, |
ἐλευθεροῦτε πατρίδ', ἐλευθεροῦτε δέ | παῖδας γυναῖκας θεῶν τε πατρῴων ἕδη |
θήκας τε προγόνων· νῦν ὑπὲρ πάντων ἀγών (*Pers.* 402–5). That passage is also
one argument in favour of Brunck's deletion of δ᾽ in 202, thus producing a
vivid asyndeton.   ἐνὶ χερσί carries more than one resonance. The fate of
Greece is 'in their hands', i.e. depends upon them, but also literally 'leans
upon' (ἐπερείδεται) the strength of their arms; in other contexts the phrase
can imply 'by martial valour', LSJ s.v. χείρ ιι 6f. We might also remember
that what Jason has just had 'in his hands' is the Fleece, and this has
become a talisman for their success and the future of their country, just
as Aeneas, in carrying his shield, is carrying *famamque et fata nepotum*
(*Aen.* 8.731).   ἑούς 'our'; elsewhere this form is used for both first
pers. singular (1.226) and second pers. plural (2.332, 3.267) possessive
pronouns, cf. 3.186n.   γεραρούς 'aged', cf. 1.683.   ἐφορμῆι '<the
success of our> raid, expedition', cf., e.g., Thucyd. 6.90.3 for this
military sense, and probably already 148; again, Jason's language suggests
preparation for an attack, not for escape, cf. 207–8n., Fränkel 1968:
468–9.   κατηφείην 'dejection', in a military context usually implying
the shame of defeat, cf. *Il.* 16.498, 17.556.   ἢ καὶ μέγα κῦδος ἀρέσθαι: καί

gives emphasis to the second alternative as the desired outcome
(Denniston 306), as does the fact that ἀρέσθαι (aor. inf. ἄρνυμαι) is a
much more natural verb with κῦδος than with κατηφείην (a 'zeugma').

206–40 The account of the Argonauts' escape is a principal source for the
description of a painting of the scene at Philostratus Iun., *Imag.* 11; many
of Ap.'s details are reproduced (nn. on 209–10, 213, 219–25).

207 θεσπέσιον μεμαῶτες 'filled with extraordinary enthusiasm', cf. Virg.
Aen. 4.581 *idem omnis simul ardor habet* and see 207–8n.

207–8 The cutting of the cables closely recalls the escape of Odysseus' ship
from the Laistrygonians (*Od.* 10.126–30). Odysseus there reports that he
urged his men to row powerfully 'in order that we might escape disaster';
Jason had spoken more inspiringly of 'winning great glory', but the
Homeric model casts a shadow over his rhetoric. In both cases escape
involves reaching the open sea (225, *Od.* 10.131). When Aeneas repeats
the actions of both Odysseus and Jason, it is to leave Carthage, but without
his 'Medea' (*Aen.* 4.579–80).   **νεώς** is an Attic form very occasionally
transmitted in Homeric manuscripts, including *Od.* 10.127, the model
passage; the normal form in *Arg.* is the epic νηός, which is metrically
impossible here.   **ἀπὸ πείσματ' ἔκοψεν**: this phrase is moved from its
initial position in the Homeric verse (*Od.*10.127); Ap. may have felt that
the separation ('tmesis') of the prefix from the verb was particularly
appropriate to the action described.

209–210 There is a memory of the dramatic close of *Odyssey* 21 when,
just after Odysseus has successfully completed the test of the bow,
Telemachus ἄγχι δ' ἄρ' αὐτοῦ | πὰρ θρόνον ἑστήκει κεκορυθμένος αἴθοπι
χαλκῶι (21.433–4). Philostratus Iun. too (cf. 206–40n.) depicts an armed
Jason standing beside Medea at the stern of the ship (*Imag.*
11.1).   **παρθενικῆς**: Medea's virginity is important to her status as
Jason's 'bride' (194–5).   **ἰθυντῆρι | Ἀγκαίωι**: cf. 1260 ἰθυντὴρ Ἀγκαῖος
in initial verse-position; the noun occurs nowhere else in *Arg.*, and the
variation of a 'formula' is typical for the Hellenistic epic.   **νηῦς** is
scanned as a single syllable ('synizesis'), cf. 226.

212–35 We are probably to understand that the Colchian discovery
came with the dawn of 183. Aietes' discovery of what has happened
and his threats of revenge were the starting point for Callimachus'
account of the rite at Anaphe in the *Aitia*, cf. fr.7.19–34, Introduction
p. 22. There is clearly a relationship between the poets here (see nn.
on 213, 229, 231–5); that Ap. is the 'borrower' is perhaps suggested
by the fact that Callimachus' narrative also seems to be echoed in
Book 3 (3.581–2n.).

213 περίπυστος occurs first here. It is used of the dream at the beginning of Callimachus' *Aitia* in an anonymous epigram (*AP* 7.42.1), and perhaps Callimachus himself had used the word. Philostratus Iun. (206–40n.) notes that Medea's deeds had become ἀνάπυστα τοῖς Κόλχοις καὶ τῶι Αἰήτηι (*Imag.* 11.1).   **ἔρως καὶ ἔργ'**: almost a hendiadys, 'the deeds caused by Medea's love'. The hiatus of καὶ ἔργ' imitates archaic epic in which the initial digamma of ἔργον is often felt. Callimachus' narrative is here very similar: ὁ δ' [sc. Αἰήτης] ὡς ἴδεν ἔργα θυγατρός, fr. 7.27.

214–19 A double simile shows the poet struggling to find the right way to convey the numberlessness of the Colchians (for which cf. 2.1205, 3.212 etc.). Virgil closely reworked this passage to describe the numberless ghosts in the Underworld (*Aen.* 6.309–12); he, like many moderns, may have read Apollonius' Colchis as a kind of Underworld (Hunter 1993: 185–6, Nelis 2001: 251–2). Bacchylides had compared the souls of the dead 'beside the streams of Cocytus' (cf. 218) to leaves in the forests of Ida (5.63–7), and this resonance gives particular point to Aietes' link to Helios (220–1): he really is a sun shining in the Underworld (cf. *Od.* 12.383). So too, the noise (κλαγγή) of the Colchians may evoke *inter alia* (219n.) the din of the numberless dead (cf. *Od.* 11.605 κλαγγὴ νεκύων ἦν οἰωνῶν ὥς). The comparison of numberless cattle to clouds driven by the winds at [Theocr.] 25.88–95 may be related to this passage (κορύσσεται in 94).

In 214–18 there is only one spondee (making the emphatic *spondeiazon* of 217); the dactylic rhythm indicates speed and number. The heavy (and unmusical) spondaic opening of 219, κλαγγῆι μαιμώοντες, thus comes with special force.

214 The first half of the verse, the *figura etymologica* ἐς δ' ἀγορὴν ἀγέροντ', repeats *Il.* 18.245 of the Trojans, thus preparing for the comparison of the two armies (nn. on 219, 238–40).

215 Assemblies are compared to countless waves at *Il.* 2.144–6 (part, as here, of a double simile), and the advance of the Greek army is compared to massed waves at *Il.* 4.422–6.   **κορύσσεται** 'rise to a peak', cf. 448, 2.71 where Σ gloss the verb as μετεωριζόμενον.

216–17 Leaves are a traditional marker of great numbers, cf. *Il.* 2.468, 800, 6.146–8 (note χαμάδις in 147), but Pollux 1.231 ascribes φυλλοχόος μήν to Hesiod (fr. 333), and φυλλοχόος μείς occurs at Call. *Hecale* fr. 69.12 H (= fr. 260.12 Pf.), where the falling leaves in that month *do not* equal the leaves with which Theseus was celebrated; Ap. may have borrowed from Callimachus here, but in any case there is a thick literary texture behind the simile.   **τεκμήραιτο** 'reckon, make an estimate of the number'. The parenthetic question, and the spondaic rhythm (214–19n.), draw sudden attention to the narrator within a multiple simile, which is very often a marked site of authorial self-consciousness (Hunter 1993: 129–38, 2006: ch. 3), and where the sense of earlier texts is palpable (previous n.).

218 ἀπειρέσιοι: the vast numbers of the Colchians is a recurrent motif, cf. 2.1205, 3.1239.

219 κλαγγῆι μαιμώοντες lit. 'raging with a din', i.e. 'shouting and raging'. At *Il.* 3.2–5 the noise of the massed Trojans is compared to that of cranes, and κλαγγή appears three times in four verses; here too the barbarians are opposed to the outnumbered Greeks who silently slip away. See further 238–40n.

219–25 The description of Aietes picks up and varies that at 3.1225–45, where he drives out to watch Jason's struggle with the bulls and the sown warriors. The concern for linguistic and thematic variation between the passages distinguishes the Hellenistic epic from its Homeric models. Aietes in his chariot is a major part of the description at Philostratus Iun., *Imag.* 11 (cf. 206–40n.).

219 εὐτύκτωι ἐνὶ δίφρωι varies εὐπηγέα δίφρον at 3.1235.

220–1 Horses were Helios' most famous attribute, and Aietes' possession of some of these reinforces the sense of the king as 'Helios on earth'. The gift of the horses varies the motif of 3.1226–7, Ares' gift to Aietes of a breastplate.

222 δινωτόν: probably 'decorated', 'carefully worked', cf. *Il.* 13.406–7 ῥινοῖσι βοῶν καὶ νώροπι χαλκῶι | δινωτήν of a shield; in the parallel passage at 3.1231 Aietes carries a πολύρρινον ... σάκος, and so, with a very sophisticated mimetic technique, both passages may pick up different elements of the same Homeric model. At 3.44 Aphrodite's chair is δινωτός, 'embossed' (cf. *Il.* 3.391). The word is normally understood here as 'round' on the basis of the bT-scholia on *Il.* 13.407 which gloss the term as περιφερῆ.

223–4 Aietes represents the same 'monstrous' threat as the dragon, cf. 127 ~ 223–4, 129 (πελώριον) ~ 224.   **πεύκην**: at an earlier Colchian assembly, Aietes had threatened to burn the *Argo* and its crew, once the bulls had killed Jason, 3.581–2.   **τετάνυστο** 'lay stretched out', the pluperfect passive of τανύω, varying τείνετο of the dragon in 127.   **πελώριον**: at 3.1232 the spear was δεινὸν ἀμαιμάκετον.

225 In the parallel passage in Book 3, Apsyrtos is called by his nickname Phaethon (3.1236), thus accentuating the connection between his father and Helios (cf. 3.242–6n.). In a further variation, Aietes himself took the reins in Book 3.   **γέντο** 'grasped', i.e. ἔλαβε, a standard meaning for this athematic aorist in Homer; see 3.1321–2n., Hopkinson on Call.

h.6.43. The current passage evokes scenes such as *Il.* 8.42–3 = 13.25–6, Zeus and Poseidon grasp (γέντο) a golden, well-fashioned (εὔτυκτον) whip and mount their chariots; at 3.1240–5 Aietes in his chariot is compared to Poseidon.   ὑπεκπρό: the force of the compound seems to be 'away from and in front [of them]'.

227 καταβλώσκοντι: the river flows 'down' into the Black Sea.

228 ἄτηι πολυπήμονι: Aietes' 'grievous disaster' is the loss of the Fleece and his daughter at the hands of those to whom he had offered hospitality.

229 If we are to think of a particular title for Zeus in this context, it may be ἐπόψιος, cf. 2.1123, 1133, 1179, Call. *fr.* 85.14–15 with Harder 2012: 2.709. Callimachus' king calls upon Helios and the Phasis (fr. 7.33–4).   ἐπιμάρτυρας: this third declension compound noun is post-Homeric (though Zenodotus read μάρτυρες for μάρτυροι in Homer), and so some editors read ἐπὶ μάρτυρας here, with the prefix in tmesis with κέκλετο, as is perhaps implied in the scholiastic gloss, μάρτυρας τῶν πεπραγμένων ἐπεκαλεῖτο; see, however, Campbell 1971: 418–19, Harder 2012: 2.629–30.

231–5 'If they did not bring him his daughter, capturing her with all speed, having found her either on land or the boat still on the swell of the navigable sea, and he did not satisfy his anger in his yearning to take revenge for all these things, they would learn at the cost of their lives the full weight of his anger and of the disaster which had befallen him, when they took these upon themselves.' Aietes' barely coherent but explosive threats (Campbell 1971: 419) are expressed through striking changes of syntax and in the indirect speech which marks the bluster and deviousness of the tyrant, cf. 3.579–605n., Hunter 1993: 147–8. In Callimachus, Aietes is given a direct speech (fr. 7.29–34).

231 Three opening spondees and a hiatus in the fifth foot introduce the harsh unmusicality of Aietes' threats.   αὐτάγρετον: one gloss for this Homeric *hapax* at *Od.* 16.148 is παραυτὰ ἀγρευόμενα, and 'caught immediately' would be appropriate here (tyrants want their orders carried out on the spot, cf. 236–8). At 2.326 the meaning must be 'brought on by oneself', and such semantic variety is a familiar feature of Ap.'s deployment of Homeric glosses (Rengakos 1994: 61–2).

232 The harsh change of object from 'her' (Medea) to 'the boat' and the forced word order are marks of Aietes' emotion.   πλωτῆς 'navigable' of the sea seems to lack point, and Campbell's πλωτήν 'floating' of the ship deserves consideration.

233 is marked by a harsh change of subject from 'the Colchians' to 'Aietes'. The verbs, like δαήσονται in 234, are vivid futures.

234–5 Sense and construction are difficult. The translation above takes χόλον and ἄτην as objects of δαήσονται, but the nouns may also be taken with ὑποδέγμενοι, 'taking on themselves the full weight of his anger', with δαήσονται used absolutely, 'they would learn a lesson'.   **κεφαλῆισιν** 'with their lives', LSJ s.v. I 3, *OLD* s.v. *caput* 4.   ἄτην closes a ring around the description of Aietes' threats (cf. 228) and the repetition perhaps suggests (again) the bullying tyrant.

236–8 The repeated 'on that very day' marks the speed with which the Colchians obey, cf. 231n.   **νηυσί** is scanned as two syllables with synizesis. The repetition after νῆας seems inelegant and Fränkel thought the verse corrupt; similar repetitions occur in Homer (Campbell 1971: 420), but Ap. has imitated and varied the language of Hes. *WD* 808 (ταμεῖν) νήϊά τε ξύλα πολλά, τά τ᾽ ἄρμενα νηυσὶ πέλονται.   **ἀνήϊον** 'were proceeding (on the open sea)'; the use of ἄνειμι in this sense is hard to parallel.

238–40 'You would not say that it was so great a naval expedition, but a vast family of birds clamouring over the seas in flocks.' **οὐδέ κε φαίης** is a Homeric form (cf. *Il.* 3.392–4, 17.366–9), but again Ap. places a marker of literary self-consciousness within a quasi-simile, cf. 216–17n., Byre 1991: 221–2, Hunter 1993: 132–3. The specific models are *Il.* 4.429–31 (the silent advance of the Greeks), οὐδέ κε φαίης | τόσσον λαὸν ἕπεσθαι κτλ., although the noise (ἐπιβρομέειν) makes us rather think of the Trojans (compared to bleating sheep immediately after, *Il.* 4.433–8), and *Il.* 2.459–65, the massed Greek army compared to ὀρνίθων πετεηνῶν ἔθνεα πολλά. Virgil imitated this potential form and this particular image at *Aen.* 7.703–5, *nec quisquam aerates acies examine tanto* | *misceri putet, aeriam sed gurgite ab alto* | *urgeri uolucrum raucarum ad litora nubem*, cf. 1300–2n., Lucan, *BC* 9.34–5.   **νηίτην στόλον**: a prosaic phrase to highlight the poetic flavour of the quasi-simile which follows: the sight was so impressive that it would make you speak like a poet.   **ἰλαδόν**: in Homer only at *Il.* 2.93 as the ἔθνεα πολλά of the Greeks rush to assembly like swarms of bees; the echo of that passage allows the poet to activate the memory of a second simile to describe numberless and noisy Colchians (*Il.* 2.96–8, cf. ἐπιβρομέειν).

241 λαιψηρά: adverbial, a variation of the Homeric λιγέων ἀνέμων λαιψηρά κέλευθα (*Il.* 14.17, 15.620).

242–3 are a careful variation of 3.1134–6, ὡς γὰρ τόδε μήδετο Ἥρη, | ὄφρα κακὸν Πελίηι ἱερὴν ἐς Ἰωλκὸν ἵκηται | Αἰαίη Μήδεια, λιποῦσ᾽ ἄπο πατρίδα γαῖαν. Both passages have a striking resemblance to a phrase in Pherecydes' summary of the story (*FGrHist* 3 F105) 'Hera put these things into Jason's mind, so that Medea might come as an evil for Pelias (ὡς ἔλθοι ἡ Μήδεια τῶι Πελίαι κακόν)'.   **Αἰαίη**: Ap. may wish to evoke a connection with the exclamation αἰαῖ, cf. 3.1133–6n.　　**Πελασγίδα**: i.e. Thessalian, from an eponymous Pelasgos, king of Thessaly, cf. 1.14, 906, 3.1323.

244–5 The Halys (mod. Kızıl Irmak) flows into the Black Sea east of Sinope, cf. 2.946–61, Delage 1930: 168–9; Strabo 12.3.12 says that the river takes its name from the salt-works (ἁλαί) alongside it. The direct distance across open sea from the mouth of the Phasis is some 300 miles, and on the outward voyage this had taken some five days; Hera makes the *Argo* travel very quickly, if not in fact supernaturally so (Casson 1971: 281–8).　　**Παφλαγόνων**: Strabo 12.3.9 makes the Halys the eastern boundary of the land of the Paphlagonians (cf. Hdt. 1.6.1); see further Delage 1930: 165–6.

246–7 ἡ γάρ: Medea, as Σ feel compelled to explain. Platt suggested τῆι 'there', but the verb requires a subject.　　ἀρέσσασθαι 'to appease, conciliate' (aor. mid. inf. of ἀρέσκομαι); Hecate must be thanked for her help.　　ἠνώγει Ἑκάτην: the hiatus imitates archaic epic; Ἑκάτη very likely began originally with a digamma.

247–8 'All that the maiden accomplished to prepare the sacrifice … '. The better attested θυηλῆι would yield ' … to prepare *for* the sacrifice'.　　πορσανέουσα: probably to be understood as a future implying purpose, cf. 3.1124, 1129, *Il.* 3.411. In a similar context at 2.719 πορσαίνοντες is 'honouring'.

248–50 For the poet's 'pious' refusal to reveal cultic secrets cf. 1.921 (rites on Samothrace), *HHDem.* 478–9. Particularly close to the present passage is Call. fr. 75.4–7, Ἥρην γάρ κοτέ φασι – κύον, κύον, ἴσχεο, λαιδρέ | θυμέ, σύ γ' ἀείσηι καὶ τά περ οὐχ ὁσίη· | ὤναο κάρτ' ἕνεκ' οὔ τι θεῆς ἴδες ἱερὰ φρικτῆς, | ἐξ ἂν ἐπεὶ καὶ τῶν ἤρυγες ἱστορίην. In both passages the poet amusingly divorces himself from his θυμός, dread rites are involved (and φρικτή might well make one think of Hecate rather than Demeter), and ἴστωρ and ἱστορίη are obviously very close; the two passages may well be related (Hunter 2008b: 119–21).　　ἴστωρ: lit. 'a knower', though Callimachus (above) makes it tempting to hear also 'a researcher, enquirer'.　　θυμός ἐποτρύνειεν: cf. *Od.* 8.45 (god allowed Demodocus to give pleasure) ὅππηι θυμὸς ἐποτρύνηισιν ἀείδειν; that the choice of song is a matter of the θυμός is a very traditional idea, cf. further Call. *h.* 4.1, Gow on Theocr. 30.11, Harder 2012: 2.587.　　ἅζομαι αὐδῆσαι: cf. Pind. *Nem.* 5.14 αἰδέομαι μέγα εἰπεῖν ἐν δίκαι τε μὴ κεκινδυνευμένον (the murder of Phokos by Peleus and Telamon), Morrison 2007: 283, 302.

250–2 The aetiology of a visible monument takes the place of divulging what must not be divulged and 'proves' the correctness of the poet's narrative; for ἐξέτι κείνου as an aetiological marker cf. 2.782, Call. *h.* 2.47,

4.275. In 251 ὅ and the second syllable of ἐπί are lengthened before initial ῥ- in imitation of Homeric practice.   γε μήν marks an opposition to what has preceded: 'I cannot tell you the rites, *but* the shrine…', cf. 277, Denniston 348, Cuypers 2005: 49.   ἕδος: it is unclear whether we are to think of a temple or just a marked sanctuary; the scholia report that Nymphis of Heraclea, probably an older contemporary of Ap. and an important source for *Arg.*, also reported that Medea founded a ἱερόν of Hecate in Paphlagonia (*FGrHist* 432 F8).   καὶ τῆμος ἰδέσθαι 'to be seen (*lit.* for the seeing) even today'. τῆμος is normally 'then, at that time', but here it must be 'now', cf. ἔτι νῦν περ in a closely analogous passage at 1.1061. This sense is found on a third-century Thessalian inscription (*IG* IX 517.44) and perhaps at Call. fr. 781; Koechly's τηλόσ' (cf. 2.807) is adopted by Fränkel, but is unconvincing.

253 αὐτίκα: we might see here the workings of Hecate in response to the honour they have paid her, but as often in *Arg.* the exact reference of this temporal adverb is rather vague, cf. 580.   ὧλλοι: an Ionic form, transmitted a number of times in *Arg.*, and read by Zenodotus at *Il.* 2.1 and 10.1 for ἄλλοι (Rengakos 1993: 53–5).

254 Cf. 2.421–2 (Phineus speaks) δαίμων ἕτερον πλόον ἡγεμονεύσει | ἐξ Αἴης. On the Argonauts' return itinerary see Introduction, pp. 7–14.

255 ἀνώιστος 'unknown, unable to be grasped'. Elsewhere in *Arg.* the sense is 'unexpected', cf. 1.680, 3.770, Rengakos 1994: 52–3.

257–93 Argos' speech forms a counterpart and contrast to Phineus' instructions for the outward voyage in Book 2 (Fantuzzi–Hunter 2004: 124–5). Whereas the prophet Phineus spoke (paradoxically) about geographical realities in the dry factual language of a *periplous*, Argos speaks in a mystical, almost inspired, manner about distant times, a world which has long been superseded, and offers the Argonauts a route founded as much in imagination as in topographical reality, cf. further Pearson 1938: 455–7. Moreover, Argos' speech distinguishes itself for its stylistic elaboration, which includes some seven *spondeiazontes*, nearly 20%, against 8% for *Arg.* overall. An important source for elements of this speech was all but certainly the Egyptian history of Hecataeus of Abdera, written in the reign of Ptolemy Soter, see notes on 262–3, 272–6, Murray 1970, Fraser 1972: I 496–505, Stephens 2003: 32–6; much of our knowledge of Hecataeus comes from Diodorus Siculus 1, for which Hecataeus was the principal source. For Virgil's use of this speech at *Aen.* 3.102–20 see Hunter 1991b: 94–9.

257–8 'We were travelling to Orchomenos, along the route which that truth-telling prophet whom you met not long ago prophesied to you'. The text is uncertain, but the necessary sense seems clear. The Argonauts need another route, and Argos knows of one from having lived in Colchis; this was the route (so we are to understand) by which Sesostris (272–6n.), using sacred Egyptian knowledge, reached the Black Sea and which Argos and his brothers were taking in order to reach Greece, when they were persuaded to join the Argonauts (note γάρ in 259). The verb in 257 must therefore be imperfect, and imperfect νίσσετο occurs at 1.741, 785, 2.824. Argos' opening words vary his explanation at 2.1153, νεύμεθ' ἐς Ὀρχομενόν κτλ., 'we *are* travelling to Orchomenos … '. The opening is however rather abrupt, and as Σ gloss his words with 'Travel in fact by the most inland route, by which we too were travelling to Orchomenos', Fränkel suggested that a verse was lost before 257.   νισόμεθ' Ὀρχομενόν: the accusative of motion towards without a preposition is common in poetry. Ap. seems to have in mind *Il.* 9.381–2 (Achilles rejecting gifts) οὐδ' ὅσ' ἐς Ὀρχομενόν ποτινίσεται, οὐδ' ὅσα Θήβας | Αἰγυπτίας, cf. 260 below.   τήν: sc. ὁδόν.

259–60 Egypt, and particularly Egyptian priests, had long been regarded as preservers of the most ancient traditions, cf. Hdt. 2, Pl. *Tim.* 21e–5d (the Nile protects Egypt from the periodic destructions of the world by fire or flood), Dio 11.37–8 (a parody of the motif), Vasunia 2001; Hecataeus of Abdera, like Herodotus before him (2.3, 54, 143), certainly used Theban priests among his sources. The scholia on these verses adduce many writers who claimed that life began in Egypt (cf. Diod. Sic. 1.9–10) and that Thebes was the first city; the antiquity of Egypt must have particularly impressed itself on the Greek inhabitants of the very new city of Alexandria.   Θήβης Τριτωνίδος 'Thebe, daughter of Triton', the eponymous heroine nymph of Egyptian Thebes; for Triton as a name for the Nile cf. 269. Why Greeks called the Egyptian city Thebes remains a puzzle (Lloyd 1976: 12–13, S. West on *Od.* 4.125–7), but the bT-scholia on *Il.* 9.383c also derive the name from 'a daughter of the Nile or Asopus or Proteus'. From a Greek perspective the inhabitants of Thebes are all 'descendants of Thebe'.

261 ἦν or some such verb must be understood; τά τ' introduces a relative clause, as regularly in Homer. An echo of *Il.* 18.485 (the Shield of Achilles), ἐν δὲ τὰ τείρεα πάντα, τά τ' οὐρανὸς ἐστεφάνωται, reinforces the point that we are before the completion of the cosmos, of which Achilles' shield was taken as an image (Hardie 1985). We are of course also a very long time before Homer and his world.   τείρεα 'constellations'.

262–3 'The sacred race of the Danaans' evokes the legend of the eponymous Danaos' move from Egypt to Argos: civilization moved outwards from Egypt to fill the rest of the world, and this was clearly

a key tenet of Hecataeus of Abdera's *Aigyptiaka*. πευθομένοις
suggests, somewhat anachronistically, the spirit of Herodotean or
Hellenistic enquiry.

263–4 The repetition ('epanalepsis') of Ἀρκάδες suggests an emotional
evocation of a legendary people. It may be relevant that the historian
Douris (*FGrHist* 76 F9) recorded a tradition of one Arkas, son of
Orchomenos, who must be the eponymous hero of the Arcadian city of
that name; that Argos comes from Boeotian Orchomenos perhaps suggests that he is being given some special connection to Arcadians, through
a mythological play with names. Ap. is fond of such repetitions of names
across verse-divisions, in imitation of a few famous Homeric examples,
cf. 764–5, 827–8, 1.87–8, 191–2, 3.1093–4, Wills 1996: 128–30, Hunter
2003a: 355–6. Dion. Perieg. 415 borrows Ἀρκάδες Ἀπιδανῆες from this
passage and combines it with a reworking of Call. *h.* 1.14–27 (Zeus's
birth and the rivers of Arcadia); he may, perhaps rightly, have seen a
connection between the two passages – the Arcadians are Ἀπιδανῆες in
line 14 of the Callimachean hymn and we are again dealing with pre-
history (οὔπω, 18). In view of the possibility of a play with 'Orchomenos', it
is curious that one of Callimachus' Arcadian rivers is the otherwise unattested Melas (line 23), which is also the name of one of Argos' brothers
(2.1156).   Ἀπιδανῆες: Ἀπία or Ἀπίς (cf. 1564n.) was believed to be
an ancient name for the Peloponnese, cf. Aesch. *Suppl.* 260, *Ag.*
256.   πρόσθε σεληναίης: that the autochthonous Arcadians lived 'before
the moon' is a tradition found from the fourth century (Eudoxus fr. 315
Lasserre, Arist. fr. 608 Gigon, Pfeiffer on Call. fr. 191.56) and perhaps
earlier (Ar. *Clouds* 398, fr. 878K–A).   ὑδέονται 'are reported', a favourite verb in such contexts with Hellenistic poets, cf. 2.528 (another passage
with close links to Callimachus), Arat. *Phain.* 257, Call. frr. 371–2 etc. If
Ap. has a particular source in mind, and the epanalepsis makes that not
unlikely, then ὑδέονται will be an 'Alexandrian footnote' of the type
discussed by Hinds 1998: 1–5, cf. 272, Harder 2012: 2.586.

265 φηγόν: acorns, traditionally primitive fare, were often associated
with the life of the 'prelunar' Arcadians, cf. Hdt. 1.66.2, Aelian, *VH*
3.39.   Πελασγίς: cf. 242–3n.

266 Deucalion was the great founder who re-established civilization after
the flood (3.1087–9n.). Jason had described him to Medea as 'he who first
made cities and built temples to the immortals and who first ruled over
men' (3.1088–9), but however economical with the truth Jason is in that
speech, his eye is very firmly on Greek civilization and there is no conflict
with the primacy of Egypt asserted here; the primitive Arcadians in any
case had no cities or temples.

267–70 'at the time when Egypt, mother of men born in earlier time, was called Eerie, rich in crops, and the broad-flowing river by which the whole of Eerie is watered <was called> Triton'. Successive *spondeiazontes* in 267–8 add a modern style to Argos' memory of a time very long ago.   **Ἠερίη**: probably 'land of mists' (with reference to the Nile valley) rather than 'land of the morning', cf. Aesch. *Suppl.* 75. Argos moves from Thessaly to Egypt and at 1.580 Thessaly had been called ἠερίη πολυλήϊος αἶα Πελασγῶν; in describing the new-old land of Egypt, Greeks 'naturally' reapplied names and descriptions from their own homelands (see further Stephens 2003: 206–8).   **πολυλήϊος**: the fertility of Egypt due to the Nile flood was very familiar to Greeks (Hunter 2003b: 156–7).   **ἐκλήϊστο** 'was celebrated as', a pluperfect passive of κληΐζω. The verb must also be understood in 269.   **Αἴγυπτος**: in Homer this was the name of both country and river (*Od.* 4.477, 581, 14.258), and so here we are dealing with a time 'two names before' Νεῖλος. The juxtaposition to Τρίτων calls attention to the play with names, cf. Lyc. *Alex.* 576 Αἰγύπτιον Τρίτωνος ... ποτόν; there is a related play at Theocr. 17.79–80 (Hunter 2003b: 157). As a name for the Nile, Triton also occurs at Lyc. *Alex.* 119, Hermippos of Smyrna fr. 103 Wehrli, Plin. *HN* 5.54; see Priestley 2014: 126–7. Rivers and name-changes were two of Callimachus' interests – known titles include 'Foundations of islands and cities and their changes of name', 'On the rivers of Europe', and 'On the name-changes of fish' – and this is another sign of a thick literary texture here.   **εὐρύρροος**: Meineke's emendation mends the metre and produces both an attractive variation on ἐυρρείτην of Egypt at *Od.* 14.257–8, where Αἴγυπτος is used in successive verses of the country and then the river, and another connection between the Nile and the 'broad' Istros (cf. 284n.).

269–78 Scraps of the beginnings of these verses are preserved in a fragment of an early seventh-century codex (Π⁷).

270–1 The rainlessness of Egypt was another very familiar fact about the country, cf. Eur. *Hel.* 1–3, Hdt. 2.13.3 (ὕεται πᾶσα ἡ χώρη τῶν Ἑλλήνων, ἀλλ' οὐ ποταμοῖσι ἄρδεται, in contrast to Egypt), Isocrates, *Busiris* 13–14 etc.   **ἅλις** 'in great quantities'. Σ notes that this could be taken with either what precedes (as in the parenthesis adopted here) or what follows. Writers about Egypt differed as to whether it received no rain at all (Hdt. 2.22.3) or just very little or some in the north but none in the south (Diod. Sic. 1.10.4). If ἅλις is taken with what follows (cf. *Il.* 14.122 ἅλις ... ἄρουραι | πυροφόροι), it will be best then to read προχοῇσιν [δ'] in a vivid asyndeton, as δέ can hardly stand in third position in its clause in such a style.   **προχοῇσι** 'because of [the river's] streams', cf. 132n. A possible alternative is 'in its channels', i.e. what were the river's channels during the flood become fields of grain, thanks to the fertile river mud. ἀνασταχύουσιν ἄρουραι 'the fields sprout up with grain', a grammatical variation of ἀνασταχύεσκον ἄρουραν of the Earthborn at 3.1354; συνασταχύοιεν ἄρουραι ends a hexameter at Arat. *Phain.* 1050.

272-6 Argos knows by report (φασι, another 'Alexandrian footnote', 263-4n.) of a great world-conqueror from Egypt; that he does not know the name adds to the sense of memories from the mists of time. As the scholiast already realized, this is Sesoosis or Sesostris or Sesonchosis whose deeds are reported at length by Hdt. 2.102-10 (on the explicit authority of Egyptian priests), and cf. also Diod. Sic. 1.53-8, following Hecataeus of Abdera. The legends of this pharaoh combined memories of more than one king of the XIIth dynasty (*c.* 1991-1786 BC) with later conquerors, notably Ramesses II, and were elaborated both to fashion a picture of the ideal ruler and as a weapon for nationalist propaganda against (particularly) the Persians,; see Murray 1970: 162-4, Lloyd 1976: 16-18, Ivantchik 1999, Stephens 2003: 34-6. As a world conqueror and civilizer, Sesostris looks back to the model of Osiris/Dionysus (cf. Diod. Sic. 1.17-20) and forwards to Alexander and then the Ptolemies; he thus straddles the human and the divine, as was becoming increasingly common in the image of Hellenistic kings.

272 At 2.103.1 Herodotus traces Sesostris' passage 'from Asia into Europe' (cf. Diod. Sic. 1.55.6). The might of Sesostris' army is stressed also in Diodorus' account (from Hecataeus), cf. 1.54. 4: 'He chose men who were outstanding in strength and he put together an army which was worthy of the greatness of his undertaking. He enlisted 600,000 footsoldiers, 24,000 cavalry and 27,000 war-chariots.'

274-5 Herodotus and Diodorus stress Sesostris' role as a builder and lawgiver in Egypt (Hdt. 2.108, Diod. Sic. 1.56-7, cf. Dicaearchus fr. 57 Wehrli, Arist. *Pol.* 7.1329b2), but as a founder of cities all over the world Sesostris is following both the specific pattern of Isis (e.g. Totti 4.13) and Osiris (Diod. Sic. 1.27.5) and a more general tradition of Egypt as a colonizing power (Diod. Sic. 1.28, 'the Egyptians say ... that very many colonies were spread out from Egypt over the inhabited world'). He also foreshadows the greatest founder of cities the Greek world had ever known, Alexander; Plutarch credits Alexander with the foundation of more than seventy cities (*Mor.* 328e), Bosworth 1988: 245-50.   ἄστη: elsewhere Ap. uses ἄστεα, but the contracted form is useful at verse-end. At Diod. Sic. 1.28.4 (from Hecataeus?) the Athenian use of ἄστυ is for the Egyptians a proof that the Athenians were colonists from Egypt, where there was a city called Astu. Ap.'s choice of word in 274 may therefore be a significant one.   νάσσατ' 'he founded', aor. mid. of ναίω.   **ναιετάουσιν** 'are inhabited', a standard meaning of the verb in Homer; νάσσατ'… ναιετάουσιν form an etymological and assonantal frame around the verse.

276 These verses will have had particular point and wit for those reading them in Alexander's most famous (new) foundation, Alexandria. Herodotus had noted that most of Sesostris' monuments are no longer to be seen (2.106.1, cf. 279–81n.), but Argos adduces the passage of time as a confirmation of his account: he has no accurate knowledge (how could he?), and the disappearance of cities is no counter-argument.   **ἄδην**: an adverbial intensifier with πουλύς, 'very much'. Σ report that Dicaearchus (fr. 58 Wehrli) dated Sesostris some 2,500 years before the sack of Troy, whereas Herodotus places him two kings before that war; for Aristotle he was 'far earlier in time' than Minos (*Pol.* 7.1329b24), see Ivantchik 1999.   **ἐπενήνοθεν**: a pluperfect which the scholia on *Il.* 2.219 connect with θέω, 'run'. The use of such a rare gloss (only here in *Arg.*, and clearly a puzzle to ancient grammarians) reinforces the sense of the passing of unfathomable time: the verb is as 'distant' as the time of which Argos speaks. See further Ardizzoni on 1.664.

277–8 The ring of Αἶα … Αἶαν emphasizes the enduring nature of that land.   **γε μήν**: cf. 250–2n.   † **ὅγε**: correction to ὅς γε would be very easy, but that combination does not appear in either Homer or *Arg.*   **καθίσσατο ναιέμεν Αἶαν** 'settled [aor. mid. καθίζω] to dwell in Aia'. That the Colchians were descended from members of Sesostris' army whom he settled there was generally accepted since Herodotus' account at 2.103–5 (cf. Diod. Sic. 1.55.4–5, Pfeiffer on Call. fr. 672).

279–81 The Colchians preserve from Sesostris' time engraved tablets showing routes around the world. It is often thought that this fancy derives from Herodotus' account of how Sesostris set up *stêlai* all over the world declaring his victories (2.102, cf. Diod. Sic. 1.55.7–8). Egypt was standardly identified as the birthplace of writing (e.g. Pl. *Phdr.* 274c5–5b2), and a written, inscribed record is fundamental both to the legends of Sesostris and to the Greek perception of Egyptian culture.   **γραπτῦς**: at the word's only appearance in Homer, γραπτῦς are 'scratches (from thorns)' against which the aged Laertes guards (*Od.* 24.229), and 'the scratches of their fathers' might precisely evoke the famous scene of Odysseus and his father; the maps or 'writings' to which Argos refers may well have been 'scratched' on metal. This rare form was also used by Eratosthenes in the *Hermes* (*SH* 397.11.2), and it may be that Hellenistic poets liked a form which defamiliarized something now as everyday as writing.   **ἕθεν**: this poetic and dialectal genitive (here plural) of the third-person pronoun is another archaizing touch in

Argos' speech.   κύρβιας is in apposition to γραπτῦς. At Athens κύρβεις were tablets erected in pyramids (ἄξονες) on which laws were inscribed, and this is another lexical rarity in Argos' speech. It is natural for us to think of the γῆς περίοδος engraved on a πίναξ of Herodotus' famous story of Aristagoras (5.49.5).   πείρατ' are probably 'conditions, circumstances of/rules for a journey', rather than 'boundaries', cf. 1201, 1.413 (Apollo showed Jason ἄνυσιν καὶ πείραθ' ὁδοῖο), 2.310; cf. perhaps the similar use of μέτρα (West on Hes. *WD* 648). If this is correct, then the tablets presumably contained writing (? hieroglyphics) as well as maps. The verse recalls the Hesiodic πάντων πηγαὶ καὶ πείρατ' ἔασιν (*Theog.* 738, 809), see Clare 2002: 130–1.   ὑγρῆς τε τραφερῆς τε πέριξ: a variation on the Homeric ἐπὶ τραφερήν τε καὶ ὑγρήν [sc. γῆν], cf. *Il.* 14.308 (with Janko's note).

282–93 Argos describes a route along the imagined path of the Istros (Danube); see Introduction, pp. 9–10. The notion that the Istros/Danube flowed not west-east (as Herodotus correctly believed), but north-south before splitting into parts, one of which emptied (as the Danube does) into the Black Sea and the other into the Adriatic (see Map), was familiar in the fourth century (cf., e.g., Arist. *HA* 7.598b17, Berger 1880: 347–50, Delage 1930: 202–3, Żmudziński 1999) and perhaps earlier (cf. Aesch. fr. 197R). Strabo 1.2.39 explicitly dismisses the idea in connection with the Argonauts.

282 ἔστι δέ τις: a standard opening in geographical descriptions, cf. 3.927–31n., *Il.* 2.811, 11.711 etc. Here the first half of the verse picks up Nestor's speech at *Il.* 11.721 ἔστι δέ τις ποταμός κτλ.   ὕπατον κέρας Ὠκεανοῖο 'most northerly branch of Ocean', or perhaps just 'most remote branch of Ocean'. All rivers are to some extent 'branches of Ocean' (cf. *Il.* 21.195–7), and so there is no real contradiction with 286–7 or need to imagine, as some commentators have done, a system of underground channels connecting the Istros to Ocean; the phrase adds to the mystery and remoteness of the journey. We may, however, momentarily be misled into thinking that Argos will propose a return for the Argonauts via Ocean, as indeed was the case in some versions (Introduction, p. 8).

283 lit. 'broad and very deep for crossing even for a trading vessel'. The river will accommodate even a laden cargo-ship, as we know the eastern reaches of the Danube actually did.

284 'They [i.e. Sesostris' army ?] have traced [its course] to a great distance, giving it the name Istros'. Herodotus (2.33.2, 4.50.1) explicitly compares the Nile and the Istros, which he calls 'the greatest of all rivers of which we know' (4.48.1), and its interest for Sesostris arose precisely because it was 'the Nile of the north'.

285–7 Argos places the source of the Istros in the very far north, in the land of the 'Hyperboreans' (Hdt. 4.13, 32–6), where Apollo was believed to pass the winter, 614n. Herodotus had placed the source of the Istros to the west, 'in the land of the Celts' (2.33.3, 4.49.3); the Danube in fact rises in the Black Forest (cf. Strabo 1.3.15, 4.6.9).   ἀπείρονα … ἄρουραν: cf. Hdt. 5.9.1 'the land beyond the Istros is deserted and boundless (ἄπειρος)'.   Ῥιπαίοις ἐν ὄρεσσιν: these 'Blast (ῥιπή) Mountains' are associated with the Hyperboreans also by Callimachus (fr. 186.8–9), and cf. already Hellanicus, *FGrHist* 4 F187, Arist. *Meteor.* 1.350b7–10, Bolton 1962: 39–44, Harder 2012: 2.996. Strabo 7.3.1 gives the Rhipaian Mountains and the Hyperboreans as two examples of 'mythical geography' arising from ignorance: the name evokes unimaginable northern distances. 287 is closely imitated by Dion. Perieg. 315.   μορμύρουσιν, 'roar', forms an expressive *spondeiazon*.

288 ἐπιβήσεται οὔρους 'enters the boundaries of … '; although the ἐπι– compound is poorly attested, it seems perfectly appropriate for the action of a river.

289–91 'there splitting in two, it empties part of its water here into the eastern sea, and sends the part behind that through the deep gulf which rises from the Trinacrian sea'. Text and detailed interpretation are difficult, though the broad sense seems clear. The remarkable word order, with διχῆι picked up by σχιζόμενος two verses later, perhaps imitates the separation of the river, but is also part of the conjuring up of a geography very far from ordinary experience.   τὸ μὲν ἔνθα … τὸ δ' ὄπισθε 'the one part … the part behind [i.e. further away]'; the description is spoken from a Colchian perspective, which is also the perspective from where the Argonauts currently find themselves. For τὸ μὲν ἔνθα cf. ἔνθα καὶ ἔνθα 'this way and that' in 325.   ἠοίην ἅλα: the 'eastern sea' must be the Black Sea, seen from a Greek perspective, cf. 2.744–5 (with Matteo's n.), Hdt. 4.100.1, Delage 1930: 200. The text cannot, however, be considered entirely certain, although the transmitted 'Ionian' seems impossible. Wilamowitz's ἡμετέρην (1924: 2.186) is an attractive alternative, which would be picked up by ὑμετέρης in 293; it would be perfectly natural for Argos to call the Black Sea 'our', for this is what he knows, just as, for a Greek, 'our sea' was the Mediterranean.   βάλλει, like ἵησι, is here apparently transitive, though both verbs can also be used intransitively of rivers emptying at their mouths (cf. ἐξανίησιν in 293).   βαθὺν διὰ κόλπον: the Adriatic is here considered a 'gulf' of the Ionian sea, because it is closed at one end, cf. 308, and 1.1360–1 for a similar conception. Argos implies that the Istros empties into the Adriatic and then continues flowing through the sea before reaching 'the Trinacrian sea'; such a conception of the continuance of rivers through the sea was not uncommon, cf. Strabo 6.2.4. πόντου Τρινακρίου: i.e. the Ionian sea off the east coast of Sicily, for which Τρινακρία ('Island of three headlands') was thought to be an old name (cf. Thucyd. 6.2.2); at 994 this is called Θρινακίης ἅλς. Callimachus mentioned the 'Trinacrian sea' in Book 1 of the *Aitia* (the book in which the Argonautic narrative occurred), but the context is not known, fr. 40, Harder 2012: 2.295. Cf. further 309–11n., 964–5n.

292–3 Argos' knowledge of the geography of Greece is limited to what he has seen on the Colchian maps, where – so we are to understand – the Achelous, Greece's largest river, was marked, as also had been the Istros. The Achelous rises in the Pindus mountains and flows into the Ionian sea in southern Acarnania, by the entrance to the Gulf of Corinth.

294 θεά: i.e. Hera, who is guiding the voyage; cf. 242, and further 1254–5n.

295 ὧι καὶ πάντες ἐπευφήμησαν ἰδόντες 'at which all shouted, when they saw it …'. ὧι is loosely instrumental. πάντες ἐπευφήμησαν occurs at *Il.* 1.22, 376 of the Greek army urging Agamemnon to respect the priest Chryses, and here too a band of Greeks shows pious respect for deity.

297 ὅπηι καὶ ἀμεύσιμον ἦεν 'where in fact they were to proceed'. ἀμεύσιμος occurs only here; ἀμεύομαι is a Doric form of ἀμείβομαι, here probably with the sense 'pass, move from one place to another' (LSJ s.v. B II 2), rather than (Fränkel 1968: 476) 'change course to'.

298 Daskylos, son of Lykos, king of the Mariandynoi, had joined the expedition at what was to become the site of Heraclea (2.802–5, 814); this is much further west than their present position, but he is left to make his own way back.

299 λαίφεσι πεπταμένοισιν 'with sails unfurled', Fantuzzi–Hunter 2004: 268.

300 Κάραμβις, modern Kerempe Burun, was imagined as a major promontory on the south coast of the Black Sea (cf. 2.361–3, 943–5, Delage 1930: 163–4, Meyer 2008: 280); Strabo notes that a line north from Karambis to the southern tip of the Crimea would divide the Black Sea into two seas or broad areas (12.3.10, cf. Dion. Perieg. 159).

302 The Danube flows into the Black Sea through a huge delta of marshland and lakes in north-eastern Romania and Ukraine.

303–6 The Colchian pursuers divide into two groups in an attempt to cut off all escape routes; the unspoken assumption is that they too know about the Istros route, for the same reason that Argos did, and that they knew that the Clashing Rocks were now stationary, as the *Argo* had successfully passed through. By having the Colchians follow two different routes, Ap. is able to include and unify different versions of the Argonauts' return; Introduction, pp. 10–11, Wilamowitz 1924: 2.176–7.

303 μαστεύοντες 'searching'. Call. fr. 10, μαστύος ἀλλ' ὅτ' ἔκαμνον ἀλητύι, all but certainly refers to one of the groups of chasing Colchians (Harder 2012: 2.163–4), and so here too there is likely to be a link to the Callimachean narrative, although Ap. does use both the verb and the noun μαστήρ elsewhere (cf. 1003 (also of Colchians), 1394, 1482).

304 'passed out from the Pontos through the Dark Rocks', cf. 1001–3n., 1.2–3. διὲκ ... ἐπέρησαν (tmesis) governs the accusative πέτρας, but also the genitive Πόντοιο, which is a natural case after διέκ.

305 ποταμὸν μετεκίαθον 'made for the river', i.e. the Istros.

306 Καλὸν δὲ διὰ στόμα πεῖρε λιασθείς 'he [i.e. Apsyrtos] passed through the Beautiful Mouth, separating himself [from the Argonauts]'; throughout this passage, the subject switches between the Colchians and their leader, Apsyrtos. That the Danube had multiple mouths into the Black Sea was a familiar fact, though there was disagreement over the number: Ap. perhaps imagines only two (cf. 309–16n.), but Herodotus (4.47.2) has five (see further Berger 1880: 344–7). Σ cites Timagetos, 'On harbours' (fr. 2 Müller = FHG IV 519) for the view that there are three mouths, one of which was 'the Beautiful Mouth'; it is likely that this work (probably fourth century) was an important source for Ap. (Introduction, p. 9). Apsyrtos is imagined to enter the river by a more southerly mouth than the Argonauts (cf. 313), and this more direct route (cf. 314) means that he reaches the Adriatic before them, although he started behind them; later geographers, however, placed the Beautiful Mouth to the north of where the Argonauts are imagined to enter the river, Delage 1930: 205.

307–8 'Therefore he anticipated them in crossing over [βαλὼν ὕπερ] the neck of land <and reaching> inside the furthest gulf of the Ionian sea.' What is in fact the huge area of central Europe between the Adriatic and the Black Sea is called 'a neck of land' in keeping with a contemporary notion that the distance was in fact quite a narrow one and that the two seas could both be seen from the top of a high mountain (cf. Theopompos, FGrHist 115 F129 = Strabo 7.5.9, [Arist.], On Marvellous Things Heard 104). **ὑπέφθη**: aorist of ὑποφθάνω. **κόλπον**: cf. 289–91n. The accusative is best understood as governed by ἔσω, cf. Il. 21.125 οἴσει ... εἴσω ἁλὸς εὐρέα κόλπον, LSJ s.v. εἴσω 1b.

309–16 Ap. imagines an island created by two mouths of the Istros; Σ cite Eratosthenes (fr. 98 Berger = 148 Roller) for the view that Πεύκη ('Pine island') was the size of Rhodes, cf. Strabo 7.3.15 ('a large island'), who however places Peuke a considerable distance into the delta. It is unclear whether in fact Ap. imagines that there are only two mouths and that Peuke is therefore a name for the entire delta. The Argonauts go around the island to the north, but the Colchians take the quicker, southerly route. See further *RE* 19.1384–90, Minns 1913: 11–13.

309–11 ἐέργεται 'is shut in', i.e. 'is surrounded by', cf. LSJ s.v. ἔργω I. **τριγλώχιν** 'three-pointed, triangular', cf. Call. fr. 1.36 (of Sicily). Homer has τριγλώχινι (dative) as an epithet for an arrow (*Il.* 5.393, 11.507), but the remarkable nominative in –ιν is first found in Simonides (*PMG* 636 = 321 Poltera); see Mineur on Call. *h.* 4.31, Harder 2012: 2.82. Given that the present passage offers a variation on 290–1 (note κόλπον, σχιζόμενος, εἰσανέχοντα), it is noteworthy that Sicily (Τρινακρία) is there evoked as 'three-pointed' (291); in using the rare τριγλώχιν of an island other than Sicily, Ap. may therefore have line 36 of the 'Reply to the Telchines' in mind.   **εὖρος μὲν … ποτὶ ῥόον** lit. 'on its broad side extending to the coastline, on its narrow point, on the other hand, facing the stream'. For ἀγκών 'angle, point', LSJ s.v. II.

312 Νάρηκος is here perhaps a genitive, 'the mouth of Narex'; the more usual name for this mouth was Narakon or Narakou.

313 ὑπὸ τῆι νεάτηι: sc. νήσωι, 'on the lowest side (of the island)', cf. 315.   **τῆιδε διαπρό** 'by this route through and in advance [of the Argonauts] … '. διαπρό occurs only here in *Arg.*, and seems more expressive than the common ἐπιπρό (Π⁷); Livrea suggested τῆσδε διαπρό, 'through this one in front (of the Argonauts)', cf. *Il.* 5.281, and Luiselli 2003: 155–7 τῆιδ᾽ ἄρ᾽ ἐπιπρό.

315–16 'The others [i.e. the Argonauts] travelled far off to the north (ὑψοῦ) by way of the tip of the island'.

316–22 The inhabitants of the land to the west of the Black Sea have never seen large ships; this is a further (cf. 1.547–52) gesture to the idea of the *Argo* as the first ship, which of course in *Arg.* it is not. Cicero similarly cites a passage from the tragedian Accius (381–94 Warmington) in which a shepherd, 'who had never seen a ship before', describes his terrified amazement at a glimpse of the *Argo* (*ND* 2.89, where see Pease's notes for the *Argo* as the first ship).

316 εἰαμενῆισι 'marshes, wetlands', very appropriate for the delta of the Danube, cf. *Il.* 15.631–2 (countless cattle) ἐν εἰαμενῆι ἕλεος μεγάλοιο.

317–18 ποιμένες ἄγραυλοι opens the Muses' address to Hesiod at *Theog.* 26; cf. Thalmann 2011: 158–9 on the clash of cultures represented by this confrontation.   **νηῶν:** as Σ explains, the shepherds are as amazed at the

Colchian ships as at the *Argo*, this seems much better than, e.g., emendation to νηός, making the reference to the *Argo* alone.   οἶά τε θῆρας | ὀσσόμενοι 'as though they were seeing beasts ... ', 400n., 1.991, Smyth §2085; other suggested construals are 'like those who see beasts ... ' and 'seeing [the ships] like beasts ... ', Ruijgh 1971: 948.

318 μεγακήτεος is already an epithet of πόντος in Homer (*Od.* 3.158); for this way of imagining the terrors of the unknown depths see Hopman 2012: ch. 3.

319 ἁλίας γε ... νῆας: γε suggests that the shepherds may (reasonably enough) have been familiar with small boats for getting around on the river.

320 Θρήϊξι: scanned as three long syllables, with –ι lengthened before initial μ-, cf. 3.1210.   **Σίγυννοι:** Herodotus 5.9, who calls them Σίγυννες, says that they live north of the Istros and stretch as far as 'the Enetoi on the Adriatic', which fits the present passage well. Strabo 11.11.8 places them much further east, see Delage 1930: 206.

321 οὔτ᾽ οὖν: the repetition of emphatic οὖν in both οὔτε ... οὔτε clauses finds no exact parallel (Denniston 419–20), although examples with εἴτε ... εἴτε occur (K– G ΙΙ 159); the repetition seems, however, meaningful in emphasizing how surprising a list this is, and neither οὔτ᾽ αὖ nor simple οὔτε (Wellauer) seems necessary.   **Τραυκένιοι:** mentioned by Steph. Byz. 631.20 as 'a tribe near the Black Sea, neighbouring the Sindoi'. The transmitted Γραυκένιοι appear nowhere else.   **Λαύριον:** this plain is mentioned only in this passage, and 326 implies that it is imagined to lie west of the division of the Istros.

322 Herodotus 5.9.1 describes the land north of the Istros as ἔρημος χώρη ... καὶ ἄπειρος, cf. 285.   **Σίνδοι:** Herodotus 4.28, 86 puts this tribe well to the west near the Crimea (and cf. Hellanicus, *FGrHist* 4 F69), but Ap. is clearly following a very different tradition. The scholia here (and for two other places in Book 4) cite a work of one Timonax, 'On the Scythians' (*FGrHist* 842 F1), which may have been Ap.'s source, but Timonax's date is quite uncertain. Why they are said 'already' to dwell on the Plain of Laurion is unclear, but Ap. may wish to reconcile variant traditions.

323–4 ἐπεί τ᾽: for this rare Homeric usage cf. 366, Ruijgh 1971: 503–4; this and the hiatus in Ἀγγούρου ὄρεος are good examples of Ap.'s sensitivity to Homeric language and his nuanced mimesis of that.   Ἄγγουρον ὄρος ... | Ἀγγούρου ὄρεος: the stylistic repetition is related to effects such as epanalepsis (263–4n.) and here gives particular emphasis to the 'romantic' name and the imagined geography of the verses, Delage

1930: 207–9. The scholia here again cite Timagetos, who may be Ap.'s source (see 306n.). Ἄγγουρον ὄρος has often been associated with an Illyrian river Angros, mentioned by Hdt. 4.49.2.   παρά is best understood as in tmesis with ἡμείψαντο in 326, 'when they had gone past', an extraordinary separation, which however helps to hold the sentence together, despite the 'interruption' of the relative clause of 325–6.   σκόπελον … Καυλιακοῖο: Ap.'s source for the 'rock of Kauliakos' is uncertain. Σ cite a work of Polemon, 'Foundations of Italian and Sicilian Cities', but the well-known periegetic writer Polemon of Ilium (cf. fr. 38 Müller = FHG III 126) was later than Ap. Hecataeus mentioned an Adriatic tribe called the Kaulikoi, and Steph. Byz. 369.12–14 associated them with Ap.'s rock.

325–6 σχίζων … ῥόον 'splits its stream', cf. Pl. Tim. 21e1-2 ἐν τῶι Δέλτα, περὶ ὃν κατὰ κορυφὴν σχίζεται τὸ τοῦ Νείλου ῥεῦμα; βάλλει is thus here intransitive (LSJ s.v. III 1), in a variation of 289. Others understand ῥόον as the object of βάλλει, in which case σχίζων would have to be an intransitive active.

ἔνθα καὶ ἔνθα | … ἁλός 'this way and that into the sea', cf. 289–91n., and for the dependent genitive cf. 3.771 ἔνθα κακῶν ἢ ἔνθα.

327 Κρονίην: the reason for this name for the northern Adriatic can only be guessed (Wilamowitz 1924: 2.191, Delage 1930: 210–11), although Aeschylus, PV 837 already refers to the same stretch of water as 'the great gulf of Rhea', and cf. 548n.   Κόλχοι ἄλαδ': the hiatus varies βάλλει ἁλός in the previous verse where –ει is correpted; in Hellenistic poetry such variety may be regarded as conscious and deliberate.

328 ὑπετμήξαντο 'they cut off'; τμήγω and its compounds are related to τέμνω, but largely restricted to hexameter poetry, cf. 28, 2.481. It becomes clear that the Colchians in fact occupy nearly all the islands near the mouths of the Istros (cf. 563–4), thus blocking exits to the open sea (335), rather than blocking every exit out of the Istros; the Argonauts succeed in leaving the river.

329 ἐκ δ' ἐπέρησαν 'and emerged [from out of the river] and passed over to … '; the preposition is appropriate and the sense clear, even if somewhat compressed. ἐκπερᾶν is normally 'pass over, through'; the closest parallel to the present usage is perhaps Eubulus fr. 9.5K–A (= 10.5 Hunter) Ἀθήνας ἐκπερᾶν, 'make [his] way to Athens'.

330 [Aristotle], On Marvellous Things Heard 105 reports that Medea built a temple to Artemis on an Adriatic island; Ap. clearly follows a different, though related, version, cf. 470n. Hyginus, Fab. 23 places the killing of Apsyrtos on an 'island of Minerva'.   Βρυγηΐδας … νήσους: the whole archipelago of islands off the modern Croatian coast is called 'Liburnian' in 564. Elsewhere we learn of Thracian (Hdt. 6.45, 7.185.2, Strabo 7.3.2) and Illyrian (Strabo 7.7.8) tribes of Βρύγοι, and the latter would be appropriate to give their name to these islands. Where precisely Ap. placed the Adriatic mouth of the Istros and hence these islands is unclear, and it is likely enough that the geography is somewhat impressionistic. Ap. makes the initial υ of Βρυγ- long, though it seems to be short elsewhere. ἀγχόθι '(lying) nearby', i.e near to where they emerged from the Istros; such 'adjectival' uses of adverbs are not uncommon, cf. K–G I 609–10.

332–3 ἐν δ' ἑτέρηι … βαῖνον 'they disembarked on to the other one'.

333 A very difficult and probably corrupt verse; the end of the verse may have been influenced by ἀγχόθι νήσους at the end of 330, and cf. 336n. It is clear that 333–4 explain why the two islands were not occupied by the Colchians; 'left' is, however, a very bald way of saying 'left unoccupied', and various suggestions have sought to remedy this (κεινάς (Huet) or κενεάς (Fränkel), 'empty', instead of κείνας, or μούνας for νήσους (Fränkel) at verse-end), although a deictic such as κείνας seems necessary. ἔνδοθι sc. ἐούσας is perhaps just possible: 'these islands, being inside [i.e. surrounded by other islands, and therefore not requiring a garrison]', but the expression is at best awkward, and ἔνδοθι νήσων (Vian after Livrea) is worth considering. A convincing solution has, however, not been found. A separate issue is whether to read the transmitted plurals, λίπον and ἁζόμενοι, referring to the Colchians, or to adopt Fränkel's singulars referring to Apsyrtos. In favour of emendation is that Apsyrtos has just been mentioned in 332, whereas the Colchians will appear in 335; stress upon Apsyrtos' piety would also help to prepare us for the impiety of his murder.

334 αὔτως: the meaning is uncertain without clarity about 333; perhaps 'of their own will'.

335 εἴρυντο 'protected, guarded', LSJ s.v. ἐρύω (B).

336 Another verse where repetition of elements (πληθὺν λίπεν ἀγχόθι νήσων) from the surrounding context suggests probable corruption. Apsyrtos stations forces not just on the islands, but also on the mainland (ἀκτάς) facing the islands; Livrea suggested ἀγχόθι νηῶν, which removes some of the repetition, but is otherwise no improvement.

337 The Salangon has been identified with the Salon, which flows into the Adriatic at Salona near Split (Barrington 20 D6). The Nestos river is almost certainly the modern Cetina, which enters the sea south of Split; for this river and the people who took their name from it see Ps.-Scylax 23, Eratosthenes fr. 112 Berger (= 145 Roller), Peretti 1979: 238–45. This area is well to the south of the Liburnian islands and the islands which became the Apsyrtides (481).

338–9 Cf. 636–42n. παυρότεροι πλεόνεσσιν begins *Il.* 13.739, Polydamas advising Hector not to continue fighting when outnumbered.

340 Ap. dispenses with any narrative about *how* the Argonauts and the Colchians reached an agreement and their respective motives; such narrative compression would be almost unthinkable in Homer. The agreement perhaps comes as a surprise, given that the situation appears to be weighted in favour of the Colchians, who may however emerge from it with nothing. The Colchians will, however, have been much more concerned with Medea than with the Fleece (cf. 231–5), and Ap.'s interest is in setting up the scene between Jason and Medea which follows.   συνθεσίην …
ἐτάμοντο 'concluded a solemn agreement'; τέμνεσθαι, with or without an object such as ὅρκια or σπονδάς, is regularly used of making an agreement, accompanied by sacrifices (LSJ s.v. 11 2). The transmitted συνθεσίηι, to be construed with μέγα νεῖκος ἀλευάμενοι, is not impossible, but the accusative seems better to introduce the account of the terms which follows. At 1.340, συνθεσίας τε μετὰ ξείνοισι βαλέσθαι, Fränkel proposed ταμέσθαι.

341–9 The terms of the agreement, with verbs in the infinitive, are given in a very dry style reminiscent of legal documents and inscribed decrees. Ap. is again experimenting with the inclusion of generically 'foreign' material into epic hexameters.

341 ὑπέστη: cf. 3.418–20.

342 οἱ 'for him', i.e. Aietes, cf. Pind. *Pyth.* 4.229–30 (Aietes speaks) τοῦτ' ἔργον … ἐμοὶ τελέσαις, 243 ἔλπετο δ' οὐκέτι οἱ κεῖνόν γε πράξασθαι πόνον. The transmitted κεῖνοι, referring to the Argonauts, seems very awkward after σφισιν immediately before and σφέας immediately following, and κείνωι (Castiglioni), referring to Aietes, equally so. The text cannot, however, be considered certain. For εἴ κεν with the optative in such clauses see Chantraine 11 277–8.

343 ἔμπεδον εὐδικίηι σφέας ἐξέμεν 'they were to have [the Fleece] with full and unchallengeable right'; ἔμπεδον also carries the resonance of 'for ever'.

344 The dichotomy 'by deceit … openly' reminds us that, although the Argonauts did have a right to the Fleece after the accomplishment of Jason's tasks, they also gained it 'by deceit/guile'; there is here very little of the moral clarity with which such legal agreements like to deal.   καί gives particular emphasis to the second possibility, cf. 202–5n.   ἀμφαδίην αὔτως 'quite openly', 'openly, just like that'.

345 τόδε, 'the fate/situation [of Medea]', cannot be considered certain, as there are other ways of adding the missing syllable to the verse; γάρ would, however, seem indispensable (contrast Fränkel 1968: 479).

346 παρθέσθαι '[they should] deposit with'. Placing Medea with 'the maiden daughter of Leto' foreshadows the importance virginity will play in Alcinous' later ruling about her fate (1106–9) and also suggests, as too does ὁμίλου, that one of the reasons for this provision is the possible impropriety of Medea staying unprotected with a group of young men. For a very similar arrangement cf. Menander, *Sikyonioi*, in which a girl whose citizen status is disputed is deposited 'for safe-keeping' with the priestess of Demeter, cf. *Sik.* 242–3 πρὸς τὴν ἱέρειαν θέσθε, καὶ τηρησάτω | ὑμῖν ἐκείνη τὴν κόρην.   ὁμίλου: i.e. the Argonauts, cf. 183n.

347 The notion seems to be that one of the local 'kings' was to adjudicate, but the concept, and the epithet θεμιστοῦχος, look forward to Alcinous' adjudication (346n.).

348–9 The repeated εἴτε … εἴτε (cf. 343–4) again evokes the language of an official document. 348a was perhaps a variant or parallel for 349 which has mistakenly entered the text; the verse is clearly in place at 2.1186 and not here, where there is a stark choice between 'Greece' and Medea's 'fatherland'. *POxy* 2691 has ..]τεμ. [, so it is unclear whether this is 348 or 348a (Haslam 1978: 65–6).

350 νόωι πεμπάσσατο 'reflected upon, considered in her mind', cf. 1748.

351 Cf. 3.113 (during Medea's first meeting with Jason) τῆς δ' ἀλεγεινόταται κραδίην ἐρέθεσκον ἀνῖαι.   μιν … κραδίην 'her in her heart', the so-called 'accusatives of part and whole', cf. 724, 3.284, *HHDem.* 40 ὀξὺ δέ μιν κραδίην ἄχος ἔλλαβεν, Smyth §985.

352 νωλεμές 'violently'; at 2.602 Σ gloss as βιαίως. This is more appropriate than the other regular meaning 'constantly, without respite'(Vian 1 274): as soon as Medea realizes the situation, she is overcome and reacts 'imme-diately' (αἶψα).

353–4 ὄφρ' ἐλίασθεν | πολλὸν ἑκάς 'until they were separated [from the others] very far away'. ἐλίασθεν is a 3rd pl. aorist, cf. 1305, 3.969.   στονόεντα 'mixed with groans/complaints'; the adjective nor-mally means 'causing grief/distress', but cf. 2.631 στονόεσσαν … νύκτα.

355–90 Medea's speech of reproach against Jason is one of the emotional high-points of the epic; the amount of necessary enjambment in the speech is a mark, not just of how far written hexameter style has moved from the Homeric pattern (Introduction, p. 26), but of Medea's rage. The most important models for Ap. were Medea's exchanges with Jason in Euripides, *Medea* (see nn. on 357–9, 368–9, 379–80), and in its turn this speech was an important model for Virgil's Dido (Nelis 2001: 160–6).

355 συναρτύνασθε: the prefix makes clear that Medea sees a plot by the Argonauts and the Colchians together.

356–7 ἦέ σε πάγχυ λαθιφροσύναις ἐνέηκαν | ἀγλαΐαι 'Have your brilliant successes completely immersed you in forgetfulness?' In her anger Medea sarcastically strains at language: λαθιφροσύνη does not occur elsewhere.   **ἐνέηκαν:** 3rd pl. aorist of ἐνίημι, LSJ s.v. 3.

357–9 Medea, like the Euripidean heroine before her (cf. esp. *Medea* 492–7), bitterly recalls Jason's past promises, particularly during their meeting in Book 3. At 3.986 Jason had appealed to Zeus as protector of suppliants and at 988 (where see n.) he pleaded that he was driven χρειοῖ ἀναγκαίηι (cf. 358); in return for her help Jason had promised her χάρις and κλέος, but not of the kind which now appears to be her fate. At 3.1079–82 he had promised never to forget her (cf. 356) and at 3.1122–30 (cf. 4.194–5) held out the hope of marriage and eternal love. Some of Medea's reproaches are repeated in her plea to the Argonauts at 1042–4.   **τῶν δ’ οὔ τι μετατρέπηι:** cf. *Il.* 1.160, Achilles charging Agamemnon with ingratitude and with reaping the benefits of others' labours, just the charges which Medea here brings against Jason. **Ἱκεσίοιο:** forms of this word can only be used in hexameters if the initial iota, short by nature, is lengthened, cf. 1043 (a variation of the present passage).

360 Medea presents her actions as a breach of κόσμος and an offence against αἰδώς, as indeed they were; for the latter theme cf. 3.653–4, 785–6 (here bitterly recalled) ἐρρέτω αἰδώς, | ἐρρέτω ἀγλαΐη· ὁ δ’ ἐμῆι ἰότητι σαωθείς κτλ.   **ἧις** 'by them', i.e. 'relying on them'.

361–2 Medea sets herself in a chain of 'tragic' women stretching back to Homer's Helen, cf. *Od.* 4.263 (Helen) παῖδά τ’ ἐμὴν νοσφισσαμένην θάλαμόν τε πόσιν τε, *Il.* 3.173–5, Eur. *Med.* 483–4, Bühler 1960: 186. The choice between being a 'Penelope' and being a 'Helen' has long been decided (Hunter 1989: 29); Greek glory (cf. 203) has proved Medea's ruin. **κλέα τε μεγάρων:** from a Colchian perspective, Medea's house was indeed one of great κλέος: her father was a king descended from Helios. τε is lengthened before initial μ-.   **ὑπέρτατα** 'most important', cf. Medea's resolution at 3.640. Fränkel 1968: 480 understands 'of the highest rank', referring to Medea's parents, but this is much less rhetorically effective.

362–3 Cf. Medea's later plea at 1040–1. The current passage has influenced Europa's lament at Moschus, *Europa* 146–8.   **λυγρῆισιν …** **ἀλκυόνεσσι:** the halcyon, a bird of romantic myth, was early identified with the kingfisher, but the original Alcyone had been transformed into a bird in her mournful searching for her lost husband Ceyx (Thompson, *Birds* 47, Bömer on Ovid, *Met.* 11.734–5). λυγρός, 'mournful, sorrowful', is perhaps used of a halcyon at Phalaecus, *AP* 13.27.6 (=*HE* 2959), probably earlier than *Arg.*, and the halcyon is already πολυπενθής in Homer (*Il.* 9.563); Ovid's Alcyone is *ales miserabilis* at the moment of transformation (*Met.* 11.733) and her cry is *maesto similem plenumque querelae … sonum* (*Met.* 11.734–5). In Medea's mouth λυγρῆισιν also carries a resonance of 'grim, hateful': she has seen all the seabirds she cares to see.   ἄμ' ἀλκυόνεσσι occurs in the same *sedes* at Alcman, *PMG* 26.3, a passage that may also be relevant at 1.1096–7.

364 μοι associates Medea with Jason's accomplishment of his tasks, without carrying the weight of 'through my efforts', as in the fuller expressions at 3.786, 1116, Eur. *Med.* 476–82.

365 ἀναπλήσειας: the optative follows on from the historic sequence of νοσφισάμην, with τηλόθι … φορεῦμαι as a kind of parenthesis.

366 ἐπεί τ' ἐπάιστον ἐτύχθη 'when the matter had become known'; Medea continued to help Jason, at enormous cost and danger to herself, even after her involvement was known (cf. 10, 84–5, 213). The text is, however, very uncertain (see apparatus); E's text, 'the fleece, which was the purpose of your expedition …' is certainly *lectio facilior*, but would not have aroused suspicion, had it been universally transmitted. The origin of the variants remains puzzling.

367–8 ματίηι 'wanton folly', cf. 1.805 (the Lemnian men); at the one Homeric occurrence of the noun there is no suggestion of 'sexual' folly (*Od.* 10.79), but Medea's self-reproaches are harshly knowing, cf. 375n. If Medea has been a Helen (361–2n.) and is momentarily to be an Andromache (next n.), here she is an adulterous Clytemnestra, cf. *Od.* 11.432–4, 'whose wicked plans poured disgrace even over women of future generations …'. Helen and Clytemnestra are paired immediately after that passage at *Od.* 11.438–9.

368–9 Not for the first time (cf. 3.732–3, with Hunter 1993: 62–3), Medea now casts herself as Andromache, cf. *Il.* 6.429–30, 'Hector, to me you are father and queenly mother and brother, to me you are my beloved bedmate'; these famous verses were imitated as early as Aesch. *Ch.* 238–43. Medea turns the Homeric rhetoric around – she, not the man, is now the subject – because it is her helpless dependence which is uppermost in her mind.   αὐτοκασιγνήτη: Medea's brother (a half-brother in fact, 3.241–3) is indeed lost to her, but soon she will lure him to a grisly death. There is a similar grim irony at Eur. *Medea* 257 where Medea complains that she has 'no mother, no brother, no relation' to help her;

there her brother had already been killed.   μεθ' Ἑλλάδα γαῖαν ἕπεσθαι
echoes the terms of the agreement (349) to stress that Jason has no real
choice here: Medea must go to Greece with him.

370 πάντηι 'in every way'.

371 ἐποιχόμενος βασιλῆας 'visiting kings', cf. 2.455 (Phineus' visitors) καί
μιν ἐποιχόμενοι κομέεσκον. The plural 'kings' suggests Medea's scorn for
Jason's apparent manoeuvrings, though she knows what is in fact going
on (377–8); there is thus no need to emend to βασιλῆα (Vian).

372–3 Medea's plea involves both δίκη, 'just agreement' (cf. the pledge
of 99–100), and θέμις, 'religious sanction' (cf. Jason's oath at 95–8).
αὔτως 'simply, without further ado'.   **συναρέσσαμεν** 'we jointly agreed',
a transitive aorist of συναρέσκω.

374 διὰ ... ἀμῆσαι 'cut through', a very expressive 'tmesis'; the aorist
infinitive is here used as an imperative.

375 'So that I may receive a reward appropriate to my wantonness'. Homer
has examples of ἐπὶ ἦρα φέρειν, with the verb in tmesis, in the sense 'render
service to', cf. 406; Aristarchus understood such cases as ἐπίηρα φέρειν, and
he seems to have been anticipated in this by poetic usage, cf. Σ *Il.* 1.572,
Rengakos 1994: 86–7, Matthews 1996: 391–2. Medea's use of ἐπίηρα as
'reward' extends the connection made by ancient grammarians (cf., e.g.,
Hesychius η 713) between the Homeric ἦρα and χάρις; the latter is what one
should receive in return for a benefaction (cf. 3.990, 1005), but death is the
χάρις she really deserves. The use of such a linguistic preciosity at a moment
of high drama and self-loathing is an effect very typical of Hellenistic
poetry.   **μαργοσύνηισιν:** cf. 367–8n., 3.797n. At 1019, in very different
rhetorical circumstances, Medea will tell Arete that it was not μαργοσύνη that
made her follow Jason, but here she again presents herself as a Helen figure,
cf. Eur. *Tr.* 992 (Hecuba to Helen) ἐξεμαργώθης φρένας, and we are perhaps
to recall *Il.* 24.30, where Aphrodite is said to have won the beauty contest
because she offered Paris μαχλοσύνη ἀλεγεινή (a verse athetized by
Aristarchus and others). μαργοσύνηισιν forms a powerful rhetorical conclusion to the idea of her own death, and hence should be followed by strong
punctuation, with σχέτλιε, addressed to Jason, introducing a new point;
contrast 388–9, where νηλεές refers back to the subject of the previous verse.

376 As transmitted, the verse is a syllable short, and this may be mended in
a number of plausible ways (see apparatus).

377 ἐπίσχετε 'you offer', i.e. 'give over'. ἐπίσχω is a reduplicated form of
ἐπέχω, but the required sense is hard to parallel and Platt proposed
ὑπίσχετε 'you submit'.

378 ἄμφω: i.e. Jason and Apsyrtos.

379–80 ἢ μάλ' εὐκλειής: for Medea's bitter irony cf. her Euripidean model at *Medea* 502–3 νῦν ποῖ τράπωμαι; πότερα πρὸς πατρὸς δόμους, | οὓς σοὶ προδοῦσα καὶ πάτραν ἀφικόμην; and Teucer's address to Ajax's body at Soph. *Ajax* 1008–9 ἢ πού <με> Τελαμών, σὸς πατὴρ ἐμός θ' ἅμα, | δέξαιτ' ἂν εὐπρόσωπος κτλ.   **οὐ … οὐ:** the 'illogical' repeated negative is a further sign of Medea's emotion, cf. *Od.* 3.27–8, Soph. *Ant.* 5–6 (with Jebb's n.), K–G II 204–5.   **ἄτην:** her cruel father would doubtless inflict horrible punishments, cf. 1043–4, 1087–8; there is no reason to refer ἄτη to the idea of exile with Jason (so Fränkel 1968: 482).   **οἷα ἔοργα:** the hiatus imitates archaic practice in which the initial digamma of the verb was often respected (e.g. *Il.* 3.57), but the harsh rhythm may also be expressively suited to Medea's wild mood.

381 ὀτλήσω … ἕλοιο: the contrast between the vivid future referring to Medea's imagined punishment and the more remote optative referring to Jason's 'sweet return' is very expressive. It has become normal to place the question-mark after ἕλοιο, with a comma after ὀτλήσω, but the older punctuation (adopted here) has much more rhetorical bite. Hellenistic poets use ὀτλέω in ways that suggest a connection with τλάω was felt.

382 τελέσειεν: Hera, like other gods, was τελεία, particularly in connection with her protection of marriage, cf. Pind. *Nem.* 10.18, LSJ s.v. τέλειος II.

383–4 The motif of 'memory' descended from the final exchange between Odysseus and Nausicaa (*Od.* 8.461–8) to Jason and Hypsipyle (1.896) and then to Jason's tender exchanges with Medea in Book 3, cf. 3.1069n. Here the mood is very different, cf. Virg. *Aen.* 4. 382–4 *spero equidem mediis, si quid pia numina possunt, | supplicia hausurum scopulis et nomine Dido | saepe uocaturum.* The whole of 383–90, with its themes of memory and Medea's magical revenge, is a revision of both the language and the subject of 3.1109–17.

384–5 It is tempting to think that these verses evoke a version in which the Fleece did just vanish, after Jason had successfully returned to Greece; Apollod. *Bibl.* 1.9.27 reports that Jason handed the Fleece over to Pelias, but nothing further is recorded of its fate.   **ἔρεβος** 'darkness'; Hesiod makes Erebos a brother of Night and child of Chaos (*Theog.* 123), and Erebos is often mentioned in connection with the Underworld. We should perhaps print Ἔρεβος here, marking Medea's knowledge of and contact with the Underworld. That the *Golden* Fleece should disappear into darkness is a very vivid wish.   **μεταμώνιον** 'turned to nothing, gone with the wind'. Dreams can fly (e.g. *Od.* 11.222) and they slip away from one's hands and memory (e.g. *Od.* 11.207–8), and so the believed connection of μεταμώνιος with ἄνεμος is relevant here.

386 σ' ἐλάσειαν: the repetition of σε can be paralleled (cf. Mastronarde on Eur. *Ph.* 497–8), and here will be dramatically effective; Fränkel deleted it as a scribal attempt to avoid (a perfectly legitimate) hiatus, just as some MSS offer ἐμαί γ'. **Ἐρινύες**: Medea evokes the situation of Orestes, driven from his homeland by his mother's Furies, cf. Aesch. *Ch.* 1062 ἐλαύνομαι δὲ κοὐκέτ' ἂν μείναιμ' ἐγώ, *Eum.* 75–7; Jason will be as guilty of causing her death as Orestes was for his mother. Jason in fact will indeed eventually be driven into exile, but *with* a living Medea. Chalciope had used a similar threat to Medea herself at 3.704. The Furies, always associated with blackness (e.g. Aesch. *Ch.* 1049, *Eum.* 52), here follow 'naturally' upon the evocation of ἔρεβος. The Furies are another theme which Virgil picked up from this passage for his Dido, cf. *Aen.* 4.384–6 (with Pease's notes, Lowe 2013), 610 *Dirae ultrices.* **οἷα**: exclamatory, 'in view of all that . . .'.

387 ἀτροπίηι 'cruelty, lack of regard', cf. 1047 (a very similar context). **τὰ μέν**: i.e. the curses and threats she has uttered.

388 ἐν γαίηι 'on to the ground', a very common compressed or 'pregnant' use of ἐν with a verb of motion, i.e. 'fall to <and rest upon> the ground', cf. 393, 771, 913, Theocr. 13.51, Smyth §1659.

389 νηλεές: cf. 375n. **θήν** marks a strong and confident assertion, cf. 1.1339, Denniston 288–9, Cuypers 2005: 60–1. **ἐπιλλίζοντες** 'winking (in mockery)', hence 'laughing at': Jason and Apsyrtos have, she implies, been making deals behind her back. At 3.791 the verb is used actively, ἐπιλλίξουσιν ὀπίσσω | κερτομίας; the present passage varies the earlier one in an excellent example of Apollonius' simultaneous evocation and avoidance of formularity. ἐπιλλίζειν was connected in antiquity with ἰλλός, 'squinting'.

390 ἔκητί γε συνθεσιάων 'as far at any rate as your agreements are concerned'; whatever else happens, this deal with Apsyrtos will do neither of them any good.

391–3 Medea's 'longing' to burn the *Argo* marks her as very much her father's daughter, cf. 223n., Hunter 1993: 61. Virgil's Dido picked up these verses also: *Aen.* 4.604–6, *faces in castra tulissem | implessemque foros flammis natumque patremque | cum genere exstinxem, memet super ipsa dedissem.* **ἀναζείουσα βαρὺν χόλον**: cf. Aesch. *PV* 370 ἐξαναζέσει χόλον; Euripides had bequeathed to the tradition a very close link between Medea and χόλος, cf. *Medea* 590. **διά τ' †ἔμπεδα πάντα κεάσσαι** 'shatter everything [. . .] in pieces'. At *Od.* 15.322, πῦρ τ' εὖ νηῆσαι διά τε ξύλα δανὰ κεάσσαι, grammarians differed as to whether the second verb meant 'burn' or 'split', *LfgrE* s.v. κεάζειν. At 1267, 'burn' is impossible and Ap. uses the simple verb in the sense of 'cut' at 2.104, 3.378; 'burn' is here not impossible, but 'break to pieces' seems much more likely (*pace* Rengakos 1994: 102); see Campbell 1971: 420, citing *Il.* 9.241–2 (about Hector) στεῦται γὰρ νηῶν ἀποκόψειν ἄκρα κόρυμβα | αὐτάς τ' ἐμπρήσειν μαλεροῦ πυρός. ἔμπεδα πάντα is impossible, and the error may have arisen from the fact that ἔμπεδα πάντα is Homeric in this *sedes*, but with quite inappropriate sense (cf. *Od.* 2.227, 11.178, 19.525). Campbell proposed ἀμφαδὰ πάντα, 'everything before their faces', cf. 3.95–6, *Od.* 19.391.

395–409 Jason responds that the pact with Apsyrtos is merely a ruse to gain time and a trick to lead him to destruction. We have no more idea than does Medea whether to understand that he is merely improvising his way out of a difficult situation (Hunter 1993: 15), but we do read his speech against his Euripidean model's plea for flexibility at *Medea* 446–64 and the hypocrisy of that speech.

395 ἴσχεο: cf. σχέο μοι at 3.386, one of a number of echoes of how Jason tried win Aietes around.   **δαιμονίη:** cf. 95, 3.1120, where again the use of this address suggests that Medea is over-reacting.

396–8 Cf. *Il.* 6.326–9 (Hector to Paris) δαιμόνι', οὐ μὲν καλὰ χόλον τόνδ' ἔνθεο θυμῶι . . . σέο δ' εἵνεκ' αὐτή τε πτόλεμός τε | ἄστυ τόδ' ἀμφιδέδηε. Hector is trying to stir Paris to fight and to keep fire from his city (cf. 6.331), whereas Jason seeks a respite from war, such as Paris is enjoying, as well as avoiding the burning of his ship. Aristarchus (and perhaps other scholars before him) wondered to what χόλον in line 326 referred (see Graziosi-Haubold ad loc.), and it is possible that Ap. does not just rewrite this exchange, with a complete reversal of the Homeric situation (Jason, after all, is more naturally a 'Paris'), but also uses the Homeric motif of χόλος more appropriately than it was believed that Homer himself had done.   **ἀμφιδέδηεν** 'blazes around', an intransitive perfect of ἀμφιδαίω; Ap. follows Homer in using it metaphorically of war, cf. previous n., *Il.* 12.35.

398–9 Neither we nor Medea have any way of knowing how much Jason knows about local attitudes to the dispute (Fränkel 1968: 485). μεμάασιν is, however, a strong word and Jason, at least, paints the situation in the blackest possible terms.

400 οἶά τε ληισθεῖσαν 'in as much as you are a captive', i.e. in the belief that the Greeks have taken Medea by force, cf. 317; in some senses, the belief is more true than they might realize, 35–40n. Jason seems to allow Medea to understand that the Colchians have falsely misrepresented the situation to the locals, a misrepresentation which would of course strengthen their case for her return. Green 1997: 310 takes the phrase to refer rather to what will happen to Medea when returned to the Colchians, but that would be much weaker rhetoric. ἄγοιτο: the better attested plural would have 'the Colchians' as subject, although the run of the sentence might suggest (absurdly) 'the locals'. The singular may be a correction designed to avoid that absurdity, but it seems a considerable improvement.

402–3 ὅ τοι καὶ ῥίγιον ἄλγος | ἔσσεται 'something which will be, believe me, an even worse grief . . .'. Jason here strikes a heroic attitude, continued in 403, by saying that the knowledge that the Argonauts were leaving Medea to her fate would make their deaths even more painful and disgraceful; the closest Homeric parallel is probably Hector's anxiety for Andromache at *Il.* 6.454–65. τοι is thus best taken as the particle 'I assure you'. More usually, Jason is understood to be saying that, if the Argonauts are killed, things will be even worse for Medea, with τοι as 'for you', cf. 407, *Il.* 1.563 (Zeus speaking harshly to Hera) τὸ δέ τοι καὶ ῥίγιον ἔσται; this has obvious rhetorical point, but places a great deal of weight upon the simple τοι. With the interpretation adopted here, Ap. pointedly varies the meaning of τοι in the Homeric model. κείνοισι: E has κύνεσσι, a memory of *Il.* 1.4, which however suggests a scribe who rightly caught Jason's heroic pose.

404 κρανέει: future of κραίνω. μιν: i.e. Apsyrtos.

405–6 βήσομεν 'we will cause him to enter', LSJ s.v. βαίνω B. οὐδ' ἄν ὁμῶς . . . ὑπὲρ σέο 'And those who dwell around will not oppose us in the same way in rendering service to the Colchians on account of you . . .'. ἀντιόωσι is best understood, despite ἄν, as the principal verb, and the meaning will be either 'oppose [us] equally' or perhaps 'aid [the Colchians] equally'; for the latter cf. 849. The present tense with ἄν is, however, hard to parallel and Diels' ἀντιόωιντο still deserves consideration, cf. 1.470 καὶ εἰ θεὸς ἀντιόωιτο (a pointed variation of *Od.* 12.88). Alternatively, ἀντιόωσι may be understood as the dative plural of the participle in agreement with Κόλχοις, to be taken with φέροιεν in 406, i.e. '. . . would not equally render service to the Colchians when they ask for assistance', cf. 703, 3.35n., LSJ s.v. ἀντιάω v. ἦρα φέροντες: cf. 375n.

407 ἀοσσητήρ 'helper', cf. 146, 785; from the point of view of the Colchians Apsyrtos has come to try to 'help' Medea, who – so they believe (400n.) – is a captive of the Greeks. There is no need (with Vian, cf. Pietsch 1999: 155) to invent a new sense 'legal protector', i.e. κύριος, for the term here.

408 †ὑπείξομαι πτολεμίζειν: the required sense is probably 'I would not refuse to fight the Colchians . . .', rather than 'I would not be defeated in battle by the Colchians . . .' (for which cf. 339). Gerhard's ὑπείξω μή is the favoured solution, but we should be cautious about introducing by emendation a breach of 'Naeke's Law' (i.e. word-division after a fourth-foot spondee, as, e.g., 971); *Arg.* breaches this rule roughly every 87 verses. Moreover, the expression, lit. 'I would not yield not to fight . . . ', is at least awkward; Brunck's ὑπείξαιμι, 'I would not withdraw from fighting . . . ' is perhaps better, but a convincing solution has yet to be found. Platt's πτολεμίζων cannot be adopted in ignorance of the preceding text.

410 ἴσκεν ὑποσσαίνων 'he spoke trying to soothe her', cf. 92, 3.396 (with Hunter and Campbell ad loc.). The participle is used of an earlier speech of Jason to Medea at 3.974.   **οὐλοὸν . . . μῦθον**: the speech will help bring about Apsyrtos' 'destruction', but the poet also passes judgement on the 'deadly' quality of what the young girl says.

411 φράζεο νῦν 'Pay attention now!' The use at 3.1026, in a similar context, is somewhat different.   **ἀεικελίοισιν ἐπ' ἔργοις**: ἐπί is probably 'on top of, in addition to' (447, 1.297, LSJ s.v. B 1e), but there is also a causal nuance 'in view of' (LSJ s.v. III).

412 τόδε: i.e. the plan she is about to propose.

413 θεόθεν: Medea now shifts responsibility, but she speaks more truly than she knows, given Hera's role in Books 3 and 4.

414 An apparently awkward verse, given that the fighting should follow the killing of Apsyrtos (cf. 420), but Medea picks up the bravado of Jason's final words of 408–9 and holds him to them.   **ἀλέξεο** 'keep off, defend yourself against'.

416 μειλίξω 'I will induce', with a suggestion of 'beguile, trick'; in the event, Medea's θέλξις (436, 442) involves the use of potions to lure Apsyrtos to her (442–4).

417 Ap. shows a very experimental technique in the handling of messengers and messenger-speeches (cf. 435–6, Hunter 1993: 144–5), but it is hard to believe that 'in the hope that I can persuade departing heralds <with the result that he> falls in with . . . ' can stand for 'in the hope that I can persuade him, through the departing heralds, to fall in with . . . '; the scholiastic paraphrase, εἴ πως . . . πείσαιμι τὸν Ἄψυρτον μόνον πρὸς μόνην ἥκειν, φιλίαν πρὸς αὐτὸν συνθεμένη, increases doubt. The compression is barely tolerable, even leaving aside the questions of the identity of the heralds (Colchian?) and the absence of any detail. It is possible that a whole verse (or verses) has fallen out after ἀπερχομένους and/or we need some word for 'despatching, sending'.

418 συναρθμῆσαι: at *Il.* 7.302 Hector suggests to Ajax that they exchange 'glorious gifts', as a mark that, though they fought, they parted ἐν φιλότητι

... ἀρθμήσαντε; Ap. echoes that passage at 1.1344 and perhaps here also. Doubt about the text of 417 makes the exact nuance uncertain: perhaps 'fall in with, unite himself to my words', but 'make an agreement < ... > through my words' cannot be ruled out.

419 οὔ τι μεγαίρω 'I do not begrudge it', i.e. 'that is fine by me', cf. 3.485.

420 κτεῖνε: the absence of an expressed object, 'Apsyrtos' or 'my brother', speaks volumes.   **ἄειρεο δηιοτῆτα** 'begin your strife with ... ', LSJ s.v. ἀείρω IV 4.

421–521 *The death of Apsyrtos.* Apsyrtos is lured to his grisly death by deceitful words, by splendid gifts and by Medea's magical powers. In earlier versions, Medea's very young brother was killed and dismembered either in the royal palace itself or during the Argonauts' flight from the city, cf. 460–1n., Pherecydes, *FGrHist* 3 F32, Soph. fr. 343R, Call. fr. 8, but it is unclear whether Ap.'s version is his own innovation. The aura of tragedy is, however, palpable in this episode; see nn. on 468, 472, 475–6, 477. Important too was probably the death of the Trojan prince Troilos, who was ambushed by Achilles at a shrine of Apollo outside the walls of Troy; the story, which is well attested in art, occurred in the *Cypria* (West 2013: 121–2, 242–3) and seems to have been dramatized by Sophocles. Such Cyclic material, with its elements of 'unheroic' strangeness (cf. 477), sits well with the obvious evocation of the death of Agamemnon, told above all in the *Nostoi* and then in Aeschylus; here and elsewhere, Ap. uses the Cycle as one of the ways in which he establishes his poetic voice against that of Homer; see 693–4n., Hunter 2008b: 143–6, Fantuzzi–Hunter 2004: 95–7, Introduction, pp. 19–21. It is, moreover, a reasonable modern speculation that Achilles fell in love with Troilos' sister, Polyxena, during this same episode, and this would then create a brother–sister lover triangle analogous to, though differently configured from, Apsyrtos–Medea–Jason. On Troilos as a model for Apsyrtos see esp. Mori 2008: 201–9, and for this episode see also Sansone 2000: 166–8, Porter 1990, Griffiths 1990, Byre 1996a, Nishimura-Jensen 1996: 168–89, Bremmer 1997, Stephens 2003: 226–9.

421 ξυμβάντε 'coming to an agreement'.   **δόλον ἠρτύναντο**: in Homer this phrase occurs only of Clytemnestra's plot against Agamemnon (*Od.* 11.439), which is to be a principal paradigm for the killing of Apsyrtos.

423–34 As in Books 1 and 3, a marvellous cloak is fraught with symbolic significance, cf. 3.1203–6n., Rose 1985; cloaks are in *Arg.* very 'significant objects' (Griffin 1980: ch. 1 on Homer), and the use of a *peplos* in this context recalls such fatal gifts as that of Deianeira to Heracles in Sophocles' *Trachiniae* and, in particular, the device by which Medea kills the young princess in Euripides' tragedy. Formally, the 'digression' to describe the history of the cloak imitates such passages as *Il.* 2.101–8 (Agamemnon's sceptre), but the history also completes some of the story of Theseus and Ariadne which Jason had dangled before Medea (and us) in Book 3, anticipates (again) what awaits Medea in Greece, and lengthens the shadow which the Lemnian episode of Book 1 casts over the whole epic (see further 3.997–1004n.). Hypsipyle's gift of a cloak to the departing Jason (for the motif cf. 2.30–2) found its Homeric model in the εἵματα θυώδεα in which Calypso clothed the departing Odysseus; Plutarch, *Mor.* 831d describes those clothes as 'fragrant of her divine skin, gifts and memorials of her love' (cf. 430–4).

425 Δίηι ἐν ἀμφιάλωι: cf. *Od.* 11.325 Δίηι ἐν ἀμφιρύτηι Διονύσου μαρτυρίηισι, in the story of Ariadne (seen by Odysseus in the Underworld), cf. 433–4n. Dia was believed to be an old name for Naxos, cf. Call. fr. 601; Diod. Sic. 5.51 records Strongule, Dia and Naxos as successive names for the island, and places the story of Theseus and Ariadne in the time of the last name. At 5.52 Diodorus explains the importance of Naxos for Dionysus: he was raised there by local nymphs, and yet another name for the island, which grows splendid wine (cf. 432), is Dionysias.   **Χάριτες:** Callimachus made the Graces children of Dionysus and a Naxian nymph called Coronis, the same name which Diodorus had given to one of the Naxian nymphs said to have raised the god (Schol. Flor. 30–2, p. 13 Pfeiffer, cf. Harder 2012: 2.138).

427–8 'and she gave this too to the son of Aison, for him to carry away, a splendid hospitality-gift together with many other fine objects'. **γλήνεσι:** a Homeric hapax: at *Il.* 24.192 Priam chooses gifts (including fabrics, 229–31) for Achilles from among the γλήνεα πολλά of his store-rooms; a standard gloss for the Homeric term is ποικίλματα (e.g. Hesychius γ 631 and the scholia here). The preciousness of Hypsipyle's gifts is marked by the rarity of the word used to denote them.

428–9 ἀφάσσων: cf. 184–6n.   **γλυκὺν ἵμερον ἐμπλήσειας:** the audience is to feel the same quasi-erotic longing as Apsyrtos and as is inscribed in the cloak's history; the audience can no more resist the gift than Apsyrtos can; see 444n., Byre 1991: 224–5. In Book 1, such addresses to the audience frame the description of Jason's marvellous cloak (1.725–6, 765–7).

430 ἀμβροσίη ὀδμή: ὀδμή | ἀμβροσίη arises from the wine with which Dionysus fills the pirate-ship in *HHDion.* 36–7. Cf. also Moschus, *Europa* 90–2 (indebted to this passage).   **ἄεν** was supplemented by Haslam 2013, and is probably to be accepted (Fränkel had conjectured πνέεν), despite the resultant double hiatus; previously the papyrus was thought to read μ[έ]νε[ν. Elsewhere Ap. uses ἄεν (an alternative imperfect of ἄημι/ἄω) only of winds, but cf. *HHDem.* 276–8 (Demeter's epiphany) περί τ' ἀμφί τε κάλλος ἄητο | ὀδμὴ δ' ἱμερόεσσα θυηέντων ἀπὸ πέπλων | σκίδνατο, with Richardson 1974: 253.

431 Νυσήϊος: Nysa was very early associated with Dionysus, but there was no agreement as to where this place was, cf. 1134, *Il.* 6.132, *HHDion.* (1) 8–9, Dodds on Eur. *Ba.* 556–9; Hesychius *v* 742 notes that it is 'a mountain, not in any one place' and enumerates 15 Nysas in various locations.

432 ἀκροχάλιξ 'tipsy, pleasantly drunk', from a believed association with χάλις 'unmixed wine'; the word is otherwise found only in an imitation of this passage at Dion. Perieg. 948, but ἀκροθώραξ means much the same (Kassel–Austin on Diphilus fr. 45.2). Gods drink nectar rather than wine (*Il.* 1.598 etc.), but – as the inventor of wine – Dionysus naturally drinks both.　　**μεμαρπώς** 'grasping, holding tight', cf. *Il.* 14.346 (another divine union) ἀγκὰς ἔμαρπτε Κρόνου πάϊς ἣν παράκοιτιν.

433–4 A variation on *Od.* 11.321–5, Ἀριάδνην, |κούρην Μίνωος ὀλοόφρονος, ἥν ποτε Θησεὺς | ἐκ Κρήτης ἐς γουνὸν Ἀθηνάων ἱεράων | ἦγε μέν, οὐδ' ἀπόνητο· πάρος δέ μιν Ἄρτεμις ἔκτα | Δίηι ἐν ἀμφιρύτηι Διονύσου μαρτυρίηισι. In Homer there is no suggestion that Theseus deliberately abandoned Ariadne (see 3.997–1004n.).　　**παρθενικῆς Μινωίδος:** the phrase occurs already at 3.998, and cf. Call. fr. 110.59 νύμφης Μινωίδος.

435–41 As elsewhere, Ap. experiments creatively with the sending of messages; here a mixture of direct and indirect speech, an almost anacoluthic parenthesis and the extraordinary postponement of a main verb until 442 create a palpable air of secrecy and deceit (Hunter 1993: 144–5).

435–8 κηρύκεσσιν ἐπεξυνώσατο μύθους | θελγέμεν ... ἐλθέμεν is best understood as 'she exchanged words with [i.e. ordered] the heralds to charm [with her gifts] <Apsyrtos> to come', or perhaps ' ... words for charming <Apsyrtos> to come ... '; θέλγειν, rather than, say, πείθειν is used because all Medea's words, as well as her gifts, carry magical force. The construction seems awkward (Fränkel proposed θέλγουσ' and Merkel θέλγε μιν), but should perhaps be accepted in view of related syntactical experiments elsewhere.

437 ἀμφιβάλησιν must here be 'envelop <them>', although the meaning is as hard to parallel as an intransitive 'fell about' <them>' would be; ἀμφιβεβήκηι would be expected, but the corruption would be very hard to explain.

438–9 3.12–13 (Hera to Athena) are verbally very close to these verses.　　**δόλον:** it is very unclear whether Π¹ did in fact have an alternative reading; see Kingston 1968: 56.

440–1 are a kind of explanatory parenthesis in direct speech: 'For, <she said>, the sons of Phrixos … '. πέρι 'very much, exceedingly', i.e. 'with irresistible compulsion', LSJ s.v. περί ε ιι. Fränkel 1964:15 suggested παρά … δόσαν 'handed over'. δόσαν ξείνοισιν ἄγεσθαι: there is perhaps a resonance of 'gave in marriage to strangers'.

442 παραιφαμένη need not imply deceit (cf. 2.287, 3.14–15n.), but here that implication is clear. θελκτήρια φάρμακ' continues the erotic atmosphere (428–9, 444n.) of Medea's 'attraction' of Apsyrtos, cf. the Nurse's φίλτρα … θελκτήρια | ἔρωτος at Eur. *Hipp.* 509–10.

444 Medea's powerful magic may remind us of Simaitha's attempts to win back (and/or destroy) Delphis in Theocritus 2 (note φάρμακα 2.15, πάσσειν 2.18–21, Έρως ἀνιαρέ 2.55, ἕλκε in the repeated refrain etc.). Both scenes evoke so-called ἀγωγή spells (cf. ἤγαγε) used to attract a desired lover to one and to separate him or her from any possible rivals (see esp. Faraone 1999); in such spells the boundary between the wish to induce desire (cf. γλυκὺν ἵμερον in 429) and the wish to destroy or inflict pain was a very fluid one, and Medea's use of erotic magic to lure Apsyrtos to his death is a new twist on that phenomenon. There is thus a very close link (normally overlooked) between these verses and the apostrophe to Eros which immediately follows.

445–9 are an invocation by the narrator to Eros in a form related to that of the ἀποπομπή or prayer to a god to leave one alone and exercise destructive powers on others, cf. Aesch. *Ag.* 1571–3 (with Fraenkel's note), Cat. 63.91–3, Fraenkel 1957: 410–11, Hunter 1993: 116–18; the chorus at Eur. *Hipp.* 525–9 express a very similar sentiment, and a comparison of these verses to the stasimon of a tragedy has often been made. This passage was to have a rich *Nachleben*, cf., e.g., Cat. 64.94–8, Virg. *Aen.* 4.412. The invocation forms the transition from the plotting of Jason and Medea to the actual killing, and this 'proemial' function increases the probability that Ap. was drawing specifically on Theognis 1231–4, verses placed (at some time) at the head of 'Book 2' of the elegiac collection: σχέτλι' Έρως, Μανίαι σ' ἐτιθηνήσαντο λαβοῦσαι· | ἐκ σέθεν ὤλετο μὲν Ἰλίου ἀκρόπολις, | ὤλετο δ' Αἰγείδης Θησεὺς μέγας, ὤλετο δ' Αἴας | ἐσθλὸς Ὀιλιάδης σῇσιν ἀτασθαλίαις. 445–9, which pick up the language of the proem of the book (cf. 1–5n., 62–3n.), have been at the centre of a debate about the extent to which *erôs* is still an important narrative driver in Book 4 (sometimes expressed as 'Does Medea still love Jason?'), cf., e.g., Fränkel 1968: 494–6, Fusillo 1985: 393n. 37, but whether we look to the longer causal chain, emanating from the god's intervention at the start of Book 3, or to the immediate context, erotic desire can hardly be written out of both the present and future stories of Jason and Medea; this is the god who 'derails the minds of just men to make them unjust and bring them to ruin' (Soph. *Ant.* 791–2). See further 446n.

445 Aratus, *Phain.* 15, χαῖρε, πάτερ, μέγα θαῦμα, μέγ᾽ ἀνθρώποισιν ὄνειαρ, has a very similar shape and expresses an almost exactly opposite emotion – grateful admiration rather than fear and loathing. As *Phain.* 15 serves to introduce a first-person statement by the poet (cf. 450–1) and comes from the proem, the probability that Ap. here echoes that verse must be considered strong.   πῆμα picks up the themes of the proem (cf. 4).

446 In one of his laments for the 'fallen' human condition, Empedocles exclaimed (fr. 124 D–K) ὦ πόποι, ὦ δειλὸν θνητῶν γένος, ὦ δυσάνολβον, | τοίων ἔκ τ᾽ ἐρίδων ἔκ τε στοναχῶν ἐγένεσθε. It was Strife (νεῖκος) which caused the unhappy human condition, but Ap. transfers this to ἔρως, the equivalent of Empedocles' φιλία or φιλότης, the alternative to Strife (Kyriakou 1994: 315). The murder of Apsyrtos and its aftermath is thus placed under the sign of Empedocles, for whom φόνος was the 'archetypal sin' (Osborne 1987: 48); cf. further 676–81, 678–80nn.   **ἔριδες:** cf. 448n. Haslam 1978: 54 argues that the reading of the papyrus is correct, with τ᾽ of the MSS being a scribal addition to avoid hiatus.   **πόνοι:** both '(physical) sufferings, toils' and 'emotional griefs', cf. 1 κάματον, 4 πῆμα δυσίμερον, Theognis 1323–4 Κυπρογένη, παῦσόν με πόνων, σκέδασον δὲ μερίμνας | θυμοβόρους, Ar. *Eccl.* 975 διά τοι σὲ πόνους ἔχω, Hunter 1993: 117n.70. The word leads into the storm imagery which follows; the 'sea of love' is a rich vein of ancient images (see, e.g., Nisbet and Hubbard on Hor. *C.* 1.5.16), particularly appropriate in an Argonautic context, and Aphrodite has by birth and cult a close association with the sea. γόοι of the MSS is also perfectly possible, and might be thought to pick up the first line of Empedocles fr. 124 (above), but adds little after στοναχαί, cf. *Od.* 16. 144 στοναχῆι τε γόωι τε, from which the MSS reading may have arisen.

447 τετρήχασι 'swirl up', an intransitive perfect of ταράσσω (or θράσσω), cf. 3.276, Philetas fr. 7.3 Powell (another passage of nautical imagery) ἀνῖαι τετρήχασιν, Campbell 1994: 244–5. The image here is of 'waves' of grief, cf. 1.1167 τετρηχότος οἴδματος, Leon. Tar. *AP* 7.283.1 (= *HE* 2351) τετρηχυῖα θάλασσα, and following note.

448 'Against my enemies' children, divine spirit, rise to a high peak … '; destructive love more often affects the young, hence 'children', but the suffering of one's children is also more painful than one's own. The image is of a monstrous wave, cf. 215, 2.70–1 κῦμα θαλάσσης | τρηχὺ θοῆι ἐπὶ νηὶ κορύσσεται, *Il.* 21.306–7 κόρυσσε δὲ κῦμα ῥόοιο | ὑψόσ᾽ ἀειρόμενος; the image was understood in antiquity as a wave rising to a peak like a helmet (κόρυς). Others take κορύσσεο here simply as 'arm yourself' (cf. δυσμενέων), but although there is certainly a resonance of war and death here, this does not do justice to the repeated imagery of the passage. Ap. has in mind the allegory of Eris at *Il.* 4.442–5, ἥ τ' ὀλίγη μὲν πρῶτα κορύσσεται ... νεῖκος ὁμοίιον ἔμβαλε ... ὀφέλλουσα στόνον ἀνδρῶν; there too the image is drawn from a wave (see Kirk on line 442). The familiar play on ἔρις ~ ἔρως is signalled by ἔριδες in 446. **δαῖμον** may refer simply to Eros' divine power to inflict both good and evil, but Ap.'s readers may also think of the Platonic explanation of Eros as a δαίμων, mediating between men and gods (*Symp.* 202d-3a).

449 στυγερὴν ... ἄτην again picks up the themes of the proem, cf. 4–5n.; at 1.802–3 Aphrodite is said to have cast θυμοφθόρον ... ἄτην upon the Lemnian men. Ap. here combines the Iliadic Eris (448n.) with 'Agamemnon's apology' for his disastrous behaviour at *Il.* 19.87–8, [Zeus and Moira and Erinys] εἰν ἀγορῇι φρεσὶν ἔμβαλον ἄγριον ἄτην.

450–1 The narrator's intrusion continues (which has led to the mistake in the papyrus in 450), but rather than the emotional and personal involvement of 445–9, we now have the poet marking the stages of his song, in a manner which places distance between himself and his material, cf. 552–6, 2.851, 1090, Theocr. 22.115 πῶς γὰρ δὴ Διὸς υἱὸς κτλ.; although such questions can be understood to be addressed to the Muse (as explicitly in Theocr. 22), the absence of any explicit reference and the 'footnote' of 451 enhance the contrast with the invocation which has immediately preceded. Morrison 2007: 302–3 understands the question to be addressed to Eros (with ἥμιν as 'the poet and Eros'), but this seems very unlikely, and ignores the progressive force of γὰρ δή, which marks a new stage in the narrative, cf. 2.852, 1090, Denniston 244.   **ἐδάμασσεν:** the subject is Medea, brought forward from 449.   **τὸ ... ἐπισχερώ ... ἀοιδῆς** 'the next part of my song', here conceived as a linear progression like a journey (Albis 1996: 50–1); we might think of this 'next part' as 'the Apsyrtos': it is framed by Ἄψυρτον (451) ~ Ἀψυρτεῦσιν (481), as the 'Hylas' is similarly framed (1.1207 ~ 1.1354), and cf. 661–2n. ἐπισχερώ is more usually an adverb.

452–4 νήσωι: there were in fact two such islands (hence Fränkel's νήῶι), but cf. 458.   **λίποντο:** the subject is probably 'the Greeks and Colchians'; it is natural that both sides would be represented, cf. Fränkel 1968: 496–7. **τοὶ μέν ... κρινθέντες** 'The others [i.e. the Greeks and Colchians] separated (κρινθέντες) and moored apart from each other (διάνδιχα) with their own ships.'

455 οὓς ἐξαῦτις ἑταίρους 'after that his [i.e. Apsyrtos'] comrades'.

458 λυγαίην 'gloomy', an appropriate atmosphere for deceitful murder. **ἐπεβήσετο:** such sigmatic aorists with 'strong' endings are found in Homer and subsequent epic, cf. 18, 1176, K–B ΙΙ 103, Chantraine I 416–17.

459 οἰόθι δ' ἀντικρὺ μετιών 'coming alone direct to [the meeting]'.

460–1 'like a tender child [tests] a winter torrent which not even men in their prime cross over'. The model is Achilles' complaint that he is to die, not heroically, but in the river ὡς παῖδα συφορβόν … χειμῶνι περῶντα (*Il.* 21.282–3). The comparison (note esp. ἀταλός) evokes the version of the story, already in Pherecydes (*FGrHist* 3 F32), in which Medea cut up her young brother to delay the Colchian pursuers, 421–521n.; such evocation of variant versions is very typical of Hellenistic and Roman poetic myth. **αἰζηοί** 'strong young men' cf. 3.518–19, 1367–8, *LfgrE* s.v.; at 268 the meaning was simply 'men'.

462–3 A pair of spondaic verses slows the narrative to prepare for Jason's sudden attack. **εἴ κε δόλον κτλ.** '[he tested her] … to see whether she would … '

464 πυκινοῦ … λόχοιο: the original sense of the adjective in this Homeric locution is perhaps 'dense', i.e. difficult to detect, but here 'clever, cunning' clearly resonates. **ἐξᾶλτο**: the transmitted ἐπᾶλτο is unmetrical. Some Homeric compounds of ἄλλομαι were understood as actually deriving from πάλλομαι (Fränkel 1923: 278–81, Bühler 149–51), and Fränkel here conjectured ἔκπαλτο, but Hölzlin's ἐξᾶλτο seems the neatest solution. Dr Benaissa informs me that ἐξᾶλτο is in fact read on an unpublished Oxyrhynchus papyrus.

466 ἔμπαλιν 'away', i.e. Medea averted her eyes, cf. 1315, Call. fr. 80.11 (with Harder 2012: 2.684). **καλυψαμένη ὀθόνηισι**: the 'fine material' here is very likely her veil (cf. 468n., καλύπτρην 473). At *Il.* 3.141 Helen feels homesick for her former life and goes to watch the fighting καλυψαμένη ὀθόνηισιν; here Medea makes a complete break with her former life and family, cf. Pavlou 2009: 194–7. The bT-scholia on the Homeric verse note that such discretion is σώφρονι γυναικὶ κόσμος, but at this moment Medea's actions are anything but σώφρων.

467 Medea tries to avoid the terrible sight, but the Erinys sees it with pitiless clarity (475–6).

468 βουτύπος is particularly used of one of the priests at a sacrifice (Σ 2.90–3, Cuypers 1997: 128), and this is appropriate here as Apsyrtos is struck down in front of a temple; Porter 1990 compares Eur. *El.* 839–43 (the 'sacrifice' of Aegisthus). The image particularly evokes the death of Agamemnon, ὥς τίς τε κατέκτανε βοῦν ἐπὶ φάτνηι (*Od.* 4.535, 11.411, cf. Aesch. *Ag.* 1126–8, Eur. *El.* 1142–4), and it is the chain of killing in the house of Atreus which is clearly Ap.'s main comparative model here, as it had already been in the *Odyssey* (Introduction, pp. 5–6); Ap. can thus both imitate the archaic epic and deepen its power through the use of earlier tragic imitations. Medea's attempt to veil her eyes has been thought to evoke a painting by Timanthes (late fifth cent.) of the sacrifice of Iphigeneia, in which Agamemnon's head was veiled (Cic. *Orat.* 74, Plin. *HN* 35.73), because his grief could not adequately be represented. According to *LIMC* ii 1.467, 'there does not seem to exist any depiction of Apsyrtos in ancient art'. κερεαλκέα 'of mighty horns', a word found only here, cf. γυιαλκής 'of strong body' (Bacchyl. 12.8). Call. *h.* 3.179 has κεραελκέες of very strong cattle (explained by Σ as 'because they drag the plough with their horns'), and one form may be a variation of the other.

469 ὀπιπεύσας 'having kept watch [for him]', cf. *Il.* 7.243 (Hector does not want to strike Ajax down) λάθρηι ὀπιπεύσας, ἀλλ' ἀμφαδόν. Others understand 'struck him, gazing at him', in contrast to Medea's averted look, but the verb regularly carries a resonance of secretive looking, *LfgrE* s.v.

470 stresses the sanctity of the place where Apsyrtos was struck down; far from building a temple of Artemis (cf. 330n.), Medea was party to a terrible crime in the enclosure of such a shrine. Temples are used to mark significant stages in the relationship of Jason and Medea: in Book 3 they met (according to Jason) 'in a holy place, where transgression would be impious' (3.981), but ἀλιτέσθαι would certainly include the murder they are about to commit. That temple was dedicated to Hecate, a goddess sometimes identified with Artemis, and Medea had been compared to Artemis as she processed to the temple (3.876–86n.); here, at a temple of Artemis, the bitter consequences of the former meeting become clear. ἀντιπέρηθεν 'from the coasts opposite', cf. 1.613 etc.

471 γνὺξ ἤριπε evokes the collapse of a sacrificial animal, cf. 2.96 (Amycus), 3.1310. λοίσθια 'at the end, at the last', an adverbial use of the neuter plural, cf. Theocr. 5.13 τὰ λοίσθια. ἥρως is used of both Apsyrtos and Jason (477) in this episode. To what extent these labels are ironized may be debated, but they do suggest the archaic 'pastness' of the events, an atmosphere confirmed by the archaic rite of *maschalismos* in 477.

472 θυμὸν ἀποπνείων 'breathing out his spirit, giving up the ghost', a Homeric locution (*Il.* 4.524, 13.654) appropriate to the distancing of the narrative. The death of Agamemnon in Aeschylus may again be relevant, cf. *Ag.* 1388–90, οὕτω τὸν αὑτοῦ θυμὸν †ὁρμαίνει† πεσών, | κἀκφυσιῶν ὀξεῖαν αἵματος σφαγήν | βάλλει μ' ἐρεμνῆι ψακάδι φοινίας δρόσου (~ 473–4). ἀναπνείων of the MSS would give the rarer phrasing, but the sense would be awkward; at 3.231, 1292 it is used of the fire-breathing bulls.

473 κατ' ὠτειλήν 'around the wound', cf. *Il.* 17.86, LSJ s.v. κατά B 2. ὑποΐσχετο 'caught from underneath', cf. 169.

473–4 καλύπτρην | ἀργυφέην καὶ πέπλον: another memory of Medea's first rendezvous with Jason, cf. 3.832–5; there (837) the narrator introduced the shadow of 'the griefs to come', and the killing of Apsyrtos is certainly one of these, but by no means the last.   **ἀλευομένης** 'as she sought to avoid it'; this present participle of ἀλέομαι is formed from the aorist ἠλευάμην, cf. West on Hes. *WD* 535.   **ἐρύθηνεν:** when Jason approached the temple of Hecate in Book 3, Medea blushed (3.963 ἔρευθος); here there is a redness of a quite different kind, cf. Rose 1985: 41. The deliberateness of Apsyrtos' staining of Medea, his marking of her with blood-guilt and with blood that will remain visible to the Fury (475–6), contrasts with the blood that covered Clytemnestra at the killing of her husband (472n.).

475–6 'With hostile glance, the subduer of all, the pitiless Erinys saw clearly what a destructive deed they had wrought.' An interwoven word order creates (as often in *Arg.*) a tension between stylistic elaboration and dread import. There may be a memory of Pind. *Ol.* 2.41–2 (Oedipus' killing of his father and the subsequent history of the house) ἰδοῖσα δ᾽ ὀξεῖ᾽ Ἐρινύς | ἔπεφνε οἱ σὺν ἀλληλοφονίαι γένος ἀρήιον.   **ὀξύ** 'sharply', hence 'clearly'.   **λοξῶι . . . ὄμματι:** the sideways glance of hostility and menace, cf., e.g., Solon fr. 34.5 West λοξὸν ὀφθαλμοῖς ὁρῶσι πάντες ὥστε δήϊον, Call. fr. 1.37–8 (with Harder 2012: 2.85–6), *Hecale* fr. 72 Hollis.   **νηλειής:** the Fury does not forgive or forget.   **Ἐρινύς** falls heavily at the end of the couplet – this is the word we have been waiting for; there is a similar effect at Soph. *El.* 489–91 (cf. Finglass on 491), and the mention of the Fury intensifies the atmosphere of tragedy. There is also a kind of tragic irony, given Medea's threats at 385–6.

477 ἥρως: see 471n.   **ἐξάργματα** 'extremities'. The reference is to μασχαλισμός, believed by later grammarians to be a rite in which murderers cut off fingers, toes etc. from their victims and hung these on a string around the neck or under the arms (μασχαλαί are armpits) to avoid vengeance and/or to cleanse themselves of guilt, cf. Ar. Byz. fr. 412 Slater, *Etym. Mag.* 118.22–36 Gaisford, Gotsmich 1955, Parker 1983: 107–8, Johnston 1999: 156–9, Ceulemans 2007. Both Aeschylus (*Ch.* 439, where see Garvie) and Sophocles (*El.* 445, where see Finglass) refer to the μασχαλισμός of the dead Agamemnon, a theme which might have appeared in the Cyclic *Nostoi*, and fr. 623 πλήρη μασχαλισμάτων suggests that it might have appeared in Sophocles' *Troilos*, as well as elsewhere in tragedy (cf. Aesch. frr. 122a, 186a R); both Agamemnon and Troilos would be appropriate here (421–521n.). Whether Alexandrian grammarians actually knew anything of the practice to which their tragic texts referred is uncertain; it may be that the explanations which have come down to us are inventions to fill a void.   **τάμνε** perhaps again (460–1n.)

evokes the version in which Medea cut up her young brother and scattered his body at the place later called Τόμοι (Tomi), cf. [Apollod.], *Bibl.* 1.9.24. The verb activates a connection between that version and the cutting involved in μασχαλισμός.

478 Ap. may again have taken the motif of spitting out blood from the murdered man from tragedy, cf. Aesch. frr. 122a, 186a R. Spitting as a means of averting evil and pollution is found in many contexts (cf. Theocr. 6.39, Diggle on Theophr. *Char.* 16.15), and three is an important number in magical rites, and one associated with Hecate and Underworld powers (Gow on Theocr. 2.43). The repetition τρὶς … τρίς suggests the careful following of ritual prescription.   **φόνου** 'some of the bloody gore', a partitive genitive, LSJ s.v. φόνος I 4.   **ἄγος** 'pollution', implying also the presence of divine anger, cf. Parker 1983: 5–12.

479 may refer to 477–8 or just to 478. The poet here lays down religious law to explain an 'archaic' practice (cf. 471n.), and one which for his readers may belong to a distant world of story-telling. It is typical of Ap. (and Hellenistic poetry more generally) to comment on or 'gloss' the narrative in a manner which is not Homeric; ἢ θέμις (ἐστίν) occurs in Homer only in the mouth of characters, never in the voice of the narrator (Griffin 1986: 38–9), but it is common in narrative in *Arg.*, cf. 694.   **δολοκτασίας**: the noun is found only here.

480 ὑγρόν 'clammy, moist', or perhaps 'limp, loose' (LSJ s.v. II), i.e. before *rigor mortis* had begun.   **κρύψεν** continues the atmosphere of secrecy and deceit; the body was 'hidden', not 'buried'.

480–1 The episode (cf. 450–1n.) is, as often, concluded aetiologically; past horror seeps into the present (Goldhill 1991: 330–2).   **Ἀψυρτεῦσιν**: i.e. the inhabitants of the Ἀψυρτίδες islands, traditionally placed in the far NE recess of the Adriatic, cf. Strabo 2.5.20, 7.5.5, Delage 1930: 212, Barrington 20 B5. It is unclear whether Ap. was the first to place the killing of Apsyrtos on those islands (Wilamowitz 1924: 2.192).

482 οἱ δ' ἄμυδις 'The other [Argonauts] all together/in a group … ', as opposed to Jason who was acting alone.

483 τέκμαρ μετιοῦσιν 'as a signal for them to come', lit. 'for them going to come'.

484 'moored (παρὰ … βάλοντο, tmesis) their ship beside the Colchian ship'.

485 Κόλχον: singular Κόλχος is not found elsewhere in the poem; it may have been chosen here to contrast with Κολχίδος immediately before, or Κόλχων should be adopted. Apsyrtos' name will be commemorated for ever (481), but the rest of the Colchians die as a nameless herd, cf. Hunter 1993: 42.

485–7 evoke the Homeric manner and also draw on specific passages, cf. *Il.* 5.161–2 ὡς δὲ λέων ἐν βουσὶ θορών κτλ., 15.323–5 οἱ δ᾽ ὡς τ᾽ ἠὲ βοῶν ἀγέλην ἢ πῶϋ μέγ᾽ οἰῶν | θῆρε δύω κλονέωσι κτλ., 22.138–44 (Achilles' pursuit of Hector); the contrast with the killing of Apsyrtos is pointed. Chiastic word order is set off by the imbalance of φῦλα πελειάων ~ μέγα πῶϋ without a dependent genitive.   **ἀγρότεροι** is here perhaps used unusually for ἄγριοι, cf. 444, 1.1244, *Il.* 24.41 (Achilles) λέων δ᾽ ὡς ἄγρια οἶδεν. ἀγρότερος is usually 'living in the fields, wild (as opposed to domesticated)', but a link with ἄγριος was familiar in the grammatical tradition (*LfgrE* s.v. ἀγρότερος), and it is used of lions already at Pind. *Nem.* 3.46.

489–91 Jason's surprisingly (cf. 491) 'late' arrival to the pitched battle (he was presumably busy with the corpse), even if not interpreted ironically, continues the distinction between the killing of Apsyrtos and the attack on the other Colchians; in the circumstances, μεμαώς, 'raging, desperate', might be thought a little strong.   **ἤντησεν** 'joined them'.

492–3 'Then they sat down and gave thought to a wise plan concerning their voyage.' For the construction cf. *Il.* 20.153–4 (perhaps echoed here) ὡς οἱ μέν ῥ᾽ ἑκάτερθε καθείατο μητιόωντες | βουλάς.

493–4 Medea is now integrated (at least temporarily) into the body of Argonauts, though the role of clever adviser falls to Peleus, as on other occasions, cf. 2.868–84, 1217–25 etc., Griffiths 2012.

496–7 εἰρεσίηι περάαν πλόον ἀντίον ὧι ἐπέχουσι | δήιοι 'row a course opposite to that which our enemies control'. The expected thing for the Argonauts to do would be to head south towards open sea, which would also make use of the prevailing wind (hence the need for rowing).   **ὧι**: i.e. κείνωι ὅν, cf. 514.   **ἐπέχουσι**: the sense is somewhere between 'control' and 'prevent [us from using]', LSJ s.v. VI.

497–9 'When at dawn they have a view of everything, I do not think that a unanimous opinion, urging them to pursue us further, will persuade them'.   **δίεσθαι**: middle inf. of δίω 'to hunt, pursue'.

500 κεδόωνται 'they will be scattered'; the form is a present passive, as though from *κεδάω (cf. Nic. *Alex.* 583 σκεδάων), which was perhaps a back-formation from the aorist ἐκέδασα; epic not infrequently uses present tenses where a future might have been expected (cf., e.g., ἀντιόω at *Il.* 13.752).

501 κεδασθέντων: the repetition from 500 carries rhetorical force – Peleus' plan envisages a 'logical' progression of events.

502 μετέπειτα κατερχομένοισι 'when we return afterwards'.

504 ἐπερρώοντ' 'exerted themselves', an imperfect of ἐπιρρώομαι, cf. 1633, 2.661, *Od.* 20.107, where the scholia gloss the form as ἐρρωμένως ἐνήργουν.

505–6 νωλεμές 'without a break' seems appropriate here, cf. 352n. Π¹ may have had a different text, but it is very unclear what that might have been (Fränkel 1964: 17, Kingston 1968: 57). **Ἠλεκτρίδα νῆσον** 'Amber island'. This island or group of islands was variously identified either in the extreme NE recess of the Adriatic or further west, near the mouth of the Eridanos (Po), where however there are no suitable islands, as Plin. *HN* 37.32 sharply points out (Delage 1930: 213, 220–1, Braccesi 1971: 223–33). ἀλλάων ὑπάτην, 'most northerly of all', might be thought to support the former placement, the reference to the Eridanos, which Ap. will indeed associate with amber (606), the latter. The point of 'most northerly', however, is to make clear that the Argonauts did indeed go in the opposite direction to what might have been expected, and Ap. is unsurprisingly impressionistic about the geography of the northern Adriatic; he may well have placed the mouth of the Eridanos further north than the mouth of the Po actually is (see next note), and so the Argonauts in fact head NW. **ποταμοῦ ... Ἠριδανοῖο:** usually identified with the Po (cf. Polybius 2.16.6 etc.), though Hdt. 3.115 regarded it as a poetic fiction (cf. Strabo 5.1.9). The Ἠριδανός was, however, also early connected with the similarly sounding Ῥόδανος, the Rhone (cf. Aesch. fr. 73a R, Wilamowitz 1924: 2.190, Delage 1930: 225–6), and Ap. will make good use of this double connection in constructing a river system embracing both.

508 δίζεσθαι ἐπέχραον 'raged to search for'. The verb (LSJ s.v. ἐπιχράω (B)) has, in *Arg.* and elsewhere, a wide range of nuance and usage, Rengakos 1994: 90, Cuypers 1997: 289–90.

509 Word order actually places 'the *Argo* and the Minyai' *inside* 'the whole sea of Kronos'; such mimetic stylistic effects, in which word order dramatizes meaning, are characteristic of Hellenistic poetry. **Κρονίης ἁλός:** cf. 327n.

511–13 The διχοστασίαι and scattering which Peleus had predicted (500) occurs, but not quite as his words would have led us to expect. Here again we are probably close to Callimachus' narrative: in fr. 10 a group of Colchians grow weary of the search (cf. 303n.), and frr. 11–12 concern Colchian colonies on the Adriatic coast. Cf. further 516–18n. **Κυταιίδος ... γαίης:** Kyta or Kytaia was thought to be a town in Colchis (cf. modern Kutaisi in Georgia), and poets used 'Kytaian' as a synonym for 'Colchian';

see Delage 1930: 186–7, Harder 2012: 2.154.   ἔμπεδον 'for the future, for all time', with ἔνασθεν.

514–15 ἧισιν ἐπέσχον 'which [the heroes] had occupied'; ἧισιν is compressed for κείναις ἅς, cf. 496.   ἐπώνυμοι Ἀψύρτοιο: a variation on 481.

516–18 refer to the Colchian foundation of Polai, the subject of Call. fr. 11, which is very close to these verses; οἱ μὲν ἐπ' Ἰλλυρικοῖο πόρου σχάσσαντες ἐρετμά | λᾶα πάρα ξανθῆς Ἁρμονίης ὄφιος | ἄστυρον ἐκτίσσαντο, τό κεν "Φυγάδων" τις ἐνίσποι | Γραικός, ἀτὰρ κείνων γλῶσσ' ὀνόμηνε "Πόλας". Callimachus' Polai is often identified with modern Pula at the tip of the Istrian peninsula (cf. Strabo 5.1.9, Hyg. *Fab.* 23.5, Barrington 20 A5), but Apollonius' settlement, which does not receive a name, clearly lies further to the south, as also in fact may Call.'s (cf. also Lyc. *Alex.* 1022–6, echoing Call. or Ap. or both), cf. Ps.-Skylax 24.2–25.1, Delage 1930: 214–16, Harder 2012: 2.169. The Encheleis were an Illyrian tribe around what is now the bay of Kotor on the coast of Montenegro (Beaumont 1936: 163); the river mentioned by Ap., probably the Rhizon, may in fact be that fjord-like bay, for which μελαμβαθέος would be very appropriate. Ap.'s failure to name the Illyrian settlement, to which attention is drawn by the fact that the other two groups of Colchians contribute to new geographical names (515, 519–21), may be making an intertextual point with or against Call. On Greek knowledge and colonization of the Adriatic see Thalmann 2011: 172–8.   Ἁρμονίης Κάδμοιό τε: after being expelled from Thebes, Cadmus and Harmonia reigned in Illyria, were transformed into snakes by Ares and then became beneficent heroes after death, cf. Hdt. 5.61.2, Dodds on Eur. *Ba.* 1330–9, Vian 1963: 122–33, Šašel Kos 1993, Harder 2012: 2.165–6, Lightfoot 2014: 350–1.   πύργον: this could refer to a fortified town or stronghold, cf. Call.'s ἄστυρον, but Ap. may actually have in mind a specific 'tower', established as a territorial marker (cf. Strabo 3.5.5).

518–21 The Keraunian mountains (Strabo 1.2.10, Barrington 49 B3) form a natural barrier between Illyria and Epiros; they run all the way down to the coast and were a famously dangerous landmark for sailors (see Nisbet and Hubbard on Hor. *C.* 1.3.20). Here they may be thought of as all the mountainous region of western Epiros, if Corcyra is considered to lie 'opposite' (see *RE* 11.268–9). Ap. derives their name from a specific incident, whereas other writers derive it from the habitually stormy nature of the area.   ἐκ τόθεν ἐξότε 'from that point forward since … ', cf. K–G 1 539 for similar combinations.   Διὸς Κρονίδαο κεραυνοί: in 509–10 Hera had, very unusually, acted by means of lightning-flashes, but there seems no reason to understand 'Zeus the son of Kronos' here as simply 'the weather' (so Paduano-Fusillo); Zeus will never be far from any place called

Keraunia.　**νῆσον ἐς ἀντιπέραιαν**: i.e. Corcyra. The Colchians would, not unnaturally, have preferred to dwell on the island, rather than in the inhospitable mountains. By this narrative device, these Colchians will not be on the island when their compatriots who pursued the Argonauts across the Mediterranean arrive there (1001–3).

522 Cf. *Od.* 4.519, ἀλλ' ὅτε δὴ καὶ κεῖθεν ἐφαίνετο νόστος ἀπήμων; as that verse refers to Agamemnon's return to Greece after the Trojan War, the echo is not very auspicious.　**ἐείσατο** 'seemed', the aorist of εἴδομαι, cf. 855; the word varies Homer's ἐφαίνετο.

523 **προμολόντες** 'proceeding, continuing their voyage', but with a resonance of 'coming out from hiding'.

524 **Ὑλλήων**: the ancients connected the name of this Illyrian tribe (Hylloi or Hyllees) with Hyllos, a son of Heracles. Ps.-Scylax 22.2 identifies them as living on a peninsula 'a little smaller than the Peloponnese', and they are usually placed on the Croatian coast between Split and Zadar, which would certainly fit the reference to the very many islands off the coast and also 563–5. γάρ perhaps implies that the Argonauts moored sooner than ideally they would have wished. Apollonius' source for this tribe may again be Timaeus (*FGrHist* 566 F77, Ps.-Scymnus 405–12, Wilamowitz 1924: II 177).　**ἐπιπρούχοντο** 'projected out (in the sea)'; προέχειν is often used of headlands 'jutting out'.

526 The Hyllees demonstrate that Jason's prediction in 405–7 has proved correct; καί is 'in fact'. Others understand 'were not hostile to the Argonauts, as also before [they had not been hostile]', with reference to alleged pro-Greek feelings stemming from their descent from Heracles, but it seems very difficult to extract this from the text.　**σφιν** is scanned long in *arsis*, cf. 535n.

527 **πρὸς δ' αὐτοὶ ἐμηχανόωντο κέλευθον** 'And, moreover, they themselves devised a route [for the Argonauts]'; the Argonauts use local knowledge in difficult sailing waters.

528 **τρίποδα μέγαν**: the final alpha is lengthened in arsis before initial μ-.

529–33 It is typical of Ap.'s narrative technique that nothing has been heard of these tripods before; they make their appearance when they have a role to play. The second tripod comes into play in the episode of Triton (1547–50, 1588–91), where the god shows the Argonauts how to get out of a lake, thus playing the same role of navigational guide as the Hyllees play here; there too the tripod subsequently disappears (ἄφαντος 536 ~ 1590). For Jason's consultation of Delphi cf. 1.209–10, 301–2, 360–1, 412–14. According to Herodotus 4.179, Jason had originally intended to take a tripod *to* Delphi before setting out on the expedition, but gave it to Triton in Libya in return for the god's help. There too the tripod is connected to the security of the land, for Triton prophesies that if any descendant of the Argonauts recovers the tripod, one hundred Greek cities will be founded around Lake Triton; as a result of the prophecy, the Libyans hid the tripod.   τηλοῦ … ἄγεσθαι '[gave them] to be transported far away', cf. 441.   περόωντι κατὰ χρέος 'who was going on a journey out of necessity'. The context, however, allows the sense 'coming to consult the oracle', like Πυθοῖ χρειομένωι at 1.413, to resonate; this is not a standard sense of κατὰ χρέος (cf. 889), though *Od.* 11.479 ἦλθον Τειρεσίαο κατὰ χρέος, may have been so understood. What follows makes the meaning clear and solves the linguistic puzzle: περόωντι κατὰ χρέος and πευσόμενος μετεκίαθε cannot be synonymous.   πέπρωτο 'it had been fated', a pluperfect passive from a presumed *πόρω, LSJ s.v. ii 4.   τήν: i.e. χθόνα.   δηίοισιν ἀναστήσεσθαι ἰοῦσι 'be ravaged by invading enemies'. For this meaning of ἀνίστημι cf. 1.1349, LSJ s.v. b ii 2; middle futures with passive sense are not uncommon, Smyth §802, 807–9. Such protective talismans are a familiar motif of cult and story; Pausanias 8.47.5 reports that Athena ensured that Tegea would be 'uncaptured for all time' and that a precinct there contained some of Medusa's hair, a gift from the goddess 'to guard the city'.

534 εἰσέτι νῦν marks, as so often, the conclusion of a cultic aetiology.

535 ἀμφὶ πόλιν: the final syllable of πόλιν is scanned long in arsis, cf. 526 (σφιν), 1229 (Κουρῆτιν); this is a variation on Homer, where ἀμφὶ πόλιν begins a hexameter but is followed by a consonant (*Il.* 9.530).   ἀγανήν 'pleasant, welcoming'. Ps.-Scymnus 407–8 reports that there are fifteen Hyllaean cities, and Steph. Byz. s.v. Ὑλλεῖς records a city Ὕλλη. Some have understood that Ἀγανή is the name of the city, but there is no other evidence for that; nevertheless, the epithet here is unusual, and textual corruption should not be ruled out.

537 οὐ μέν corrects the expectation created by the previous verses that the Argonauts will have met the eponymous Hyllos, Denniston 362.

538 Μελίτη: cf. 542–3n.

539 δήμωι Φαιήκων: the Homeric Scherie, long since identified with Corcyra, mod. Corfu; Ap. does not use the name Scherie for the island, only Drepane. See further 540n., 990–1n.   Ναυσιθόοιο: in the *Odyssey*, Nausithoos, Alcinous' father, was the founder of Scherie (*Od.* 6.7–12, 7.56–63 etc.); in *Arg.*, Alcinous is already king, though relatively young (there is no Nausicaa), and Heracles is at the end of his labours (cf. 1477–8on.). If we assume that (the relatively young) Heracles' visit to

Corcyra, for which there is no other surviving evidence, was imagined immediately after the killing of his children and before his canonical labours, then there is some consistency in the mythic chronology. Ap. is here presumably drawing upon mythical traditions developed and preserved on Corcyra.

539a is best explained as a makeshift by someone working with a text lacking lines 540–7, which could easily have dropped out by homoioteleuton (Ναυσιθόοιο at end of 539 and 547); the verse assumes that ὁ γάρ in 539 refers to Hyllos, whereas in fact it refers to Heracles (Fränkel 1964: 37). Brunck moved 539 and 539a to follow 543; hence the subsequent gap in line-enumeration.

540 Μάκριν: Makris was, as we learn in 1131–40, a figure of Euboean myth, whose traditions then moved to Corcyra; on Euboea she had been entrusted with care of the baby Dionysus. Callimachus uses Makris as a name for Euboea (*h.* 4.20, cf. Ps.-Scymnus 568, Hesychius μ131), and by the evocation of Euboea Ap. is clearly setting a mythological and geographical puzzle: εἰσαφίκανε at first suggests that Μάκριν is a place (Euboea?), not a person, and Διωνύσοιο τιθήνην could readily be applied to either (cf. 991 Φαιήκων ἱερὴ τρόφος of Drepane). The puzzle is only solved some 600 verses later. The scholia on 540–9 claim that Makris was an old name for Scherie, but this may be simply an (erroneous) inference from the text, and 990 is equally ambiguous.

541 We may infer that Makris had a special role to play in Heracles' cleansing, but there is no other evidence for this.

542–3 Cf. 1149–50. Ap. is our only source for this river on Corcyra (Steph. Byz. s.v. Ὑλλεῖς derives from *Arg.*).   **νηιάδα Μελίτην**: the final syllable of νηιάδα is lengthened before initial μ, as often. Μελίτη gave her name to a mountain on the island (1150), and was also the name of an island to the north, mod. Mljet off the Croatian coast. In 1131–7 we are to learn that honey (μέλι) played an important role in the legend of Makris.

547 ὑπ' ὀφρύσι 'under the (haughty) gaze of'; ὑπ' ὀφρύσι is a familiar (formulaic) phrase referring to facial gesture (3.371, 1024, *Il.* 13.88 etc.), here given new metaphorical life, under the influence of the common use of ὀφρῦς with reference to pride (LSJ s.v. 1). The implication of internal dissonance leading to emigration follows a very familiar pattern in stories of colonization; Nausithoos seems very happy to help Hyllos to leave (549–50).

548 Hyllos here replays what Nausithoos had done in the *Odyssey* (6.4–10), by leaving an unsatisfactory situation to found a new colony.   **αὐτόχθονα** poses an immediate puzzle for readers of Homer, but it is subsequently (991–2) explained that the people of Drepane ('sickle') descended from the blood of Ouranos when he was castrated by Kronos; it is hard to resist the sense that Ap. is also hinting here at an explanation for the name 'sea of Kronos', 327n. As with Makris (540n.), Ap. is setting mythological puzzles which he will later solve; we are being trained *how* to read poetry of this kind.   λαὸν ἀγείρας: cf. 2.520–1, also in the context of colonization.

550 τόθι δ' εἵσατο 'and there [i.e. in the land to be called after him] he settled'. The verb is an aorist middle of ἵζω, LSJ s.v. III 1.

551 Μέντορες: an Illyrian tribe further to the north; Ps.-Scylax 21.2 refers to νῆσοι Μεντορίδες, which are usually identified with Cissa (mod. Pag) and nearby islets (Barrington 20 B5).   ἀλεξόμενοι: for such stories cf., e.g., 1488, *Od.* 11.401–3. Cattle-rustling belongs to the heroic, epic world and is not to be considered 'dishonourable'. The transmitted ἀλεξόμενον is certainly possible, but it is perhaps slightly more probable that it was the newcomers from the south who were doing the rustling, not *vice versa.*

552–6 The poet asks the Muses (cf. 450–1) to explain why there are Argonautic legends and traces in the western Mediterranean and the west coast of Italy, although the heroes are currently in the Adriatic. Here the Muses, functioning almost metonymically for 'received traditions' and 'written records' (554n.), are used to allow the poet to combine various versions of the Argonauts' return; see Introduction pp. 10–11, 557n.

552 ἀλλὰ, θεαί, πῶς: Σ paraphrase as 'the poet asks the Muse', but that does not necessarily mean that they had a text with θεά rather than θεαί. Callimachus begins the *aition* of the rite at Anaphe (cf. 1727–30), and his whole Argonautic narrative, with κῶς δέ, θεαί (fr. 7.19), and there is very likely an intertextual relation between the two passages. For such questions cf. further Call. *h.* 3.186, Theocr. 22.116.   τῆσδε παρὲξ ἁλός 'beyond that sea'. Ap. also uses παρέξ with the accusative (2.1010) and adverbially; early epic has παρὲξ ἅλα, which Ap.'s phrase varies. The usage was discussed by grammarians (cf. Σ *Od.* 12.443, *Il.* 9.7), and for the use of παρέξ in general see K–G I 528.

552–4 γαῖαν | Αὐσονίην: i.e. Tuscany and Campania. The Ausones (Lat. *Aurunci*) were an Oscan-speaking people long known to the Greeks, cf. Hecataeus, *FGrHist* 1 F61, Hellanicus, *FGrHist* 4 F79(b), Arist. *Pol.* 7.1329b20. Strabo 5.3.6 notes that the 'Sicilian' sea is called the 'Ausonian' (cf. 660), though the Ausones never lived on the coast. The evocative name is common in Lycophron's *Alexandra*, and cf. Call. *Hecale* fr. 18.14 Hollis, with Hollis' note. Σ interestingly note that Ap. had been criticized for anachronism: Ausonia derived from Auson, a son of Odysseus and Calypso (cf., e.g., Ps.-Scymn. 230), and therefore the name was not in use at the time of the Argonauts; the scholia offer the (reasonable) defence that it is the poet, not the Argonauts, using the term (Nünlist 2009: 118–19). Dion. Hal., *AR* 1.35.3 notes that Italy was successively called Hesperia, then Ausonia, and finally Italia by the Greeks. An alternative genealogy made Auson the son of Odysseus and Circe (e.g. *Et. Mag.* s.v. Αὔσονες). νήσους τε Λιγυστίδας: the 'Ligurian' islands, we will discover (649–50), are placed near the mouth of the Rhone, and are usually identified with the modern Îles d' Hyères off Toulon. The Ligurians were conceived as living to the south of the Celts and as occupying the whole coastal area east of Marseilles, rather than the more limited Italian area of modern Liguria, cf. Hecataeus, *FGrHist* 1 F55, Hdt. 5.9.3 ('the Ligurians living inland above Marseilles'), Ps.-Scylax 4, Delage 1930: 234–6. καλέονται | Στοιχάδες: the name 'Ligurian islands' does not occur elsewhere, and Stoichades ('the islands in a row') appears first here; island-names and how they changed was a subject of great interest to the Alexandrians – Callimachus wrote a 'Foundations of islands and cities and their name-changes' and cf. also his *Hymn to Delos* – and it is very likely that Ap. is here referring to a written source now lost to us. See further 267–70n.

554 περιώσια σήματα 'very many signs', cf. 2.394 περιώσια φῦλα. Fränkel suggests rather a connection with περιεῖναι, 'surviving signs', but this seems to add less to the question to the Muses. Ap. may here in fact be echoing his sources (552–6n.): [Arist.], *Marvellous Things Heard* 105 notes that ἄλλα τεκμήρια οὐκ ὀλίγα are adduced to prove the Argonauts' presence in the Adriatic, Diod. Sic. 4.56.5 cites Timaeus (*FGrHist* 566 F85) and others for the fact that there are ἐμφανῆ σημεῖα of the Argonauts in the western Mediterranean, and cf. Strabo 1.2.39.

555 νημερτὲς πέφαται 'make infallible appearances' or 'are claimed with all truth'; the perfect passive verb could be derived from φαίνω (cf. 2.853 ἔτι σήματα φαίνεται, Rengakos 1994: 148) or from φημί (cf. 1.988, 2.500); in Homer, the form belongs to a third root and means 'has been killed'. The linguistic uncertainty is playfully signalled by νημερτές 'with full truth'. ἀπόπροθι τόσσον 'so far away'. ἀνάγκη: the 'necessity and need' is in fact the poet's (Hunter 2008b: 139).

556 αὖραι: winds would normally be a serious problem for anyone wishing to sail from the Illyrian coast to the western Mediterranean, but Hera solved the problem (578–80). The question also evokes the Odyssean motif of winds blowing a heroic expedition off course, thus allowing unexpected events to occur.

557 που both marks the poet's refusal to claim infallible knowledge of Zeus's mind (cf., e.g., 1.996, Feeney 1991: 65) and emphasizes the fact that the otherwise amazing presence of Argonautic traces in the west is perfectly understandable, once Zeus's anger is taken into account. Σ see the poet as suddenly inspired after his question, and Fränkel 1968: 502 develops a similar idea. Here, as elsewhere, however, we are not to see the Muses taking over the poet's voice; invocations such as 552–6 rather mark significant turns in the narration. It is important that in 552–6 the poet does not say, in contrast, for example, to Homer at *Il.* 2. 486, that he is ignorant of the answers to the questions he is posing. For the use of που more generally see Hunter 1993: 108–9, Cuypers 2005: 41–5, Morrison 2007: 275–9.   **μεγαλωστὶ δεδουπότος** 'fell dead in his tall stature', cf. the Homeric μέγας μεγαλωστί (*Il.* 16.776 etc.). For the participle cf. 1.1304. δουπεῖν originally referred to the clashing sound of a warrior falling dead in his armour, but a passage such as *Il.* 13.424–6 (ἵετο ... αὐτὸς δουπῆσαι ἀμύνων λοιγὸν Ἀχαιοῖς) could easily have been understood as showing that Homer too used this simply as a verb for 'to die/be killed'. The matter was discussed both by the grammarians called Γλωσσογράφοι (fr. 8 Dyck, Dyck 1987: 138–9) and by Aristarchus; a sense of violent death seems still to resonate in *Arg.* (Rengakos 1994: 71–2).

558 reworks the reaction of Proitos to Anteia's slander of Bellerophon, ὡς φάτο· τὸν δὲ ἄνακτα χόλος λάβεν, οἷον ἄκουσεν (*Il.* 6.166); see Clare 2002: 136–7.   **οἷον ἔρεξαν**: an echo of 475 suggests that the Erinys and Zeus work together, cf. 713–14n.

559 Αἰαίης ... Κίρκης: in the *Odyssey* Circe lives on Αἰαίη νῆσος (10.135 etc.), but in *Arg.* she lives in the west, cf. 3.311–13, 1071–4nn. Κίρκη ... Αἰαίη is a Homeric collocation (*Od.* 12.268, 273), but here it draws particular attention to the links between Circe and her niece, Αἰαίη Medea (243, 3.1136). **δήνεσι** 'counsels, skills', cf. 3.661n.; the wide semantic range of the term is illustrated by the difference between this use and that in 1. The verse reverses *Od.* 10.289, ὀλοφώϊα δήνεα Κίρκης: here Circe's δήνεα are beneficial, and it is her visitors who have ὀλοὸν αἷμα on their hands.

560 evokes the Odyssean pattern of great suffering before return, cf. *Od.* 1.4, 9.532–5 (the Cyclops' prayer to Poseidon). There may, however, be a further point to Zeus's double decision. In the *Eumenides*, Orestes seems to undergo both purification at Delphi (693–4n.) and an exhausting series of wanderings which have helped to wear away the stain of blood, cf. *Eum.* 75–9, Taplin 1977: 382–3. Just so, Jason and Medea will be purified by Circe and endure wanderings and terrible πόνοι in the Libyan deserts.

561 In contrast to Odysseus who heard the Cyclops' prayer (previous note), the Argonauts had no inkling of what was in store; Odysseus was later to have another divine informant in Calypso (12.389–90).

562 ἐξανιόντες 'putting out to sea from', LSJ s.v. ἄνειμι 2.

563–5 Cf. 334–6.   ἐξείης, 'in turn, in succession', is probably to be taken with πλήθοντο rather than with ἀπέλειπον.   Λιβυρνίδες: Ap. seems to use 'Liburnian' quite broadly of the very many islands off the Croatian coast, rather than just of islands to the north of the Hyllaean land, cf. Strabo 2.5.20, 7.5.5, distinguishing Issa etc. from the Liburnians, Delage 1930: 218; Ap.'s picture of these islands is not to be pushed too hard against modern geographical knowledge. Issa, a Syracusan colony, seems to be mod. Vis (cf. Ps.-Scylax 23.2, Beaumont 1936: 188–9, Wilkes 1992: 115–16), Dyskelados and Pityeia cannot be identified, but seem likely to be two out of Brattia (mod. Brac), Pharos (mod. Hvar), and Olunta/ Sollentia. Whether Dyskelados has anything to do with the *Celadoussae* islands named at Plin. *HN* 3.152 is uncertain.   ἱμερτὴ Πιτύεια: verses consisting of three names, only the third of which has an epithet, are common (*Il.* 2.647, 656 etc.); here Ap. may have in mind Odysseus' description of Δουλίχιόν τε Σάμη τε καὶ ὑλήεσσα Ζάκυνθος (*Od.* 9.24).

566 ἐπὶ τῇσι 'after these', cf. 572.   Κέρκυραν: 'Black Corcyra' (571), mod. Korčula, originally a Knidian colony or a joint enterprise from Knidos and the better known Κέρκυρα (Beaumont 1936: 174–5, Wilkes 1969: 8–9, 1992: 114).

567 Ἀσωπίδα ... κούρην: Kerkyra's father was the Asopos which flowed south from Sicyon and passed very close to Phleious, in the northern Peloponnese. Diod. Sic. 4.72.1–3 names Κόρκυρα among a list of Asopos' daughters, and notes that she gave her name to (the well known) Corcyra, cf. also Hellanicus, *FGrHist* 4 F77. Ap. keeps the story, but moves it to 'Black Corcyra', thus drawing attention to his avoidance of that name for the island of Alcinous, cf. 539n., 540n.   νάσσατο 'settled'.

568 ἠύκομον: the epithet appears only here in *Arg.* and has a special point. The island was to get its name from a combination of the nymph's name and its lush vegetation, but the nymph herself already had 'beautiful hair', and κόμη is regularly used of tree-foliage (LSJ s.v. ii), just as ἠύκομος may be used of trees (Empedocles fr. 127.2 D–K); in another context, ἠύκομον Κέρκυραν could easily be the island, not the nymph. The point is not just to strengthen the identification of nymph and island (cf. 540n. on Makris), but also to evoke different ways, including rationalization, of interpreting myth: did the island or the eponymous nymph come first?

570 κελαινῆι πάντοθεν: a breach of Naeke's Law, cf. 608 (κελαινῆς), 408n.

571 For the role of sailors in naming cf. Pind. *Paean* 7b.48M καλέοντί μιν Ὀρτυγίαν ναῦται πάλαι, Call. *h.* 4.51–4; in Callimachus the island (Delos) is οὐκέτ' ἄδηλος, whereas Corcyra is μελαινομένη: some intertextual link is possible.

572 Μελίτην: cf. 542–3n. Grammatical sources (see Pfeiffer on Call. fr. 579) sometimes confuse this Melite with another one, mod. Malta; 574–5n.   λιαρῶι 'warm, balmy'.

573 Κερωσσόν: unidentified.   ὕπερθε δὲ πολλὸν 'much further on', or perhaps rather 'much further out to sea', cf. the disputed πανυπερτάτη at *Od.* 9.25.

574–5 A rewriting of *Od.* 7.245–6, ἔνθα μὲν Ἄτλαντος θυγάτηρ, δολόεσσα Καλυψώ, | ναίει ἐυπλόκαμος. In Homer Calypso lives on Ogygia, 'where is the navel of the sea' (*Od.* 1.50), which at least does not suggest an offshore island; Ogygia is 'far away' (5.55, 100–2, 7.244–7), and Odysseus is swept for nine days from Scylla and Charybdis to reach it (12.447–8). Some placed Ogygia near Crete, perhaps Kaudos to the south, but various western locations were also championed (cf. Ps.-Skylax 13.5 (off the SW Italian coast), *RE* 10.1784, Dufner 1988: 69–70, 358–61); in one poem (Pfeiffer on fr. 470) Callimachus might have placed Calypso on Gaulos, mod. Gozo off Malta, and it is therefore of some interest that here too Calypso's island was somewhere near another 'Melite' (572n.). Once again, Ap. is presumably being playful with the names of islands. There was, at least later (Caesar, *BC* 3.26, Plin. *HN* 3.144), a harbour called Nymphaeum near Lissos (Barrington 49 B2), but where Ap. imagined Νυμφαίη must remain a secret (as he perhaps intended); Vian suggests the tiny island of Sason (mod. Sazon), but the fact that the Argonauts thought they could see the Keraunian mountains (575–6) does not mean that Ap. placed Νυμφαίη right up against those mountains.

575–6 λεύσσειν |... **δοιάζοντο** 'they imagined that they saw', i.e. they were unsure whether they did or did not see the mountains, cf. 1478–9 εἴσατο ... ἰδέειν (Lynkeus and Heracles).   οὔρεα ... Κεραύνια: cf. 518–21n. The sight of these mountains would have meant that they were sailing back into 'Greek' waters. For the motif cf. *Od.* 10.29–30: Odysseus' beloved homeland was coming into view when disastrous winds struck. Odysseus was sailing from the west towards Ithaca, and the Argonauts' southerly voyage would eventually have brought them to Ithaca; the two epic voyages are here closely intertwined, 579n.

577 Ζηνός: the genitive is to be taken with both 'plans' and 'anger'; for the position of τε in such a case cf., e.g., Aesch. *Ag.* 589 φράζων ἅλωσιν Ἰλίου τ' ἀνάστασιν.

578 τοῖο πλόου: i.e. the voyage necessitated by Zeus's plan of 559–61; τοῖο is demonstrative, 'that voyage'. Hera wants to get the Argonauts to the west coast of Italy as quickly as possible.

579 Cf. *Od.* 10.48 (the Aeolus episode) τοὺς δ'αἶψ' ἁρπάξασα φέρεν πόντονδε θύελλα, 23.316–17 (Odysseus' narrative to Penelope) ἀλλά μιν αὖτις ἀναρπάξασα θύελλα | ... φέρεν βαρέα στενάχοντα; once again the Argonautic expedition is made both to echo and foreshadow its Homeric model.   **ταῖς** 'by which'. This is slightly preferable to the alternative τοὶ δ', 'and they [were swept]', as it keeps the focus on Hera's deliberate actions.

580 νήσου . . . Ἠλεκτρίδος: cf. 505–6n.   **αὐτίκα:** the implication seems to be that the miraculous voice spoke when they were near the island, but as often the chronological nuance of this adverb is somewhat vague, cf. 253.

581–3 are very like 1.525–7, and 583 is identical to 1.527, a very rare case of a repeated verse in *Arg*. The first passage marks the start of the expedition, the second the start of a voyage which the Argonauts neither planned nor wanted. That the *Argo* could speak was a traditional feature of Argonautic myth, cf. Aesch. fr. 20R, Pherecydes, *FGrHist* 3 F111(a), Call. fr. 16, Lyc. *Alex.* 1320–1 (very close to this passage) φθογγὴν ἐδώλων Χαονιτικῶν ἄπο | βροτησίαν ἱεῖσαν.   **μεσσηγὺ θεόντων** 'as they were speeding along', cf. 584–5n.   **αὐδῆεν γλαφυρῆς νηὸς δόρυ** 'speaking plank of the hollow ship'. The juxtaposition νηὸς δόρυ plays with the use of δόρυ for 'ship' (LSJ s.v. I 2).   **στεῖραν** 'keel'. The word appears twice in Homer (*Il.* 1.482, *Od.* 2.428), together with ἴαχε, describing a ship running fast with a following wind; that Homeric motif is here reworked into something supernatural and unsettling.   **Δωδωνίδος . . . φηγοῦ:** at the sanctuary of Zeus at Dodona in Epiros, oracles were given (*inter alia*) by a sacred oak, cf. *Od.* 14.327–8 = 19.296–7, Aesch. *PV* 832 (αἱ προσήγοροι δρύες). It is thus appropriate that it is this plank which informs the Argonauts of Zeus's anger.

584–5 Cf. *Od.* 9.256–7 (the Cyclops) ἡμῖν δ' αὖτε κατεκλάσθη φίλον ἦτορ | δεισάντων φθογγήν τε βαρὺν αὐτόν τε πέλωρον.   **μεσσηγὺ δέος λάβεν εἰσαΐοντας** 'fear gripped them while in the very act of hearing'; word-order emphasizes the simultaneity of hearing and fear. Ap. is fond of the construction of μεσσηγύ with a participle, cf. 581, 602–3, 1362.   **φθογγήν:** word order suggests that this may be Zeus's voice, as well as that of the *Argo*, cf. 577n. Our uncertainty as to the origin of the voice matches that of the Argonauts.

586 πόνους picks up μυρία πημανθέντας in 560. The alternative πόρους produces an Apollonian catchphrase, cf. 1556, 1.21 δολιχῆς τε πόρους ἁλός, 361 etc., and is more likely to have arisen through error than πόνους.

588–9 Castor and Polydeuces were traditional protectors of sailors in storms (cf. *Hom. Hymn* 33, Theocr. 22.8–22), and the current episode will almost provide an aetiology for that role (593n., 650n.).   ἀθανάτοισι θεοῖς: Castor and Polydeuces do not (yet) belong to that company (note Τυνδαρίδαι in 593), and would never in fact be 'deathless' in the full sense, cf. *Il.* 3.236–44, Pind. *Nem.* 10.73–91.

589–90 κελεύθους | Αὐσονίης ἔντοσθε … ἁλός 'pathways inside the Ausonian sea', i.e. pathways which would bring them into the Ausonian sea (552–3n.).

591 δήουσιν 'they will find', a vivid present with future reference, LSJ s.v. δήω.   Πέρσης: Circe's mother Perse was a daughter of Okeanos, cf. *Od.* 10.135–9.

592 κνέφας: the Argonauts have had a very long day, first sailing south a long way (562–76), and then being blown right back to the north of the Adriatic.

593 Castor and Polydeuces here behave in just the way that sailors in trouble were later to pray to them, cf. *Hom. Hymn* 33.8–11. There is thus an implicit aetiology: every time sailors call upon the (now divine) Tyndaridai, they are re-enacting what the Tyndaridai themselves did to save the Argonauts and earn their divinity. In Call. fr. 18 the Tyndaridai seem to pray to the immortals in the Anaphe-episode; the latter part of that fragment is clearly related to 1701–10 (cf. 1701–5n.), and it may well be that there is a link between fr. 18.1–4 and the current passage; cf. Introduction, pp. 22–3, Harder 2012: 2.186–7. That one Callimachean passage corresponds to two different Apollonian episodes might be thought to make Ap. more likely to be the imitator.

594 τὰ ἕκαστα: the Tyndaridai carried out their instructions to the letter.

595 πολλὸν ἐπιπρό 'far further on', cf. 141.

596 ἐς δ' ἔβαλον 'they entered, passed into', cf. 639, 826, LSJ s.v. εἰσβάλλω II 3.   μύχατον ῥόον Ἠριδανοῖο 'the deepest [i.e. most remote] course of the Eridanos', 505–6n.

597–611 The Eridanos had long since been identified as where Phaethon fell to earth from the chariot of the sun, killed by Zeus in order to protect the earth from a natural calamity, and where his sisters wept tears which turned to amber (Barrett 1964: 300–1, Leigh 1998: 88–90). For the myth of Phaethon in general see Diggle 1970: 3–32; the narrative given by the scholia on *Od.* 17.208 (Diggle 1970: 31) is quite close to *Arg.* In paying for the killing of one descendant of the sun called 'Phaethon' (3.242–6n.),

the Argonauts' first encounter is with his ghostly namesake; see further
Fusillo 1985: 42–3.

597 κεραυνῶι: Zeus blasted Phaethon to save the earth, cf., e.g., Pl. *Tim.*
22c7, [Arist.] *Marvellous Things Heard* 81 (599–603n.), Ov. *Met.* 2.311–13.

598 ἡμιδαής begins a hexameter at *Il.* 16.294 (the fire at the ships). Virgil
borrowed from this passage to describe the giant Enceladus trapped
beneath Etna, *semustum fulmine*, *Aen.* 3.578; like Phaethon, the giant
sends up smoke and vapours (Nelis 2001: 50–1).

599–603 Places or people struck by lightning tend never to lose the marks
of what has happened, cf., e.g., Eur. *Ba.* 7–9 (Semele's smoking house),
with Dodds's n. on 6–12. For Phaethon's lake cf. [Arist.] *Marvellous Things
Heard* 81, 'There is also a lake, as it seems, near the river [i.e. the Eridanos],
containing hot water; a noisome (βαρεῖα) and unpleasant smell rises from
the lake, and no animal drinks from it nor does any bird succeed in flying
over it, but they drop down dead. It has a circumference of 200 stades and
a breadth of 10. The locals tell the story that Phaethon fell into this lake
when he was blasted by the thunderbolt.' It is more likely that [Arist.] and
Ap. here share common sources (? Timaeus, cf. Polybius 2.16.15) than
that either depends upon the other. Plutarch (*Mor.* 665c) notes that,
because it is believed that the bodies of those killed by lightning do not
putrefy, some found fault with Euripides for making Clymene, Phaethon's
mother, lament that her son's body lies 'unwashed and rotting (σήπεται)',
fr. 786K = 3 Diggle. Ap. perhaps leaves unclear whether the terrible
stench (cf. 620–3) is that of sulphur or rotting flesh or both.

599 ἡ δ' ἔτι νῦν περ: cf. 2.1211–14 describing Typhaon, another victim of
Zeus's thunderbolt and, like Phaethon, still (i.e. to the time of the narrator) lying in a lake.

600 τραύματος αἰθομένοιο 'from his smoking wound', an ablatival
genitive.   **βαρύν** 'hard to bear, disgusting', cf. 620–3 (βαρύθοντες 621),
[Arist.] cited in 599–603n., Soph. *Phil.* 1330 νόσος βαρεῖα.

601–3 Such 'no go' areas for birds as a result of noxious vapours are a
familiar ancient idea, the most famous being Lake Avernus (Ἄορνος), cf.
Lucr. 6.818–29, Virg. *Aen.* 6.239–40 *quam super haud ullae poterant impune
uolantes | tendere iter pennis*, Nelis 2001: 244–5.   **διὰ … τανύσσας:** tmesis;
the compound is found only here, cf. 771. In this heavy atmosphere
no wings will be sufficiently 'light' or 'swift'.   **βαλέειν ὕπερ** 'to pass
over' (anastrophic tmesis), LSJ s.v. ὑπερβάλλω III 1a.   **μεσηγύς …
πεποτημένος** 'in mid-flight', cf. 584–5n.   **ἐνιθρώισκει:** cf. Lucretius
6.824–5 (the bird above Avernus) *cadat … corruit*. The transmitted
ἐπιθρώισκει is not impossible, but that compound would more naturally

suggest a rising up, of smoke etc. Fränkel suggested φλογμὸς ἐπιθρώισκει πεποτημένωι, but it is not flames which rise up to attack the bird (cf. 600), and the marvel is the observable movement of the bird, not that of the vapours.

603–4 Unlike Apsyrtos, Phaethon is mourned for ever by his sisters. The metamorphosis of Phaethon's (half-)sisters into poplars and of their tears into droplets of amber were a familiar part of the myth from an early date. Plin. *HN* 37.44 (cf. 606n.) explains the link between amber and the Po from the fact that the women of the region use amber for both decorative and medicinal purposes. In an alternative aetiology, amber was formed from tears shed for Meleager by his sisters, who were turned into μελεαγρίδες, 'guinea-fowl', cf. Soph. fr. 830a R, Ov. *Met.* 8.536–46, Strabo 5.1.9 (associating the story with the Electrides Islands near the mouth of the Eridanos), Thompson, *Birds* 198–9. **κοῦραι | Ἡλιάδες**: cf. 629–30n. **†ἀείμεναι**: the correct reading is completely uncertain; 'battered by winds inside their poplars' is not a happy idea. In a passage imitating this one, Dion. Perieg. 292 has the Celts ὑφήμενοι αἰγείροισι, 'sitting under poplars', to collect amber and it is tempting to transfer that reading, or something like it, to this passage; it has been observed that this would suit the fact that the Heliades cannot here have actually been metamorphosed, as they are still mourning and have eyelids. This, however, may be too literal an approach to poetic images, and Ap. is clearly describing a scene imagined as contemporary with himself as much as with the Argonauts; the relation between the girls and their trees must remain as uncertain as the text. Gerhard's ἐελμέναι would be 'shut inside' (εἴλω), cf. 1.870.

605 Ovid has an extended description of this mourning at *Met.* 2.340–6. **ἐκ** is probably best taken in tmesis with προχέουσιν, though it also governs βλεφάρων. **φαεινάς**: an appropriate commemoration for Phaethon. One of the Heliades was named Phaethousa (cf. *Od.* 12.132, Ov. *Met.* 2.346), and a catalogue of their names at Hyginus, *Fab.* 154 includes a Lampetie.

606 Amber is fossilized tree resin, and technical writing uses δάκρυον and similar words to describe such substances, LSJ s.v. 2. The fullest ancient account of amber is Plin. *HN* 37.30–47; Pliny's account of how Baltic amber 'is hardened by heat or the action of the sea when a swelling tide carries the tree-gum off from the islands, and it is washed up on the shores' (37.42) is not unlike 607–9. Cf. further 625–6n., Cunliffe 2001: ch. 7.

607 τερσαίνονται 'are dried out'; more commonly, the exuded resin is said to 'harden' or 'turn to stone', cf. [Arist.] *Marvellous Things Heard* 81 ἀποσκληρύνεσθαι ὡσανεὶ λίθον, Ps.-Scymnus 392 δάκρυον ἀπολιθούμενον, Ov. *Met.* 2.364 *sole rigescunt.*

608–9 'But when the waters of the dark lake wash on to the banks, stirred by the blast arising from the roaring wind ... '.   κελαινῆς ὕδατα: cf. 570n.   πνοιῆι πολυηχέος ἐξ ἀνέμοιο offers a sort of combination of πνοιῆι ἀνέμοιο and πολυηχέος ἐξ ἀνέμοιο.

610 A wholly dactylic verse, the first since 600 and marked off by the initial spondee of 611, imitates the rapid action of the waters. A similar effect with κυλίνδετο in Hom. *Od.* 11.598 was later discussed by Dion. Hal., *Comp. uerb.* 20.16, and Ap. may (though need not) here be reflecting discussion of Homeric poetic effects.   ἐς Ἠριδανόν: it remains unclear whether the lake is to be imagined as standing alongside the river, but not actually part of it, or whether the river in fact flows through the lake.   ἀθρόα πάντα marks the sudden swiftness with which all the amber is swept into the river, cf. 3.1361.

611–17 There is no other evidence for this 'Celtic' version of the origin of amber or for an association between the story of Apollo and Coronis and amber. In the familiar version (cf. Hesiod frr. 50–60, where however the reconstruction is fraught with difficulty, Pind. *Pyth.* 3, Eur. *Alc.* 2–7, 121–6), Zeus blasted Apollo's son by Coronis, Asclepius, because he used his skill to raise men from the dead, and in anger Apollo then killed the Cyclopes who had fashioned Zeus's thunderbolt; Apollo was punished for this by Zeus with a period of exile and servitude in Thessaly. For the association of amber with the Celts more generally cf. Dio Chrys. 79.4.

611 ἐπὶ βάξιν ἔθεντο: the nuance of the compound verb (in tmesis) is uncertain: 'added', i.e. to the canonical account, and 'forged, invented' are the regular interpretations, but the use is very hard to parallel. 619–26 do, however, certainly suggest that the Celtic version is false.

612–13 τάδε δάκρυα: English would render 'these are the tears which ... ', but Greek uses a more compact construction.   πάροιθεν 'on a previous occasion'.

614 Apollo is the god most closely connected with the legendary Hyperboreans of the far north; he visited them regularly (cf. 2.675, Alcaeus 307c V, Pind. *Pyth.* 10.34–6, Diod. Sic. 2.47.6), and every year they sent offerings to Delos, cf. Hdt. 4.33–5, Call. fr. 186. These people were evoked also at 286 (cf. 285–7n.), and we are here far to the west of that description, but the Hyperboreans are imagined to occupy the whole space of the north (see in general Romm 1992: 60–7). Here Apollo leaves Olympus for one of his favourite haunts (cf. 616–17n.), not for Thessaly, as in the usual story.

615 αἰγλήεντα: according to the fourth-century paean of Isyllos (*CA* pp. 133–4), Coronis' real name was Αἴγλα, but there is perhaps no more than coincidence here, cf. 958.   **ἐνιπῆς** 'threat, angry rebuke'.

616–17 seem to offer a compressed version of the traditional story. The principal difficulty, which led Fränkel to propose a lacuna after 615, is that Apollo's anger (χωόμενος) is relevant in two places in the story: anger at Coronis' unfaithfulness (cf. Pind. *Pyth.* 3.11 χόλος), and then at Zeus's killing of Asclepius (cf. Hes. fr. 51.3 θυμόν, Eur. *Alc.* 5 χολωθείς). Here, however, Apollo's anger seems to be contemporary with, or even the cause of, his departure from Olympus. Such narrative unclarity is by no means unique in *Arg.*, but one might consider χωομένου, explaining why *Zeus* was angry (cf. Hes. fr. 51.2 χώσατ' of Zeus's anger against Asclepius), or perhaps we are to understand a rather different version in which an angry Apollo voluntarily withdraws from Olympus; this would explain why he goes to his beloved Hyperboreans, rather than to rural Thessaly. The motif of divine withdrawal is most familiar from Demeter's withdrawal after the loss of her daughter.   **Λακερείηι:** a Magnesian town near Larissa, where Coronis lived, cf. Pind. *Pyth.* 3.33.   **Κορωνίς:** perhaps in different poems, Hesiod might have called Asclepius' mother both Coronis and Arsinoe (cf. frr. 50, 60M–W, West 1985: 69–72, Hirschberger 2004: 334–5, D'Alessio 2005: 208–10); Ap. would have had very good reasons for avoiding the latter. Ap.'s language here is very close to that of a *Homeric Hymn* to Asclepius, υἱὸν Ἀπόλλωνος τὸν ἐγείνατο δῖα Κορωνίς | Δωτίωι ἐν πεδίωι κούρη Φλεγύου βασιλῆος (16.2–3); both λιπαρῆι and δῖα would be appropriate to an encomiastic resonance as Asclepius is evoked.   **προχοῆις:** cf. 132n.   **Ἀμύροιο:** a river flowing into Lake Boibais near Coronis' home; this was a traditional element of the Coronis story, cf. Hes. fr. 59.3M–W, Pherecydes, *FGrHist* 3 F3.

618 Ap. teases us with the identity of his source for the Celtic version; whether his ancient readers were better informed than we are is yet another puzzle. For similar closing formulas cf. 1216, 1.1309 = Call. fr. 126; here the spondaic ending adds to the sense of closure.   **κεκλήισται** 'related, spread around', a perfect passive of κληίζω; Ap. uses the pluperfect ἐκλήιστο in the sense 'called' (267) or 'celebrated' (1202).

619–26 After the lengthy excursus on the myths of Phaethon, we now return to the experiences of the Argonauts, who (so we are to understand) know nothing of Phaethon or why they are surrounded by stench and lamentation; the narrative effect is as eerie as the landscape in which they find themselves; see Byre 1996b.

620 νόος ἐτράπετ': the transmitted τράπετο νόος has the final syllable of τράπετο lengthened in arsis before initial ν, cf. 125, and Homer has τρέπεται νόος at this place in the hexameter (*Od.* 3.147); Ap.'s expression would then be a refinement of Homer. Homer does, however, also have νόος ἐτράπετ᾽ αὐτοῦ at the end of a hexameter (*Il.* 17.546, cf. *Od.* 7.263), and Hermann's restoration of rhythmical 'normality' is an easy change.

621 στρεύγοντο 'they were sickened'.   **περιβληχρόν** 'to the point of great weakness', an adverbial neuter, probably to be construed with both verb and participle. The sense is, however, awkwardly compressed, and Madvig's περιβληχροί deserves consideration.

622 ἄσχετον 'ceaselessly, without a break'; the regular sense in *Arg.* is 'irresistible', and here the word is normally understood as 'intolerable', cf. 2.272 ὀδμὴ δυσάσχετος [δυσάνσχετος Ernesti], but that would add little which is new. For further discussion see Rengakos 1994: 59–60.

623–6 A series of repetitions and variations from earlier in the episode mark closure: 622–3 ~ 596–600, 624–5 ~ 604–5, 626 ~ 613.

623 τυφομένου Φαέθοντος depends upon ἐξ- in the verb.

624–6 Virgil seems to have used this passage in describing the night Aeneas and his men spend near Etna, *noctem illam tecti siluis immania monstra | perferimus, nec quae sonitum det causa uidemus* (*Aen.* 3.583–4); Virgil had used this same Apollonian episode a few verses earlier (598n.). These verses are closely reworked at Dion. Perieg. 289–93.   **νύκτας** need not imply that the Heliades mourn only at night when the Argonauts are said to hear them, cf. Σ *Od.* 17.208 ἡμέρας ἀδιαλείπτως καὶ νύκτας [Hermann: νυκτός], Ov. *Met.* 2.342 *nocte dieque*.   **ὀξύν** 'shrill, sharp', appropriate to the male perception of female lamentation.

625–6 are, if pushed, somewhat inconsistent with 607–11, but hardly problematically so.   **δάκρυα μυρομένηισιν**: a reworking of *Il.* 17.437–9 (Achilles' horses mourning for Patroclus) δάκρυα δέ σφιν | θερμὰ κατὰ βλεφάρων χαμάδις ῥέε μυρομένοισιν | ἡνιόχοιο πόθωι; the Heliades are mourning for another lost charioteer, Phaethon. Ap. may have already been thinking of this Homeric passage at 606.   **οἷον ἐλαιηραὶ στάγες**: amber may be roughly the colour of olive oil. Ap. is here varying a Homeric image of how oil floats on the top of water (*Il.* 2.754), but he may also be poeticizing 'technical' discussions of amber, cf. Plin. *HN* 37.42 (Baltic amber) 'seems to hang [in the water] and not settle on the bottom'.

627–39 On the imagined geography cf. 505–6n., Delage 1930: 224–36 and Introduction pp. 9–10. The dangerous confluence of the rivers is marked by verbal evocation of Circe's description of the rivers of the Underworld at *Od.* 10.513–15; cf. further 629–30n.

627 ἐκ δὲ τόθεν 'from there'.   **εἰσεπέρησαν** 'they proceeded into'.

628 ἄμμιγα 'coming together, mixing', i.e. ἀνάμιγα with apocope of the disyllabic preposition and subsequent assimilation.

629 βέβρυχε 'roars', a perfect describing a continuous state; Homer also uses this verb of the confluence of streams of water (*Il.* 17.264).

629–30 γαίης | ἐκ μυχάτης 'from the deepest recess of the earth'; the river system is imagined to rise from within the earth and then split into three branches.   **πύλαι καὶ ἐδέθλια Νυκτός**: from a Greek perspective, Night might be expected to dwell in the far north and west (cf., e.g., Strabo 1.2.28), and this would fit with the imagined geography of the Argonauts' return. Ap. is clearly using Hesiod's conception of the grim (possibly underground) house and threshold of Night (*Theog.* 736–57, cf. Stesichorus, *PMG* 185 = 8a Finglass), but of particular importance is the evocation of the proem of Parmenides' poem (fr. 1 D–K), in which Parmenides, picking up the Hesiodic motifs, imagines himself riding, like (though more successfully than) Phaethon, in a chariot, escorted by Ἡλιάδες κοῦραι (cf. 603–4) προλιποῦσαι δώματα Νυκτός, and he describes the place where are the πύλαι Νυκτός. In a passage which is an extraordinary mixture of 'science' and poetic myth, Ap. evokes a poem which itself thematizes the distinction between ἀληθείη and 'the opinions of mortals in which there is no true reliance' (lines 29–30). Ap. will return to the Presocratic imagination when describing the nightmarish creatures which surround Circe, cf. 672–5n.

631–4 Ap. conjures an enormous tripartite river system. One branch flows north to Ocean (cf. 637–9); this will be what we would call the Rhine, and if Ocean has any 'modern' geographical analogue, it may be the Atlantic. Another flows east and empties into the Adriatic ('the Ionian sea', cf. 289–91n.); this is the Eridanos along which the Argonauts have travelled. The third, which we would call the Rhone, flows south into the western Mediterranean. Cf. further Introduction, pp. 9–10. **ἐπερεύγεται ἀκτάς** 'empties with a roar on to the shores', cf. 1242. At *Il.* 15.621 κύματα ... προσερεύγεται ἀκτῆι Ap. may have known the reading ἀκτήν (Rengakos 1993: 135).   **Σαρδόνιον πέλαγος** is used of the Mediterranean west of Italy and near Sardinia and Corsica, cf. Hdt. 1.166.2, Strabo 5.2.1, Gow on Theocr. 16.86.   **ἀπείρονα κόλπον**: the 'boundless gulf' is usually understood to be the Golfe du Lion, the Γαλακτικὸς κόλπος (Strabo 4.1.6 etc.), into which the Rhone empties west of Marseilles, though it might be a more general reference to the huge expanse of the Mediterranean.   **ἑπτὰ διὰ στομάτων**: the number of mouths of the Rhone was very variously given in antiquity, cf. Strabo 4.1.8. Seven mouths allows one to be 'midmost' (649).   **ἱεὶς ῥόον**: βάλλει must be understood with this third branch as well. The alternative ἵει ῥόον occurs in this *sedes* in Homer (*Il.* 12.25), where the verb is imperfect; Ap. might be varying Homer by using ἵει as a present, but it is very easy to understand βάλλει from 632. ἵει may be either a memory of Homer or a misguided attempt to mend syntax.

635–6 The vast 'wintry lakes' are presumably a vague allusion to the lakes of North Italy and Switzerland. **εἰσέλασαν** 'entered by rowing'. **ἀθέσφατον** 'over indescribable distances'; the adverbial neuter is preferable to the more obvious ἀθέσφατοι.

636–42 Epic is fond of grim counterfactuals, especially at moments of high drama, which broaden the texture by suggesting narrative paths not actually taken by the poet, cf. 20–4, 338–9, 903–6, 1305–8, 1651–3, 1.1298–1301, 2.985–95, *Il* 3.373–4, 7.104–6, de Jong 2004: 68–81, Nesselrath 1992. Very often, as here, it is divine action which prevents the potential events from actually occurring.

637 φέρε 'led to, ran into', intransitive, LSJ s.v. vii 1. The imperfect does not imply that the situation no longer exists, but the vivid focus is on what mattered at the time, cf. ἐξανίεσκον in 622. **τις ἀπορρώξ** 'one branch' of the three.

638–9 The poet does not stop to tell us why the Argonauts would have taken the stream to the north; perhaps we are to understand that it was the first way out of the lakes which they discovered, cf. 643–4. **εἰσβαλέειν:** cf. 596n. **ἐξεσάωθεν:** third plural aor. pass. of ἐκσαόω, used like (ἐκ–) σώιζεσθαι, 'to escape safely, reach home'; at *Od.* 3.185 the simple ἐσάωθεν means 'got home safely'. Timaeus (and perhaps others) had brought the Argonauts home via Ocean (*FGrHist* 566 F85, Introduction pp. 7–8), and so there is a literary game with Ap.'s predecessors here also (Romm 1992: 195–6).

640–2 vary the scream of the *Argo* itself at 580–5; there too a scream led to a complete change of direction by the Argonauts.

640 ἀλλ' Ἥρη: cf. *Od.* 12.72 (the *Argo*'s escape from the Clashing Rocks) ἀλλ' Ἥρη παρέπεμψεν, ἐπεὶ φίλος ἦεν Ἰήσων. There too Hera intervened in a 'counterfactual' construction (cf. 12.69), but she here averts the danger from a great crag, whereas in the *Odyssey* it was great rocks which posed the danger. **σκοπέλοιο καθ' Ἑρκυνίου** 'down from the Herkynian crag'. The 'Herkynian' mountains and/or forests were imagined in the far north, somewhere in modern Germany (perhaps the Black Forest), cf. Eratosthenes III B 118 Berger, Arist. *Meteor.* 1.350b5–6, Delage 1930: 232. [Arist.] *Marvellous Things Heard* 105 reports the view that the Istros rises in the 'so-called Herkynian forests' before splitting into two (cf.

282–93n.), and that passage shows that the name was connected with the Argonautic voyage before Ap.

641 οὐρανόθεν προθοροῦσα: the lack of preparation for Hera's intervention – no planning on Olympus *uel sim.* – heightens the narrative sense of suddenness and danger. ἐτίναχθεν: τινάσσεσθαι, 'quake, be shaken', is not commonly used of men, and momentarily we might think that it is the timbers of the *Argo* itself which shake.

642 ἐπὶ ... ἔβραχεν: tmesis; the simple verb, common in Homer, and its compounds appear only in the aorist.

643 παλιντροπόωντο: an unaugmented imperfect with 'diectasis' to preserve the metrical value of the original: –άοντο > – ῶντο > – όωντο. Ap. uses such artificial forms as part of his imitation of Homeric language. θεᾶς ὕπο 'with the goddess' help'.

644 'that [τήν demonstrative] route by which there was safe return for them on their journey'; this is the river (the Rhone) of 633–4. περ καί is a common combination in relative clauses (Denniston 490), and for the present case see Ruijgh 1971: 945.

645 ἁλιμυρέας 'washed by the sea', cf. 1.913, 2.554. In addition to ἁλιμυρής, Ap. uses, as does Homer, ἁλιμυρήεις of rivers 'flowing into the sea' (2.936).

647 Λιγύων: cf. 552–3n. The order of names, 'Celts and Ligurians', follows the sequence of the Argonauts' voyage south. ἀδήϊοι 'unmolested, unharmed', a remarkable event given the warlike nature of the Celts. αἰνήν is usually a negative term, 'terrible, dread', but here it is intensive, 'very thick' cf. 3. 211 ἠέρα πουλύν, *Od.* 7.15 πολλὴν ἠέρα, but also with a resonance of 'supernatural, eerie' (Fränkel 1968: 611).

648 The Homeric model is the mist which Athena pours around Odysseus as he approaches Alcinous' palace, *Od.* 7.14–15, but Ap. has produced a careful variation of his earlier imitation of that Homeric passage at 3.210–11, τοῖσι δὲ νισομένοις Ἥρη φίλα μητιόωσα | ἠέρα πουλὺν ἐφῆκε δι' ἄστεος, where see the notes of Hunter and Campbell. There the Argonauts are not seen by Κόλχων μυρίον ἔθνος, cf. 646–7. ἠέρα ... θεά evokes, but avoids, the familiar link between Ἥρη and ἀήρ (3.210–14n.).

649 διὰ ... βαλόντες 'passing through' (tmesis), LSJ s.v. διαβάλλω I 2.

650 Στοιχάδας ... νήσους: cf. 552–3n. ὅσοι εἵνεκα κούρων | Ζηνός: the phrase recalls the role of the Dioscuri as θεοὶ σωτῆρες, cf. Alcaeus 34.7 V ῥύεσθε, *Hom. Hymn* 33.6, Eur. *El.* 1348–53, Sens on Theocr. 22.6. Ptolemy I and Berenice were also θεοὶ σωτῆρες, and there is here a resonance of the importance of the Dioscuri in Ptolemaic cult (Cameron 1995: 433–6).

Through their actions the Tyndaridai of 593 have become 'the sons of Zeus', honoured in cult, and it is not hard to see here a reflection of and model for Hellenistic ruler cult, in which great men did earn divinity both by the power they held and by their 'saving' actions (Fränkel 1968: 513–16, Harder 2012: 2.187). This new role for the Dioscuri had already been foreshadowed at 2.806–10 where Lycus says that he will establish cult and a ἱερόν to the Tyndaridai, for the special attention of sailors, because of Polydeuces' killing of Amycus. The Argonauts owed their safety, of course, as much (if not more) to Hera as to the Dioscuri, but it is the latter upon whom cultic honours are bestowed; whether we should see here a measure of irony in the treatment of 'ruler cult' may be debated. The change of name from Tyndaridai to Dioscuri is made explicit in the Argonautic narrative at Diod. Sic. 4.48.6 (= Dionysius Scytobrachion fr. 30 Rusten).

651 These signs of cult are part of the σήματα of 554. Diod. Sic. 4.56.4 notes that 'not a few both of the ancient historians and of those who came after, one of whom is Timaeus (*FGrHist* 566 F85)' adduce as part of the evidence for the Argonauts' return via Ocean (Introduction p. 8) the fact that 'the Celts who dwell along the Ocean reverence the Dioscuri most of any gods, for they have a tradition handed down from ancient times that these gods appeared among them from Ocean'. Ap. may therefore have here again borrowed from Timaeus, but transferred the cult to the Mediterranean.   ὅ 'for which reason', LSJ s.v. ὅς Ab IV 2.

652–3 ἔμπεδον (cf., e.g., 343) functions as an aetiological marker, like the common ἔτι καὶ νῦν etc.   οὐδ' ... ναυτιλίης 'And they followed as watchers not only of that expedition ... '. 'Following' is what the Dioscuri will habitually do; whether we should see a specific reference to St Elmo's Fire, that 'electrical discharge which plays about the masts and rigging of vessels' (Page 1955: 267) and which was identified with the Dioscuri, is uncertain, cf. *Hom. Hymn* 33.12–13, Alcaeus fr. 34.11–12 V.   ἐπίουροι 'watchers, protectors', cf. 3.1179–82n.   πόρε 'entrusted'; the scholiast sees an ellipse of σώιζειν with the verb. Zeus here performs his traditional role of distributing spheres of action to new gods, as in Hesiod's *Theogony*.

654–5 Αἰθαλίην ... | νῆσον: Elba, off the Tuscan coast. Steph. Byz. s.v. Αἰθάλη connects the name, 'Sooty Island', with iron-working conducted there. Stone on Elba was indeed rich in iron and hence brownish in colour (*RE* 9.1090–1), a colour which Ap.'s aetiological story will explain, but αἰθαλόεις can mean 'burnt-coloured' (LSJ s.v. II 2), and so, as often, Ap. may here gesture towards competing aetiologies.

655 ἀπωμόρξαντο: the Argonauts used pebbles as strigils to clean the oil, sweat and dirt off their bodies (next note), and despite the textual difficulties of the following verses it seems all but certain that this is the aetiology of the colour of Elba's stones. The 'logic' is very typical of aetiological stories: a one-time event coloured some stones on the island, and henceforth all stones (new and old) bear that colour. Other reports of this aetiology suggest that it was not the stone-strigils themselves which explain the colour, but rather the dirt and sweat which the Argonauts scraped off (ἀποστλεγγίσματα) and which subsequently congealed into stones, cf. Lyc. *Alex.* 874–5, [Arist.] *Marvellous Things Heard* 105, Strabo 5.2.6.   **καμόντες** 'after their exertions'. This is often taken to refer to the journey from the Stoichades, but cf. 2.86–7 (Polydeuces and Amycus boxing) ἀπωμόρξαντο μετώπων | ἱδρῶ ἅλις, καματηρὸν ἀυτμένα φυσιόωντε. This passage confirms, as do the use of strigils and the σόλοι of 657, that we are to understand that the Argonauts competed in athletic contests on the island; see further Fränkel 1968: 516–17 on how Ap. spreads athletic events through his epic, rather than concentrating them in one major episode, as Homer and Virgil do. The elliptical narrative style is very typical of *Arg.*, and entirely unlike Homeric narrative. Athletes oiled their bodies before competition, and then cleaned themselves with strigils afterwards.

656–7 The transmitted text, with εἴκελαι for εἴκελοι, must mean 'and they [i.e. the stones] are strewn over the beach like skin-colour' or perhaps ' . . . like in colour' [either to the original stones or to the Argonauts' sweat]. This is just about comprehensible, but Fränkel's lacuna is an attractive solution. Another possibility, with or without the lacuna, is ποικίλοι for εἴκελοι, as this is the word which both [Aristotle] and Strabo (cf. 655n.) use to describe the colour of the island's stones.

σόλοι 'weights for throwing', whether like a discus or a modern shot-put, cf. 851, *Il.* 23.826. The latter passage gave rise to a debate about the material of which such weights were composed (see Erbse on Σ *Il.* 23.826), and Ap. provokes us to wonder what these σόλοι were made of, on an island where the stones contained a great deal of iron, two of the materials involved in the debate about Homeric σόλοι. At 3.1365–6 a great rock is described as a 'terrible σόλος of Ares'.   **τρύχεα** means 'rags, tatters', and it is not easy to believe that Ap. is alleging that the island preserves bits of Argonautic clothing. Some have therefore understood the term metaphorically, 'vestiges, traces', but parallels are very hard to find; Livrea 1984 understands 'miraculous rags' as a humorous reference to the pebbles of 655. The alternative τεύχεα, 'arms, equipment', seems very weakly general. We would expect something specific and non-metaphorical to match σόλοι.

658 λιμὴν Ἀργῷος: Portoferraio, on the north coast of Elba. The name (cf. 1620), like the stones and the weights, is yet another aetiological 'sign'

that the Argonauts did indeed visit the west, cf. Diod. Sic. 4.56.5, probably
again from Timaeus (*FGrHist* 566 F85).

659–60 The Argonauts travel roughly SE, from Elba to 'Monte Circello'
between Rome and Naples (Barrington 44 D3), where Circe's western home
('Aiaie') had been identified, cf. 3.311–13n.   **Αὐσονίης**: cf. 552–3n.

661–2 pick up *Od.* 10.135–6 Αἰαίην δ᾽ ἐς νῆσον ἀφίκομεθ᾽· ἔνθα δ᾽ ἔναιε | Κίρκη
ἐυπλόκαμος; Ap. might have read the end of line 135 as δὲ ναῖε.   **λιμένα
κλυτόν**: a Homeric phrase (*Od.* 10.87, the Laistrygonians, the episode
immediately preceding Circe (cf. 673–4n.), 15.472), here given new
point: Circe's harbour is 'famous' (from the perspective of Ap.'s audience)
because of the *Odyssey*. This is the first of several places where Ap. will
exploit the temporal fracture by which his Argonauts visit Circe both
before and 'after' Odysseus and his men do, cf. 667, 693–4, 784nn. In
Homer, Odysseus arrives ναύλοχον ἐς λιμένα on Circe's island (*Od.* 10.141),
where ancient scholars debated the meaning of the epithet.   **πείσματ᾽**:
i.e. stern-cables, πρυμνήσια (840, 857), Casson 1971: 48.   **σχεδόθεν** probably means 'at once, without delay', cf. 1081 and αὐτοσχεδόν in 101; speed
is important to this episode – in contrast to the Homeric episode, the
Argonauts come upon Circe as soon as they arrive, and they are keen to
get on with things. Others understand '[they attached the ropes] from
near at hand', marking the fine quality of the harbour; this could perhaps
be understood as picking up (and explaining) ναύλοχον in Homer, but it is
hard to see the point of such a detail.   **Κίρκην**: as with the 'Apsyrtos
episode' (cf. 450–1n.), the 'Circe episode' is framed by her name, cf. 752.
On Ap.'s reuse of and difference from Homer in this episode see Knight
1995: 184–200, Plantinga 2007.

663–4 Water, and particularly the water of the 'ever-flowing' sea, was
perhaps the most common of all sources of purification, cf. Eur. *IT* 1193
θάλασσα κλύζει πάντα τἀνθρώπων κακά, Parker 1983: 226–7. This is one of
several motifs shared between this episode and Eur. *IT*, in which 'a couple,
stained ... with the blood of a relative of one of them, come at the
command of a divine voice to receive purification. The purifier, who is
related to murderer and victim, is forewarned of the arrival in a dream'
(Hunter 1987: 131n.17). The motif of such purification after a troubling
dream is familiar from fifth-century drama, cf. Aesch. *Pers.* 201–2 (with
Garvie's n. on 201–4), Ar. *Frogs* 1338–40. Of particular importance is Aesch.
Ch. where Clytemnestra, 'disturbed' (ἐπτοημένη *Ch.* 535, cf. ἐπτοίητο in 664
here), sends propitiatory offerings to Agamemnon's tomb, cf. also Soph.
El. 405–27; here, then, another motif from the tragic versions of the story
of the House of Atreus has been redistributed as part of the large-scale
analogy which Ap. builds between the killing of Apsyrtos and the killing of

Agamemnon (Introduction pp. 5–6. As in tragedy, Circe's dream here is symbolic in its foreshadowing, even if the element of the strange and uncanny is greatly increased in Circe's dream over those of her tragic forebears. On Circe's purifications see further 693–4n.   εὗρον is another fragment of the Homeric Circe-episode, cf. *Od.* 10.210. κάρη: washing κατὰ κεφαλῆς, 'from the head down', is elsewhere found in purificatory contexts, cf. Theophr. *Char.* 16.14, *LSC* 55.4, *LSS* 65.8. ἐπιφαιδρύνουσαν: the hiatus after κάρη perhaps makes ἐπι- more probable than περι-; there seem to be the same set of variants at 3.832. The description of Circe and her animals is marked by a very high ratio of spondaic verses: 9 in the 23 verses from 662–684, including 3 pairs, i.e. 39%, as against the 8% for the poem overall; after this description, the next *spondeiazontes* are 693, 702 and 731. This strange, almost 'pre-historic' scene is described in a very modern style.   νυχίοισιν ὀνείρασιν: in Homer, Circe had been forewarned by Hermes that Odysseus would visit her (*Od.* 10.330–2), and as Hermes is closely associated with dreams, we might see here a variation on and/or interpretation of the Homeric motif, as well as the important debt to tragedy.

665 The Homeric model for Circe's vision is that of the seer Theoclymenus, who sees the suitors shrouded in night and tear-stained, αἵματι δ᾽ ἐρράδαται τοῖχοι καλαί τε μεσόδμαι (*Od.* 20.354); in that same vision, Odysseus' palace is 'full of ghosts (εἴδωλα) hastening to Erebos and the darkness'. Circe's animals may owe something to those εἴδωλα, particularly as Empedocles seems to have described the creatures of the second stage of 'evolution' as εἰδωλοφανεῖς, cf. 31 A 72 D–K, cited in 672–5n. Here the blood both signifies the killing of her nephew and foreshadows the presence in her house of blood-stained murderers.   ἕρκεα 'court-yards'.

666 The symbolic significance of the fire which devours Circe's potions – presumably in some sense another foreshadowing of the presence of those stained with blood-guilt – may be debated; there is perhaps an association with the hearth which will occupy a central role in the supplication scene (693, 723), or with the blazing torch which was doused in sacred water as a preliminary to purificatory sacrifice (Eur. *HF* 928–9). Fire itself was a purifying agent, Eur. *HF* 937, Parker 1983: 217. The closest tragic equivalent to Circe's dream is perhaps Hecuba's dream in Euripides' *Alexandros* that she gave birth to a torch (Paris) which consumed her city. The present dream certainly threatens the very identity of Circe πολυφάρμακος (*Od.* 10.276). See further Walde 2001: 184–92.

667 is best understood as an explanatory intrusion by the narrator, rather than as an element from within the dream.   πάρος points to the fact (cf. 661–2n.) that we are 'before' the *Odyssey* in terms of mythological chronology and 'after' it in terms of literary history; Roman poetry was to be very fond of such effects (Barchiesi 1993).

668 φονίωι … αἵματι 'blood of a killed victim'; the rite of purification will wash away blood with blood, cf. Heraclitus fr. 5 D–K 'They purify themselves by staining themselves with another shedding of blood, as if someone were to step into mud and then wash it off with mud', Eur. *IT* 1223–4, Parker 1983: 371–2. The phrase may evoke again the proscriptions of Presocratics: Empedocles noted that in the period of Love ταύρων δ' ἀκρήτοισι φόνοις οὐ δεύετο βωμός (fr. 128.3 D–K), Osborne 1987: 48. There is a similar paradoxical reciprocity in the fact that it is the killer's 'blood-stained' hands which must be sprinkled with sacrificial blood (705 ~ 716, cf., e.g., Eur. *HF* 1145, 1324, Pl. *Laws* 9.864e4). **πορφύρουσαν:** this verb is properly applied to the sea, cf. *Il.* 14.16 ὡς δ' ὅτε πορφύρηι πέλαγος μέγα κτλ., where Aristarchus seems to have understood the meaning as 'grow black (μελανίζειν)', cf. 152–3n., and μέλας is a regular scholarly gloss for πορφύρεος in Homer, an adjective applied to both blood (e.g. *Il.* 17.360–1) and death (*Il.* 5.83). Here Ap. may reflect predecessors of the Aristarchan view: that the fire should darken makes perfect sense, given the association of blackness with death. The usual interpretation is 'seething, surging', cf. 1.935 of the Hellespont.

669 χερσὶν ἀφυσσαμένη, 'drawing it off with her hands', almost suggests that Circe kept a supply of blood ready to hand. This detail is perhaps connected with the rite of 706–7, but the details of the correspondence are hazy, as dreams often are.

670–1 offer a close reprise and variation of 663–4, perhaps as a marker of difference from Homeric style in a scene describing a character drawn from Homer: ἐπιπλομένης ἠοῦς … ἐγρομένη ~ νυχίοισιν ὀνείρασιν, νοτίδεσσι θαλάσσης ~ ἁλὸς νοτίδεσσι, πλοκάμους ~ κάρη, φαιδρύνεσκε ~ ἐπιφαιδρύνουσαν. **ἐγρομένη:** cf. 1352n. **πλοκάμους** alludes to ἐυπλόκαμος, a Homeric epithet of Circe (*Od.* 10.36 etc.). **φαιδρύνεσκε:** it is very common in poetry for an uncompounded verb to pick up a preceding compound and carry the same sense as the compound, Renehan 1976: 11–27.

672–5 In place of the bewitched animals who fill the Homeric Circe's woods (cf. *Od.* 10. 212–15) and the men metamorphosed into pigs while retaining human minds (10. 239–40), Circe is here accompanied by creatures composed of a jumble of different limbs, apparently put together at random. They resemble (676–81) creatures from a time before life had been organized into species and limbs arranged to create unified forms. Ap.'s debt here to the zoogony of Empedocles (for which cf. Sedley 2005) has long been recognized, cf. 31 A 72 D–K: 'Empedocles held that the first generations of animals and plants were not complete (μηδάμως ὁλοκλήρους) but consisted of separate limbs not joined together (ἀσυμφυέσι τοῖς μορίοις διεζευγμένας); the second, arising from the joining of these limbs, were like creatures in dreams (συμφυομένων τῶν μερῶν εἰδωλοφανεῖς); the third was the generation of whole-natured forms (τῶν ὁλοφυῶν) … ' (trans. KRS p. 303). A surviving fragment of Empedocles' poem on the history of the world (perhaps entitled Περὶ φύσεως or Φυσικά) records that 'many creatures were born with faces and breasts on both sides, man-faced ox-progeny (βουγενῆ ἀνδρόπρωιρα), while others again sprang forth as ox-headed offspring of man (ἀνδροφυῆ βούκρανα), creatures compounded partly of male, partly of the nature of the female, and fitted with shadowy parts (σκιεροῖς … γυίοις)' (fr. 61 D–K, trans. KRS p. 304), and another that 'many faces without necks sprang up (ἐβλάστησαν), arms wandered without shoulders, unattached, and eyes strayed alone, in need of foreheads' (fr. 57 D–K, trans. KRS p. 303). The clear implication is that Circe's 'dream-like' creatures were the result of her bewitching magic: she turned her visitors back to the creatures of a time even before there were 'creatures', and this is part of how in book 4 the Argonauts are made to confront the whole of human history (Hunter 1993: 164–6). The choice of Empedocles, like that of Parmenides earlier (cf. 629–30n.), suggests that Ap. uses what we call the 'Presocratics' to conjure up an earlier world 'before history'; already in Book 1, Empedoclean cosmology had been used in the song which Orpheus sings to calm disputes in the group (1. 496–511), cf. further 693–4n., Kyriakou 1994.

672 οὐ θήρεσσιν ἐοικότες: a witty reuse of a phrase Homer applies to Eumaeus' guard-dogs (*Od.* 14.21). In Homer, the wild animals in Circe's forests are compared to dogs fawning around their master (*Od.* 10.216–19), and Eumaeus' dogs fawn around Telemachus when he arrives at the farm (*Od.* 16.4–6); Ap.'s allusion to *Od.* 14.21 draws a link between the two Homeric scenes and prepares for the simile of 674–5.

673–4 Cf. *Od.* 10.120 (the Laistrygonians) μυρίοι, οὐκ ἄνδρεσσιν ἐοικότες, ἀλλὰ Γίγασιν; for an earlier evocation of this episode cf. 661–2n. Odysseus' men meet a Laistrygonian girl drawing water at a spring (*Od.* 10.105–13), and Ap. has included touches from that episode within his reworking of the Homeric Circe.   **ὅλον δέμας** 'in their body as a whole', an accusative of respect. ὅλον picks up Empedocles' references to 'whole' forms, cf. A 72 D–K (672–5n. above), fr. 62.4 D–K, οὐλοφυεῖς … τύποι. The alternative, ὁμὸν δέμας, offers the choicer word and a similar sense, but without the Empedoclean allusion; Hölzlin suggested ὁμοί, but this adjective is not otherwise constructed with the dative.   **ἄλλο δ᾽ ἀπ᾽ ἄλλων | συμμιγέες μελέων** 'a mixture in different parts [ἄλλο adverbial neuter] from different limbs', cf. 898–9, 2.1240–1. The phrase is reworked in 677. The sense seems rather awkward, as even 'whole' creatures are composed of 'different' limbs, and ἄλλων can hardly mean 'coming from different creatures'. Fränkel therefore proposed γενέων, 'from different species', cf. Lucr. 5.880 (there never existed creatures) *ex alienigenis membris compacta*. This, however, does not take account of the obvious *uariatio* in 677, and – if change is needed – an alternative would be μερέων, the word Empedocles uses for the 'bits' out of which the first creatures were formed, cf. A 72 D–K, cited in 672–5n.

674–5 vary *Od*.10. 216–19 in which Circe's bewitched animals are compared to fawning dogs, cf. 672n.; the closest parallel in *Arg.* is 1.575–80, the fish hearing Orpheus' music compared to flocks returning to their stall.   ἅλις 'in crowds, *en masse*', cf. μυρία at 1.576.

676–81 Circe's creatures are compared to the earliest forms of life to emerge from the primeval slime. Ap.'s debt to the cosmology and cosmogony of Empedocles continues, though the idea of primeval mud or slime was very common in cosmologies of all types; see Pfeiffer on Call. fr. 493, Nisbet and Hubbard on Hor. *C.* 1.16.14. That both our physical environment and all living things were formed as the result of a combination of pressure upon this mud, the action of the sun and then evaporation was common to more than one cosmological theory, cf., e.g., Arist. *Meteor.* 2.353b7–13, Diod. Sic. 1.7, Lucr. 5.480–94, Ov. *Met.* 1.416–37 (with Barchiesi's n. on 416–51). These verses find a place for all four of Empedocles' original elements – water, earth, air and sun (cf. 31B 71 D–K). In comparing Circe's creatures to the visions of Presocratic science Ap. contributes to a debate about the kind of traces of 'history' which poetry preserves; our fullest ancient source for that debate is the discussion of Homer in Book 1 of Strabo's *Geography*, but there is little doubt that it was an active debate in third-century Alexandria. We may also think of this as an alternative model to allegorization for how poetry was to be understood (above pp. 6–7); Circe was one of the most allegorized of all Homer's characters (Kaiser 1964: 197–213).

676 ἰλύς is the *mot juste* for primeval ooze, cf., e.g. 'Orpheus' 1B 13.24 D–K, Archelaos, 60 A 1 D–K τὰ ζῶια ἀπὸ τῆς ἰλύος γεννηθῆναι, 60 A 4.5 D–K, Diod. Sic. 1.7.1.   ἐβλάστησε: cf. Empedocles fr. 57.1 D–K, cited in 672–5n. βλαστάνω and βλαστέω are more usually intransitive, as in Empedocles, but cf. 1517.

677 ἀρηρεμένους 'fitted out with, composed of', pf. pass. participle of ἀραρίσκω. Ap. may here again be close to an Empedoclean phrase, cf. fr. 35.16–17 D–K, ἔθνεα μυρία (~ 646) θνητῶν,| παντοίοις ἰδέῃσιν ἀρηρότα, θαῦμα ἰδέσθαι (~ 682).

678–80 'when [the earth] had not yet been compressed by the parched air nor yet received sufficient moisture through the action of the scorching sun'. The reference seems to be to a time before the formation of both firm land (678) and the oceans (679–80); the sun is relevant to the latter process, because – in a common theory of the formation of the world – the oceans were formed either after moisture evaporated from the primeval slime and then fell again as rain, or resulted from the moisture 'sweated' out of the slime by the action of the sun, cf., e.g., Empedocles, 31 A 66, B 55 D–K. This seems the best explanation of a very difficult passage. Wilamowitz suggested αἰνυμένου, 'of the sun which received/took up moisture', in which case πιληθεῖσα would go with both ἠέρι and βολαῖς; the run of the sentence, however, strongly leads us to expect two nominative participles in co-ordination.   **πιληθεῖσα** 'condensed, made solid', another term of science, cf., e.g. Parmenides 28 A 37 D–K, Empedocles 31 A 49, 66 D–K, Pl. *Tim.* 58b4, 76c3.   **ἰκμάδας:** this noun seems to have had an important place in Presocratic theories; Aristophanes' Socrates reports, alluding to the theories of Diogenes of Apollonia, that 'the earth violently draws (ἕλκει) towards itself the moisture (ἰκμάδα) of thought' (*Clouds* 232–3, where see Dover's note).

680–1 'The stretch of time ordered these things [i.e. the first creatures] and brought them into species'.   **στίχας** is here used for what are more commonly called τάξεις, cf., e.g., Pl. *Tim.* 30a5; τάξεις is a standard gloss for Homeric στίχες (Erbse 1953: 176).   **συγκρίνας** is another term borrowed from Presocratic science; it denotes ordered rearrangement of parts, cf. Empedocles 31 A 37, 43 D–K, and the entries συγκρίνειν and σύγκρισις in the Index in D–K vol. III.

681 τώς, 'thus, just so', probably picks up 676–7, rather than taking the narrative back to the comparison of 674–5 (with ἕποντο picking up ὀπηδεύοντα); in the latter case, 676–81 would be treated as a parenthetic digression.   **φυὴν ἀίδηλοι** 'ill-defined/unclear in their form'; for ἀίδηλοι cf. 47n., 3.1132n.; at 1157 the sense is 'unexpected'.

682 θάμβος: in Homer it was fear which the sight of Circe's animals produced (*Od.* 10.219); the difference may be suggestive of Hellenistic curiosity about marvels.

683 φυήν 'physical appearance, stature'.   **ὄμματα:** the explanation follows at 727–9, a postponement typical of *Arg.* Cf. also 3.885–6n.   **παπταίνοντες:** Ap. constructs ἕκαστος with both singular and plural verbs, cf. 185, 1291–2, Smyth §951.

685 ἀπὸ ... πέμψεν: tmesis. Fränkel proposed πέμψατ', cf. Eur. *Hec.* 72 ἀποπέμπομαι ἔννυχον ὄψιν, but there seems no reason to insist on the middle.

686 ἀπέστιχε is used of Circe at *Od.* 12.143, the end of the episode in Homer: here we are at the beginning. Circe's return to her house marks also a return to her 'normal' behaviour.   ἕπεσθαι: the echo of 681 suggests what happens to those who do 'follow' Circe; in Homer, those who followed (ἕποντο, *Od.* 10.230) were indeed metamorphosed.

687 χειρὶ καταρρέξασα: Homer has six instances of the verse χειρί τέ μιν κατέρεξεν ἔπος τ᾽ ἔφατ᾽ ἔκ τ᾽ ὀνόμαζεν, and memory of that verse marks Circe's silence here, and the eerie silence which hangs over the whole episode. Here there can be no physical contact (contrast the Homeric 'stroked with the hand'), and so Ap. innovates with an intransitive use, 'making a gesture (of invitation) with her hand'. We catch a glimpse here of the post-Homeric representation of Circe as a dangerously sexy courtesan; see Kaiser 1964: 201–2, [Heraclitus], *On unbelievable things* 16, 'Circe was a hetaira. She bewitched (κατακηλοῦσα) strangers and at first made them well-disposed to her by performing every kind of service . . . '. In Homer, Circe invited (κάλει) Odysseus' men inside (*Od.* 10.231), and, from one perspective, such an invitation by a woman, in breach of all normal decency, could mean only one thing, cf., e.g., Theocr. 2.101, 116; what Ap.'s depiction in fact owes to contemporary discussion of the Homeric text is harder to determine.   δολοφροσύνηισιν: at the corresponding moment of the *Odyssey*, Eurylochos waits behind because he thinks Circe's invitation is a δόλος (*Od.* 10.232); cf. 10.339 δολοφρονέουσα.

689 μίμνεν: E's μίμνον may be correct, but there is the same phenomenon at 1.239, where the singular also has the support of a third-century papyrus.   ἀπηλεγέως 'without paying attention (to Circe)'; the etymology from ἀλέγω is important here. Cf. further 1469n.

690 ἑσπέσθην: aorist dual of ἕπομαι.   αὐτὴν ὁδόν: i.e. the same route as Circe had taken.

691–2 Circe acts again like her Homeric model, cf. *Od.* 10.233, εἷσεν δ᾽ εἰσαγαγοῦσα κατὰ κλισμούς τε θρόνους τε.   λιπαροῖσι 'splendid'. ἀμηχανέουσα κιόντων 'at a loss at (the reason for) their coming'; κιόντων functions like a genitive absolute.

693–4 Jason and Medea rush to seize the hearth, as the special place of protection for suppliants (Gould 1973: 97–8), before they can be prevented from doing so. The obvious Homeric parallel is *Od.* 7.153–4, where Odysseus places himself 'in the dust at the hearth beside the fire', after he has made his plea to Arete, but of particular importance (again) is the story of Orestes in Aeschylus. In the *Eumenides*, the priestess reports that she found Orestes at the *omphalos*, his hands dripping with blood and holding a sword (*Eum.* 40–3); later, Orestes claims that he was cleansed

of his pollution 'at the hearth of the divine Apollo by pig-killing purifications' (*Eum.* 282–3), cf. 705–6n.; when he arrives in Athens he takes his
seat by the statue of Athena which the goddess describes as 'near my
hearth' (*Eum.* 440). Most striking of all, Orestes notes that until he is
purified, 'it is the law that the murderer is to be speechless', ἄφθογγον εἶναι
τὸν παλαμναῖον νόμος (448); 693–4 look like a transcription into epic style of
Eum. 448 (cf. also 709n.), and this would be one of the most striking
textual links between the killings of Agamemnon and Apsyrtos (cf. further
712–13n.). Secondly, coming after the 'Empedoclean' passage of 672–81,
the description of the rite of purification can hardly fail to evoke
Empedocles' Καθαρμοί, which seems to have contained advice on ritual
and other forms of purification and cleanliness, and may or may not have
been a different poem from the poem on nature (see, e.g., Osborne 1987,
Sedley 1998: 2–8, Martin-Primavesi 1998: 118–19); purification through
blood sacrifice would not, however, have been something which
Empedocles, with his views on the transmigration of souls, would have
recommended, cf. 668n. Whether or not Ap.'s pattern of Φυσικά surrounded by two different sorts of Καθαρμοί, first of Circe herself and then
of Jason and Medea, reflects his own belief in the number of Empedocles'
poems must remain conjectural, but it is striking that Ap. presents three
related ways of considering the death of Apsyrtos and its aftermath, as
analogous to Cyclic, rather than Homeric epic (cf. 421–521n.), as like the
tragic representation of the murder of Agamemnon and its aftermath, and
like the grim Empedoclean world of Strife.

　　After Ap., Aristarchus was to hold the view that ritual purification for
murder was not known in the heroic age (see Schmidt 1976: 228–9,
T-schol. on *Il.* 11.690), and it is noteworthy that the exegetical scholia
explain the simile of *Il.* 24.480–2, in which Priam's appearance in Achilles'
tent is compared to the arrival of a murderer at the house of a rich man in
a foreign land, as the case of a man who comes 'to be purified and takes
his seat at the hearth' (T-scholia on 24.480–2a), although Homer says
nothing about purification. Ap. has of course a model in tragedy for the
retrojection of purification into the heroic age, but – if a debate about
purificatory rites in the heroic age goes back to his time – then he gains a
particularly pointed fracturing of time (cf. 667n.) by having a Circe, who
is both pre- and post-Homeric, performing rites which were believed to
post-date even Homer's heroes. On Homer's apparent silence about
purification for murder see Parker 1983: 130–43; it is known, however,
that the motif occurred (perhaps twice) in the *Aithiopis*, and this then
would be another link between Ap.'s presentation of the killing of Apsyrtos
and its aftermath and the Epic Cycle, cf. 421–521n. ἄνεωι καὶ ἄναυδοι:
cf. 3.502–4n. For the ritual silence of those who have killed, cf. (in

addition to Aesch. *Eum.* 448–50 above) Eur. fr. 1008K, *HF* 1218–19, Σ *Il.* 24.482, Parker 1983: 371.   ἥ τε δίκη: for such explanatory glosses by the narrator cf. 479n. Verbally close is [Hes.] *Aspis* 85 ἣ δίκη ἔσθ᾽ ἱκέτηισι.   λυγροῖς 'wretched, in misery'.

695 Medea hides her face in her hands in a gesture of grief and supplication; 'placing her forehead on her hands', rather than *vice versa*, stresses that she lowers her head rather than raising her hands.

696 Cf. Aesch. *Eum.* 40–3 (693–4n.); we are perhaps to understand that the sword too needs to be cleansed (Lorimer 1921). In Homer Odysseus confronted Circe with a sword (*Od.* 10.321), but in very different circumstances.

697 πάϊν is an accusative found only here in *Arg.*, formed on the analogy of the epic nominative πάϊς, which Ap. uses freely; the rare form perhaps adds to the formal solemnity of the moment.

697–8 'They never raised their eyes (kept) behind their eyelids (to look) directly (at Circe)'.

699 φύξιον οἶτον 'their fate as exiles'. Φύξιος was an epithet of Zeus as the helper of exiles (cf. Lyc. *Alex.* 288); it was to this Zeus that Phrixos had sacrificed the golden ram (119n., 2.1147), and the following verse and 708–9 show that epithets of Zeus were in Ap.'s mind here.

700 Cf. 2.1131–3, *Od.* 14.283–4 (the 'Cretan tale' to Eumaeus) Διὸς δ᾽ ὠπίζετο μῆνιν | Ξεινίου, ὅς τε μάλιστα νεμεσσᾶται κακὰ ἔργα. Like Croesus confronted with Adrastos (Hdt. 1.35.1), Circe performs the purificatory rites before asking the names of her visitors.

701 Cf. 2.215–16, Ἱκεσίου πρὸς Ζηνός, ὅ τις ῥίγιστος ἀλιτροῖς | ἀνδράσι, Aesch. *Suppl.* 616–17 ἱκεσίου Ζηνὸς κότον | μέγαν. Zeus's help to murderers consists in the existence of purificatory rites, which often involve, as here, sacrifices to Zeus himself; a fifth-century lead tablet from Selinous seems to prescribe the sacrifice of a piglet to Zeus for the purification of someone who has shed blood (Jameson–Jordan–Kotansky 1993, Robertson 2010). There may be a particular reference to a tradition that Zeus instigated those rites himself, in order to purify Ixion for the killing of his father-in-law, cf. Aesch. *Eum.* 717–18, Pherecydes, *FGrHist* 3 F 51b, Blickman 1986: 196–7. If so, it is noteworthy that reference is made to this in the *Eumenides*, which is so important for this whole scene in *Arg.* Moreover, those requiring purification are merely a sub-group of suppliants (Parker 1983: 134), and as such it is indeed the Zeus Hikesios of 700 who 'brings great help to murderers'.   ἀνδροφόνοισιν is the object of both verbs.

702–3 These are the rites called τὰ νομιζόμενα in the story of Croesus and Adrastos (Hdt. 1.35.2). Sacrifices were a central part of many rites of purification.   ἀπολυμαίνονται is taken from *Il.* 1.313–14 where the verb appears in successive verses; in Homer it seems to be middle, 'purify oneself', and may be so here, but Ap. may rather intend the passive.   †νηληεῖς†: the reading is very uncertain. We expect the meaning 'wretched, miserable' or 'guilty', and so any form of νηλεής 'pitiless' seems improbable; Race's 'ruthless suppliants', explained as a 'brachylogy for ruthless men who come as suppliants', does not convince. *Od.* presents three instances of a verse describing women αἵ τέ σ' ἀτιμάζουσι καὶ αἳ νηλίτιδές εἰσιν (16.317, 19.498, 22.418); the adjective of unknown meaning already has variant forms and spellings in Homeric MSS, but Aristarchus took the meaning to be 'having committed many crimes', whereas others understood 'guiltless', cf. *Et. Mag.* 603.49–58 Gaisford, Matthews 1996: 271–2. If some form like this is adopted for *Arg.*, e.g. νηλητεῖς or νηλειτεῖς, then Ap. too will presumably have interpreted the Homeric adjective in a similar way, and this would not be the only case where Ap. seems to reflect views which were later held by Aristarchus (Rengakos 2008: 250–2).   ὅτ' ἐφέστιοι ἀντιόωσι 'when they make supplications at the hearth'. The Ionic form ἐπίστιος occurs more than once in the story of Croesus and Adrastos (Hdt. 1.35.3, 44.2).

704 ἀτρέπτοιο: the meaning is uncertain: 'which cannot be undone' makes good sense, though clear parallels are lacking. Alternatively, Fränkel 1968: 482–3 suggests a connection with ἀτροπίη (387, 1047), so that the phrase will be the equivalent of φόνον … νηλέα in 587–8.

705–6 The description of the sow evokes the detailed prescriptions of sacral laws; on purification for murder more generally see Wächter 1910: 64–76. For the use of piglets in such purifications cf. Aesch. *Eum.* 283 (693–4n.), fr. 327 (where it is again the hands of the murderer which are to be sprinkled with blood), and the 'purification text' from Selinous (701n.). The purification of Orestes by the blood of a piglet held above him (cf. καθύπερθε) is shown on several South Italian vases, see Dyer 1969: *Plates* II 1 (= *LIMC* VII 2, 'Orestes 48'), I 2, IV 6; noteworthy also in these representations are Orestes' lowered head and eyes (cf. 697–8, 726), the fact that he is always holding a sword (cf. 696–7), and the presence of the Erinyes (cf. 714).   καθύπερθε 'above (Jason and Medea)'.   πλήμυρον 'were full, flowed (with milk)'.   λοχίης ἐκ νηδύος lit. 'from a stomach which had given birth'; this remarkable phrase more probably gives the reason why the sow's teats are full than that ἐκ implies 'hanging from'.   χεῖρας: cf. 668n.

707 ἐπιτμήγουσα 'cutting, gashing'; Ap. is fond of the form τμήγω for τέμνω.

708 μείλισσεν 'made propitiatory offerings'; contrast the use at 416. The verb may evoke another common epithet of Zeus, Μειλίχιος (cf. Jameson-Jordan-Kotansky 1993: 81–103), and perhaps suggests, by popular etymology, that the offerings (see next n.) included honey, μέλι.   **χύτλοισι** '(poured) offerings', particularly associated with chthonic powers and the dead, cf. 1.1075, 2.926.   **Καθάρσιον** is a common title of Zeus in such situations, cf., e.g., Hdt. 1.44.2.

709 παλαμναίων τιμήορον ἱκεσιάων 'who brings aid [LSJ s.v. τιμήορος II] to the supplications of murderers'; the genitive, rather than ἱκεσίηισι, is the expected case after τιμήορος. The text must, however, be considered uncertain, and the variants suggest that corruption set in early. παλαμναῖον, '[Zeus] of those who have killed', would give a run of epithets in an indirect description of a prayer which is of a common type (cf. 146–8n., 3.861–3 with 3.862n.), and Zeus has just been closely associated with murderers at 701 (where see n.); for this title of Zeus cf. [Arist.] *De mundo* 401a23, a list of epithets of Zeus 'from the poets', καθάρσιός τε καὶ παλαμναῖος καὶ ἱκέσιος καὶ μειλίχιος.

710 ἐκ ... ἔνεικαν: tmesis, with ἐκ also governing δόμων.   **λύματ'** are the 'leftovers' of the ritual (cf. *Il.* 1.314), which are themselves to be properly disposed of, as in the text prescribing purificatory rules at Cyrene (Rhodes–Osborne no. 97, lines 26–9); here they will include the body of the piglet and the remains of the χύτλα. We are perhaps also to understand that, although there is no indication in the text, the blood will have been washed off the hands of Jason and Medea with water, and that this 'foul' liquid will also have to be removed (cf. Dorotheus *ap.* Ath. 9.410a-b = *FGrHist* 356 F1).

711 In Homer Circe has four ἀμφίπολοι whose domestic tasks Odysseus describes in surprising detail at *Od.* 10.352–9. Some of these come 'from springs and holy rivers' (350–1), where the scholia explain that these are naiads and dryads. νηιάδες πρόπολοι and ἕκαστα are pointed compressions of *Od.* 10.348–51 and 10.352–9 respectively; Homer, we are to understand, is taken as read.   **πόρσυνον** varies the Homeric πένοντο (*Od.* 10.348).

712–13 πελανούς: mixtures of meal, honey and oil, of varying consistencies, shown by the fact that πελανοί may be poured (Aesch. *Ch.* 92) or thrown on the fire, as here (cf. Aesch. *Pers.* 204); full discussion in Amandry 1950: 86–103. The word is particularly associated with rites for the dead (cf., e.g., Aesch. *Pers.* 523–4). At Aesch. *Eum.* 107–8 Clytemnestra reminds the Erinyes (cf. 714) that she has offered them χοάς τ᾽ ἀοίνους, νηφάλια μειλίγματα, | καὶ νυκτίσεμνα δεῖπν᾽ ἐπ᾽ ἐσχάραι πυρός; just as *Eum.* 107 is very close to Ap. here (see below), so it is tempting to see πελανούς as an explanatory gloss on νυκτίσεμνα δεῖπν᾽; if so, we would have here another rewriting of the *Eumenides*, cf. 693–4n. Whereas in Aeschylus Clytemnestra's ghost recalls past sacrifices in order to rouse the sleeping Furies' vengeful anger, here Circe performs the rites to put an end to their anger.   **μείλικτρά τε νηφαλίηισι … ἐπ᾽ εὐχωλῆισι** 'offerings accompanied by wineless prayers'; μείλικτρα and related words are particularly associated with offerings to chthonic powers and the dead, cf. Aesch. *Pers.* 610, *Eum.* 107 (previous note). Dread gods such as the Eumenides/Erinyes standardly received libations of milk and honey, but not wine, cf. Soph. *OC* 100 (with Σ ad loc.), 481, Call. fr. 681 (with Pfeiffer's note), Henrichs 1983, esp. 91–2. Henrichs notes that νηφάλιος is often used of parts of the ritual, or those performing it, other than the offerings which are strictly 'wineless', and so we need not insist that here νηφαλίηισι must be transferred to εὐχωλῆισι by 'hypallage'.

713–14 Cf. *HHDem.* 349–51 (Hermes tells Hades that he must let Persephone go) ὄφρα ἑ μήτηρ | ὀφθαλμοῖσιν ἰδοῦσα χόλου καὶ μήνιος αἰνῆς | ἀθανάτοις παύσειεν; as 713–17 must be understood as a report of what Circe actually said in her prayer, both passages are addressed to Underworld powers, but Ap. has completely rearranged the import of the different elements. Contextually closer is Soph. *OC* 486–8 (Oedipus receives instructions for ritual purification) ὡς σφας καλοῦμεν Εὐμενίδας, ἐξ εὐμενῶν [~ εὐμειδής] | στέρνων δέχεσθαι τὸν ἱκέτην σωτηρίους | αἰτοῦ κτλ., cf. 715n.   **αὐτός**: i.e. Zeus. This form of designation is suggestive of Zeus as 'the Erinyes' master' (LSJ s.v. αὐτός I 1); this sits well with the switch from the Fury at 475–6 to Zeus at 558.

715 εὐμειδής occurs elsewhere only at Call. *h.* 3.129, also of a divinity looking favourably upon humans. In juxtaposition to Ἐρινύας, the word may evoke εὐμενής, an epithet of Zeus found in association with the Eumenides on the 'purification text' from Selinous (701n.).

716–17 As happens very often in prayers, Circe covers all possibilities, cf. 1412–13 and (in a very different prayer) Theocr. 2.44 (Simaitha prays that Delphis will forget his new love) εἴ τε γυνὰ τήνωι παρακέκλιται εἴ τε καὶ ἀνήρ. Between them, Jason and Medea in fact cover the possibilities raised in Circe's prayer.   **ὀθνείωι … αἵματι** 'blood of a stranger, of someone from outside the family'.   **ἐμφύλωι**: cf. 1.865, Pind. *Pyth.* 2.32 ἐμφύλιον αἷμα of Ixion killing his father-in-law, Blickman 1986.   **προσκηδέες**: the meaning is uncertain. It is often understood as 'full of cares', like πολυκηδέος in 734, 1073; the only Homeric occurrence of the adjective, ξεινοσύνης προσκηδέος (*Od.* 21.35), is however similarly opaque, *LfgrE* s.v. A possible alternative is 'as relatives' (cf. κῆδος), in which case προσκηδέες will belong with 717 only. Cf. further Levin 1950. **ἀντιόωσιν**: Wilamowitz proposed the more expected ἀντιόωιεν, but there seems no reason to deny Ap. the use of a very vivid indicative.

719 The narrative model is *Od.* 12.34 (Odysseus and Circe) εἷσέ τε καὶ προσέλεκτο (~ 720) καὶ ἐξερέεινεν ἕκαστα (~ 721), and cf. also *Od.* 10.365–6, but equally important is the scene in book 7 in which Alcinous raises Odysseus from the hearth (7.167–71), cf. 693–4 for the influence of Odysseus' arrival inside Alcinous' hall on the present narrative. **ξεστοῖσιν**, 'made smooth, polished', replaces ἀργυροήλου (7.162) and φαεινοῦ (7.169) in the scene of Odysseus and Alcinous.

721 χρειώ ναυτιλίην τε 'their purpose and voyage', i.e. 'the purpose of their voyage', cf. 2.8–9 χρειώ .... ναυτιλίης. Very similar are Philoctetes' questions to Neoptolemus, τίς προσήγαγεν | χρεία; τίς ὁρμή;, Soph. *Phil.* 236–7. **διακριδόν** 'in detail', cf. ἕκαστα at *Od.* 10.14 (Aeolus questioning Odysseus), 12.34 (Circe questioning Odysseus) and 730 below.

722 ὁπόθεν should mean 'from where', which would evoke the standard questions which a Homeric host asks a visitor (e.g. *Od.* 3.80 etc.). 'From what cause' is, however, a likely alternative here, and πόθεν very commonly means 'why?', LSJ s.v. Ι 4.

723 αὔτως 'just like that', a reference back to their 'dash' for the hearth at 693–4.

724 ἀεικελίη: cf. 4–5n. **δῦνεν φρένας ὁρμαίνουσαν** 'entered her mind as she reflected'; the participle here takes the place of the proper name which is more usual with such double accusatives of 'part and whole' (351n., Smyth §985). The construction is found with this verb already in some texts of *Od.* 18.348 = 20.285, and cf., e.g., [Hes.] *Aspis* 41 κραδίην πόθος αἴνυτο ποιμένα λαῶν.

725 'She was longing to know the voice of a girl of her [i.e. Circe's] race'; the adjective colours κούρης by a kind of hypallage. ἐμφυλίου might make the sense clearer, but is probably an unnecessary change. As ἴδμεναι is normally not just 'to hear' (as the scholiast interprets it), others understand 'to know the girl's native language', but once Circe has seen Medea's eyes, she knows at once what that language is; ἴδμεναι suggests both 'hearing' and 'understanding'. We may again be reminded of Sophocles' Philoctetes, φωνῆς δ' ἀκοῦσαι βούλομαι ... (*Phil.* 225).

726 ἐνόησεν 'saw (and therefore understood the identity of)'. **λαβοῦσαν**: the transmitted βαλοῦσαν would be very hard to parallel for 'raising' the eyes (contrast 1.790 ἐγκλιδὸν ὄσσε βαλοῦσα, 3.1008), and the aorists of βάλλειν and λαμβάνειν are regularly confused in manuscripts; for the opposite action cf. Eur. *Ion* 582 τί πρὸς γῆν ὄμμα σὸν βαλὼν ἔχεις. Fränkel noted the possibility of a different interpretation: when Medea uncovered her face (cf. 695), she nevertheless understandably kept her eyes lowered, allowing the gleam of her eyes to reflect on the floor around her, and he therefore proposed ἐπ' οὔδεος (which Dr Benaissa informs me is in fact read on an unpublished Oxyrhynchus papyrus). Nevertheless, the clear contrast between the scene of purification (with lowered, covered eyes) and the scene of conversation seems to require a stronger contrast than this. Some doubt about the true text must, however, remain.

728–9 ἦεν: the past tense does not necessarily imply that all descendants of Helios have died out, but rather it helps the audience understand an unfamiliar detail of this narrative set in the past.   **ἐπεί ... αἴγλην** 'since through the gleaming of their eyes into the distance they sent out a radiance in front of them as if of gold'.   **μαρμαρυγῆισιν**: later scientific and physiognomic texts use μαρμαρυγαί to describe an alleged real feature of some people's eyes, cf. 'Damianus', *Optics* 2, Adamantius 1.16 (I 331 Foerster = Repath 2007: 508).

730 τὰ ἕκαστα διειρομένηι 'asking about everything in detail', cf. 3.493–4, *Il.* 1.550.

731–6 Medea answers Circe's desire by speaking Colchian, thus of course excluding Jason; this, together with the use of indirect speech and the fact that what we receive is inevitably a transcription into Greek of what was said (Hunter 1993: 146–7), strongly marks her reply as very much her own 'Colchian' version of events. The narrative form then allows Ap., with his constant search for variety, to present a similar speech of Medea in direct form at 1018–28. It is noteworthy that non-Greek language has an important role in another version of the Argonautic story: at Diod. Sic. 4.48.1 (perhaps Dionysius Scytobrachion = fr. 26 Rusten), Medea fools those guarding the Fleece by speaking to them in their native 'Tauric language'; it is possible that Ap. has taken over the motif of non-Greek speech from another part of the story. For Dionysius Scytobrachion see Rusten 1982, Hunter 1989: 20.

731 γῆρυν: the only instance of this word in Homer is also in a context of linguistic difference, *Il.* 4.437, see Knight 1995: 193.   **βαρύφρονος** marks the contrast between the grim father and the 'gentle' speech of the daughter; the epithet also reminds us of what might lie in store for Medea (cf. 735–6).

732 στόλον ἠδὲ κελεύθους, a variation on χρειὼ ναυτιλίην τε in Circe's questioning (721), refers at least primarily to the outward voyage (and its purpose) to Colchis; the report of Medea's speech broadly follows the chronology of the narrative.

733 θοοῖς ... ἀέθλοις 'strenuous challenges'; the exact nuance of the adjective is, however, unclear, as neither 'swift' nor 'sharp' is really appropriate. Pindar celebrates Aeacid heroes for their success νικαφόροις ἐν ἀέθλοις ... καὶ θοαῖς | ... ἐν μάχαις (*Pyth.* 8.26–7). The 'challenges' are most naturally taken to be those which Aietes imposed and which Jason performed in book 3.

734–5 The repeated ὥς τε imitates the manner of Homeric indirect narratives, cf. *Od.* 23.312, 314, 318 (Odysseus' summary to Penelope). **πολυκηδέος**: cf. 717n. Arete uses this word of Medea herself at 1073. **ἤλιτε** is to be understood as (a Greek translation of) Medea's own Colchian term, cf. 1023; the reference will be to Medea helping Jason in the contest of the bulls and the earthborn warriors.　**βουλαῖς** is suitably vague: Chalciope did indeed ask Medea to help the Greeks, but Medea wanted to be asked and gave her sister every opportunity to do so (cf. 3.688–98).　**ἀπονόσφιν ἄλυξεν ὑπέρβια δείματα πατρός** 'she fled far away [adverbial] from the violent terrors of her father', i.e. from the appalling things her father threatened, almost as though Medea had heard the threats (δεινά) of 230–5. Why in fact Medea left Colchis has been an issue since 5 and 14–15. The scholia see here invention on Medea's part (ἐπλάσατο).

736–7 Medea did indeed leave 'with the sons of Phrixos', but that is hardly the full story, cf. 20–3n.　**παισὶ Φρίξοιο**: initial Φρ- here lengthens the vowel at the end of the preceding word, cf. 3.330; contrast 119.　**φόνον δ' ... τὴν δ' οὔ τι νόωι λάθεν**: the Homeric model is Nausicaa and her father, αἴδετο γὰρ θαλερὸν γάμον ἐξονομῆναι | πατρὶ φίλωι· ὁ δὲ πάντα νόει κτλ., *Od.* 6.66–7. Nausicaa has been a central model for Medea throughout, but there is a world of difference between γάμος and φόνος; the Homeric reminiscence also draws our attention to Medea's silence about her relationship to the man sitting beside her (he has already promised γάμος).　**νόωι** 'in her [i.e. Circe's] mind'. The construction is somewhat awkward, and Fränkel suggested τῆς δ' οὔ τι νόον. Our uncertainties as to how much Circe knew and when she knew it add to a striking 'atmosphere of edgy uncertainty' (Green 1997: 323) throughout this scene.　**ἀλλὰ καὶ ἔμπης** 'but even so', cf. 880.

738 ἐπί is adverbial, 'in addition' (LSJ s.v. ε I), rather than in tmesis with ἔειπεν.

739 σχετλίη: very different in character is σχέτλιοι, the first word Circe addresses to Odysseus and his men on their return from the Underworld (*Od.* 12.21).   **μήσαο**: uncontracted 2nd pers. sing. aor. of μήδομαι. **νόστον** 'voyage', rather than 'return', cf. 822, 1473, LSJ s.v. 2. In an epic context, however, it is hard not to feel resonances from the *Odyssey*, and the implication might be: '*your nostos* to Greece is disgraceful, unlike the *nostos* with which everyone (who knows their Homer) is familiar'.

741 For this possibility cf. 1103. Herodotus reports that 'the Colchian king sent a herald to Greece to seek justice for the abduction and to demand back his daughter' (1.2.3).   **καί** 'even'.

742 ἄσχετα ἔργα 'intolerable actions'.

743 ἔπλευ, 'you are', a contracted 2nd sing. aor. of πέλομαι, cf. 1.414, LSJ s.v. B 3; the form is transmitted in Homeric MSS, where however some modern editors read ἔπλε(ο).

744 seems to hint darkly that Circe could turn them all, like her previous visitors (hence the point of ἐνθάδ᾽ ἰούσηι), into the 'creatures' they have already seen. This is the extent of Circe's pity (738).

745–52 Circe's harsh dismissal and its effect are modelled on Aeolus' dismissal of Odysseus, after he has turned up at Aeolus' island for the second time, *Od.* 10.72–6 ἔρρ᾽ ἐκ νήσου θᾶσσον κτλ.

746 ἄιστον 'unknown'. The barb is a sharp one, given that in the *Odyssey* Circe knew who Jason was and described the *Argo* as πᾶσι μέλουσα (*Od.* 12.69–72).   **ἀείραο** 'you have carried off (like a prize)', a 2nd sing. aor. middle of ἀείρω, cf. 171n. The variant ἀνείραο would mean 'you have fastened to yourself' (ἀνείρω). Köchly, pointing to εὗρε in Nausicaa's speech at *Od.* 6.277, suggested ἀνεύραο 'discovered, dug up'.   **πατρός ἄνευθεν** probably suggests both 'without your father's permission' and '[carried off] far from your father'.

747 γουνάσσηαι: a 2nd sing. uncontracted aor. subj. The closest Homeric model is Achilles' harsh words to Hector, *Il.* 22.345 μή με, κύον, γούνων γουνάζεο.

748 βουλάς τε σέθεν: a very pointed variation on Medea's claim at 734. The implication that the killing of Apsyrtos was indeed Medea's βουλή is hardly an unfair interpretation, cf. 411–20.   **ἀεικέα φύξιν**: a forceful ring-composition (cf. 739), but Circe's words also give a very clear view on the question posed in the proem of the book cf. 4–5n.

749–50 Scenes of women mourning while covering their face with their robe are very common in Greek art.   **ἀμέγαρτον** 'great, unrestrained', cf. 3.631, Fränkel 1968: 527–8.

COMMENTARY: 751–761   189

751 Cf. *Od.* 15.465.   ἐπισχόμενος 'grasping hold of', constructed here
with the genitive, as, e.g., λαβόμενος; contrast 1609.

752 δείματι: Medea's fears go back both to the threat from her father
(740–2) and to the uncertainty of her future.   λεῖπον δ' ἀπό: anastrophic tmesis.   Κίρκης: cf. 661–2n.

753–4 Just so, the Argonauts' departure before the parallel episode of
the Symplegades 'did not escape Athena's notice' (2.535); Hera and
Athena are the two great goddesses working for the Argonauts' successful
return (cf. 959–60). Iris was last seen in the episode of the Harpies in Book
2. Her role here as Hera's servant finds a close analogy in Callimachus'
Hymn to Delos, where she and Ares keep watch to prevent Leto finding a
place to give birth (Hunter 1993: 96). The immediate model of the
present scene is, however, *Il.* 24.74–92, in which Iris fetches Thetis to
Olympus, but for Zeus, not Hera. After completing that mission, Iris
is then dispatched to Priam (lines 143–88); here Hera outdoes her
husband by sending Iris on a triple mission, without a pause between the
legs of her trip.

756 ἐποτρύνουσ': cf. *Il.* 24.143 Ἶριν δ' ὤτρυνε Κρονίδης.   ἀγόρευεν: verbs
of speaking, calling (cf. 843), ordering etc. regularly appear in the imperfect, rather than the aorist, to convey a sense of duration and process
(Chantraine II §286).

757 When mortals ask a god for favours, they standardly remind the god of
services they have offered in the past (cf. *Il.* 1.39 εἴ ποτέ τοι κατὰ πίονα μηρί'
ἔκηα) or of previous occasions on which they have had the god's help
(cf. Sappho fr. 1.5 V ἀλλὰ τυίδ' ἔλθ', αἴ ποτα κἀτέρωτα κτλ. ~ 1.25 ἔλθα μοι καὶ
νῦν); here the urgency of Hera's request (which is actually an order) is
amusingly evocative of such prayers.

758 μετοιχομένη 'going off (on a mission to fetch, μετ-)'.

760 Cf. *Il.* 10.118 = 11.610 χρειὼ γὰρ ἱκάνεται οὐκέτ' ἀνεκτός. κιχάνεται offers
a phonic echo of ἱκάνεται, and the memory of the Homeric οὐκέτ' ἀνεκτός
amusingly emphasizes Hera's need – for Thetis, of all gods! αὐτὰρ ἔπειτα:
there is to be no rest for Iris.

761–2 Ap. places Hephaistos' forge among the volcanic Aeolian islands
(cf., e.g., Thucyd. 3.88.3), which in fact lie off the NE coast of Sicily, but
which are here equated with the 'Wandering Islands' imagined to lie,
where Timaeus too had placed them (Σ 786–7 = *FGrHist* 566 F86), in the
Strait of Messina; at 3.42 the forge is located in 'the deep recess of
Wandering Island', and Ap. is probably thinking of the island of Hiera
('Sacred (to Hephaistos)', mod. Vulcano), which is indeed not far from

the strait, cf. 3.38–42n. Σ 761–5b cites Agathocles of Cyzicus (*FGrHist* 472 F8), said to have been a pupil of Zenodotus, for the view that the two actively volcanic islands belonged to Hephaistos (Hiera) and Aeolus (Strongule); this fits Ap.'s picture very well, but it is not necessary to infer that he is following Agathocles. Already Thucydides calls the group 'islands of Aeolus' (3.88.1, cf. Strabo 6.2.10); cf. further 764–5n. ἐλθεῖν: an imperatival infinitive, cf. 764, 766, Smyth §2013. Rzach proposed ἐλθέμεν (cf. 438, 3.622), but there is no reason to insist on this form at verse opening, cf. 1723.   ἄκμονες Ἡφαίστοιο: Callimachus has a similar verse-end at *h.* 3.48 (cf. also fr. 115.17), and there may be an intertextual link between that description of Hephaistos' forge, there placed on the island of Lipari itself, and the present passage. In particular, 762, which evokes the noise of the forge, may compress various elements of *h.* 3.59–61, ῥαιστῆρας 'hammers', χαλκόν, τετύποντες (~ τυπίδεσσιν); cf. further 776n. τυπίδεσσιν 'hammers', cf. Call. fr. 110.50.

763 φύσας πυρός 'blasts of fire', a poeticization of ἀναφυσήματα, the normal prose term for volcanic eruptions, cf., e.g., Pl. *Phd.* 113b5–6, Arist. *Meteor.* 2.367a15, Diod. Sic 5.7. 3 πυρὸς … ἀναφυσήματα μεγάλα on the Lipari islands, LSJ s.v. Strabo 6.2.10 refers to ἀναπνοὰς τρεῖς on Hiera and Ps.-Scymnus 260 to διαπύρων εἰς ὕψος ἀναβολαὶ μύδρων; Strabo also (13.4.11) reports that three collapsed craters in Mysia were called φῦσαι. In poetry, the φῦσαι of Hephaistos would normally be his bellows, cf. *Il.* 18.412, 468–70, Call. *h.* 3.56, and that usage is here evoked and avoided.

764–5 In Homer Aeolus lives 'on a floating (πλωτή) island', or perhaps 'an island called Πλωτή' (*Od.* 10.3), and so it was hardly difficult to locate his home in 'the islands of Aeolus' (cf. 761–2n.) and/or among the 'Wandering Islands'; Strongule was usually the favoured choice, though Aeolus was sometimes placed on Lipari. Hephaistos and Aeolus were associated together in the cult life of the islands (cf. Diod. Sic. 20.101.2), and this was confirmed at the level of natural science and popular belief in the view that volcanic and wind activity were intimately linked (Strabo 6.2.10). For Iris' traditional association with winds cf. *Il.* 23.198–211, West on Hes. *Theog.* 266, Hunter 1993: 81–2.   Αἴολον … Αἴολον: cf. 263–4n.   ὅς τ' … ἀνάσσει: a gloss and expansion of the Homeric ταμίης ἀνέμων (*Od.* 10.21).   αἰθρηγενέεσσιν 'born in the upper air', a Homeric epithet for Boreas (*Il.* 15.171 = 19.358). The meaning of the word was debated in antiquity (*LfgrE* s.v.), and some understood it as 'producing cold', which would be appropriate for Boreas; Ap.'s extension to all the winds suggests that he at least used it in the way modern scholars understand it. Cf. ὑπ' ἠέρι in 767, which perhaps indeed glosses αἰθρηγενέεσσιν.

767 ἀπολλήξειεν is here transitive (contrast 1.1154, 1353), as the simple λήγω sometimes is in Homer.   ὑπ' ἠέρι: cf. 764–5n. Ap. normally does not make the Aristarchan distinction between ἀήρ (the lower air) and αἰθήρ (the upper air) (see Rengakos 1994: 37–9), and there is no need to think that Hera here means only 'the lower atmosphere' (as Erbse 1963a: 21).

768 Ζεφύρου: the Argonauts will first sail down the west coast of Italy and through the Strait before (as Hera hopes) heading east to Drepane (Corcyra); in the *Odyssey* also it was a favourable west wind which was carrying Odysseus home towards Ithaca from the island of Aeolus when disaster struck (*Od.* 10.25–6). It is very likely that Ap. imagines the Italian coast to run much more west-east than north-south; the west wind will therefore be what is required for the whole trip to Drepane. It may also be relevant that Strabo 6.2.10 (quoting Polybius) notes that the west wind gives the best sailing conditions in the Aeolian islands, as the south wind produces a thick mist and the north wind increases volcanic activity; Ap.'s Hera understands the micro-climate.   ἀήτω: 3rd sing. imperative of ἄημι.

770–2 Cf. *Il.* 24.78–9 'Iris leapt (ἔνθορε) into the dark sea between Samos [i.e. Samothrace] and rocky Imbros'; Ap., however, will tease us by not saying where in the Aegean the house of Nereus is to be found. In Homer also its location is quite unspecific (*Il.* 18.140–1).   τέμνε 'cut (the air)', cf. 2.1244 for a similar omission of the object.   ἐνὶ πόντωι: the so-called 'pregnant construction': 'fell (into and remained) in the sea', cf. 388n.

773–4 In Homer (cf., e.g., *Il.* 24. 88, 171–87) Iris would have been given direct speech to Thetis; Ap. constantly varies the Homeric pattern for messenger-scenes.   Ἥρης ἐννεσίηις 'under Hera's influence', an unusual use of this common type of phrase in the context of carrying out Hera's orders.   ὦρσεν replaces ὄρσο at *Il.* 24.88.   μιν εἰς ἕ occurs in Homer only at *Il.* 23.203, where Iris is visiting the winds, as she is about to visit Aeolus; this is a very nice example of Ap.'s sensitivity to Homeric language and his technique of stylistic mimesis.

776 ῥίμφα 'quickly', i.e. 'on the spot, forthwith'.   σιδηρείων τυπίδων: iron was the one feature of Callimachus' description of Hephaistos' forge (*h.* 3.60) which had not yet figured in Ap.'s text, and that gap is here made good. Ps.-Scymnus 261 (about Hiera) σιδήρειός τε ῥαιστήρων κτύπος is perhaps indebted to this passage.

777 αἰθαλέοι πρηστῆρες 'sooty bellows', a phrase derived from *Il.* 18.471 where Hephaistos' bellows (φῦσαι) are described παντοίην εὔπρηστον ('strongly blown') ἀυτμὴν ἐξανιεῖσαι. Anaximander may have used πρηστήρ for bellows (cf. fr. 4 D–K, Diels 1929: 26), and note 3.1301 ὅτ' αὖ λήγουσιν αὐτμῆς of bellows (φῦσαι). πρηστῆρες are normally 'tornadoes' or fiery winds which set things alight (Arist. *Meteor.* 3.371a18, Strabo 13.4.11, West on Hes. *Theog.* 846), and some have understood the latter to be the sense here; it is, however, not the fiery blasts which stop instantly, but rather work in the forge (cf. *Il.* 18.412), and when the Argonauts finally arrive the sea is still giving off θερμήν ... αὐτμήν (929).

778 καὶ τῶι 'to him also'.

779 Iris takes a well-earned break (something Homer certainly does not tell us about), and Ap. parades his presentation of simultaneous events.

782–841 On the exchange between Hera and Thetis see esp. Herter 1959, Hunter 1993: 97–100, Mori 2012. Over the exchange hovers that between Zeus and Thetis in *Iliad* 1: there Zeus had complained about Hera and how Thetis' request would get him into trouble with his wife (517–23). Here, Hera wants Thetis to understand that she is her closest friend and benefactor.

782 ἆσσον ἑοῖο παρεῖσε 'sat [Thetis] down near her'; παρεῖσε is the aorist of transitive παρίζω.   **φαῖνέ τε μῦθον**: cf. *Od.* 8.499 φαῖνε δ' ἀοιδήν. At *Il.* 3.312 μύθους καὶ μήδεα πᾶσιν ἔφαινον, the verb is only weakly attested (for ὕφαινον), but probably correct.

783 Θέτι δῖα: an ingratiating address (though cf. 932); in Homer, Thetis can be δῖα θεάων (*Il.* 19.6, 24.93), but the adjective is never attached to her name.

784 οἶσθα μέν: Hera treats Thetis as a confidante, but in fact there is no sign that Thetis has any interest in the Argonauts; it is tempting to see here an allusion (by Hera) to the one passage of the *Odyssey* which declared the *Argo* to be πᾶσι μέλουσα 'known to all', and asserted Hera's favour to Jason (*Od.* 12.69–72); see Introduction, pp. 14–15. This would be a very particular case of *Arg.* being both 'before and after' Homer.

786 presents probably the most difficult and intriguing textual problem in the whole poem. Hera can hardly say that she 'saved' the Argonauts on the passage through the Planktai when this lies in front of them, however the episodes of the Symplegades and the Planktai are shaped as parallel obstacles on the outward and return journey. Even if 'Planktai' were here a unique term for the Clashing Rocks of Book 2, it was Athena, not Hera, who saw the heroes safely through that obstacle, although Hera might of course just be lying; the firestorms of 787, however, make it plain that Hera is referring to the Planktai which lie ahead (cf. *Od.* 12.68). It is therefore most likely that ἐσάωσα refers to Hera's 'saving' actions in the past (e.g. 640–4, the events of book 3) and that a passage has fallen out in which Hera sets out for Thetis the current situation. Some, following Giangrande 1973: 37, understand the verb as a potential 'I would/could save them', with or without Hart's κε for τε (which produces an unconvincing asyndeton), and with or without οἵη ('by myself') rather than οἵη; the aorist (rather than the imperfect) with reference to the present or future, though certainly not impossible (cf. K–G I 214–16, Vian III 42–3) would however be a very odd way for Ap. to express this notion (916 is importantly different in this regard, being a statement by the narrator about the past). This approach does, however, at least have the merit of focusing attention on the crucial narrative question: *Why* does Hera need Thetis and the Nereids? Of the two routes open to the *Argo*, as to Odysseus 'after' them, Hera has neutralized part of the danger posed by the Planktai through the aid of Hephaistos and Aeolus, but she can apparently do nothing about the waves and the rocks themselves (cf. 823–4); so too, she can (apparently) do nothing about Scylla and Charybdis who lie outside her control (825–32). What she needs, then, are marine deities who will be able to steer a path through the Rocks, while keeping well clear of Scylla and Charybdis; Thetis and the Nereids had long had an important role in both literature and cult as protectors of sailors, cf., e.g., Sappho fr. 5 V, Eur. *Helen* 1584–7, Barringer 1995: 55–6. In the event, Ap. will make the Rocks the centrepiece of his narrative, in counterpoise to Homer, who put Scylla and Charybdis, not the alternative Planktai route, at the centre, but the danger posed by Scylla and Charybdis remains, should the Argonauts rely merely on mortal steersmen. νῦν δέ in 789 has been thought corrupt (Fränkel suggested τῇ δέ 'by the other route'), but in fact helps to explain why Thetis is needed, and should remain in the text, particularly with the assumption of a lacuna after ἐσάωσα. It may also be thought that, without the assumption of a lacuna, Hera's introduction of the Planktai at the start of her speech is very sudden, even if Thetis was as concerned with the fate of the Argonauts as Hera makes out. For the view that Hera is in fact here simply 'citing' *Od.* 12.69–72 cf. Green 1997: 324–6.

787–8 Cf. *Od.* 12.68 (about the Planktai) κύμαθ' ἁλὸς φορέουσι πυρός τ' ὀλοοῖο θύελλαι. **περιβλύει** 'seethe around'. **σκληρῇσι … σπιλάδεσσι**: cf. 2.550 τρηχείῃς σπιλάδεσσιν of the Clashing Rocks.

789–90 Cf. 786n. These verses combine *Od.* 12.430 ἦλθον ἐπὶ Σκύλλης σκόπελον δεινήν τε Χάρυβδιν with echoes of the swimming Odysseus hearing the waves crash on the reefs of Scherie in *Od.* 5, σπιλάδεσσι (401, 405), δεινὸν ἐρευγόμενον (403). **δέχεται ὁδός** 'the route lies in wait (for them)', LSJ s.v. δέχομαι II 2.

790–817 Hera interrupts her account of the Argonauts' situation to press the fact that Thetis 'owes her' as a result of past benefactions: how could Thetis refuse this request? Here, as with the subsequent account of Thetis' abandonment of Peleus, Ap. is very likely drawing heavily, not just on Hera's claims about her care for Thetis at *Il.* 24.59–63 (cf. 791, 797, Hunter 1993: 97), but on the Epic Cycle, notably the *Cypria* (cf. 792–3n.), and Ap. again (cf. 421–521n.) looks to the Cycle as one of the ways to mark out his difference from Homer.

790 γάρ is 'anticipatory' and explains why Hera is asking Thetis (Denniston 68–9).

791 νηπυτίης is probably an adjective, 'since [you were] very young', rather than an otherwise unattested noun, 'childhood'. **τρέφον ἠδ' ἀγάπησα**: cf. *Il.* 24.60 (Hera about Thetis) θρέψα τε καὶ ἀτίτηλα καὶ ἀνδρὶ πόρον παράκοιτιν. The alternation of imperfect and aorist stresses the length of time involved in 'rearing' a child. Why Hera raised Thetis is not recorded.

792–3 Hera's appeal is complicated by verbal echoes of Thetis' complaint in *Il.* 18. 432–4 of how she has suffered at the hands of Zeus, ἐκ μέν μ' ἀλλάων ἁλιάων ἀνδρὶ δάμασσεν, | Αἰακίδη Πηλῆι, καὶ ἔτλην ἀνέρος εὐνήν | πολλὰ μάλ' οὐκ ἐθέλουσα. We wonder how the silent Thetis is receiving Hera's appeal.   **οὕνεκεν** 'for which reason, because of which'; West 2013: 70 n.11 notes the possibility of emending to τούνεκεν. Hera's account seems to follow that of the *Cypria*, as probably given by Apollod. *Bibl.* 3.13.5: 'Some say that Thetis did not wish to sleep with Zeus as she had been reared (τραφεῖσαν) by Hera ... '; Philodemus reports simply that in the *Cypria* Thetis avoided sex with Zeus 'out of *charis* to Hera' (fr. 2 West, cf. 796). Others understand οὕνεκεν here as 'because', with no strong punctuation after 792; in this case the aorist ἀγάπησα is to be taken strictly of a one-time event: 'I conceived great love for you because ... '. This would find a close parallel in the story of Asterie in Callimachus' *Hymn to Delos*, 247–8 (Hera speaks) ἀλλά μιν ἔκπαγλόν τι σεβίζομαι, οὕνεκ' ἐμεῖο | δέμνιον οὐκ ἐπάτησε, Διὸς δ' ἀνθείλετο πόντον.   **ἔτλης** 'had the recklessness to ... ', a variation on ἔτλην in the Homeric model (above), 'endured, had to suffer'.

794 λέξασθαι 'to lie, sleep' (λέχομαι).

795 We think particularly of Zeus's catalogue of his divine and mortal conquests at *Il.* 14. 315–28, cf. 315 οὐ γάρ πώ ποτέ μ' ὧδε θεᾶς ἔρος οὐδὲ γυναικός κτλ.   **ἠὲ ... ἠέ**: Ap. contrives to vary the scansion within the one verse; for such effects see Hopkinson 1982.

796 τε is hard to defend in this position and may have been added to avoid hiatus (Wilamowitz suggested γ'), but ἀλλ' ἐμέ τ' εἰσορόων begins a hexameter at *Il.* 10.123, and emendation seems unwise.

797 ἠλεύω 'you shunned him', 2nd sing. aor. of ἀλέομαι.   **πελώριον ὅρκον**: a step beyond μέγας ὅρκος (Hes. *Theog.* 400, 784). The story of Zeus's oath too seems to be drawn from the *Cypria*, cf. fr. 2 West.

799–804 Hera creates a fusion of the two standard explanations for Zeus's abandonment of the pursuit of Thetis, thwarted desire and information from Themis. The latter is first attested for us in Pindar, *Isthmian* 8 (where both Zeus and Poseidon pursued the Nereid); Themis' knowledge is the secret harboured by Prometheus, Themis' son, in Aeschylus' 'Prometheus' trilogy. The narrative link is created by the fact that even after his oath Zeus still had designs on Thetis.

799 ὀπιπεύων almost amounts to 'ogling', cf. *Od.* 19.67 (Melantho to Odysseus) ὀπιπεύσεις δὲ γυναῖκας. Hera's scorn for her sex-mad husband is palpable.   **ἀέκουσαν** evokes (again) Thetis' very different complaint at *Il.* 18.434 (792–3n. above).

800 πρέσβειρα varies the Hesiodic αἰδοίη for Themis (*Theog.* 135). **ἕκαστα**: ἅπαντα may be correct, but cf. 730.

801–2 Cf. Pind. *Isthm.* 8.32–3 (Themis declares) εἵνεκεν πεπρωμένον ἦν, φέρτερον πατέρος | ἄνακτα γόνον τεκεῖν | ποντίαν θεόν, Aesch. *PV* 768. **πέπρωται** 'it was fated', LSJ s.v. *πόρω II. For the role of fate in this matter cf., e.g., Aesch. *PV* 518–19.   **λιλαιόμενος** 'despite his desire'.

803–4 'Out of fear that another one of the immortals, a match for himself, should rule, but that he should guard his power forever'. There is a slight syntactical awkwardness as the second clause does not express Zeus's fear, but rather what he actually wants to happen, as an alternative to what he fears.   **ἀντάξιος** 'as good as, worth the same as' here almost amounts to 'a rival'.

805 At *Il.* 24.61 Hera describes Peleus, to whom she gave (πόρον) Thetis, as περὶ κῆρι φίλος . . . ἀθανάτοισιν, and at Pind. *Isthm.* 8.40 he is εὐσεβέστατος; that was little consolation to the Thetis of *Il.* 18.434–5.

806 θυμηδέος: Thetis' account in *Il.* 18 is very different, cf. 792–3n. **γάμου . . . ἀντιάσειας** is a striking variation on Hera's declaration at *Il.* 24.62 πάντες δ' ἀντιάασθε, θεοί, γάμου (i.e. of Peleus and Thetis).

807 τέκνα: although Achilles is the only child of which we know anything, the Hesiodic *Aigimios* told how Thetis threw her children into boiling water 'to discover whether they were mortal'; after the death of 'many' children,

Peleus prevented a similar fate for Achilles (fr. 300M–W). According to
Lyc. *Alex.* 178 (where see Σ), Achilles was the only one of seven children to
survive. Hera's plural may therefore (again) cause Thetis mixed feelings.
At *Pyth.* 3.100 Pindar describes Achilles as 'whom alone immortal Thetis
bore in Phthia'; some scholia (II 88 Drachmann) explain that Achilles
was the only one to survive, but in an encomiastic context Pindar may
well be reacting against the Hesiodic tradition and mean that Achilles
really was 'an only child'.   **δαῖτα**: this feast on Mt Pelion was a standard
element of literary references to the wedding of Peleus and Thetis
(*Il.* 24.62–3, Pind. *Pyth.* 3.93, Eur. *IA* 707, 1041) and seems to have been
described at length in Pindar's *First Hymn*. There was presumably a description of it in the *Cypria*.

808–9 Hera, having raised Thetis, played the role of mother of the bride
at the wedding, cf. Eur. *Ph.* 344–6; as goddess of marriage, Ζυγίη (cf. 96),
this was a very appropriate role for her. Thetis' true parents, Nereus and
Doris, figure little, if at all, in descriptions of the wedding; at Eur. *IA* 703
Zeus acts as 'father' for Thetis in the matter of her marriage (ὁ κύριος).
Whether or not the detail of the torch is an 'invention' of Ap.'s Hera, we
cannot say.   **ἀγανόφρονος εἵνεκα τιμῆς** 'as a result of the kindly-minded
honour (you did me)', a reference back to Thetis' refusal of Zeus's
advances.

811 Hera moves effortlessly to Achilles' afterlife, thus eliding entirely the
life of grief that he and his mother will endure. In Homer, only Menelaos
is promised an afterlife in Elysium, 'because Helen is his wife and he is
Zeus's son-in-law' (*Od.* 4.569). Achilles is the son of a god and, as Hera has
presented it, virtually her own grandson. In later literature, Elysium is
often run together with the 'Isles of the Blessed' where Hesiod placed
some heroes of the Heroic Age after death (*WD* 171, where see West's
note); it is there that Pindar, *Ol.* 2.79–80 places Achilles (together with
Peleus). In the Cyclic *Aithiopis* Thetis took Achilles' body to the legendary
island of Leuke in the Black Sea (cf. Eur. *Andr.* 1260–2, Paus. 3.19.11–13),
but the scholia on 814–15 report that both Ibycus (*PMG* 291) and
Simonides (*PMG* 558 = 278 Poltera) had Achilles marrying Medea in
Elysium, and cf. also Lyc. *Alex.* 174–5 (with Σ). On Elysium and ideas of
hero-cult see further Sourvinou-Inwood 1995: 32–56.

812 That Achilles had been brought up by Cheiron had been in the
tradition at least since *Il.* 11.832, cf. 1.553–8, Hes. fr. 204.87–9, Pind.
Nem. 3.43–58, Jouan 1966: 87–92. Why Thetis is not looking after her son
we shall learn in 869–79.

813 Νηιάδες: usually identified as Cheiron's wife Chariclo and his
mother Philyra, cf. 2.1239 (Philyra is an Oceanid), Hes. fr. 42 (Cheiron

married a Naiad), Pind. *Pyth.* 4.102–3 (Chariclo and Philyra raised Jason). λίπτοντα 'desiring, feeling the lack of', another detail which might cause Thetis mixed feelings. Hera does not say whether Achilles is being fed on the milk of another woman, but a persistent tradition (from the Cycle?) had it that Cheiron raised Achilles on a meat diet, which gave rise to an etymology of his name from ἀ-χεῖλος, 'he who did not put his lips to the breast', cf. 816n., Euphorion fr. 62 van Groningen (= 81 Lightfoot), Apollod. *Bibl.* 3.13.6, Σ *Il.* 1.1h Erbse, *Et. Mag.* 181.27–30.

815 Cf. 811n. In another version (Paus. 3.9.11–13) Achilles married Helen on Leuke (cf. 811n.). Hera appeals to the fact that Thetis is to be Medea's mother-in-law; whether or not Medea is a 'dream daughter-in-law' might be debated, but relations between a mother-in-law and a daughter-in-law might be proverbially bad, *itaque adeo uno animo omnes socrus oderunt nurus* (Ter. *Hec.* 201, cf. Herter 1959: 50–2). περ might be strengtheningly affirmative – 'you are her mother-in-law, after all' – but the possibility of taking it concessively – 'though you are her mother-in-law' – is always there for the reader (and Thetis). Throughout this speech we must ask why Ap. makes Hera speak, often through allusion, in a manner which is open to 'misinterpretation',

816 Thetis' anger can be as 'firmly set' as that of her son Achilles will prove, cf. Mori 2012: 319–21; the spondaic ending of the verse is also perhaps expressively 'firm'. In the *Iliad*, Achilles claims that the Myrmidons reproved him with the words 'Your mother reared you on *cholos*' (16.203), cf. 813n. There is a certain irony in Hera's question of course: she herself was notoriously a goddess who nursed grudges, against Heracles and Pelias, for example, cf. 1138.

817 That *âtê* affects even the gods is a lesson which Hera takes from 'Agamemnon's apology' at *Il.* 19.88–131. Once again, Hera's Homeric allusion is ambivalent in its possible effects: the context of Agamemnon's *âtê* was a terrible wrong to Thetis' son, which led to the whole grim story of the *Iliad*, and Zeus's *âtê* involved being tricked by Hera about the future of his son: how deceptive is Hera being now? In the parallel story in the *Homeric Hymn to Demeter* (cf. 869–79n.), Metaneira too was the victim of *âtê* in 'rescuing' young Demophon from the fire (lines 246, 258).

819 πρήσσοντα 'firing, setting alight'; the verb occurs, however, nowhere outside *Arg.*, and here and at 1537 Brunck suggested the more regular πρηθ-. If sound, πρήσσω (or πρήσω) is perhaps a back formation from ἔπρησα, the aorist of πίμπρημι.

820 ἄϊκας 'gusts, rushes'; the noun, to be connected with ἀΐσσω, appears only here, but κατάϊξ (or κατᾶιξ) occurs at 1.1203, Call. fr. 238.29 (where see Pfeiffer's n.), *h.* 3.114. Homer has the form ἀϊκή, also with both initial vowels long, at *Il.* 15.709.

821 ἐυσταθέος 'steady, well settled in'.

823–4 Cf. 786n.   **τρέψαιο** stands here apparently for ἀποτρέψαιο, 'avert'. For similar uses of the simple for the compound cf. ἕλοντο in 901, στείλαντας in 3.514, Vian 1975: 84.

825 ἀμηχανέοντας '(when they are) unable to do anything about it'.

826 ἀναβρόξασα 'sucking them down', cf. *Od.* 12.240 (Charybdis) ἀναβρόξειε … ὕδωρ. The variant ἀναβρώξασα may derive from an attempt to connect the verb with βιβρώσκω (cf. 2.271), as though Charybdis was gaining some of the features of Scylla.

827 In Homer Circe advised Odysseus to take the lesser evil of Scylla, rather than Charybdis, but here both are to be avoided, as the chosen route will be through the Planktai.   **νέεσθαι:** sc. ἐάσῃις.

828 Σκύλλης: for the 'epanalepsis' of the name cf. 263–4n. Scylla is 'Ausonian' (cf. 552–3n.) because she was normally placed on the Italian side of the strait. Hopman 2012: 160–70 discusses a set of oppositions between Thetis and Scylla, visible in both literature and art.   **Φόρκωι:** the more common form of the name is Φόρκυς (cf. 1598), and Wellauer proposed Φόρκυϊ here, but this would produce a very unusual synizesis at the end of the verse. For the form Φόρκος cf., e.g., Soph. fr. 861R.

829 Scylla's parentage was very variously recorded (cf., e.g., Σ *Od.* 12.124), but in Homer her mother is Krataiis (*Od.* 12.124). Another tradition made her mother Hecate (Hes. fr. 262, Acusilaos of Argos, *FGrHist* 2 F42), and, with the sensitivity typical of a Hellenistic poet, Hera combines these variants into one, by treating Krataiis, 'the powerful one', as a suitable name for Hecate, who was indeed a goddess with many names.   **νυκτιπόλος:** cf. 148, 1020.

830 σμερδαλέηισιν: Homer uses this adjective to describe Scylla's heads (*Od.* 12.91), cf. 154n.   **ἐπαΐξασα** varies the Homeric ἐφορμηθεῖσα (*Od.* 12.22).

831 A heavy spondaic opening emphasizes the threat which Scylla poses. At *Od.* 12.246 Odysseus describes Scylla's victims as 'the best (of my men) in strength of arm and might'. Does Hera have anyone specific in mind here? Peleus, perhaps? Or is she just (once again) echoing the Homeric narrative?

831–2 'But hold the boat in that direction where there is an escape, narrow though it be, from death'.   **παραίβασις** does not occur previously in this sense.

833–41 Thetis' silence about her anger and about Peleus speaks volumes.

834 Thetis' response picks up fragments of Hera's speech (πυρὸς μένος, cf. 819, θύελλαι, cf. 787), as one of the ways in which Ap. advertises his difference from Homeric technique.

836 καὶ κύματος ἀντιόωντος 'even if the wave should oppose us'.

837 σαωσέμεναι: a future infinitive with Aeolic ending. The form occurs at *Il.* 13.96, also in the context of saving ships.   **Ζεφύρου λίγα κινυμένοιο:** cf. *Od.* 4.567 Ζεφύρου λιγὺ πνείοντας ἀήτας, in the description of the Elysium which awaits Menelaos; the echo reinforces the positive connotations of the west wind in this context (cf. 768n.). Aristarchus read πνείοντος ἀήτας in the *Odyssey*-verse, and it has been argued that 837 must also assume that reading, cf. Call. *h.* 2.82, Rengakos 1993: 100. Strabo 1.2.21 alludes to *Od.* 4.567 with λίγα rather than λιγύ, but he may just be paraphrasing.   **λίγα:** Homer uses λιγύς both of winds which are fierce and hostile (e.g. *Od.* 3.289) and of favourable 'stiff' breezes (e.g. *Od.* 4.357); the latter is obviously appropriate here, cf. λαιψηροῖο in 886.

838 The tone of Thetis' reference to the 'long, unspeakably long' journey ahead of her is hard to catch (Hunter 1993: 100), but at the very least it does not thank Hera for entrusting her with this task. The length of the journey certainly means that there is no time for further discussion about the other matters which Hera had raised.

840 'and (to travel to the place) where the ship's cables are attached'.

841 ὑπηῶιοι 'in the morning, when dawn comes'; Greek often uses an adjective in such cases where English prefers an adverb or phrase, cf. 7n.   **μνησαίατο:** the epic and Ionic 3rd pers. pl. aor. mid. opt., instead of –ντο.   **νόστον ἑλέσθαι** 'to resume their voyage (home)'. The phrase is hard to parallel in this sense, but if one can 'take away' someone's νόστος (e.g. 901 (cf. 823–4n.), *Od.* 13.132), then presumably one can also 'pick it up'. The simple ἑλέσθαι is used here somewhat like ἀναλαμβάνειν 'to resume'.

842 αἰθέρος ἔμβαλε δίναις ends a hexameter at Empedocles fr. 115.11 D–K.

843 κάλει: cf. 756n.

845 ἤντεον ἀλλήλῃσι 'they met each other' reads oddly in English, and there is a slight narrative unclarity. 780 might have suggested that all the Nereids were in one place (i.e. 'Thetis met the rest of the group'), but ἄλλοθεν ἄλλαι at 930 suggests otherwise, and it is better to understand that the Nereids were scattered around the sea when they answered Thetis' call, so that the phrase amounts to 'they came together'. If we wish to tie up

loose ends, we can say that some, but not all, of her sisters were with
Thetis in their father's house at 780. For such a βοή for assistance cf.,
e.g., *Od.* 9.399–401, the Cyclopes gather in one place ἄλλοθεν ἄλλος
from their various caves 'when they heard his shout'. Everything is happening at great speed in this narrative. For the form ἤντεον (from ἀντάω)
cf. 1183–5n.

847–8 A double comparison shows the poet struggling to convey the speed
of divine movement; cf. the speed of Athena compared to that of shifting
thoughts at 2.541–8. Fränkel 1968: 538–9 suggested that 848 alluded to
the importance that contemporary science gave to the fact that the sun's
first rays illuminated everything at once, rather than there being a gradual
illumination, as a marker of the inexpressible speed of light, cf. Lucr.
2.147–9. There is however little (if any) evidence for a Greek background
to Lucretius' observation (Fowler 2002: 210–13), and just as ἀμάρυγμα,
'flash of light', focuses on light in motion, so dawn is the obvious time at
which the sun's rays may be seen to 'move'; it is thus not clear that Ap.
required scientific 'sources' for this image.   περαίης ... γαίης 'the land
on the other side [sc. of the sea]' must here be the horizon, cf. περάτηθεν in
54. This strikingly unusual expression suggested to Fränkel 1968: 458 that
Ap. must have understood the curvature of the earth, i.e. he knew that
beyond the sea out of which the sun seems to rise there were indeed other
lands. ὑψόθι γαίης ends a hexameter also at Arat. *Phain.* 558 in a context of
the zodiac and the rising of the sun.

849 σεύατ' ἴμεν 'hastened on her journey', cf. 2.540 also of a god, LSJ s.v.
σεύω II 2.   λαιψηρά is the neuter plural used adverbially.

850 Cf. 660–1, 3.312 ἀκτὴν ἠπείρου Τυρσηνίδος. The present verse, with its
chiastic arrangement and spondaic ending, might be thought quintessentially Hellenistic.

851–2 The language is of a common type (cf. the athletic pursuits of
the enforcedly idle Myrmidons at *Il.* 2.773–5), but it is difficult not to
recall the Greek ambassadors arriving at the tent of Peleus and Thetis' son,
τὸν δ' ηὗρον φρένα τερπόμενον φόρμιγγι λιγείῃ.   σόλωι: cf. 656–7n.

852–3 The sequence is common in divine apparitions in Homer and
reinforces the echo of Athena's epiphany to Achilles at *Il.* 1.197–8, στῆ δ'
ὄπιθεν ... | οἴωι φαινομένη, τῶν δ' ἄλλων οὔ τις ὁρᾶτο. Dr Benaissa informs me
that στῆ, conjectured by Fränkel, is in fact read on an unpublished
Oxyrhynchus papyrus.   ὀρεξαμένη 'touching', rather than 'reaching
for', cf. D-Schol. on *Il.* 6.466, LSJ s.v. 2a.   ὁ γάρ ῥά οἱ ἦεν ἀκοίτης, 'he
was, after all, her husband', explains the verbal gesture, but also draws
attention to the gulf between them: Peleus was her ἀκοίτης in name only.

854 ἔμπεδον 'clearly, without possibility of error', cf. 1429–30. The word catches mortal uncertainty about divine epiphany: how can one ever be 'certain'?

855 ἐείσατο: cf. 522n.

856–64 Thetis and Peleus also confront each other at the end of Eur. *Andr.*, where the goddess appears *ex machina*; the effect there is, however, very different. Thetis there speaks of the χάρις arising from their previous relationship (1231, 1253) and promises that she will make Peleus a god and that they will live happily together ever after (1253–8). She commands him to cease from λύπη, an injunction which he obeys (1270, 1276). Here her appearance brings only ἄχος (866).

856 ἦσθε 'sit (idly)'.

857 θοῆς ... νηός is a very common Homeric syntagm, but in *Arg.* (cf. 101n., 2.533, 895) it evokes the etymology of Ἀργώ as 'the swift (ἀργός) ship'; at 1.111, αὐτὴ γὰρ καὶ νῆα θοὴν κάμε, σὺν δέ οἱ Ἄργος, Ap. alludes to two different etymologies in one verse, cf. *Et. Mag.* 136.32–4.

859 πασσυδίηι 'all together', but here the other sense, 'with all speed', may also resonate.   **ἀντιόωσι** 'come together'.

860 In *Od.* Circe tells Odysseus that Planktai is what the gods call (καλέουσι) the Rocks (12.61); she does not say whether mortals have a name for them, cf. Clay 1972. So here, Thetis assumes ignorance on Peleus' part; the textual problems of 786 make it unwise to assume that Hera did not need to explain the name to Thetis, a fellow god. Grammarians variously associated the name with πλήσσεσθαι, because of the beating of the waves against the Rocks, or with πλάζεσθαι, because the rocks 'wandered' (Σ *Od.* 12.61, Heubeck on *Od.* 12.55–72).

861 ῥυσόμεναι 'to protect' [future participle of purpose] the ship on its passage through the Rocks.   **ἐναίσιμος**: in fact, of course, the route is a deliberate choice by the poet; for such wry comments on narrative choice cf. 1226–7n.

862–4 imply that the Argonauts will see the Nereids when they arrive to help (cf. 933–8, Cat. 64.14–21), and that Peleus might be tempted to point Thetis out; given her feelings about Peleus and her union with him, this would be a source of great shame to her.   **ἀντομένην** 'coming (to your aid)'.   **νόωι δ' ἔχε** 'keep it to yourself', i.e. keep my identity to yourself, when you see me at the Rocks. Others understand 'bear in mind' (what I am telling you now), but this seems a more awkward sequence.   **ἀπηλεγέως** 'heedlessly, without paying me due regard', cf. 689.

865 ἀΐδηλος ἐδύσατο 'invisible she plunged into … ', i.e. she plunged into … and became invisible. ἀΐδηλος here means ἄδηλος, cf. 47n., Soph. *Ajax* 607 (with Finglass' note), Hesychius α1773 ἀΐδηλον· ἄδηλον, ἀφανές. ἄφαντος at 1590 is exactly synonymous.   **βένθεα πόντου** occurs also at 1.922, but is not in Homer or Hesiod; in view of the coming debt to the *Homeric Hymn to Demeter* (cf. 869–79n.), it is likely that Ap. here echoes lines 38–40 of that poem, ἤχησαν … βένθεα πόντου | … τῆς δ᾿ ἔκλυε πότνια μήτηρ. | ὀξὺ δέ μιν κραδίην ἄχος ἔλλαβεν (~ 866). Here, however, it is the father who feels ἄχος, and the mother who has given up her own child.

866 ἄχος αἰνόν: cf. 868n.   **οὐκέτ᾿ ἰοῦσαν** suggests that Thetis would sometimes visit Peleus after abandoning him, but had not done so for a long time. With πάρος, however, the sense is compressed and a bit awkward, and Lloyd-Jones's οὔποτ᾿ is attractive (cf. *Od.* 6.325). Fränkel proposed οὐ μετιοῦσαν.

868 Ἀχιλῆος immediately after ἄχος activates the etymology of the hero's name from that noun, cf., e.g., Σ *Il.* 1.1h Erbse, *Et. Mag.* 181.25–7, Nagy 1999: 69–83, Mirto 2011. For allusion to another etymology cf. 813n. Mirto 2011, noting that αἰνὸν ἄχος is what Aphrodite feels in *HHAphr.* because she has been made to share a mortal's bed (lines 198–9), discusses analogies between the goddess' situation and that of Thetis in the current episode.

869–79 The description, told as a kind of flashback of what passes through Peleus' mind, of Thetis' attempts to make Achilles immortal, of Peleus' intervention, and of her abandonment of husband and son may draw on the *Cypria*, though there is no clear evidence that it does (Burgess 2009: 9–19); it certainly, however, makes extensive use of the parallel scene in the *Homeric Hymn to Demeter* in which Metaneira's intervention spoils Demeter's plan to make Demophon immortal (Richardson 1974: 237–8). It would be very characteristic for Ap. to combine an archaic version of the story he is telling with reminiscences of another, parallel archaic episode; for the different version of the Hesiodic *Aigimios* cf. 807n. The view that Homer did not know of the 'divorce' of Peleus and Thetis and that this was a motif of οἱ νεώτεροι (including the Cycle?) goes back at least to Aristarchus (Severyns 1928: 254–9); whether or not Ap. took this view, the prominent place he gives to non-Homeric, and possibly Cyclic, material is again noteworthy. Slatkin 1991: 88–105 discusses a much wider pattern of analogy between Thetis and Demeter, centring around their anger and their power to bring the cosmic order to a halt.

869 περί is probably adverbial, '(the flesh) around him', rather than in tmesis with ἔδαιε. For anthropological parallels for this story of 'putting children in the fire' see Frazer 1921: II 311–17.

870 Cf. *HHDem.* 239 νύκτας δὲ κρύπτασκε πυρὸς μένει.

871 Cf. *HHDem.* 237 χρίεσκ᾽ ἀμβροσίηι. βροτέας in 869 activates the etymology of ἀμβροσίη as 'non-mortal'. Beyond *HHDem.*, another important model here is *Il.* 23. 185–7, Aphrodite's protection for the body of Achilles' enemy Hector (note ἄλαλκε in 185). Once again, Ap. runs together two analogous, but actually very different, archaic models.

872 Cf. *HHDem.* 242 καί κέν μιν ποίησεν ἀγήρων τ᾽ ἀθάνατόν τε κτλ.

873 In contrast to *HHDem.* 243–5, Ap. does not tell us why Peleus 'leapt up' on one particular occasion (note αἰεί in 869), and in his telling of the story, which may depend on *Arg.* or the Cycle or both, Apollodorus is compelled to add an explanation, which he may in fact have borrowed from *HHDem.*, for it would not suit Ap.'s narrative: 'Peleus kept watch … ', Πηλεὺς δὲ ἐπιτηρήσας κτλ. (*Bibl.* 3.13.6). In *Arg.*, the narrative gap advertises what is important. An obvious reason why Peleus might have leapt up would be that Achilles screamed (cf. Theocr. 24.22–40), but Achilles is not that kind of baby: he only screams when he is taken *out of* the fire (876). Rather, it is Peleus himself who is 'the big baby', μέγα νήπιος (875).

874 σπαίροντα is a later form for the Homeric ἀσπαίρω, which is used of the baby Demophon in the archaic narrative (*HHDem.* 289).   ἧκε δ᾽ αὐτήν: cf. *HHDem.* 245 κώκυσεν of Metaneira.

875 ἡ δ᾽ ἀίουσα: cf. *HHDem.* 250 τῆς δ᾽ ἄιε δῖα θεάων.

876 Thetis acts more violently than does Demeter at 253–4 of the *Hymn*.   ἁρπάγδην: lit. 'snatchingly', i.e. 'snatching him from the fire'.   κεκληγῶτα gives an expressively heavy, spondaic ending to the verse, as the baby cries. Just as Demophon cried when he was abandoned by the goddess and objected to being looked after by 'worse nurses' (*HHDem.* 284–91), so the infant Achilles wishes he was still in the fire.

877 A double comparison in asyndeton gives a more mannered verse than merely 'like a breeze or a dream', cf. *HHHermes* 147 αὔρηι ὀπωρινῆι ἐναλίγκιος ἠΰτ᾽ ὀμίχλη. At *Od.* 6.20 Athena rushes to Nausicaa's bed ἀνέμου ὡς πνοιή and appears to her in a dream (στῆ δ᾽ ἄρ᾽ ὑπὲρ κεφαλῆς κτλ.). The detail of δέμας perhaps hints at Thetis' powers to change shape: in one familiar version of the story, Peleus was advised by Cheiron how to catch her, despite the various metamorphoses she would employ (cf. Menelaos and Proteus). Any passing breeze might of course be a god: can one ever be sure? Did Peleus merely dream the whole thing – both his marriage and his wife's sudden reappearance? Cf. further 880n.

878 Cf. *HHDem.* 281 (the angry Demeter) βῆ δὲ διὲκ μεγάρων. Unlike Demeter, however, Thetis disappears without a word.

879 picks up 866 to close the analeptic flashback.   **χωσαμένη**: *HHDem.*
251 χολωσαμένη, 254 κοτέσασα μάλ᾽ αἰνῶς.

880 We are now back in the time of 865 (ἀμηχανίη, 'helpless depression', varies ἄχος), but the reaction could indeed have been that of Peleus to Thetis' first disappearance; sophisticated narrative technique runs the two events together, just as Peleus' mind has run them together.

882 μεσσηγύς 'in the middle (of the games)'.

884 νύκτ᾽ ἄεσαν, 'slept through the night', a Homeric phrase (e.g. *Od.* 3.490, 15.88). The verb (with initial long α) occurs only in this aorist; ancient grammarians traced it back to various putative presents (ἄω, αὔω etc.), *LfgrE* s.v.

885 describes not 'first light', but the time when the whole sky is illumined. The reference to Dawn will be picked up at 981, to mark the trip from Circe to Drepane as an episode of one full day and night.

886 κατηλυσίηι: winds are naturally thought to 'descend' from, or originate in (cf. 764–5n.), the air above us, cf. 1.1274 πνοιαὶ δὲ κατήλυθον (a departure scene), Thucyd. 2.25.4 etc. The dative is best understood as 'accompanying circumstance' (Smyth §1527).

887–90 For this description of departure cf. Antipater of Sidon, *AP* 10.25–7 (=*HE* 442–4) τοὔνεκα μηρύσασθε διάβροχα πείσματα, ναῦται, | ἕλκετε δ᾽ ἀγκύρας φωλάδας ἐκ λιμένων, | λαίφεα δ᾽ εὐυφέα προτονίζετε, Theocr. 13.68–9.

887 κληῖδας 'rowing-benches', LSJ s.v. κλείς IV.

888 εὐναίας 'anchor-stones', called in Homer εὐναί. These 'beds' were heavy flat stones through which a hole was bored so that cables could be attached to them; many ancient examples have been recovered from the seabed; see Casson 1971: fig. 187. This detail varies the description of the tying of the stern-cables on arrival (661–2); the poet avoids repetitiveness by distributing these habitual actions across departure and arrival.   **περιγηθέες** is picked up by κεχαρμένοι in 980, as part of the ring around the episode of the voyage from Circe's home, cf. 885n. The Argonauts' happiness here is presumably at the promise of the Nereids' help.

889 ἄρμενα μηρύοντο 'they stowed the tackle'. The verb is used of 'furling' sails at its only appearance in Homer, as here immediately before the episode of the Sirens (*Od.* 12.170); Antipater (887–90n.) uses it of winding ropes, but here it is probably more general in application, 'stowed, made ready'.   **κατὰ χρέος** 'in due order, appropriately'.

890 τανύσαντες ἐν ἱμάντεσσι κεραίης 'stretching (the sail) tight on the lifts of the yard-arm'; for these sailing-terms see Casson 1971: 230–2, 260–3.

891–919 Only our knowledge of previous literature, most notably *Od.*, leads us to expect an encounter with the Sirens; unlike Odysseus, Jason and his crew have not been forewarned. Although the principal intertext for Ap.'s Sirens episode is the corresponding encounter in *Od.* 12 (Goldhill 1991: 298–300, Knight 1995: 200–6), it is almost certain that Ap. inherited the contest of Orpheus and the Sirens from earlier treatments, whether lyric (cf. Simonides, *PMG* 567, 595, West 2005: 46–7, Power 2010: 276–7) or epic or both. A (probably fourth-century) terracotta group of Orpheus and two Sirens is preserved from Tarentum (West 1983: pl. 4). On the Sirens in general see *LIMC* (Suppl.) s.v. Seirenes, pp. 1093–4.

891–2 εὐκραής 'brisk', cf. 2.1228 where sailing speed is also emphasized. The word probably derives from a misdivision of ἀκραής (cf. 1224) as ἀ-κραής 'unmixed', rather than ἀκρ-αης. **νῆσον ... Ἀνθεμόεσσαν**: in Homer the Sirens live on an island (*Od.* 12.167), but also 'sit in a meadow' (12.45, 159). Odysseus tells his men of the Sirens' λειμῶν' ἀνθεμόεντα (12.159, a detail Circe had not in fact told him), and Hesiod seems, like Ap., to have called the island Ἀνθεμόεσσα (fr. 27M–W); whether the Homeric adjective was the origin of the name or rather alludes to it is hard to say. This island had been subsequently placed at more than one point off the Italian south coast or even at the entrance to the Strait of Messina; this last, though not entirely excluded, here seems improbable, and it is very likely that Ap. would have placed the Sirens near the later Sorrento and Capri, perhaps on Rocks called 'Seirenoussai' (mod. 'Li Galli', Barrington 44 F4), cf. Strabo 1.2.12–14, 18, Delage 1930: 241.   **λίγειαι**: cf. 914. The Sirens'song is λιγυρή at *Od.* 12.44, 183, and Λίγεια is one of the reported names of the Sirens (Σ *Od.* 12.39, Σ Lyc. *Alex.* 715).

893 Ἀχελωίδες: cf. 895–6n.   ἡδείηισι creates a spondaic close to the verse; whether there is a deliberate effect of 'sweetness' is difficult to say, but 893–9 contain 4 *spondeiazontes* in 7 verses, and this may be part of the characterization of the Sirens as expert poets. This rhythmical 'nest' is notably isolated: the previous spondaic verse was 876, and the next is 937.

894 rewrites *Od.* 12.40 ἀνθρώπους θέλγουσιν, ὅ τίς σφεας εἰσαφίκηται. θέλγειν is almost the *uox propria* for the effect of the Sirens, cf. also *Od.* 12.44. One of the names of the Sirens was Θελξιέπεια or Θελξινόη (Σ 892, Σ *Od.* 12.39); whether Σ 892 had any authority for claiming Μόλπη as another Siren name we do not know.   **παρὰ ... βάλοιτο** 'threw ashore', tmesis; contrast 484 where the verb means 'moor'.

895–6 Σ *Od.* 12.39 explicitly notes that Homer does not give any genealogy for the Sirens; Ap. makes good that deficiency. Achelous is the most commonly named father (Lyc. *Alex.* 712 etc.), though Soph. fr. 861R names Phorkos. The name of the mother is more varied. Σ *Od.* 12.39 also name Terpsichore, but may in fact be indebted to this passage; μελῳδοῦ μητρός at Lyc. *Alex.* 713 suggests the Muse Melpomene, rather than Terpsichore whom the scholia on that passage name.

896–9 The Sirens had once been Persephone's playmates and/or maids; it is noteworthy that this myth is introduced so soon after an extended reworking of material from *HHDem.* In the *Hymn*, Persephone is playing with daughters of Ocean when she is abducted (line 5, cf. Richardson 1974: 140), and it is a small step from there to having her playing with 'daughters of Achelous' when Hades struck; Ov. *Met.* 5.552–5 seems already to have taken that step, or indeed to have interpreted the present passage as implying it, and ἀδμῆτ᾽ ἔτι makes that indeed an easy enough interpretation. The Sirens are already associated with Persephone at Eur. *Helen* 167–78. Later texts offer various explanations for the metamorphosis of the Sirens into part-birds. They were punished by Demeter for failing to protect her daughter (Hyg. *Fab.* 141), or they themselves asked for metamorphosis in order to continue to look for her (Ov. *Met.* 5.552–63), or they were punished by Aphrodite for choosing to remain virgins (Σ *Od.* 12.39; παρθενικῆις in 899 and παρθενίην in 909 may evoke this aetiology, and in 917–19 Aphrodite intervenes to deprive the Sirens of a victim). The mixture of a female head and a bird body is standard in artistic representations of the Sirens; *LIMC* (Suppl.) s.v. Seirenes.

897 θυγατέρ᾽ ἰφθίμην: Homer uses θυγατέρ᾽ ἰφθίμηι in the dative (*Od.* 10.106, 15.364), a nice example of Ap.'s 'imitation with difference' of Homeric language. The adjective is standardly understood in antiquity to mean 'strong, powerful', and that would fit the other examples in *Arg.*, though Zenodotus understood it to mean ἀγαθός; *LfgrE* s.v., Erbse on Σ *Il.* 1.3. **πορσαίνεσκον** 'looked after, cared for', cf. Pind. *Ol.* 6.33, LSJ s.v. πορσύνω III.

898 ἄμμιγα μελπόμεναι 'playing alongside her'. For μέλπεσθαι and μολπή in this sense cf. 1728, 3.897, 949–50, *Od.* 6.101; no doubt this 'play' did involve μολπή in the sense of 'singing'. Aristarchus was later to restrict μολπή in Homer to the meaning παιδιά (Rengakos 1994: 115–16).

898–9 Cf. Ov. *Met.* 5.552–3, *uobis, Acheloides, unde | pluma pedesque auium, cum uirginis ora geratis?*, a passage very likely echoing the present one.

900 εὐόρμου . . . ἐκ περιωπῆς 'from a lookout point with a good anchorage'; the anchorage for passing boats is important to the Sirens' evil plans.

COMMENTARY: 901–907   207

There are famous paintings from the classical period of the Sirens sitting
on cliff-tops, which are indeed perfect 'lookouts', cf., e.g., *LIMC* s.v.
Odysseus nos. 152, 155.

901 ἢ θαμὰ δή: such explicit emotional involvement by the narrator with
his story is typical of Hellenistic poetry (cf., e.g., 1242, 1.631, 3.954,
Cuypers 2005: 54–5), and very un-Homeric.   **μελιηδέα** occurs in the
Homeric Sirens' episode – at *Od.* 12.48 it is used of wax. Homer has
νόστον ... μελιηδέα at *Od.* 11.100.   **ἕλοντο** 'took away'; the simple verb
is here used for a compound with ἀπο-, cf. 916, 823–4n.

902 τηκεδόνι φθινύθουσαι: lit. 'causing them to waste with melting'. The
noun here suggests both the 'wasting desire' induced by the lovely voices
(cf. the fate of Boutes) and the physical wasting (cf. *Od.* 11.201), which is
what happens to the Sirens' victims; both τηκεδών and φθίσις can be used of
'consumption', the 'wasting disease'. The Homeric Sirens are surrounded
by 'a heap of the bones of rotting men' (*Od.* 12.45–6).   **ἀπηλεγέως:**
perhaps 'without caring' (that these are the Argonauts), but the meaning
is uncertain; 'immediately' and 'unceasingly' have also been suggested.

903 Cf. *Il.* 3.152 (the Trojan elders compared to cicadas), δενδρέωι
ἐφεζόμενοι ὄπα λειριόεσσαν ἱεῖσιν; both cicadas and Sirens are (for different
reasons) devoted to song, but Ap. gives the description a strikingly different context.   **λείριον** and λειριόεις were as mysterious in antiquity as they
are today, cf. West on Hes. *Theog.* 41, Egan 1985. The connection with lilies
leads to glosses such as ἀνθηρόν and εὐανθές (Σ *Il.* 3.152, 13.830), which
would suit the name of the Sirens' island, but other ancient glosses such as
ἡδεῖα and ἐπιθυμητής, 'full of desire', would also be very appropriate here.

904–5 For such counterfactuals cf. 636–42n. Orpheus is the obvious
opponent for the Sirens (cf. 891–919n.), as θέλγειν is also his hallmark,
cf. 1.27, 31.   **ἔμελλον** here amounts to 'were making preparations to ...'.
Οἰάγροιο πάϊς: cf. 1.24–5, 570 etc. Oiagros is the name of Orpheus' Thracian
father as early as Pind. fr. 128c.11M, cf. *RE* 17.2082–5.

906 Βιστονίην ... φόρμιγγα: cf. 2.704. The Bistones were a Thracian
tribe of the coastal region south of the Rhodope mountains (Barrington
51 D2). Roman poets regularly use 'Bistonian' as a learned word for
'Thracian' (cf. Lyne on [Virg.], *Ciris* 165), perhaps in imitation of Ap.
ἐνὶ χερσὶν ἑαῖς ... τανύσσας: lit. 'stringing ... in his hands', i.e. 'taking his
lyre in his hands and stringing it (or tightening the strings)'; for the verb
cf. *Od.* 21.407, *HHHermes* 51.

907–9 Two wholly dactylic verses, imitating the speed of Orpheus' playing,
are brought to a jolting close by κρεγμῶι, which suggests the loudness of
the playing. Orpheus' performance is that of a virtuoso kitharode, but the

effect of the clash of 'swift-rolling' sound and a lovely female choir is
anything but harmonious (Hunter 1996: 146–9). It is unclear whether
we are to imagine Orpheus' performance as purely instrumental, but the
emphasis is certainly on his playing rather than on any singing.

907 'caused to sound out the swift melody of a fast-running
song'. εὐτροχάλοιο, like the Homeric εὔτροχος, would properly be
used of a chariot or cart (cf. 3.889 etc.), but is used of a ball at 3.135,
and here it denotes the speed, and perhaps swift changes, of Orpheus'
virtuoso playing; Eur. *Ba.* 268 εὔτροχον γλῶσσαν, 'a fluent tongue', is
perhaps the closest analogue (cf. also *IG* v 1.264).

908–9 lit. 'so that as he confounded (the Sirens by playing) simulta-
neously, (the Argonauts') ears would ring with the knocking (of his
plectrum).' The use of κλονεῖν, 'to harass, confound', of Orpheus' playing
leads to a difficult compression of meaning. Glei–Natzel-Glei 1996 understand 'so that when he struck the strings all at the same time, their ears . . .',
but this seems difficult to get from the Greek. Whereas Odysseus' men
pass the Sirens without hearing anything at all, the Argonauts are bom-
barded with a superfluity of sound.   ἐπιβρομέωνται ἀκουαί: cf. 16–17n.
Echoes of Sappho in a context where what matters is the loud clashing of
dissonant sound are wrily pointed (Goldhill 1991: 300).   κρεγμῶι:
cf. 1194 φόρμιγγος ἐϋκρέκτου.   παρθενίην δ' ἐνοπὴν ἐβιήσατο φόρμιγξ
'the lyre overpowered/did violence to the virgin voices'; there is a clear
suggestion of rape which perhaps picks up the Sirens' role in the story of
Persephone (896–9n.).

910 reminds us that conditions are quite different from the weird calm
which descended upon Odysseus' boat as soon as it was near the Sirens'
island (*Od.* 12.168–9).

911 ἄκριτον: 'indistinct' seems more pointed here than 'without stopping'.
The Sirens have to compete not only with Orpheus, but also the wind and
the waves. Although we know what the Homeric Sirens sang, we shall never
know 'what song the Sirens sang' (cf. Suet. *Tib.* 70.3) to the Argonauts.

912–19 The Sirens' one victim is the Athenian Boutes (cf. 1.95–100),
whose name evokes the legendary ancestor of the priestly family of the
Eteoboutadai. This ἥρως (cf. Paus. 1.26.5) is here brought together with a
Sicilian ἥρως of the same name, who seems to have been a kind of Adonis
figure and lover of Aphrodite; their child, Eryx, founded what was to
become a very famous and rich temple to his mother on the mountain-
top named after him (mod. Erice) at the NW tip of Sicily, cf. Thucyd. 6.46,
Theocr. 15.101, Call. fr. 43.53, Diod. Sic. 4.23.2, 83.1–4, Harder 2012:
2.331–2. The original running together of the two homonymous figures is

COMMENTARY: 912–920 209

often thought to date to the first alliance of Athens and Segesta in the middle of the fifth century; see, e.g., Wilamowitz 1924: 2.180–1. Virgil has the temple founded rather by Aeneas, *Aen.* 5.759–60.

912 The ancestor of the Eteoboutadai is normally said to be a son of Pandion, but Teleon is one of the Athenian descendants of Ion at Eur. *Ion* 1579, where however most editors adopt Canter's Γελέων.

913 προφθάμενος: it is unclear when exactly Boutes leapt in, or indeed whether that is a question we are intended to ask. Vian suggests that 912–14 take us back to 902–3, i.e. to before Orpheus started playing, but it may rather be that the reference of προφθάμενος is somewhat vague, 'before they had got safely away': Boutes leapt, despite Orpheus' playing and the sound of the wind and the waves. πόντωι: cf. 388n.

914 θυμὸν ἰανθείς 'warmed in his heart' by erotic longing (cf. 902). This is a very different kind of 'warming' than occurs in the Homeric episode (*Od.* 12.175).

915 πορφυρέοιο 'surging'.

916 σχέτλιος: cf., e.g., 1524, 1.1302, 3.1133n.   ἤ τέ οἱ: it is difficult to give the precise nuance of τε in this collocation; see Ruijgh 1971: 795–803, 959–60, pointing out that Homer uses ἤ τε almost exclusively in character speech, whereas Ap. uses it freely in narration, as here and 1524. Schaefer suggested κε for τε, but the omission of the modal particle is well paralleled (cf. 786n.).   κατ᾽ αὐτόθι 'on the spot', cf. 1409.

917 Ἔρυκος: the reference to the temple, to be built only by Boutes' son (912–19n.), is not 'anachronistic', as it helps to fill out the narrative of Aphrodite's rescue; the temple is one of the end points towards which the narrative moves.

918 ἀνερέψατο 'snatched up', cf. 1.214, 2.503; whether this or ἀνερείψατο is the correct form is quite uncertain, cf. West on Hes. *Theog.* 990. Ap. may have in mind Hes. *Theog.* 989–901: Aphrodite 'snatched up' the young Phaethon, and established him in her temple as a δαίμονα δῖον, as Boutes too has plainly become.

919 πρόφρων ἀντομένη 'coming kindly (to his aid)', cf. 121, 863. Λιλυβηίδα ναιέμεν ἄκρην '[saved him], to dwell on the height of Lilybaeum'. Boutes is established as a hero at Lilybaeum (mod. Marsala), whereas his son will found the famous temple to the north at Mt Eryx.

920 is an Apollonian version of a familiar Odyssean motif, 'moving on, while lamenting those who have been lost', cf. *Od.* 9.62–3, 105,

565–6 etc. ὅπαζον 'pressed upon', i.e. followed soon after, cf. 1.614, LSJ s.v. IV.

921 '[other things] worse (than the Sirens), destructive of ships … ' μιξοδίηισιν ἁλός: the Strait of Messina is where seas meet: to the north, the Tyrrhenian, to the east the Sicilian, to the south the African or Libyan. Like a cross-roads, the meeting point of seas is to be a place of danger and decision. Analogously, the Symplegades are placed 'where the sea contracts', ἁλὸς ἐν ξυνοχῆισι, 2.318.

922–4 Scylla and Charybdis lie in wait on either side of the narrow point of the strait between Italy and Sicily, where the Homeric στεινωπός (*Od.* 12.234) had long been identified; 922–3 in fact rewrite *Od.* 12.235–6. Also somewhere (the vague ἄλλοθι in 924) in the strait are the Planktai (cf. 761–2n., Thalmann 2011: 184), and it is the Nereids' task to get the boat through the 'small passage' (832) which will keep it clear of Scylla and Charybdis, though an encounter with the Planktai cannot be avoided.

922 begins with four spondees; according to La Roche 1899: 190, there are only three such verses in *Arg.* (cf. 2.13, also introducing a serious danger, 3.700, a moment of great solemnity). λισσή 'smooth', cf. *Od.* 12.79 (Scylla's rock) πέτρη γὰρ λίς ἐστι, περιξέστηι ἐικυῖα, but probably also 'sheer', cf. 956, 2.730–1.

923 ἀναβλύζουσα: cf. *Od.* 12.104, 236–9; for the noise of Charybdis cf. *Od.* 12.242.

924–6 rewrite *Od.* 12.59–60, in the Homeric description of the Planktai. ἀπέπτυεν, 'spat out' (intransitive), has no real parallel and Fränkel's ἀνέπτυεν would bring the sentence very close to 2.569–70; an alternative would be to read πυριθαλπέας … πέτρας in 926, cf. Strabo 6.2.10 (about Hiera) μύδρους αἱ φλόγες ἀναφέρουσιν. Nevertheless, Homer has two examples of ἀποπτύει, and one, *Il.* 4.426 ἀποπτύει δ᾽ ἁλὸς ἄχνην, occurs in a simile which is as close to a 'Planktai' description as the *Iliad* comes; Ap. may have taken over the verb and used it intransitively.

927 Strabo 6.2.10 describes how, when the north wind is going to blow, a cloud of mist (ἀχλὺν ὁμιχλώδη) descends over Hiera, and Ap. may here be indebted to one of Strabo's predecessors.

928 ἔδρακες: for such 2nd person addresses to the reader cf. 238–40n., 1.765, Byre 1991.

929 Pytheas of Massalia (late fourth century) reported that the sea around the Aeolian islands boiled (ζεῖν), fr. 15 Mette; cf. 955n. κήκιε is almost used for ἀνεκήκιε, cf. 600.

930–8 The intervention of the Nereids was used by Virgil at *Aen.* 10.215–27 to describe Aeneas' ship surrounded by the nymphs who had once been his own ships, cf. Nelis 2001: 224–5.

930 ἄλλοθεν ἄλλαι: cf. 845n.

931 πτέρυγος … πηδαλίοιο 'the blade of the rudder', a technical term rather than a poetic image (Casson 1971: 224 n. 2).

932 δῖα Θέτις: cf. 783n. Thetis' role as divine steersperson corresponds to the forward shove which Athena gave the *Argo* through the Symplegades (2.598–600). **ἔρυσθαι** 'to guide, watch over', cf. 1.401, a rather different meaning than the Homeric νῆας ἔρυσθαι, which is 'to watch over the ships' when they are moored or beached (*Od.* 9.194, 10.444 etc.). The transmitted ἐρύσσαι, 'to draw', does not make much sense in the context of steering the rudder.

933–6 The comparison of the Nereids to dolphins owes little to extant archaic models (*Il.* 21.22–4, [Hes.], *Scut.* 209–12), but it was important for Moschus' description of the marine parade at *Europa* 115–19. The triple anaphora of ἄλλοτε catches the familiar phenomenon of dolphins appearing, then disappearing, and then appearing off another part of the boat. Unsurprisingly, Nereids and dolphins regularly appear together in art.

933 ὑπὲξ ἁλὸς εὐδιόωντες 'enjoying the good weather (and coming) up out of the sea', cf. 1.572–4.

936 παρβολάδην 'alongside, parallel to the ship'. Ap. probably borrowed the term from Aratus, *Phain.* 318, where it appears in the description of the constellation of the Dolphin. **ναύτηισι:** both specific (the Argonauts) and general (all sailors). **χάρμα:** gambolling dolphins are a delightful sight and they were thought to be the sea-animals closest and most beneficial to man, as well as having a special relationship with the divine (Thompson, *Fishes* 52–3). The appearance of dolphins was almost certainly also a good omen for any voyage, cf. Pacuvius 353–60 Warmington, though whether they were thought to signal the accompaniment of Apollo Δελφίνιος is very uncertain (Graf 1979). Dolphins were reputed to move with amazing rapidity (cf., e.g., Arist. *HA* 8.631a21–4), so that any boat which kept up with them was making excellent progress (cf. σπερχομένην in 934).

937–8 ὑπεκπροθέουσαι 'running up out (of the water) and in advance (of the *Argo*)'. ὑπεκ– picks up ὑπὲξ ἁλός, ἐπήτριμοι, 'all in a group, in ranks', varies ἀγεληδόν, the verb (ἑλίσσεσθαι) is repeated, and περί with the dative varies περί with the accusative. For the very close matching of tenor to vehicle in Apollonius' similes see Hunter 1993: 129–32.

939 ἐνιχρίμψεσθαι 'crash into'. Both future and aorist infinitive are possible after ἔμελλον. **ἔμελλον**: the subject is the Argonauts; this is very easy to understand, but Fränkel suggested ἔμελλεν, i.e. the ship of 938.

940 πέζας: cf. 46, 3.874–5 (Medea's maids); the principal archaic model is probably *HHDem.* 176 ὧς αἱ ἐπισχόμεναι ἑανῶν πτύχας ἱμεροέντων κτλ. (with Richardson 1974: 204). It might be thought that gods would not need to execute this quintessentially female gesture to ensure ease of movement and speed (cf. Theocr. 14.35), but the flowing chitons of the Nereids are very prominent in art – cf. the 'Nereid monument' from Xanthos, Barringer 1995: pl. 63–6 – and the poet is already preparing for the simile of 948–52. ἐπί 'on' indicates that the dresses were lifted 'up to', but not further than, the knees.

941 κύματος ἀγῆς 'the shoreline, where the wave breaks', cf. 1.554, Numenius, *SH* 584.5.

942 ῥώοντ' 'moved nimbly', almost 'danced'; Homer uses the verb of nymphs (*Il.* 24.616) and Hesiod of the Muses (*Theog.* 8). Elsewhere Ap. uses the compound ἐπιρρώομαι. **διασταδὸν ἀλλήλῃσι** 'standing at intervals from each other'.

943 τὴν δὲ παρηορίην κόπτεν ῥόος 'The current jolted it (i.e. the ship) from side to side', a difficult and very mannered phrase which draws on the familiar analogy between horses, chariots and ships. The adjective παρηόριος is connected with παρήορος, the 'trace-horse' on a chariot, but was also used to mean 'crazy, unhinged' (cf. *Il.* 23.603, Theocr. 15.8); so here the word suggests the erratic movements of a wave-tossed ship. κόπτειν in this sense is otherwise only used of the effect of the irregular movement of horses on their riders, 'jolt', LSJ s.v. 1 11.

944 ἐπικαχλάζεσκεν provides an expressive spondaic close to the description of the wild water.

945–7 pose an important and difficult problem. The vertical movement of the Planktai, which contrasts with the horizontal movement of the Symplegades in Book 2, would explain their 'wandering' name, in accordance with a view ascribed in Σ *Od.* 12.61 to οἱ νεώτεροι, who 'interpret Planktai as "wandering", because they wander into the heights and the depths (πλάζεσθαι εἰς ὕψος καὶ βάθος)'; see Rengakos 1994: 130–1. The rise and fall of the Rocks would also explain the wild waves of the area, for which no other explanation is offered, particularly as the winds have dropped (cf. 767–8, 2.580–1, the huge waves which accompany the Symplegades). Such moving geographical entities have a surprisingly prominent role in Hellenistic poetry; see, e.g., Nishimura-Jensen 2000. On the other hand, a significant case can be made (Fränkel 1968: 543–8) that the movement of the Rocks in these verses is how the sailors see them, as mountainous waves rise and fall around them; the movement is in fact an illusion. The strongest argument for this is the fact that nothing is elsewhere said about the rocks' vertical movement, certainly not by Hera to Thetis (at least in the text of that speech as we have it), or indeed by Circe to Odysseus, and one might have thought that Hephaistos would not have established his forge in an island which constantly rose and fell, or that he would have chosen the top of such a rock from which to watch the spectacle (956–8). The problem of the name remains, however, and it may be that we will have to accept some apparent awkwardness in the narrative here. One possibility perhaps worth considering is that Ap. envisages the Planktai as rocks close to, but not identical with, the volcanic islands on which Hephaistos operates, despite the fact that in Bk 3 his forge is on a νῆσος Πλαγκτή (3.42) and that in the *Od.* 'gusts of destructive fire' seem to be a hallmark of the Rocks (12.68). The problem is particularly important because it touches our view of the whole conception (and state of completion) of Book 4; see Introduction, p. 2.

945 αἱ δ': sc. Πλαγκταί, the rocks of the previous verse; cf. further 948n.   **ἠέρι κῦρον** 'reached to the sky', cf. 2.363, Call. *h.Dem.* 37.

947 ἠρήρειν: if correct, this 3rd pers. plural pluperfect passive may belong to ἀραρίσκω, 'were fitted, attached to', or, perhaps more probably, to ἐρείδω, 'were pressed down', cf. 3.1398 and esp. 2.320–2 (the Symplegades) οὐ γάρ τε ῥίζηισιν ἐρήρεινται νεάτηισιν | ... ὕπερθε δὲ πολλὸν ἁλὸς κορθύεται ὕδωρ. The form, instead of ἠρήρειντο, will be on the analogy of forms such as ἠείδειν in 1700; in other parts of the Greek verb system, e.g. the strong aorist, first person singular and third person plural forms coincide. The reading, and the text of the opening of the verse, remain however rather uncertain; moreover, clarity about the movement of the Rocks (945–7n.) does not depend upon decision between ἀραρίσκω and ἐρείδω.

948–55 The Nereids transport the *Argo* through the dangerous waves like girls playing with a ball on the seashore. The principal archaic models are *Il.* 15.362–4 (a child knocking over a sandcastle), *Od.* 6.100–1 (Nausicaa and her friends playing ball), 8.372–80 (Phaeacian ball-playing and dancing). That the Nereids are compared to girls playing ball, when girls (Nausicaa and friends) playing ball are in fact a primary literary model, demonstrates again the intimate connection in Hellenistic and Roman poetry between similes and intertextual allusion; see Hunter 2006: ch. 3.

948 αἱ δ': the Nereids are now introduced exactly as the Rocks in 945; corruption in either place seems unlikely (Merkel suggested αἵ θ' in 945), but the parallelism is one further slight awkwardness in this episode.

949 δίχα: interpretation is uncertain. The adverb has traditionally been understood with the participle, though it is hard to see exactly what it would then mean; Vian understands 'in two groups' of the girls, i.e. they divide into two teams. This makes good sense, but the expression is then awkwardly compressed and the word order somewhat surprising.   **ἐπ' ἰξύας** 'to their waists', i.e. higher than the modest Nereids of 940 and more adventurous than Nausicaa and her group who merely discard their veils (*Od.* 6.100). Cf. further Hunter 1991a.

950 The text at the end is quite uncertain; E's τήν would refer to the ball, but like αἱ, looks like an attempt to mend the sense. The real problem is ἔπειτα, which has not been satisfactorily explained; none of the usages under LSJ s.v. II fits the present case.

951 ὑπ' . . . δέχεται: tmesis.

952 μεταχρονίην came, perhaps through a misunderstanding, to be used as a synonym of μετέωρος, cf. 1385, West on Hes. *Theog.* 269, *LfgrE* s.v. So too at the Symplegades the *Argo* was ὑψοῦ μεταχρονίη (2.587), as well as μετήορος after Athena had given it a helping shove (2.600).   **οὐ ποτε πίλναται οὔδει**: a striking reuse of the Homeric description of Ἄτη, who never touches the ground (*Il.* 19.92–3); like the young girls, Ate has ἁπαλοὶ πόδες.

953–4 Once again (cf. 937–8n.), tenor and vehicle are closely matched. **πέμπε**: a plural verb is more common with such expressions as ἄλλοθεν ἄλλη, cf. K–G I 286–7.   **διηερίην ἐπὶ κύμασιν** 'lifted into the air on top of the waves'; the Nereids skim the boat from one to another through the Rocks. διηερίην varies μεταχρονίην and picks up ἐς ἠέρα in the description of the girls playing.

955 σφιν seems to refer to the Nereids rather than to the Rocks, cf. *Il.* 18.66–7 of Thetis and the Nereids, περὶ δέ σφισι κῦμα θαλάσσης | ῥήγνυτο.   **ζέεν** 'seethed' (cf. Hdt. 7.188.2), lit. 'boiled', and the literal meaning resonates here, cf. 929n. The transmitted θέεν presumably arose under the influence of θέουσαν in 953.

956 ἄναξ is almost a title for Hephaistos (though not, of course, for him alone), cf., e.g., *Il.* 15.214, 18.137, *Od.* 8.270, Archilochus fr. 108.1 W.   **κορυφῆς ἐπὶ λισσάδος ἄκρης** 'on the topmost sheer peak'; for the feminine adjectival form λισσάς cf. 1717, 2.731. Later at least, λισσάς was also used as a noun, and 'on the peak at the top of the sheer rock' is possible here.

957 ὀρθός, 'upright', is not the posture we expect from Hephaistos, both because of his limping gait, and because he is normally working at his smithy. Here he rests his 'heavy shoulder' (the muscular shoulder of a blacksmith) on one of his tools, like Heracles resting on his club in the famous 'Farnese Heracles' statue; the implication may be that Hephaistos always carries one of his tools to support himself. At *Il.* 18.416 he takes a 'stout staff' when he goes to greet Thetis, and the scholia explain that he needs this for support (πρὸς τὸ ἐπερείδειν) because he is lame. Hephaistos is regularly depicted in art as carrying a long-handled axe or a hammer (*LIMC* s.v. Hephaistos 5, 44, 164b, 166, 172b etc.).

958–60 Hera and Athena are 'ideal' spectators, whose emotional engagement with the narrative is both a model for Ap.'s audience, and also wrily distanced from that audience.   **αἰγλήεντος ὕπερθεν | οὐρανοῦ** 'above the glittering heaven', i.e. on the top of Olympus.

961–2 'As much as the measure of a day is lengthened out in springtime, for just that time did they labour … ', i.e. the task took the time by which spring days are longer than winter ones. This interpretation is consistent both with the speed with which the Nereids work and with the fact that the current day, which began at 885, included the voyage past the Sirens and the Cattle of the Sun (cf. 979). This is, however, at best a vague measure of time, and the alternative interpretation, that the verses refer to the full length of a spring day, is not lightly to be discarded, despite the (? slight) inconsistency and the fact that we might have expected the Nereids to complete the task more quickly. There seems no reason why μηκύνεται, 'is stretched out', should not refer to the full length of the day, and the Homeric model, Odysseus' proposed agricultural contest in springtime 'when the days become long', certainly does envisage a full day's labour (*Od.* 18.366–70). Nevertheless, the scholia on *Od.* 18.367 show that scholars puzzled over why 'spring days' were said to be long, and one explanation at least was that the Homeric verb πέλονται means 'become' rather than 'be'; Ap. may therefore be making a point of Homeric interpretation in these verses (and the very rare τοσσάτιον, unique in *Arg.*, may point in the same direction). Also to be considered is Call. *h.* 3.170–82, which draws on the same Homeric passage: there Helios stops his chariot to watch the nymphs' dance 'and the days lengthen out' (μηκύνονται). That passage has in common with *Arg.* a god stopping his normal work to watch from on high nymphs (or Nereids) and the lengthened days; it is very likely that Call. and Ap. have an intertextual relationship here.

962 ὀχλίζουσαι, 'heaving', lit. 'levering up', offers a spondaic close expressive of the Nereids' effort. There is, throughout this passage, a witty tension between the Nereids' hard efforts (note also μογέεσκον) and the ease of divine working, particularly when the gods are like young girls playing ball.

964–5 In *Od.* the cattle of the sun graze on an island called Θρινακίη, which, like the very similar Τρινακρία (cf. 289–91n.), had been identified with Sicily, probably long before Ap., cf. 994, *RE* 6A. 601–7; Odysseus' boat reaches the island 'immediately' after leaving Scylla and Charybdis (*Od.* 12.261), cf. ὦκα in 964, 968–9n. There is, however, a mismatch between the apparently small Homeric island and Sicily, on which so many Odyssean adventures had been located; one scholarly way out was to identify the Homeric νῆσος as in fact one small Sicilian peninsula, that of Mylai (mod. Milazzo) on the NE coast (cf. *RE* 6A. 606). Once, however, Scylla, Charybdis and the Planktai are placed at the narrows of the Strait of Messina, this location for the cattle is impossible, and Ap. (or a predecessor) has solved the problem in a different way: Thrinakie is now the name of well-watered meadow (presumably somewhere on the east coast of Sicily), which is not only appropriate for cattle-grazing, but also suits the Homeric descriptions of Thrinakie (*Od.* 12.305–6, 317–18).

966–7 Cf. *Od.* 5.352–3 (Leucothoe, another helpful marine goddess) αὐτὴ δ' ἂψ ἐς πόντον ἐδύσετο κυμαίνοντα | αἰθυίηι εἰκυῖα.   **αἰθυίηισι:** 'shearwaters' is the conventional translation, but the word may not always be as specific as that (Harder 2012: 2.987).   **πόρσυνον:** Platt suggested the aorist πόρσυναν, but the pluperfect is the required sense, and no such form of πόρσυνω is known.

968–9 Cf. *Od.* 12.265–6, μυκηθμοῦ τ' ἤκουσα βοῶν αὐλιζομενάων | οἰῶν τε βληχήν. At *Od.* 12.262–6 the animals are βόες, μῆλα, βόες again, and then ὄιες; Aristophanes of Byzantium and Aristarchus were later to rule that μῆλα in Homer referred only to small animals (i.e. sheep and goats), whereas οἱ νεώτεροι used μῆλα for 'flocks' of any kind (Slater on Ar. Byz. frr. 118–19). That μῆλα and ὄιες were synonymous would have been a reasonable inference from that Homeric passage (and cf. also *Od.* 12.136), but it is unclear whether Ap. is here making a philological point.   **ἄμυδις:** probably 'suddenly, immediately', rather than 'simultaneously' of the noise of sheep and cattle.   **αὐτοσχεδόν** 'close by, near at hand'.

970 τὰ μέν: sc. μῆλα.   **δρία** 'wooded pastures', only here in *Arg.* and once in Homer (*Od.* 14.353), cf. 2.1003–4 οὐδὲ μὲν οἵ γε | ποίμνας ἐρσήεντι νομῶι ἔνι ποιμαίνουσιν.

971–4 Homer (*Od.* 12.132–3) had reported the name of the girls' mother (Neaira), but not their respective ages (Phaethousa was named first) or tasks. That the younger daughter looks after the sheep and goats and is equipped with a less valuable staff than is her older sister fits conventional notions of the relative value of cattle and sheep (Hunter on Theocr. 1.80).

972 χαῖον 'a shepherd's crook', cf. Call. *Hecale* fr. 65.2 Hollis (= 292.2 Pf.), Gow on Theocr. 4.49. **πηχύνουσα**: probably not just an ornate synonym of ἔχουσα, but suggestive of the way that shepherds twine their arm around a crook and lean upon it.

973 ἐπὶ βουσίν: not just 'over the cattle', but, particularly in juxtaposition to her name, 'in charge of the cattle', cf. *Od.* 20.209, 221, *Il.* 6.25, LSJ s.v. ἐπί III 6. **ὀρειχάλκοιο φαεινοῦ**: cf. [Hes.] *Aspis* 122. 'Orichalc', 'mountain-copper', was a mythical metal of fabulous value. Pl. *Critias* 114e3–5 reports that it belonged to the distant past and is 'now only a name'; cf. Bulloch on Call. *h.* 5.19, Olson 2012: 283–4.

974 καλαύροπα: a staff associated with the herding of cattle, which could be thrown when necessary, cf. 2.33 (Amycus, who is associated with cattle), *Il.* 23.845–6, Matthews 1996: 200–2. **αὐτοί**: i.e. the Argonauts, who saw but, unlike Odysseus' men, did not touch. The apparently superfluous emphasis perhaps serves to stress the Argonauts as observers and hence the very pictorial detail of the description we have just read.

975 ποταμοῖο: no river is mentioned on Thrinakie in Homer, but there is a supply of fresh water (*Od.* 12.306).

977–8 Homer had said nothing about the colour of the cattle, but gleaming white animals were naturally associated with, and sacrificed to, Helios, cf. *Il.* 3.103–4 (with Σ), Stengel 1910: 187–8. The cattle had been allegorized, as the days of the year, at least as early as Aristotle (cf. Σ *Od.* 12.128, 129 = fr. 398 Gigon, Buffière 1956: 243–5), and became the subject of a famous mathematical problem associated with Ap.'s younger contemporary, Archimedes of Syracuse. That the cattle have more than one colour is central to the problem, and lines 5–6 of *SH* 201, the extant elegiac poem devoted to the problem, τὸ μὲν λευκοῖο γάλακτος, | κυανέωι δ' ἕτερον χρώματι λαμπόμενον, may perhaps be indebted to *Arg.* There seem to be no echoes of these interpretative traditions in *Arg.*, although the emphatic statement that all the cattle were white might be taken as a denial of the possibility of the 'cattle problem' (Knight 1995: 216–20). Interestingly close to these verses, however, is [Theocr.] 25. 129–33, twelve snow-white cattle of Helios, the strongest of which is called Phaethon; it is very likely that the two poems are intertextually linked here (note line 133 γαυριόωντο ~ κυδιάασκον), as elsewhere, cf. 3.242–6n., 3.1306–25n. **χρυσέοισι κεράασι**: gold is the precious metal we have been waiting for since the mention of silver and 'orichalc'. κεράασι, in which the first α is long, has analogies in forms such as κεράατος at Arat. *Phain.* 174 and κεράατα at Nic.

Ther. 291; χρυσέοις κεράεσσι (with a short α) would require the final ι to be lengthened by position to create a fourth-foot spondee followed by word-break, a breach of 'Wernicke's Law' (cf. 3.515–20n.).

979 καὶ μέν: the only example of 'progressive' (Denniston 390) καὶ μέν in *Arg.*; τὰς μέν is certainly possible, but may be the result of corruption to a more familiar form.   **παράμειβον**: unlike Odysseus' men.

980–1 Cf. 885, 888nn. The Argonauts now sail the open sea between Sicily and Greece, and arrive (993) at Drepane, Homer's Scherie, which had long since been identified with Kerkyra, mod. Corfu (cf. Thucyd. 1.25.4).

982–1223 On the episode on Drepane see Hunter 1993: 68–71, 161–2, Knight 1995: 244–57, Mori 2008: 127–39. As with 'Apsyrtos' and 'Circe' (cf. 450–1n., 661–2n.), the 'Drepane episode' is bounded by allusions to the island's name.

982–3 follow a familiar Homeric pattern, cf. *Od.* 4.354–5 νῆσος ἔπειτά τις ἐστι πολυκλύστωι ἐνὶ πόντωι | Αἰγύπτου προπάροιθε, Φάρον δέ ἑ κικλήσκουσι, 4.944–7, 7.244, 19.172–3 Κρήτη τις γαῖ’ ἔστι μέσωι ἐνὶ οἴνοπι πόντωι, | καλὴ καὶ πίειρα, περίρρυτος.   **πορθμοῖο παροιτέρη Ἰονίοιο** 'in front of the Ionian strait', i.e. at the entrance to the crossing from Epirus to the heel of Italy, cf. Pind. *Nem.* 4.53 Ἰόνιον πόρον.   **ἀμφιλαφής** probably means simply 'large, expansive', cf. 1366 (a large horse), 2.733 (plane trees), Theocr. 24.66 (a παστάς), Hopkinson on Call. *h.* 6.26. The scholia, however, understand the word to refer to Corcyra's multiple harbours (cf. 1125–6n., Thucyd. 3.72.3) and cite Call. fr. 15 ἀμφίδυμος Φαίηξ, but that adjective appears to refer to harbours with more than one entrance, rather than to the existence of multiple harbours, cf. 1.940, *Od.* 7.847, Harder 2012: 2.177–8. Σ also note that some took ἀμφιλαφής to mean 'well-wooded'; cf. perhaps Call. *h.* 6.25–6 ἄλσος ... δένδρεσιν ἀμφιλαφές. **πίειρα** is true both of Homer's Scherie (cf. esp. *Od.* 7.112–32) and of Corcyra (Xen. *Hell.* 6.2.6 etc.).   **Κεραυνίηι ... ἁλί** will denote the sea between the Keraunian mountains (518–21n.) and the Italian coast.

984–92 The poet offers two *aitia* (cf. 603–18) for the name of the island Drepane, 'Sickle'; the island is never called Scherie in *Arg.* This name for Corcyra, which does indeed resemble a sickle in shape, is first attested in Hellanicus (*FGrHist* 4 F77), and Ap. is clearly drawing on a very rich mythical tradition; the story of Ouranos' castration was associated with the island from an early date, cf. 991–2n. There seems to have been another version, probably in Timaeus (*FGrHist* 566 F79, cf. Lyc. *Alex.* 761–2), in which it was in fact Kronos who was castrated by his son, Zeus. A number of other places in the Greek world were associated with the sickle with which Kronos castrated Ouranos, notably Zankle-Messina in

Sicily, cf. Call. fr. 43.70–1, and it is very likely that Ap. here has his eye on that passage (Harder 2012: 2.347–8, Hunter 2015). Elsewhere, Call. too seems to have used the name Drepane for Corcyra (fr. 14), though fr. 12.4 uses the name Κέρκυρα in association with the Argonauts (Harder 2012: 2.172–3).

In both Hesiod (*Theog.* 181 ἤμησε) and Callimachus (fr. 43.70 ἀπέθρισε) the action of the sickle had been suitably described as 'harvesting'. Ap. does not follow suit, but rather allows 'reaping' to re-enter the narrative through a second *aition*; this is a virtuoso mimetic technique which clearly aims to trump what has gone before. The scholia cite a story from Aristotle's 'Constitution of the Corcyreans' (fr. 157 Gigon = 512 Rose) linking Demeter to the island and explaining the name Scherie, and then another story, just possibly still from Aristotle but more likely from another unknown source (there is a lacuna in the text), which is very like Ap.'s: '[the island is called Drepane] because Demeter requested a sickle from Hephaistos and taught the Titans to harvest, and then she hid it on the coast of the island; when the sea washed against it, the shape of the land became like a sickle'. The double explanation in this last version is very typical of ancient aetiology, but unfortunately the identity of the citation, and therefore of Ap.'s probable source, is lost. For the Hellenistic interest in name-etymology and aetiology more generally see O'Hara 1996: 21–42.

984–5 The poet apologises to the Muses, who are delicate ladies, for staining his poem with such an impious story, one lacking in τὸ πρέπον of any kind, and claims that he is merely following 'earlier' tellers (Hunter 2008b: 118–19); that the story comes from the Muses' own poem, Hesiod's *Theogony*, is an important part of the wit. For such apologies and disclaimers of responsibility cf. 2.708–10 (Orpheus' song), Arat. *Phain.* 637–8 (Orion's attack on Artemis) Ἄρτεμις ἱλήκοι· προτέρων λόγος κτλ., Call. *h.* 5.56 (address to Athena) μῦθος δ' οὐκ ἐμός, ἀλλ' ἑτέρων (see Bulloch ad loc.). Hesiod stands at the head of the πρότεροι, but the reference will embrace many others also, including probably Timaeus and perhaps Callimachus. The stop-start rhythm of 984–6, all of which have a very strong break after the fourth foot, is perhaps expressive of the poet's hesitancy.   **οὐκ ἐθέλων**: the poet poses as the 'servant of truth', compelled to tell everything, rather than as a poet making narrative and aetiological choices at every turn; cf. n. on νηλειῶς below.

985–6 Cf. Hes. *Theog.* 180–1 φίλου δ' ἀπὸ μήδεα πατρός | ἐσσυμένως ἤμησε; this passage is also imitated at Antimachus fr. 51 Matthews.   **νηλειῶς**, instead of the Hesiodic ἐσσυμένως, is precisely one of those choices that show us the 'unwilling' poet in operation.

987 χθονίης refers to Demeter as an agricultural goddess, cf. Nicarchos, *AP* 6.31.2 (= *HE* 2752). Paus. 2.35.4–8 tells us that Χθονία was a name for Demeter at Hermione in the Argolid; at her annual festival, the Χθόνια, animals were slaughtered with a sickle, but this may simply be coincidence.

989 Call. *h.* 6.19–21 is suggestively similar to this verse; it would certainly not surprise to find Call. involved in both of Ap.'s *aitia*. Τιτῆνας: this version envisages the Titans as 'pre-historic' inhabitants of the island; this provides a link between the two *aitia*, as it takes us back to the time of Kronos. στάχυν ὄμπνιον 'rich crop'. The scholia imply that the phrase occurred in Philitas' glossographical work (fr. 44K), and it is obviously tempting to wonder whether his *Demeter* is echoed here. The adjective ὄμπνιος, 'rich, nourishing', is particularly associated with Demeter and agriculture, cf. Call. fr. 1.10, *Hec.* fr. 111 Hollis (with Hollis 1990: 295), Dettori 2000: 113–24, Spanoudakis 2002: 143–4, 369–70.

990 Μάκριδα: cf. 540n., 1131–40n; this form varies the accusative Μάκριν of 540. Ap. is again playing with uncertainty as to whether Makris is a name for the island or for a nymph or both. In the latter cases, we know nothing else about Demeter's relationship with her, unless it is a natural sympathy for Dionysus' nurse (cf. Call. *h.* 6.70–1).

990–1 Without the benefit of modern punctuation, it is (deliberately) unclear whether Δρεπάνη ... τροφός continues the second *aition* or takes us back to the first, as 991–2 would suggest, cf. Thalmann 2011: 178. This is part of Ap.'s knowing exploitation of the fact that aetiologies can always be multiplied and bleed into each other; the choice of one over the other is not necessarily driven by a search for 'historical truth'. τόθεν: 'for that reason' is more likely than 'since then', as for neither *aition* have we been told how and why the sickle was buried. ἐκλήϊσται varies the reduplicated perfect form at 618. Fränkel suggested emending to the pluperfect, as the island had undergone more than one further name-change by Ap.'s time. Ap. however, elides those names and uses Kerkyra of another island (567n.); for poets Drepane *is* a name for the island. Φαιήκων: Ap. preserves the Homeric name for the inhabitants of the island (cf. 537–51), although the traditional etymology for that name was from Phaiax, the son of Poseidon and Kerkyra, a story which Ap. has transferred to 'Black Kerkyra' (567n.). The repetition of the name in 991–2 both reminds us of the *aition* which Ap. has omitted and makes clear that the Phaeacians are not associated with 'Kerkyra' (or Scherie) but with 'Drepane'.

991–2 Cf. 548n. This tradition goes back at least to Acusilaos (*FGrHist* 2 F4) and is also reported for Alcaeus (441 V). In Hesiod, the drops of

Ouranos' blood bring forth Furies, Giants, and the nymphs called Meliai (*Theog.* 185–7), and it may be relevant that in other traditions the Phaeacians were linked to the Giants (*Od.* 7.79, 206); at *Od.* 5.35 the Phaeacians are 'close to the gods'. **αἵματος Οὐρανίοιο γένος** 'by race [acc. of respect] from the blood of Ouranos'.

993–4 As often, it is the *Argo* itself which is the focus of the narrative, rather than the Argonauts she is carrying, cf. 1327–8, Fränkel 1968: 550–1. **τούς ... ἵκετ'** 'reached ... them', acc. of motion without a preposition. **ἐνισχομένη** 'held back by, delayed by'; the *Argo* had been close to Drepane when Hera's action imposed a huge detour (575–6). **Θρινακίης ... ἐξ ἁλός**: cf. 289–91n. **ἀγανῆισιν** 'pleasing' (to the gods), cf., e.g., *Il.* 9.499.

995–7 The Argonauts receive a welcome which belies the inhospitable reputation that the Phaeacians carry in the *Odyssey* (6.273–85, 7.32–3). This is part of the stress in this episode on the bonds of 'Greekness' which bind the Argonauts and the inhabitants of the island (see Introduction, p. 4); the Argonauts are all but 'home' (cf. 999–1000), though this is to prove a false ending. **δειδέχατ'** 'greeted, welcomed', a 3rd pers. plural past form inherited from Homer (e.g. *Il.* 9.671), and probably connected with δειδίσκομαι (Beekes s.v., *LfgrE* s.v. δειδέχεται); cf. 1.1179–80 (a very similar context). **ἀσπασίως** reinforces the sense of an ending, cf. 1781n., *Od.* 23.296. **ἐπὶ δὲ σφισι**: the variant περί may be correct, though the repetition of ἐπί is not 'inelegant' as it might appear to modern readers. **καγχαλάασκε**: at 3.124, 286 this verb (Halliwell 2008: 57) suggests laughter at another's discomfort, but not here, cf. *Cat.* 31.13–14 (another poem of arrival) *o Lydiae lacus undae | ridete quidquid est domi cachinnorum.* **φαίης κεν**: cf. 238–40n. There is perhaps a memory of Arat. *Phain.* 196 φαίης κεν ἀνιάζειν ἐπὶ παιδί (a very different context), but Eumaeus' pleasure at Telemachus' safe return, 'as when a loving father greets his son who has returned from a distant land in the tenth year' (*Od.* 16.17–18), is not far away here.

998–1000 Cf. 2.441–2, *Od.* 10.419–20 (Odysseus' men greeting him on his return from Circe) ὡς ἐχάρημεν, | ὡς εἴ τ' εἰς Ἰθάκην ἀφικοίμεθα πατρίδα γαῖαν. **κεχάροντο**: reduplicated aor. middle of χαίρω, cf. 2.1157, *Il.* 16.600. **τῶι ἴκελοι οἷόν τε** 'like to that [situation] as if ... '; the neuter ἴκελον, co-ordinate with οἷον, would give a more expected construction (Ruijgh 1971: 949). **Αἱμονίηι** 'the land of Haimon', i.e. Thessaly, cf. 1034, 1075, 3.1090n., Harder 2012: 2.154–5. **μέλλον** is almost 'it was their destiny to ... '; Ap. inherited such narrative devices from Homer (de Jong 2004: 86–7), but they become another marker, like narrative 'need' (555n.), of how the narrator moves his story along (Hunter 1995:

26).   **βοῆι ἔπι** 'for combat'; βοή is the 'cry' which marks the start of hostilities, cf. Theocr. 16.97.

1001–3 reintroduce the other party of Colchian pursuers who passed out of the Black Sea (303–4) and, we are to understand, have sailed across the Aegean and around the Peloponnese. Echoes of 303–4 (μαστῆρες, ἐπέρησαν) mark the picking-up of this narrative thread, but there is also a striking verbatim repetition of 1.2–3 which announced the outward journey of the Argonauts; the Colchians, μαστῆρες ἀριστήων, are 'on their tracks', but in reverse. Whether we are to see irony in the echo of 1.2–3 (the Argonauts' great achievement has in fact worked against them, so Fränkel 1968: 553) seems uncertain.   **ὧδε μάλ᾽ ἀγχίμολον** 'so very close at hand'; Vian prefers to see here another case of an adverb of place used with temporal sense, 'so suddenly'.   **στρατὸς ἄσπετος**: the huge numbers of the Colchians (cf. 239–40) is an important element in continuing the theme of the Argonautic expedition as a foreshadowing of the conflict of Greece and Persia, cf. 202–5n., 1101–3n.

1004 **ἔξαιτον** appears only here in *Arg.*, and the meaning is uncertain. The normal Homeric sense is 'picked out, choice'; this is inappropriate, but if a link with ἐξαιτέω is felt, then the word may indicate that, as in the previous agreement of 340–9, Medea is singled out as the only object of Colchian demand, so 'special'.

1005 **ἀπροφάτως**: probably 'without further ado, without discussion/negotiation', cf. 2.62. Elsewhere (1.1201, 2.580, 3.1117) the adverb means 'suddenly, unexpectedly'.

1006 **χαλεπῆισιν … ἀτροπίηισιν** 'with persistent harshness', lit. 'with difficult unturningness', is better taken with ὁμόκλεον than with νωμήσειν; the Colchians would not give way on their demand. For the sense of inflexibility cf. Theognis 218 (the octopus) κρέσσων τοι σοφίη γίνεται ἀτροπίης.

1007 'there and then and at a later date in conjunction with an expeditionary force under Aietes' (Campbell 1976: 337n.15); for this latter threat cf. 741n. The Colchian threat will carry weight with Alcinous (1102–3).   **κελεύθωι**: for this sense cf. Aesch. *Pers.* 758 (the Persian invasion of Greece), *Ag.* 127.

1008–10 We later learn that an agreement has been reached to allow Alcinous to decide the matter (cf. 1176, 1205); memory of the earlier agreement to allow a βασιλεύς to decide Medea's fate (347) makes the compressed narrative here easier to follow. Here, as there (κούρη 350, 1010), the agreement is followed by an alarmed speech from Medea.   **σφεας** is scanned as a single syllable by synizesis.   **ὑπέρβια νείκεα λῦσαι**: in Homer this is a characteristic activity of Arete (*Od.* 7.74), and this scene will show us how Arete 'operates'. The phrase however also introduces the idea of Alcinous as a Hesiodic 'just king', cf. 1100n., *Theog.* 87.

1012 Some critics see significance in the fact that Medea now turns, not to Jason, but to his comrades; this does not, however, merely vary Medea's earlier speech of protestation, but also shows her increasing desperation – now she must clutch at any straw she can.

1013 Medea supplicates Arete as Odysseus was to do (*Od.* 7.142, see Plantinga 2000: 123–6). The omission of any initial verb of speaking to introduce her speech dramatizes her urgency.

1014 Cf. *Od.* 6.149 (Odysseus' first words to Nausicaa) γουνοῦμαί σε, ἄνασσα· θεός νύ τις ἦ βροτός ἐσσι; ἵλαθι 'show favour', a prayer normally addressed to a god (1600, 2.693 etc.) or greater being (1773), thus picking up the rhetoric of Odysseus' approach to Nausicaa.

1015 ὦι πατρί 'my father', cf. οὕς in 1036, *Od.* 9.28, 13.320, LSJ s.v. ὅς III.

1016–17 Medea presents her situation as the sort of thing that happens all too often to mortals – it is nothing exceptional.   φέρβεαι 'you are nourished', i.e. 'you exist/live', cf. 2.393.   κούφηισι ... ἀμπλακίηισιν, 'light mistakes', suggests both 'slight, venial' errors (cf. Pl. *Laws* 9.863c3 κούφων ἁμαρτημάτων) and also mistakes which come all too 'easily'; the literal sense of 'light' is felt after ὠκύτατος.

1018 Medea suffered from a failure of judgement, nothing worse, cf. 3.286–90n.   ἐκ ... ἔπεσον: tmesis.

1019 μαργοσύνης: Medea tailors her defence to her audience, cf. 367–8n., 375n. This denial reintroduces the theme of the cause of Medea's flight (2–5): μαργοσύνη is a harsh equivalent of ἄτης πῆμα δυσίμερον, just as 1022–3 evoke φύζα ἀεικελίη.

1019–20 Medea's oath embraces the sun above (a very common witness of oaths, cf. 229) and the very goddess of darkness, Hecate; she is granddaughter of one and priestess of the other. At *Il.* 19.258–62 Agamemnon swears by Zeus, Earth, Helios and the Erinyes that he has not had sexual relations with Briseis.   ἴστω: the asyndeton and hiatus before ἱερόν, both removed by ἴστω δ' of *m*, add a great solemnity to the oath.   νυκτιπόλου: cf. 148, 829.   Περσηίδος 'daughter of [the Titan] Perses', cf. 3.467, Hes. *Theog.* 409–11.

1021–2 μή with the indicative is standard in solemn oaths, Smyth §2705. Whether or not Medea left 'willingly' has been a contested issue ever since the opening of the book, cf. her very different rhetoric to Jason at 360,

Hunter 1987. It is tempting to believe that Medea here echoes the oath which Berenice's lock of hair swears to the young queen in Callimachus' poem for her (fr. 110); the verses survive only in Catullus' translation, *inuita, o regina, tuo de uertice cessi,* | *inuita* (Cat. 66. 39–40). The echo would suit the many suggestions that one of the patterns for Ap.'s Arete and Alcinous is a Ptolemy and his queen, and would also suit a relatively late date for book 4 (see Introduction, pp. 1–2). Virgil's famous imitation of Catullus (*Aen.* 6.458–60) would then show him 'epicizing' his witty predecessor in imitation of Ap.'s 'epicizing' of the Callimachean oath (Hunter 1987: 39, 1995: 24–5). Behind this rich later tradition may lie an archaic lyric such as Sappho fr. 94.5 V Ψάπφ᾽, ἦ μάν σ᾽ ἀέκοισ᾽ ἀπυλιμπάνω. σὺν ἀνδράσιν ἀλλοδαποῖσι: cf. 3.891–2.

1023–4 Cf. 1019n.   ἥλιτον: cf. 734; as there, Medea means the help she offered to her sister's sons and hence to Jason.   μῆτις 'plan', i.e. there was nothing else she could do in the circumstances other than leave with the Argonauts; the poet does not need to repeat the matter of Aietes' grim threats, cf. 379–81, 735–6. Medea's words echo those of Penelope telling the disguised Odysseus of her plight, now that the suitors have uncovered her trick with Laertes' shroud, νῦν δ᾽ οὔτ᾽ ἐκφυγέειν δύναμαι γάμον οὔτε τιν᾽ ἄλλην / μῆτιν ἔθ᾽ εὑρίσκω, *Od.* 19.157–8; Medea is presenting herself as a 'Penelope' who was certainly not seeking 'marriage'.

1024 μίτρη 'my virgin's girdle', which a husband would remove on the wedding-night, cf. 1.288, Call. fr. 75.45, LSJ s.v. I 2. Archaic and classical poetry prefers ζώνη in this sense.

1025 The twinned synonyms produce a very solemn pronouncement, cf. 2.502 παρθενίη καὶ λέκτρον ἀκήρατον.

1026–8 rework Odysseus' famous wish for Nausicaa at *Od.* 6.180–2. We know from Homer that Arete did come to enjoy the personal blessings of which Medea speaks, but the final wish, for 'the glory of an unsacked city', takes us to the problematic fate of the Phaeacians: at *Od.* 13.170–83 we leave them sacrificing anxiously to Poseidon, and at least one scholiast (on line 185) had no doubt as to their fate, 'they were wiped out'.   τελεσφόρον 'full', i.e. a life which, by reaching its proper *telos*, contains all that a life should contain; such a life will inevitably be 'long', but the adjective conveys more than just this.   ἀγλαΐην contains the ideas of both happiness and of public esteem, such as the Homeric Arete notably enjoyed, *Od.* 6.303–15, 7.53–7.   παῖδας: in Homer Arete and Alcinous have five sons (*Od.* 6.62–3, 7.70), and at least one daughter (Nausicaa); children are implied in Odysseus' wish for 'a husband and an *oikos*' for Nausicaa at *Od.* 6.181. One of Arete's future children will be a principal literary model for both Medea and the Apollonian Arete, but no wish for 'children' in Medea's mouth can fail to be coloured by our knowledge of the future (Hunter 1993: 70).

1029 δάκρυ χέουσα: Dr Benaissa informs me that δακρυόεσσα is read on an unpublished Oxyrhynchus papyrus, but the more emotional expression is perhaps appropriate here.

1030 ἐναμοιβαδίς, 'in turn', is also transmitted at 1.380 (and cf. ἀμοιβαδίς in 199); E's ἐπαμοιβαδίς may be correct, but the form in ἐν– is perfectly credible.

1031–52 Medea's speech to the Argonauts carries many echoes and revisions of her earlier reproaches to Jason (355–90). Although we are told that this is a speech delivered to individual Argonauts (1030, 1053–4), plural forms are used throughout, as in the opening address.

1031–2 pose a difficult textual problem, not least because the scholia may suggest a text somewhat different from what has been transmitted. The standard interpretation of the transmitted text is that ἀτύζομαι governs first the genitive ὑμέων (cf. 2.635) and then ἀμφί τ' ἀέθλοις, with οὕνεκεν added 'pleonastically' to the preposition, which is a well attested prose idiom (cf. K–G I 529, LSJ s.v. ἕνεκα I 4). The only other poetic example to be cited, however, is Soph. *Phil.* 554, where the construction is preserved by no recent editor. It is, then, more likely that οὕνεκεν is an intrusion, intended to explain the construction of ὑμέων (the scholia gloss ἕνεκα τῶν ὑμετέρων ἄθλων), which has ousted something such as ἥδ' ἐγώ (cf. 1036) or νῦν ἐγώ (Fränkel); the scholiastic paraphrase uses ἐγώ.   **ὦ πέρι δή μέγα φέρτατοι:** cf. 1383 (where see n.), in the voice of the narrator; if the text is sound (Fränkel reads ὑμείων πέρι δή, μέγα φέρτατοι), Medea's address carries more than a touch of bitter irony. πέρι δή is 'exceedingly', LSJ s.v. περί E II, Bulloch on Call. *h.* 5.58.

1033–4 ἐκ ... κείρατε: tmesis.   **ἧς εἵνεκεν:** a powerfully scornful variation on ἧς ἰότητι in 1032. For this claim cf. 364–5.   **Αἰμονήνδε:** cf. 998–1000n.

1035 rounds off a fine piece of rhetoric with a ringing *spondeiazon*: Medea is responsible for their *nostos*, cf. 366–7, 381.

1036 Cf. 361–2.   **οὕς:** cf. 1015n.

1038–41 The pattern of necessary enjambment with strong punctuation after the first word of the verse suggests the vehemence of Medea's emotion; see Wilamowitz 1924: II 203–4.

1038 ὕμμι: Campbell's ὕμμε is based on Soph. *OT* 720–1, ἐκεῖνον ἤνυσεν | φονέα γενέσθαι, but the dative also seems perfectly in order.

1039 γλυκεροῖσιν: one's eyes are 'sweetened' at the sight of parents (cf. *Od.* 9.34–5); this is not just a case of an epithet transferred from the noun to which it properly belongs to another ('hypallage'), and it also differs from the familiar observation that one's eyes are 'sweet' or 'precious' (Headlam on Herodas 6.23).

1040 ἀπό … εἵλετο: tmesis.

1041 ἀγλαΐας: a bitter echo of 357 (and cf. also 3.786). One of Medea's models, Penelope, had also complained of the loss of ἀγλαΐη, cf. *Od.* 18.180–1, 19.81–2. Verbally, however, these verses seem rather to recall Eumaeus' prayer for Odysseus' return at *Od.* 17.243–6 (note δαίμων, ἀγλαΐας, ἀλαλήμενος).   **σὺν ὀθνείοις ἀλάλημαι:** an almost mocking reprise of 363 λυγρῆισιν κατὰ πόντον ἄμ' ἀλκυόνεσσι φορεῦμαι; the Argonauts are no better company than seabirds. Cf. also 1021.

1042 Cf. 359, 385–6.

1043–4 εἰς χεῖρας … δηιωθῆναι 'if I fall into Aietes' hands to be killed with horrible suffering'; ἰούσης is the most attractive and simplest emendation, though some doubt about the true text must remain. The transmitted ἰοῦσαν offers no satisfactory sense or syntax; Fränkel punctuates strongly after θεῶν and reads ἰοῦσα, but the sequence of thought with the following negatives is then very awkward.   **δηιωθῆναι** rounds off a powerful verse with a strong spondaic close. For such 'final' infinitives cf., e.g., 1188, 3.1236, Smyth §2008.

1045–6 Cf. 368–71. Medea's use of asyndeton and anaphora pulls out all the rhetorical stops.   **προτιβάλλομαι** is apparently used with the sense of προβάλλομαι, 'hold out as/look to for protection', LSJ s.v. προβάλλω B III 1; there seems to be an imitation at Oppian, *Hal.* 4.626 μαψιδίην φυλακὴν προτιβάλλεται. The usage may have arisen from discussion of προτιβάλλεαι at *Il.* 5.879, which was sometimes understood as προβάλληι, though in a quite different sense from the present passage.

1047 brings together a number of 'fragments' from Medea's earlier speech, cf. 376, 387, 389.   **ἀτροπίης:** genitive of cause in an exclamation, cf. Eur. *Alc.* 741 σχετλία τόλμης, Smyth §1407.

1049 ἀμήχανον 'in my helplessness', with μ' in 1048. Platt punctuated here with a question-mark, and the proposal is worth consideration; such a question would make Medea's efforts to shame the Argonauts more pointed.

1049–51 If Medea's scorn has a specific target, it is best taken to refer to the bravado shown when the Argonauts first met the sons of Phrixos at 2.1219–25, words which of course Medea did not 'actually' hear.

1052 ἠνορέης picks up ὑπερήνορι with bitter sarcasm.   **ὅτε μοῦνοι ἀποτμηγέντες ἔασιν** 'now that they are cut off without reinforcements'. ἀποτμηγέντες is the aorist passive participle.

1054 ὅς 'that man' (LSJ s.v. ὅς A 1), picking up ὅν τινα.   **ἐρητύων ἀχέουσαν** 'seeking to restrain/calm her in her anguish'.

1056 φάσγανά τ' ἐκ κολεῶν 'and swords [which they had drawn] from their scabbards'.

1057 ἀντιάσειεν: the plural would stress the bond between Medea and the Argonauts, but the singular ('should Medea meet with . . . ') comes better with the promise of 'help'.

1058–67 Medea's tortured sleeplessness picks up the similar scene in book 3 (cf. 3.744–51n.) and is one of the markers of how the narrative has moved on, but not in the directions she might have hoped. Her situation contrasts not only with that of the royal couple (1068–1110), but also of the Argonauts who have just been so keen to offer their assistance: they presumably have no trouble sleeping (note ἄνδρεσσ· in 1059).

1058 στρευγομένης: i.e. Medea. The transmitted dative plural, to be taken with ἄνδρεσσι, makes no sense with ἀν' ὅμιλον, even if it could just mean 'worn out'.

1062–5 express Medea's sense of loneliness and abandonment by comparing her to a poor widow, forced to work through the night to support herself and her children. This simile forms a doublet with 3.291–5, where the beginning of Medea's love for Jason is compared to the fire kept alive by a poor woman so she can spin by its light, cf. 3.291–5n., Fantuzzi 1988: 142–5, Campbell 1994: 264–5. Both similes derive from *Il.* 12.433–5, where the even balance of battle is compared to the even scales held by a poor spinning woman 'so that she can gain a miserable payment for her children', and both illustrate the Hellenistic interest in depicting the straitened lives of the humble (Call. *Hecale*, Leonidas, *AP* 7.726 (= *HE* 2411–20, on a poor spinning-woman) etc.). Two other passages which may be evoked here are *Od.* 8.523–31 (the weeping Odysseus compared to a woman mourning over her husband who has been killed in war) and 20.25–30 (the sleepless and plotting Odysseus compared to a man turning a sausage over a fire).

1062 κλωστῆρα 'spindle', though Gow on Theocr. 24.70 understands 'yarn'.   **ταλαεργός,** 'hard working/long suffering', here evokes ταλασία, 'spinning', cf. 3.292 ταλασήϊα ἔργα; both expressions may derive by phonic echo from τάλαντα at *Il.* 12.433, thus marking their common ancestry. In early epic the adjective is used only of mules.

1063–4 The woman is forced to work through the night because she is a widow; τῆι δ' ἀμφὶ κινύρεται ὀρφανὰ τέκνα is thus a kind of parenthesis. More than one punctuation of these verses is however possible: Platt placed strong punctuation after τέκνα, but this would leave δ' almost impossibly late.

1065 μυρομένης: cf. Il. 24.794, Hes. WD 206 (a passage which may have been in Ap.'s mind, cf. 1067n.). Choice between this and μνωομένης, 'remembering, thinking over', is not easy.   **ἐπισμυγερή:** some older editors adopted (from m) ἐπὶ σμυγερὴ λάβεν, with the compound verb in tmesis, cf. 3.751.

1067 εἰλεῖτο 'revolved, twisted', imperfect passive of εἰλέω (LSJ s.v. εἴλω C), picks up and varies ἑλίσσει in 1062. MSS are very inconsistent with the aspirate on this verb.   **πεπαρμένον ἀμφ' ὀδύνηισι** 'pierced through with pains', cf. Il. 5.399 ὀδύνηισι πεπαρμένος, Hes. WD 205 (the nightingale) πεπαρμένη ἀμφ' ὀνύχεσσι (with West's note), Archil. fr. 193.2–3W χαλεπῆισι θεῶν ὀδύνηισιν ἕκητι | πεπαρμένος δι' ὀστέων. πεπαρμένος is the perfect passive participle of πείρω. At Empedocles fr. 112. 12 D–K χαλεπῆισι πεπαρμένοι < ἀμφ' ὀδύνηισιν> is an attractive supplement.

1068–1110 The peaceful and amusing scene of Alcinous and Arete in their marital bed (cf. Alcmena and Amphitryon in Theocr. 24) contrasts strikingly with Medea's anguish, which has just been compared to that of a widow. Homer had shown us the royal couple settling down together (Od. 7.346–7), but Ap. goes one better and imagines their 'pillow talk'; see Hunter 1993: 71–3, 161–2. This scene also shows us how Arete exercises that influence which Homer had described so memorably (Od. 6.310–15, 7.66–77) but which was never really seen in action. The closest analogue to this scene in extant literature is Hdt. 3.134, where Atossa pleads in bed with her husband Darius on behalf of the doctor Democedes; such scenes must have found a nuanced reception at the court in Alexandria where influential queens were very familiar (see further Priestley 2014: 174–5).

1068 ὡς τὸ πάροιθεν marks the normality of royal life, in contrast to Medea's terrible situation; the phrase may also remind us that we have seen this couple in bed before, in the Odyssey (previous n.).

1069 A humorously grand verse: this is how the royal family spends its evenings.

1071 ἐνὶ λεχέεσσι: the second syllable of ἐνί is lengthened in arsis before initial lambda, cf. 1085.   **οἷα** generalizes the situation – this is what all husbands and wives do – marking again the 'ordinariness' of this night for the royal couple.

1072 allows us to sense that Arete is not just using rational argument to persuade her husband: this is a couple who, at this rate, very soon will have children ... θαλεροῖσι is commonly used of a spouse or of marriage (LSJ s.v. 1), hence of a speech 'affectionate, loving'.   προσπτύσσετο 'entreated', but the sense 'embrace, hold tight' is not far away here, cf. 94.

1073 ναί 'Please!', cf. 3.467, Call. *Epigr.* 32.4 (= *HE* 1074) ναὶ φίλε. φίλος: nominative for vocative, as not infrequently in urgent requests, cf. Theocr. 1.61, Crinagoras, *AP* 9.559.5 (= *GP* 1959), West 1967: 139–44. πολυκηδέα: cf. 716–17n.

1074–5 The young queen deploys arguments from international strategy.   Μινύαισι 'descendants of Minyas', a standard description of the Argonauts; in *Arg.* Jason is Minyas' great-grandson, cf. 3.265–7n., 578n.   ἐγγύθι δ' Ἄργος: Fränkel's deletion of δ' (as an addition to prevent hiatus) is unnecessary. Arete uses Ἄργος for Greece generally; that Homer had used Ἄργος to refer to the Peloponnese as a whole was familiar lore, cf., e.g., Σ^A *Il.* 6.152d, Strabo 8.6.7, Kirk on *Il.* 2.108, just as the Greeks in Homer were Ἀργεῖοι. Arete is not here showing her geographical ignorance, but speaking like a character from the imagined Bronze Age; in responding to her, Alcinous' 'Greece' (1103) varies her 'Argos'.   Αἱμονιῆες: cf. 998–1000n.

1076–7 The dismissive anaphora of Αἰήτης helps us to imagine this speech in performance. Behind Arete's words lie Homer's admission and plea to the Muses at *Il.* 2.486 ἡμεῖς δὲ κλέος οἶον ἀκούομεν, οὐδέ τι ἴδμεν; there can be no certainty at all about Aietes, whose very name (it is suggested) is connected with ἀίω, whereas Medea is a very real presence (note ἥδε). Arete's scorn for things Colchian is the 'Greek version' of Chalciope's dismissal of Orchomenos at 3.265–6.

1078 αἰνοπαθής: in Homer only at *Od.* 18.201 of Penelope.   κατά ... ἔκλασεν: the sense is less 'broken' so much as 'won over', i.e. 'broke my resistance', cf. Call. *h.* 4.107.

1079 ἄναξ is both a vocative address to her husband and carries the sense 'do not, in the exercise of your royal power ... '.   ἐς πατρὸς ἄγεσθαι repeats Medea's plea to her at 1015, but in the words that Medea had used to the Argonauts (1004), cf. next note.

1080–1 We do not know how Arete learned about Medea's potions in book 3; we can imagine (if we wish) that much more of the backstory was bruited about on Drepane than the poet makes explicit, but throughout Arete's speech it is more important that there are suggestions that she has been reading the *Argonautica* itself. Her character does not just follow the familiar pattern of the youth of a character whose future is already written (e.g. the Cyclops in Theocritus 11, Barchiesi 1993), but she is also conscious of the poem in which she currently finds herself.   ἀάσθη: cf. Medea's explanation at 1016. Medea had argued that 'all mortals' do this; an echo of 817 (Hera to Thetis) reminds us that the same is true of gods.   βοῶν θελκτήρια: a witty echo of *Od.* 1.337, βροτῶν θελκτήρια of songs.

1081–2 again present Medea's error as almost proverbially ordinary, just as Medea had presented it to Arete; for the idea of trying to heal one ill by another cf., e.g., Hdt. 3.53.4, Soph. *Ajax* 362–3 (with Finglass' n.).   σχεδόθεν 'right after that', cf. 662, 1110 ἐπισχεδόν. ἀμπλακίῃσιν: cf. 1017.   ἀκειομένη 'trying to cure'.

1083 Arete may claim that they know nothing certain about Aietes, but she knows very well how the poem has presented him, cf., e.g. 9, 231–5, 3.336–8.

1084–5 Arete also knows the earlier part of book 4 well.   ὡς ἀίω suggests the listening and gossiping networks that men imagine women to use constantly, but also marks Arete's reference to a specific moment in the poem: 194–5 where Jason promised to make Medea precisely his ἄκοιτιν / κουριδίην.   ἐξ ἔθεν 'since that time', i.e. the time of Medea's escape.   ἐνὶ μεγάροισιν: the second syllable of ἐνί is lengthened in arsis before initial μ-, cf. 1071.

1086 αὐτός appeals to Alcinous' strong sense of justice (cf. 1100), as, until the enjambed θείης, it is almost as if Arete is telling her husband not to break his own oath (αὐτὸς ἑκών); the transmitted αὐτόν, with Αἰσονίδην, adds little, except an otherwise obvious contrast with Medea herself.   ἑκὼν ἐπίορκον ὀμόσσαι prepares for the Hesiodic flavour of Alcinous' coming speech, cf. *Theog.* 232, *WD* 282; the Hesiodic echoes carry their own implicit warnings to the king about the fate of those who break their oaths.

1087–8 ἄσχετα: Arete's word conjures up Medea's fears as to the punishments which Aietes will inflict (379–81), but we also think of 742, where Circe uses this same word of Medea's actions.   δηλήσαιτο gives an emphatic, spondaic close to the verse. The verb is constructed with two accusatives (ἄσχετα, παῖδα), as, e.g., in the common κακὰ πράττειν τινα etc.

1089 Fathers over-react when their daughters become involved (in any sense) with men.   δύσζηλοι 'harmfully jealous'. The Homeric model is *Od.* 7.307 (Odysseus to Alcinous, precisely in the context of Alcinous and his daughter) δύσζηλοι γάρ τ' εἰμὲν ἐπὶ χθονὶ φῦλ' ἀνθρώπων.

1090–5 Like all good orators (and poets), Arete can also produce (from her reading?) appropriate mythological exempla to suit her case, or rather exempla that can be presented in the most helpful light. There is an amusingly ironic implication in the first two examples that Jason is somehow like Zeus.

1090 The story of Antiope of Thebes had many variants, but what is most important here is that she was impregnated by Zeus (in the form of a satyr) and then escaped her father Nykteus' wrath by fleeing to Sicyon; Nykteus died before he could inflict the desired punishment upon her (the careful Arete says only μήσατο), but the sons she bore to Zeus, Amphion and Zethos, later took vengeance upon Nykteus' brother Lykos and his wife Dirce for their maltreatment of her, cf. Apollod. *Bibl.* 3.5.5, Vian 1963: 194–201, Kannicht's introduction to the fragments of Eur. *Antiope*. The prologue of Euripides' tragedy was presumably an important source for later mythographers (including the scholiast on the present passage). That harsh physical maltreatment was part of Antiope's story is suggested by ἠικίζετο in Apollod. loc. cit., and cf. κακοῦν at Paus. 2.6.2. At 1.735 Ap. had used an alternative version (cf. *Od.* 11.260) which made Antiope the daughter of the river Asopos, but here the 'darkness' of Nykteus' name suits Arete's rhetoric.

1091 Akrisios of Argos locked his daughter Danae in a bronze tower because he had received an oracle that he would be killed by a grandson. After she had borne a son (Perseus) to Zeus, who had visited her in a shower of gold, Akrisios set mother and child afloat on the sea in a box; Σ cite a full account from Pherecydes, *FGrHist* 3 F10.

1092–5 If Antiope and Danae are figures of past 'myth', known to Arete perhaps from a standard educational diet of tragedy, Echetos, an obscure figure who makes one appearance in Homer, is a 'contemporary' who shows the queen's command of the wilder fringes of 'history'; Arete's point is 'Why recite old myths? Just look at contemporary events under your nose ... '. At *Od.* 18.83–7 Antinoos threatens Iros that, if Odysseus beats him in their boxing-match, he will send him to the mainland (or 'to Epiros', which is certainly 'not far' from Drepane) where King Echetos, 'who destroys all men', will mutilate him horribly; a certain rhetorical force is added to Arete's exemplum by our memory of Aietes' threat at 3.378–9 that he might cut out the tongues of the sons of Phrixos and chop off their hands. Σ here say that the story of Echetos is to be found in a work of Lysippos of Epiros (date unknown) entitled 'Catalogue of Wrongdoers', and the scholia on the Homeric passage offer the following version: 'Echetos ... blinded his daughter, called Metope or Amphissa, after she had been seduced by Aimodikos, and compelled her to grind grains of iron, telling her that she would get her eyes back when she had finished the grinding; he invited Aimodikos to a feast, mutilated him, and cut off his genitals [as in Homer]'. The method of blinding which Arete here claims – pins in the eyes – recalls tragic stories such as the self-blinding of Oedipus and Hecuba's blinding of Polydorus in Eur. *Hecuba.* χάλκεα ... χαλκόν: this emphasis might reflect knowledge that the use of bronze preceded that of iron (contrast the story told by the scholia above, West on Hes. *WD* 150); Hesiod's Bronze Age was characterized by 'warfare and ὕβριες' (*WD* 145–6), which suits ὑβριστὴς Ἔχετος. On the other hand, Σ 1.430 reports that in a grammatical work 'Apollonius' (identity unclear) claimed that 'the ancients called iron bronze'; there seems, in any case, some particular point to Arete's repetition. κάρφεται 'is withered away', both literal (she starves and endures the hardest of labour) and metaphorical (cf. Hes. *WD* 7).

1095 'grinding bronze in a dark barn'; it is dark because her eyes have been put out.

1096 φρένες ἰαίνοντο: cf. 3.1019. Here the expression denotes 'pleasure' at what his wife said (cf. 2.639), and also reminds us of the erotic framing of the speech. It is clear that Alcinous has already reached a decision with which his wife will not disagree.

1098 καί κεν σὺν τεύχεσιν ἐξελάσαιμι 'also with arms I could drive [the Colchians] away'; the καί marks that this would be an alternative to the agreement which has been reached.

1099 Alcinous picks up Arete's words at 1074.

1100 Alcinous plays the role of the Hesiodic king who delivers straight justice and puts an end to νείκεα, cf. *Theog.* 86–7. This 'Hesiodic' presentation probably takes off from a recognition of the similarities between the description of Arete at *Od.* 7.66–74 and that of 'the good king' at Hes. *Theog.* 81–93. A light humour plays over the entire 'Hesiodic' presentation of Alcinous in these scenes; the humour is slightly broader for the king of the Mossynoikoi at 2.1026–7.

1101–3 Like his wife, Alcinous deploys arguments from international strategy. The verses emphasize Aietes' likeness to the Great King of Persia, who certainly did bring war against Greece; Alcinous, again like his wife, identifies himself with 'Greece', cf. 1074–5n. λώιον '[is it] better', i.e. advantageous, cf. 3.527. ἄγοιτο: the standard verb in such expressions is ἀείρειν, but ἄγοιτο emphasizes the notion of 'bringing' warfare from far away, and cf. Pind. *Pyth.* 9.31.

1104–5 Like a good politician, Alcinous is concerned both with the substance of his decisions, and how they will be received. The Hesiodic flavour continues, cf. *WD* 279–80.

1106–8 There were of course, throughout historical times, real 'legal' issues when a girl ran off with a man without her father's permission, particularly of course if the girl was no longer a virgin; 'bridal theft' is a familiar institution in societies which otherwise impose the strictest segregation and one which is often accepted by both sides, as (under certain circumstances) it allows honour to be preserved all round (Campbell 1964: 129–31, Green 1997: 335–6, Mori 2006: 114–15).

1106–7 'If she is a virgin, I propose | my decision is to return her to her father.' The difficulty lies less in the present tense of ἰθύνω (Fränkel proposed an otherwise unattested future ἰθυνέω), than in the sense of ἰθύνω with an infinitive; the normal meaning of the verb is 'direct, govern, steer', and it is not usually used of individual judgements or decisions. It has perhaps here drawn close to ἰθύω with the infinitive, 'desire, long to' do something, perhaps under the influence of ἰθεῖαν in 1100, or we might indeed read ἰθύω, in which case the present tense is the natural one. There is a close paraphrase of Aietes' decision and the subsequent events at Hyg. *Fab.* 23.2–3.   ἀπὸ . . . κομίσσαι: tmesis.

1108 γενέθλην 'a child', cf. LSJ s.v. I 2.

1109 The identity of the 'enemies of Medea's children' is to become a central issue of her whole story.

1110 We sense that Alcinous knows exactly what will happen when his eyes are closed.   εὔνασεν ὕπνος: contrast Medea's sleeplessness, expressed in the same words, at 1060.

1111 πυκινόν is a conventional epithet in such circumstances, but here it makes us wonder again how knowing was Alcinous' 'wise' response.

1113 δέσποιναν ἑὴν μέτα ποιπνύουσαι 'bustling after their mistress'; ποιπνύειν is used of Hephaistos' mechanical ἀμφίπολοι at *Il.* 18.421. The meaning of the verb was debated in antiquity, with the two standard glosses being διακονεῖν 'to serve' and ἐνεργεῖν 'to be busy, work' (*LfgrE* s.v., Dyck 1987: 154–5, Rengakos 1994: 131), but here there is a strong sense of movement.

1114–20 In another variation on the messenger-scene (cf. 417n., Hunter 1993: 145), Medea's instructions to her herald are first given in indirect speech, and then an explanatory parenthesis switches to direct narrative which we can, if we wish, understand as part of what Medea said to the herald. The forced syntax emphasizes the atmosphere of secrecy and concealment.

1114–16 'Summoning her herald in silence, she addressed him, with the purpose of encouraging in her wisdom the son of Aison to have intercourse with the girl … '; the apparent awkwardness of the construction is a further sign of Ap.'s experimental approach to the narratology of the messenger-scene.	ᾗσιν ἐπιφροσύνῃσιν: in the description of Arete at *Od.* 7.74, Eustathius (*Hom.* 1568.29) preserves ᾗσιν ἐυφροσύνῃσιν as a variant for the beginning of the verse, from which Voss conjectured ᾗσιν ἐπιφροσύνῃσιν; there is, therefore, a slight chance that Ap. here evokes a disputed Homeric passage. The echo would be appropriate as the Homeric context is Arete's ability to 'put an end to quarrels', which is precisely what she is planning here.	ἐποτρυνέουσα: the future, which has been simplified to the present participle in a few late MSS, expresses Arete's purpose.	μιγῆναι to refer to sex is perfectly at home in epic (LSJ s.v. B 4), but it here contrasts with the 'euphemism' of 1107 (cf. 1119) to emphasize that Jason should 'get on with it' as soon as possible; the contrast is strengthened by the syntactic change from 1114–15 to 1117–20. Similarly at 1164 the straightforward μιγῆναι contrasts with γάμον … τελέσσαι in 1161, to emphasize that what matters is not the married state, but Medea's virginity. Σ 1153–4 reports the locations where Timaeus (cf. 1128–1200n.) and Dionysius Scytobrachion placed the wedding (τοὺς γάμους ἀχθῆναι), whereas in Antimachus (fr. 75 Matthews = 64W) the couple had sex (μιγῆναι) 'beside the river in the land of the Colchians'; the wording is not to be pressed, but there may be a distinction drawn also in the scholium between the physical act and a formal celebration.

1117 τὸ γὰρ αὐτὸς ἰὼν Κόλχοισι δικάσσει 'for he himself [she said] will go to deliver judgement to the Colchians that … ': there is no need to waste time beseeching Alcinous, for he himself will come out of the palace to do what is necessary.

1118–20 repeat 1106–8, but with verbal variation to mark the difference from Homeric technique; in 1120 κουριδίης … φιλότητος, an apparently innovative phrase (cf. κουριδίοιο φίλοιο of a husband at *Od.* 15.22), may reflect a 'female' spin on Alcinous' more legalistic decision (1108). That Arete apparently did not repeat Alcinous' reference to potential children (1108–9) is, however, a way of drawing our attention to the importance of that theme (cf. 1109n.), rather than a matter of female delicacy.

1122 ἐναίσιμον: probably 'which boded well', cf. 1.438 (a favourable omen), 717 ἐναίσιμος … μῦθος (also of the speech of a messenger); the sense here will overlap with ἑαδότα 'pleasing' in 1127, just as θυμηδές at 1.714 corresponds to ἐναίσιμος.

1123 θεουδέος, 'god-respecting', refers back to 1100. At *Od.* 7.231 Alcinous is θεοειδής, 'god-like', and the shift is lightly ironic.

1125–6 Ὑλλικῶι ἐν λιμένι: for the eponymous hero Hyllos, son of Heracles, cf. 534–43. This harbour, presumably identical with that called Ὑλλαϊκός at Thucyd. 3.72.3, may well be the present-day harbour of Corfu town, cf. Gomme 1956: 370–3. The specificity of the name contributes to literary *enargeia*: even if we have never been to Corcyra, the name encourages us to imagine the topography. σχεδὸν ἄστεος: Ps.-Scylax 29 notes that Corcyra has 'three harbours near the city', and σχεδὸν ἄστεος may reflect something Ap. found in such a geographical source. Σ Dion. Perieg. 492 names two harbours, 'of Hyllos' and 'of Alcinous'.   πᾶσαν ... ἀγγελίην draws attention to the fact that, unlike Homeric practice, we have not heard 'the whole message'.

1128–1200 Before Ap., both Timaeus (*FGrHist* 566 F87, but location unspecified) and Philitas (fr. 9K = 22 Spanoudakis, 'in the house of Alcinous') had placed the wedding on Corcyra (Spanoudakis 2002: 309); it is unclear whether Callimachus alluded specifically to the wedding on Corcyra in the course of his Argonautic *aition*, although frr. 9 and 21 make it not unlikely. Virgil was to take the Apollonian narrative of a double celebration, first a 'secret' one in a cave during which the 'marriage' was consummated and then a more public situation, as the starting point for his narrative of the 'marriage' of Dido and Aeneas (Hunter 1993: 182, Nelis 2001: 148–52).

1128–9 Libations and sacrifices were standard accompaniments of weddings; see, e.g., Men. *Sam.* 674–5, Call. fr. 75.10–11, Oakley-Sinos 1993: 11–12.   αὐτίκα: the Argonauts waste no time (cf. also αὐτονυχί in 1130). The remarkable brevity of the description of the sacrifice (contrast, e.g., 1.406–36) both emphasizes the speed with which Arete's advice was carried out and also shows Ap.'s avoidance of the formularity of Homeric scenes of sacrifice (for which see Arend 1933: 64–8, Kirk 1981: 62–70).   κρητῆρα κερασσάμενοι 'mixing a mixing-bowl', i.e., by a very common idiom, mixing wine and water in a mixing-bowl, cf., e.g., *Od.* 3.393, 7.179.   εὐαγέως: cf. 2.699 in a similar scene of sacrifice. ἐπιβώμια μῆλ' ἐρύσαντες 'dragging sheep to the altar'. ἐρύειν is also used in this context at 1.407; whether the use of this verb gestures towards the idea of the 'consenting victim' of sacrifice (these animals have to be dragged) is uncertain, but we are to envisage the procession of animals to the altar which was a standard feature of Greek sacrifice (cf., e.g., Burkert 1985: 56).

1130 The preparation of the nuptial bed was an important ceremonial moment, cf. e.g., Call. fr. 75.16, Theocr. 17.133 (with Hunter 2003b: 194), Moschus, *Europa* 164; at *Od.* 23.289–91 the preparation of the bed adds to the sense that the reunion of Odysseus and Penelope is a second 'wedding'.

1131–40 The consummation of the union takes place in the cave of Makris, whose story, briefly alluded to before (cf. 540n.), is now filled out. Caves were standardly associated with supernatural beings, particularly nymphs (see in general Ustinova 2009), and this cave-wedding probably owes something to descriptions of the wedding of Peleus and Thetis in Cheiron's cave on Pelion.

1131 ἄντρωι ἐνὶ ζαθέωι: there is almost nothing to choose between this reading from a papyrus of the late first century BC, and ἄντρωι ἐν ἠγαθέωι of the manuscript tradition (cf. 3.981 χώρωι ἐν ἠγαθέωι at verse-beginning); Quint. Smyrn. 10.127 ἄντρον ὑπὸ ζάθεον perhaps looks to this passage (the context is Selene and Endymion, cf. 57–8). The variation (and cf. also 1132) cautions more generally against over-confidence in the transmitted text, see further Campbell 1971: 421.

1132–3 Part of the story of Aristaeus, son of Apollo and Cyrene (and thus of great interest in Alexandria), is told at 2.506–30 in connection with the *aition* of the etesian winds. His role as the 'first inventor' of bee-keeping and honey-making, which he learned from nymphs who brought him up, was told by Aristotle in the *Constitution of the Ceans*, cf. fr. 516 Gigon, Diod. Sic. 4.81.2; it is most familiar to us from Virgil, *Georgics* 4. The invention of many agricultural and rural skills was ascribed to him, including the making of olive-oil, cf., e.g., Nonnus, *Dion.* 5.229–79 (drawing on both of Ap.'s accounts of Aristaeus). Diod. Sic. 4.82 records extensive travels of Aristaeus, including to various islands, and these, we must assume, included Euboea. **περίφρονος** 'wise', because of his many contributions to human life; in the account in Book 2 he is also a healer and a prophet. In the bulk of the tradition περίφρονος has been ousted by μελίφρονος, 'whose care was honey' or 'sweet-minded', under the influence of what follows, see Vian II x. **πολυκμήτοιο ... πῖαρ ἐλαίης** 'the rich oil of the olive which requires much labour'.

1134–5 Cf. 540n. **πάμπρωτα**: cf. 1693 παμπρώτιστα. Makris had the honour of being the very first to receive the baby Dionysus in her arms. Dionysus appears at several important moments in the story of Jason and Medea, in particular to mark Ariadne as a model for Medea (3. 997–1004) and in the history of the cloak with which Apsyrtos is lured to his death (423–34). **Διὸς Νυσήιον υἷα** expands and evokes Διόνυσον, cf. 431n. **Ἀβαντίδος**: the Abantes were believed to be the ancient population of Euboea, cf. *Il.* 2.536. Ap. uses Ἀβαντίς as an epithet of Euboea, whereas Hesiod (fr. 296) reported that this was the previous name of the island; Call. *h.* 4.20 calls Euboea Μάκρις Ἀβαντιάς.

1137 ἐκ πυρός: i.e. the fire which consumed his mother Semele after she had asked to see Zeus in his full glory, a ploy which was put down to the hostility of Hera, cf. Eur. *Ba.* 8–9, Apollod. *Bibl.* 3.4.3, Ovid, *Met.* 3.259–315.

1138 χολωσαμένη: Hera's anger against Zeus's girlfriends and their offspring was notorious, cf. 816n.

1139–40 Makris had status on Corcyra as a beneficent 'heroine'; Corcyra was indeed a very rich and well-stocked island. It is possible that behind this story of Makris' move from Euboea lies a belief in early Euboean colonization of Corcyra and the nearby coasts (Thalmann 2011: 180).

1141 picks up 1130 to mark the story of Makris as a parenthesis.

1142–3 Cf. Pind. *Pyth.* 4.230–1 ἄφθιτον στρωμνὰν … κῶας αἰγλᾶεν χρυσέωι θυσάνωι. The idea of the fleece as a bed-covering is here literalized: the Pindaric scholiast notes (II 153 Drachmann) that 'in olden times men slept on (or under) fleeces', as indeed quite regularly happens, e.g., in the *Odyssey*, cf. 16.47, 19.101.   ἀοίδιμος occurs only here in *Arg.* and in Homer (excluding the *Hymns*) only at *Il.* 6.357–8, where Helen laments that Zeus has brought about all the troubles of Paris and herself 'so that in the future also we might be ἀοίδιμοι for men who come after'. The most 'glorious and sung-about' γάμος was probably that of Peleus and Thetis (cf. 1131–40n.), but here the fact that we are in a poem which precisely 'sings of' the γάμος of Jason and Medea confirms the success of the Argonauts' plan; so too, does the close rewriting, and hence evocation, of Pindar: both the Fleece and this wedding did indeed become 'sung about'. At such metapoetic moments, it is perhaps unwise to ask how 'deliberate' was the Argonauts' strategy, i.e. how much 'purpose' is there in ὄφρα, but epic heroes are always conscious of how the future will remember them.   ἄνθεα: flowers served several purposes at weddings, as garlands (cf. Men. *Sam.* 190, 731), to decorate the bridal chamber, and also perhaps to throw upon the happy couple, cf. Stesichorus, *PMG* 187 (= 88 Finglass).

1144 The appeal to sensuous colour heightens the 'lyric' atmosphere. Sappho fr. 122V, ἄνθε᾽ ἀμέργοισαν παῖδ᾽ ἄγαν ἀπάλαν, is not necessarily a 'model' here, but Sappho was *the* poet of wedding-songs.

1145–6 The gleam of the Fleece was central to the scene of its acquiring, cf. 167, 172–3, 178, 185; that scene is recalled as Jason and Medea finally consummate their union. The gleam perhaps replaces the torches which were normal at wedding-celebrations.   πυρός: the second syllable is lengthened before ὥς in imitation of archaic practice, cf. 1.1247.   χρυσέων θυσάνων 'golden fringes/tassels', cf. Pind. *Pyth.* 4.231 (1142–3n.).

1147 δαῖε: the subject is the Fleece.   γλυκερὸν πόθον: for the erotic power of the Fleece cf. 185–6. Hypsipyle's cloak, with its sensuous, erotic past, is described in very similar terms at 428–9, and already at 181 Jason cannot resist 'touching' the Fleece; here the erotic role of the Fleece lies, not in the past, but in the immediate future. The principal model is (again) Pind. *Pyth.* 4.184–5, τὸν δὲ παμπειθῆ γλυκὺν ἡμιθέοι- | σιν πόθον ἔνδαιεν Ἥρα | ναὸς Ἀργοῦς.

1148 αἰδώς continues the erotic atmosphere, as this is precisely what should restrain young girls when they feel πόθος, cf. 3.652–3; the extraordinary power of the gleaming Fleece makes us both want and not want to touch it.   ἱεμένην περ ὅμως 'despite desiring to do so', cf. 3.949, West on Hes. *WD* 20.

1149–51 Greek poets are fond of catalogues of different nymphs, cf. 1.1222–9, 3.881–3. The division into nymphs of the rivers, the mountains, and the groves or forests is a common one, cf. *Od.* 6.123–4, *Il.* 20.8–9, *HHAphr.* 97–9. Here the catalogue form suggests the very large number of nymphs present, as also does the verbal variation, καλέοντο ~ ἀμφενέμοντο ~ ἔσαν. The nymphs here take the place of the bride's female friends and former playmates, who have an important role at weddings, cf., e.g., Theocritus 18.

1149 Cf. 542–3n.

1150 There is no other evidence for 'the mountain of Melite', but Melite was a naiad daughter of the river Aigaios (542–3), and so the topographical traditions of the island are interlinked.

1151 Cf. 1.1066 νύμφαι ... ἀλσηίδες.

1152 Hera acts both as goddess of marriage and as Jason's chief protector.

1153–4 Whether or not 'Medea's Cave' was indeed on show for visitors to Corcyra we do not know, but there is nothing improbable about the idea.   ὅθι ... ἔμιξαν 'where [the nymphs] joined them together/caused them to have intercourse', cf. 1114–16n. The use of the transitive verb in this sense is very unusual, and reinforces the 'involuntary' nature of the union, cf. 1161–9.

1155 τεινάμεναι ἑανοὺς εὐώδεας 'by spreading out fragrant cloths', either to seal off the entrance to the cave, thus creating a θάλαμος, or by fashioning a kind of bridal canopy (παστός) over the bed, cf. Xen. Eph. 1.8.2.

1155–60 Following upon the aetiology of the name of the cave (cf. perhaps 'Helen's tree' in Theocr. 18), the description of a choir of armed men, garlanded (amusingly?) with branches, also has the feeling of a ritual aetiology, even if this is not spelled out: it is easy enough to imagine a Callimachus asking the Muses 'Why on Corcyra do men carry arms while singing the marriage-hymn?'.

1156 πρίν: i.e. before the marriage was completed, which would mean that Medea could stay with the Argonauts.   **ἐς ἀλκήν** 'for battle', cf. LSJ s.v. ἀλκή III.

1157 Cf. 1.678–9 αἴ κεν ἐπιβρίσηι Θρήιξ στρατὸς ἠέ τις ἄλλος | δυσμενέων. **ἀίδηλος** 'unexpected', cf. 1.298. Ap. here produces a typical variation on *Od.* 23.303 where ἀίδηλον ὅμιλον refers to the 'appalling/unspeakable group' of suitors. Cf. further 47n.

1158 κράατα is an epic plural connected with κράς, 'head', also found at 1.1010 and 2.1013.

1159–64 Debiasi 2003 notes that a number of features of these verses are shared with the fragments of hexameters on an Argonautic theme preserved on *POxy* 3698, which Debiasi suggests belong to Eumelos' *Korinthiaka* (see Introduction, p. 15).

1159 ἐμμελέως 'harmoniously', of the Argonauts' song, cf. 2.162 (another rustic celebration), ἐς ἓν μέλος at Theocr. 18.7.   **ὑπαί** 'to the accompaniment of', cf. 1194, LSJ s.v. ὑπό A 5. Brunck proposed ὑπό on the basis of instances of ὑπὸ λιγ- where the second syllable of the preposition is lengthened before initial λ.

1160 νυμφιδίαις … ἐπὶ προμολῆισιν 'at the entrance to the bridal chamber'; for the noun cf. 3.215, Call. *h.* 3.142.

1161–4 Jason and Medea had wanted a 'proper' wedding, with the bride received into the bridegroom's house, but events forced a different plan.   **μενέαινε**: unaugmented imperfect.   **μιγῆναι**: cf. 1114–16n.

1165–9 A first-person *gnōmē* on the human condition in the voice of the narrator owes more to the lyric tradition than to that of archaic epic; it is Homer's characters, rather than Homer himself, who dispense such wisdom. Even in *Arg.*, however, the technique is rare (cf. 2.541–3), and here it draws very striking attention to the shadow that hung over Jason and Medea even at what should have been a moment of great happiness and celebration. The thought itself, though here expressed in an innovative extended metaphor, is not an unusual one, cf. esp. *Il.* 24.527–30 (Zeus's jars), Call. *Hecale* fr. 115 Hollis (= 298 Pf.) 'god never allows wretched mortals to laugh without tears', Ov. *Met.* 7.453–4 etc.

1165 ἀλλὰ γάρ 'for, as a matter of fact ... ', cf. Denniston 100–6.   **δυηπαθέων** occurs first here; in earlier poetry ὀιζυρός and δειλός are standard epithets in generalizing statements describing the human condition.

1166 τερπωλῆς ἐπέβημεν ὅλωι ποδί 'enter upon [gnomic aorist] delight with whole foot', i.e. find completely unalloyed delight. Ap. has here literalized a Homeric metaphor, cf. *Od.* 22.424 (the wicked maids) ἀναιδείης ἐπέβησαν, LSJ s.v. ἐπιβαίνω A I 4. The *Suda* ο 190 glosses ὅλωι ποδί as ὅληι δυνάμει, but that is not quite how Ap. uses the phrase here. For similar expressions see LSJ s.v. πούς 6f, Headlam on Hds. 8.60.

1167 παρμέμβλωκεν 'travels alongside', a perfect of παραβλώσκω, continues the image of a path; the perfect, as regularly, conveys a habitual state, cf. *Il.* 4.11, 24.73.

1168 φιλότητι 'love-making', cf. the more explicit description of sexual 'warming' at Theocr. 2.140–1.

1169 'Fear gripped them, as to whether Alcinous' decision would be put into effect.'

1170–5 Life stirring at the coming of dawn is a familiar subject for poetic description, cf. Eur. *Phaethon* fr. 773.19–42K [= 63–86 Diggle], Call. *Hecale* fr. 74.24–8 H (with Hollis 1990: 254); 3.824 κίνυντο δ'ἀνὰ πτολίεθρον ἕκαστοι gestures towards the theme, but without elaboration, in part because of the extended description of the coming of night with which that scene begins (3.744–50).

1170 varies the familiar Homeric verse, ἦμος δ' ἠριγένεια φάνη ῥοδοδάκτυλος ἠώς, which occurs at *Od.* 8.1, as Alcinous gets out of bed (as here) to proceed to the public assembly. Ap.'s concern throughout for verbal variation is well seen by putting 1170–3 alongside 1.1280–2. For such descriptions in *Arg.* in general see Fantuzzi 1988: 121–32.

1171 ἐγέλασσαν: this common metaphorical usage may have begun with the sense 'shine', cf. *Il.* 19.362, *HHDem.* 13–14, West on Hes. *Theog.* 40, but Ap. will certainly have felt the resonance 'smiled, laughed', which is also in keeping with the fact that Alcinous' decision will favour the Greeks; nature responds to the human mood, in a kind of 'pathetic fallacy'.

1173 θρόος: noise is a standard element in descriptions of the start of a new day; contrast 3.749–50 (night comes on) οὐ θρόος ἦεν | ἠχήεις.

1174 κίνυντ': unaugmented imperfect of κίνυμαι, an epic form of κινέομαι.

1175 We cannot be sure where Ap. envisages the 'peninsula of Makris, in the distance', but it has often been identified with Palaiopoli, the peninsula on which the modern city stands. The point of mentioning the Colchians is that they have been asleep, while the Greeks have been very busy.   **χερνήσοιο**: this shorter form substitutes for χερσόνησος, which cannot be used in a hexameter, cf. 1.925.

1176 μετεβήσετο: the exact nuance of the prefix is uncertain, perhaps 'moved from one place to another' or 'got underway'; he is of course going to the place of public assembly, as at the opening of *Od.* 8. For the form of the verb cf. 458n.   **συνθεσίηισιν**: cf. 1008–10n.

1178 χρυσοῖο: gold here marks authority, though golden sceptres are found in various contexts, cf. *Il.* 1.15 (Chryses), *Od.* 11.91 (Teiresias). **δικασπόλον**: used at *Il.* 1.238 of those who hold the sceptre, rather than of the sceptre itself. Ap. has here combined that passage with the very similar Hes. *Theog.* 84–6: what we are about to see is a case of 'Hesiodic' dispute-settlement (cf. *Theog.* 87).   **λαοί** is found (presumably as a conjecture) only in the *editio princeps*, but it has much more point than the transmitted πολλοί, cf. Hes. *Theog.* 84 (λαοί at verse-end in a passage which was clearly in Ap.'s mind), *Od.* 7.71 (Arete). πολλοί may perhaps have arisen under the influence of the ending of δικασπόλον, and cf. 2.1027 (a very similar context) ἰθείας πολέεσσι δίκας λαοῖσι δικάζει.

1179 '[by which the people] received straight judgements'. Ap. seems to have run together two ideas to produce a variation on traditional expression: the people have *disputes* settled (διακρίνεσθαι νεῖκος, cf. Hes. *WD* 35), whereas kings pass down *decisions* (διακρίνειν θέμιστας, cf. 1169 διάκρισις, Hes. *WD* 221, West on Hes. *Theog.* 85–6), but here the two ideas are combined.

1180 τῶι δὲ καὶ ἑξείης 'following after him also'.

1181 Φαιήκων οἱ ἄριστοι is a Homeric phrase, but from a very different context, the peaceful dancing and games on Scherie, *Od.* 8.91, 108. **ὁμιλαδόν** suggests, as also does the verb which follows, the great numbers of the Colchians pursuing the Argonauts, cf. 238–40 etc.   **ἐστιχόωντο**: the Homeric scholia regularly gloss this verb as 'followed', and that is how it is used here, cf. *Il.* 15.277 ὁμιλαδὸν αἰὲν ἕποντο, 17.730.

1182–1200 Fränkel suggested transposing these verses to follow 1169, so that the whole description of the wedding forms one block; the cause of the textual dislocation would be Ἀλκινόοιο at the end of both 1169 and 1200. The separation of the two parts of the wedding, or indeed almost the two 'weddings', however, emphasizes how one was conducted hurriedly under cover of darkness and the other, corresponding to celebrations which did indeed regularly take place on the morning after the 'wedding-night', was an open ceremony shared with the women, who would of course only leave the city when day came, and the rural inhabitants; the men of the city went to listen to Alcinous' judgement. The two-part ceremony corresponds also to the revelation of Alcinous' decision – first in bed with only Arete as audience, and then publicly and formally. For other objections to Fränkel's proposal see Erbse 1963b: 246–51.

1182 γυναῖκες ἀολλέες occurs at *Od.* 22.420 of the wicked maids who are about to be killed horribly; reuse of the phrase in a completely different context well illustrates the challenges which Ap.'s *mimesis* of Homer (deliberately) poses.

1183–5 σὺν ... ἤντεον: tmesis. The form with –εον is an imperfect of ἀντᾶν inherited from the epic language, cf. 845, 931, *Il.* 7.423 etc.   εἰσαΐοντες 'when they heard' the news, rather than the sound of the women moving through countryside.   βάξιν: the report which Hera spread around was one of the starting points for Virgil's famous passage on *Fama* at *Aen.* 4.173–97.   ἐπιπροέηκεν: aorist of ἐπιπροίημι. It is typical of Ap.'s technique that we do not learn in any detail *how* Hera spread this rumour; Ap. is much less specific about how gods work than is Homer. Here we might contrast *Od.* 8.7–15 where Athena takes the appearance of Alcinous' herald and we are given the speech with which she roused the Phaeacian men to attend the assembly.

1185–6 ἔκκριτον ἄλλων | ἀρνειὸν μήλων 'a ram picked out from all the rest of the flocks'; a ram is both a very precious animal and also, because of its association with fertility, an appropriate gift for a wedding. Elsewhere Ap. uses ἀρνειός for 'sheep' more generally, cf. 3.1032–4n.   ἀεργηλήν: a young heifer is again both appropriate to a wedding, and avoids the killing of a working beast. In three places in *Il.* 6 (94, 275, 309) reference is made to the sacrifice of βοῦς ... ἤνις ἠκέστας; the first adjective is glossed in the D-scholia on 10.292 as 'yearling, young', cf. 174, and the second (on 6.94) as 'not whipped, untamed'. It is not improbable that ἀεργηλήν also looks to these Homeric glosses.

1187 ἐπισχεδόν 'near at hand'.

1188 κίρνασθαι 'for the mixing', an infinitive of purpose (Smyth §2008).   θυέων δ' ἀπό 'and from the sacrifices ... '; the preposition here follows the noun ('anastrophe'), cf. 1.437 in a very similar scene. Others understand ἀποτήλοθι, 'the smoke of the offerings billowed far away'; there is a similar problem at 1208.

1189 οἷα γυναῖκες 'as women do', a reference to the gifts that a new bride would be offered after her wedding-night (Oakley-Sinos 1993: 44).

1190–1 μείλιά τε χρυσοῖο 'gifts made of gold', presumably jewellery. At *Il.* 9.147 (cf. 289) Agamemnon offers one of his daughters in marriage to Achilles and adds ἐγὼ δ' ἐπὶ μείλια δώσω; that passage (where Aristarchus read ἐπιμείλια) will be the origin of this usage (Rengakos 1994: 112–13). Elsewhere Ap. uses μείλια of children's toys (3.135, 146) and propitiatory offerings (1549); the last meaning stresses the connection with μειλίσσω. Knight 1991 argues that these gifts look forward to the treacherous gifts which Medea will send to Jason's new bride in Eur. *Med.*   **ἀλλοίην ἐπὶ τοῖσιν | ἀγλαΐην** 'in addition to these other kinds of adornment'. **ἐντύνονται** 'wear, are dressed in', cf. 1.235 ὅσσα περ ἐντύνονται ... νῆες. Elsewhere (1.354, 3.293 etc.) the middle of this verb means 'make ready'; if it is passive, οἵην will be a kind of retained accusative, Smyth §1621, 1632.

1191–3 is the only example in *Arg.* of three successive *spondeiazontes*; for other examples in Greek poetry cf. Gow on Theocr. 13.42.

1192 θάμβευν: the only example of this Doric imperfect in *Arg.*

1193 εἴδεα καὶ μορφάς: the scholia seek to draw a clear distinction between the two nouns ('face and appearance'), but cf., e.g., 2.37 οὐ δέμας οὐδὲ φυήν, *HHAphr.* 84–5 (a similar context) θαύμαινέν τε | εἶδός τε μέγεθός τε καὶ εἵματα σιγαλόεντα. Such doublets belong to the formal stylization of epic poetry.

1194 ὑπαί: cf. 1159n.   **ἐυκρέκτου** 'tuneful', lit. 'well struck with the plectrum'.

1195 σιγαλόεντι, 'shining', continues the perspective of the admiring women; this common Homeric epithet for clothes or textiles is usually glossed as ποικίλον or λαμπρόν (*LfgrE* s.v.), but the latter is appropriate here, particularly as the sandal is moving and thus catching the light. At *HHAphr.* 84–6, a passage which may have been in Ap.'s mind (cf. 1193n.), εἵματα σιγαλόεντα seems to be explained by line 86, and the explanation again looks to dazzling brightness, πέπλον μὲν γὰρ ἕεστο φαεινότερον πυρὸς αὐγῆς.   **πέδον ... πεδίλωι:** the jingle evokes the repetitive and rapid beating of Orpheus' foot.   **κρούοντα:** choice between this and κροτέοντα (cf. Theocr. 18.7), which would produce a fast, wholly dactylic verse (cf. 907–9n.), is not easy. Nonnus may have read κρούοντα, cf. *Dion.* 40.240, Βασσαρὶς οἰστρήεντι πέδον κρούουσα πεδίλωι.

1196 ἄμμιγα πᾶσαι 'all together'. ἄμμιγα picks up the variety of nymphs who here come together (cf. 1149–51); it does not mean 'mingled in with the men'.   **ὅτε μνήσαιτο γάμοιο** 'whenever [Orpheus] mentioned marriage'; the nymphs sing in response at appropriate moments of Orpheus' song, as well (1197–8) as performing circular dances by themselves. The Argonauts too may be singing (cf. 1159–60), and certainly are with the transmitted μνήσαιντο, but the change of subject is then a harsh one (if not impossibly so), and Brunck's emendation seems to bring much gain at little cost (Hunter 1996: 144–5).

1197 ἱμερόενθ᾽ ὑμέναιον 'the lovely wedding-song'. ἱμερόεις is a standard epithet of song or dance (*Il.* 18.603, 18.570, *Od.* 1.421, 17.529 etc.), though it gains particular resonance in the context of a wedding-song; the epithet is used of marriage itself at *Il.* 5.429, *HHAphr.* 141 etc.

1198 The nymphs sing in honour of Hera, goddess of marriage, and also perform a circular dance, typical of young women, cf. Eur. *IA* 1055–7 (the wedding of Peleus and Thetis) εἱλισσόμεναι κύκλια | πεντήκοντα κόραι Νηρέως | γάμους ἐχόρευσαν. The verses convey a strong sense of the Hellenistic envisioning of the lyric past, as in the wedding-song of Theocr. 18.

1199 The poet's second-person address to the goddess in the midst of his narrative is hymnic and encomiastic in style. The sudden revelation of Hera's role in Arete's ploy is in keeping both with Ap.'s innovative narrative technique, which gives the gods far less prominence than in Homer, cf. 3.818n., Feeney 1991: 89, and with Hera's controlling role throughout these episodes; by the familiar idea of epic 'double motivation', Hera's role does not turn Arete into a puppet of the goddess, but rather shows us a character whose independent actions are also part of a divine plan. This is, however, Hera's last appearance in the poem, and after this the Argonauts must seek assistance elsewhere.   **σὺ γὰρ καί** 'for you in fact ... '. We do not have to assume that the nymphs knew of Hera's role or that they celebrated Hera both as goddess of marriage and as the helper of the Argonauts in this instance. Rather, the poet finds a particular appropriateness in the nymphs' song; the switch from the perspective of the nymphs to that of the narrator is marked by the sudden intrusion of second-person apostrophe.

1200 picks up 1111 to mark the success of Arete's (and Hera's) plan.   **φάσθαι:** i.e. to the Argonauts.

1201–3 'As for Alcinous, as he had at first publicly proclaimed the terms of his straight judgement – and the consummation of the marriage was now well known – so did he respect [the decision] to the end without wavering ... '. The correlative pair ὥς... ὥς..., 'just as/in the manner in which ... so ... ', is interrupted by a parenthesis, which is decisive for the future course of events: according to Alcinous' judgement, the wedding means that Medea will now stay with her husband. When we last saw Alcinous, he was on his way to give his judgement (1175–81); it is typical of Ap.'s technique that the public announcement is not actually narrated: why repeat a message which we have already had twice (1106–9,

1118–20)? This use of ὥς…ὥς… is not to be confused with the famous and much imitated temporal construction of *Il.* 14.294, for which cf. Bühler 1960: 119–20.   πείρατ᾽ 'terms, conditions', cf. 279–81n.   ἀλέγυνε: an unusual use without an object. The basic sense of the verb is 'prepare, make ready', but at 3.1105 συνημοσύνας ἀλεγύνειν is 'to respect agreements', and this is clearly the sense here; there may be some influence from ἀλεγίζειν, 'to pay heed to, care for'.

1204 ἐπήλυθον 'attacked, came over [Alcinous]', LSJ s.v. ἐπέρχομαι 2. 'Fear' is an entirely regular subject for such a verb, but μήνιες less so, and so many editors adopt Madvig's ὑπήλυθον, 'crept over', cf., e.g., 3.1077 ὑπήϊε … ἔρως; there seems, however, no reason why Ap. should not have slightly extended the usual range of ἐπέρχομαι, particularly if we understand '<thoughts of> Aietes' anger'.

1205 'and he had bound <them> by unbreakable oaths', i.e. to respect his decision; again (cf. 1201–3n.), these oaths have not actually been mentioned before, but they are almost a natural concomitant of the decision-making process. For the common periphrasis of ἔχειν with a participle see Smyth §§599b, 1963, K–G II 61–2; the periphrasis has particular point here, as the idea of 'unbreakable bonds' allows the literal sense of ἔχειν, 'hold, grip', to resonate.

1206 'Therefore, when the Colchians realized that they were making their request in vain … '. For the adverb (only here in *Arg.*) see Hopkinson on Call. *h.* 6.90.

1208 λιμένων: cf. 1125–6n. Fränkel 1968: 577–8 sees in this verse a threat by Alcinous to impose a commercial embargo on trade with all Colchians (cf. perhaps the terms of the 'Megarian Decree' forbidding access to 'harbours in the Athenian empire' (Thucyd. 1.67.4, 139.1)), but this can hardly be extracted from the text; Alcinous is basically telling the Colchians to accept the judgement or 'go away', and there is no thought that they will simply move on to ambush the Argonauts elsewhere.

1209–10 'then, they requested him [μιν] to receive them as allies, as they were afraid of their king's threats'. Like the other group of their compatriots (511–13), the Colchians judge exile preferable to returning to face Aietes. The fate of this group of Colchians was also briefly narrated by Callimachus in his Argonautic *aition*, cf. fr. 12, Harder 2012: 2.170–6; behind Ap. here lie perhaps both Timaeus and Callimachus.   μειλίξαντο: for the construction cf. 1.650 Ὑψιπύλην μειλίξατο δέχθαι ἰόντας.   συνήμονας occurs certainly only here, but for the noun συνημοσύνη cf. 1.300, 3.1105; a συνήμων is someone with whom you have a pact or agreement. Fränkel 1968: 579n.272 suggested

supplementing συνήμονες ('they became συνήμονες of the Phaeacians') at
Call. fr. 12.2.   αὖθι 'there'.

1211 δὴν μάλα 'for a very long time'.

1212 Βακχιάδαι: an aristocratic clan which governed Corinth between
roughly 750 and 660; they were finally driven out by Cypselus and, by
tradition, moved in exile to Corcyra, where they had previously founded a
colony under Chersicrates *c.* 734/3, cf. Hdt. 5.92.2–4, Hammond 1967:
414–19.   **Ἐφύρηθεν**: Ephyra was perhaps originally believed to have
been a town of the Argolid separate from Corinth (cf. Strabo 8.3.5, *Il.*
6.152 with Kirk and Graziosi-Haubold ad loc.), but from an early date the
name was used as an archaic and poetic name for Corinth, and taken to be
the name of an eponymous heroine (Eumelos fr. 1 Davies, cited by Σ
1212–14). Debiasi 2003 suggests that Ap. is here indebted to Eumelos.

1213–14 μετὰ χρόνον: cf. 1216n.   **περαίην | νήσου** 'the mainland oppo-
site the island', which would be the natural immediate destination for
anyone exiled from Corcyra, cf. 1.1112–13 περαίη | Θρηικίης. The trans-
mitted περαίην νῆσον could only mean 'the island opposite/on the other
side', and no appropriate sense can be given to this; there are a few tiny
islands to the NW of Corcyra which hardly fit the bill. The paraphrase of
the scholia, 'to the island nearby', shows just how difficult the transmitted
phrase is.

1214–15 μέλλον conveys the sense of a long historical process: change
does happen, if you take the long view; the verb thus prepares for
1216.   **Κεραύνια ... Ἀμάντων | οὔρεα**: cf. 518–21n. The Amantes were
an Illyrian tribe of the area around Oricum to the north of Corcyra (cf. Ps.-
Scylax 27.1, Plin. *HN* 3.145, Steph. Byz. s.v. Ἀμαντία, Barrington 49 B3),
and in his narrative of these events Call. refers to Ἀμαντίνην ... Ὠρικίην (fr.
12.5). The similarity of the name to Ἄβαντες, the early inhabitants of
Euboea (1134–5n.), clearly led to aetiological connections being created
between the two peoples (Steph. Byz. reports that Amantia was founded
by 'Abantes returning from Troy'), but Ἀβάντων would here have less point
than Ἀμάντων, despite traditions of Euboean migrations to Epiros (Lyc.
Alex. 1042–3, Paus. 5.22.4).   **Νεσταίους**: cf. 337n.   **Ὤρικον**: this port,
protected from the elements by the promontory of Acroceraunia, is also
identified as a Colchian foundation by Plin. *HN* 3.145.

1216 'But these things took place in the ceaseless march of time', cf. 276,
1764, *Il.* 12.34–5, *Od.* 8.510. Timaeus reported that the Bacchiadai colonized Corcyra '600 years after the Trojan War' (*FGrHist* 566 F80). Call.'s
brief account of these same events probably concluded with the verse καὶ
τὰ μὲν ὡς ἤμελλε μετὰ χρόνον ἐκτελέεσθαι (fr. 12.6), which Ap. uses at 1.1309

to conclude the narrative of the future fate of the Boreads. An intertextual relationship binding these three passages seems certain, particularly as 1.1309 is the only occurrence of the form ἤμελλε in *Arg.*; whatever reconstruction of the relationship is adopted (cf. Harder 2012: 2.175), it is clear at least that Ap. consciously alludes to the relationship, as μετὰ χρόνον appears immediately above in 1213, and nowhere else (apart from 1.1309) in *Arg.*

1217-19 Timaeus (*FGrHist* 566 F88) reported that Medea established altars on Corcyra to the Nymphs and the Nereids as a memorial to her marriage, 'near the sea, not far from the city'. Ap. has probably substituted the Moirai for the Nereids, because of their close association with weddings (as with all significant 'life-changing' moments), cf. Pollux 3.38 (sacrifices to Hera, Artemis, and the Moirai at weddings), *RE* 15.2486-7, Dunbar on Ar. *Birds* 1734-5. This is the only occurrence of the plural Moirai in *Arg.*, and there was correspondingly only one in Homer (*Il.* 24.49). Altars to the Nymphs celebrate their role at Medea's wedding.   κεῖσε 'there', with little sense of 'movement towards', cf. 1.955, 1224, LSJ s.v. ἐκεῖσε II.   Νομίοιο ... Ἀπόλλωνος: for this cult, appropriate here because of the rustic audience for the wedding (1183-8), cf., e.g., Call. *h.* 2.47-54, [Theocr.] 25.21; later texts identify the cult as native to Arcadia (Cic. *ND* 3.57, Clement, *Protrep.* 28.13 Marcovich). Νόμιος was also a title of Apollo's son Aristaeus (1132-3n.), cf. 2.506-7, Pind. *Pyth.* 9.59-65, Diod. Sic. 4.81.2, and this too is clearly appropriate: if the cave of Makris has become the 'cave of Medea', not all traces of Makris, daughter of Aristaeus, have disappeared.

1219-22 The Argonauts receive going-away gifts, just as did Odysseus (*Od.* 13.10-15, 217-18 etc.). As in the *Odyssey*, Alcinous and his wife give their gifts separately.   πολλά ... πολλά: the anaphora here stresses multiplicity, cf. 1011-12, Call. *h.* 5.125.   δυώδεκα ... | ... δμωάς: Medea can now travel 'decently' on the *Argo*, and the number matches those of Medea's attendants back in Colchis (3.838-40); Callimachus too seems to have referred to these Phaeacian maids (fr. 21.5-7). In the *Odyssey*, Arete dispatched maids to carry her gifts to the boat (13.66-9), but Odysseus could hardly be given maids to accompany him.

1224 ἀκραής 'brisk', cf. 891-2n.   ὑπεύδιος 'in a clear sky'.

1226-7 Successive *spondeiazontes* mark a major junction in the narrative, where Ap. joins two Argonautic itineraries which had previously been separate, cf. Introduction pp. 10-11. αἴσιμον 'permitted by fate'. The decision, so it has been suggested (560-1), was Zeus's, but it is the poet making the choices; there are similar effects at 555-6, 861.   Λιβύης here designates North Africa as a whole, not just the territory around

Cyrene.	ὀτλήσειαν: the intransitive use is very rare; contrast 381, 3.769.

1228–31 The Argonauts retrace Odysseus' steps as he was safely transported south from Scherie (Corcyra) to Ithaca, but their troubles are far from over. The comparable 'nearly at home' experience for Odysseus is not the journey from Scherie, but rather after leaving Aeolus' island, cf. *Od.* 10. 28–49, esp. 37 τῆι δεκάτηι δ' ἤδη ἀνεφαίνετο πατρὶς ἄρουρα.	†ποτί is impossible; παρά (Campbell 1973: 86) offers possible sense, 'already <they had travelled> past … ', and cf. *Od.* 15.298 (a passage perhaps in Ap.'s mind), but the corruption seems hard to explain; other suggestions (ποθι, ποτε) seem mere gap-fillers.	κόλπον ἐπώνυμον Ἀμβρακιήων: the 'Ambracian Gulf' is the great, almost enclosed bay, in NW Greece above Acarnania; its entrance was the site of the Battle of Actium. Ps.-Scylax 33.2 marks Ambracia as the place where 'Hellas' begins to be continuous all the way around to Magnesia (Shipley 2011: 114, Lightfoot 2014: 355); the Argonauts really are 'all but home', when disaster strikes again.	Κουρῆτιν … χθόνα: the final syllable of Κουρῆτιν is lengthened in arsis at the caesura. The Kouretes are here associated with Acarnania (cf. Strabo 7.7.2, 10.3.2), rather than Aetolia (*Il.* 9.529 etc.), where the scholarly tradition usually placed them in the area around Pleuron on the Corinthian Gulf.	στεινὰς … νήσους '[some] tiny islands, together with the Echinades themselves'. The Echinades (cf. *Il.* 2.625) are a group of small islands just off the mainland east of Ithaca; to the south at the mouth of the Corinthian Gulf lie the Oxeiai ('Pointed Islands'), which were identified with the νῆσοι θοαί (or Θοαί) of *Od.* 15.299 (Telemachus' return journey), cf. Strabo 8.3.26, 10.2.19, *RE* 18.2003–4, and from where the Peloponnese would certainly be visible. If indeed it is these which are Ap.'s 'tiny islands', then this would give point to αὐταῖς, as the Oxeiai are conceived as a kind of adjunct to the main Echinades. Some have looked here for a reference to islands such as Leukas and Ithaca, but it is hard to see how they could be described as στειναί, unless that is to be understood as 'close-set together', rather than 'narrow'.

1232–4 Cf. *Od.* 10.48 (after Odysseus' crew has opened the bag of winds) τοὺς δ' αἶψ' ἁρπάξασα φέρεν πόντονδε θύελλα, 4.515–16 (Agamemnon swept off course). Odysseus' travails began when he too was swept off course by the north wind and carried for nine days ὀλοοῖσ' ἀνέμοισι to the land of the Lotus-eaters (*Od.* 9.80–4). This people was traditionally placed on or off the North African coast (Hdt.4.176–8, Ps.-Scylax 110.1, *RE* 13.1507–8), and often in the area of the Syrtis, though more usually the 'Little Syrtis' to the west of where the Argonauts land (1235n.), cf. Polyb. 1.39.2, Strabo 17.3.17. Like the Lotus-eaters (*Od.* 9.97, 102), the Syrtis apparently ends any chance of νόστος (1235). In Herodotus' account (4.179), Jason was

swept away by the north wind to Libya when he was travelling, before
the expedition for the Golden Fleece, to Delphi; he was stranded in the
shoals of Lake Triton and saved by the intervention of the local deity
(Introduction, p. 8).   μεσσηγύς 'in mid-course'.   μέχρις occurs only
here in *Arg.*; Homer uses μέχρι(ς) twice as a preposition (*Il.* 13.143,
24.128), never as a conjunction (LSJ s.v. iii). Ap.'s use is a typical variation
on Homeric language.

1235 προπρὸ μάλ' ἔνδοθι Σύρτιν 'very far advanced into the Syrtis', i.e.
already deep in the shoals and far from the open sea. All but certainly, Ap.
here refers to the southernmost part of 'Great Syrtis', i.e. the Gulf of Sidra
west of Cyrene (see Map), cf. Delage 1930: 255–61; this is what Ps.-Scylax
(109.3) calls 'the most hollow part of the Syrtis, the innermost recess
(μυχός)', cf. 1243, Strabo 17.3.20. In the literate imagination, this was a
desolate landscape of marshland, treacherous tides and trackless sand,
where ships were wrecked and venomous serpents lurked everywhere,
cf. Diod. Sic. 20.41.42 (Ophellas' march 'through a waterless land infested
by beasts'), *RE* 4A.1826–8; Lucan 9.303–47 describes the Syrtis as a paradox, caught somewhere between land and sea, and belonging properly
to neither. If the area was in fact not quite as desolate as some ancient
accounts depict it (cf. Ps.-Scylax 109.3, Strabo 17.3.20), there is little
doubt that this was not an area where any traveller wished to land; see
further Green 1997: 340.

1236 βιώιατο 'they are forced', an epic 3rd plural optative medio-passive;
at *Il.* 11.467 this form takes an object, 'they were pressing [him] hard'.
Here, as elsewhere, Strabo's account of the Syrtis is quite close: 'In many
places [in the Syrtes], the waters have shallows (τεναγώδης ἐστὶν ὁ βυθός,
cf. 1237, 1264–5), and because of the ebbings and in-rushings of the tide
(κατὰ τὰς ἀμπώτεις καὶ τὰς πλημμυρίδας, cf. 1241–3, Dion. Perieg. 202–3), it
happens that men end up in the shallows and are stuck, and very few
boats get away safe. For this reason men sail along the coast at quite a
distance, taking care not to be caught unawares by winds and driven into
these gulfs' (17.3.20). It is not improbable that Strabo and Ap. have
sources in common.

1237–44 The present tenses and the parenthetic explanation of 1241–3
mark this as a description of the Syrtis not just as the Argonauts confronted
it, but also as Ap.'s readers would find it; the mixing of narrative tenses
in 1241–4 breaks down the barriers between us and the time of the
Argonauts.

1237–8 The anaphora of πάντηι emphasizes the unending sameness of
the bleak landscape, and the contrast of τέναγος ~ βυθοῖο (cf. Strabo cited
in 1236n.) marks the paradox and weirdness of the place.   **μνιόεντα**

βυθοῖο | τάρφεα lit. 'seaweedy clumps of the deep', i.e. 'clumps of seaweed from the depths', a very strange phrase to match the strangeness of the landscape. μνιόεις does not occur elsewhere.   κωφή ... ὕδατος ἄχνη 'noiseless foam of water', cf. 153; ὕδατος ἄχνην ends a hexameter at Call. *h.* 4.4.

1239 ἠερίη δ' ἄμαθος παρακέκλιται: the meaning is uncertain. The scholia understand ἠερίη as 'in vast quantity', perhaps rightly, cf. 1246–7, Diod. Sic. 1.33.3 (sand-dunes containing ἄμμου μέγεθος ἀέριον), but 'in the mist' would also make excellent sense in such a landscape. It may, however, be that 'in the air' heightens the sense of weird paradox, cf. Lucan 9. 341–2 (about the Syrtis) 'far from the cultivated fields, a rampart of dry sand, untouched by the water, rises on the back of the sea'; so the sense might be 'sand stretches away, raised into the air' (i.e. above the waterline).

1240 ἀείρεται is properly appropriate only to ποτητόν, not ἑρπετόν, by the figure called 'zeugma', but the fact that no land-animal or bird 'rises to view' is not an unnatural expression. The figure also helps to push us away from understanding ἑρπετόν as 'reptile', which would not in fact be very appropriate for the Syrtis.

1241 πλημυρίς: cf. 1236n.   καὶ γάρ τ' 'for in fact', Ruijgh 1971: 956; this seems preferable to linking καί to the καί of the following verse.

1242 ἢ θαμὰ δή: cf. 901n. Here the narrator's engagement adds to the vividness of the description and marks this tidal movement as a natural marvel.

1243–4 μυχάτηι ... ἠιόνι 'the innermost shore', cf. 1235n.   ἐνέωσε: aorist of ἐνωθέω.   τάχιστα: the variant ἄγεσθαι looks a gap-filler; τάχιστα, on the other hand, has real point: the tide moves so swiftly that one can do nothing about it. λάβρον ... τάχιστα frame *Od.* 15.293 in a context of sailing.   μάλ' ... παῦρον 'very little'.   ἔλειπτο may be an aorist or a pluperfect passive, cf. 1.45, 824, Griffith 1968: 173.

1246 νῶτα χθονός is attested before *Arg.*, but here it evokes and varies the Homeric νῶτα θαλάσσης, to mark the interchange of land and sea. This is a landscape where it is very difficult to distinguish sea, land and sky.

1247 διηνεκές: the neuter is here used adverbially.

1247–9 The empty landscape evokes and reverses the lush pleasure of Homer's deserted 'Goat Island' (*Od.* 9.116–65), where there is a rich supply of water and food and an excellent harbour for boats (Introduction, p. 12). For specific echoes cf. lines 119 οὐ μὲν γὰρ πάτος ἀνθρώπων ἀπερύκει (~ 1248), 122 (no flocks or agricultural land) ~ 1248–9, 145 κατείχετο δὲ νεφέεσσιν ~ 1249. As with the Syrtis, Odysseus' men run ashore before they

realize what is happening (lines 146–9).   οὐδέ τιν’ ἀρδμόν: cf. Strabo
17.3.20 on the Syrtis, 'watering-places are scarce'.   πάτον 'path',
'ground marked by the tread of men'.   κατείχετο: cf. Call. *h.* 5.74
(another supernatural and threatening landscape) πολλὰ δ’ ἀσυχία τῆνο
κατεῖχεν ὄρος.

1251–2 The double question evokes the standard question of the *Odyssey*,
τίς πόθεν εἰς ἀνδρῶν; πόθι τοι πόλις ἠδὲ τοκῆες; (1.170, 10.325 etc.), but here
there is no prospect of human intercourse. The Argonauts' position is
far worse than that of Odysseus, returned to Ithaca (though he does not
know it), cf. *Od.* 13.200 ὦ μοι ἐγώ, τέων αὖτε βροτῶν ἐς γαῖαν
ἱκάνω;   εὔχεται: sc. εἶναι. It is people who normally 'boast of' or 'claim'
lineage and identity (*Il.* 5.246, 13.54, *Od.* 14.199, 20.192 etc.), and here
there is despairing sarcasm in the epic expression.   ξυνέωσαν varies
ἐνέωσε of 1243.   ἀφειδέες 'without thought for, disregarding'.

1253 The Argonauts do not know that the Symplegades are now fixed
immovably.   διαμπερές, 'straight through', governs πετράων.

1254–5 are a 'counterfactual' wish expressed with ἄν and the past indicative, cf. *Il.* 5.201. At their lowest ebb, the Argonauts express the most
traditional of heroic desires, cf. *Il.* 22.304–5 (Hector facing death), *Od.*
5.306–12 (Odysseus in the storm).   ἤ τ’ imitates Homeric usage,
cf. 916n.   καὶ ὑπὲρ Διὸς αἶσαν ἰοῦσι 'even were we to go against Zeus's
will'. The Argonauts know that Zeus is watching them (584–5), but if this
phrase has a specific sense, we may rather understand that (quite reasonably) they took the omen of 296–7 concerning the route they were to take
as coming from Zeus, when in fact it came from Hera. It may, however, be
that the phrase is simply an expression of the depth of their conviction.
Phrases such as ὑπὲρ αἶσαν and ὑπὲρ μόρον (cf. 20–3n.) are common in
Homer, always with reference to unrealized possibilities, but ὑπὲρ Διὸς
αἶσαν occurs only once, *Il.* 17.321 from the narrator; here the unique
phrase is given to characters.   μενοινώοντας: the accusative is influenced by the infinitive which follows, despite the preceding ἰοῦσι,
cf. 1262–3.

1256–7 Cf. *Il.* 19.90 (Agamemnon's apology) ἀλλὰ τί κε ῥέξαιμι; θεὸς διὰ
πάντα τελευτᾶι. It is typical of both the theological and the geographical
slant of *Arg.* that it is not the gods, but the natural environment against
which the Argonauts protest.   ἐρυκόμενοι 'if we are constrained ... ';
elsewhere in *Arg.* ἐρύκεσθαι with the infinitive means 'be prevented' from
doing something. ἐρητύεσθαι shows a similar variation, cf. *Il.* 13.280.

1257–8 'How deserted is the shoreline of this vast land which spreads
out before us!' πέζα 'shoreline', LSJ s.v. II 2.   διωλυγίης: some ancient

grammarians understood this word as σκοτεινός, and the actual meaning was unclear from a relatively early date (Danielsson 1905/6: 144–9).   ἀναπέπταται: pf. pass. of ἀναπετάννυμι.

1259 ἀμηχανίηι κακότητος: the more common expression is ἀμηχανέων κακότητι (2.410, 1140, 3.423), and Fränkel proposed reading that here.

1260 After the Argonauts in general have expressed their helplessness, the expert steersman confirms the hopelessness of their position. ἀκηχεμένοις: pf. pass. participle from ἀχέω.

1261 δῆθεν adds a touch of resigned indignation.

1262 πάρα δ᾽ ἄμμι τὰ κύντατα πημανθῆναι 'What remains for us is to experience the very worst of sufferings'. The spondaic close of the verse adds to the effect of helpless despair.

1263 τῆιδ᾽ ὑπ᾽ ἐρημαίηι πεπτηότας 'having fallen into/happened upon this desert'; the preposition and the participle are best taken as in tmesis. Others understand ὑπό as 'at the edge of' or emend to ἐπ᾽, but the usage does not seem difficult, even if hard to parallel.

1264 χερσόθεν: even winds from the south will not help them. ἀμπνεύσειαν: aor. opt. of ἀναπνέω, with 'apocope' (shortening) and assimilation of the disyllabic prefix.   τεναγώδεα: acc. sing. with ἅλα, cf. 1236n. The key word is moved to the front of the clause to stress its importance.

1264–72 The central part of Ankaios' speech varies the narrator's description of the Syrtis at 1235–44, in another experimental variation of Homeric technique.

1265 ἤλιθα 'to no purpose, uselessly (for us)', cf. 2.283: there is water, but it is not going to get the *Argo* refloated. An alternative interpretation, and the standard meaning of the adverb in Homer, is 'in vast quantity' (cf. 176–7n.), i.e. as far as one can see, cf. 1237–9, which this passage varies. See further Bulloch on Call. *h.* 5.124, Rengakos 1994: 96.

1266 ξαινόμενον 'broken up', lit. 'carded, mangled', a metaphor from wool-working; the reference is to the foam of 1238, cf. Oppian, *Hal.* 5.306 (the dying whale) διαξαίνει ... θάλασσαν.   ἐπιτροχάει varies ἐπιβλύει of 1238.

1267–9 Only the incoming tide which has pushed them so deep into the Syrtis has prevented the break-up of the boat.   διὰ ... κεάσθη: cf. 391–3n. νηῦς is scanned as a single syllable by synizesis.   χέρσου πολλὸν πρόσω 'very far from (real) land'.   πλημυρὶς ἐκ πόντοιο is taken from *Od.* 9.486 – a moment of very great danger in the attempt to escape from the Cyclops. The middle syllable of πλημυρίς is here short, but long in 1241; for such variation as part of the display of poetic artistry see Hopkinson 1982.   **μεταχρονίην** 'raised up', i.e. 'afloat', cf. 952n.

1270–1 οἰόθι δ᾽ … ἔχουσα 'and nothing but sea-water on which one cannot sail swirls around, barely rising above the land'.   **ὕπερ … ἔχουσα:** tmesis.   **ὅσσον** 'barely, a little', cf. 1.183, Gow on Theocr. 9.20, and the common οὐδ᾽ ὅσον (1.482, 3.519 etc.).

1272 ἀπ᾽ … κεκόφθαι: tmesis. This seems to be the earliest occurrence of ἀποκόπτειν ἐλπίδα; at Polyb. 3.63.8 Hannibal tells his men 'all hope [of turning around and returning] is cut off', and, like Hannibal's men, the Argonauts are literally and metaphorically 'cut off'. Cf. also Plut. *Pyrrhos* 2.3.

1274 φαίνοι ἐήν: Madvig's emendation has been universally accepted, though Campbell 1973: 85 notes that the correption of optative –οι in this place is without parallel, and he tentatively suggested φαίνειεν (Schwyzer I 796–7).   **οἰήκεσσι** 'the tiller bars', by which a steersman controlled the rudders, cf. Casson 1971: 224–8.

1275 κομιδῆς 'safe return'.   **οὐ μάλα** 'not at all'.

1276 ἐφ᾽ probably means 'after', but the nuance may be 'in return for, at the price of', LSJ s.v. ἐπί B III 4. Ankaios returns at the end to the despair with which his speech began.

1279 παχνώθη κραδίη: more than one emotion can 'freeze the heart', cf. *Il.* 17.111–12 (a disappointed lion), Aesch. *Ch.* 83 (the grieving and sympathizing chorus), West on Hes. *Theog.* 360. Here it is fear, also marked by the pale χλόος of their faces, cf. 2.1216, *Il.* 3.35; the chill and paleness of fear lead into the comparison of the Argonauts to men resembling 'lifeless phantoms', thus breaking down the formal barrier between narrative and simile.

1280–9 The despairing Argonauts are compared to men who have been led by omens to expect some great catastrophe and thus roam their city aimlessly. There are some formal similarities to the similes at *Il.* 10.5–8 and 17.547–52 (a τέρας presaging war or freezing winter), but this remarkable passage is essentially a new creation; see Faerber 1932: 25–7. The most important Homeric model is Theoclymenus' vision of impending disaster for the suitors at *Od.* 20.350–7, which shares with *Arg.* motifs of darkness, the failure of the sun, blood, groaning and εἴδωλα (Hunter 1993: 135–6); that scene had already been used in the description of Circe's ominous dream (665n.). Whereas the suitors remain blissfully unaware of their coming doom, the Argonauts have resigned themselves to death. The portents themselves find many parallels, both specific and general, in history and poetry, cf., e.g., Hdt. 6.27, 7.37, 140, Cic. *ND* 2.5.14, *De Div.* 1.97, Virg. *G.* 1.476–83 (which seems indebted to *Arg.*), Tib. 2.5.71–8, Plut. *Pyrrhos* 31.3 (a city facing destruction), but it seems very likely that Ap. and his readers will have thought of specific (and relatively recent) parallels; Σ 1284 gives as an example of sweating statues what happened at Thebes before the Battle of Chaironeia (cf. Plut. *Demosthenes* 19), but it is tempting to connect this passage rather with the omens at Thebes reported by Diodorus before the city's sack by Alexander: ' . . . the statues in the market-place sweated and were covered in large drops . . . the marsh at Onchestos emitted a sound like bellowing, and at Dirke a blood-filled ripple ran along the surface of the water. . . . The temple which the Thebans had dedicated from Phocian spoils at Delphi was seen to have blood on the roof . . . Those whose business it was to interpret signs said that . . . the sweating of the statues indicated an overwhelming disaster and the appearance of blood in several places indicated that there would be great slaughter in the city' (Diod. Sic. 17.10.4–5). Ap.'s readers, for whom the possibility of such omens was more real than it is for many modern readers, will have had the despair of the Argonauts vividly brought home to them; as such, the evocation of believed historical events serves the *enargeia* of the simile (Hunter 2006: 92–3). So too, at one level, does the remarkable accumulation of alternatives marked by ἢ . . . ἤ; the poet is giving us every chance to visualize the remarkable narrative and the remarkable simile.

1280 An opening likeness colours both the Argonauts (cf. 1279n.) and the city-dwellers of the simile.   ἀψύχοισιν . . . εἰδώλοισιν: εἴδωλα are themselves the stuff of omens, and by comparing those in receipt of dread signs to 'lifeless phantoms' the poet blurs further the line between sign and effect, thus increasing the eerie weirdness of this simile. The juxtaposition εἰδώλοισιν ~ ἀνέρες marks the point of the likeness.

1281–3 ἢ πολέμοιο | ἢ λοιμοῖο τέλος: the assonance of the nouns (cf. *Il.* 1.61) adds to the uncanniness. As the men are expecting a disaster, τέλος with the genitive means principally 'doom of, outbreak of' (LSJ s.v. I 4), but the periphrasis is chosen to evoke τέλος as 'end, climax'.   ὄμβρον: in an essentially agricultural world, the destruction wrought by floods, which might themselves bring the λιμὸς καὶ λοιμός of Hes. *WD* 243, is on a par with that of war, cf. 3.1399–1404, Virg. *G.* 1.481–3, Hor. *C.* 1.2 (with Nisbet and Hubbard's commentary).   βοῶν . . . ἔργα are primarily 'fields worked by cattle', cf. *Od.* 10.98 and the imitation of this passage at Virg. *G.* 1.324–6 *ruit arduus aether | et pluuia ingenti sata laeta boumque labores | diluit*, but the phrase also suggests the laborious efforts of the cattle, as at Hes. *WD* 46.   μυρία marks the extent of the devastation; Fränkel's μυρίος (cf. 2.1120) removes the hiatus before ἔκλυσεν (and note *ingenti* at Virg. *G.* 1.325 above), but adds very little after ἄσπετον.

1284–5 The omens are divided into a couplet of earthly signs and a couplet of heavenly ones, and a pair of *spondeiazontes* marks the eeriness of the signs on earth.   ἢ ὅταν: these verses must form not an alternative to 1280–3, but rather give the reasons for the citizens' despair; ἢ ὅταν has, therefore, regularly been replaced by Wilamowitz's ὁππότ' ἄν (the error might have arisen from miscopying of ἤ from the head of 1282), but ἢ ὅταν may be a mannered variant for ὅταν ἤ (cf. *Od.* 22.97, Eur. *Med.* 846–8), and ἠέ in 1286 is usually preceded by ἤ. It seems therefore best to allow the text to stand.   αὐτόματα is strictly redundant, but increases the sense of strangeness. Here and elsewhere in this passage Ap. has in mind (*inter alia*) Hephaestus and the marvels of his house in *Il.* 18: cf. lines 372 τὸν δ' ηὗρ' ἱδρώοντα, ἑλισσόμενον περὶ φύσας, 376 αὐτόματοι. Both passages describe θαύματα (cf. line 377 with bT-schol.), but of very different kinds.   αἵματι is placed in significant 'unnecessary' enjambment, as statues can sweat liquids other than blood, cf. 1280–9n.   καί: Fränkel proposed ἤ on the basis of a paraphrase in the scholia, but sweating statues and phantom bellowings in shrines (σηκοί) belong together.   φαντάζωνται: both here and in 1287 the choice between the vivid indicative and the subjunctive is not straightforward; a variation of mood between the two verbs would be in the Hellenistic style.

1286–7 Eclipses belong to the most universal and powerful of portents.   φαείνει: cf. previous note.

1288 πρόπαρ 'along the length of', cf. 1.454, Mastronarde on Eur. *Ph.* 120.

1289 Cf. *Il.* 24.12 (the distraught Achilles) δινεύεσκ' ἀλύων παρὰ θῖν' ἁλός, *Od.* 13.219–20 (the grieving Odysseus who does not realize that he has reached home) ἑρπύζων παρὰ θῖνα κτλ.   ἑρπύζοντες denotes slow and laboured movement, and it too, like ἀλύειν, is used of the grieving Achilles (*Il.* 23.225, where see the bT-scholia).

1290 ἐλεεινά 'piteously', adverbial neuter.   σφέας 'each other', cf. σφίσι at 2.128, 3.1023.

1291–2 The group becomes again a disparate collection of individuals, and that communal solidarity which has always differentiated the ethos of the Argonauts from that of Odysseus' adventures dissolves.   δακρυόειν ἀγάπαζον 'greeted each other tearfully', i.e. said tearful farewells. δακρυόειν is a rare alternative for δακρυόεν, cf. 2.404, K–B 1 529; the latter could only appear in hexameters if followed by a consonant.   ἕκαστος followed by a plural verb is already familiar in Homer, cf., e.g., *Il.* 1.606, 9.656–7, K–B 1 286–7.

1293 ἑκαστέρω 'further away' (cf. 2.855), with the implication 'deeper into the Syrtis', a true mark of the abandonment of hope. Next to ἄλλυδις ἄλλος, the form resonates with ἕκαστος in 1291 to emphasize the break-up of the group.

1294 Mourning is regularly accompanied by covering of the head, cf. 1.264 (Jason's father), 2.861–2 (the Argonauts at the death of Tiphys), *Il.* 24.162–3 (Priam).

1295 ἄκμηνοι καὶ ἄπαστοι 'without food or nourishment'; ancient grammarians explain the two adjectives as virtual synonyms; see *LfgrE* s.v. ἄκμηνος, Pfeiffer on Call. fr. 312 (= *Hecale* fr. 120 H). The model here is Achilles who grieves for Patroclus ἄκμηνος καὶ ἄπαστος (*Il.* 19.346); ἄκμηνος occurs a further three times in *Il.* 19 and nowhere else in Homer. Achilles is indeed a heroic model of grief, but the Argonauts are mourning for themselves.   **ἐκείατο**: epic-ionic third pl. imperfect, cf. the present κείαται in 481.

1296 φάος: i.e. the following morning.   **οἰκτίστωι θανάτωι** occurs twice in *Od.* of the death of Agamemnon (11.412, 24.34), but here it refers to the special awfulness of death by starvation, cf. *Od.* 12.342 (Eurylochos about the Cattle of the Sun) λιμῶι δ᾽ οἴκτιστον θανέειν καὶ πότμον ἐπισπεῖν.   **νόσφι** 'apart, separately'.

1297 The Phaeacian maids (cf. 1221–2) form a kind of chorus to respond to Medea's lamentations, cf. the female laments for Hector at *Il.* 24.722, 746.

1298–1304 Comparisons of the mourning women to two very different sets of 'mourning' birds (Hunter 1993: 136–7).

1298–9 evoke both Achilles' comparison of himself to a mother-bird at *Il.* 9.323–5 and also the comparison of Artemis fleeing the battlefield to a dove seeking refuge from a hawk in a rock (*Il.* 21.493–6). The comparison puts the helplessness and exposure of the girls into stark relief.   **ἐρημαῖοι** 'abandoned', or rather 'deserted', which catches the resonance, reinforced by an echo of 1263, of 'in the desert'; the word thus forms a strong link between the fate of the girls and that of the young birds.   **πέτρης | χηραμοῦ** 'a hollow rock'. At *Il.* 21.494–5 the rock in which the dove seeks shelter is κοίλην . . . πέτρην | χηραμόν, where the scholia note that κοίλην . . . πέτρην explains χηραμόν, i.e. the latter gloss is regarded as a noun, cf. Arist. *HA* 8.614b35. At 1452 χηραμόν is certainly a noun, but at *Il.* 21.495 it may well have been taken by some as a two-termination adjective, and that is how it seems to be used here. To offer in the same poem one example each of the two possible interpretations of a Homeric rarity is very typical of Hellenistic style. Whereas Artemis and the dove

escape, the girls and the chicks are utterly exposed.   ἀπτῆνες … νεοσσοί
'chicks which cannot fly', cf. *Il.* 9.323, but these chicks have no mother
to protect them; ἀπτῆνες resonates with πεπτηότες to suggest that they
'fall' because they cannot fly. An etymological connection between
πίπτω and πέτομαι is accepted by both ancient (*Etym. Mag.* 673.4–12)
and modern scholars.

1300–2 The mourning girls are compared to swans at the lush meadows
of the Pactolus in Lydia (Barrington 56 F/G 5), cf. Call. *h.* 4.249–50;
conditions in the Syrtis, however, are very different indeed. Swans were
thought to sing most sweetly before their death, to mourn themselves as
it were, and so there is a particular pathos to the image; see Thompson,
Birds 181–2, Arnott 1977. Whereas the similarity of the girls to the
chicks of 1298–9 is very clear, the swan-simile marks difference as much
as similarity, and we may see here Ap. exploiting ancient discussion
of Homeric similes which was much concerned with how extensive the
analogies between vehicle and tenor were or should be; cf. further
1338–43n. The principal Homeric model is the comparison of the mas-
sing troops to swarms of birds, including swans, at the Cayster (another
Lydian river) at *Il.* 2.459–63; Virgil combines the Homeric and Apollonian
passages at *Aen.* 7.699–702 (immediately followed by a rewriting of
Arg. 4.238–40).   καλά: adverbial neuter. The Pactolus was believed
to flow with gold dust brought down from the Tmolus mountains,
and was also known as Χρυσορρόας, *RE* 18.2439.   ὀφρύσι 'raised
banks'.   κινήσωσιν ἐὸν μέλος 'set their own song in motion'. The aorist
subjunctive varies the present indicative of 1299; the variant κινήσουσιν is
taken by some as a rare form of the subjunctive (Chantraine I 454–5), but
it is hard to see that it could be understood as anything but a future tense.
The choice of verb is often explained by the belief (by no means universal
in antiquity) that the song of the swan was produced by the beating of
its wings (Arnott 2007: 123), but the expression, though unparalleled,
does not seem difficult enough to warrant this explanation, particularly
if Ap. is pointedly varying the Homeric κινεῖν μέλος, where the noun means
'limb' (*Od.* 8.298, *HHAphr.* 234, Campbell 1971: 421–2).   βρέμεται
'resound, ring with noise', a variation of σμαραγεῖ at *Il.* 2.463.

1304 A heavy spondaic close and the remarkable assonance of ἐλεεινὸν
ἰήλεμον evoke the sound of the girls' lamentation.

1305–7 Cf. 636–42n.   ἀπὸ ζωῆς ἐλίασθεν: this expression for death does
not seem to occur before this passage.   νώνυμνοι is normally understood as 'nameless, leaving no name', cf. 2.982, Call. fr. 43.55, but the
word is twice used in *Il.* of the Achaeans being wiped out (12.70, 13.227),
and some grammarians associated it in those places with ὕμνος, so 'without

lamentations, unmourned'. This would not fit here, but 'without ὕμνοι' certainly would: if the Argonauts had perished in the desert, there would have been no epics through which 'mortals learn' of them, they would not be ἀοίδιμοι, cf. 1319–21n., Morrison 2007: 304. For the styling of *Arg.* as a hymn cf. esp. 1773–5.

1308 σφεας is scanned as a single long syllable by synizesis.

1309–36 The 'heroines' were local deities worshipped across a wide area of Libya, cf. Call. fr. 602 δέσποιναι Λιβύης ἡρωίδες, αἳ Νασαμώνων | αὖλιν καὶ δολιχὰς θῖνας ἐπιβλέπετε (which suggests an area close to where the Argonauts are imagined to be stranded, cf. Pfeiffer ad loc.), Nicaenetus, *AP* 6.225 (= *HE* 2689–94, perhaps indebted to *Arg.*). They here play the saving role associated with minor deities such as Leukothea in *Od.* 5, cf. 1318n. Call. fr. 37, from *Aetia* 1, consists of a hexameter cited by Steph. Byz. joined (by Pfeiffer) to two verses preserved in a papyrus commentary, οἵη τε Τρίτωνος ἐφ᾽ ὕδασιν Ἀσβύσταο | Ἡφαίστου λόχιον θηξαμένου πέλεκυν | βρέγματος ἐκ δίοιο σὺν ἔντεσιν ἧλαο πατρός; there is an obvious intertextual relation between that passage and 1309–11; 1310–11 are *spondeiazontes*, as is the corresponding Callimachean verse.

1309 The shape of the verse is similar to that of *Il.* 2.547 (the – interpolated – passage about Athena and the autochthonous Athenians), δῆμον Ἐρεχθῆος μεγαλήτορος ὅν ποτ᾽ Ἀθήνη, and if this is deliberate, the point may be not merely to do honour to Athena, but also to colour the subsequent description of the heroines as χθόνιαι, cf. 1322n., Griffiths 2012: 24.   ἡρῶσσαι: the 'correct' form would be ἡρῶισσαι, but the form without iota, which dominates the tradition here and elsewhere, is well attested in inscriptions and papyri, cf. Call. fr. 66.1.   τιμήοροι 'protectors', cf. 1730.

1310 θόρε perhaps alludes, as does ἧλαο at Call. fr. 37.3, to one ancient etymology of the name Παλλάς, i.e. because she 'leapt' (cf. πάλλειν etc.) from Zeus's head, cf. *Etym. Mag.* 649.53–4.   παμφαίνουσα 'glittering' (in her armour), σὺν ἔντεσιν in Call. fr. 37.3; cf. Stesichorus, *PMG* 233 (=270a Finglass), Pind., *Ol.* 7.35–7 etc. In Hesiod, *Theog.* 924–6, Athena is born ἐκ κεφαλῆς from Zeus, but nothing is said about her being armed; for the myth in general see West on *Theog.* 886–900.

1311 Athena's birth beside one of the several rivers and lakes named after Triton is commonly attested, first perhaps in Hes. fr. dub. 343.11–12, cf. Harder 2012: 2.290–1; this was one of the explanations for her title Τριτογένεια. Apollonius placed the North African lake, which had long been connected with Argonautic legend (cf. Pind. *Pyth.* 4.21, Hdt. 4.179.2–3), near the coast just northeast of Euhesperides/Berenice (cf., e.g., Strabo 17.3.20), but imagined locations differed according to the mythic version being narrated, and the lake was often placed much further west, cf. Ps.-Scylax 110.8, Delage 1930: 261–70, Ferri 1976, Peyras-Trousset 1988, Malkin 1994: 198–9. Hdt. 4.188 reports that the tribes around this lake are particularly devout towards Athena, and Ps.-Scylax places a sanctuary of the goddess there.   ἐφ' ὕδασι: Campbell (1969: 284) proposed ἐν, as better suited to χυτλώσαντο, but the phrase goes as much with the participle as with χυτλώσαντο, and the bathing may have taken place 'beside' the lake. In view of Call. fr. 37, any change seems dangerous. Cf. further 3.876–7n.   χυτλώσαντο 'bathed, washed', cf. Call. h. 1.17; at its only occurrence in Homer (Od. 8.60), the meaning must be 'anoint oneself [after washing]'.

1312–14 The appearance of the heroines to Jason is halfway between a typical epic dream sequence (Arend 1933: 61–3, Vian III 192–3) and the hallucination of a desert mirage in circumstances of severe heat, solitude, lack of food, and physical and psychological stress. On ancient ideas of hallucination see Harris 2013.   ἔνδιον ἦμαρ 'the middle part of the day', cf. Od. 4.450, Call. fr. 260.55, Hollis on Call. Hecale fr. 18.1. The middle of the day was a common and often a very dangerous time to meet gods (cf. Theocr. 7.21, Hopkinson on Call. h. 6.38, Papanghelis 1989), but here what is relevant is the intense heat and brightness appropriate for seeing mirages.   ὀξύταται: the variant ὀξύτατοι would be an example of a superlative treated as a two-termination adjective (Hunter 1999: 167), and it may be correct.

1314 The unveiling allows Jason, and Jason alone (cf. 1315), to see the goddesses.   ἠρέμα marks the goddesses' concern, cf. 1351.

1315 εἰς ἑτέρωσε παλιμπετὲς ὄμματ' ἔνεικε 'turned back his eyes aside'; we are to understand that Jason had at first raised his eyes to the heroines when they uncovered his head. For the expression cf. 466.

1316 αὐτόν reinforces οἷον in the sense 'alone', cf. Od. 14.450, LSJ s.v. αὐτός I 3. αὐτόν νιν as a strengthened accusative pronoun occurs on a healing record from Epidauros (IG IV 952.47), and cf. Il. 11.117.   ἀμφαδόν: cf. ἔμπεδον in the very similar sequence at 854–5.

1318 Cf. Od. 5.339–40 (Leukothea to Odysseus) κάμμορε, τίπτε τοι ὧδε Ποσειδάων ἐνοσίχθων | ὠδύσατ' κτλ.; like the heroines, Leukothea speaks out of pity (line 336). Like Odysseus, Jason too is 'shipwrecked', but in a very different sense; see further Clare 2002: 154–9.   κάμμορε 'ill-fated, long-suffering', an apocopated form of κατάμορε.   βεβόλησαι: pf. pass. of βολέω, with the same sense as βάλλω, and the same metaphorical meaning as this form has in Homer.

1319–21 The heroines rework the claim to knowledge with which the Sirens tempt Odysseus (*Od.* 12.189–91), but they want to help, not destroy, the hero (Hunter 1993: 126, Feeney 1991: 91–2). The episode of the Sirens showed Odysseus at his most intellectually curious and heroic; this episode, in which he is unable to solve the riddle the heroines pose for him, shows Jason at his most ἀμήχανος. Some have suggested that we are to understand that the source of the heroines' knowledge comes from their association with Athena, but that seems an unimaginatively 'rationalized' explanation. Rather, the verses, with their strong recall of the proem to Book 1 and their foreshadowing of the close of the poem (esp. 1776), suggest that *Arg.* itself is the source of their knowledge; this is a typically self-conscious variation on the verses of the Homeric Sirens, which suggest that their knowledge comes from epic poetry on the theme of the Trojan War. Albis 1996: 109–10 argues that the principal model for the epiphany of the heroines is the appearance of the Muses to Hesiod at the opening of *Theog.*

1319 ἐποιχομένους: sc. ὑμᾶς.

1320 ἐπὶ χθονὸς ὅσσα τ' ἐφ' ὑγρήν: although emendation to ὑγρῆς would be very easy (cf. 1359), the variation of case after the preposition is elegant. The division into sufferings on 'land' and on 'sea' evokes the opening of the *Odyssey*.

1321 πλαζόμενοι κατὰ πόντον refers to the labours both on land and on sea, as the former were endured during stops along the way.   ὑπέρβια 'overwhelming, amazing'.

1322 οἰοπόλοι 'solitary, living in the loneliness', cf. 1333 ἐρημονόμοι, 1413; at Pind. *Pyth.* 4.28 Triton is an οἰοπόλος δαίμων and the scholia there gloss the phrase as ὁ μόνος ἀναστρεφόμενος θεός. Σ here, however, understand the word to mean 'shepherds' and identify them with nymphs known from later texts as Ἐπιμηλίδες. Ambiguity would certainly suit the riddling style in which the heroines speak, and χθόνιαι which follows is also capable of more than one interpretation. Cf. further 1412–14n., Livrea 1972: 238–40.   χθόνιαι 'of the land', i.e. native, indigenous, cf. 2.504 (also of Libyan nymphs). In other contexts the word can of course mean 'born from the soil' (cf. 1398), and the fact that they claim to be 'daughters of Libya' does indeed make them γηγενεῖς in a special sense, cf. 1309n.   αὐδήεσσαι 'speaking with a human voice', and hence intelligible to mortals. In *Od.* this epithet is used of Circe (10.136, 11.8, 12.150) and Calypso (12.449), and in *Arg.* it is only minor divinities who address mortals directly. Leukothea, however, who is a principal model for the heroines (1318n.), had been a βροτὸς αὐδήεσσα before she became a sea-god (*Od.* 5.334). Aristotle (fr. 394, 1 Gigon) had discussed the Homeric epithet and proposed (humorously?) in the case of Calypso and Circe emending the text to αὐλήεσσα, 'because they were solitary', and for Leukothea to οὐδήεσσα, meaning ἐπίγειος, 'terrestrial'. It is certainly tempting to believe that this verse at least gestures towards Aristotle's discussion; see further *LfgrE* s.v. αὐδήεις.

1323 That the heroines are both protectors and daughters of Libya plays with the name as both that of a land and of its eponymous nymph, cf. 1742; the style is again somewhat oracular and riddling.

1324 ἀκάχησο: a passive imperative connected with ἄχομαι or ἀκαχίζομαι.

1325–6 εὖτ' ἄν ... αὐτίκα 'as soon as ... '.   Ἀμφιτρίτη is wife of Poseidon (cf. 1371) and mother of Triton (Hes. *Theog.* 930–1), and so there is a special appropriateness to her in this connection. She is often depicted in vase-painting driving the god's chariot (cf. *LIMC* s.v. 25–8), and that role is also relevant here. The name is also (principally in later texts) used by metonymy for water or the sea (Hunter 2006: 77–8), and 'when Amphitrite releases ... ' thus continues the heroines' riddling: is this Poseidon's wife or the sea (cf. 1365)?

1327 σφετέρηι 'your', cf. 3.186n.

1328 ὧν: i.e. ἐκείνων ἅ; κάμνειν is normally followed by the accusative. κάματος may be applied to the pains of childbirth (Soph. *OT* 174 etc.), and that sense resonates in the verb here.   κατὰ νηδύος 'in the depths of her stomach'; the *Argo* has looked after the Argonauts as a mother's womb protects the unborn.

1329 A closural *spondeiazon* lends weight to the hope which the heroines hold out.

1330–1 ἄφαντοι ... παρασχεδόν 'immediately disappeared together with their voices, on the spot where they had stood'.   ὁμοῦ governs the preceding φθογγῆι, LSJ s.v. I 3.

1332 ἀν' ... ἕζετ' 'sat up' (tmesis).

1333 ἐρημονόμοι: cf. 1322n.   κυδραί does not correspond to anything the heroines themselves said: it is Jason's acknowledgement of their power.

1334–5 οὔ τι μάλ' ἀντικρὺ νοέω lit. 'not at all do I completely understand', i.e. 'I do not at all understand'; this seems more apt for Jason's ἀμηχανίη than 'I do not completely understand ... '. In 1356 the adverbial phrase is varied by οὐ πάγχυ.   ἑταίρους | εἰς ἓν ἀγειράμενος marks the reassertion of the Argonautic ethos after the crisis of 1290–3.

1335–6 τέκμωρ … κομιδῆς 'an indication of [how to] return', 'way of achieving return'. At *Od.* 4.373–4, 466–7 'unable to find a τέκμωρ' is used to mean much the same of Menelaos stuck on Pharos.   **δήωμεν:** subjunctive from δήω.   **πολέων δέ τε μῆτις ἀρείων** marks the gulf which separates the Argonautic ethos from that of the relationship between πολύμητις Odysseus and his crew, cf. 3.171–5, Hunter 1988: 441–2. Formally, the expression seems to be a variation of *Il.* 12.412 (Sarpedon calling for aid from his Lycian troops) πλεόνων δέ τοι ἔργον ἄμεινον.

1337 ἐπὶ μακρὸν ἀΰτει varies μακρὸν ἀΰτει at the end of *Il.* 20.50, and ἐπὶ μακρὸν ἀυτεῖ (present tense) ends a hexameter at Hermesianax fr. 7.5 Powell.

1338 αὐσταλέος combines 'dried (by heat)' and 'filthy', an easy combination for Greeks who associated bodily cleanliness with moisture and the use of oil, cf. 1.1175, 2.200. Both αὐχμῶν and κατάξηρος are found as glosses for αὐσταλέος, *LfgrE* s.v.

1338–43 Jason is compared to a lion whose roar as it searches for its mate fills the landscape and terrifies the domestic animals and their herdsmen. Jason's roar does not, however, terrify his comrades. At one level the simile illustrates the closeness of the bond between Jason and the other Argonauts; pairs of lions are common in Homeric similes (cf. *Il.* 5.554–60, 10.297–8 etc.), but the nearest analogy to the present passage is *Il.* 18.318–23, where Achilles' mourning for Patroclus is compared to that of a lion searching for its cubs which a hunter has taken away, and there too the emotional weight of the simile lies not in the principal formal point of contact between tenor and vehicle, namely the sound of mourning and the lion's roaring, but in the angry grief of both Achilles and the lion. 1342b-3, however, seem to suggest a potential likeness, here denied, between the Argonauts and the terrified animals and herdsmen. That denial of similarity amounts to a failure of the very structure of the epic simile (see, e.g., Goldhill 1991: 307–8), one appropriate to the desolation of the terrain in which the Argonauts find themselves, but it is best understood against the background of ancient discussion of Homeric similes, which was much concerned with how extensive were the points of contact between tenor and vehicle (Nünlist 2009: 287–8). 1339b-42a has no proper counterpart in the narrative and is thus a descriptive extension, rather than an integral part of the simile; this therefore, unlike *Il.* 18.318–23, is not a ὅλον πρὸς ὅλον simile (cf. bT-scholia on vv. 318–22). Although Libya is indeed a place where lions might be expected, the effect of 'dissimilarity' is increased by the stark difference between the landscape of the Syrtis, where there are certainly no grazing cattle (cf. 1247–9), and the agricultural landscape of the simile. From this perspective, 1342b-3 can be considered a kind of 'scholiastic' explanation of why the preceding verses are not in fact integral: this is, then, a simile composed not merely against the background of scholarly discussion, but one which provides its own interpretation. As with dream sequences and the retelling of narratives (cf. 1347–62n.), the Libyan wasteland proves fruitful terrain for the exploration of epic technique.

1339 σύννομον ἦν 'its mate'. At Soph. *Phil.* 1436 λέοντε συννόμῳ suggests rather 'two lions working as a team'.   **ὠρύεται**: this verb is first found of lions here.   **βαρείῃ** 'deep, low' of sound, LSJ s.v. III 1.

1340 ὑποβρομέουσιν 'resound, rumble with sound'; the alliteration with β enacts the meaning of the sentence, and the prefix indicates the source of the noise. The much better attested ὑποτρομέουσιν gives a picture of nature responding to the terrifying sound (Campbell 1971: 422), but the position of δείματι perhaps suggests that it is here where the idea of fear is first introduced.

1341 πεφρίκασι: the perfect of φρίσσειν is commonly used with present meaning, cf. 1.689, *Il.* 24.775, Call. *Hecale* fr. 113.2 Hollis (= 291.2 Pf.). At *Il.* 11.383 Paris describes the Trojans' fear of Diomedes, οἵ τέ σε πεφρίκασι λέονθ᾽ ὡς μηκάδες αἶγες.

1342 βουπελάται: the noun occurs first here.

1343 ῥιγεδανή occurs only here in *Arg.*, and only once in Homer (*Il.* 19.325 of Helen). The D-scholia on the latter passage gloss the word as χαλεπῆς, φρικτῆς and φοβερᾶς, and so the epithet may form a strong bond to πεφρίκασι in the simile.   **φίλοις ἐπικεκλομένοιο** 'calling to his friends'. At 3.85 this verb is followed by the dative in the sense 'instruct', but cf. *Il.* 8.346 'encouraging each other'; φίλους may, however, be correct, cf. 1717, 1.410, 2.493.

1344 κατηφέες 'with their heads down', cf. 3.123–4n., Campbell 1994: 113.

1345 The mingling of the sexes indicates the breakdown of all conventional niceties under the pressure of their extraordinary situation.

1347–62 Jason's report varies Homeric technique by containing a mixture of repetition, variation, and new detail.

1347 κλῦτε φίλοι introduces a dream narration at *Il.* 2.56 and *Od.* 14.485.   **τρεῖς ... θεάων** 'three from among the goddesses'; for this genitive see Smyth §1317, K–G I 339. The expression, rather than 'three goddesses', conveys Jason's wonder: there are so many gods all around us. That the heroines were three in number is a new detail.

1348–9 The narrator had not told us how the heroines were dressed. στέρφεσιν αἰγείοις ἐζωσμέναι 'girt with skins of goats', cf. Nicaenetus, *AP* 6.225.2 [= *HE* 2690] (the heroines) αἰγίδι καὶ στρεπτοῖς ζωσάμενοι θυσάνοις; στέρφος is a very rare noun, cf. Lyc. *Alex.* 1347, Leonidas, *AP* 6.298.1–2 [= *HE* 2307–8]. ἠύτε κοῦραι: in Homer gods normally appear in dreams in the guise of mortals, but Jason here seems to refer to a believed characteristic of Libyan girls, cf. Hdt. 4.189.1–2: 'The Greeks have taken over the dress and aegis of representations of Athena from the Libyan women; the two are identical, except that the dress of Libyan women is made of leather and the tassels on the aegis are thongs rather than snakes ... Libyan women wear tasseled goatskins from which the fleece has been removed ...'. West (on Hes. *Theog.* 346) suggests that κοῦραι in fact means 'nymphs', but that seems to lack point, and the passages he cites do not show that the bald κοῦραι can easily be understood in that sense. The poet seems rather to allow Jason to speak with more knowledge of Libyan customs and of where he actually is than 'in reality' he could possibly have; perhaps, however, the emphasis is less on the goatskin than on the fact that the skins fall around the back and waist, as girls' tunics do.

1350 ὑπὲρ κεφαλῆς: this is typical of dream appearances (e.g. *Il.* 2.20, *Od.* 6.21), contrast 1313–14; Jason's report of his experience assimilates it more closely to an epic dream than does the narrator's account, perhaps because the event was so strange that he 'translates' it into the familiar language of dreaming, cf. 1361–2n. ἄν is the apocopated form of ἀνά, here in tmesis with ἐκάλυψαν, 'they uncovered [me]'; the variant ἐκ presumably arose through misunderstanding of ἄν.

1351 varies 1314.

1352 ἔγρεσθαι: ἔγρω is a later by-form of ἐγείρω, cf. 671. It perhaps arose as a back-formation from the Homeric aorist ἔγρετο, but the aorist ἔγρεσθαι at *Od.* 13.124 may have been taken as a present. The verb may be addressed both to those who are awake (cf., e.g., 1.666, 2.884) and to sleepers, and thus it continues the ambivalent uncertainty of what is being described.

1353–6a rewrites 1325–8, but with a different ordering (Amphitrite here comes at the end), and Jason says nothing about return to Achaea. σφετέρηι 'our'; repetition from 1327 is here in fact variation. μενοεικέα is added by Jason himself and takes its cue from *Il.* 23.650 σοὶ δὲ θεοὶ τῶνδ' ἀντὶ χάριν μενοεικέα δοῖεν, cf. *Od.* 12.382 εἰ δέ μοι οὐ τείσουσι βοῶν ἐπιεικέ' ἀμοιβήν. The adjective here probably simply means 'abundant', rather than 'which will please them'; δαψιλής and πολλή are among the glosses found for this term, cf. *LfgrE* s.v.

1354 A virtually repeated verse (cf. 1358 ~ 1323) is used to call attention to the overall departure from the Homeric technique.

1355 λύσηισιν varies λύσηι and εὔτροχον occupies a different position than in 1326.

1356b–7a rewrites 1333–4, with variation of virtually every word.   ἴσχω followed by an infinitive is essentially the same as ἔχω with the infinitive, 'be able to . . . ', LSJ s.v. ἔχω A III 1.

1357–60 rewrites 1319–23, but again with a different ordering (the heroines' claim to knowledge is here placed second) and a mixture of repetition and variation.

1359 ἐφ᾽ ὑγρήν: ἐφ᾽ ὑγρῆς would produce a variation on 1320 and may be correct; ἐφ᾽ ὑγρήν is the standard Homeric verse-ending.

1360 διίδμεναι occurs only here in *Arg.* and never in Homer; the compound varies the repeated simple verb of 1319.   εὐχετόωντο 'they claimed'.

1361–2 vary 1330–1. Whereas the narrator had reported that the heroines 'disappeared', Jason uses the language of ἀχλύς and νέφος which is standard in epic for distortions of vision and for death; at *Il.* 15.668 νέφος ἀχλύος over the eyes prevents characters from seeing, and cf. also *Il.* 5.127. Here again, Jason is struggling to understand what has happened to him – hence the alternatives τις ἀχλύς and νέφος – and translates his experience into the language of Homeric convention, cf. 1350n.   μεσσηγὺ φαεινομένας 'in the very midst of their apparition', cf. 584–5n.

1364 μήκιστον, lit. 'furthest, longest', here functions as a synonym of μέγιστον, LSJ s.v. 2.

1365–8 form a vivid pictorial vignette ('ecphrasis') focalized by the Argonauts, as Μινύαισιν suggests; the partly overlapping adjectives, πελώριος . . . ἀμφιλαφής, mark the heroes' amazement at the size of the horse. The Libyans were famed as rearers of horses and the whole land was thought sacred to Poseidon (cf. Hdt. 2.50.2–3, Ottone 2002: 363–8).   πελώριος 'huge', but with a resonance of the supernatural, following τεράων.   ἔκθορεν: the variant ἄνθορεν may be correct (cf. Faerber 1932: 15), but ἐκ– is perhaps a better fit with 'towards the mainland'.   ἀμφιλαφής 'large, massive'. One of the explanations in Σ is 'covered with hair [i.e. a mane] on both sides', which presumably derives from the use of the adjective to describe abundant foliage or hair, and Nonnus, *Dion.* 1.318–19 seems to play with such a sense in evoking this passage; Ap. too may be playing with an ambiguity.   χρυσέηισι μετήορος αὐχένα χαίταις 'its neck and golden mane held high', lit. 'raised as to its neck with its golden mane'. Gold is the colour always most associated with divinity, but it is particularly relevant that Poseidon's horses, like Zeus's (*Il.* 8.42–3), have manes of gold and live in his 'gleaming golden palace' in 'the depths of a lake' (*Il.* 13.21–6). νήχυτον 'copious', from a supposed intensive force of νη- and χέω, cf. 3.530, Pfeiffer on Call. fr. 236.3.

1368–79 As before (cf. 2.868–84, 1217–25, 3.502–4n.), Peleus plays an important role at a critical moment; for his role in *Arg.* see Griffiths 2012. Peleus had received horses from the gods, notably from Poseidon (*Il.* 16.867, 17.443–4, 23.277–8), and so is a very appropriate Argonaut to understand what has happened.

1370 ἄρματα varies the singular at 1326, 1356.

1372–3 'I declare that our mother is none other than the ship herself'. προτιόσσομαι: the normal sense is 'foretell, foreshadow', but here 'declare, interpret'.　ἦ γάρ 'for indeed'.

1373–4 The text is uncertain as both αἰὲν ἔχουσα | ἡμέας and ἄμμε φέρουσα | νωλεμές are possible and Apollonian; the former, however, is closer to previous expressions (1328, 1354), and Ap.'s fondness for *uariatio* favours the text printed here. Fränkel adopts αἰὲν ἔχουσα | νωλεμές, but an expressed object seems necessary.　καμάτοισιν: cf. 1328n.

1375, like 1384, evokes a heroic ethos for what will be the most amazing of all the feats in the poem.

1376 ὑψόθεν ἀνθέμενοι 'putting her aloft [on us]', LSJ s.v. ἀνατίθημι B 1.　ἔνδοθι governs the genitive (cf. 508, 1385), but here with some sense of motion, 'towards the interior of ...'.

1377 'where in front of us the swift horse has driven his hooves'. Others interpret ἤλασεν intransitively, 'where in front of us the swift-footed horse has proceeded', and as 'ride' is a common meaning of ἐλαύνειν, there is certainly some linguistic play in the verse.

1378 οὐ γὰρ ὅ γε ξηρὴν ὑποδύσεται 'for he will not plunge into dry land'. The verb suggests entry into water (LSJ s.v. II c), and so the verbal paradox emphasizes the truth of Peleus' observation.

1379 σημανέειν: what the Argonauts most need in a featureless landscape are 'signs', Thalmann 2011: 80–1.　τιν' ... μυχὸν καθύπερθε θαλάσσης 'some gulf of the sea above [i.e. to the north of] us'. The horse has apparently headed south into the interior, but Peleus, who understands that a horse of Poseidon will always seek open water, expresses the hope that it will lead them to a gulf of the Mediterranean extending into Libya

from which they can make their escape. In the event the horse leads them
NE to Lake Triton.

1380 ἐπήβολος: probably 'appropriate, advantageous', though, as at 1.694,
the exact nuance is uncertain.

1381–7 Confronted with the most extraordinary achievement of the
Argonautic story, the poet stresses his reliance on the tradition ('the
Muses') which he has inherited; see Fusillo 1985: 372–4, Hunter 2008b:
124–5. The poet is forced to tell what he tells, but this time (contrast 984–5
with n. ad loc.) he does not need to apologize to the goddesses. The poet's
amazed apostrophe to his heroes may be a poeticization of prose sources:
Diod. Sic. 4.46.3 reports that some writers, including Timaeus (*FGrHist*
566 F85), recorded that, by their return, the Argonauts 'accomplished an
extraordinary (παράδοξον) feat deserving of being remembered'. The
carrying of the *Argo* had long been an element in the story. In *Pythian* 4,
Medea reports that the Argonauts carried the ship 'from Ocean over the
desert stretches of the land for twelve days' (25–6), and Σ 4.257–62b tells
us that this Pindaric version, in which they reached (the south of) Libya by
means of Ocean, and then transported the *Argo* to the Mediterranean,
appeared also in Hesiod (fr. 241M–W) and Antimachus (fr. 76 Matthews);
see Introduction, p. 8). Processions in which boats were carried towards
temples were a familiar element of Egyptian cult, and this episode has
been interpreted as one of the places in the epic where Greek and
Egyptian culture come together, and the validity of Greek (i.e.
Ptolemaic) claims to North Africa are confirmed; see Mori 2008: 13–18.

1381 The distinction between Μουσάων and ἐγώ at the head of the two
halves of the verse suggests a distinction between subject matter (the
μῦθος) and its verbal form, for which the poet is responsible; this reverses
the close of the proem (1.20–2), however that is interpreted, where the
poet (ἐγώ) takes responsibility for the matter of the song and asks
the Muses to be ὑποφήτορες ... ἀοιδῆς. See further Morrison 2007:
305.   **ὑπακουός** 'a listener to', i.e. 'obedient to'. As often in
Hellenistic poetry (cf., e.g., Bruss 2004), there is a suggestion of oral
transmission (cf. also 1382), whereas in fact Ap.'s information will come
from previous texts. ὑπακουός is not attested elsewhere (ὑπήκοος being the
regular form), but the idea that poets are the 'mouthpiece' (ὑποφήτης etc.)
of the Muses is very common (Sens 1997: 156).

1382 Πιερίδων: Pieria, the wooded coastal region north of Mt Olympus,
was the birthplace of the Muses (Hes. *Theog.* 53) and is closely associated
with Orpheus (1.31–4).   **πανατρεκές** 'exactly [as I repeat it]', adverbial
neuter.   **ὀμφήν** is often used of a divine voice, and here it is a synonym
of φάτις, 'story [imparted by a divine voice]'.

1383 Cf. 1031. The story of the carrying of the *Argo* excites even the poet who enthusiastically addresses his heroes; the informality of ὦ marks his emotional involvement (contrast Giangrande 1968: 55).   ἀνάκτων: probably 'gods', rather than just 'kings', cf. 1389, 1773, 2.1223, 3.366; at 1411 Orpheus addresses the Hesperides as ἄνασσαι.

1384 ἦι βίηι, ἦι ἀρετῆι: the asyndeton, assonance and awkward rhythm (correption followed by hiatus) all contribute to the sense of the poet's excitement.   θῖνας ἐρήμους ' desert sand-dunes', cf. Pind. *Pyth.* 4.26 νώ-| των ὕπερ γαίας ἐρήμων. Call. fr. 602 (cf. 1309–36n.) refers to the 'stretching dunes' of this area, and Ps.-Scylax 109.3 places 'Dunes of Heracles' between Euhesperides and the Syrtis.

1385 μεταχρονίην: cf. 952n.   ἄγεσθε is best taken as an unaugmented imperfect. The transmitted ἄγεσθαι would be an example of the verb of a subordinate clause attracted into the infinitive in indirect speech (Smyth §2631), but may have arisen from a misunderstanding of ἄγεσθε.

1386 Cf. 1375–6: the Argonauts carry out Peleus' instructions to the letter.   δυοκαίδεκα πάντα 'for a full twelve ... '.

1387–8 The description of the Argonauts' sufferings is beyond any poet, cf. Call. *h.* 1.92–3, 'Who could sing of Zeus's deeds? No one.' γε μέν marks an opposition (Denniston 387): '[this is what you did], *but* who could tell ... ?'.

1389–90 ἔμπεδον 'truly, assuredly'.   οἷον ... ἔργον '[given] what a deed they accomplished', a common use of οἷον, which offers an exclamatory justification for the preceding assertion.

1390–2 'Far further forward, with great joy at the waters of Lake Triton, as they had been carrying it, just so did they enter [the waters] and set it down from their stout shoulders.' The mannered word order and the ὡς ... ὥς correlative pair are further markers of the poet's vivid imagining of this heroic action; Fränkel's suggestion, however, to transpose 1391 and 1392 deserves serious consideration.   ἀσπασίως, as often, refers to the pleasure that attends the end of an ordeal, cf. 1781n.   Τριτωνίδος ὕδασι λίμνης: cf. 1311n.   εἰσβάντες: in other contexts, 'embarking' would be a regular sense, and the choice of this word marks the paradox of what happens: the Argonauts carry, rather than drag, their boat into the lake.

1393 Cf. *Il.* 17.725–6. The comparison suggests the frenzy of rabies-infected dogs; raging thirst affects both infected dogs and those they have bitten, and it is not clear that a link had been drawn already by Ap.'s time between the bite of rabid dogs and human 'hydrophobia'; see Baumann 1928, Merlen 1971: 70–81.

1394–5 Lake Triton contained salt water and was undrinkable.   ἐπί ...
ἔκειτο 'lay on/oppressed [them]', with the following datives giving the
reason for their thirst; others understand '[thirst] was added to their
[suffering]', but this is not the normal meaning of the compound verb.
γάρ is here unusually delayed to third position, but this is well paralleled in
high poetry (Denniston 96).

1396–1460 The Garden of the Hesperides ('the daughters of Evening')
was usually placed, together with Atlas, in the extreme west, but Ap. places
it, like Lake Triton, near Euhesperides/Berenice; Ps.-Scylax 108.4 has a
rich description of the vegetation of the garden, which he however places
near Cyrene; see further Stucchi 1976a, Shipley 2011: 189, *LIMC* s.v.
Hesperides, Fowler 2013: 291–9. A very different tradition placed the
Garden in the far north among the Hyperboreans, cf. Apollod. *Bibl.*
2.5.11. Lucan has used this passage in his account of the Garden at *BC*
9.355–67.

1396 ἱερὸν πέδον: the Garden is imagined as a sanctuary, with the
Hesperides as cultic attendants, cf. Virg. *Aen.* 4.484–6.   Λάδων: this is
the only text to give the dragon of the Hesperides a name. 'Ladon' is most
plausibly connected with the (underground and/or Underworld) river
Λάθων or Λήθων which was believed to flow in the area, cf. Strabo 17.3.20,
Lucan, *BC* 9.355, Hunter 1993: 31, Ottone 2002: 332–5, *LIMC* s.v. Ladon
I, Ogden 2013: 33–40. The brutal, but unnarrated, killing of Ladon
contrasts with the earlier detailed description of the lulling to sleep of
the Colchian serpent; in Greek art 'Ladon seems always to be shown alive',
whereas in the Roman period he is often 'lifeless, his head hanging limply'
(*LIMC* s.v. Ladon I, 179).

1397 εἰσέτι που χθιζόν 'until yesterday (as it were)', i.e. very recently,
cf. 1436. This seems better than to take που, as at 557 (where see n.), as
an authorial refusal of omniscience (so Cuypers 2005: 45) or as marking a
conclusion drawn by the Argonauts themselves (Fränkel); 1457 shows
yet another nuanced use of this particle. χθιζόν here functions as the
adverb χθές, cf. *Il.* 19.195.   παγχρύσεα ῥύετο μῆλα varies Hes. *Theog.*
335 παγχρύσεα μῆλα φυλάσσει. Stesichorus, *SLG* S8 (= *Geryoneis* fr. 10
Finglass) may have made the homes of the Hesperides παγχρύσεα.

1398 Ἄτλαντος: Atlas is associated with the singing Hesperides as early as
Hes. *Theog.* 517–18, cf. Eur. *Hipp.* 742–51; the Hesperides were in fact
often identified as Atlas' daughters. Atlas and the Atlas mountains were,
like the Hesperides, more usually placed far to the west.   χθόνιος 'born
from the earth', as in one sense all Libyan snakes were (cf. 1513–17); the
word, however, also activates the Underworld associations of the name

Ladon (1396n.). Σ cite 'Peisander' (*FGrHist* 16 F8 = Peisander of Camira fr. dub. 3 Davies) for the birth of the snake ἀπὸ τῆς γῆς, but Hesiod made it the child of Keto and Phorkys (*Theog.* 335), whereas Pherecydes (*FGrHist* 3 F16b) seems to have made its parents Typhon and Echidna. The final syllable of χθόνιος is lengthened in arsis.

1399 ποίπνυον 'worked, busied themselves'. If the verb was understood as a synonym of διακονεῖν (cf. 1113n.), this would suit the sense of the Garden as a sanctuary with attendants.   **ἀείδουσαι**: the only example in *Arg.* of ἀειδ– in the present tense with a long first syllable; there is one apparent Homeric example (*Od.* 17.519), but the phenomenon is common elsewhere in Hellenistic poetry. Beautiful singing is a characteristic of the Hesperides as early as Hes. *Theog.* 275, 518, cf. Eur. *HF* 394 ὑμνῳδούς τε κόρας.

1400 The text of the opening part of the verse must be considered uncertain: the variant δὴ τότε δὴ τῆμος is impossible, but τῆμος is a favourite Apollonian word.   **Ἡρακλῆϊ**: securing the golden apples of the Hesperides was traditionally Heracles' last (or penultimate) labour, after which his immortality on Olympus was not long delayed, cf. Pherecydes, *FGrHist* 3 F16–17, Diod. Sic. 4.26.2–4, Bond on Eur. *HF* 394–9. The killing of the dragon was a traditional part of the labour; Panyassis fr. 10 Davies, Soph. *Tr.* 1099–1100, Eur. *HF* 397–9, Verbanck-Gilis 1998.   **δαϊχθείς** 'pierced' [by Heracles' arrows], the aor. pass. participle of δαΐζω.

1401–2 μήλειον βέβλητο ποτὶ στύπος 'it lay dying [lit. had been struck] against the trunk of the apple-tree'; for the preposition see LSJ s.v. πρός C I 2. Ogden 2013a: 38 understands στύπος as 'stump' ('Heracles evidently having cut the tree down'), but cf. 1428, 1.1197.   **οἰόθι δ' ἄκρη | οὐρὴ ἔτι σπαίρεσκεν** 'only the tip of its tail still writhed'; with ἄκρηι | οὐρῆι the subject of the verb will be the dragon. σπαίρεσκεν is the expected verb here (cf. 874, *Il.* 12.203 of a snake carried by an eagle); the transmitted σκαίρεσκεν, 'danced', seems overly frenetic in the context and is not adequately defended by ἀνασκαίρειν of a warrior hit by arrows at Quint. Smyrn. 8.320–1.

1403 ἄχρις ἐπ' ἄκνηστιν 'all along/to the very tip of the spine'. ἄκνηστις occurs only here in *Arg.* and only once in Homer, *Od.* 10.161, where the correct reading is probably κατὰ κνῆστιν; the form was discussed by Aristarchus and probably grammarians before him. The Homeric context, Odysseus' spearing of a huge deer on Circe's island, suggests a parallelism between that deer, described as δεινοῖο πελώρου (line 168) and μέγα θηρίον (171), and the serpent slain by Heracles' arrows. The actions of both

Heracles and Odysseus (cf. lines 174–5) save their comrades from death; cf. further 1458n.

1404 That Heracles dipped his arrows in the venom of the Lernaean hydra after he had killed it was a familiar element of the story of Heracles' adventures, cf. Soph. *Tr.* 573–4. Lerna is on the coast of the gulf south of Argos.   χόλον 'venom'.

1405 πυθομένοισιν reminded Σ of the etymology of the 'Pythian' serpent slain by Apollo (cf. *HHAp.* 363–74); the intense heat of the sun 'rotted' that dead snake (*HHAp.* 369–74), and in the context of the burning Libyan desert, Ap. may well have the *Homeric Hymn* in mind here.   τερσαίνοντο 'were withering', lit. 'drying out'. This seems the best explanation of a very puzzling verb: the flies which came to feed on the gore were unable to drink and so were killed off by the poison. Livrea suggests that there is a reference to the believed spontaneous generation of flies from the combination of liquid and heat in the corpse, but it is very hard to see how this can be derived from the text. No suggested emendation carries any plausibility.

1406–7 evoke and vary the grieving of Medea and her maids at 1303–4: the 'beautiful singing' (1399) of the Hesperides has turned to lamentation. Many fourth-century vases show the Hesperides attending to the snake and giving it food and water (cf. *LIMC* s.vv. Hesperides, Ladon), and this close bond is reflected in their grief at what has happened. The Hesperides place their hands on their heads in a gesture of grief which is very familiar in pictorial representations, cf., e.g., Alexiou 1974: fig. 1, Garland 1985: 29 with fig. 7. The epithets in 1407 indeed suggest the pictorialism of art (see next note); several vase-paintings precisely highlight the white flesh of the Hesperides.

1408–9 ἄφνω ... αἶψα ... ἐσσυμένως: the emphasis on haste as the narrative resumes intensifies the sense of the previous description as an ecphrastic 'pause'. Here again, the speed of the disappearance reminds us of a mirage: were the Hesperides really ever there, or did the thirst-crazed Argonauts imagine them? κατaυτόθι 'on the spot'.   νώσατο: a contracted form of νοήσατο; such Ionic forms are common in Herodotus and poetry, cf. Call. fr. 353, Gow on Theocr. 12.35.

1410 τέρα: a contracted neuter plural, for τέραα (cf. *Od.* 12.394) or τέρεα (Hdt. 8.37.2).   †τὰς δέ σφι†: if correct, this would have to mean '[exhorted] them on their [i.e. the Argonauts'] behalf'. τὰς δέ σφε as a compound accusative might be defended by τὴν δέ μιν, which is transmitted at 3.741 but commonly emended away. E's στάς seems very weak. παρηγορέεσκε 'exhorted, sought to win over'.

1411 ὦ is postponed in a solemn address to divinities, cf., e.g., *PMG* 1018b.5, Call. *h.* 4.325, Giangrande 1968: 54, Harder 2012: 2.775.

1412–14 As part of their encomiastic strategy, prayers regularly seek to cover all possible 'bases': the current location of the god (e.g. Theocr. 1.123–6), what name the god wishes to be addressed by (cf. καλέεσθε), or (as here) the very identity of the god, cf. 1597–9, Norden 1913: 144–7, Burkert 1985: 74–5, Pulleyn 1997: 100–15; Orpheus is a 'religious expert' who understands such things. Orpheus' division is into 'heavenly' (i.e. Olympian) goddesses, chthonic powers, and then – in place of a generalized 'earthly' divinities – he specifies local nymphs of the kind the Argonauts have just experienced and who indeed identified themselves (1322n.) as χθόνιοι. As it turns out, the Hesperides are 'tree nymphs' (of a kind). Σ see here a division into three classes of nymphs (cf. 1149–51n.), but that cannot be right. οἰοπόλοι: cf. 1322n. The story of the Hesperides and their apples was, at least later, rationalized as the story of a shepherd called Δράκων and his sheep (μῆλα), cf. Diod. Sic. 4.26–7, 'Palaephatus' 18, 'Agroitas' *FGrHist* 762 F3, Ottone 2002: 321–36; it is not impossible that Ap. knew such a rationalization, and the possibility that the Hesperides are οἰοπόλοι may allude to this.

1414 Orpheus senses that they are nymphs and uses the fact that all nymphs are descended from Ocean (Hes. *Theog.* 346–66) and have a special connection with water to press his case.

1416 χύσιν ὕδατος: the same phrase appears in this metrical position at Arat. *Phain.* 393.

1417–18 ἀπό . . . λωφήσομεν: tmesis.   αἰθομένην ἄμοτον 'insatiably burning'; the D-scholia gloss adverbial ἄμοτον at *Il.* 4.440 as ἀπληρώτως.

1418–21 Such promises of *post factum* reward are very common in literary prayers, cf. 1704–5, *Od.* 12.346–7 (a perverted form of the idea). εἰλαπίνας 'ritual feasts', 'feasts accompanied by sacrifices'.   εὐμενέοντες recalls the opening εὔφρονες of the goddesses, to mark the promised reciprocity.

1422 λισσόμενος: the final syllable is lengthened in arsis at the caesura. ἀδινῆι: cf. 3.616n. This adjective is often associated with lamentation (29, 1.269, *Il.* 24.747 etc.), and Rengakos 1994: 35 understands it here as 'piteous', but, despite ἐλέαιρον, Orpheus' speech seems rather 'pressing, fervent', and the commonly intensifying force of the adjective, cf. πυκνός, *LfgrE* s.v., justifies such an interpretation. See further Fantuzzi 2008: 238.

1423 ἐγγύθεν: 'nearby' could be construed either with the verb or the participle, but in either case the sense is weak. Vian understands the adverb temporally, 'soon, without delay'; ἐγγύθι δ' ἠώς at *Il.* 10.251 is an inadequate defence, but Ap. does seem to use adverbs of place temporally (cf. Vian II 121–2), and this may be the best explanation.   **ἐξανέτειλαν** 'caused to shoot up'.

1424 ποίην here refers to the low 'shoots' which will eventually become trees, rather than to 'grass'.   **γε μέν** marks the next in a sequence of events, cf. 1466; the anaphora ποίην ... ποίης ('from the shoots') also draws attention to the ordered sequence of the metamorphosis.

1425 ἔρνεα 'young trees, saplings'.

1427–8 Hesiod perhaps named the Hesperides as Aigle, Erytheia, and Hesperethousa (fr. dub. 360, cf. Apollod. *Bibl.* 2.5.11); Erytheia (here Erytheis) was the mother of Erytion, slain by Heracles in Stesichorus' *Geryoneis.* Just as the number of Hesperides varies widely, so many other names, often suggestive of brightness or gleaming light, are known from vase-paintings; *LIMC* s.v. Hesperides 395, 406.

1427 is structured as an elegant chiasm.   **αἴγειρος** '(black) poplar'. Plin. *HN* 37.38 preserves a myth in which the Hesperides in North Africa are like the Heliades (603–4n.) and collect amber which drips from poplar trees into a lake called Electrum ('Amber').   **ἔγεντο:** this syncopated form first occurs in Hesiod (cf. West on *Theog.* 199), and is common in Hellenistic poetry.

1428 ἰτείης ἱερὸν στύπος: the circumlocution varies the simple nouns of the previous verse.

1429 οἷαι ἔσαν, τοῖαι πάλιν ἔμπεδον αὔτως 'back again in the same certain form they had before'; for ἔμπεδον, 'certainly, palpably', cf. 854n.

1430 θάμβος περιώσιον: the so-called 'accusative in apposition to the sentence', cf. 3.602n.

1431 ἀμειβομένη χατέοντας 'answering them in their need'.

1432–49 Aigle's response mixes bitterness and sarcasm in laying emphasis upon the bestial and comic aspects of Heracles (whom she cannot recognize); see Hunter 1993: 30. There is a witty disjunction between the style of her speech and how we imagine this lovely tree-nymph to look.

1432 μέγα πάμπαν 'altogether great, very great indeed'.

1433 ὁ κύντατος 'that scoundrel'; the Hesperides do not know who Heracles is, but Aigle's description of him will leave us in no doubt.

Cf. further 1441-3n.   ἀπούρας 'having deprived', a Homeric aorist
participle of uncertain etymology, cf. 3.173-5n. The postponement of
the genitive ζωῆς momentarily evokes the idea that Heracles stole, rather
than killed, the serpent, just as he carried off Cerberus from the
Underworld.

1434 θεάων: the apples were traditionally given by the Earth to Hera at
her marriage to Zeus, and according to Pherecydes (*FGrHist* 3 F16c) she
then planted them 'in the garden of the gods near Atlas'; Stesichorus (*SLG*
S8 = *Geryoneis* fr. 10 Finglass) perhaps placed the Hesperides on a 'very
beautiful island of the gods'. Aigle seems here to refer to the apples as the
joint possession of Hera and other Olympian goddesses, but the rhetorical
point is clear: Heracles' action was both brutal and impious.

1435 The expression of grief evokes some of the most familiar laments for
the dead; cf. the parody at Ar. *Frogs* 1353 ἐμοὶ δ' ἄχε' ἄχεα κατέλιπε.

1437 δέμας: Campbell 1971: 423 suggested μένος, but Heracles' body did
no doubt seem ὀλοώτατος to the lovely nymphs.   **βλοσυρῶι** 'terrible,
fear-inspiring', cf., e.g., *Il.* 15.607-8, [Hes.], *Aspis* 145-8. Callimachus
uses the superlative of the gaze of a lion (*h.* 6.52), that animal with
which Heracles is most associated.   **ὑπέλαμπε:** cf. 16-17n.

1438 ἀμφὶ ... ἔστο 'he wore', a pluperfect middle of ἀμφιέννυμι.

1439 ὠμόν, ἀδέψητον 'untreated, untanned'; the implication is that
Heracles skinned the lion himself and then put on the skin, as at
[Theocr.] 25.275-9. The words also suggest that Heracles himself is as
'uncouth' as the garment he wears. [Theocr.] 25 also plays with the idea
of someone who does not recognize Heracles, and there may be an
intertextual connection between this passage and the Theocritean
poem.   **ἐλαίης:** in [Theocr.] 25 the club is made of wild olive (lines
208-10, 257); elsewhere the club is often said also to have knots of metal
embedded in it, cf. 1.1196.

1440 πέλωρ seems a strange word to use of the Hesperides' beloved
dragon (cf. *HHAp.* 374 of the Pythian serpent), but the repetition from
πελωρίου in 1438 stresses (again) Heracles' affinity to the bestial world.

1441-3 vary 1393-5 (πίδακα μαστεύεσκον ~ ὕδωρ ἐξερέων); κἀκεῖνος points
the parallelism. In its only other appearance in *Arg.*, καρχαλέος is used of
dogs (3.1058), and this also binds the passages together: Heracles ὁ
κύντατος (1433) is as 'dog-like' as the Argonauts (1393-4). Lucan uses
these passages on δίψη in his description of the effect of the bite of the
διψάς (*BC* 9.749-50).   **ἤλυθε δ' οὖν:** the narrative resumes (cf. ἤλυθε in
1436) after what amounts to a parenthetic ecphrasis; for δ' οὖν marking

such a resumption see Denniston 463–4. **κἀκεῖνος**: cf. 1731n. **ἅ τε χθόνα πεζὸς ὁδεύων** 'as you would expect of someone travelling on foot across the land'.

1442 Despite her bitterness, Aigle's language is very 'choice': καρχαλέος παίφασσε juxtaposes two words which each only occur once in Homer. **δίψηι καρχαλέος**, 'rough/harsh with thirst', repeats a unique Homeric verse-beginning (*Il.* 21.541), where the scholia explain that 'great thirst makes the tongue dry and rough', cf. Virg. *G.* 3.434 *asper siti*, Rengakos 1994: 101. **παίφασσε**: the D-scholia on *Il.* 2.450 gloss this verb as 'rushing enthusiastically' (cf. Hesychius π108), and 'rushed over, scoured' is probably the meaning here, cf. ἀΐσσοντες in 1393; the verb was also understood in antiquity as 'look around everywhere, scan in all directions' and, though ἰδέσθαι does not prove the case, this sense (or a combination of them) is also possible (Rengakos 1994: 124–5).

1443 τὸ μὲν οὔ ποθι μέλλεν ἰδέσθαι 'that [i.e. water] he was not likely to see anywhere', a sarcastic reference to the desert all around them; it is part of the aura of uncertainty surrounding the whole meeting with the Hesperides (cf. 1408–9n.) that, despite the sacred apple-tree and the trees into which the nymphs turn, there is no visible source of fresh water. μέν is picked up by δέ in the following verse.

1444–6 As one of his services to mankind (and here to the Argonauts), Heracles was often associated with the creation of rivers and springs, cf., e.g., Pausanias 2.32.4 (Troezen), *CEG* II 822 (a fountain dedicated to Heracles). We do not know whether there was in fact a spring near Euhesperides named for Heracles, but everything about Aigle's narrative suggests an *aition*. Diod. Sic. 4.17–18 reports that Heracles civilized Libya and brought the land under cultivation.

1444 ἥδε functions as a kind of demonstrative, 'but here ... '; we may imagine that Aigle points in the appropriate direction.

1445 Aigle seeks to minimize Heracles' achievement and, at the same time, likens him to the savage Cyclops, cf. *Od.* 9.339 (the Cyclops brings all his flock into the cave) ἤ τι ὀϊσάμενος ἢ καὶ θεὸς ὣς ἐκέλευσεν. ἢ καί regularly marks the more likely or privileged of two alternatives (cf. 202–5n.): in Aigle's view, it is unlikely that her visitor had the intelligence to find the spring himself.

1446 The expressive dactyls may mimic the speed of Heracles' action and of the bubbling up of the spring. Many stories told of springs created or found in this way, but Ap. seems here indebted to Arat. *Phain.* 219–20 (the creation of Hippocrene) ἀλλ' Ἵππος μιν [sc. Helicon] ἔτυψε, τὸ δ' ἀθρόον αὐτόθεν ὕδωρ | ἐξέχυτο πληγῆι προτέρου ποδός. The story of the creation of

Bourina at Theocr. 7.6–7 may also be relevant: note ἐνερεισάμενος ~ ἐρείσας (1447) and the poplars and elms of line 8 (~ 1427). This passage seems in turn to have been imitated at Lyc. *Alex.* 245–8 (the spring created by Achilles' leap from his ship on to the beach at Troy). Cf. further 1454n. λὰξ ποδί, 'kicking with the foot', is a Homeric doubling (e.g. *Il.* 10.158, *Od.* 15.45).

1448 ῥωγάδος ἐκ πέτρης 'from the broken rock', cf. Theocr. 24.95.

1449 νηδύν accusative of respect. **φορβάδι ἶσος ἐπιπροπεσών:** Heracles is to be imagined, not as flat on his stomach, but probably on his knees with his hands on the ground and upper chest pressed low to the ground (cf. 1447), to enable him to get at the water coming out of a cleft low in the rock; this is not exactly the position adopted by cattle to drink from a pond or stream, but a little zoological inaccuracy is a small price to pay to cast Heracles once again with the dumb animals. Vian prefers to punctuate after ἶσος, so that the comparison refers not to Heracles' position, but rather to his filling of his great belly; this seems to make the text far less vivid, and two imitations in Nicander (*Ther.* 340–2, *Alex.* 495–6) also suggest the traditional punctuation.

1450 ἀσπαστόν 'gladly', an adverbial neuter, cf. [Hes.] *Aspis* 42. Others understand it as an adjective with πίδακα, but this seems rather understated for the plight in which the Argonauts find themselves.

1451 τῆι, 'in that direction', picks up ἵνα. **ὄφρ'** 'until'.

1452–6 The Argonauts are compared to ants, which do not figure in Homeric simile, and flies, which do (cf. *Il.* 2.469–71, 16.641–3); both would be quite at home in the desert in which the heroes find themselves (cf. 1405). The two similes are carefully varied and matched, both in vocabulary and word order, with an attention to stylistic detail typical of Hellenistic poetry; see further Faerber 1932: 22–3.

1452 χηραμόν: cf. 1298–9n.

1453 γειομόροι 'which dwell in/work the land', cf. 1.1214 (an ox), Harder 2012: 2.216; the adjective evokes the busy activity of a swarm of ants. The variant γειοτόμοι and Vian's γειοτόροι, 'earth-piercing', are not impossible, but may be thought more obvious than γειομόροι. It may only be a curious coincidence that Philip, *AP* 9.438 (= *GP* 2987–94) describes how ants were stealing honey: βωλοτόμοι μύρμηκες, ὁ γῆς στρατός, ἡνίκα τένδον | γειομόρου μελιχρὴν σμηνοδόκου χάριτα κτλ. **ὁμιλαδόν:** cf. *Il.* 16.641, 644, where ὁμίλεον is used of warriors busying themselves around a corpse and they are compared to flies around milk-pails.

1454 λίβα 'a drop'; the nominative *λίψ does not actually occur. Call. *h.* 2.112 describes the water which 'bees' bring to Demeter as bubbling up πίδακος ἐξ ἱερῆς ὀλίγη λιβὰς ἄκρον ἄωτον; immediately before Apollo has kicked (ποδί τ' ἤλασεν) Phthonos out of the way, cf. Heracles' creation of the spring at 1446. This passage of the Libyan episode thus interestingly shares language and motifs with the *sphragis* of a Callimachean poem celebrating Cyrene and its god; if there is an intertextual relationship, the scattering of the shared material would normally suggest Ap. as the borrower.   **πεπτηυῖαι** 'falling [on the honey]', a perfect participle of πίπτειν, cf. 3.973, Campbell on 3.321. This form could also derive from πτήσσω, but that verb hardly makes sense for flies. At *Il.* 18.552 and 19.226 forms of ἐπήτριμοι are associated with forms of πίπτειν.

1455 μεμάασιν 'rage furiously', from μέμονα; more usually this is followed by an infinitive.   **ἐπήτριμοι**, 'in a swarm', varies ὁμιλαδόν, as at 937–8 it varies ἀγεληδόν.

1456 δινεύεσκον: the spondaic ending matches εἱλίσσονται in the first verse of the simile.

1457–60 As often in Homer (see de Jong 1987, Beck 2012: 47–56), an unnamed observer (τις) comments on the situation which has unfolded. Ap. here innovates in three ways from the Homeric model. που shows the narrator imagining his characters, just as his readers do; they are 'real', and the aorist, rather than the Homeric frequentative, emphasizes that this was actually said: it is not just the sort of thing which might have been said (cf. also 2.144, and contrast the effect of the plural verb at Hdt. 5.1.3). Finally, the τις speech here leads to a development in the action, whereas in Homer, as also elsewhere in *Arg.* (cf. 2.144–53, where see Matteo's n.), such speeches comment on, but do not affect, the narrative.

1457 διεροῖς 'wet', cf. Williams on Call. *h.* 2.3, Rengakos 1994: 69–70.

1458 ὦ πόποι ἦ begins a τις speech at *Il.* 2.272 in praise of the 'countless good things' which Odysseus has done for the Greeks; in saving his comrades (cf. 1403n.), Heracles proves more successful than Odysseus.

1459 εἴ πως with the optative expresses a wish, 'if only … '.

1460 δι' ἠπείροιο more naturally goes with κιόντες than with στείχοντα, cf. 1482.

1461–2 'As they [i.e. all the Argonauts] conversed, those who were fitted for this task leapt up and separated themselves off in different directions to search [for him]'. This seems the best interpretation of a difficult sentence: ἀμειβομένων is a genitive absolute (cf. 2.449), and ἦσαν is to be understood after οἵ τ' (Ruijgh 1971: 942). Alternatively, ἀμειβομένων refers to the same subset as οἵ τ' ἄρμενοι, either 'of those who conversed, the fittest … ', or 'as those who were fittest … conversed, they … ', with the genitive absolute taking the place of a nominative participle, for which cf. K–G II 110. It seems, however, more natural that all the Argonauts should express the wish to find Heracles, but then only a small group act upon this wish.   **ἄρμενοι**: a syncopated aorist middle participle of ἀραρίσκω, LSJ s.v. B V.   **ἀναΐξας**: the Argonauts are on the ground drinking, so those who go in search of Heracles must 'leap up'.   **ἐρεείνειν**: infinitive of purpose (Smyth §2008).

1463 ἐπηλίνδητ' 'had been effaced', lit. 'had been rolled over', a pluperfect passive of ἐπαλινδέομαι. Schneider suggested ἀπηλίνδητ', as a more fitting compound.

1464–5 The Boreads had wings on their ankles and (perhaps also) on their temples, cf. 1.211–23; they contribute not just speed, but also the possibility of an aerial view in the search for Heracles.

1466–7 Euphemos, who will soon play a very important role in the foundation narrative of Cyrene, was 'the most swift-footed' and could skim over water (1.179–84); Ap. follows Pindar (*Pyth.* 4.44–6) in making him the son of Poseidon and Europa, daughter of Tityos, but Hesiod (fr. 253) named his mother as Mekionike, the daughter of the Spartan river Eurotas (Hirschberger 2004: 452–4). Lynceus was the son of Aphareus and brother of his fellow Argonaut Idas (cf. Theocritus 22); he was said to be able to see even beneath the earth (1.153–5, picking up Pind. *Nem.* 10.62–3), and his sharp vision plays an important role in the poetic tradition as early as *Cypria* fr. 13 Davies. It is also important that Lynceus' speed is emphasized in the tradition, cf. *Cypria* fr. 13.2 Davies ποσὶν ταχέεσσι πεποιθώς (which is precisely said of Euphemos here), Pind. *Nem.* 10.63, Theocr. 22.139. Both Lynceus and Kanthos of Euboea here make their first entries in the poem since the catalogue of Book 1. The latter's death in Libya is already foretold in the Catalogue (1.77–85), but we know virtually nothing of the links to Polyphemos which prompted him to join the search (Vian I 45–6); the different style in which he is introduced here marks him as the one searcher without supernatural powers, and also the one who will not return.   **ὀξέα**: adverbial neuter.   **βαλεῖν** must depend upon πίσυνος, 'trusting in [his ability] to cast his glance … '; such a construction is very rare, but it is eased by the fact that πίσυνος has already been followed by the expected dative.   **μετὰ σφίσιν** 'along with them', LSJ s.v. μετά B II.

1468 αἶσα θεῶν: cf. 1.79–80 of Kanthos' fate.   **ἠνορέη**: although Kanthos' purpose was to find out about Polyphemos, only heroic bravery would allow someone to set off into the trackless desert.

1469 ἀπηλεγέως: a favourite word of Ap.; here perhaps 'without reserve', i.e. 'in full truth', cf. 2.845, 3.19, Rengakos 1994: 53–4.

1470 It was the Argonauts themselves, not Heracles, who had abandoned Polyphemos, son of Eilatos (cf. 1.1283 λιπόντες), but Kanthos quite naturally (though wrongly) assumes that Heracles and Polyphemos travelled on together after they had been left behind in Mysia, as the Hylas-narrative implies a special friendship between the two (cf. 1.1240–2). **μέμβλετο γάρ οἱ**: Ap. has moved this phrase from its Homeric position at the head of a verse (*Il.* 21.156).

1471 οὗ ἕθεν 'his own, of himself', cf. 1.362; this double genitive form occurs first in *Arg.*

1472–7 Some details of Polyphemos' future were foretold by Glaukos at 1.1321–3 and by the narrator at 1.1345–7. After the loss of Hylas, Heracles rushed off looking for him, but Polyphemos at first stayed in the area and (like a good Greek) founded a city, Kios (mod. Gemlik), named from the river which flowed there into the Propontis (Barrington 52 E4), cf. 1. 1346 ἐπώνυμον ἄστυ.

1472 ἐπικλεὲς ἄστυ varies περικλεὲς ἄστυ at 1.1322; the former epithet occurs first here.

1473 νόστου κηδοσύνῃσιν 'out of yearning for the expedition', cf. 739n.

1475 The Chalybes were a fierce tribe renowned as ironworkers and/or the inventors of ironworking, cf. 2.374–6, 1001–8, Call. fr. 110.47–9 with Harder 2012: 2.819. Aesch. *PV* 716 describes them as 'unfriendly to strangers', and this will help to explain Polyphemos' fate. Ap. clearly places them, as most sources do, on the south coast of the Black Sea between Sinope and Trabizon (Barrington 87 BC 3–4), which implies that Polyphemos walked some 600 km from where he had been abandoned (τῆλε δι' ἠπείροιο). The Chalybes were, however, sometimes placed in Scythia (Aesch. *Sept.* 728, *PV* 714–16, Σ 1.1321–3), and thus ἀγχιάλων probably evokes a disagreement about their location. Σ 1470 cites Nymphodorus for the story of Polyphemos' death 'fighting against the Chalybes'. If this is N. of Amphipolis, whose 'Barbarian Customs' probably belongs to the early third century (*RE* 17.1623–5), then that might be Ap.'s source; if, however, it is N. of Syracuse (*FHG* 11 380), then this will not be Ap.'s source, as that writer seems to belong to the end of the century. **καί** is postponed, 'and there … '.

1476 βλωθρὴν ἀχερωΐδα 'a tall (?) white poplar'; the meaning of this epithet of trees was disputed in antiquity, but 'tall' seems the likeliest sense here, *LfgrE* s.v. Ap. recalls a repeated Homeric simile in which a falling warrior is compared to τις δρῦς ... ἠ᾽ ἀχερωίς | ἠὲ πίτυς βλωθρή (*Il.* 13.389–90, 16.482–3); the echo of Homeric death makes this tree a very appropriate grave-marker. Pausanias 5.14.2 connects ἀχερωίς with the Underworld river Acheron and also with Heracles, Polyphemos' friend. This σῆμα is proof of the narrative, but also a typical challenge to the reader: if you make the very long trip to the Black Sea, can you find this poplar 'a little way from the sea'?

1477–80 The last we and the Argonauts see of Heracles is merely a possible glimpse, visible only to the sharp-sighted Lynceus, as he disappears 'far away across the boundless land'; we are to understand that Heracles is on his way to Olympus, just as in the Underworld Odysseus found only an εἴδωλον of the hero (*Od.* 11.601–26). This is the last of the several 'visions' in the Libyan desert which may or may not be mirages. Virgil's famous imitation of this passage to describe Aeneas' sighting of Dido in the Underworld (*Aen.* 6.452–6) may help with some of the details of the simile, but Virgil himself will have innovated on his model.

1478 μοῦνον: choice between this and μοῦνος is not easy. The latter stresses that Heracles was so far away that even Lynceus was unsure whether he really saw him. With μοῦνον, which is preferred here, the stress is on the distance Heracles has now placed between himself and the Argonauts, and indeed us also; μοῦνον also seems to sit better with the following expression of distance. Whichever text Virgil read, he innovated by giving Dido a partner in her pain (*Aen.* 6.473–4): she was not 'alone'.   **ἀπειρεσίης τηλοῦ χθονός**: the genitive is loosely attached to the adverb, cf. Ar. *Clouds* 138 τηλοῦ ... τῶν ἀγρῶν, where Dover ad loc. compares the use of πόρρω with the genitive (LSJ s.v. πρόσω B I).   **εἴσατο** 'thought, believed', from εἴδω, cf. 1.718, 1024, Rengakos 1994: 75.

1479 νέωι ἐνὶ ἤματι 'on the first day of the month', when the moon offers no reflected light at all; Arat. *Phain.* 781–2 suggests that it is worth looking for weather-signs from the moon only on the third or fourth day of the month. The last day of the lunar month was ἔνη καὶ νέα (Dover on Ar. *Clouds* 1131), and the first day, which is here evoked by Ap.'s expression, was νουμηνία, cf. also Pl. *Laws* 8.849b1–2 μηνὸς τῆι νέαι, 'on the first <day> of the month'. The apparent difficulty of Ap.'s expression has led some to see a reference here to the morning, when the outline of the moon is often still visible, but 'new day' would be a very surprising way of expressing that; Fränkel emended to νέης, 'on the day of the new <moon>', but that is unnecessary. For the counting of days in the lunar month cf. Arat. *Phain.* 778–818.

1480 The aorists are gnomic.   **ἐπαχλύουσαν** 'obscured', presumably by clouds, although the word would not be inappropriate to the faint image of the new moon itself. Ap. may have in mind the description of obscured stars at Arat. *Phain.* 893–906 (where forms of ἀχλύς appear three times).

1481–2 echo and prove false the hopes of 1459–60.   μυθήσατο is here followed by μή with the future infinitive, a construction familiar from oaths (Smyth §2716); Lynceus' news amounts to a strong assertion or promise.   στείχοντα refers to Heracles, as at 1460.

1484 The episode of the Hesperides and Heracles ends with a closural spondaic verse.   μεταμώνια 'in vain', with a pun on the etymology from ἄνεμος, which is very appropriate to the sons of Boreas, cf. Apollonius Soph. 112.3 Bekker, 3.1121n.

1485–1536 The paired deaths of Kanthos (cf. 1466–7n.) and Mopsus match those of the other seer Idmon and the steersman Tiphys, killed respectively by a wild boar and a 'brief illness', on the outward voyage (2.815–63).

1485 presents the only example of apostrophe by the narrator to one of his characters, rather than to the collective of Argonauts (1383–7, 1773–81). In the *Odyssey* only Eumaeus is apostrophized by the poet, some fifteen times in speech introductions, whereas in the *Iliad*, Patroclus is apostrophized eight times in Book 16 (including line 787 as 'the end of his life appeared'), Menelaos seven times, Achilles once (20.2), and a minor character once (15.582); see Grillo 1988: 59–65. The scholia on *Il.* stress that this form shows the poet's emotional sympathy for the character apostrophized (cf. Σ *Il.* 4.127, 146, 16.692–3, 787), and Ap.'s engagement with the fate of Kanthos and Mopsus was already advertised through a *gnômê* on the human condition when their fates were foreshadowed at 1.82–5.   Κῆρες: cf. 1665n.

1486–8 ἀνήρ | αὐλίτης 'a man of the sheepfold (αὐλή, αὖλις)', i.e. a shepherd; outside the lexicographers, αὐλίτης otherwise occurs only at Soph. fr.502.1R, but it is here a further marker of the fact that we have now left behind the 'nothingness' of the Syrtis, contrast 1248–9. Rustling, such as Kanthos attempted, is a familiar feature of the epic–heroic world.   τόφρ' ἑτάροισι | δευομένοις κομίσειας 'while you were wanting to/seeking to bring them to your needy (i.e. hungry) comrades'. For temporal τόφρα cf., e.g., 1617; the optative is best understood as expressing a wish, equivalent to ἐβούλου κομίζειν (Gow 1938, Gow on Theocr. 15.70–1).

1489 λᾶϊ: dat. sing. λᾶας, 'a stone'.   μέν is emphatic, '(not) at all', cf. Denniston 362.   ἀφαυρότερος: cf. *Il.* 15.11 (Hector, having also been hit by a stone) αἷμ' ἐμέων, ἐπεὶ οὔ μιν ἀφαυρότατος βάλ' Ἀχαιῶν, where there is a very weakly attested variant ἀφαυρότερος. The regular sense of ἀφαυρός is

'physically weak' (cf. 1496 κρατερόν τε Κάφαυρον, *LfgrE* s.v.), but some
understand here 'of humbler birth (than Kanthos)', as Hesych. α 8576–
7 glosses the adjective as ταπεινός and the following verses are concerned
with his divine genealogy.

1490 The four-word hexameter, largely consisting of names, continues
the impressive introduction for this grandson of Apollo.   **Λυκωρείοιο:**
Lycoreia was identified with Delphi, whether as the summit of Parnassus
or as a village on the mountain; see Williams on Call. *h.* 2.19. It is noteworthy that that poem gives such prominence to Cyrene, and it is a pity
that we do not know in what context Call. mentioned Lycoreia in *Aitia*
Book 3 (fr. 62).   **Κάφαυρος:** the name seems to resonate punningly with
ἀφαυρότερος. The variant Κάφαυλος seems also to lie behind Hyginus, *Fab.*
14.28, where Kanthos is killed (according to the transmitted text) *a pastore
Cephalione.*

1491–3 Minos' daughter Akakallis, one of whose children is said to have
been Kydon, the eponymous hero of Cretan Kydonia, is used as a key
figure around whom complex legendary links between Crete and North
Africa can gather, cf. Hdt. 4.151, 154–61, Agroitas, *FGrHist* 762 F1–2,
Ottone 2002: 295–320; Battos himself, the founder of Cyrene, was
believed to be of Cretan descent (Hdt. 4.150, 155), and one tradition
made Apollo take the maiden Cyrene to Crete before they came to North
Africa (Agroitas, *FGrHist* 762 F1). A very rich body of myth grew up around
Akakallis: Anton. Lib. 30, for example, tells how Minos tried to rape her
son by Apollo, Miletos, i.e. his own grandson (though he did not know
that), and she was subsequently grandmother to the incestuous Byblis
and Kaunos. The current, and clearly different, story rather resembles
that of Coronis in Pind. *Pyth.* 3, though αἰδοίης makes clear that Akakallis
was blameless.

1491 Cf. *Od.* 11.322–3 (Ariadne, another daughter of Minos who fell out
with her father) κούρην Μίνωος ὀλοόφρονος, ἥν ποτε Θησεύς | ἐκ Κρήτης ἐς
γουνὸν Ἀθηνάων κτλ.; the end of the verse finds a close parallel at Call.
h. 3.190–1 (Britomartis) ἧς ποτε Μίνως | πτοιηθεὶς ὑπ' ἔρωτι κτλ.

1492 ἀπένασσε 'removed to, settled in', from ἀποναίω.   **θεοῦ βαρὺ κῦμα
φέρουσαν:** cf. Pind. *Pyth.* 3.15 (Coronis, also pregnant by Apollo) φέροισα
σπέρμα θεοῦ καθαρόν.   **βαρύ:** the exact resonance is uncertain. Is the
unborn child 'heavy' because its father is divine, or because it is nearly
ready to be born? Cf. Call. *h.* 4.212 (the birth of Apollo) 'τί μητέρα, κοῦρε,
βαρύνεις;'.

1494 The double name (cf. 1513–14) for Akakallis' son may be intended
to be understood, not as a reference to an inconsistency in Ap.'s sources,

but as a Greek name and a local one for the eponymous hero of the Garamantes, a tribe of the deep desert to the south of where the Argonauts find themselves (Hdt. 4.174, 183).   κικλήσκουσιν refers to previous written traditions, but we cannot know to which ones Ap. is referring; Ottone 2002: 312 suggests Agroitas.

1496 Νασάμωνα: the eponymous hero of the Nasamones, a Libyan nomad tribe of the desert south of the Syrtis (Hdt. 4.172, 190).

1497 ῥήνεσσιν 'sheep'. *ῥήν first occurs here and otherwise, outside the lexicographers, only Nic. *Ther.* 453; it is perhaps a back formation from Homeric πολύρρηνος.

1498–1501 present a very rapid narrative of the consequences of Kanthos' death; Ap. does not dwell on how the Argonauts found out what had happened, though the verses suggest that a search-party was sent out to look for him. Textual corruption also obscures the sequence of events.

1499 ἀνάειραν ὀπίσσω: 'raised up <and carried> back' is the most probable interpretation, though 1501 might be thought to suggest that the burial took place away from the main body of the Argonauts.

1500 †πυθόμενοι†, 'having found out', is unmetrical and weak and repetitive after μάθον; πευθόμενοι solves the first but not the second problem. Wifstrand's πυθόμενον, 'rotting', seems to be an unfortunate anticipation of 1530–1, but is not impossible; Giangrande 1973: 45–6 proposed κευθόμενον. Fränkel 1968: 603–5 suggested that μυρόμενοι (1501) actually began 1500, on the pattern of the parallel passage at 2.833–4 (death of Idmon) τὸν δ' ἕταροι ἐπὶ νῆα φέρον ψυχορραγέοντα | ἀχνύμενοι; cf., however, the parallel honours for Mopsus at 1535.

1501 μετὰ σφέας is regularly taken to mean 'to the main body of the Argonauts', but the expression is decidedly odd; μετὰ σφέων (with synizesis) may be worth considering, despite the breach of Naeke's Law. Cf. further 1593.

1502–36 The death and burial of the seer Mopsus, son of Ampyx, is briefly described at Lyc. *Alex.* 881–6, in a passage indebted to *Arg.*

1503 ἀδευκέα was normally explained (*LfgrE* s.v.) as either 'bitter' or 'unexpected', and both may resonate here and at 1.1037 in a similar context (Rengakos 1994: 33); 'unexpected' would make a particular point with μαντοσύναις. At *Od.* 10.245 ἀδευκέα πότμον refers to what Circe did to Odysseus' men, and the scholia there offer both 'bitter' and 'unexpected' as glosses.

1504 Cf. 2. 815–17: μαντοσύναι also failed to save Idmon.

1505–31 What we learn of the snake which killed Mopsus suggests that, as was to become common also in, e.g., Nicander and Lucan, *BC* 9, the characteristics of more than one venomous snake, as analysed in technical writing, have here been combined; see Morel 1928: 362–4, Green 1997: 348–51. The description in 1506–12 is, as with many of Nicander's descriptions, intended to provoke us to try to identify it; the Egyptian cobra (ἀσπίς) has here made the principal contribution. Ap. will have drawn on medico-zoological works about snakes (Jacques 2002: xxv-xliv), as well perhaps as on the poetic *Theriaca* of Noumenios of Heraclea (*SH* 589–94, cf. 1680n., Jacques 2002: xliv-v). Ap. in turn became a source for Nicander's *Theriaca*, cf. 1541n.

1505–6 Cf. 2.818 (the death of Idmon) κεῖτο γὰρ εἰαμενῆι κτλ.; the parallel led Fränkel to propose κεῖτο γὰρ ἐν ψαμάθοισι here. Although this is unnecessary, the deaths of the two seers are clearly set in counterpoint: one takes place in wetlands, the other in the desert; the boar attacks Idmon unprovoked, whereas the snake acts in self-defence. Ap. evokes also the mysterious snake of the apocalyptic scene near the end of Hesiod's *Catalogue*, εἰσι]ν ἀ[λυσ]κάζων καὶ ἀπεχθαίρων πάτον ἀνδρῶν ... δεινὸς ὄφις (fr. 204.132–6). **ἐνὶ** is preferable to ἐπί as the snake is trying to escape from the heat. It is, however, unnecessary to conclude that Ap. is thinking of the sand-coloured snake called ἀμμοδύτης (Strabo 17.1.21, Lucan, *BC* 9.715–16, Philoumenos 22.1–2W). **νωθής** '(too) sluggish'; for this use of the positive in place of the comparative see K–G II 10–11. Sluggishness is not a characteristic of only one snake (cf., e.g., Aelian, *HA* 15.13 of the 'blood-letter'), but it is very likely that Ap. here has the Egyptian cobra in mind, cf. Nic. *Ther.* 158, 162–3, Helvius Cinna fr. 10 Courtney *somniculosam ut Poenus aspidem Psyllus* (probably misunderstood by Aulus Gellius 9.12.12 and many modern editors). **ἑκὼν ἀέκοντα:** a kind of 'polar' expression emphasizing that the snake will not attack unprovoked; most people are 'unwilling' to be attacked by a cobra. **χαλέψαι:** the nearest parallel for χαλέπτειν in such a context is Dosiadas, *Altar* 13 χάλεψε γάρ νιν ἰῶι of the snake which bit Philoctetes; the chronology of Dosiadas is uncertain, but the *Altar* is on an Argonautic theme.

1507 ὑποτρέσσαντος: genitive absolute. **ἐνωπαδὶς ἀίξειεν** 'would launch an open assault on, would dart frontally upon'.

1508 μελάγχιμον: the colour of death, cf. 1516. **ἐνείη:** aor. opt. ἐνίημι.

1509–12 are imitated by Euphorion fr. 50 Powell (= 70 Lightfoot) to describe the effect of the Lernaean hydra's poison. See further Hunter 1993: 31–2.

1510 '[For that creature] the path to Hades is not even a cubit in length'. Hecataeus (*FGrHist* 1 F27) had rationalized Cerberus as a δεινὸς ὄφις (cf. 1506), which was called 'Hades' dog' because its bite led to immediate death. οὐδ' ὁπόσον πήχυιον: such expressions, more commonly with οὐδ' ὅσον, are standardly followed by the accusative, cf. Headlam on Herodas 7.33. οὐδ' ὅσον itself means 'not even a little', cf. 1700, 2.181, 190. Snakes are standardly measured in spans or cubits (cf., e.g., Philoumenos 16.1–2W of cobras), and πήχυιον may be a poetic reapplication from the snake to its effect; Strabo 17.2.4 notes that there are two kinds of Egyptian cobra, of which one measures only a span, but it 'brings death more quickly', whereas the other measures a full fathom (cf. Nic. *Ther.* 169).

1511 Παιήων: a healing god often identified with Apollo, but – as Homeric scholars acknowledged (cf. Σ *Il.* 5.899, *Od.* 4.232) – separate from him still in Homer, and cf. also Hes. fr. 307. Such hyperboles (cf. Headlam on Herodas 2.90) are a feature of 'popular speech', and here the poet, confronted with the horror of this snake, falls back on the vividness of popular expression.

1512 ἐνιχρίμψῃσιν 'bite, attack'.

1513–17 Ap. seems to have related this same *aition* in the 'Foundation of Alexandria' (fr. 4 Powell, cf. Fränkel 1968: 606–7, Barbantani 2014); if that poem, as seems likely, preceded *Arg.* 4, then we would have here a case of self-citation, and both Perseus' double name and the absence of anything like 'for they say that . . . ' may wittily point to that other passage. No earlier extant source offers this version of the origin of snakes, but the Colchian dragon arose from the Earth where drops of Typhon's blood had landed (2.1209–13), and already in Euripides' *Ion* Creusa possesses a deadly poison from the Gorgon's blood (lines 1003–19, 1264–5); the origin of the Prometheion root from the ichor of Prometheus at 3.851–3 bears a general resemblance. Akousilaos is reported to have traced the origin of 'all biting things' to Typhon's blood (*FGrHist* 51 F14), and Nicander seems to claim that Hesiod (fr. 367) traced the origin of snakes to the blood of the Titans (*Ther.* 10–11). Ap.'s verses are very likely a principal source for Ov. *Met.* 4.617–20; Lucan, *BC* 9.619–99 treats this *aition* much more elaborately. The Gorgons were normally placed in the extreme west, often on an island in Ocean, and so Perseus will have passed over Libya on his way back to Greece.

1513–14 ἰσόθεος: Perseus was a son of Zeus, but was also believed to be worshipped at Chemmis in Egypt (Hdt. 2.91), where he was clearly identified with a local god (Lloyd 1969); ἰσόθεος, 'equal to the gods', may therefore have a particular point here. Hdt. 2.91.6 reports that Perseus visited Chemmis on his trip bringing the Gorgon's head from Libya. As an ancestor of the Macedonian Argeads, Perseus will have been a mythical figure of interest to Ptolemaic culture (Barbantani 2014: 218–20). **Περσεύς | Εὐρυμέδων**: double names are familiar in epic tradition (cf. 1494, *Il.* 6.402–3), but presentation in asyndeton such as this is very rare; we are perhaps momentarily tempted to take εὐρυμέδων as an epithet. The reason why Danae called her son by this name may have been given in the 'Foundation of Alexandria', cf. 1513–17n. Euphorion fr. 18, 86 Powell (=19a.41–5 Lightfoot) probably followed Ap. in adopting this double name for the hero.

1515 βασιλῆι: Polydektes of Seriphos who forced himself on Perseus' mother Danae; Perseus offered to bring him the Gorgon's head as a wedding present, and then turned him and his people to stone. Σ cites Pherecydes, *FGrHist* 3 F51 for the story.

1516–17 Cf. Hes. *Theog.* 183–4 (the castration of Ouranos) ὅσσαι γὰρ ῥαθάμιγγες ἀπέσσυθεν αἱματόεσσαι, | πάσας δέξατο Γαῖα. **κυανέου** varies the Homeric epithets for blood, μέλαν and κελαινόν. **κείνων** may carry a particular point: Ap. does not say 'all snakes', cf. 1513–17n. **ἐβλάστησαν**: cf. 676n.

1518 ἐνεστηρίξατο 'pressed down on'; the simple στηρίζομαι is commonly used of supporting one's weight on something. In the 'Kanobos' Ap. described the death of Menelaos' steersman from the bite of a αἱμορροΐς ('blood-letter'), cf. fr. 3 Powell, adding perhaps Aelian, *HA* 15.13. Both Nicander, *Ther.* 312–19, presumably indebted to Ap. (note εἰ ἔτυμον in line 309, perhaps pointing an allusion), and Aelian loc. cit. say that Helen punished the snake by cracking its spine; how she did so is not stated, but the possibility that she trod on it is at least worth considering. If so, the manner of Mopsus' death may contain another allusion by Ap. to his own poetry, just as the *aition* for these snakes seems to have done (1513–17n.). On the 'Kanobos' see van Krevelen 1961, Krevans 2000.

1519 λαιὸν ... ταρσὸν ποδός 'the left sole of the foot' is a poeticism, with the figure of 'hypallage', for 'the sole of the left foot', cf. K–G I 263. The nearest Homeric model is *Il.* 11.377 ταρσὸν δεξιτεροῖο ποδός, where Paris shoots Diomedes in the foot with an arrow (ἰός): is there a play here on two of the senses of ἰός?

1520–2 Cf. Lucan, *BC* 9.738 (the fate of Aulus) *torta caput retro dipsas calcata momordit.* **κερκίδα καὶ μυῶνα πέριξ** 'around the lower leg and calf-muscle'; πέριξ is less likely to be in tmesis with ἑλιχθείς, as the compound verb is normally followed by the dative or by repeated περί. κερκίς for the lower part of the leg, more usually κνήμη, appears only here in poetry;

Herophilus is reported to have used the word to refer to the tibia (fr. 129 von Staden). μυών, lit. 'muscle', may owe something to *Il.* 16.314–15 πρυμνὸν σκέλος, ἔνθα πάχιστος | μυὼν ἀνθρώπου πέλεται. **σάρκα** is the object of both participle and verb. **Μήδεια**: most commentators explain that Medea, with her specialist knowledge of poisons, understands instantly what has happened; perhaps, however, the poet presents a 'female' reaction to the appearance of a very nasty snake. Medea's flight contrasts with Nausicaa's endurance in a similar, but amusingly different, situation (*Od.* 6.138–9).   **ἄλλαι … ἀμφίπολοι** 'her maidservants as well', cf. *Od.* 6.84, 19.601, LSJ s.v. ἄλλος II 8.

1523 ὑπέρβιον is best taken adverbially, 'excessively'.   **ἄλγος** is the simplest substitute for the transmitted ἕλκος, which seems all but impossible after 1522, and which may have arisen either from there or from *Il.* 16.510–11 τεῖρε γὰρ αὐτόν | ἕλκος. A repeated ἕλκος in Noumenios' *Theriaca*, a poem which Ap. may have known (cf. 1505–31n.), is also regularly emended away (*SH* 590); Meineke suggested οἶδος, 'swelling', in both places.

1524 ἤ τε: cf. 916n.   **κῶμα**: for this effect from a cobra bite cf. Nic. *Ther.* 188–9, 'the man dies without distress, and a sleepy lethargy (ὑπνηλὸν νῶκαρ) brings on the end of life', Lucan, *BC* 9.701 *aspida somniferam*, 816–18, Philoumenos 16.3W (symptoms include numbness (νάρκα), lethargy (νωθρία), and a sleeplike collapse (καταφορὰ ὑπνώδης)).

1525 evokes death in Homeric battle (*Il.* 5.696, 16.344, *Od.* 22.88 etc.), but for ἀχλύς of the effects of snakebite cf. Arist. fr. 270.9 Gigon, Aelian, *HA* 15.18; Lucan's *caligo* following a cobra-bite (*BC* 9.817) probably translates ἀχλύς.

1526–7 For such descriptions cf. Nic. *Ther.* 247–55 (the effects of a viper-bite).   **ψύχετ' ἀμηχανίηι** 'grew cold, completely powerless'; Nicander uses ἀδρανίη for such powerlessness (*Ther.* 248). For coldness as the result of snakebite cf., e.g., Nic. *Ther.* 251–5, Diod. Sic. 17.103.5 (arrows tipped with snake venom), Philoumenos 16.3W (κατάψυξις).

1528 ἀδινῆι: cf. 1422n.; a connection with 'lamentation' would obviously be appropriate here, 'his sad fate', but the word may also be intensive, 'his very terrible fate'.

1529 οὐδὲ μὲν οὐδ': an emphatic double negative, cf. 1.224.

1530–1 offer a poetic version of the fact that some powerful snake venom does indeed break down body tissue, appearing (to the naked eye) to 'rot' the flesh (Green 1997: 350–1). The rotting is most frequently associated with the snake called σήψ or σηπεδών (cf. Nic. *Ther.* 320–33, Lucan, *BC*

9.762–88). For hair loss as a result of snakebite cf. Aelian, *HA* 17.4 (the πρηστήρ), Philoumenos 23.2W (σήψ), 31.2W (βασιλίσκος). There is a striking parallel at Aelian, *HA* 15.18, where the effect of a σηπεδών-bite is described: 'the hair too turns clammy (μυδῶσα) and disappears (ἀφανίζεται) ... darkness (ἀχλύς) covers the eyes ... '; Aelian is explicitly paraphrasing Nic. *Ther* 320–33, but these details come rather from *Arg.* or from a common source, which Jacques 2002: xxxiii-vii identifies as the works of 'Apollodorus', Nicander's principal source. Lucian, *Philopseud.* 11 describes the victim of the bite of an ἐχίδνη: his leg was rotting, he was near death and 'clammy' (μυδῶντα) all over. The rotting of Mopsus' flesh horribly reverses the divine preservation of the corpses of Patroclus and Hector, cf. *Il.* 19.38–9, 23.184–91, 24.410–23; Hector's body was, unlike Mopsus', protected from the effects both of the sun and of rotting. From another perspective, Mopsus' death and subsequent decay may be seen as retributive justice for Heracles' killing, with arrows dipped in snake venom, of the serpent of the Hesperides (Hunter 1993: 31–2). **ἄφαρ:** cf. 1510. Aelian (previous note) says that the venom (ἰός) of the σηπεδών spreads over the body 'with irresistible speed (τάχει ἀμάχωι)'.

1532 χαλκείηισι adds epic/heroic colouring.

1533–4 ἐμοιρήσαντο δὲ χαίτας 'cut locks of hair', an apparent reference to a rite such as that of *Il.* 23.135–6 where locks of hair are thrown on to Patroclus' corpse; LSJ offers no parallel for μοιρᾶσθαι in such a context. **κοῦραι:** the context perhaps evokes an etymological connection with κείρω, cf. *Et. Mag.* 534.3–4.

1535 Cf. 1.1059–60, *Il.* 23.13–14. 'Three' is a very common number in rites of all kinds.

1536 εὖ κτερέων ἴσχοντα '[the corpse] which received a proper share of funeral honours', cf. 2.838 τάρχυον μεγαλωστί. ἴσχειν here functions like intransitive ἔχειν (LSJ s.v. III), and for εὖ followed by the genitive in such expressions see Smyth §1441. **χυτὴν ἐπὶ γαῖαν ἔθεντο** 'placed heaped earth on [it]', cf. *Il.* 23.256, *Od.* 3.258.

1537 πρήσσοντος 'blowing'; the correct form of this verb is uncertain, cf. 819n.

1538 νοτίοιο: the rise of a south wind, which would take the Argonauts in the direction of Greece, encourages them to embark and set sail. **ἀπετεκμαίροντο** 'were trying to discover'; this compound does not appear elsewhere. Vian notes that, if the transmitted aorist is retained, the sense might rather be 'failed to discover', with ἀπο- functioning as, for example, in ἀπογιγνώσκειν.

1540 ἀφραδέως 'aimlessly'.

1541–7 The *Argo*'s aimless searching for a way out of the lake is compared to the hurried 'sidewinding' of a snake heading for its hole in order to escape the burning sun. The closest Homeric parallel is *Il.* 22.93–6, Hector waiting for Achilles compared to a vicious snake waiting 'by its hole' to attack a man; this snake, however, like the Argonauts, is a picture of agitated motion. Following immediately upon the death of Mopsus from snakebite, this is an extraordinary narrative sequence, emphasizing the prevalent importance of snakes in this part of Libya; Lucan was certainly to take the hint. The principal animal-similes of the Libyan episode give pride of place to the animals for which Libya was best known – lions (1338–43), snakes (1541–7) and horses (1604–10).

1541 σκολιήν ... οἶμον: cf. Nic. *Ther.* 267 (the 'sidewinding' of the *kerastes*) οἶμον ὁδοιπλανέων σκολιήν; that passage compares the motion of that snake to a ship battling into the wind, thus reversing the tenor and vehicle of Ap.'s simile, cf. Magnelli 2006: 194–5.   **εἰλιγμένος**: cf. Hes. fr. 70. 23M–W, εἰλιγμένος εἶσι δράκων ὥς.

1543 ῥοίζωι was used of the sound of the Colchian dragon at 129, 138; here of a quieter, but no less malevolent, hiss.

1543–4 Cf. 1.1296–7, the angry Telamon. The snake's eyes blazed as do those of warriors in early epic: the end of 1543 is identical with *Il.* 19.16 where χόλος enters Achilles (cf. the snake at *Il.* 22.94) and his eyes blaze at the sight of the new armour. Snakes' eyes are often said in poetry to be fiery (cf. Hes. *Theog.* 826–7), and this may be connected with the link between δράκων and δέρκομαι (cf. 128n.), but Virgil seems to have (*inter alia*) the current passage in mind at *G.* 3.432–3, *flammantia lumina torquens* | *saeuit agris asperque siti atque exterritus aestu* of the *malus anguis*.   **πυρός**: the final syllable is lengthened in arsis at the caesura.   **μαιμώοντι** agrees with οἱ, 'in its fury'.

1545 λάμπεται: cf. 16–17n.   **ῥωχμοῖο** 'a crack [in the ground]'. **ὄφρα** is usually taken as 'until', but it may rather introduce a purpose clause loosely dependent on μαιμώοντι, 'in its furious eagerness to slip into ... '.

1546–7 vary 1538–40.   **ἀμφεπόλει**, 'roamed about', has no exact parallel in this sense; the compound normally means 'attend, accompany, serve', but Ap's innovation lays emphasis on the second half, LSJ s.v. πολέω I.   **αὐτίκα** has, as often, a rather vague temporal sense. If correct, 'suddenly' might suggest the intervention of the divine; Orpheus' 'bright idea' shows his understanding of higher powers (cf. 1412–14n.).

1548 τρίποδα: cf. 529–33n. This tripod had long been embedded in different versions of the Libyan episode, cf. Hdt. 4.179 (where it was intended to be a dedication *to* Apollo), Timaeus, *FGrHist* 566 F85 (a gift of thanks to Triton), and was a powerful symbol of Greek claims to North Africa; see Introduction, pp. 8–9. In Lyc. *Alex.* 886–96, Medea rather gives Triton a golden mixing-bowl, which the local people then hide in order to prevent subsequent Greek occupation.

1549 ἐγγενέταις 'local, native'.   **μείλια:** cf. 1190–1n.

1550 κτέρας 'possession', but here rather 'gift'.

1551 The pattern is familiar from early epic, cf., e.g., *Il.* 16.715 (Apollo and Hector), *Od.* 10.277–9 (Hermes and Odysseus). In Pind., *Pyth.* 4 the god appears to the Argonauts 'looking like a man' (lines 21, 28–9).

1552–3 Cf. Pindar, *Pyth.* 4.34–5.   **Τρίτων εὐρυβίης** is how the god is introduced at Hes. *Theog.* 931.   **βῶλον:** the clod of earth, which is to play such an important role in the future history of North Africa (1731–64n.), seems originally to have belonged to a different version of the story from that of the tripod, cf. Vian III 58–60, Jackson 1993: 49–58, Introduction, p. 14). Whether or not the combination is original to Ap. is unknown.   **ξείνι'** 'as a guest-gift', cf. Pind., *Pyth.* 4.35 προτυχὸν ξείνιον.

1554–5 'since I do not have [ἐστί understood] here and now an outstanding gift to grant to my visitors'.   **περιώσιον,** 'exceptional', here functions as a synonym of περισσόν. Others understand 'superior [to this clod]', cf. 1.466 for such a comparative sense.   **ἀντομένοισιν:** 'visitors' seems a more probable sense than 'suppliants', particularly in the lightly amused, teasing style in which the god speaks; cf. Pind., *Pyth.* 4.30 ξείνοις ... ἐλθόντεσσιν.

1556–7 The god knows of course exactly what they want.   **μαίεσθ'** is here constructed with the accusative, but with the genitive in 1275.   **οἷά τε πολλά ... περόωντες:** for such generalizations cf. 2.540–1, *Od.* 9.128–9, both in the mouth of the narrator.   **ἐπ' ἀλλοδαπῆι** 'over a foreign land'; ἐν ἀλλοδαπῆι would be more usual (cf. 2.870), but cf., e.g., *Il.* 4.443 ἐπὶ χθονὶ βαίνει. 'To a foreign land' would perhaps make most contextual sense, but that would seem to require ἐπ' ἀλλοδαπήν.

1558 ἐπιίστορα 'knowledgeable (about)', cf. 89, 2.872.

1560–1 For such formulas of introduction, which place a certain emphasis on the importance of the named individual, cf., e.g., 3.362–3, Call. fr. 64.5; *Od.* 15.403, *HHAphr.* 111 use the related formula εἴ που ἀκούεις. When used to introduce oneself, the tone is of polite self-depreciation.   **ἀκούετε νόσφιν ἐόντες** ends a hexameter at *Od.* 3.193

(Nestor telling Telemachus of the fate of the Greeks).   Εὐρύπυλον:
Eurypylos was by tradition an early or the first king of Cyrene, and a figure
with a rich cultic and mythic tradition; see *RE* 6.1349, Ferri 1976: 14–16,
Ottone 2002: 285–9. He too was a son of Poseidon and some traditions
made him Triton's brother, rather than this being an identity the god
assumed. In Pind. *Pyth.* 4, Medea recalls that the god (never explicitly
identified) who appeared to the Argonauts 'said that he was Eurypylos
son of Poseidon' (line 33), and Ap.'s version is therefore a 'natural'
interpretation of Pindar, and one shared by the Pindaric scholia (II
102–4 Drachmann).   θηροτρόφωι: the Argonauts will naturally think
of snakes (cf. Nic. *Ophiaka* fr. 32.3 Σύρτις ... θηροτρόφος), but we will
recall the story of how Eurypylos' kingdom was ravaged by a lion which
was finally killed by the maiden Cyrene, cf. Call. *h*.2.92, Akesandros,
FGrHist 469 F4; the ambiguity is in keeping with the tone of Eurypylos'
speech. Ap. may have used πολύθηρος of Libya in the 'Foundation of
Alexandria' (Fränkel 1968: 606–7). The variant μηλοτρόφωι is used of
Libya in an oracle at Hdt. 4.155.3.

1562 ὑποέσχεθε: cf. *Il.* 7.188; this aorist is found only in poetry, LSJ s.v.
*σχέθω. The transmitted ὑπερ- would mean 'held his hands over ...', which
seems much less appropriate.   **χεῖρας:** Platt's χεῖρα (cf. Pind. *Pyth.* 4.37)
is unnecessary.

1563 Εὔφημος: cf. 1466–7n. Why Euphemos took the clod from the god
is a scholarly 'problem' discussed in the scholia to Pindar's *Pythian* 4 (II
105–6 Drachmann). He, like Triton, was a son of Poseidon, but the real
reason of course is that the future history of Cyrene demands this narrative, cf. 1731–64n., Introduction, p. 14); Euphemos may have appeared in
this role already in Pindar (D'Alessio 2005: 195–9). A Roman copy of a
bronze group, going back perhaps to the later third century, has been
thought to show Euphemos with the clod in his hand and carrying Triton
on his back (*LIMC* s.v. Argonautai, no. 37).

1564 Ἀπίδα 'the Peloponnese'. Apis was a figure from the earliest legends
of the Peloponnese; the normal form in which the land commemorates
his name is Ἀπία (first attested in Aesch. *Suppl.* 260, 777), but for the
form Ἀπίς cf. [Theocr.] 25.183, Nic. fr. 104.5. The Argonauts know that
they are on the Libyan coast, and Crete and the Peloponnese are the
closest parts of Greece; they will in any case have to sail around the
Peloponnese to reach home. The transmitted Ἀτθίδα is a puzzle: did it
arise from ignorance of the reference of Ἀπίδα? **πέλαγος Μινώιον** 'the
Cretan sea'. Ap. places Minos before or contemporary with the Argonauts,
cf. 2.299, 3.998.   **ἥρως:** Euphemos knows that Eurypylos is (at least) a
son of Poseidon, so that this is the very least he can call him.

1565 ἔνισπε: aor. imperative ἐνέπω, cf. 3.1; at *Od.* 4.642 this form is guaranteed, but ἔνισπε and ἐνίσπες are regular variants at line-end in *Il.*

1567 ἐνὶ πείρασι: ἐπὶ πείρασι might have been expected in this expression (Λιβύης ἐνὶ πείρασι at 1.81 is much easier), but ἐγχρίμπτω is a standard verb for 'approach, draw near to', and this may have influenced the choice of preposition.

1568–9 μεταχρονίην: cf. 952n., 1385.　　　**τόδε λίμνης | χεῦμα** 'this flowing lake', lit. 'this channel of lake'.

1570 'where the route leads out <to allow us> to reach the land of Pelops'. **πλόος:** cf. Lyc. *Alex.* 889 (the same context) πλωτὴν οἶμον.　　　**ἐξανάγει** is probably a conjecture, but the noun ἐξαγωγή occurs in exactly this context at Hdt. 4.179.2, just as πόντοιο διήλυσις in 1573 seems to reflect διέκπλοον at Hdt. 4.179.3. The transmitted ἐξανέχει would be 'extends into', cf. 1578.

1571–2 innovate as a speech introduction; the emphasis is on Triton's gesture, not on the verb of speaking.　　　**ἀγχιβαθές** alludes to *Od.* 5.413, ἀγχιβαθὴς δὲ θάλασσα, in Odysseus' monologue as he seeks for an ἔκβασις ... ἁλός in order to reach land; his situation is thus exactly the reverse of that confronting the Argonauts. Grammarians (cf. *LfgrE* s.v.) understood the Homeric epithet to mean 'deep beside the land', i.e. the sea did not taper towards the land, thus making Odysseus' task even harder. That sense would also suit here, cf. 1574–5n.　　　**στόμα λίμνης:** στομαλίμνης, 'lagoon', is a variant verse-ending at *Il.* 6.4, and it has been argued that Ap. here reflects that text (Rengakos 1993: 154–5).

1573 κείνη functions as a kind of demonstrative, cf. 1577.　　　**πόντοιο διήλυσις:** cf. 1570n.

1574–5 Cf. *Il.* 7.63–4, where armed ranks, ἀσπίσι καὶ κορύθεσσι καὶ ἔγχεσι πεφρικυῖαι, are compared to the ripple as the sea grows black under the west wind; here it is not the wind (note ἀκίνητον), but the depth of the water, which causes the blackening. See further LSJ s.v. φρίξ I.　　　**μελανεῖ:** some grammarians understood μελάνει at *Il.* 7.64 as an intransitive present, and that accentuation is also part of the transmission here; Ap. may, however, have read μελανεῖ in Homer, and it seems safer to keep that form here.　　　**ῥηγμῖνες φρίσσουσι διαυγέες** 'gleaming breakers ripple'; the surf is visible in the distance against the black of the water-surface, cf. further 152–3n.

1577–8 'There the sea stretches through the mist to the holy land of Pelops beyond Crete'.　　　**θείην:** Triton's father, Poseidon, was a very important deity in the Peloponnese, and Euphemos, whom Triton is addressing, was himself from Tainaron.

1578–81 'When you exit from the lake into the open sea, steer to the right, keeping very close to the land itself, for as long as it heads north'. **εἰς ... βάλητε:** tmesis, cf. 639, LSJ s.v. εἰσβάλλω II 1.   **τόφρ᾽** is co-ordinate with **ἔστε.**   **ἐεργμένοι:** lit. 'constrained, held in'. Triton advises them to 'hug the coastline'.

1581–2 περιρρήδην δ᾽ ἑτέρωσε | κλινομένης χέρσοιο 'when the land swings in a curve around in the other direction', i.e. when the land drops away to the south. Triton is all but certainly describing the headland at Cape Phykous (probably mod. Ras Sem) above Cyrene (Barrington 38 C1), believed to be the most northerly point of the Libyan coast; this would indeed be the starting point for a trip to Crete and Greece, and the geography would have been familiar to many of Ap.'s readers. Strabo 17.3.20 makes the distance from Berenice, near where Ap. seems to have placed Lake Triton, to Cape Phykous some 1000 stades. See further Goodchild 1976: 249, Stucchi 1976: 20–3.   **περιρρήδην** must mean 'in a curve', κατὰ περιφέρειαν as Σ gloss it. The Homeric περιρρηδής (*Od.* 22.84) is picked up at 1.431 (Rengakos 1994: 128).   **ἀπήμων** is a common word in *Arg.*, but at Hdt. 4.179.2 Triton sends the Argonauts on their way ἀπήμονας; Ap. certainly knew these chapters of Hdt. well.

1583 'lies stretched out for you as you head away from the jutting headland'. The text must be regarded as at least uncertain; ἰθύς may have come in from 1580, but other scenarios are also possible.

1584–5 Syntax and sense are disputed. Either 'Let there be no toilsome pain to weary limbs resplendent with youth' or 'Let there be no pain arising from your labours, that limbs resplendent with youth should labour' seems possible; Triton is either wishing them a trouble-free trip (which will, of course, not happen) or observing that they are strong enough to survive the exertions of the trip.   **κεκασμένα:** perf. pass. participle from καίνυμαι, cf. 2.816.

1586 ἴσκεν 'he spoke', cf. 3.396n.

1589 ἀνθέμενος 'gathering up', apparently used here as a synonym of ἀνελόμενος; 189 shows a related, but rather different, use of this compound. **εἴσατο** 'seemed', from εἴδομαι, cf. 855, 1733.

1590 οἷον, '<given> how ... ', introduces a clause which is part exclamation, part explanation (Smyth §2685).

1591 σχεδόν 'suddenly'.

1592 ἐναίσιμος 'favourably disposed', though the resonance of 'boding well, of good omen' is also present.

1593 μήλων ὅ τι φέρτατον ἄλλων 'the finest of all [the other] sheep'; such superlative expressions with ἄλλος are very common (K–G 1 23, Smyth §1434). The superlative here also carries some of the force of the comparative, cf., e.g., *Il.* 1.505 (Achilles) ὠκυμορώτατος ἄλλων.

1594 ἐπευφημῆσαι 'to say prayers over [the sacrifice]'.   ἑλόντα seems rather weak (Fränkel suggested ἐπευφημεῖν ἀνελόντα, cf. *Od.* 3.453), but the active may here serve for the middle ἑλόμενον, 'choosing', cf. ἐκρίνατο in the following verse.

1596 σφάξε: the temporal relation between this verse and 1601–2 (where see n.) is somewhat unclear, and Fränkel proposed the imperfect σφάζε, 'prepared to sacrifice'.   **ἐπὶ δ' ἔννεπεν εὐχωλῇσι** fulfils the suggestion of ἐπευφημῆσαι, as σφάξε picks up ῥέξαι. ἐπί is best taken adverbially, 'and in addition he spoke in prayer'; others understand a tmesis of a compound ἐπεννέπειν, cf. 3.780 ποῖον δ' ἐπὶ μῦθον ἐνίψω;, or take ἐπί ... εὐχωλῇσι together, 'in prayer'.

1597–1600 Cf. 1412–14n.

1598–9 The variety of construction in the text adopted here, 'whether you are Triton ... or the daughters call you ... ' seems preferable to the uniformity of reading σέ γε Τρίτων', cf. 1411–14.   **Φόρκυν:** Nereus' brother, though often in fact identified with him, cf. Hes. *Theog.* 233–9, with West's n. on 237. Ap. perhaps alludes to the variability of the genealogical relationship by offering the two alternatives here; the 'sea-dwelling daughters' must be the Nereids (cf. 1743), so the question is by what name they call their father.   **ἁλοσύδναι:** an epithet of Thetis at *Il.* 20.207, where Ap. presumably understood it as do the D-scholia, ἐναλίας ... ἐν θαλάσσηι κατοικούσης, and apparently of another sea-goddess at *Od.* 4.404.

1600 Cf. 1.249.

1601–2 Cf. 1595n. The act of 'throat-cutting' is not different from that of 'sacrificing' (cf. 2.840), and so 1601–2 essentially summarize 1595–1600. This is one of the passages which raise the possibility that Ap. never gave Book 4 a final revision (Introduction, p. 2).

1603 ἐτήτυμος: the early emendation ἐτήτυμον would be adverbial, 'how he was in truth for the seeing'. For Triton's appearance cf. 1610–16n.

1604–10 Triton leads the *Argo* to the exit to the open sea as a man leads in a racehorse to the arena. This joyful simile contrasts with the worried menace of the snake-simile at 1541–7, when the Argonauts were unable to find a way out. 'Ships are the horses of the sea' (*Od.* 4.708–9, cf. Artemidorus 1.56), and the two are commonly compared in ancient poetry; the closest Homeric models for the present passage are *Il.* 15.679–84 (leaping from ship to ship compared to trick-riding) and *Od.* 13.81–3 (the Phaeacian ship compared to chariot-horses). This simile has elements in common with that of 3.1259–61.

1604 ἀγῶνος 'racecourse', cf. LSJ s.v. I 2.

1605 στέλληι: 'sends' here amounts to 'leads'; we are to imagine that the man is on foot beside the horse, holding it by its mane.   **ὀρεξάμενος** 'having grasped'; as regularly with such verbs, the relevant part of the body is in the genitive.

1606 εἶθαρ: the normal sense is 'immediately', but here 'quickly' would seem most appropriate.   **ἐπ᾽ αὐχένι γαῦρος ἀερθείς:** a standard sign of a proud or pleased horse is a raised neck, cf. 3.1261, *Il.* 6.509 (where κυδιόων is like γαῦρος here), Xen. *Eq.* 10.3–4, 13, 16 (γαυριώμενος). The syntax, however, is obscure: some understand 'proudly exalted because of its neck' or a variation for ἐπ᾽ αὐχένι γαῦρος ἀερθέντι 'proud in its raised neck'; ἐπ᾽ αὐχένι γαύρωι ἀερθείς would be much easier, but both word order and the rare fifth-foot correption (2.57, Campbell 1973: 89) enjoin caution.

1607 ἕσπεται is a metrically useful variant for ἕπεται, cf. 1.103, 3.615; such forms may have arisen from understanding certain Homeric past tenses as presents.

1607–8 'the gleaming bit clanks beside its mouth as it champs at both ends'.   **ἀργινόεντα** stresses the impressive appearance of the proud horse. Others understand that the bit is white from the horse's foaming mouth, cf. Virg. *Aen.* 4.135 *frena ferox spumantia mandit.*   **χαλινά:** for the design of different types of bit see Delebecque 1978: 81–5, with fig. 3.   **παραβλήδην** 'on the two sides (of its mouth)'. Arat. *Phain.* 535 uses παραβλήδην of two parallel lines, and the present usage is not far from that; cf. further 936n.

1609 ἐπισχόμενος 'taking hold of', cf. 751.   **ὁλκήϊον** perhaps refers to butts protruding beyond the ship from a through-beam (Casson 1971: 46 n.20); this would offer a close analogy to the horse being led by the mane, and cf. 1.1314 where Glaukos seizes νηίου ὀλκαίοιο. Others take the reference to be to the stern-post or even the rudder, as the scholia gloss ἐφόλκαιον at *Od.* 14.350 (where see the nn. of Hoekstra and Bowie).

1610–16 Triton is standardly represented in human (or divine) form as far as the waist, which then joins the long (cf. 1614), curling tail of a sea serpent, cf. *LIMC* s.v. Triton.

1612 'was exactly (ἀντικρύ) like in extraordinary appearance to the blessed ones'.   **ἔϊκτο**: in form this is a pluperfect passive of *ἔϊκω (ἔοικα), cf. 2.39, *Il.* 23.107.

1613 ὑπαί is the best attested form here, but it may (as also ὑπέκ) have arisen from a failure to understand that G's ὑπό would scan (the second syllable being lengthened before initial λ-), cf. 1735.   **δίκραιρα** 'with two forks, bifurcated'. In representations of Triton the two 'flukes' of his tail, shaped (as Σ note) like two crescent moons, are very prominent; cf. next n.

1614–16 ἀλκαίη 'tail', cf. Oppian, *Hal.* 5.264, 331 of a whale, Harder 2012: 2.454.   **ἀκάνθαις** apparently refers to Triton's dorsal fins or spines (cf. Diod. Sic. 3.41.4), although it is hard to believe that the image of crescent moons in 1616 refers to anything but the two flukes of his tail, cf. Ov. *Met.* 3.681–2 (transformation into dolphins) *falcata nouissima cauda est, | qualia diuiduae sinuantur cornua lunae*, and κόπτε would indeed be an appropriate verb for the action of the tail. Perhaps, then, the Argonauts see only the spines or fins which appear to end in the crescent-shaped extremities. Aelian, *HA* 15.4, however, describes a 'moon-fish', whose dorsal fins, when it dives down, 'divide out and give the form of a semi-circle, and it is like looking at the shape of a half-moon'; if Ap. is referring only to dorsal spines, which are indeed prominent in some representations of Triton, then the κέντρα may be the individual 'needles' which make up what seems to be one fin, but which at the bottom divide. At *Imag.* 2.15.6 Philostratus describes Glaukos' curling tail (in an Argonautic scene) as μηνοειδές. The interpretation of Ap.'s description remains uncertain.   **αἵ τε**: for such epic usages see Ruijgh 1971: 942.   **ἐπινειόθι**: if correct, this adverbial form must mean 'below, at the base'. Others interpret as σκολιοῖς ἐπὶ νειόθι κέντροις, 'with curving needles below'.   **ὡς** is strictly 'unnecessary', as ἐειδόμεναι means 'appearing like to', cf. *Il.* 23.430.   **διχόωντο**: διχάω is the standard term for 'bisect, divide' in, e.g., Arat. *Phain.* (cf. line 799 of the moon), and that astronomical resonance is important here; Ap. may in fact remember line 856 which ends ἑλισσόμεναι διχόωνται (note ἔνθα καὶ ἔνθα in line 855).

1617–18 'He led [the boat] until he sent her on her way travelling over the open sea'.   **μέγαν**: the variant μέσον may be correct.

1619 τέρας: cf. 1598: Jason's surmise has proved correct.   **αἰνόν** here combines resonances of 'strange', 'supernatural' and 'beyond (human) comprehension'.

1620–2 Cf. 655–8 for another 'harbour of the *Argo*' and physical signs of the Argonauts' presence. This harbour is presumably placed at the mouth of the entrance to Lake Triton; Strabo 17.3.20 notes a 'harbour of the

Hesperides' near the lake and into which the river Lathon (cf. 1396n.) empties (although λίμνη is often adopted in the text of Strabo in place of the transmitted λιμήν). Although 1617–18 seemed to suggest that the Argonauts headed off immediately, we now learn that in fact they paused to commemorate the divine help they had received.   σήματα νηός are not more closely identified; are we to think of some kind of monument marked by an oar, as the end of Odysseus' travels was marked by an oar planted in the ground and sacrifices to Poseidon (*Od.* 11.129–30)? ἰδέ, a metrically useful alternative for ἠδέ, occurs only here in *Arg.*   ἐπέσχεθον 'they made a pause', cf. LSJ s.v. ἐπέχω IV 2.

1623–4 They carry out Triton's instructions to the letter, cf. 1578–80. αὐτήν, 'the same', implies that they kept the land 'constantly' close on the right-hand side.

1625–6 'On the following dawn they saw the headland and the deepest recess of the sea bending away beyond the jutting headland'. See 1581–3n. for this geography.   μυχάτην τε θάλασσαν is a difficult phrase. Perhaps, as they reach the headland they are granted a view of the whole expanse of the Mediterranean as it spreads towards its eastern edges where it is sealed off, hence μυχάτην. Others understand the reference in a more limited way, namely to the bay of Apollonia that swings away to the east beyond the headland.

1627–8 πρυμνήταο νότου 'a southwind blowing from the stern', i.e. a wind that will propel the *Argo* northwards. There is no other attestation for πρυμνήτης referring to a wind, but the variant ἀργεστᾶο may be readily explained as a memory of *Il.* 11.306, 21.334. Vian, however, notes that the Argonauts must have been propelled by a SW wind, as they arrive at Karpathos, and the proper name for the SW wind from Africa (cf. *GGM* II 473.10 = Timosthenes of Rhodes fr. 6 Wagner) was λευκόνοτος, which, in accordance with contemporary scholarship (cf. Strabo 1.2.21, bT-Σ on *Il.* 11.306), was to be identified with the Homeric νότος ἀργέστης. The argument is clever, but perhaps over-precise (the Argonauts did row for two days before reaching Karpathos), and it is very hard to explain the origin of πρυμνήταο, except as the original reading. West 1963: 12 proposed ἀργέστης for ζέφυρος in 1627.   χήραντο: aorist middle of χαίρω, cf. 55, *Il.* 14.270.   ἰωῆι 'at the rustling (of the wind)', cf. *Il.* 4.276, 11.308.

1629–30 Cf. Call., *SH* 259.5–6 = fr. 54c.5–6 Harder (the 'Victoria Berenices') ἀστὴρ δ' εὖτ'] ἄρ' ἔμελλε βοῶν ἄπο μέσσαβα [λύσειν | αὔλιος], ὃς δυθμὴν εἴσιν ὑπ' ἠελίου. Both Ap. and Call. offer the same gloss on αὔλιος, namely the evening star that brings an end to ploughing for the day, and 1630 is close to the explanation of the epithet (εἰς ἀνάπαυσιν ἄγων τὰ ζῶια) in the A-scholia to *Il.* 11.62 where, as the poets presumably knew, it is a variant for οὔλιος (Rengakos 1993: 133–4, Harder 2012: 2.441–2). Σ here connect the epithet with αὐλίζεσθαι and αὐλή. As Call.'s poem almost certainly belongs to the later 240s (Harder 2012: 2.390), the nature of the intertextual relationship here between Call. and Ap. is both unclear and particularly interesting, given the probable date of *Arg.* 4; see Introduction, pp. 1–2. For such time-descriptions cf. 1.1172–8, 3.1340–4, Fantuzzi 1988: 121–54.   ἀνέπαυσεν: gnomic aorist as at *Il.* 17.550, which is clearly in Ap.'s mind. Although the star marks rest for ploughmen, for the Argonauts the hard labour of rowing is just beginning. Ploughing and rowing ('ploughing the sea') are often compared, cf. 1.1167–8, Virg. *Aen.* 2.780, Pfeiffer on Call. fr. 572, McKeown on Ov. *Am.* 2.10.33.

1631 λιπόντος: intransitive, cf. 1.607.

1633 Cf. 504n., *Il.* 7.5–6 ἐπεί κε κάμωσιν ἐυξέστηις ἐλάτηισιν | πόντον ἐλαύνοντες.

1634 well captures the monotony of rowing.   ἐπ' ἤματι δ' 'and after that day ... ', cf. 2.631, 660, 945.

1635–6 ὑπέδεκτο δ' ἀπόπροθι 'received them far off [i.e. from where they had started]', cf. 1.954. It is clear from what follows that the Argonauts decided not actually to stop for any length of time at Karpathos, perhaps because of the difficulty of access (παιπαλόεσσα). The expression is, however, a difficult one and other interpretations have been suggested: 'awaited them in the distance', i.e. they saw Karpathos but never headed for it (Fränkel 1968: 612–13), or 'appeared next in the distance' (Hopkinson 1988: 195), cf. LSJ s.v. ὑποδέχομαι IV 2.   παιπαλόεσσα | Κάρπαθος varies Κάρπαθος ἠνεμόεσσα at *HHAp.* 43 (where παιπαλόεις is used of Mimas in 39).   περαιώσεσθαι ἔμελλον 'they had in mind to cross over to', followed by the simple accusative rather than ἐς Κρήτην.

1637 ὑπερέπλετο, 'surpassed', is of uncertain meaning. Crete is certainly the largest Aegean island, and the meaning might be that the Argonauts chose Crete because of its size (cf. Hopkinson 1988: 196) or because its mountains rose above those of other islands; this would allow the past tense to carry its expected significance. More commonly, however, the verb is taken to refer to Crete's position 'furthest' out to the open sea, from the perspective of the Greek homeland, cf. *Od.* 13.256 where Crete is described as τηλοῦ ὑπὲρ πόντου; at 9.25–6 Odysseus describes Ithaca as lying πανυπερτάτη ... πρὸς ζόφον, a description which was debated in antiquity almost as fiercely as it has been in modern times. Ap. seems to use καθύπερθε, 'above', to mean 'out at sea' at 1.924, 928.

1638–88 *The Talos episode.* The bronze man who guarded Crete first appears in the fragments of early epic (Cinaethon fr. 1 Davies) and of

Simonides (*PMG* 568 = fr. 286 Poltera) and Sophocles (frr. 160–1 R), and is clearly associated with the Argonauts already in fourth-century vase-painting, though in what appears to be a very different version than that given by Ap. It is clear that there was no single canonical version of the episode and Ap.'s 'sources' remain uncertain. Apollod. *Bibl.* 1.9.26 gathers different versions together: 'Some say that Talos belonged to the Bronze Race, but others that he was given to Minos by Hephaistos; he was a man of bronze, but some say that he was a bull. He had a single vein extending from his neck to his ankles, and at the end of the vein was fitted a bronze nail. This Talos watched over the island by running around it three times each day ... He died having been deceived by Medea, sent mad, as some report, by her drugs, whereas others report that she promised to make him immortal and drew out the nail, so that he died when all his ichor flowed out. Some, however, say that Poias killed him by shooting him in the ankle.' Hesychius τ 87 records that ταλῶς (accented thus) is 'the sun', and this *might* suggest some connection between Ap.'s figure and the bronze statue of Helios, the 'Colossus of Rhodes', which stood some 33m high and seems to have collapsed 'broken at the knees' in the 220s (Strabo 14.2.5, cf. Pliny, *HN* 34.41). The pseudo-Platonic *Minos* rationalizes Talos as a judge who travelled 'three times a year' around Crete with the laws inscribed on bronze tablets. On the Talos-episode see Paduano 1970/1, Robertson 1977, Hopkinson 1988: 194–200, Dickie 1990, Buxton 1998, *LIMC* s.v. Talos I, Schaaf 2014: 311–29.

1638 ἀπὸ στιβαροῦ σκοπέλοιο 'from a massive/beetling vantage-point'; the adjective is perhaps transferred from the rock out of which the vantage-point is made to the point itself.

1639 Talos is one of the 'Cyclops' figures of *Arg.*, cf. *Od.* 9.481–3; whereas, however, the Cyclops sought to drive Odysseus' ship back to land, Talos seeks to keep the Argonauts away. Cf. further 1657n.

1640 'as they reached the Dictaean shelter of an anchorage'. 'Dictaean' is often used to mean 'Cretan' in a general sense, but Ap. refers specifically to Mt Dikte at the extreme east of the island near Itanos, cf. Strabo 10.4.12, Σ Arat. *Phain.* 30–3 (p. 86 Martin). The far east of Crete was a centre for Ptolemaic influence (there was a naval base at Itanos), and this will have given the legends of this area a certain topical interest for Ap.'s readers (see Hunter 2011).   ἐπιωγήν appears in Homer only at *Od.* 5.404, where Odysseus is trying to reach Scherie; here too the Argonauts cannot land, but not because of the geography of the island. The Homeric scholia explain that ἐπιωγή refers to a sheltered mooring where there is not actually a proper harbour.

1641 μελιηγενέων: according to Hesiod, *WD* 143–5 the violent Bronze Race, which preceded the race of ἡμίθεοι to which the Argonauts belong (though Hesiod does not mention the Argonauts), was born ἐκ μελιᾶν, 'from ash-trees' or 'from ash-tree nymphs', cf. the nn. of West and Ercolani ad loc.

1642 ῥίζης, 'stock' (LSJ s.v. ΙΙ 1), here replaces γένος, the standard Hesiodic term for the Races.

1643 This version is found elsewhere only in Σ *Od.* 20.302 and Eustath. *Hom.* 1893.30; we are perhaps to think that Zeus gave Talos to Europa after he had made love to her, cf. Moschus, *Europa* 165–6.   **νήσου … οὖρον** 'watcher over the island', a witty variant of ἔμμεναι οὖρον, 'to be a boundary-marker', at the end of *Il.* 21.405. Elsewhere Ap. uses the compound ἐπίουρος, cf. 652, 1.87, 3.1180.

1644 Cf. 1.1059. In the most common version attested after Ap., Talos runs three times *per day* around Crete, cf. Agatharcides fr. 1.7 (*GGM* I 115.25–6), Apollod. *Bibl.* 1.9.26 (1638–88n.), and Fränkel therefore suggested ποσὶν ἤματι for Κρήτην ποσί; Κρήτην after νήσου in the previous verse may also be thought inelegant, and the text must be considered suspect.

1645 Cf. *Il.* 23.454–5 (a horse, another creature which races in circles) ὃς τὸ μὲν ἄλλο τόσον φοίνιξ ἦν, ἐν δὲ μετώπωι | λευκὸν σῆμ᾽ ἐτέτυκτο; δέμας is there a weakly attested variant for τόσον, cf. 1.731–2, Ap. Soph. 164.29 Bekker, Rengakos 1993: 136–7. Moschus, *Europa* 84–5 combines this passage with its Homeric model.   **δέμας καὶ γυῖα:** accusatives of respect.

1647–8 σῦριγξ αἱματόεσσα 'a blood-filled vein'; the model is *Il.*2.267 σμώδιγξ δ᾽ αἱματόεσσα. In the sense 'vein', σῦριγξ is largely a medical and technical term, cf. LSJ s.v. ΙΙ 3; Talos in fact has ichor, rather than blood, in his vein.   **†αὐτὰρ ὁ τήν γε† … θανάτοιο:** the transmitted text can only mean 'but a fine membrane held/covered it [the vein], the difference between life and death', with ζωῆς … πείρατα καὶ θανάτοιο 'in apposition'. This hardly seems possible, and it is much more natural for ἔχε to govern πείρατα. Of the suggested emendations, Fränkel's is the most attractive, 'but around [the vein] a fine membrane held the difference between life and death'.   **ζωῆς … πείρατα καὶ θανάτοιο:** πείρατα are here the 'determining conditions' between life and death, cf. Sotades fr. 4c Powell, Meleager, *AP* 12.158.8 (= *HE* 4503).

1650 νῆα … ἀνακρούεσκον 'pushed the ship back'; the middle ἀνακρούεσθαι is not uncommonly used of 'backing water'.

1651–3 For such counterfactuals at crucial narrative moments cf. 636–42n. Successive spondaic verses in 1651–2 perhaps evoke the

Argonauts' weariness.   ἠέρθησαν, aorist passive of ἀείρω, most likely means 'would have been carried away, transported'; αἴρειν is, however, used of launching ships (LSJ s.v. 1 5), and 'would have set off' is a possible alternative.   λιαζομένοις 'as they were departing'; the variant λιλαιομένοις, 'in their eagerness/need', may have arisen from the parallel instances at 256 and 1.350, but it is not impossible.

1654 μούνη 'by myself [i.e. without further help]', rather than 'alone [of all us]'. Medea's conquest of Talos is a very unusual version of Iliadic single-combat.

1655–6 Cf. *Il.* 20.102, about Achilles, another character vulnerable only in his foot.   ὁππότε μή οἱ ἐπ' ἀκάματος πέλοι αἰών 'provided that he does not enjoy unwearying life', i.e. provided that he is in fact mortal. ἀκάματος is appropriate for Talos who spent his life in almost constant motion, cf. 1687.   οἱ ἐπ' ... πέλοι 'is upon him'; there is a kind of tmesis, though ἐπιπέλω does not otherwise occur.

1657 αὐτοῦ 'here'.   θελήμονες 'relaxed, in calm', i.e. not rowing with exertion, cf. 2.557, West on Hes. *WD* 1 18–19.   ἐρωῆς 'range', lit. 'force, motion', cf. *Il.* 15.358–9 ὅσον τ' ἐπὶ δουρὸς ἐρωή | γίνεται. Behind this passage lies *Od.* 9.480–92, where, as a result of the Cyclops' rock-throwing, Odysseus has to push the boat away from the land and his men row furiously, anything but θελήμονες.

1659–60 'And they held the ship with the oars out of reach of the missiles ... '. ὑπὲκ βελέων ἐρύσαντο: in Homer this would mean 'dragged away from the missiles', cf. *Il.* 18.152, 232, but Ap. varies the Homeric model by using ἐρύομαι in the sense 'hold, protect' (LSJ s.v. ἐρύω (B)), rather than 'drag' (LSJ s.v. ἐρύω (A)), cf. 2.1282; the imperfect ἐρύοντο may be correct. If the verb is understood as 'dragged, moved', i.e. LSJ s.v. ἐρύω (A), ἐπ' ἐρετμοῖσιν is very difficult to construe: Vian suggests 'they drew the boat out of range of the missiles <in order to hold it> with the oars'.

1661 μῆτιν: another evocation of the Homeric episode of the Cyclops. For the link between Μήδεια and μῆτις cf. 3.825–7n., 1133–6n.

1661–2 is perhaps the most striking case of alliteration in *Arg.*, cf. 1100, 3.71n. In part this derives from the Homeric model, *Il.* 5.315–16 (Aphrodite protecting Aeneas) πρόσθε δέ οἱ πέπλοιο φαεινοῦ πτύγμ' ἐκάλυψεν | ἕρκος ἔμεν βελέων, but in part it perhaps signals the 'uncanniness' of what we are about to witness. Medea acts not principally to create a 'closed ritual space' from which to operate (Paduano 1970/1: 58), but rather to protect the Argonauts from the maleficent power which she is about to exert through her eyes (1664–72n.); it is clear that the sight of

Medea's eyes is not *always* dangerous (cf. 1669), but caution in exposure to them is always advisable, cf. 3.885–6.

1663 ἐπ' ἰκριόφιν 'on to the deck', cf. 80; this is very likely the stern deck (Casson 1971: 179–80). -φι(ν) is an old instrumental ending which is used for the genitive already in Homer.   **μεμαρπώς**: perfect participle of μάρπτω, 'seize', constructed as regularly with the accusative and the genitive of the part of the body taken.

1665–72 Medea's magical destruction of Talos recalls her invocations to put the Colchian dragon to sleep, 145–8. Here Medea puts the 'evil eye' on Talos, with the result that he has an accident which proves fatal. Ap.'s description of how Medea operates has several features in common with the discussion of the 'evil eye' in Plutarch, *Sympotic Questions* 5.7, most notably the explanation of this in terms of 'emanations' (ἀπόρροιαι or εἴδωλα) from one person to another, a familiar element of Presocratic thought, particularly of Empedocles (cf. fr. 89 D–K) and Democritus; one of the guests in Plutarch's essay cites Democritus' explanation (68 A77 D–K) as follows: 'Democritus says that the envious send out (ἐξιέναι) images (εἴδωλα), which are not completely without perception or purpose (ὁρμή), and which are full of wickedness and envy from those who emit them (τῶν προιεμένων). The images and their envy establish themselves in and cling permanently to the objects of envy and confound and damage both their bodies and their minds' (682f–3a), cf. further *Mor.* 735a-b, Dickie 1990, Powers 2002.

1665 'There, she made propitiations in song, and hymned the Keres ... '.   **μέλπε**: the variant θέλγε, 'sought to win over', is not impossible (and cf. λιταῖς in 1669), and prayer and incantation blend into each other in the performance of magic (cf. 1668–9), but θέλγε is perhaps less natural with Κῆρας as the object. Some editors adopt the emendation τε for δέ, so that Κῆρας is the expressed object of both verbs, but this is unnecessary.   **Κῆρας**: spirits of death, the children of Night, cf. 1485, 1.690, Hes. *Theog.* 217 Κῆρας ... νηλεοποίνους (with West's n.); [Hes.] *Aspis* 248–57 offers a bloodily grim picture of them at work. They are often virtually identified with the Erinyes, who are also invoked in the practice of magic (cf. *PGM* v 193, *Orph. Lith.* 588–92), and who are regularly imagined as 'dogs' (cf. next n.).

1666 θυμοβόρους: the Keres 'eat away at one's life'. This, like the phrase which follows it, is to be understood as taken from what Medea 'actually said'; for such mingling of direct and indirect speech in the narrative of invocations cf., e.g., 146–8n., 708–9.   **Ἀίδαο θοὰς κύνας** fuses two ideas. (i) The servants of gods are regularly called 'dogs', cf. 2.289, LSJ s.v. κύων III. (ii) The Erinyes and the Keres are commonly represented as hunting-dogs or as having dog-faces, cf., e.g., Aesch. *Eum.* 131–2, 246–51, Soph. *El.* 1387–8, Eur. *El.* 1252. Medea's invocation of the Keres as infernal dogs is very like that of Lyssa at Eur. *HF* 870–860 (with Jackson's transposition).

1667 ἐπὶ ζωοῖσιν ἄγονται 'are set upon mortals'; ἐπάγειν is used of setting hunting-dogs on their prey, cf. *Od.* 19.445, LSJ s.v. 2. Powers 2002 compares the language of atomist accounts of the εἴδωλα around us.

1668–9 'Three' is a very common number in rituals of all kinds, particularly those associated with the Underworld, cf. 1535n., Gow on Theocr. 2.43; the anaphora, the distinction between ἀοιδαί and λιταί, and the formal structure of the verses all suggest the need for 'correct' practice in magic.   ἀοιδαῖς is here probably used for ἐπαοιδαῖς, 'incantations', cf. 42, 59, Pind. *Pyth.* 4.217 (Aphrodite taught Jason) λιτάς τ᾽ ἐπαοιδάς. θεμένη δὲ κακὸν νόον 'making her mind malevolent', cf. 3.641 θεμένη κύνεον κέαρ, Theognis 89. It seems clear that we are to understand that Medea is able to control the effects of her eyes, so that they are only truly dangerous when she wants them to be; this seems also to be the implication of Democritus 68 A77 D–K (1665–72n.).   ἐχθοδοποῖσιν 'hostile'; this form is rarer than ἐχθοδαποῖσιν, and Homer has only the verb ἐχθοδοπέω (*Il.* 1.518).

1670 is framed by two words for 'eyes', to emphasize that Medea's dangerous power moves 'eye to eye'. Talos' eyes were presumably also of bronze, though Ap.'s readers will have been familiar with bronze statues in which the eyes were made from a variety of materials – glass, bone, ivory – and then inset into the statue (Mattusch 1996: 24, 1997: 33); mention of Talos' eyes will have conjured a very vivid picture.   ἐμέγηρεν 'she bewitched', a unique use of μεγαίρειν for βασκαίνειν; intransitive μεγαίρειν is commonly used for φθονεῖν, 'to be envious'. Later texts attest Μέγαιρα as the name of one of the Furies (alongside Tisiphone and Allecto), and this may have influenced Ap.'s use of the verb here, cf. Apollod. *Bibl.* 1.1.4, Virg. *Aen.* 12.846.

1671–2 Medea's dominant motive is anger, rather than the envy which is more usually associated with the evil eye, but the two emotions overlap importantly, and other texts too associate the 'evil eye' with anger, cf. Plin. *HN* 7.16.   λευγαλέον δ᾽ ἐπὶ οἷ πρῖεν χόλον 'she gnashed terrible anger against him', a strikingly compressed version of 'she gnashed her teeth in anger against him', cf. Ar. *Frogs* 927. There seems no reason to understand this as purely metaphorical; Medea concentrates all the powers at her disposal.   ἀΐδηλα | δείκηλα 'terrible fantasms/visions', though the sense 'unseen, invisible' also resonates in the adjective, cf. 47n., 3.1132n., Powers 2002. Democritus seems to have used δείκελον as one of his words for 'bodily emanations' (fr. 123 D–K).   ἐπιζάφελον: adverbial neuter.

1673–5 The poet expresses his amazed wonder that someone can damage us from afar by magical powers such as that of the evil eye. Plutarch too introduces his discussion of this phenomenon by stressing the element of τὸ θαυμάσιον, and by noting that there are many recorded παράδοξα which seem to lack a rational explanation (*Mor.* 680c-d); for this theme cf. also Apul. *Met.* 1.3. In describing Medea's actions in terms of Presocratic science and in making them an example of something which might strike any of us at any time, Ap. emphasizes their strange reality; it is often thought that these verses are 'tongue in cheek' and represent the scepticism of the educated man in the face of folkloric superstition, but even today very many intelligent and otherwise 'rational' people believe in 'the evil eye' (or something like it), and there is no reason to assume that Ap. would not have regarded it as a serious phenomenon; see further 3.531–3n.

1673 ἄηται 'blows (like a wind)', cf. 3.288, 688 also of emotional disturbance. The Homeric model is *Il.* 21.386, δίχα δέ σφιν ἐνὶ φρεσὶ θυμὸς ἄητο.

1674–5 νούσοισι τυπῆισί τε embodies paired oppositions, 'unseen ~ seen' and 'non-violent ~ violent', which (one might have thought) embraced all the ways in which we could be destroyed; Medea's powers, however, prove otherwise. Crucial is ἀπόπροθεν: to catch a disease or to be killed by a blow we need to be close to the source of the danger, but the evil eye can affect us from a very great distance.   **ἀντιάει** 'comes upon (us)'.

1676 ὑπόειξε δαμῆναι: cf. 1658: Medea's promise is coming true.

1677 βρίμηι: a virtually unique occurrence of this noun (cf. *Hom. Hymn* 28.10). The scholia gloss it as 'strength' (ἰσχύς), whereas Hesychius β 1161 offers 'threat' (ἀπειλή).   **ἄν:** apocopated form of ἀνά, in tmesis with the following ὀχλίζων.

1678 ἐρυκέμεν: infinitive of purpose (Smyth §2008), 'to prevent them from ...'.

1679 πετραίωι στόνυχι 'the edge/sharp point of a rock', cf. Eur. *Cycl.* 401 πρὸς ὀξὺν στόνυχα [Scaliger: γ᾽ ὄνυχα] πετραίου λίθου. The scholia here claim that στόνυξ properly refers to a spear-point.   **χρίμψε** 'knocked', lit. 'brought near to'. This verb is more usually intransitive, though Homer uses ἐγχρίμπτω transitively.   **ἰχώρ** is what flows in the veins of gods (*Il.* 5.339–40), Titans such as Prometheus (3.853n.), and giants (Strabo 6.3.5). The word is also used more generally of any pus or sluggish liquid (LSJ s.v. II), and we should perhaps not enquire too closely as to what flowed in Talos' vein.

1680 τηκομένωι ἴκελος μολίβωι: 'molten lead' is an appropriate comparison for a man of bronze. Noumenios, *SH* 591 refers to ichor μολίβωι ἐναλίγκιον εἶδος as a result of snakebite, and the two passages can hardly be unconnected (cf. 1505–31n.). The form μόλιβος appears once in Homer (*Il.* 11.237) and here only in *Arg.*

1682–8 Talos' collapse is compared to that of a tree which has been half-chopped by woodcutters and which collapses overnight from the force of the winds. The passage evokes Homeric similes comparing the fall of warriors to the collapse of trees (*Il.* 4.482–7, 13.389–91 = 16.482–4), thus continuing the presentation of Medea's triumph as a single-combat (cf. 1654n.), but the two-stage collapse is, as far as we know, original to Ap. The passage has contributed to several famous later similes, notably Cat. 64.105–10, Virg. *Aen.* 2.626–31.

1682 ἐν ὄρεσσι: the position on the mountains matches that of Talos on his high vantage-point; for the close matching of vehicle and tenor in this simile see Hunter 1993: 130.

1683 τήν τε: for this 'generalizing' use of τε in relative clauses see Ruijgh 1971: 944.   **ἡμιπλῆγα** is found only here in Greek literature.

1686 πρυμνόθεν 'at the base', cf. Call. *h.* 4.35. At Aesch. *Suppl.* 71, 1056 the adverb rather means 'from the base up', i.e. 'utterly'.   **ἐξαγεῖσα**: aorist passive participle of ἐξάγνυμι.

1687 ἀκαμάτοις: his feet are not exhausted, but his life-force is flowing away, cf. ἀμενηνός in the following verse.   **ἐπισταδὸν ἠιωρεῖτο**, 'swayed [while still] standing', contrasts with the collapse in the following verse. In Homer the basic sense of ἐπισταδόν is 'successively' (*Od.* 12.392, 13.54), and so some understand here 'on one foot, then the other', but 'standing' is rather the sense required. See further LSJ s.v. αἰωρέω II 2.

1689 ἐνί is probably in tmesis with ηὐλίζοντο (cf. Hdt. 1.181.5 νύκτα οὐδεὶς ἐναυλίζεται), rather than to be taken, as most MSS take it, in anastrophe as Κρήτηι ἔνι. See further Matteo on 2.908.

1691 'Minoan' is not otherwise attested as a cult-title of Athena, and it is uncertain of which (if any) shrine Ap.'s readers would here be reminded; the NE part of Crete was, however, a centre of Athena's worship, cf. 1693n.

1692 εἰσαφύσαντο: the simple ἀφύσσομαι is more common in this sense, e.g. *Od.* 9.85.

1693 παμπρώτιστα 'at the very earliest opportunity'; this unparalleled superlative expresses the Argonauts' eagerness now that they are all but 'home'. Homer has the simple πάμπρωτος.   **βάλοιεν ὑπέρ** 'round',

anastrophic tmesis, cf. LSJ s.v. ὑπερβάλλω III 1b.   **Σαλμωνίδος ἄκρης**
probably refers to Cape Sidero, the NE tip of Crete above Itanos; this
headland is also referred to as Σα(μ)μωνίς, and was the site of a cult of
Athena 'Samonia' or 'Salmonia', *RE* 1A.1986–9.

1694–1730 The Argonauts are saved from an impenetrable, supernatural
darkness by the intervention of Apollo, who reveals an island to them,
which they name Anaphe ('Revelation') in honour of Apollo's help, and
on which they found a shrine of Apollo Aigletes ('the Gleamer'). Mocking
banter between the Argonauts and Medea's maids is the aetiology for
humorous abuse which still characterizes Apollo's cult on the island.
One Homeric seed for this episode is *Od.* 14.301–9, storm and darkness
just off Crete 'where no other land could be seen'; cf. the impenetrable
darkness of the storm which wrecked Phrixos' sons, 2.1103–5, and the
dark storm of Virg. *Aen.* 3.192–204 which is indebted to this passage.
Another Homeric model is the dark fog which Zeus pours around the
combatants in *Il.* 17 and which Ajax prays to him to disperse so that they
can continue properly to fight (lines 645–70), see Fantuzzi–Hunter 2004:
105–6. Ap.'s narrative is very close in some details to what we can reconstruct of Callimachus' treatment of the episode in *Aitia* 1, cf. 593n.,
Introduction, pp. 24–5. Callimachus' whole Argonautic narrative is
intended to answer the question why the rites of Apollo on Anaphe involve
scurrilous abuse (fr. 7.19), and frr. 18–21 suggest a sequence very like
Ap.'s, cf. fr. 18.8 ἀμιχθαλόεσσαν … ἠέρα, 21c.3–4 Harder (repeated
σκοτίαν); in two later versions the Argonauts suffer only a 'very severe
storm' (Apollod. *Bibl.* 1.9.26, Conon, *FGrHist* 26 F1.49, cf. 1700–1n.).

1694 αὐτίκα 'suddenly'.   **Κρηταῖον**: the 'Cretan sea' is that part of the
Mediterranean stretching north of Crete to the Cyclades and Sporades. It
is perhaps relevant to the terror faced by the Argonauts that this is a part of
Greek waters where one can be out of sight of any land for a long time, cf.
Od. 14.301–2, Green 1997: 356–7.

1695 κατουλάδα: 1696 suggests a connection with ὀλοός, and this is one of
several etymologies found in the ancient lexicographers, cf. Radt on Soph.
fr. 433; other explanations include a connection with κατίλλω and/or
κατειλέω, hence 'enshrouding, wrapping up'.   **κικλήσκουσι**: unfortunately we do not know to whom Ap. is referring; the only attestation earlier
than Ap. is Soph. fr. 433R. The scholarly 'footnote' increases the sense of
uncanny menace in this darkness.

1696 διίσχανεν 'pierced, separated', imperfect of διισχάνω, a unique
alternative for διέχω. Call. too (fr. 17 Harder) seems to have drawn
attention to the absence of stars which made navigation impossible,
cf. 1700–1n.

1697 χάος suggests the primeval 'nothingness' from which Hesiod's cosmogony begins and which is the father of 'Erebos and black Night' (*Theog.* 123), cf. Detienne–Vernant 1978: 156–7, Hunter 1993: 167. χάος is also often used of the 'emptiness' of space between earth and heaven, cf. Ar. *Clouds* 424, *Birds* 1218.   **ἠέ τις ἄλλη κτλ.**: the poet's ignorance of the source of the blackness is not merely a technique for suggesting the 'historicity' of the event, but also increases the atmosphere of dread. Fränkel's ἠδέ for ἠέ would destroy the opposition between 'heaven' and 'the lowest pits'.

1698 ὠρώρει: an intransitive pluperfect connected with ὄρνυμι, cf. *Il.* 18.498; the origin of Ap.'s usage is the Homeric formula ὀρώρει δ' οὐρανόθεν νύξ (*Od.* 5.294, 9.69, 12.315, all of storms at sea).   **βερέθρων**: an epic form of βαράθρων, cf. 2.642 διὲξ Ἀΐδαο βερέθρων.

1699 Hiatus at the central caesura marks a strong opposition between the two possibilities. The Argonauts' position is even worse than that of Odysseus and his crew who lose all sense of geographical direction before reaching Circe's island (*Od.* 190–2).

1700–1 Ignorance is also a theme in Call.'s version of these events, cf. fr. 17.8–9 Harder, 'he did not know (ἠδμώλει) where ... Tiphys should steer'. The rare gloss ἠδμώλει, rather than Ap.'s ᾔείδειν οὐδ' ὅσσον, is a nice marker of stylistic difference between the two passages.   **ᾔείδειν**: cf. 947n.   **οὐδ' ὅσσον**: cf. 1510n.   **ἀμηχανέοντες ὅπηι φέροι** 'not knowing where it would direct them'. Conon, a mythographer of the time of Augustus, reports that the Argonauts were struck by χειμὼν ἄφατος καὶ ἀμηχανία πᾶσα, *FGrHist* 26 F1.49 (Brown 2002: 338–43); it is clear, however, that he is following a version different from Ap.'s. At Call. *h.* 4.191–4 the unborn Apollo describes Asterie-Delos as διειδομένη τις ἐν ὕδατι νῆσος ἀραιή, which floats ὅπηι φορέηισι θάλασσα; the similarity to 1701 would be unremarkable, but for the fact that this small island, like Anaphe, has a name denoting brightness and a very close connection to Apollo. Ap. may, then, have combined two Callimachean stories about the appearance of islands. For a possible play on Δῆλος and Ἀνάφη in *Orph. Arg.* see Paschalis 1994.

1701–5 Cf. Call. fr. 18.5–8 ἀλλ' ὅ γ'ἀνι]άζων ὃν κέαρ Αἰσονίδης | σοὶ χέρας ἠέρ-]ταζεν, Ἰήιε, πολλὰ δ' ἀπείλει | ἐς Πυθὼ πέ]μψειν, πολλὰ δ' ἐς Ὀρτυγίην, | εἴ κεν ἀμιχθαλόεσσαν ἀπ' ἠέρα νηὸς ἐλάσσηις. Both poets give Jason's prayer in indirect speech, and both poets apostrophize the god. In lines 9–14 Call. seems to explain that Jason called upon Apollo, because it was that god who was responsible for the whole expedition; Jason's action is here not explained, whereas Apollo's responsibility is made clear in the parallel passage at 1.411–19 before the expedition sets out, cf. 1704–5n. Ap. may, therefore, have framed the expedition with two 'Callimachean' prayers, with internal repetition marking 'external' borrowing.

1704–5 Cf. 1.419–20 (Jason praying to Apollo in direct speech) ἄλλα δὲ Πυθοῖ, | ἄλλα δ' ἐς Ὀρτυγίην ἀπερείσια δῶρα κομίσσω. The anaphora of πολλά perhaps evokes one of the most common etymologies of Apollo's name.   Ἀμύκλαις: site of a famous sanctuary of Apollo and of the festival of the Hyakinthia south of Sparta.   Ὀρτυγίην here almost certainly refers to Delos, cf. 1.419 (above), 537, Call. fr. 18.7 (above), Harder 2012: 2.194. The two seem to be different places at *HHAp.* 16 (Richardson ad loc.), but are identified as early as Pind. *Paean* 7b.48. Later sources offer two explanations of the name: Leto took the shape of a quail (ὄρτυξ) to hide from Hera on the island (Σ Call. *Ap.* 59) or the island was colonized from Ortygia in Aetolia (Nicander, *FGrHist* 271–272 F5).

1706 Λητοΐδη: the poet's apostrophe is a mark of his piety, which joins that of his character.   **πέτρας**: accusative of motion without a preposition.

1707 Μελαντείους: cf. Call. fr. 19 Μελαντείους δ' ἐπὶ πέτρας, which has (not unreasonably) been thought to derive from this same episode. The darkness (μέλας) of the name is important – the Argonauts will be saved by the appearance of a bright light – although the grammatical tradition (cf. Σ here) associates the name with Melas, the son of the eponymous founder of Naxos. Strabo 14.1.13 locates the Μελάνθιοι σκόπελοι near Samos, but Ap. is presumably thinking of somewhere closer to Anaphe: Barrington 61 B5 identifies them with the islets of Pachia and Makra south of Anaphe, cf. Green 1997: 357.   **ἀριήκοος** 'in answer', 'having heard'; at Call. *h.* 4.308 the meaning rather is 'famous, heard about'.

1709 The famous image of Apollo on Delos held the bow in the left hand (as at 2.678) and the Graces in the right (Call. fr. 114, with Pfeiffer's nn.), although [Plut.] *De mus.* 14 (*Mor.* 1136a) describes a Delian image with the bow in the right hand, as here; [Plut.] may just have made a mistake, or his text may be emended, but there seems in any case a strong possibility that Ap. is here evoking an image of the god familiar to his readers.

1710 As at 2.669–80 the epiphany of Apollo is the coming of light in darkness. Apollo's final epiphany reverses his first appearance 'like night' in the *Iliad* (1.47).   **ἀπέλαμψε**: the transitive use innovates on Homer who only uses this verb intransitively.   **βιός** varies τόξον in the previous verse.   **περὶ πάντοθεν** 'all around on all sides'.

1711 The gleam from the divine bow allows them to make out the island of Anaphe. In the version of Conon (cf. 1700–1n.), the island seems rather to rise up from the depths of the sea when Apollo raises his bow; if Ap. knew such a version, one reason why he might have avoided it was that he is about to tell of Thera's 'rising' from the sea (1757–8).   τόφρ' presumably means 'at that time', but an exact parallel is not forthcoming. At 1.1207, Call. fr. 21.3, 260.7 (= *Hecale* fr. 70.12 Hollis) the meaning seems rather to be 'meanwhile'; it is noteworthy that Call. fr. 21.3 is in the Anaphe-episode and in a verse about the coming of dawn.

1712 ἰδεῖν: epexegetic infinitive, 'appeared ... for the seeing'.   ὀλίγης varies βαιή in the previous verse.   Ἱππουρίδος: the identity of this 'small island' is uncertain; suggestions include mod. Amorgopoula between Anaphe and Amorgos to the north, Pachia to the south (cf. 1707n.), or a tiny islet between Anaphe and Pachia and Makra (so Barrington 61 B5).

1713 εὐνάς 'anchor-stones', cf. 888n.

1714–18 The shrine to Apollo 'the Gleamer' (cf. Strabo 10.5.1), here (as also in Callimachus) said to have been founded by the Argonauts, was on the eastern edge of Anaphe, an appropriate position to greet the gleaming dawn (McNeal 1967, Chuvin 2003: 215–17). The cult title Αἰγλήτης is attested as early as the fifth century (*IG* XII 3, 259–60, 412), and also appears in the second century in the form Ἀσγελάτας (*IG* XII 3, 248), with an accompanying festival, the Ἀσγέλαια (*IG* XII 3, 249). The history and inter-relations of the two forms of the name are disputed (Burkert 1992: 78–9, Bremmer 2005).

1714 ἀγλαόν 'glorious', but 'shining, bright' must resonate in the present context, and ancient etymologists indeed connected the adjective with αἴγλη, cf. *LfgrE* s.v. ἀγλαός, Giangrande 1977: 102–3.

1715 †σκιόεντά† is an impossible repetition. στιόεντα (Campbell), 'made of pebbles', cf. 1.1123, 2.694–5, 1170–2, would make excellent sense, but the first syllable of that word should be long, and a short syllable is required here; such variation in length does not seem impossible, but uncertainty is too great to place this word in the text. Livrea 2006 argues that Call. fr. 118, which refers to the building of a temple to Apollo, belongs at the corresponding point of the Callimachean narrative.

1716 εὐσκόπου 'far-seen, clearly visible', a variation on μαρμαρέην in 1710. The more common sense of the adjective is 'keen-sighted' and/or 'with a good aim, shooting well', and it is applied, *inter alios*, to Apollo (cf. LSJ s.v.); that latter sense is evoked also here, and it draws attention to Ap.'s innovation.

1717–18 Φοῖβον ... Φοῖβος: the repetition allows the accepted meaning of the title as λαμπρός, through a connection with φάος, to resonate, cf., e.g., *Et. Mag.* s.v. Φοῖβος Ἀπόλλων.   **κεκλόμενοι**: cf. 162–3n.   **λισσάδα**

'craggy, sheer', a very appropriate description of (particularly) Mt Kalamos at the eastern end of the island, where the temple of Apollo was situated.

1719–20 Cf. 2.688–9 (following Apollo's previous epiphany) τὰ δὲ ῥέξομεν οἷα πάρεστιν, | βωμὸν ἀναστήσαντες ἐπάκτιον.   **ῥέζον δ' οἷά κεν κτλ.** 'they sacrificed with such things as … '; it is clear from what follows that the Argonauts did not have wine left with which to conduct the sacrifice, but there is no reason to think that they did not have a sheep to be killed (cf. 1593–1602). In Conon's narrative (1701n.), the Argonauts and the maids have a jolly, and rather alcoholic, party (παννυχίς).   **ῥέζειν |…** **ἐφοπλίσσειαν** 'could prepare for sacrifice', i.e. 'could provide themselves with for sacrifice'.   **ὅ** 'as a result of which', see LSJ s.v. ὅς, ἥ, ὅ A b IV 2.

1721 Odysseus' men too use water instead of wine when they make sacrifices after the killing of the Cattle of the Sun (*Od.* 12.362–3), but that model merely points up the Argonauts' piety. It is very likely that we are to understand that libations of water also had a part in the later rite at Anaphe (1727–30).

1722 Cf. 1222. There seems to have been a very similar sequence in Call., cf. fr. 21.5–7, δμωῆισι … ξείνιον Ἀλκιν[ο … Φαιηκίδας (almost certainly in the same *sedes*).

1723 **γέλω**: this accusative is found as a variant for γέλων in some passages of Homer, cf. K–B I 516. Chuvin 2003: 219–20 suggests that the sound of this verse evokes the title Ἀσγελάτας (1714–18n.) and connects it with γέλως; cf. further Halliwell 2008: 184.   **οἷα**, 'in as much as', gives the following participle an explanatory force, Smyth §2085.   **θαμειάς** 'lavish', lit. 'crowded', i.e. involving the sacrifice of many cattle. For the lavishness of Alcinous' hospitality cf. *Od.* 8.59–60.

1724 **ὀρόωσαι**: the present participle has a durative or frequentative force, cf. K–G I 135–6; this was something which the maids were accustomed to see.

1725–30 The mutual raillery of the men and women is, as also apparently in Call., an aetiology of the ritual scurrility with which Apollo the Gleamer is still worshipped on Anaphe. Many Greek cults, particularly agrarian rituals, were characterized by aischrology and the exchange of abuse; the most familiar example is the banter exchanged *en route* to the celebration of Demeter's mysteries at Eleusis, and Call. indeed seems to have compared the rite at Anaphe to the Eleusinian mockery (fr. 21.8–12 Harder). See in general Richardson 1974: 213–17, Bremmer 2005, Halliwell 2008: 160–91, esp. 184–6 on the Anaphe rite. Richardson 1974: 217 notes that 'laughter is often a symbol of rebirth, or of restoration of the dead to life', and this certainly fits the case of the Argonauts after their dread experience with infernal darkness.

1725 αἰσχροῖς: cf. Call. fr. 7.19, where this word seems to appear in the poet's question to the Muses about the rite at Anaphe.   **ἐπεστοβέεσκον** 'mocked', cf. 3.663. Such frequentative forms are regularly unaugmented in Homer, and two witnesses to the text here present ἐπιστοβ-; certainty is not possible.

1726 χλεύηι 'jesting, mockery', cf. Call. fr. 21.8–9. The corresponding verb is used of Iambe's jesting at *HHDem.* 202 in what was almost the authorizing epic text for ritual mockery, cf. Ar. *Frogs* 375; Ap. has used the *mot juste* for banter of this kind.   **γλυκερή** forms a striking oxymoron with the nouns which follow.   **ἀνεδαίετο** 'flared up'; the verb continues the sense of warmth in γλυκερή. Vian suggested ἐνεδαίετο, which is clearly correct at 3.286, but there seems no need for change here.   **μέσσωι** 'in their midst', cf. *Il.* 4.444 (Eris) ἥ σφιν καὶ τότε νεῖκος ὁμοίιον ἔμβαλε μέσσωι. The variant τοῖσι would fulfil the function of σφιν in the Homeric verse, but the sense is very clear without it, and μέσσωι seems unlikely to have arisen as a memory of Homer.

1727 νεῖκος ἐπεσβόλον 'abusive dispute'; Call. used the noun ἐπεσβολίη to describe the Eleusinian banter to which he compared the rites at Anaphe (fr. 21.11 Harder, with Harder 2012: 2.207–8, D'Alessio 2014: 495–7). The adjective is used of Thersites at *Il.* 2.275, and the standard ancient etymology was ἔπεσσι βάλλων with the gloss λοίδορος, cf. the D-scholia ad loc., Ap. Soph. 71.18 Bekker, Rengakos 1994: 83–4; this would certainly suit the present context. νεῖκος too is at the heart of the Thersites-scene: there is a pointed contrast between that angry scene and the light-hearted Argonautic exchange, but whether Ap. wishes to trace, as some modern scholars have wished to do, a line of descent from the Thersites-scene to other forms of 'ritualized' abuse must remain unclear.

1728–9 μολπῆς 'game', 'playfulness'; cf. 3.897, 949–50. Aristarchus was later to hold that this was the only permissible meaning of μολπή in Homer, cf. Rengakos 1994: 116.   **τοῖα . . . δηριόωνται** 'dispute in such a way', i.e. as the maids and the Argonauts had done.

1730 A spondaic verse once again concludes an episode. The very first words of Calliope's Argonautic narrative in Call. are Αἰγλήτην Ἀνάφην τε (fr. 7.23), and this correspondence of a beginning in the *Aitia* and an end in *Arg.* can hardly be coincidence; Ap. perhaps places a Callimachean seal upon his narrative to acknowledge his principal source.   **τιμήορον** 'protector', 'guardian of', cf. 1309.

1731–64 *The history of Thera.* As they leave Anaphe, Euphemos recalls a
dream he had had that night in which he was told to cast the clod which
Triton had given him (1552–63) into the sea; Jason is able to link this
dream to prophecies from Apollo: the clod will become an island where
Euphemos' descendants will dwell. The poet then explains that this will be
Kalliste, which later received colonists from Sparta led by Theras and
changed its name to Thera. Among Ap.'s sources, two major texts are
still extant. In *Pythian* 4, Medea prophesies at Thera that Libya will be
colonized from there by a descendant of Euphemos; this will, however, be
delayed until the seventeenth generation because the Argonauts had
carelessly allowed the clod to be washed overboard, rather than guarding
it so that Euphemos could offer it to Poseidon at his home at Tainaron in
Laconia. We then learn that the Lemnian descendants of the Argonauts –
in Pindar the stop on Lemnos comes at the end, not the beginning, of the
expedition (Braswell 1988: 347–8) – settled Kalliste, via Lacedaimonia,
and from there Libya was colonized. Secondly, Herodotus 4.145–58
relates how the Lemnian descendants of the Argonauts were driven out
of the island by Pelasgians and went to Sparta where they were eventually
accepted and intermarried. After various troubles, however, these Minyai
joined the colonizing expedition of Theras to Kalliste, and from there
Libya was eventually colonized under Battos, who was thus ultimately a
descendant of Euphemos. On these legends see Corsano 1991, Jackson
1993: 49–58, Ottone 2002: 225–60, Calame 2003: 35–119. Whether or
not the actual creation of Thera out of the clod and Euphemos' dream are
Ap.'s own invention, we cannot say. Callimachus traces much the same
itinerary (Sparta – Thera – Cyrene) for the cult of Apollo Karneios at
Call. *h.* 2.72–6. The creation of Thera, another island sacred to Apollo
and one for which he is responsible (cf. 1747), forms a diptych with the
'revelation' of Anaphe; in an important sense, *Arg.* both begins (1.1) and
ends with Apollo.

What is perhaps most striking about Ap.'s version is that it concludes with the establishment of Euphemos' descendants on Thera
and nothing is said about the subsequent colonizing of Libya and the
founding of Cyrene. This has often been seen as a very political
silence: Ap. thus refuses to acknowledge the legitimate claims of the
Battiad clan to rule Cyrene, and this will have been very welcome to
his Ptolemaic patrons. Ap. has, however, very clearly evoked the narratives of Pindar and Herodotus and none of his readers will have
been unaware of 'what happened next'; see Stephens 2008: 100–3,
Stephens 2011. What Ap. explicitly offers instead is a diptych of 'island
creation' – first Anaphe, and then Thera – and this sense of the
creation of the Greek homeland is for his poem as important as the
fact that Euphemos' action 'activates the chain of events that

guaranteed the subsequent Greek return to North Africa' (Stephens 2000: 202); see further Hunter 1993: 168.

1731 κἀκεῖθεν 'from there also', i.e. as well as from Crete. The MSS of *Arg.* regularly present such forms (i.e. καὶ ἐκεῖθεν with crasis, cf. 1441), although Ap. seems only to use κει- rather than ἐκει- forms, when not preceded by καί; both Zenodotus and later Aristarchus insisted on καὶ κει- in the text of Homer, and some editors print that everywhere in *Arg.* also. **ὑπεύδια:** the adjective here functions adverbially.

1732 well captures the fact that memory of dreams is indeed often delayed.

1733 ἀζόμενος Μαίης υἷα κλυτόν: Hermes, 'the glorious son of Maia', is the god most closely associated with dreaming (he is the ἡγήτωρ ὀνειράτων, *HHHermes* 14), and Euphemos presumably 'shows reverence for' the god by remembering this significant dream; had he forgotten it (as dreams are very often forgotten), not only would Thera never have been created, but a blessing of Hermes would have been callously disregarded.

1733–45 Euphemos dreamed that he breast-fed the clod which then turned into a young maiden; he had sex with her and then lamented that he had slept with his own daughter. The maiden then revealed that she was in fact the child of Triton and Libya, and would be the 'nurse' of his descendants; if he dropped the clod (i.e. herself) into the sea, she would return to the sunlight 'ready for his descendants'. This is a dream which would have been classified by our principal surviving text of dream interpretation, the *Oneirokritika* of Artemidorus (2nd cent. AD), as 'allegorical', i.e. as a dream which indicates its meaning through 'riddles' (αἰνίγματα), cf. 1.2, 4.1. Artemidorus knows of dreams in which men have milk in their breasts (1.16) and in which men sleep with their daughters (1.78). Euphemos' actions will create Thera, and thus she is symbolically his 'daughter', but it is his descendants who will people the island and make it prosper. See further Walde 2001: 196–202.

1734 δαιμονίη βῶλαξ, both 'the clod given by a *daimon*' (cf. 1549, 1597) and 'the marvellous clod', is taken from Pind. *Pyth.* 4.37; the Pindaric 'fragment' is placed at a moment of maximum difference from the Pindaric narrative.   **ὧι ἐν ἀγοστῶι:** the Homeric ἀγοστός (cf. 3.1393–8n.) was very variously interpreted, but both 'palm of the hand' and 'elbow, cradle of the arms' (ἀγκών, ἀγκάλη) would suit a dream experience in which a clod of earth is breast-fed and becomes human; Ap. may thus evoke more than one current interpretation of the Homeric gloss (Livrea 1972: 232–7).

1735 ἄρδεσθαι is more appropriate to the earth than to feeding a baby, but it is 'watering' which makes the land fertile.   **ὑπό:** the second syllable is lengthened before initial lambda, cf. 1613n.; ὑπαί will arise from failure to understand the scansion, unless ὑπό itself is a learned emendation.

1738 ἄσχετον ἱμερθείς 'seized by irresistible desire'.   ὀλοφύρετο: the imperfect is perhaps to be preferred as signalling an ongoing event in the dream, i.e. 'he was lamenting ... when the maiden addressed words of consolation ... '.   ἠύτε, 'because, on the grounds that', followed by a participle, is here used in place of ὡς (cf. 1349), perhaps to evoke and vary Achilles' famous description of Patroclus as a weeping girl at *Il.* 16.7. The use of ἠύτε at 3.460–1 is more usual but not too far from the present instance, ὀδύρετο δ᾽ ἠύτε πάμπαν | ἤδη τεθνειῶτα.

1742 οὐ κούρη 'not your daughter'.   Λιβύη is again (cf. 1323) both the land and the eponymous heroine.

1743 Νηρῆος ... παρθενικῇσιν 'the virgin daughters of Nereus' functions here almost as a metonymy for 'the sea', cf. 1599, but the clod-maiden wishes to be 'entrusted' to those like her (cf. 1737); the riddling periphrasis suits the mystery of the dream.

1744 The future Thera describes herself as 'close to Anaphe'; Call.'s Kalliope, by contrast, describes Anaphe as 'neighbour to Laconian Thera' (fr. 7.23); see Introduction, p. 25 n.72.

1745 μετόπισθε 'at a future time'.   τεοῖς νεπόδεσσιν, 'your descendants', varies (and is explained by) τεῶν ... παίδων from 1741 and also places an emphatic ring around the maiden's speech: Euphemos' dream of sex will certainly produce offspring. For νέποδες cf. Theocr. 17.25, Call. fr. 222.2, Harder 2012: 2.534. At *Od.* 4.404 Proteus' seals are νέποδες καλῆς ἁλοσύδνης, and ancient scholarship variously understood this gloss as 'offspring' or 'footless' or 'swimming (νήχεσθαι) with the foot'; it is perhaps appropriate that the clod-maiden should recall a Homeric scene connected with an island and the sea, but such a rare Homeric gloss is certainly at home in the mysterious dream-narrative.

1746 'Euphemos cast memory of these things upon his heart'; the expression is unusual and somewhat mannered, but it builds on locutions such as Aesch. *PV* 705–6 τοὺς ἐμοὺς λόγους | θυμῶι βάλ᾽, Soph. *OT* 975, and there seems no reason to adopt Campbell's ἐνί or Vian's λάβεν. With τῶι δ᾽ ... κραδίη the meaning would be 'his heart cast memory upon him ... '.   ἔκ τ᾽ ὀνόμηνεν 'and he recounted [it] ... '.

1747 θεοπροπίας Ἑκάτοιο: these oracles were presumably delivered during Jason's original consultation of Delphi, cf. 529–33n. This is the first we have heard that Apollo touched upon this subject: the silence suggests that

Jason had long forgotten the god's words until Euphemos' dream acti-
vated his memory as well.

1748 πεμπάζων 'thinking over'; Ap. uses the middle of this verb in
350.   **ἀνενείκατο φώνησέν τε**: cf. *Il.* 19.314, also in a context of memory
(μνησάμενος); there the context and following utterance are sad, and Ap.
uses ἀνενείκατο with an object (μῦθον, φωνήν) in sad contexts at 3.463, 635.
Ancient scholars understood ἀνενείκατο in Homer to refer either to
'bringing the voice up from the chest' or to 'sighing' (Bühler 1960:
66–7); here the most likely reference is to the fact that Jason speaks
slowly and deliberately after a long pause for reflection, but his words
are anything but sad.

1749 ὦ πέπον: an affectionate address, stressing the bond between the
two Argonauts, cf. 1.1337. ὦ πόποι would rather emphasize Jason's surprised realization; this may be correct, but it may also have arisen from
memory of a very common Iliadic verse-opening.   **σε … ἔμμορε** 'has
fallen to your lot', an unparalleled construction, perhaps deriving from
uses of λαγχάνειν such as Theocr. 4.40 τῷ σκληρῷ μάλα δαίμονος ὅς με
λελόγχει. The usual construction would be ἔμμορες κύδεος, cf. 62, 3.4.

1750 βώλακα … βαλόντι suggests an etymological connection, cf. *Et. Mag.*
217.47 Gaisford. The etymology has a point: Euphemos' action will reveal
the 'true meaning' of the βῶλος.   **πόντονδε βαλόντι**: Jason expresses
himself much more prosaically than did the maiden in the dream
(1743–4).

1752–4 Jason's words do not mean that he has only just realized that it
was Triton who handed them the clod; rather, he has been pondering
Apollo's (doubtless riddling) oracle, and we might infer that Apollo
referred to the sea-god in a way which only now becomes clear. Jason's
mental process of 'putting two and two together' is evoked by the use
of 'fragments' from Triton's appearance, cf. ξεινήιον (~1555), ἐγγυάλιξε
(~ 1554), ἀντιβολήσας (~ 1551).   **Λιβυστίδος**: for this form of the adjective, rather than Λιβυστικός (1233), cf. Call. fr. 676.

1755–64 give the future history of the clod in a brief narrative framed by
Euphemos' name (1756, 1764). The style of the narrative, with its pointed
repetitions (Λῆμνον … Λήμνου, Σπάρτην … Σπάρτην, Θήρας … Θήρα),
emphasizes historical sequence: Lemnos, then Sparta, and finally Thera.

1755 ἁλίωσεν 'brought to naught', 'made ineffectual'.   **ὑπόκρισιν**
'interpretation'; this is not the normal meaning of this noun (only
here in *Arg.*), but both ὑποκρίνειν and ὑποκριτήρ are used of dream-
interpretation (LSJ s.vv.), and at its only occurrence in *Arg.* ὑποκρίνεσθαι
is used of the interpretation of an omen.

1757 ἧκεν ὑποβρυχίην 'dropped it [so that it was] submerged', the third different way in which Ap. has expressed this idea within a short space (cf. 1743–4, 1750).   ἔκτοθι here functions as the equivalent of ἐκ, cf. 1.1291.

1758 confirms the claim of 1741.   Καλλίστη: the old name of Thera, cf. Pind. *Pyth.* 4.257, Hdt. 4.147, Call. fr. 716; the name-changes of lands, particularly islands, are a frequent theme of Hellenistic poetry, cf. 267–70n., 1.624, 2.296–7, Pfeiffer on Call. fr. 601. Καλλιστώ, Καλλίστη, and Καλλίστιον are all attested female names, and so this is appropriate to the island which appeared as a maiden in Euphemos' dream; Ap. however plays with the name, as the Greek could (and, in one sense, does) mean 'a very beautiful island arose'.   ἱερή: at Pind. *Pyth.* 4.7 Thera is ἱερὰν | νᾶσον, and the Pindaric scholia (II 97 Drachmann) suggest that the epithet refers either to the fertility of the island or to the cults of Poseidon, Athena and Apollo there.

1759 Σιντηίδα: cf. 1.608. The Sinties were believed to be early inhabitants of Lemnos, cf. *Il.* 1.593–4 (with Σ), and Strabo 12.3.20 identifies them as a Thracian people; the standard ancient etymology was from σίνεσθαι, and various explanations of the 'damage' which the Sinties did survive (cf. Hellanicus, *FGrHist* 4 F71).

1760 Τυρσηνοῖσι: a people often connected or identified with the Pelasgians, by whom Hdt. 4.145 has the Minyai driven out of Lemnos, cf. Thucyd. 4.109.4 (with Hornblower's note), Soph. fr. 270.4R, Dion. Hal. *AR* 1.25.2, 1.28.3; for the Pelasgian/Tyrrhenian occupation of Lemnos cf. Hdt. 5.26, 6.137–40. To what extent the Tyrrheni of the eastern Aegean are to be identified with the Etruscans remains a matter of considerable debate; see De Simone 1996.

1761 ἐφέστιοι is glossed as ἔποικοι in Σ, but the narrative in Hdt. would allow either 'as fellow residents', i.e. 'in order to dwell with them', or 'as suppliants', and the latter seems more likely, cf. 703, 723, 3.584–8n.

1762 Theras' father, Autesion, was a Theban descendant of Oedipus, through Polynices, cf. Hdt. 4.147.1, Call. *h.* 2.74, Paus. 9.5.15, Vian 1963: 218–20. There is further (cf. 1758n.) play here on the name of the island: Ap. encourages us to see that the words might suggest 'the excellent son of Autesion led them to the very beautiful island of Thera', rather than 'Theras, the excellent son of Autesion, led them to the island Kalliste'.

1763–4 The printed text is based on a paraphrase in Σ: 'The island of Kalliste changed its name and was called Thera after you, o Theras son of Autesion, for you established a Spartan colony there and remained'. The poet thus apostrophizes the island's colonizer as a mark of honour. Even with the middle ἀμείψατο, the transmitted text would seem to mean 'and he changed the name of Thera from his own <name>'. In a passage rich in wordplay, however, an element of uncertainty about text and interpretation remains. ἀλλὰ τὰ μὲν μετόπιν κτλ.: cf. 1216n. Εὐφήμοιο: the episode closes with a *spondeiazon*.

1765-72 The final event of the poem is the *aition* of the Aeginetan 'Hydrophoria', as almost the final event for Pindar's Argonauts was athletic contests on Lemnos (*Pyth.* 4.253). The Aeginetan *aition* was also the subject of Callimachus' *Iambus* 8. Only the first verse of Call.'s poem survives, Ἀργὼ κοτ' ἐμπνέοντος ἥκαλον νότου, 'The *Argo* once when the south wind was blowing gently', but the ancient summary (διήγησις) survives entire (Pfeiffer I 195, Kerkhecker 1999: 198–9): 'An epinician for Polycles of Aegina who won the double-lap "amphora race" in his homeland. The contest is as follows. At the end of the stadium is an amphora full of water; a contestant runs empty-handed up to it, picks it up and turns around, and the one who arrives first (προφθάσας) wins. The origin <of the contest> is as follows. When the Argonauts landed on Aegina, they competed with each other in quickness to fetch water. The contest is called Hydrophoria.' Athletic contests were so central to Greek identity that the small episode truly marks the return of the Argonauts to a familiar world, but it is likely enough that the passage also allows Ap. to mark his debt to Call. in the very last event of his poem; see Cameron 1995: 251–3.

1765 ἀπτερέως 'quickly'; the adverb, first at Hes. fr.204.84, occurs only here in *Arg.*, but 'swift' is a standard explanation of Homeric ἄπτερος (*LfgrE* s.v.). As oars are 'the wings of a ship' (*Od.* 11.125, LSJ s.v. πτερόν III 1), Ap. may also be telling us that they travelled 'quickly', because 'without oars', i.e. there was a southerly wind blowing (cf. 1769). διὰ ... ταμόντες: tmesis. The transmitted διὰ ... λιπόντες might mean 'leaving behind a gap of a great expanse ... ', but the expression seems very awkward and διαλείπειν is not otherwise found in such contexts. λιπόντες may have arisen from λιπόντας in 1761.

1767 ὑδρείης πέρι 'to fetch water', lit. 'concerning water-fetching'. ἀμεμφέα marks this intra-group competition as entirely harmless. Ap. may have in mind *Od.* 8.76–8, the contrastingly unedifying quarrel of Odysseus and Achilles, marked by δηρίσαντο ... δηριόωντο, which was to mark the πήματος ἀρχή (line 81); here we are at the very end of πήματα.

1768 'to see who could draw water and get back first to the ship'. φθαίη: cf. προφθάσας in the Callimachean *diēgēsis* (1765–72n.). μετὰ νῆάδ': the nearest Homeric model for this 'pleonastic' form is perhaps πρὸ φόωσδε at *Il.* 16.188, 19.118; Ap. is fond of compound prepositions and

this double form may be seen as an extension from such uses, cf. ἀπ'
Αἰγίνηθεν in 1777.

1769 The Argonauts hurried both because of their need for water and
because they wanted to take advantage of a strong wind blowing in their
favour. The 'gentle south wind' of the opening verse of Call.'s poem
(1765–72n.) might be the wind that brought them to Aegina or the
wind that was going to take them away; in Ap.'s narrative we are invited
to understand that this was one and the same wind, and the Argonauts
merely made a very quick stop for fresh water.

1770 ἔνθ' ἔτι νῦν: a familiar aetiological marker.

1771 ἄφαρ, 'quickly', reinforces κούφοισιν ... πόδεσσι.

1772 Μυρμιδόνων: i.e. the Aeginetans. A story, first attested in Hes. fr. 205,
explains the name from the fact that Zeus turned the ants (μύρμηκες) of the
island into men in order to keep Aiakos, the son of the eponymous Aigina,
company, cf. Ov. *Met.* 7.614–60, Hirschberger 2004: 375–6. In Homer, the
Myrmidons are Thessalian followers of Achilles, and a link was drawn
between the two groups through Achilles' father, Peleus, who had been
exiled from Aegina; cf., e.g., Strabo 9.5.9, Apollod. 3.13. It is tempting to
believe that Call. alluded to the myth in *Iambus* 8.

1773–81 The poet bids farewell to the Argonauts in a hymnic style which
matches that of the opening of the poem; although their 'heroic' status is
in one sense the result of their birth (1773), it is their deeds which are
really responsible for this, as marked here by the transition from
παλαιγενέων ... φωτῶν in 1.1. It is, however, the poet's celebration of
those deeds which, in annual repetition, will keep their *kleos* alive
(Hunter 1993: 127–9). The wish for the heroes' continued *kleos* is thus
also a wish for the survival of *Arg.* and the poet's ever-increasing *kleos* 'year
after year', cf. Call. fr. 7.13–14 (an address to the Graces at the conclusion
of the first *aition*) ἔλλατε νῦν, ἐλέγοισι δ' ἐνιψήσασθε λιπώσας | χεῖρας ἐμοῖς, ἵνα
μοι πουλὺ μένωσιν ἔτος, a passage which Ap. may have in mind (see Hunter
2008b: 122, Harder 2012: 2.134). We may also compare the farewell to
Hecale at Call. *Hecale* fr. 263 (= 80 Hollis), πολλάκι σεῖο, | μαῖα, ... φιλοξείνοιο
καλιῆς | μνησόμεθα, a farewell which, like the end of *Arg.*, looks forward to
the afterlife of both the poem and its central character (McNelis 2003).

1773–5 Cf. Cat. 64.22–5 (also addressing the Argonauts) *o nimis optato
saeclorum tempore nati | heroes, saluete, deum genus! o bona matrum | progenies,
saluete iter<um ... > | uos ego saepe, meo uos carmine compellabo.*   ἵλατ' both
bids farewell to the Argonauts and begs them to be understanding if he is
now going to stop his poetic celebration of them, cf. 984, 1333,
2.693.   ἀριστῆες, μακάρων γένος 'heroes, offspring of the gods', as at

Cat. 64.23 above. The Argonauts belong to the Hesiodic race of ἡμίθεοι (*WD* 156–73, cf. Pind. *Pyth.* 4.12); cf. 1.548–9 (the start of the expedition), the gods look down on ἡμιθέων ἀνδρῶν γένος, οἳ τότ' ἄριστοι | πόντον ἐπιπλώεσκον. Elsewhere Ap. stresses their descent from gods (2.1223, 3.366, 402 etc.); in her first words, Pindar's Medea addresses the Argonauts as παῖδες ὑπερθύμων τε φωτῶν καὶ θεῶν (*Pyth.* 4.13). Ap. seems to use μάκαρες only of gods, and so the transmitted text, in which the Argonauts are either 'a race of *makares* heroes' or 'the offspring of *makares* heroes', would be surprising.   εἰς ἔτος ἐξ ἔτεος evokes the annual repetition of festivals, perhaps – given the context – of hero-cult; Giangrande 1968: 56 suggests an allusion to *HHAp.* 169–73 in which the singer commends the sweetness and supremacy of his verses. For phrases of this type cf. 1.861 εἰς ἦμαρ... ἐξ ἤματος, Theocr. 18.15 (with Gow's n.), Headlam on Hds. 5.85.   γάρ: the poet explains the double wish for the understanding of his heroes and the *kleos* of his own poem.

1775–6 The end of 'your labours', for which Ἀργοναυτικά would be a close synonym, is also the end of the poet's task – there is nothing left to report, see Goldhill 1991: 294–5.

1777 ἀπ' Αἰγίνηθεν: for such a double form cf. 1768 μετὰ νῆάδ', 2.586 ἐκ πρύμνηθεν, *Il.* 8.304 ἐξ Αἰσύμηθεν, [Theocr.] 25.180 οὕς Ἑλίκηθεν. ἀνερχομένοισιν: 'on your return home', rather than 'as you departed from', is the most likely nuance of this compound, cf. 1.442, 821, 2.674.

1778 ἀνέμων ἐριῶλαι 'wind-storms'.   ἐνέσταθεν: the scholia paraphrase as ἐκινήθησαν καὶ ἔπνευσαν, which allows either of the transmitted alternatives. ἐνέσταθεν in the particular meaning of 'blocked your way' (LSJ s.v. B IV 1) gives, however, a more specific sense than the more general 'arose', and this is perhaps to be preferred.

1779–80 From Aegina they headed east and then north to sail up the channel separating Euboea from the mainland; the voyage took them past the coasts of Attica, then Boeotia (Aulis) and then eastern Locris. Aulis is on the mainland where the channel is at its narrowest. 1780 alludes to and reverses the frame of *Il.* 2.535, Λοκρῶν, οἳ ναίουσι πέρην ἱερῆς Εὐβοίης.   γαῖαν Κεκροπίην: i.e. Attica.   παρά ... μετρήσαντες: tmesis. Εὐβοίης ἔντοσθεν perhaps goes more closely with the participle than with Αὐλίδα: the Argonauts sailed 'inside Euboea', i.e. between Euboea and the mainland, not on the side of the open sea. If taken closely with Αὐλίδα, the phrase is best understood as 'on this side of Euboea', i.e. on the mainland side, cf. LSJ s.v. ἐντός 1 2, and the use of πέρην in *Il.* 2.535 above. Ὀπούντιά τ' ἄστεα Λοκρῶν, 'Opuntian cities of the Locrians', amounts to 'Opus (the chief city) and the other Locrian cities'; for a list of these cities in heroic times cf. *Il.* 2.531–3, with Kirk's n. The area referred to lies on the mainland opposite the NW coast of Euboea.

1781 Cf. *Od.* 23.238 (Penelope weeping with joy compared to shipwrecked sailors who have made it to shore) ἀσπάσιοι δ' ἐπέβαν γαίης, κακότητα φυγόντες, Hunter 1993: 119–20; the triple repetition of ἀσπάσιος and ἀσπαστός in that passage (233, 238, 239) will have made it particularly memorable. ἀσπάσιος and related words are frequently found as markers of narrative closure or homecoming, cf. 996, 1391, 1.1173, *SH* 947.4, Dufner 1988: 212–18. One instance of this is *Od.* 23.295–6 (Odysseus and Penelope) οἱ μὲν ἔπειτα | ἀσπάσιοι λέκτροιο παλαιοῦ θεσμὸν ἵκοντο, which Ap. perhaps echoed at 2.728. *Od.* 23.296 is where, as the Homeric scholia tell us, Aristophanes of Byzantium and Aristarchus identified the πέρας or τέλος of *Od.*; what these scholars actually meant by this judgement has generated a large bibliography (see Heubeck's n. on line 297, Pfeiffer 1968: 175–7, Hunter 1993: 120 n.77), but it was suggested long ago that 1781 evokes this Homeric verse, from which we may infer that this 'Alexandrian end' of *Od.* had been identified before Aristophanes, perhaps as early as Zenodotus (Rossi 1968, Rengakos 1993: 92–3). That Ap. should end his poem with an allusion to a scholarly theory about a Homeric 'ending' would certainly not surprise, but 1781 is in fact not particularly like *Od.* 23.296 (*Od.* 23.238 is certainly closer), and the two verses would probably never have been brought together but for the note in the Homeric scholia; the possibility intrigues, but no convincing case based on stylistic likeness has been made. For a different approach to closure in *Arg.* see Theodorakopoulos 1998.   ἀκτὰς Παγασηίδας: the Argonauts disembark exactly where they set off, cf. 1.237–8, 317–18; Ap. treats 'the Pagasean shores' as the port of Iolkos.

WORKS CITED

Acosta-Hughes, B. 2010. *Arion's lyre*, Princeton

Albis, R. V. 1996. *Poet and audience in the Argonautica of Apollonius*, Lanham MD

Alexiou, M. 1974. *The ritual lament in Greek tradition*, Cambridge

Amandry, P. 1950. *La mantique apollinienne à Delphes*, Paris

Arend, W. 1933. *Die typischen Scenen bei Homer*, Berlin

Arnott, W. G. 1977. 'Swan songs', *Greece & Rome* 24: 149–53
  2007. *Birds in the ancient world from A to Z*, London

Asper, M. 2008. 'Apollonius on poetry' in Papanghelis–Rengakos 2008: 167–97

Barbantani, S. 2014. 'Mother of snakes and kings: Apollonius Rhodius' *Foundation of Alexandria*', *Histos* 8: 209–45

Barchiesi, A. 1993. 'Future reflexive: two modes of allusion and Ovid's *Heroides*', *Harvard Studies in Classical Philology* 95: 333–65

Barrett, W. S. 1964. *Euripides, Hippolytos*, Oxford

Barringer, J. M. 1995. *Divine escorts. Nereids in archaic and classical Greek art*, Ann Arbor

Baumann, E. D. 1928. 'Über die Hundswut im Altertume', *Janus* 32: 137–51

Beaumont, R. L. 1936. 'Greek influence in the Adriatic sea before the fourth century B.C.', *Journal of Hellenic Studies* 56: 159–204

Beck, D. 2012. *Speech presentation in Homeric epic*, Austin TX

Berger, H. 1880. *Die geographischen Fragmente des Eratosthenes*, Leipzig

Betz, H. 1992. *The Greek Magical Papyri in translation*, 2nd edn, Chicago

Blickman, D. R. 1986. 'The myth of Ixion and pollution for homicide in archaic Greece', *Classical Journal* 81: 193–208

Bolton, J. 1962. *Aristeas of Proconnesus*, Oxford

Bosworth, A. B. 1988. *Conquest and empire*, Cambridge

Braccesi, L. 1971. *Grecità adriatica*, Bologna

Braswell, B. K. 1988. *A commentary on the Fourth Pythian Ode of Pindar*, Berlin/New York

Bremer, J. M. 1987. 'Full moon and marriage in Apollonius' *Argonautica*', *Classical Quarterly* 37: 423–6

Bremmer, J. N. 1997. 'Why did Medea kill her brother Apsyrtus?' in J. J. Clauss and S. I. Johnston eds., *Medea. Essays on Medea in myth, literature, philosophy, and art* (Princeton) 83–100 [= Bremmer 2008: 320–34]
  2005. 'Anaphe, aeschrology and Apollo Aigletes: Apollonius Rhodius 4.1711–1730' in A. Harder and M. Cuypers eds., *Beginning from Apollo. Studies in Apollonius Rhodius and the Argonautic tradition* (Leuven) 18–34 [= Bremmer 2008: 249–65]

2008. *Greek religion and culture, the Bible and the ancient Near East,* Leiden

Brown, M. K. 2002. *The narratives of Konon,* Leipzig

Bruss, J. S. 2004. 'Lessons from Ceos: written and spoken word in Callimachus' in M. A. Harder, R. F. Regtuit and G. C. Wakker eds., *Callimachus II* (Leuven) 49–69

Buffière, F. 1956. *Les mythes d'Homère et la pensée grecque,* Paris

Bühler, W. 1960. *Die Europa des Moschos,* Wiesbaden

Burgess, J. S. 2009. *The death and afterlife of Achilles,* Baltimore

Burkert, W. 1985. *Greek religion,* Oxford

1992. *The orientalising revolution,* Cambridge MA

Buxton, R. 1998. 'The myth of Talos' in C. Atherton ed., *Monsters and monstrosity in Greek and Roman culture* (Bari) 83–112

Byre, C. S. 1991. 'The narrator's addresses to the narratee in Apollonius Rhodius' *Argonautica*', *Transactions of the American Philological Society* 121: 215–27

1996a. 'The killing of Apsyrtus in Apollonius Rhodius' Argonautica', *Phoenix* 50: 3–16

1996b. 'Distant encounters: the Prometheus and Phaethon episodes in the *Argonautica* of Apollonius Rhodius', *American Journal of Philology* 117: 275–83

Calame, C. 2003. *Myth and history in ancient Greece,* Princeton

Cameron, A. 1995. *Callimachus and his critics,* Princeton

Campbell, J. K. 1964. *Honour, family and patronage,* Oxford

Campbell, M. 1969. 'Critical notes on Apollonius Rhodius', *Classical Quarterly* 19: 269–84

1971. 'Further notes on Apollonius Rhodius', *Classical Quarterly* 21: 402–23

1973. 'Notes on Apollonius Rhodius, Argonautica II', *Revue de Philologie* 47: 68–90

1976. Review of Livrea 1973, *Gnomon* 48: 336–40

1994. *A commentary on Apollonius Rhodius, Argonautica III 1–471,* Leiden

1995. 'Hiatus in Apollonius Rhodius' in M. Fantuzzi and R. Pretagostini eds., *Struttura e storia dell'esametro Greco* (Rome) I 193–220

Casson, L. 1971. *Ships and seamanship in the ancient world,* Princeton

Ceulemans, R. 2007. 'Ritual mutilation in Apollonius Rhodius' Argonautica. A contextual analysis of IV, 477–9 in search of the motive of the μασχαλισμός', *Kernos* 20: 97–112

Chuvin, P. 2003. 'Anaphé, ou la dernière épreuve des Argonautes' in D. Accorinti and P. Chuvin eds., *Des Géants à Dionysos. Mélanges de mythologie et de poésie grecques offerts à Francis Vian* (Alessandria) 215–21

Clare, R. J. 2002. *The path of the Argo,* Cambridge

Clauss, J. J. 2000. 'Cosmos without imperium: the Argonautic journey through time' in Harder–Regtuit–Wakker 2000: 11–32

Clay, J. 1972. 'The Planktai and Moly: divine naming and knowing in Homer', *Hermes* 100: 127–31

Corsano, M. 1991. 'Il sogno di Eufemo e la fondazione di Cirene nelle *Argonautiche* di Apollonio Rodio', *Rudiae* 3: 57–72

Cunliffe, B. 2001. *The extraordinary voyage of Pytheas the Greek*, London

Cuypers, M. 1997. *Apollonius Rhodius, Argonautica 2.1–310, A commentary*, Dissertation Leiden

  2005. 'Interactional particles and narrative voice in Apollonius and Homer' in A. Harder and M. Cuypers eds., *Beginning from Apollo. Studies in Apollonius Rhodius and the Argonautic tradition* (Leuven) 35–69

D'Alessio, G. B. 2005. 'The *Megalai Ehoiai*: a survey of the fragments' in R. Hunter ed., *The Hesiodic Catalogue of Women: constructions and reconstructions* (Cambridge) 176–216

  2014. Review of Harder 2012, *Mnemosyne* 67: 492–9

Danielsson, O. A. 1905/6. 'Zu Thukydides VII 75, 4', *Eranos* 6: 136–49

Debiasi, A. 2003. '*POxy* LIII 3698: Eumeli Corinthii fragmentum novum?' *Zeitschrift für Papyrologie und Epigraphik* 143: 1–5

Delage, E. 1930. *La Géographie dans les Argonautiques d'Apollonios de Rhodes*, Bordeaux

Delebecque, E. 1978. *Xénophon. De l'art équestre*, Paris

De Simone, C. 1996. *I Tirreni a Lemnos*, Florence

Detienne, M. and Vernant, J.-P. 1978. *Cunning intelligence in Greek culture and society*, Hassocks, Sussex

Dettori, E. 2000. *Filita grammatico*, Rome

Dickie, M. 1990. 'Talos bewitched. Magic, atomic theory and paradoxography in Apollonius *Argonautica* 4.1638–88', *Papers of the Leeds Latin Seminar* 6: 267–96

Diels, H. 1929. *Doxographi Graeci*, 2nd edn, Berlin

Diggle, J. 1970. *Euripides, Phaethon*, Cambridge

Dufner, C. M. 1988. *The Odyssey in the Argonautica: reminiscence, revision, reconstruction*, Dissertation Princeton

Dyck, A. R. 1987. 'The glossographoi', *Harvard Studies in Classical Philology* 91: 119–60

  1989. 'On the way from Colchis to Corinth: Medea in Book 4 of the "Argonautica"' *Hermes* 117: 455–70

Dyer, R. R. 1969. 'The evidence for Apolline purification rituals at Delphi and Athens', *Journal of Hellenic Studies* 89: 38–56

Egan, R. B. 1985. 'Λειριόεις κτλ. in Homer and elsewhere', *Glotta* 63: 14–24

Eichgrün, E. 1961. *Kallimachos und Apollonios Rhodios*, Dissertation Berlin

Erbse, H. 1953. 'Homerscholien und hellenistische Glossare bei Apollonios Rhodios', *Hermes* 81: 163–96

  1963a. Review of Fränkel 1961, *Gnomon* 35: 18–27

1963b. 'Versumstellungen in den "Argonautika" des Apollonios Rhodios', *Rheinisches Museum* 106: 229–51

Faerber, H. 1932. *Zur dichterischen Kunst in Apollonios Rhodios' Argonautica*, Dissertation Berlin

Fantuzzi, M. 1988. *Ricerche su Apollonio Rodio*, Rome

2007. 'Medea maga, la luna, l'amore (Apollonio Rodio 4, 50–65)' in A. T. Cozzoli and A. Martina eds., *L'epos argonautico* (Rome) 77–95

2008a. '"Homeric" formularity in the Argonautica of Apollonius of Rhodes', in Papanghelis–Rengakos 2008: 21–41

2008b. 'Which magic? Which eros? Apollonius' Argonautica and the different narrative roles of Medea as a sorceress in love' in Papanghelis–Rengakos 2008: 287–310

Fantuzzi, M. and Hunter, R. 2004. *Tradition and innovation in Hellenistic poetry*, Cambridge

Faraone, C. A. 1999. *Ancient Greek love magic*, Cambridge MA

Feeney, D. C. 1991. *The gods in epic*, Oxford

Ferri, S. 1976. 'Fenomeni ecologici della Cirenaica costiera nel II millennio a.C. Nuovi dati archeologici su gli Argonauti a Euesperide' in Stucchi 1976b: 11–17

Fowler, D. 2002. *Lucretius on atomic motion*, Oxford

Fowler, R. L. 2013. *Early Greek mythography*, Vol. II, Oxford

Fränkel, H. 1923. 'Homerische Wörter' in *ANTIΔΩPON. Festschrift Jacob Wackernagel* (Göttingen) 274–82

1961. *Apollonii Rhodii Argonautica*, Oxford

1964. *Einleitung zur kritischen Ausgabe der Argonautika des Apollonios*, Göttingen

1968. *Noten zu den Argonautika des Apollonios*, Munich

Fraenkel, E. 1957. *Horace*, Oxford

Fraser, P. M. 1972. *Ptolemaic Alexandria*, 3 vols., Oxford

Frazer, J. G. 1921. *Apollodorus. The Library*, London

Fusillo, M. 1985. *Il tempo delle Argonautiche*, Rome

Gantz, T. 1993. *Early Greek myth. A guide to literary and artistic sources*, Baltimore

Garland, R. 1985. *The Greek way of death*, London

Giangrande, G. 1968. 'On the use of the vocative in Alexandrian epic', *Classical Quarterly* 18: 52–9

1973. *Zu Sprachgebrauch Technik und Text des Apollonios Rhodios*, Amsterdam

1977. 'Polisemia del linguaggio nella poesia alessandrina' *Quaderni Urbinati di Cultura Classica* 24: 97–106

Glei, R. and Natzel-Glei, S. 1996. *Apollonios von Rhodos, Das Argonautenepos*, Vol. II, Darmstadt

Goldhill, S. 1991. *The poet's voice*, Cambridge

Gomme, A. W. 1956. *A historical commentary on Thucydides*, Vol. II, Oxford

Goodchild, R. G. 1976. *Libyan studies*, London

Gotsmich, A. 1955. 'Der Maschalismos und seine Wiedergabe in der griechischen Kunst' in *Monumentum Bambergense. Festgabe für Benedikt Kraft* (Munich) 349–66

Gould, J. 1973. 'Hiketeia', *Journal of Hellenic Studies* 93: 74–103

Gow, A. S. F. 1938. 'Apollonius Rhodius IV.1486ff.', *Classical Review* 52: 215–16

Graf, F. 1979. 'Apollon Delphinios', *Museum Helveticum* 36: 2–22

Graz, L. 1965. *Le feu dans l'Iliade et l'Odyssée*, Paris

Green, P. 1997. *The Argonautika by Apollonios Rhodios*, Berkeley

Griffin, J. 1980. *Homer on life and death*, Oxford

1986. 'Words and speakers in Homer', *Journal of Hellenic Studies* 106: 36–57

Griffith, A. 1968. Review of A. Ardizzoni, *Le Argonautiche, libro* I (Rome 1967), *Journal of Hellenic Studies* 88: 173–5

Griffiths, F. T. 1990. 'Murder, purification, and cultural formation in Aeschylus and Apollonius Rhodius', *Helios* 17: 25–39

2012. 'Claiming Libya: Peleus and the Ptolemies in Apollonius Rhodius' *Argonautica*' in C. Cusset, N. Le Meur-Weissman, F. Levin eds., *Mythe et pouvoir à l'époque hellénistique* (Leuven) 1–35

Grillo, A. 1988. *Tra filologia e narratologia*, Rome

Groningen, B. A. van 1953. *La poésie verbale grecque*, Amsterdam

Halliwell, S. 2008. *Greek laughter*, Cambridge

Hammond, N. G. L. 1967. *Epirus*, Oxford

Harder, A. 2002. 'Intertextuality in Callimachus' Aetia' in *Callimaque, Entretiens sur l'antiquité classique* xlviii (Vandoeuvres-Geneva) 189–233

2012. *Callimachus, Aetia*, 2 vols., Oxford

Harder, A., Regtuit, R. F., Wakker, G. C. eds. 1998. *Genre in Hellenistic poetry*, Groningen

2000. *Apollonius Rhodius*, Leuven

2006. *Beyond the canon*, Leuven

2014. *Hellenistic poetry in context*, Leuven

Hardie, P. 1985. 'Imago mundi: cosmological and ideological aspects of the shield of Achilles', *Journal of Hellenic Studies* 105: 11–31

Harris, W. V. 2013. 'Greek and Roman hallucinations' in W. V. Harris ed., *Mental disorders in the classical world* (Leiden) 285–306

Haslam, M. W. 1978. 'Apollonius Rhodius and the papyri', *Illinois Classical Studies* 3: 47–73

2013. 'Ap. Rhod. *Argon.* 4.430', *Zeitschrift für Papyrologie und Epigraphik* 184: 116

Henrichs, A. 1983. 'The "sobriety" of Oedipus: Sophocles *OC* 100 misun-
derstood', *Harvard Studies in Classical Philology* 87: 87–100
Herter, H. 1959. 'Hera spricht mit Thetis', *Symbolae Osloenses* 35: 40–54 [=
Kleine Schriften (Munich 1975) 433–44]
Hinds, S. 1998. *Allusion and intertext*, Cambridge
Hirschberger, M. 2004. *Gynaikon Katalogos und Megalai Ehoiai*, Leipzig
Hollis, A. S. 1990. *Callimachus, Hecale*, Oxford
Hopkinson, N. 1982. 'Juxtaposed prosodic variants in Greek and Latin
poetry' *Glotta* 60: 162–77
  1984. *Callimachus, Hymn to Demeter*, Cambridge
  1988. *A Hellenistic anthology*, Cambridge
Hopman, M. G. 2012. *Scylla. Myth, metaphor, paradox*, Cambridge
Hunter, R. 1987. 'Medea's flight: the fourth book of the *Argonautica*',
  Classical Quarterly 37: 129–39 [= Hunter 2008a: 42–58]
  1988. '"Short on heroics": Jason in the *Argonautica*', *Classical Quarterly*
  38: 436–53 [= Hunter 2008a: 59–85]
  1989. *Apollonius of Rhodes, Argonautica Book III*, Cambridge
  1991a. '"Breast is best": Catullus 64.18', *Classical Quarterly* 41: 254–5
  1991b. 'Greek and non-Greek in the *Argonautica* of Apollonius' in
  S. Said ed., *ΕΛΛΗΝΙΣΜΟΣ. Quelques jalons pour une histoire de l'identité
  grecque* (Leiden) 81–99 [= Hunter 2008a: 95–114]
  1993. *The Argonautica of Apollonius: literary studies*, Cambridge
  1995. 'The divine and human map of the *Argonautica*', *Syllecta Classica* 6:
  13–27 [= Hunter 2008a: 257–77]
  1996. *Theocritus and the archaeology of Greek poetry*, Cambridge
  1999. *Theocritus, a selection*, Cambridge
  2003a. 'Aspects of technique and style in the *Periegesis* of Dionysius' in
  D. Accorinti and P. Chuvin eds., *Des Géants à Dionysos. Mélanges de
  mythologie et de poésie grecques offerts à Francis Vian* (Alessandria)
  343–56 [= Hunter 2008a: 700–17]
  2003b. *Theocritus, Encomium of Ptolemy Philadelphus*, Berkeley
  2006. *The shadow of Callimachus*, Cambridge
  2008a. *On coming after. Studies in post-classical Greek literature and its
  reception*, Berlin
  2008b. 'The poetics of narrative in the Argonautica' in Papanghelis–
  Rengakos 2008: 115–46 [= Hunter 2008a: 343–77]
  2009. *Critical moments in classical literature*, Cambridge
  2011. 'Festivals, cults, and the construction of consensus in Hellenistic
  poetry' in G. Urso ed., *Dicere laudes. Elogio, communicazione, creazione del
  consenso* (Pisa) 101–18
  2015. '*Aetia fr.* 43 and 178' in D. Sider ed., *Hellenistic Greek poetry: a
  selection*, Ann Arbor

forthcoming. 'Notes on the ancient reception of Sappho' in T. S. Thorsen ed., *The reception of Sappho in Rome*

Hutchinson, G. O. 1988. *Hellenistic poetry*, Oxford

Huxley, G. L. 1969. *Greek epic poetry from Eumelos to Panyassis*, London

Ivantchik, A. I. 1999. 'Eine griechische Pseudo-Historie. Der Pharao Sesostris und der skytho-ägyptische Krieg', *Historia* 48: 395–441

Jackson, S. 1993. *Creative selectivity in Apollonius' Argonautica*, Amsterdam

Jacques, J.-M. 2002. *Nicandre. Oeuvres Tome II. Les Thériaques*, Paris

Jameson, M. H., Jordan, D. R., Kotansky, R. D. 1993. *A Lex Sacra from Selinous*, Durham NC

Janko, R. 1982. *Homer, Hesiod and the Hymns*, Cambridge

Janni, P. 1984. *Il mappa e il periplo*, Rome

Johnston, S. I. 1999. *Restless dead: encounters between the living and the dead in ancient Greece*, Berkeley

Jong, I. de 1987. 'The voice of anonymity: tis-speeches in the *Iliad*', *Eranos* 85: 69–84

2004. *Narrators and focalizers. The presentation of the story in the Iliad*, 2nd edn, London

Jouan, F. 1966. *Euripide et les légendes des Chants Cypriens*, Paris

Kaiser, E. 1964. 'Odyssee-Szenen als Topoi', *Museum Helveticum* 21: 109–36, 197–224

Kerkhecker, A. 1999. *Callimachus' Book of Iambi*, Oxford

Keyes, C. W. 1929. 'Papyrus fragments of extant Greek literature', *American Journal of Philology* 50: 255–65

Kingston, P. 1968. '2694. *Argon.* ii 917–53, iv 317–22, 416–61, 468–512' in *The Oxyrhynchus Papyri* XXXIV (London) 49–58

Kirk, G. S. 1981. 'Some methodological pitfalls in the study of ancient Greek sacrifice (in particular)' in *Le sacrifice dans l'antiquité* (Vandoeuvres-Geneva) 41–80

Knight, V. 1991. 'Apollonius, *Argonautica* 4.167–70 and Euripides' *Medea*', *Classical Quarterly* 41: 248–50

1995. *The renewal of epic*, Leiden

Krevans, N. 2000. 'On the margins of epic: the foundation-poems of Apollonius' in Harder–Regtuit–Wakker 2000: 69–84

Kyriakou, P. 1994. 'Empedoclean echoes in Apollonius Rhodius' "Argonautica"', *Hermes* 122: 309–19

La Roche, J. 1899. 'Der Hexameter bei Apollonios, Aratos und Kallimachos', *Wiener Studien* 21: 161–97

Lefkowitz, M. 2008. 'Myth and history in the biography of Apollonius' in Papanghelis–Rengakos 2008: 51–71

Leigh, M. 1998. 'Sophocles at Patavium (*fr.* 137 Radt)', *Journal of Hellenic Studies* 118: 82–100

Lehrs, K. 1882. *De Aristarchi studiis Homericis*, 3rd edn, Leipzig

Leumann, M. 1950. *Homerische Wörter*, Basel

Levin, S. 1950. 'ΠΡΟΣΚΗΔΗΣ, "mournful"', *Classical Philology* 45: 110–11

Lightfoot, J. L. 2014. *Dionysius Periegetes, Description of the known world*, Oxford

Livrea, E. 1972. 'Una "tecnica allusiva" apolloniana alla luce dell'esegesi omerica alessandrina', *Studi Italiani di Filologia Classica* 44: 231–43

   1973. *Apollonii Rhodii Argonauticon Liber Quartus*, Florence

   1984. 'Il sudore degli Argonauti all'Elba' in *Lirica greca da Archiloco a Elitis. Studi in onore di F. M. Pontani* (Padua) 205–11 [= Livrea 1991: 131–6]

   1987. 'L'episodio libyco nel quarto libro delle "Argonautiche" di Apollonio Rodio', *Quaderni di Archeologia della Libia* 12: 175–90 [= Livrea 1991: 137–56]

   1991. *Studia Hellenistica* I, Florence

   2006. 'Il mito argonautico in Callimaco. L'episodio di Anafe' in G. Bastianini and A. Casanova eds., *Callimaco: cent'anni di papiri* (Florence) 89–99

Lloyd, A. B. 1969. 'Perseus and Chemmis (Herodotus II 91)', *Journal of Hellenic Studies* 89: 79–86

   1976. *Herodotus Book II. Commentary 1–98*, Leiden

Lorimer, H. L. 1921. 'Note on *Eumenides* 41–2', *Classical Review* 35: 143

Lowe, D. 2013. 'Women scorned: a new stichometric allusion in the *Aeneid*', *Classical Quarterly* 63: 442–5

Luiselli, R. 2003. 'Papiri greci riutilizzati per la manifattura di un *cartonnage* di legatura', *Zeitschrift für Papyrologie und Epigraphik* 142: 147–62

Magnelli, E. 2006. 'Nicander's chronology: a literary approach', in Harder–Regtuit–Wakker 2006: 185–204

Malkin, I. 1994. *Myth and territory in the Spartan Mediterranean*, Cambridge

Marcotte, D. 2000. *Géographes grecs*, Vol. 1, Paris

Martin, A. and Primavesi, O. 1998. *L'Empédocle de Strasbourg (P. Strasb. gr. inv. 1665–1666)*, Berlin

Mastronarde, D. 2002. *Euripides, Medea*, Cambridge

Matthews, V. J. 1996. *Antimachus of Colophon*, Leiden

Mattusch, C. 1996. *Classical bronzes*, Ithaca NY

   1997. *The victorious youth*, Los Angeles

McKay, K. J. 1967. 'Door magic and the epiphany hymn', *Classical Quarterly* 17: 184–94

McNeal, R. A. 1967. 'Anaphe. Home of the Strangford Apollo', *Archaeology* 20: 254–63

McNelis, C. 2003. 'Mourning glory: Callimachus' *Hecale* and heroic honours', *Materiali e Discussioni* 50: 155–61

Merlen, R. H. A. 1971. *De canibus. Dog and hound in antiquity*, London

Meuli, K. 1921. *Odyssee und Argonautika*, Berlin

Meyer, D. 2008. 'Apollonius as a Hellenistic geographer' in Papanghelis–Rengakos 2008: 267–85

Minns, E. H. 1913. *Scythians and Greeks*, Cambridge

Mirto, M. S. 2011. 'Il nome di Achille nelle *Argonautiche* tra intertestualità e giochi etimologici', *Rivista di Filologia e di Istruzione Classica* 139: 279–309

Morel, W. 1928. 'Iologica', *Philologus* 83: 345–89

Mori, A. 2008. *The politics of Apollonius Rhodius' Argonautica*, Cambridge
2012. 'Reconciliation and ceaseless wrath: paradoxical Hera in Apollonius and Callimachus' in C. Cusset, N. Le Meur-Weissman, F. Levin eds., *Mythe et pouvoir à l'époque hellénistique* (Leuven) 319–36

Morrison, A. D. 2007. *The narrator in Archaic Greek and Hellenistic poetry*, Cambridge

Mugler, C. 1959. 'Sur l'origine et le sens de l'expression καθαιρεῖν τὴν σελήνην', *Revue des Études Anciennes* 61: 48–56

Müller, W. 1968. 'Griechische literarische Texte auf Papyrus und Pergament', *Forschungen und Berichte (Berlin), Archäologische Beiträge*, 10: 113–32

Murray, J. 2012. 'Burned after reading: the so-called list of Alexandrian librarians in *P. Oxy.* X 1241', *Aitia* 2 [http://aitia.revues.org/544]
2014. 'Anchored in time: the date in Apollonius' Argonautica' in Harder–Regtuit–Wakker 2014: 247–77

Murray, O. 1970. 'Hecataeus of Abdera and pharaonic kingship', *Journal of Egyptian Archaeology* 56: 141–71

Nagy, G. 1999. *The best of the Achaeans*, 2nd edn, Baltimore

Natzel, S. 1992. *Κλέα γυναικῶν. Frauen in den "Argonautika" des Apollonios Rhodios*, Trier

Nelis, D. 1991. 'Apollonius Rhodius, *Argonautica* 4.12', *Classical Quarterly* 41: 250–1
2001. *Vergil's Aeneid and the Argonautica of Apollonius Rhodius*, Leeds

Nesselrath, H.-G. 1992. *Ungeschehenes Geschehen*, Stuttgart

Nishimura-Jensen, J. 1996. *Tragic epic or epic tragedy: narrative and genre in Apollonius of Rhodes' Argonautica*, Dissertation Wisconsin-Madison
2000. 'Unstable geographies: the moving landscape in Apollonius' *Argonautica* and Callimachus' *Hymn to Delos*', *Transactions of the American Philological Association* 130: 287–317

Norden, E. 1913. *Agnostos theos*, Stuttgart

Nünlist, R. 2009. *The ancient critic at work*, Cambridge

Oakley, J. H. and Sinos, R. H. 1993. *The wedding in ancient Athens*, Madison

Ogden, D. 2013a. *Drakon. Dragon myth and serpent cult in the Greek and Roman worlds*, Oxford
2013b. *Dragons, serpents, and slayers in the classical and early Christian worlds. A sourcebook*, Oxford

O'Hara, J. J. 1996. *True names*, Ann Arbor

Olson, S. D. 2012. *The Homeric Hymn to Aphrodite and related texts*, Berlin

Osborne, C. 1987. 'Empedocles recycled', *Classical Quarterly* 37: 24–50

Ottone, G. 2002. *Libyka*, Rome

Paduano, G. 1970/1. 'L'episodio di Talos: osservazioni sull'esperienza magica nelle *Argonautiche* di Apollonio Rodio', *Studi Classici e Orientali* 19/10: 46–67

Page, D. L. 1955. *Sappho and Alcaeus*, Oxford

Papanghelis, T. 1989. 'About the hour of noon: Ovid, *Amores* 1, 5', *Mnemosyne* 42: 54–61

Papanghelis, T. and Rengakos, A. eds. 2008. *Brill's companion to Apollonius Rhodius*, 2nd edn, Leiden

Parker, R. 1983. *Miasma*, Oxford

Paschalis, M. 1994. 'Anaphe, Delos and the Melantian Rocks (Ap. Rhod. *Arg.* 4, 1694–1730 and *Orph. Arg.* 1353–1359)', *Mnemosyne* 47: 224–6

Pavlou, M. 2009. 'Reading Medea through her veil in the Argonautica of Apollonius Rhodius', *Greece & Rome* 56: 183–202

Payne, M. 2013. 'Aristotle on poets as parents and the Hellenistic poet as mother' in V. Zajko and E. O'Gorman eds., *Classical myth and psychoanalysis* (Oxford) 299–313

Pearson, L. 1938. 'Apollonius of Rhodes and the old geographers', *American Journal of Philology* 59: 443–59

Peretti, A. 1979. *Il periplo di Scilace*, Pisa

1983. 'I peripli arcaici e Scilace di Carianda' in F. Prontera ed., *Geografia e geografi nel mondo antico* (Rome) 71–114

Peyras, J. and Trousset, P. 1988. 'Le lac *Tritonis* et les noms anciens du Chott El Jerid', *Antiquités africaines* 24: 149–204

Pfeiffer, R. 1968. *History of classical scholarship from the beginnings to the end of the Hellenistic age*, Oxford

Pietsch, C. 1999. *Die Argonautika des Apollonios von Rhodos: Untersuchungen zum Problem der einheitlicher Konzeption des Inhalts*, Stuttgart

Plantinga, M. 2000. 'The supplication motif in Apollonius Rhodius' Argonautica' in Harder–Regtuit–Wakker 2000: 105–28

2007. 'Hospitality and rhetoric: the Circe episode in Apollonius Rhodius' *Argonautica*', *Classical Quarterly* 57: 543–64

Porter, J. R. 1990. 'Tiptoeing through the corpses: Euripides' *Electra*, Apollonius, and the *bouphonia*', *Greek, Roman, and Byzantine Studies* 31: 255–80

Power, T. 2010. *The culture of Kitharôidia*, Washington DC

Powers, N. 2002. 'Magic, wonder and scientific explanation in Apollonius, Argonautica 4.1638-93', *Proceedings of the Cambridge Philological Society* 48: 87–101

Priestley, J. 2014. *Herodotus and Hellenistic culture*, Oxford

Pulleyn, S. 1997. *Prayer in Greek religion*, Oxford

Raman, R. A. 1975. 'Homeric ἄωτος and Pindaric ἄωτος. A semantic problem', *Glotta* 53: 195–207

Renehan, R. 1976. *Studies in Greek texts*, Göttingen

Rengakos, A. 1992. 'Zur Biographie des Apollonios von Rhodos', *Wiener Studien* 105: 39–67

1993. *Der Homertext und die hellenistischen Dichter*, Stuttgart

1994. *Apollonios Rhodios und die antike Homererklärung*, Munich

2004. 'Die *Argonautika* und das "kyklische Gedicht". Bemerkungen zur epischen Erzähltechnik' in A. Bierl, A. Schmitt and A. Willi eds., *Antike Literatur in neuer Deutung* (Leipzig) 277–304

2008. 'Apollonius Rhodius as a Homeric scholar' in Papanghelis–Rengakos 2008: 243–66

Repath, I. 2007. 'The Physiognomy of Adamantius the Sophist' in S. Swain ed., *Seeing the face, seeing the soul* (Oxford) 487–554

Richardson, N. J. 1974. *The Homeric Hymn to Demeter*, Oxford

Robertson, C. M. 1977. 'The death of Talos', *Journal of Hellenic Studies* 97: 158–60

Robertson, N. 2010. *Religion and reconciliation in Greek cities*, New York

Roller, D. W. 2006. *Through the Pillars of Herakles*, New York

Romm, J. S. 1992. *The edges of the earth in ancient thought*, Princeton

Rose, A. 1985. 'Clothing imagery in Apollonius's *Argonautika*', *Quaderni Urbinati di Cultura Classica* 21: 30–44

Rossi, L. E. 1968. 'La fine alessandrina dell'*Odissea* e lo ζῆλος Ὁμηρικός di Apollonio Rodio', *Rivista di Filologia e Istruzione Classica* 96: 151–63

Ruijgh, C. J. 1971. *Autour de "τε épique"*, Amsterdam

Rusten, J. S. 1982. *Dionysius Scytobrachion*, Opladen

Sansone, D. 2000. 'Iphigeneia in Colchis' in Harder–Regtuit–Wakker 2000: 155–72

Šašel Kos, M. 1993. 'Cadmus and Harmonia in Illyria', *Arheoloski Vestnik* 44: 113–36

Schaaf, I. 2014. *Magie und Ritual bei Apollonios Rhodios*, Berlin

Schade, G. and Eleuteri, P. 2008. 'The textual tradition of the Argonautica' in Papanghelis–Rengakos 2008: 29–50

Schmidt, M. 1976. *Die Erklärungen zum Weltbild Homers und zur Kultur der Heroenzeit in den bT-Scholien zur Ilias*, Munich

Sedley, D. 1998. *Lucretius and the transformation of Greek wisdom*, Cambridge

2005. 'Empedocles' life cycles' in A. L. Pierris ed., *The Empedoclean κόσμος: structure, process and the question of cyclicity* (Patras) 331–71

Sens, A. 1997. *Theocritus: Dioscuri (Idyll 22)*, Göttingen

2000. 'The particle ἤτοι in Apollonian narrative' in Harder–Regtuit–Wakker 2000: 173–93

Severyns, A. 1928. *Le cycle épique dans l'école d' Aristarque*, Paris

Shipley, G. 2011. *Pseudo-Scylax's Periplous. The circumnavigation of the inhabited world*, Exeter

Slatkin, L. 1991. *The power of Thetis*, Berkeley

Sourvinou-Inwood, C. 1995. *'Reading' Greek death*, Oxford

Spanoudakis, K. 2002. *Philitas of Cos*, Leiden

Stengel, P. 1910. *Opferbräuche der Griechen*, Leipzig/Berlin

Stephens, S. 2000. 'Writing epic for the Ptolemaic court' in Harder–Regtuit–Wakker 2000: 195–215

2003. *Seeing double. Intercultural poetics in Ptolemaic Alexandria*, Berkeley

2008. 'Ptolemaic epic' in Papanghelis–Rengakos 2008: 95–114

2011. 'Remapping the Mediterranean: the Argo adventure in Apollonius and Callimachus' in D. Obbink and R. Rutherford eds., *Culture in pieces* (Oxford) 188–207

Stucchi, S. 1976a. 'Il giardino delle Esperidi e le tappe della conoscenza della costa cirenaica' in Stucchi 1976b: 19–73

ed. 1976b. *Cirene e la Grecia*, Rome [= *Quaderni di Archeologia della Libia* 8]

Thalmann, W. G. 2011. *Apollonius of Rhodes and the spaces of Hellenism*, Oxford

Theodorakopoulos, E. 1998. 'Epic closure and its discontents in Apollonius' Argonautica' in Harder–Regtuit–Wakker 1998: 187–204

Ustinova, Y. 2009. *Caves and the ancient Greek mind*, Oxford

Van Krevelen, D. A. 1961. 'Bemerkungen zum "Kanobos" des Apollonios von Rhodos', *Rheinisches Museum* 104: 128–31

Vasunia, P. 2001. *The gift of the Nile: Hellenizing Egypt from Aeschylus to Alexander*, Berkeley

Vatin, C. 1970. *Recherches sur le mariage et la condition de la femme mariée à l'époque hellénistique*, Paris

Verbanck, A. and Gilis, E. 1998. 'Héraclès, pourfendeur de dragons' in C. Bonnet, C. Jourdain-Annequin, V. Pirenne-Delforge eds., *Le bestiaire d' Héraclès* (Liège) 37–60

Vian, F. 1963. *Les origines de Thèbes. Cadmos et les Spartes*, Paris

1975. 'Notes critiques au Chant II des "Argonautiques" d' Apollonios de Rhodes', *Revue des Études Anciennes* 75: 82–102

1987. 'Poésie et géographie: les retours des Argonautes', *Comptes rendus des séances de l'Académie des Inscriptions et Belles-Lettres* 131: 249–62

Wächter, T. 1910. *Reinheitsvorschriften im griechischen Kult.* Giessen

Wackernagel, J. 1920. *Vorlesungen über Syntax*, Basel

2009. *Lectures on syntax*, ed. D. Langslow, Oxford

Walde, C. 2001. *Die Traumdarstellungen in der griechisch-römischen Dichtung*, Leipzig

Weinreich, O. 1929. 'Türöffnung im Wunder-, Prodigien- und Zauber-glauben der Antike, des Judentums und Christentums', *Tübinger Beiträge zur Altertumswissenschaft* 5: 200–464

West, M. L. 1963. 'Critical notes on Apollonius Rhodius', *Classical Review* 13: 9–12

1967. 'Epica', *Glotta* 44: 135–48

1982. *Greek metre*, Oxford

1983. *The Orphic poems*, Oxford

1985. *The Hesiodic Catalogue of Women*, Oxford

2003. *Greek epic fragments*, Cambridge MA

2005. '*Odyssey* and *Argonautica*', *Classical Quarterly* 55: 39–64 [= *Hellenica I* (Oxford 2011) 277–312]

2013. *The Epic Cycle*, Oxford

Wilamowitz-Moellendorff, U. von. 1924. *Hellenistische Dichtung in der Zeit des Kallimachos*, Berlin

Wilkes, J. J. 1969. *Dalmatia*, London

1992. *The Illyrians*, Oxford

Williams, M. F. 1991. *Landscape in the Argonautica of Apollonius Rhodius*, Frankfurt

Wills, J. 1996. *Repetition in Latin poetry*, Oxford

Żmudziński, M. 1999. 'Konnten die Argonauten vom Schwarzen Meer zur Adria durch die Donau fahren?', *Eos* 86: 19–24

INDEXES

Atlas 1398
Ausonia, Ausones 552–3

Bacchiadai, Corinthian clan 1212
Bacchylides 214–19
Battos 1731–64
Berenice 1021–2
Bistones, Thracian tribe 906
Boreas 764–5
Boutes 912–19, 918
bronze 1092–5
Brugoi, Illyrian tribe 330

Cadmus 516–18
Callimachus *1, 2, 7, 16, 17, 20, 21–5,
25–26, 213,* 263–4, 267–70, 289–91,
425, 511–13, 552, 552–3, 571,
574–5, 753–4, 761–2, 776, 982–3,
984–92, 1021–2, 1155–60, 1209–10,
1454, 1490, 1629–30, 1694–1730,
1700–1, 1730, 1731–64, 1773–81. *See
also* Index of passages discussed
Calliope 22–5
Calypso 574–5
Cattle of the Sun 964–5, 977–8
Catullus 1021–2
Celts 611–17
Cerberus 1510
Chalybes 1475
Charybdis 786, 826, 922–4
Cheiron 812, 813, 877
Circe *3, 6, 14–15, 16,* 559, 661–2,
663–4, 672–5, 686, 687, 693–4, 746
cloaks, descriptions of 423–34,
428–9
Clytemnestra *5–6,* 367–8, 421, 473–4,
663–4
Colossus of Rhodes 1638–88
Conon, mythographer *24,* 1700–1,
1711, 1719–20
Coronis 611–17, 615, 616–17
counterfactual statements 636–42,
1651–3
Cretan Sea 1694
Crete 1637, 1638–88, 1640, 1691, 1693
Cycle, Epic *6, 19,* 421–521, 477, 693–4,
790–817, 792–3, 869–79
Cyclops 1639, 1657, 1661
Cyrene 1454, 1466–7, 1490, 1491–3,
1563, 1731–64

Danae 1091
Danaos 262–3
Danube, river *See* Istros

deer 12–13, 174–5
Delos 1700–1, 1704–5
Demeter 869–79, 984–92, 987, 989,
1725–30
Democritus 1665–72, 1671–2
Deucalion 266
Dikte, Mt 1640
Dionysius Periegetes 285–7, 432,
603–4, 624–6
Dionysus 425, 431, 1134–5
Dioscuri 588–9, 593, 650, 652–3
dolphins 933–6, 936
door-magic 41
dragons 128, 145–66, 1396, 1513–17
dreams 663–4, 666, 669, 1312–14,
1350, 1731–64, 1733–45
Drepane (Corcyra) 539, 548, 768,
980–1, 984–92, 990–1, 1125–6

Echetos 1092–5
Echinades, islands 1228–31
Egypt, Egyptian traditions 259–60,
267–70, 270–1, 274–5, 279–81
Elysium 811
Empedocles *3, 6, 16,* 446, 448, 665,
668, 672–5, 673–4, 676–81, 693–4,
1665–72
Encheleis, Illyrian tribe 516–18
Endymion 54–65, 57–8
enjambment *26,* 355–90, 1038–41
epanalepsis 263–4, 323–4, 828
Ephyra, name for Corinth 1212
Erato 1–5
Eratosthenes 7
Eridanos (Po) *10,* 505–6, 597–611,
603–4, 631–4
Erinyes 386, 475–6, 712–13, 713–14,
1665, 1666, 1670
ἔρως, Eros 445–9
Eryx 912–19, 917
Euboea 540, 1139–40, 1214–15,
1779–80
Eumaeus 672
Eumelos *15,* 1212
Euphemos *14,* 1466–7, 1563, 1577–8,
1731–64
Euphorion 1513–14
Euripides *Andr.* 856–64; *Antiope*: 1090;
IT: 663–4; *Medea*: *4–5, 20,* 1–5, 32–3,
35–40, 95–8, 355–90, 357–9, 368–9,
379–80, 391–3, 395–409, 423–34
Eurypylos 1560–1
eye, evil *6,* 1665–72, 1671–2, 1673–5,
1674–5